Social Research Methods

Social Research Methods

Alan Bryman

OXFORD

UNIVERSITY PRESS

OXFORD

UNIVERSITY PRESS

Great Clarendon Street, Oxford OX2 6DP

Oxford University Press is a department of the University of Oxford.
It furthers the University's objective of excellence in research, scholarship,
and education by publishing worldwide in

Oxford New York

Athens Auckland Bangkok Bogotá Buenos Aires Calcutta
Cape Town Chennai Dar es Salaam Delhi Florence Hong Kong Istanbul
Karachi Kuala Lumpur Madrid Melbourne Mexico City Mumbai
Nairobi Paris São Paulo Shanghai Singapore Taipei Tokyo Toronto Warsaw

with associated companies in Berlin Ibadan

Oxford is a registered trade mark of Oxford University Press
in the UK and in certain other countries

Published in the United States
by Oxford University Press Inc., New York

British Library Cataloguing in Publication Data

Data available

Library of Congress Cataloging in Publication Data

Data available

ISBN 0–19–874204–5
ISBN 0–19–924698–X (hb)

3 5 7 9 10 8 6 4

Typeset in ITC Stone
by RefineCatch Limited, Bungay, Suffolk
Printed in Great Britain by
The Bath Press, Bath

Acknowledgements

Many people have helped me with this book, many of them unwittingly. Generations of research methods students at Loughborough University have plied me with ideas through their questioning of what I said to them. I wish to thank several people at or connected with OUP: Tim Barton for suggesting to me in the first place that I might like to think about writing a book like this; Angela Griffin for her editorial help during the book's passage; Miranda Vernon for her firm but fair grip on the book's production; Angela Martin for her imaginative cartoons; and Hilary Walford for her astute, careful, and tireless copy-editing. I also wish to thank Alan Beardsworth for his helpful and always constructive comments on drafts of the book and Michael Billig for valuable comments on part of the book. As usual, Sue and Sarah have supported me in many ways and put up with my anxieties and with my sudden disappearances to my study. When Sarah became a university student herself, she gave me many insights into a consumer's perspective on a book like this, for which I am grateful. Everyone except me is, of course, absolved of any responsibility for any of the book's substantive deficiencies.

Contents

Part Four

Abbreviations

ASA	American Sociological Association
BCS	British Crime Survey
BFI	British Film Institute
BHPS	British Household Panel Study
BPS	British Psychological Society
BSA	British Sociological Association
BSE	bovine spongiform encephalopathy (mad cow disease)
CA	conversation analysis
CAQDAS	computer-assisted qualitative data analysis software
CV	curriculum vitae
DA	discourse analysis
ECA	ethnographic content analysis
EFS	Expenditure and Food Survey
ENT	ear, nose, and throat
ESRC	Economic and Social Research Council
FES	Family Expenditure Survey
FIAC	Flanders Interaction Analysis Categories
GHS	General Household Survey
HALS	Health and Lifestyle Survey
HRT	hormone replacement therapy
IBSS	International Bibliography of the Social Sciences
ICI	Imperial Chemical Industries
ISSP	International Social Survey Programme
LFS	Labour Force Survey
NCDS	National Child Development Study
NFS	National Food Survey
ORACLE	Observational Research and Classroom Learning Evaluation
SCELI	Social Change and Economic Life Initiative
SCPR	Social and Community Planning Research
SRA	Social Research Association
SSCI	Social Sciences Citation Index
TDM	Total Design Method
WERS	Workplace Employee Relations Survey

Guide to the Book

Focus of the book

This book has been written with two groups of readers in mind. First, undergraduates in subjects such as sociology, social policy, human geography, and education who at some point in their degree take a course, and often more than one course, in the area of research methods. The book covers a wide range of research methods, approaches to research, and ways of carrying out data analysis, so it is likely to meet the needs of the vast majority of students in this position. Research methods are not tied to a particular nation; many if not most of the principles transcend national boundaries. However, in writing the book, I have given it a decidedly British emphasis. This means that I have used British examples of research whenever possible or appropriate.

The second group, which in most cases overlaps with the first, comprises undergraduates who do a research project as part of the requirement for their degree programmes. This can take many forms, but one of the most common is that a small-scale research project is carried out and a dissertation based on the investigation is presented. In addition, students are often expected to carry out mini-projects in relation to certain modules. The accent on the chapters in Parts Two and Three is on the practice of social research and as such will be extremely useful in helping students make informed decisions about doing their research. In addition, when each research method is examined, its uses and limitations are explored in order to help with students' decisions. In Part Four, Chapter 23 provides advice on writing up research. But most signficantly, Chapter 25 has been written specifically for students doing research projects.

In addition to providing students with practical advice on doing social research, the book also explores the nature of social research. This means that it attends to issues relating to fundamental concerns about what doing social research entails. For example:

- Is a natural science model of the research process applicable to the study of people and society?
- If not, why not?
- Why do some people feel it is inappropriate to employ such a model?
- If we do use a natural science model, does that mean that we are making certain assumptions about the nature of social reality?
- Equally, do those writers and researchers who reject such a model have an alternative set of assumptions about the nature of social reality?
- What kind or kinds of research findings are regarded as legitimate and acceptable?
- To what extent do values have an impact on the research process?
- Should we worry about the feelings of people outside the research community concerning what we do to people during our investigations?

These and many other issues impinge on social research in a variety of ways and will be confronted at different stages throughout the book. While knowing how to do research—how best to design a questionnaire, how to observe, how to analyse the mass media, and so on—is crucial to an education in research methods, so too is a broad appreciation of the wider issues that impinge on the practice of social research.

The structure of the book

Social research has many different traditions, one of the most fundamental of which is the distinction between quantitative and qualitative research. This distinction lies behind much of the book in terms of its structure and the way in which issues and methods are approached.

This book is divided into four parts.

Part One comprises two scene setting chapters. It deals with basic ideas about the nature of social research. Chapter 1 examines such issues as the nature of the relationship between theory and research and the degree to which a natural science approach is an appropriate framework for the study of society. It is here that the distinction between quantitative and qualitative research is first encountered. They are presented as different research strategies with different ways of conceptualizing how people and society should be studied. It is also shown that there is more to the distinction between them than whether an investigation includes the collection of quantitative data. In Chapter 2, the idea of a research design is introduced. This chapter allows an introduction to the basic frameworks within which social research is carried out, such as social survey research, case study research, and experimental research. These two chapters provide the basic building blocks for the rest of the book.

Part Two contains ten chapters concerned with quantitative research. The first chapter explores the nature of quantitative research and as such provides a context for the later chapters. The next four chapters are largely concerned with aspects of social survey research. Chapter 4 deals with sampling. Chapter 5 is concerned with the kind of interviewing that takes place in survey research. Chapter 6 covers the design of questionnaires. Chapter 7 examines the issue of how to ask questions. Chapter 8 covers structured observation, which is a method that has been developed for the systematic observation of social behaviour. Chapter 9 presents content analysis, a method that provides a rigorous framework for the analysis of a wide range of documents. Chapter 10 deals with the analysis of data collected by other researchers and by official bodies. The emphasis then switches to the ways in which we can analyse quantitative data. Chapter 11 presents a range of basic tools for the analysis of quantitative data. The approach taken is non-technical. The emphasis is upon how to choose a method of analysis and how to interpret the findings. No formulae are presented. Finally, Chapter 12 shows you how to use computer software—in the form of SPSS, the most widely used software for analysing quantitative data—in order to implement the techniques you learned in Chapter 11.

Students pursuing a module in just quantitative research would need to read all of the chapters to this point. Students pursuing a module in survey research would need to read Chapters 2–7, along with Chapters 11 and 12 if the course includes data analysis.

Part Three contains eight chapters on aspects of qualitative research. Chapter 13 has the same role in relation to Part Three as Chapter 3 has in relation to Part Two. It provides an overview of the nature of qualitative research and as such provides the context for the other chapters in this part. Chapter 14 is concerned with ethnography and participant observation, which are the source of some of the best known studies in the social sciences. The two terms are often used interchangeably and refer to the immersion of the researcher in a social setting. Chapter 15 deals with the kinds of interview that qualitative researchers conduct. Chapter 16 explores the focus group method, whereby groups of individuals are interviewed on a specific topic. Chapter 17 examines two ways in which qualitative researchers analyse language: conversation analysis and discourse analysis. Chapter 18 deals with the examination of documents in qualitative research. The emphasis then shifts to the analysis of qualitative data. Chapter 19 explores some approaches to the analysis of qualitative data. Chapter 20 shows you how to use computer software—a relatively new development in qualitative research—to assist with your analysis.

It is striking that certain issues recur across Parts Two and Three: interviewing, observation, documents, and data analysis. However, as you will see, quantitative and qualitative research constitute contrasting approaches to such activities.

Part Four contains chapters that go beyond the quantitative/qualitative contrast. Chapter 21 deals with some of the ways in which the distinction between quantitative and qualitative research is less fixed than is sometimes supposed. Chapter 22 presents some ways in which they can be combined to produce what is referred to as multi-strategy research. Chapter 23 has been included to help with writing up research. Chapter 24 considers the ways in which ethical issues impinge on researchers and the kinds of principles that are involved. Chapter 25 offers advice on doing your own research project.

Special features of the book

Several special features have been included in order to make the book helpful.

- *Examples*. It is often said that the three most important features to look for when buying a house are location, location, location. I think that a parallel for the teaching of research methods is examples, examples, examples. I have always learned a lot by reading research and finding out how others have carried out research and what lessons they seem to have learned. In view of this, the book is full of examples. I have tried to illustrate most of my major points with an example and often more than one.

- *Boxes*. The text is full of boxes. These do a variety of things. Sometimes they provide examples; sometimes they define key terms (What is . . .); sometimes they list series of important points. They help to break up the text and to provide a focus for definitions and for key examples.

- *Reader's guide.* Each chapter begins with a reader's guide that takes you through the main areas to be covered in each chapter. They are meant to provide you with a route map of what is to follow.

- *Key points.* At the end of each chapter there is a set of significant points that are particularly crucial for you to take note of. They are meant to alert you to issues that are especially important and to jog your memory about the areas that have been covered.

- *Revision questions.* At the end of each chapter there is also a series of questions to help you to test your understanding of key concepts and ideas.

- *Glossary.* At the end of the book is a glossary of definitions of central terms. Many repeat definitions in the What is . . . boxes, but they also provide a convenient way of knowing what is meant by key terms.

The book is supplemented by a website containing additional material for students and lecturers, including a powerpoint lecture series:

www.oup.com/uk/best.textbooks/sociology/bryman

Part One

Part One of this book is concerned with two ideas that will recur again and again during the course of this book—the idea of research strategy and the idea of research design. Chapter 1 outlines a variety of considerations that impinge on the practice of social research and relates these to the issue of research strategy. Two research strategies are identified: quantitative and qualitative research. Chapter 2 identifies the different kinds of research design that are employed.

These chapters provide some basic conceptual building blocks that you will return to at many points in the book. Some of the issues may seem remote from research practice but they are in fact important aspects of how we think about social research.

1 Social research strategies

Reader's guide

The chief aim of this chapter is to show that a variety of considerations enter into the process of doing social research. The distinction that is commonly drawn among writers on and practitioners of social research between *quantitative research* and *qualitative research* is explored in relation to these considerations. This chapter explores:

- the nature of the relationship between theory and research, in particular whether theory guides research (known as a *deductive* approach) or whether theory is an outcome of research (known as an *inductive* approach);

- *epistemological* issues—that is, ones to do with what is regarded as appropriate knowledge about the social world, one of the most crucial aspects is the question of whether or not a natural science model of the research process is suitable for the study of the social world;

- *ontological* issues—that is, ones to do with whether the social world is regarded as something external to social actors or as something that people are in the process of fashioning;

- the ways in which these issues relate to the widely used distinction in the social sciences between two types of *research strategy*: quantitative and qualitative research; there is also a preliminary discussion, which will be followed up in Chapter 21, that suggests that, while quantitative and qualitative research represent different approaches to social research, we should be wary of driving a wedge between them;

- the ways in which *values* and *practical issues* also impinge on the social research process.

Introduction

This book is about social research. It attempts to equip people who have some knowledge of the social sciences with an appreciation of how social research should be conducted and what it entails. The latter project involves situating social research in the context of sociology, which in turn means attending to the question of its role in the overall enterprise of the discipline. It would be much easier to 'cut to the chase' and explore the nature of methods of social research and provide advice on how best to choose between and implement them. After all, many people might expect a book with the title of the present one to be concerned mainly with the ways in which the different methods in the social researcher's arsenal can be employed.

But the practice of social research does not exist in a bubble, hermetically sealed off from the social sciences and the various intellectual allegiances that their practitioners hold. Two points are of particular relevance here. First, methods of social research are closely tied to different visions of how social reality should be studied. Methods are not simply neutral tools: they are linked with the ways in which social scientists envision the connection between different viewpoints about the nature of social reality and how it should be examined. However, it is possible to

overstate this point. While methods are not neutral, they are not entirely suffused with intellectual inclinations either. Secondly, there is the question of how research methods and practice connect with the wider social scientific enterprise. Research data are invariably collected in relation to something. The 'something' may be a burning social problem or, more usually, a theory.

This is not to suggest that research is entirely dictated by theoretical concerns. One sometimes finds simple 'fact-finding' exercises published. Fenton *et al.* (1998) conducted a quantitative content analysis of social research reported in the British mass media. They examined national and regional newspapers, television and radio, and also magazines. They admit that one of the main reasons for conducting the research was to establish the amount and types of research that are represented. Sometimes, such exercises are motivated by a concern about a pressing social problem. McKeganey and Barnard (1996) conducted qualitative research involving observation and interviews with prostitutes and their clients in Glasgow. One factor that seems to have prompted this research was the concern about the role of prostitutes in spreading HIV infection (McKeganey and Barnard 1996: 3). Another scenario occurs when research is done on a topic when a specific opportunity arises. The interest of Westergaard *et al.* (1989) in the effects of redundancy seems to have been profoundly motivated by the opportunity that arose when a Sheffield steel company, which was close to their institutional base at the University of Sheffield, made a large number of people redundant. The firm's management approached the authors a year after the redundancies to conduct research on what happened to the individuals who had been made redundant. The authors conducted social survey research using a structured interview approach on most of those made redundant. Of course, the authors were influenced by theories about and previous research on unemployment, but the specific impetus for the research on the effects of redundancy was not planned. Yet another stimulus for research can arise out of personal experiences.

Lofland and Lofland (1995) note that many research publications emerge out of the researcher's personal biography, such as Zukin's (1982) interest in loft living arising out of her living in a loft in New York City. Certainly, my own interest in Disney theme parks can be tracked back to a visit to Disney World in Florida in 1991 (Bryman 1995, 1998), while my interest in the representation of social science research in the mass media (Fenton *et al.* 1998) can almost certainly be attributed to a difficult experience with the press reported in Haslam and Bryman (1994).

By and large, however, research data achieve significance in sociology when viewed in relation to theoretical concerns. This raises the issue of the nature of the relationship between theory and research.

Theory and research

Characterizing the nature of the link between theory and research is by no means a straightforward matter. There are several issues at stake here, but two stand out in particular. First, there is the question of what form of theory one is talking about. Secondly, there is the matter of whether data are collected to test or to build theories.

What type of theory?

The term 'theory' is used in a variety of different ways, but its most common meaning is as an explanation of observed regularities, for example, why sufferers of schizophrenia are more likely to come from working-class than middle-class backgrounds, or why work alienation varies by technology. But such theories tend not to be the stuff of courses in sociological theory, which typically focus much more on theories with a higher level of abstraction. Examples of such theories include structural-functionalism, symbolic interactionism, critical theory, poststruc-

turalism, structuration theory, and so on. What we see here is a distinction between theories of the former type, which are often called *theories of the middle range* (Merton 1967), and *grand theories*, which operate at a more abstract and general level. According to Merton, grand theories offer few indications to researchers as to how they might guide or influence the collection of empirical evidence. So, if someone wanted to test a theory or to draw an inference from it that could be tested, the level of abstractness is likely to be so great that the researcher would find it difficult to make the necessary links with the real world. There is a paradox here, of course. Even highly abstract ideas, such as Parsons's notions of 'pattern variables' and 'functional requisites', must have some connection with an external reality, in that they are likely to have been generated out of Parsons's reading of research or his reflections upon that reality or others' writings on it. However, the level of abstractness of the theorizing is so great as to make it difficult for them to be deployed in research. For research purposes, then, Merton argued that grand theories are of limited use in connection with social research, although, as the example in Box 1.1 suggests, an abstract theory like structuration theory (Giddens 1984) can have some pay-off in research terms. Instead, middle-range theories are 'intermediate to general theories of social systems which are too remote from particular classes of social behavior, organization and change to account for what is observed and to those detailed orderly descriptions of particulars that are not generalized at all' (Merton 1967: 39).

By and large, then, it is not grand theory that typically guides social research. Middle-range theories are much more likely to be the focus of empirical enquiry. In fact, Merton formulated the idea as a means of bridging what he saw as a growing gulf between theory (in the sense of grand theory) and empirical findings. This is not to say that there were no middle-range theories before he wrote: there definitely were, but what Merton did was to seek to clarify what is meant by 'theory' when social scientists write about the relationship between theory and research.

Middle-range theories, unlike grand ones, operate in a limited domain, whether it is juvenile delinquency, racial prejudice, educational attainment, or the labour process (see Box 1.2). They vary somewhat in their range of application. For example,

labelling theory represents a middle-range theory in the sociology of deviance. Its exponents sought to understand deviance in terms of the causes and effects of the societal reaction to deviation. It was held to be applicable to a variety of different forms of deviance, including crime and mental illness. By contrast, Cloward and Ohlin's (1960) differential association theory was formulated specifically in connection with juvenile delinquency and in subsequent years this tended to be its focus. Middle-range theories, then, fall somewhere between grand theories and empirical findings. They represent attempts to understand and explain a limited aspect of social life.

Even the grand/middle-range distinction does not entirely clarify the issues involved in asking the deceptively simple question of 'what is theory?'. This is because the term 'theory' is frequently used in a manner that means little more than the background literature in an area of social enquiry. To a certain extent, this point can be taken to apply to fact-finding exercises such as those referred to above. The analysis of the representation of social research in the media by Fenton et al. (1998) was undertaken against a background of similar analyses in the USA and of studies of the representation of natural science research in the media in several different countries. In many cases, the relevant back-

Box 1.1 Grand theory and social research

Giddens's (1984) structuration theory represents an attempt to bridge the gulf between notions of structure and agency in social life and was the theoretical backcloth to an article by Layder et al. (1991). The empirical focus of research was the transition from school to work among British 18–24 year olds from four different labour markets. Data were generated through structured interviews and were quantitative. The data allowed the researchers to tease out the relative influence of structural variables (such as, class, gender, and unemployment levels) and individual variables (such as whether the individual had A levels, attitudinal factors such as whether or not respondents considered their futures when choosing jobs, and behavioural factors like a

willingness to travel or use informal job search methods). The authors found that the relative importance of structural and individual (agency) variables differed between the six different job segments identified by the authors (for example, clerical, skilled, semi-skilled, and unskilled segments). The authors had hypothesized, on the basis of structuration theory, that individual variables would be more significant in connection with higher socio-economic segments and that structural variables would be more significant for lower segments. In fact, the pattern of findings proved more complicated than this and cast some doubt on aspects of the theory. For example, gender was found to be an important factor among all job segment levels.

Box 1.2 Labour process theory: A middle-range theory

In the sociology of work, labour process theory can be regarded as a middle-range theory. The publication of *Labor and Monopoly Capital* (Braverman 1974) inaugurated a stream of thinking and research around the idea of the labour process and in particular on the degree to which there has been an inexorable trend towards greater and greater control over the manual worker and deskilling of manual labour. A conference volume of much of this work was published as *Labour Process Theory* (Knights and Willmott 1990). P. Thompson (1989) described the theory as having four elements: the principle that the labour process entails the extraction of surplus value; the need for capitalist enterprises constantly to transform production processes; the quest for control over labour; and the essential conflict between capital and labour. Labour process theory has been the focus of considerable empirical research (e.g. Knights *et al.* 1985).

---

ground literature relating to a topic fuels the focus of an article or book and thereby acts as the equivalent of a theory, as with the research referred to in Box 1.3.

In articles or books like Sullivan's (1996) article reported in Box 1.3, there are no, or virtually no, allusions to theories. Instead, the literature in a certain domain acts as the spur to an enquiry. The literature acts as an impetus in a number of ways: the researcher may seek to resolve an inconsistency between different findings or between different interpretations of findings; the researcher may have spotted a neglected aspect of a topic (in a sense, this is what Duncombe and Marsden (1993) did, and which influenced Sullivan—see Box 1.3); certain ideas may not previously have been tested; the researcher may feel that existing approaches being used for research on a topic are deficient, and so provides an alternative approach; and so on.

Social scientists are sometimes prone to being somewhat dismissive of research that has no obvious connections with theory—in either the grand or middle-range senses of the term. Such research is often dismissed as naive *empiricism* (see Box 1.4). It would be harsh, not to say inaccurate, to brand as naive empiricism the numerous studies in which the publications-as-theory strategy is employed, simply because their authors have not been preoccupied with theory. Such research is conditioned by and directed towards research questions that arise out of an interrogation of the literature. The data collection and analysis are subsequently geared to the illumination or resolution of the research issue or

---

Box 1.3 Background literature as theory: The case of 'emotion work' among couples

Sullivan (1996) collected data from 380 heterosexual couples concerning the amounts of time they spent in different activities either separately or together. The data were derived from a technique known as time use diaries, which are used rather infrequently by social scientists. She wanted to collect data that were concerned not just with the domestic division of labour between husbands and wives (who does what in the household?) but also with levels of enjoyment. Her findings show that many couples derive particular emotional satisfaction from those activities conducted together. While research into the relationship between women's paid and unpaid work and into the domestic division of labour provided important components of the concerns of Sullivan's research, of particular significance was Duncombe and Marsden's (1993) article, which argued that, unlike their North American counterparts, British sociologists have been relatively indifferent to intimacy and hence to the emotional dimensions of households. The findings are taken to suggest that 'certain activities are . . . more enjoyed when done together' (Sullivan 1996: 96) and are interpreted in terms of the existing literature.

Box 1.4 ⌁◠⌁ *What is empiricism?*

The term 'empiricism' is used in a number of different ways, but two stand out. First, it is used to denote a general approach to the study of reality that suggests that only knowledge gained through experience and the senses is acceptable. In other words, this position means that ideas must be subjected to the rigours of testing before they can be considered knowledge. The second meaning of the term is related to this and refers to a belief that the accumulation of 'facts' is a legitimate goal in its own right. It is this second meaning that is sometimes referred to as 'naive empiricism'.

problem that has been identified at the outset. The literature acts as a proxy for theory. In many instances, theory is latent or implicit in the literature.

Indeed, research that appears to have the characteristics of the 'fact-finding exercise' should not be prematurely dismissed as naive empiricism either. McKeganey and Barnard's (1996) research on prostitutes and their clients is a case in point. On the face of it, even if one strips away the concern with HIV infection, the research could be construed as naive empiricism and perhaps of a rather prurient kind. However, this again would be a harsh and probably inaccurate judgement. For example, the authors relate their research findings to the literature reporting other investigations of prostitutes in a number of different countries. They also illuminate their findings by drawing on ideas that are very much part of the sociologist's conceptual tool kit. One example is Goffman's (1963) notion of 'stigma' and the way in which the stigmatized individual seeks to manage a spoiled identity; another is Hochschild's (1983) concept of 'emotional labour', a term she coined to denote the way in which airline flight attendants contrive a demeanour of friendliness when dealing with passengers, some of whom may be extremely difficult.

It is not possible to tell from McKeganey and Barnard's (1996) report whether the concepts of stigma

and emotional labour influenced their data collection. However, raising this question invites consideration of another question: insofar as any piece of research is linked to theory, what was the role of that theory? Up to this point, I have tended to write as though theory is something that guides and influences the collection and analysis of data. In other words, research is done in order to answer questions posed by theoretical considerations. But an alternative position is to view theory as something that occurs after the collection and analysis of some or all of the data associated with a project. We begin to see here the significance of a second factor in considering the relationship between theory and research—whether we are referring to deductive or inductive theory.

Deductive and inductive theory

Deductive theory represents the commonest view of the nature of the relationship between theory and social research. The researcher, on the basis of what is known about in a particular domain and of theoretical considerations in relation to that domain, deduces a hypothesis (or hypotheses) that must then be subjected to empirical scrutiny. Embedded within the hypothesis will be concepts that will need to be translated into researchable entities. The social scientist must both skilfully deduce a hypothesis and then translate it into operational terms. This means that the social scientist needs to specify how data can be collected in relation to the concepts that make up the hypothesis.

This view of the role of theory in relation to research is very much the kind of role that Merton had in mind in connection with middle-range theory, which, he argued, 'is principally used in sociology to guide empirical inquiry' (Merton 1967: 39). Theory and the hypothesis deduced from it come first and drive the process of gathering data (see Box 1.5 for an example of a deductive approach to the relationship between theory and data). The sequence can be depicted as one in which the steps outlined in Figure 1.1 take place.

The last step involves a movement that is in the

Box 1.5 A deductive study

Kelley and De Graaf (1997) show that a number of studies have examined the factors that have an impact upon individuals' religious beliefs, such as parents, schools and friends, but they also argue that there are good grounds for thinking that the nation into which one is born will be an important cross-cultural factor. These reflections constitute what they refer to as the 'theory' that guided their research and from which the following hypothesis was derived: 'People born into religious nations will, in proportion to the orthodoxy of their fellow-citizens, acquire more orthodox beliefs than otherwise similar people born into secular nations' (1997: 641). There are two central concepts in this hypothesis that would need to be measured: national religiosity (whether it is religious or secular) and individual religious orthodoxy. The authors hypothesized further that the religious orientation of the individual's family (whether devout or secular) would affect the nature of the relationship between national religiosity and religious orthodoxy.

To test the hypotheses a secondary analysis was conducted on large sample survey research from fifteen nations. UK readers will be interested to know that the British and Northern Irish (and Irish Republic) data were derived from the British Social Attitudes survey for 1991 (Jowell *et al*. 1992). Religious orthodoxy was measured by four survey questions concerned with religious belief. The questions asked about (1) whether the person believed in God, (2) their past beliefs about God, (3) how close the individual felt to God, and (4) whether he or she felt that God cares about everyone. To measure national religiosity, the fifteen nations were classified into one of five categories ascending from secular to religious. The classification was undertaken according to 'an unweighted average of parental church attendance . . . and religious belief in the nation as a whole' (1997: 647). Family religious orientation was measured on a scale of five levels of parental church attendance. The hypotheses were broadly confirmed and the authors conclude that the 'religious environment of a nation has a major impact on the beliefs of its citizens' (1997: 654). Some of the implications of the findings for theories about international differences in religiosity are then outlined.

1. Theory
   ↓
2. Hypothesis
   ↓
3. Data collection
   ↓
4. Findings
   ↓
5. Hypotheses confirmed or rejected
   ↓
6. Revision of theory

Fig. 1.1 The process of deduction

opposite direction from deduction—it involves *induction*, as the researcher infers the implications of his or her findings for the theory that prompted the whole exercise. The findings are fed back into the stock of theory and the research findings associated with a certain domain of enquiry. This can be seen in the case of Layder *et al*.'s (1991) final reflections on the implications of their findings for structuration

theory (see Box 1.1): 'Thus we conclude that empirically structure and action [i.e. agency] are interdependent . . . but partly autonomous and separate domains. In this respect our findings lead us to conclude that the empirical applicability of structuration theory concerning the interconnection between structural and individual variables is somewhat more limited than has hitherto been acknowledged' (Layder *et al*. 1991: 461). However, while this element of inductiveness undoubtedly exists in the approach outlined, it is typically deemed to be predominantly deductive in orientation. Moreover, it is important to bear in mind that, when this deductive approach, which is usually associated with quantitative research, is put into operation, it often does not follow the sequence outlined in its pure form. As previously noted, 'theory' may be little more than the literature on a certain topic in the form of the accumulated knowledge gleaned from books and articles. Also, even when theory or theories can be discerned, explicit hypotheses are not always deduced from them in the way that Kelley and De Graaf (1997) did in Box 1.5. A further point to bear in mind is that the deductive process appears very linear—one step follows the other in a clear, logical sequence. However, there are many instances where this is not the case: a researcher's view of the theory or literature may have changed as a result of the analysis of the collected data; new theoretical ideas or findings may be published by others before the researcher has generated his or her findings; or, as in the case of Layder *et al.* (1991), the relevance of a set of data for a theory may become apparent *after* the data have been collected.

This may all seem rather surprising and confusing. There is a certain logic to the idea of developing theories and then testing them. In everyday contexts, we commonly think of theories as things that are quite illuminating but that need to be tested before they can be considered valid or useful. In point of fact, however, while the process of deduction outlined in Figure 1.1 does undoubtedly occur, it is better considered as a general orientation to the link between theory and research. As a general orientation, its broad contours may frequently be discernible in social research, but it is also the case that we often find departures from it.

However, in some research *no* attempt is made to follow the sequence outlined in Figure 1.1. Some researchers prefer an approach to the relationship between theory and research that is primarily *inductive*. With an inductive stance, theory is the *outcome* of research. In other words, the process of induction involves drawing generalizable inferences out of observations. To put it crudely, whereas deduction entails a process in which

theory → observations/findings

with induction the connection is reversed

observations/findings → theory.

However, just as deduction entails an element of induction, the inductive process is likely to entail a modicum of deduction. Once the phase of theoretical reflection on a set of data has been carried out, the researcher may want to collect further data in order to establish the conditions in which a theory

will and will not hold. Such a general strategy is often called *iterative*: it involves a weaving back and forth between data and theory. It is particularly evident in *grounded theory*, which will be examined in Chapter 19, but in the meantime the basic point is to note that induction represents an alternative strategy for linking theory and research, although it contains a deductive element too.

However, as with 'theory' in connection with the deductive approach to the relationship between theory and research, we have to be cautious about the use of the term in the context of the inductive strategy too. While some researchers undoubtedly develop theories, equally it is necessary to be aware that very often what one ends up with can often be little more than empirical generalizations of the kind Merton (1967) wrote about. In Box 1.6 is an example of research that can be classified as inductive in the sense that it develops a theory out of interview data deriving from men suffering from chronic illness concerning what determines successful coping mechanisms for males afflicted with such a condition. In fact, the analytic strategy adopted by the author (Charmaz 1997) was grounded theory, and it is certainly the case that many of the most prominent examples of inductive research derive from this tradition (see the other chapters in Strauss and Corbin, 1997, from which Charmaz's example was taken).

Charmaz's (1997) research is an interesting illustration of an inductive approach. Two points are particularly worth noting about it. First, as previously noted, it uses a grounded theory approach to the analysis of data and to the generation of theory. This approach, which was first outlined by Glaser and Strauss (1967), is often regarded as especially strong in terms of generating theories out of data. This contrasts with the nature of many supposedly inductive studies, which generate interesting and illuminating findings but whose theoretical significance is not entirely clear. They provide insightful empirical generalizations, but little theory. Secondly, in much the same way that the deductive strategy is associated with a quantitative research approach, an inductive strategy of linking data and theory is typically associated with a qualitative research approach. It is

---

Box 1.6 An inductive study

Charmaz (1991, 1997) has been concerned to examine a number of aspects of the experiences of people with chronic illness. One phase of her research has entailed the examination specifically of men with such a condition. In one of her reports (Charmaz 1997), she discusses the results of her research into twenty men suffering from chronic illness. The bulk of her data derive from semi-structured interviews. In order to bring out the distinct-iveness of men's responses, she compared the findings relating to men with a parallel study of women with chronic illness. She argues that a key component of men's responses is that of a strategy of *preserving self*. Although the experience of chronic illness invariably necessitates a change of lifestyle that itself occasions a change in personal identity, the men sought to preserve their sense of self by drawing on 'essential qualities, attributes, and identities of [the] past self' (1997: 49). By contrast, women were less reliant in their strategies of preserving self on the recapturing of past identities. She relates her theoretical reflections of her data to her male respond-ents' notions of masculine identity. Her emphasis on the idea of preserving self allows her to assess the factors that lie behind whether a man with chronic illness will 'reconstruct a positive identity or sink into depression' (1997: 57). If they were unable to have access to actions that would allow their sense of past self to be extended into the future (for example, through work), the prob-ability of their sinking into depression was enhanced.

---

not a coincidence that Charmaz's (1997) research referred to in Box 1.6 is based on in-depth, semi-structured interviews that produced qualitative data in the form of respondents' detailed answers to her questions. However, as will be shown below, this characterization of the inductive strategy as associated with qualitative research is not entirely straight-forward: not only does much qualitative research *not* generate theory, but also theory is often used at the very least as a background to qualitative investigations.

It is useful to think of the relationship between theory and research in terms of deductive and inductive strategies. However, as the previous dis-cussion has implied, the issues are not as clear-cut as they are sometimes presented. To a large extent, deductive and inductive strategies are possibly bet-ter thought of as tendencies rather than as a hard-and-fast distinction. But these are not the only issues that impinge on the conduct of social research.

Epistemological considerations

An epistemological issue concerns the question of what is (or should be) regarded as acceptable know-ledge in a discipline. A particularly central issue in this context is the question of whether the social world can and should be studied according to the same principles, procedures, and ethos as the natural sciences. The position that affirms the importance of imitating the natural sciences is invariably associated with an epistemological position known as *positivism* (see Box 1.7).

A natural science epistemology: positivism

The doctrine of positivism is extremely difficult to pin down and therefore to outline in a precise man-ner, because it is used in a number of different ways by authors. For some writers, it is a descriptive category—one that describes a philosophical pos-ition that can be discerned in research—though there are still disagreements about what it comprises;

Box 1.7   What is positivism?

Positivism is an epistemological position that advocates the application of the methods of the natural sciences to the study of social reality and beyond. But the term stretches beyond this principle, though the constituent elements vary between authors. However, positivism is also taken to entail the following:

1. Only phenomena and hence knowledge confirmed by the senses can genuinely be warranted as knowledge (the principle of *phenomenalism*).

2. The purpose of theory is to generate hypotheses that can be tested and that will thereby allow explanations of laws to be assessed (the principle of *deductivism*).

3. Knowledge is arrived at through the gathering of facts that provide the basis for laws (the principle of *inductivism*).

4. Science must (and presumably can) be conducted in a way that is value free (that is, *objective*).

5. There is a clear distinction between scientific statements and normative statements and a belief that the former are the true domain of the scientist. This last principle is implied by the first because the truth or otherwise of normative statements cannot be confirmed by the senses.

---

for others, it is a pejorative term used to describe crude and often superficial data collection.

It is possible to see in the five principles in Box 1.7 a link with some of the points that have already been raised about the relationship between theory and research. For example, positivism entails elements of both a deductive approach (2) and an inductive strategy (3). Also, a fairly sharp distinction is drawn between theory and research. The role of research is to test theories and to provide material for the development of laws. But either of these connections between theory and research carries with it the implication that it is possible to collect observations in a manner that is not influenced by pre-existing theories. Moreover, theoretical terms that are not directly amenable to observation are not considered genuinely scientific; they must be susceptible to the rigours of observation. All of this carries with it the implication of greater epistemological status being given to observation than to theory.

It should be noted that it is a mistake to treat positivism as synonymous with science and the scientific. In fact, philosophers of science and of the social sciences differ quite sharply over how best to characterize scientific practice, and since the early 1960s there has been a drift away from viewing it in positivist terms. Thus, when writers complain about the limitations of positivism, it is not entirely clear whether they mean the philosophical term or a sci-

entific approach more generally. *Realism* (in particular, *critical realism*), for example, is another philosophical position that purports to provide an account of the nature of scientific practice (see Box 1.8).

The crux of the epistemological considerations that form the central thrust of this section is the rejection by some writers and traditions of the application of the canons of the natural sciences to the study of social reality. A difficulty here is that it is not easy to disentangle the natural science model from positivism as the butt of their criticisms. In other words, it is not always clear whether they are inveighing against the application of a general natural scientific approach or of positivism in particular. There is a long-standing debate about the appropriateness of the natural science model for the study of society, but, since the account that is offered of that model tends to have largely positivist overtones, it would seem that it is positivism that is the focus of attention rather than other accounts of scientific practice (such as critical realism—see Box 1.8).

Interpretivism

Interpretivism is a term given to a contrasting epistemology to positivism (see Box 1.9). The term subsumes the views of writers who have been critical of

Box 1.8 What is realism?

Realism shares two features with positivism: a belief that the natural and the social sciences can and should apply the same kinds of approach to the collection of data and to explanation, and a commitment to the view that there is an external reality to which scientists direct their attention (in other words, there is a reality that is separate from our descriptions of it). There are two major forms of realism:

- *Empirical realism* simply asserts that, through the use of appropriate methods, reality can be understood. As such, it 'fails to recognise that there are enduring structures and generative mechanisms underlying and producing observable phenomena and events' and is therefore 'superficial' (Bhaskar 1989: 2). This is perhaps the most common meaning of the term. When writers employ the term 'realism' in a general way, it is invariably this meaning to which they are referring.

- *Critical realism* is a specific form of realism whose manifesto is to recognize the reality of the natural order and the events and discourses of the social world and holds that 'we will only be able to understand—and so change—the social world if we identify the structures at work that generate those events and discourses. . . .

These structures are not spontaneously apparent in the observable pattern of events; they can only be identified through the practical and theoretical work of the social sciences' (Bhaskar 1989: 2).

Critical realism implies two things. First, it implies that, whereas positivists take the view that the scientist's conceptualization of reality actually directly reflects that reality, realists argue that the scientist's conceptualization is simply a way of knowing that reality. As Bhaskar (1975: 250) has put it: 'Science, then, is the systematic attempt to express in thought the structures and ways of acting of things that exist and act independently of thought'. Secondly, by implication, critical realists unlike positivists are perfectly content to admit into their explanations theoretical terms that are not directly amenable to observation. As a result, hypothetical entities to account for regularities in the natural or social orders (the 'generative mechanisms' to which Bhaskar refers) are perfectly admissible for realists, but not for positivists. What makes critical realism *critical* is that the identification of generative mechanisms offers the prospect of introducing changes that can transform the status quo.

---

the application of the scientific model to the study of the social world and who have been influenced by different intellectual traditions, which are outlined below. They share a view that the subject matter of the social sciences—people and their institutions—is fundamentally different from that of the natural

Box 1.9 What is interpretivism?

Interpretivism is taken to denote an alternative to the positivist orthodoxy that has held sway for decades. It is predicated upon the view that a strategy is required that respects the differences between people and the objects of the natural sciences and therefore requires the social scientist to grasp the subjective meaning of social action. Its intellectual heritage includes: Weber's notion of *Verstehen*; the hermeneutic–phenomenological tradition; and symbolic interactionism.

sciences. The study of the social world therefore requires a different logic of research procedure, one that reflects the distinctiveness of humans as against the natural order. Von Wright (1971) has depicted the epistemological clash as being between positivism and *hermeneutics* (a term that is drawn from theology and that, when imported into the social sciences, is concerned with the theory and method of the interpretation of human action). This clash reflects a division between an emphasis on the *explanation* of human behaviour that is the chief ingredient of the positivist approach to the social sciences and the *understanding* of human behaviour. The latter is concerned with the empathic understanding of human action rather than with the forces that are deemed to act on it. This contrast reflects long-standing debates that precede the emergence of the modern social sciences but find their expression in such notions as the advocacy by Max Weber (1864–1920) of a *Verstehen* approach.

Weber described Sociology as a 'science which attempts the interpretive understanding of social action in order to arrive at a causal explanation of its course and effects' (1947: 88). Weber's definition seems to embrace both explanation *and* understanding here, but the crucial point is that the task of 'causal explanation' is undertaken with reference to the 'interpretive understanding of social action' rather than to external forces that have no meaning for those involved in that social action.

One of the main intellectual traditions that has been responsible for the anti-positivist position has been *phenomenology*, a philosophy that is concerned with the question of how individuals make sense of the world around them and how in particular the philosopher should bracket out preconceptions in his or her grasp of that world. The initial application of phenomenological ideas to the social sciences is attributed to the work of Alfred Schutz (1899–1959), whose work did not come to the notice of most English-speaking social scientists until the translation from German of his major writings in the 1960s, some twenty or more years after they had been written. His work was profoundly influenced by Weber's concept of *Verstehen*, as well as by phenomenological philosophers, like Husserl. Schutz's position is well captured in the following passage, which has been quoted on numerous occasions:

The world of nature as explored by the natural scientist does not 'mean' anything to molecules, atoms and electrons. But the observational field of the social scientist— social reality—has a specific meaning and relevance structure for the beings living, acting, and thinking within it. By a series of common-sense constructs they have pre-selected and pre-interpreted this world which they experience as the reality of their daily lives. It is these thought objects of theirs which determine their behaviour by motivating it. The thought objects constructed by the social scientist, in order to grasp this social reality, have to be founded upon the thought objects constructed by the common-sense thinking of men [and women!], living their daily life within the social world.   (Schutz 1962: 59)

Two points are particularly noteworthy in this quotation. First, it asserts that there is a fundamental difference between the subject matter of the natural and the social sciences and that an epistemology is required that will reflect and capitalize upon that difference. The fundamental difference resides in the fact that social reality has a meaning for human beings and therefore human action is meaningful— that is, it has a meaning for them and they act on the basis of the meanings that they attribute to their acts and to the acts of others. This leads to the second point—namely, that it is the job of the social scientist to gain access to people's 'common-sense thinking' and hence to interpret their actions and their social world from their point of view. It is this particular feature that social scientists claiming allegiance to phenomenology have typically emphasized. In the words of the authors of a research methods text whose approach is described as phenomenological: 'The phenomenologist views human behavior ... as a product of how people interpret the world. ... In order to grasp the meanings of a person's behavior, *the phenomenologist attempts to see things from that person's point of view'* (Bogdan and Taylor 1975: 13–14, emphasis in original).

In this exposition of *Verstehen* and phenomenology, it has been necessary to skate over some complex issues. In particular, Weber's examination of *Verstehen* is far more complex than the above commentary suggests, because the empathetic understanding that seems to be implied above was not the way in which he applied it (Bauman 1978), while the question of what is and is not a genuinely phenomenological approach to the social sciences is a matter of some dispute (Heap and Roth 1973). However, the similarity in the writings of the hermeneutic– phenomenological tradition and of the *Verstehen* approach, with their emphasis upon social action as being meaningful to actors and therefore needing to be interpreted from their point of view, coupled with the rejection of positivism, contributed to a stream of thought often referred to as interpretivism (e.g. J. A. Hughes 1990).

Verstehen and the hermeneutic–phenomenological tradition do not exhaust the intellectual influences on interpretivism. The theoretical tradition in sociology known as *symbolic interactionism* has also been regarded by many writers as a further influence. Again, the case is not clear-cut. The implications for empirical research of the ideas of the founders of symbolic interactionism, in particular George Herbert Mead (1863–1931), whose discussion of the way in which our notion of self emerges through an appreciation of how others see us, have been hotly debated. There was a school of research, known as the Iowa school, that has drawn heavily on Mead's concepts and ideas, but has proceeded in a direction that most people would prefer to depict as largely positivist in tone (Meltzer *et al.* 1975). Moreover, some writers have argued that Mead's approach is far more consistent with a natural science approach than has typically been recognized (McPhail and Rexroat 1979). However, the general tendency has been to view symbolic interactionism as occupying similar intellectual space to the hermeneutic–phenomenological tradition and so broadly interpretative in approach. This tendency is largely the product of the writings of Herbert Blumer, a student of Mead's who acted as his mentor's spokesman and interpreter, and his followers (M. Hammersley 1989; R. Collins 1994). Not only did Blumer coin the term symbolic interaction; he also provided a gloss on Mead's writings that has decidedly interpretative overtones. Symbolic interactionists argue that interaction takes place in such a way that the individual is continually interpreting the symbolic meaning of his or her environment (which includes the actions of others) and acts on the basis of this imputed meaning. In research terms, according to Blumer (1992: 55), 'the position of symbolic interaction requires the student to catch the process of interpretation through which [actors] construct their actions', a statement that brings out clearly his views of the research implications of symbolic interactionism and of Mead's thought.

It should be appreciated that the parallelism between symbolic interactionism and the hermeneutic–phenomenological tradition should not be exaggerated. The two are united in their antipathy for positivism and have in common an interpretative stance. However, symbolic interactionism is, at least in the hands of Blumer and the many writers and researchers who have followed in his wake, a type of social theory that has distinctive epistemological implications; the hermeneutic–phenomenological tradition, by contrast, is best thought of as a general epistemological approach in its own right. Blumer may have been influenced by the hermeneutic–phenomenological tradition, but there is no concrete evidence of this. There are other intellectual currents that have affinities with the interpretative stance, such as the working-through of the ramifications of the works of the philosopher Ludwig Wittgenstein (Winch 1958), but the hermeneutic–phenomenological, *Verstehen*, and symbolic interactionist traditions can be considered major influences.

Taking an interpretative stance can mean that the researcher may come up with surprising findings, or at least findings that appear surprising if a largely external stance is taken—that is, a position from outside the particular social context being studied. Box 1.10 provides an interesting example of this possibility.

Of course, as the example in Box 1.10 suggests, when the social scientist adopts an interpretative stance, he or she is not simply laying bare how members of a social group interpret the world around them. The social scientist will almost certainly be aiming to place the interpretations that have been elicited into a social scientific frame. There is a double interpretation going on: the researcher is providing an interpretation of others' interpretations. Indeed, there is a third level of interpretation going on, because the researcher's interpretations have to be further interpreted in terms of the concepts, theories, and literature of a discipline. Thus, taking the example in Box 1.10, Foster's (1995) suggestion that Riverside is not perceived as a high crime area by residents is her interpretation of her subjects' interpretations. She then had the additional job of placing her interesting findings into a social scientific frame, which she accomplished by relating them to existing concepts and discussions in criminology of such things as informal social control, neighbourhood watch schemes, and the role of housing as a possible cause of criminal activity.

The aim of this section has been to outline how epistemological considerations—especially those

---

Box 1.10 **Interpretivism in practice**

Foster (1995) conducted ethnographic research using participant observation and semi-structured interviews in a housing estate in East London, referred to as Riverside. The estate had a high level of crime, as indicated by official statistics on crime. However, she found that residents did not perceive the estate to be a high crime area. This perception could be attributed to a number of factors, but a particularly important reason was the existence of 'informal social control'. People expected a certain level of crime, but felt fairly secure because informal social control allowed levels of crime to be contained. Informal social control comprised a number of different aspects.

One aspect was that neighbours often looked out for each other. In the words of one of Foster's interviewees: 'If I hear a bang or shouting I go out. If there's aggravation I come in and ring the police. I don't stand for it'. Another aspect of informal social control was that people often felt secure because they knew each other. Another respondent said: 'I don't feel nervous . . . because people do generally know each other. We keep an eye on each others properties . . . I feel quite safe because you know your neighbours and you know they're there . . . they look out for you' (Foster 1995: 575).

---

relating to the question of whether a natural science, and in particular a positivist, approach, can supply legitimate knowledge of the social world—are related to research practice. There is a link with the earlier section in that a deductive approach to the relationship between theory and research is typically associated with a positivist position. Box 1.7 does try to suggest that inductivism is also a feature of positivism (third principle), but, in the working-through of its implementation in the practice of social research, it is the deductive element (second principle) that tends to be emphasized. Similarly, the third level of interpretation that a researcher engaged in interpretative research must bring into operation is very much part of the kind of inductive strategy described in the previous section. However, while such interconnections between epistemological issues and research practice exist, it is important not to overstate them, since they represent tendencies rather than definitive points of correspondence. Thus, particular epistemological principles and research practices do not necessarily go hand in hand in a neat unambiguous manner. This point will be made again on several occasions and will be a special focus of Chapter 21.

Ontological considerations

Questions of social ontology are concerned with the nature of social entities. The central point of orientation here is the question of whether social entities can and should be considered objective entities that have a reality external to social actors, or whether they can and should be considered social constructions built up from the perceptions and actions of social actors. These positions are frequently referred to respectively as *objectivism* and *constructionism*. Their differences can be illustrated by reference to two of the most common and central terms in social science—organization and culture.

Objectivism

Objectivism is an ontological position that implies that social phenomena confront us as external facts that are beyond our reach or influence (see

Box 1.11). We can discuss organization or *an* organization as a tangible object. It has rules and regulations. It adopts standardized procedures for getting things done. People are appointed to different jobs within a division of labour. There is a hierarchy. It has a mission statement. And so on. The degree to which these features exist from organization to organization is variable, but in thinking in these terms we are tending to the view that an organization has a reality that is external to the individuals who inhabit it. Moreover, the organization represents a social order in that it exerts pressure on individuals to conform to the requirements of the organization. People learn and apply the rules and regulations. They follow the standardized procedures. They do the jobs to which they are appointed. People tell them what to do and they tell others what to do. They learn and apply the values in the mission statement. If they do not do these things, they may be reprimanded or even fired. The organization is therefore a constraining force that acts on and inhibits its members.

The same can be said of culture. Cultures and subcultures can be viewed as repositories of widely shared values and customs into which people are socialized so that they can function as good citizens or as full participants. Cultures and subcultures constrain us because we internalize their beliefs and values. In the case of both organization and culture, the social entity in question comes across as something external to the actor and as having an almost tangible reality of its own. It has the characteristics of an object and hence of having an objective reality. To a very large extent, these are the

'classic' ways of conceptualizing organization and culture.

Constructionism

However, we can consider an alternative ontological position—*constructionism* (Box 1.12). This position challenges the suggestion that categories such as organization and culture are pre-given and therefore confront social actors as external realities that they have no role in fashioning.

Let us take organization first. Strauss *et al.* (1973), drawing on insights from symbolic interactionism, carried out research in a psychiatric hospital and proposed that it was best conceptualized as a 'negotiated order'. Instead of taking the view that order in organizations is a pre-existing characteristic, they argue that it is worked at. Rules were far less extensive and less rigorously imposed than might be supposed from the classic account of organization. Indeed, Strauss *et al.* prefer to refer to them as 'much less like commands, and much more like general understandings' (1973: 308). Precisely because relatively little of the spheres of action of doctors, nurses, and other personnel was prescribed, the social order of the hospital was an outcome of agreed-upon patterns of action that were themselves the products of negotiations between the different parties involved. The social order is in a constant state of change because the hospital is 'a place where numerous agreements are continually being terminated or forgotten, but also as continually being established, renewed, reviewed, revoked, revised. . . . In any pragmatic sense, this is the hospital at the moment: this is its social order' (Strauss *et al.* 1973: 316–17). The authors argue that a preoccupation with the formal properties of organizations (rules, organizational charts, regulations, roles) tends to neglect the degree to which order in organizations has to be accomplished in everyday interaction, though this is not to say that the formal properties have *no* element of constraint on individual action.

Much the same kind of point can be made about the idea of culture. Instead of seeing culture as an

---

Box 1.11 🔆 *What is objectivism?*

Objectivism is an ontological position that asserts that social phenomena and their meanings have an existence that is independent of social actors. It implies that social phenomena and the categories that we use in everyday discourse have an existence that is independent or separate from actors.

Box 1.12 ⌇👁⌇ *What is constructionism?*

Constructionism is an ontological position (often also referred to as constructivism) that asserts that social phenomena and their meanings are continually being accomplished by social actors. It implies that social phenomena and categories are not only produced through social interaction but that they are in a constant state of revision.

In recent years, the term has come also to include the notion that researchers' own accounts of the social world are constructions. In other words, the researcher always presents a specific version of social reality, rather than one that can be regarded as definitive. Knowledge is viewed as indeterminate. The discussion of postmodernism in Chapter 23 further examines this viewpoint. This sense of constructionism is usually allied to the ontological version of the term. In other words, these are linked meanings.

Both meanings are antithetical to *objectivism* (see Box 1.11), but the second meaning is also antithetical to *realism* (see Box 1.8). The first meaning might be thought of usefully as constructionism in relation to the social world; the second as constructionism in relation to the nature of knowledge of the social world (and indeed the natural world).

Increasingly, the notion of constructionism in relation to the nature of knowledge of the social world is being incorporated into notions of constructionism, but in this book I will be using the term in relation to the first meaning, whereby constructionism is presented as an ontological position in relating to social objects and categories—that is, one that views them as socially constructed.

---

external reality that acts on and constrains people, it can be taken to be an emergent reality in a continuous state of construction and reconstruction. Becker (1982: 521), for example, has suggested that 'people create culture continuously. . . . No set of cultural understandings . . . provides a perfectly applicable solution to any problem people have to solve in the course of their day, and they therefore must remake those solutions, adapt their understandings to the new situation in the light of what is different about it.' Like Strauss *et al.*, Becker recognizes that the constructionist position cannot be pushed to the extreme: it is necessary to appreciate that culture has a reality that 'persists and antedates the participation of particular people' and shapes their perspectives, but it is not an inert objective reality that only possesses a sense of constraint: it acts as a point of reference but is always in the process of being formed.

Neither the work of Strauss *et al.* nor that of Becker pushes the constructionist argument to the extreme. Each admits to the pre-existence of their objects of interest (organization and culture respectively). However, in each case we see an intellectual predilection for stressing the active role of individuals in the social construction of social reality. Not all writers

adopting a constructionist position are similarly prepared to acknowledge the existence or at least importance of an objective reality. Walsh, for example, has written that 'we cannot take for granted, as the natural scientist does, the availability of a preconstituted world of phenomena for investigation' and must instead 'examine the processes by which the social world is constructed' (1972: 19). It is precisely this apparent split between viewing the social world as an objective reality and as a subjective reality in a continuous state of flux that Giddens sought to straddle in formulating his idea of structuration (see Box 1.1).

Constructionism also suggests that the categories that people employ in helping them to understand the natural and social world are in fact social products. The categories do not have built-in essences; instead, their meaning is constructed in and through interaction. Thus, a category like 'masculinity' might be treated as a social construction. This notion implies that, rather than being treated as a distinct inert entity, masculinity is construed as something whose meaning is built up during interaction. That meaning is likely to be a highly ephemeral one, in that it will vary by both time and place. This kind of stance frequently displays a concern

Box 1.13 Constructionism in action

Lantz and Booth (1998) have shown that breast cancer can be treated as a social construction. They note that US data show a rise in the incidence of the disease since the early 1980s, which has led to the depiction of the trend as an epidemic. The authors examined a variety of popular magazines using qualitative content analysis (see Box 9.1, p. 180), for a brief description of this method). They note that many of the articles draw attention to the lifestyles of modern women, such as delaying first births, diet and alcohol consumption, and having careers. The authors argue that the articles

ascribe blame to individual behaviors by listing a wide array of individual risk factors (many of which are not behaviors of 'traditional' women), and then offering prudent prescriptions for prevention. Women are portrayed as victims of an insidious disease, but also as victims of their own behaviors, many of which are related to the control of their own fertility. . . . These articles

suggest that nontraditional women experience pathological repercussions within their bodies and, in turn, may be responsible for our current epidemic of breast cancer. (Lantz and Booth 1998: 915–16)

This article suggests that, as a social category, the breast cancer epidemic is being represented in popular magazines in a particular way—one that blames the victims and the lifestyles of modern women in particular. This is in spite of the fact that fewer than 20 per cent of cases of breast cancer are in women under the age of 50. Lantz and Booth's study is fairly representative of a constructionist ontology in suggesting that the epidemic is not simply being construed as a social fact but is being ascribed a particular meaning (one that blames the victims of the disease). In this way, the representation of the disease in popular magazines forms an important element in its social construction.

with the language that is employed to present categories in particular ways. It suggests that the social world and its categories are not external to us, but are built up and constituted in and through interaction. This tendency can be seen particularly in discourse analysis, which is examined in Chapter 17. As Potter (1996: 98) observes: 'The world . . . is *constituted* in one way or another as people talk it, write it and argue it.' This sense of constructionism is highly antithetical to realism (see Box 1.8). Constructionism frequently results in an interest in the representation of social phenomena. Box 1.13 provides an illustration of this idea in relation to the representation of the breast cancer epidemic in the USA.

Constructionism is also frequently used as a term that reflects the indeterminacy of our knowledge of the social world (see Box 1.12 and the idea of constructionism in relation to the nature of knowledge of the social world). However, in this book, I will be using the term in connection with the notion that social phenomena and categories are social constructions.

Relationship to social research

Questions of social ontology cannot be divorced from issues concerning the conduct of social research. Ontological assumptions and commitments will feed into the ways in which research questions are formulated and research is carried out. If a research question is formulated in such a way as to suggest that organizations and cultures are objective social entities that act on individuals, the researcher is likely to emphasize the formal properties of organizations or the beliefs and values of members of the culture. Alternatively, if the researcher formulates a research problem so that the tenuousness of organization and culture as objective categories is stressed, it is likely that an emphasis will be placed on the active involvement of people in reality construction. In either case, it might be supposed that different approaches to the design of research and the collection of data will be required.

Research strategy: quantitative and qualitative research

Many writers on methodological issues find it helpful to distinguish between quantitative and qualitative research. The status of the distinction is ambiguous, because it is almost simultaneously regarded by some writers as a fundamental contrast and by others as no longer useful or even simply as 'false' (Layder 1993: 110). However, there is little evidence to suggest that the use of the distinction is abating and even considerable evidence of its continued, even growing, currency. The quantitative/qualitative distinction will be employed a great deal in this book, because it represents a useful means of classifying different methods of social research and because it is a helpful umbrella for a range of issues concerned with the practice of social research.

On the face of it, there would seem to be little to the quantitative/qualitative distinction other than the fact that quantitative researchers employ measurement and qualitative researchers do not. It is certainly the case that there is a predisposition among researchers along these lines, but many writers have suggested that the differences are deeper than the superficial issue of the presence or absence of quantification. For many writers, quantitative and qualitative research differ with respect to their epistemological foundations and in other respects too. Indeed, if we take the areas that have been the focus of the last three sections—the connection between theory and research, epistemological considerations, and ontological considerations—quantitative and qualitative research can be taken to form two distinctive clusters of *research strategy*. By a research strategy, I simply mean a general orientation to the conduct of social research. Table 1.1 outlines the differences between quantitative and qualitative research in terms of the three areas.

Thus, quantitative research can be construed as a research strategy that emphasizes quantification in the collection and analysis of data and that:

- entails a deductive approach to the relationship

Table 1.1 Fundamental differences between quantitative and qualitative research strategies

	Quantitative	Qualitative
Principal orientation to the role of theory in relation to research	Deductive; testing of theory	Inductive; generation of theory
Epistemological orientation	Natural science model, in particular positivism	Interpretivism
Ontological orientation	Objectivism	Constructionism

between theory and research, in which the accent is placed on the testing of theories;

- has incorporated the practices and norms of the natural scientific model and of positivism in particular; and

- embodies a view of social reality as an external, objective reality.

By contrast, qualitative research can be construed as a research strategy that usually emphasizes words rather than quantification in the collection and analysis of data and that:

- predominantly emphasizes an inductive approach to the relationship between theory and research, in which the emphasis is placed on the generation of theories;

- has rejected the practices and norms of the natural scientific model and of positivism in particular in preference for an emphasis on the ways in which individuals interpret their social world; and

- embodies a view of social reality as a constantly shifting emergent property of individuals' creation.

There is, in fact, considerably more to the quantitative/ qualitative distinction than this contrast. In Chapters 3 and 13 the nature of quantitative and then qualitative research respectively will be outlined in much greater detail, while in Chapters 21 and 22 the contrasting features will be further explored. In particular, a number of distinguishing features flow from the commitment of the quantitative research strategy to a positivist epistemology and from the rejection of that epistemology by practitioners of the qualitative research strategy. In other words, the three contrasts in Table 1.1 are basic, though fundamental, ones.

However, the interconnections between the different features of quantitative and qualitative research are not as straightforward as Table 1.1 and the last paragraph imply. While it is useful to contrast the two research strategies, it is necessary to be careful about hammering a wedge between them too deeply. It may seem perverse to introduce a basic set of distinctions and then suggest that they are problematic. A recurring theme of this book is that discussing the nature of social research is just as complex as conducting research in the real world. You may discover general tendencies, but they are precisely that—tendencies. In reality, the picture becomes more complicated the more you delve.

For example, it is common to describe qualitative research as concerned with the generation rather than the testing of theories. However, there are examples of studies in which qualitative research has been employed to test rather than to generate theories. For example, Adler and Adler (1985) were concerned to explore the issue of whether participation in athletics in higher education in the USA is associated with higher or lower levels of academic achievement, an issue on which the existing literature was inconsistent. This is an illustration of the use of the existing literature on a topic being employed as a kind of proxy for theory. The first author was a participant observer for four years of a basketball programme in a university and both authors carried out 'intensive, taped interviews' with players. The authors' findings do lead them to conclude that athletic participation is likely to result in lower academic achievement. This occurs because

the programme participants gradually drift from idealistic goals about their academic careers, and a variety of factors lead them to become increasingly detached from academic work. For example, one student is quoted as saying: 'If I was a student like most other students I could do well, but when you play the calibre of ball we do, you just can't be an above-average student. What I strive for now is just to be an average student. . . . You just can't find the time to do all the reading' (Adler and Adler 1985: 247). This study shows how, although qualitative research is typically associated with generating theories, it can also be employed for testing them.

Moreover, it is striking that, although the Adler and Adler study is broadly interpretivist in epistemological orientation, with its emphasis on how college athletes view their social situation, the findings have objectivist, rather than constructionist, overtones. For example, when the authors describe the students' academic performance as 'determined less by demographic characteristics and high school experiences than by the structure of their college experiences' (Adler and Adler 1985: 249), they are positing a social world that is 'out there' and as having a formal, objective quality. It is an example of qualitative research in the sense that there is no quantification or very little of it, but it does not have *all* the other features outlined in Table 1.1. Similarly, the previously mentioned study by Westergaard *et al.* (1989) of the effects of redundancy was a quantitative study in the sense of being concerned to measure a wide variety of concepts, but exhibited little evidence of a concern to test theories of unemployment or of a stressful life event like redundancy. Instead, its conclusions revolve around seeking to understand how those made redundant responded to the experience in terms of such things as their job-search methods, their inclination to find jobs, and their political attitudes. As such, it has interpretivist overtones in spite of being an exercise in quantitative research.

The point that is being made in this section is that quantitative and qualitative research represent different research strategies and that each carries with it striking differences in terms of the role of theory, epistemological issues, and ontological concerns.

However, the distinction is not a hard-and-fast one: studies that have the broad characteristics of one research strategy may have a characteristic of the other. Not only this, but many writers argue that the two can be combined within an overall research project, and Chapter 22 examines precisely this possibility.

Influences on the conduct of social research

We are beginning to get a picture now that social research is influenced by a variety of factors. Figure 1.2 summarizes the influences that have been examined so far, but has added two more—the impact of *values* and of *practical considerations*.

Values

Values reflect either the personal beliefs or the feelings of a researcher. On the face of it, we would expect that social scientists should be value free and objective in their research. After all, one might want to argue that research that simply reflected the personal biases of its practitioners could not be considered valid and scientific because it was bound up with the subjectivities of its practitioners. Such a view is held with less and less frequency among social scientists nowadays. Émile Durkheim (1858–1917) wrote that one of the corollaries of his injunction to treat social facts as things was that all 'preconceptions must be eradicated' (1938: 31). Since values are a form of preconception, his exhortation was at least implicitly to do with suppressing them when conducting research. His position is unlikely to be regarded as credible nowadays, because there is a growing recognition that it is not feasible to keep the values that a researcher holds totally in check. These can intrude at any or all of a number of points in the process of social research:

- choice of research area;
- formulation of research question;
- choice of method;
- formulation of research design and data collection techniques;
- implementation of data collection;
- analysis of data;
- interpretation of data;
- conclusions.

There are, therefore, numerous points at which bias and the intrusion of values can occur. Values can materialize at any point during the course of research. The researcher may develop an affection or sympathy, which was not necessarily present at the outset of an investigation, for the people being studied. It is quite common, for example, for researchers working within a qualitative research strategy, and in particular when they use participant observation or very intensive interviewing, to develop a close affinity with the people that they study to the extent that they find it difficult to disentangle their stance as social scientists from their subjects' perspective. This possibility may be exacerbated by the tendency that Becker (1967) identified for sociologists in particular to be very sympathetic to underdog groups. Equally, social scientists may be repelled by the people they study. The social anthropologist Colin Turnbull (1973) reports the results of his research into an African tribe known as the Ik. Turnbull was appalled by what he witnessed: a loveless (and for him unlovable) tribe that left its young and very old

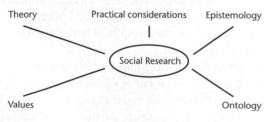

Fig. 1.2 Influences on social research

to die. While Turnbull was able to point to the conditions that had led to this state of affairs, he was very honest in his disgust for what he witnessed, particularly during the period of his initial sojourn among the tribe. However, that very disgust is a product of Western values about the family and it is likely, as he acknowledged, that these will have influenced his perception of what he witnessed.

Another position in relation to the whole question of values and bias is to recognize and acknowledge that research cannot be value free but to ensure that there is no untrammelled incursion of values in the research process and to be self-reflective and so exhibit *reflexivity* about the part played by such factors. As Turnbull (1973: 13) put it at the beginning of his book on the Ik: 'the reader is entitled to know something of the aims, expectations, hopes and attitudes that the writer brought to the field with him, for these will surely influence not only how he sees things but even what he sees.' Researchers are increasingly prepared to forewarn readers of their biases and assumptions and how these may have influenced the subsequent findings. There has been a growth since the mid-1970s of collections of inside reports of what doing a piece of research was really like, as against the generalities presented in social research methods textbooks (like this one!). These collections frequently function as 'confessions', an element of which is often the writer's preparedness to be open about his or her personal biases. This point will be taken up further in Chapter 23.

Still another approach is to argue for consciously value-laden research. This is a position taken by some feminist writers who have argued that only research on women that is intendedly *for* women will be consistent with the wider political needs of women. Mies (1993: 68) has argued that in feminist research the 'postulate of *value free research*, of neutrality and indifference towards the research objects, has to be replaced by *conscious partiality*, which is achieved through partial identification with the research objects' (emphases in original).

The significance of feminism in relation to values goes further than this, however. In particular, several feminist social researchers around the early 1980s proposed that the principles and practices associated with quantitative research were incompatible with feminist research on women. For writers like Oakley (1981), quantitative research was bound up with male values of control that can be seen in the general orientation of the research strategy—control of the research subject/respondent and control of the research context and situation. Moreover, the research process was seen as one-way traffic, in which researchers extract information from the people being studied and give little or more usually nothing in return. For many feminists, such a strategy bordered on exploitation and was incompatible with feminism's values of sisterhood and non-hierarchical relationships between women. The antipathy towards quantitative research resulted in a preference for qualitative research among feminists. Not only was qualitative research seen as more consistent with the values of feminism; it was seen as more adaptable to those values. Thus, feminist qualitative research came to be associated with an approach in which the investigator eschewed a value-neutral approach and engaged with the people being studied as people and not simply as respondents to research instruments. The stance of feminism in relation to both quantitative and qualitative approaches demonstrates the ways in which values have implications for the process of social investigation. In more recent years, there has been a softening of the attitudes of feminists towards quantitative research. Several writers have acknowledged a viable and acceptable role for quantitative research, particularly when it is employed in conjunction with qualitative research (Jayaratne and Stewart 1991; Oakley 1998). This issue will be picked up in Chapters 13, 21, and 22.

There are, then, different positions that can be taken up in relation to values and value freedom. Far fewer writers overtly subscribe to the position that the principle of objectivity can be put into practice than in the past. Quantitative researchers sometimes seem to be writing in a way that suggests an aura of objectivity (Mies 1993), but we simply do not know how far they subscribe to such a position. There is a greater awareness today of the limits to objectivity, so that some of the highly confident, not to say naive, pronouncements on the subject, like

Durkheim's, have fallen into disfavour. A further way in which values are relevant to the conduct of social research is through the following of ethical principles or standards. This issue will be followed up in Chapter 24.

Practical considerations

Nor should we neglect the importance and significance of *practical issues* in decisions about how social research should be carried out. There are a number of different dimensions to this issue. For one thing, choices of research strategy, design, or method have to be dovetailed with the specific question being investigated. If we are interested in teasing out the relative importance of a number of different causes of a social phenomenon, it is quite likely that a quantitative strategy will fit our needs, because, as will be shown in Chapter 3, the assessment of cause is one of its keynotes. Alternatively, if we are interested in the world views of members of a certain social group, a qualitative research strategy that is sensitive to how participants interpret their social world may be the direction to choose. If a researcher is interested in a topic on which no or virtually no research has been done in the past, the quantitative strategy may be difficult to employ because there is little prior literature from which to draw leads. A more exploratory stance may be preferable and, in this connection, qualitative research

may serve the researcher's needs better, since it is typically associated with the generation rather than the testing of theory (see Table 1.1) and with a relatively unstructured approach to the research process (see Chapter 13). Another dimension may have to do with the nature of the topic and of the people being investigated. For example, if the researcher needs to engage with individuals or groups involved in illicit activities, such as violence (Patrick 1973), pilferage (Ditton 1977), or drug dealing (P. A. Adler 1985), it is unlikely that a social survey would gain the confidence of the subjects involved or achieve the necessary rapport. It is not surprising, therefore, that researchers in these areas have tended to use a qualitative strategy. By contrast, it does not seem likely that the hypothesis in the research described in Box 1.5 could have been tested with a qualitative method like participant observation.

While practical considerations may seem rather mundane and uninteresting compared with the lofty realm inhabited by the philosophical debates surrounding such discussions about epistemology and ontology, they are important ones. All social research is a coming together of the ideal and the feasible. Because of this, there will be many circumstances in which the nature of the topic or of the subjects of an investigation and the constraints on a researcher loom large in decisions about how best to proceed.

Key points

- Quantitative and qualitative research constitute different approaches to social investigation and carry with them important epistemological and ontological considerations.

- Theory can be depicted as something that precedes research (as in quantitative research) or as something that emerges out of it (as in qualitative research).

- Epistemological considerations loom large in considerations of research strategy. To a large extent, these revolve around the desirability of employing a natural science model (and in particular positivism) versus interpretivism.

- Ontological considerations, concerning objectivism versus constructionism, also constitute important dimensions of the quantitative/qualitative contrast.

- Values may impinge on the research process at different times.

- Practical considerations in decisions about research methods are also important factors.

- Feminist researchers have tended to prefer a qualitative approach, though there is some evidence of a change of viewpoint in this regard.

Revision questions

Theory and research

- If you had to conduct some social research now, what would the topic be and what factors would have influenced your choice? How important was addressing theory in your consideration?
- Outline, using examples of your own, the difference between grand and middle-range theory.
- What are the differences between inductive and deductive theory and why is the distinction important?

Epistemological considerations

- What is meant by each of the following terms: positivism; realism; and interpretivism? Why is it important to understand each of them?
- What are the implications of epistemological considerations for research practice?

Ontological considerations

- What are the main differences between epistemological and ontological considerations?
- What is meant by objectivism and constructionism?
- Which theoretical ideas have been particularly instrumental in the growth of interest in qualitative research?

Research strategy: Quantitative and qualitative research

- Outline the main differences between quantitative and qualitative research in terms of: the relationship between theory and data; epistemological considerations; and ontological considerations.
- To what extent is quantitative research solely concerned with testing theories and qualitative research with generating theories?

Influences on the conduct of social research

- What are some of the main influences on social research?

2 Research designs

Reader's guide

In focusing on the different kinds of research design, we are paying attention to the different frameworks for the collection and analysis of data. A research design relates to the criteria that are employed when evaluating social research. It is, therefore, a framework for the generation of evidence that is suited both to a certain set of criteria and to the research question in which the investigator is interested. This chapter is structured as follows.

- Reliability, replication, and validity are presented as criteria for assessing the quality of social research. The latter entails an assessment in terms of several criteria covered in the chapter: measurement validity; internal validity; external validity; and ecological validity.

- The suggestion that such criteria are mainly relevant to quantitative research is examined, along with the proposition that an alternative set of criteria should be employed in relation to qualitative research. This alternative set of criteria, which is concerned with the issue of *trustworthiness*, is outlined briefly.

- Five prominent research designs are then outlined:
  - experimental and related designs (such as the quasi-experiment);
  - cross-sectional design, the most common form of which is social survey research;
  - longitudinal design and its various forms, such as the panel study and the cohort study;
  - case study design;
  - comparative design.

- Each research design is considered in terms of the criteria for evaluating research findings.

Introduction

In the previous chapter, the idea of *research strategy* was introduced as a broad orientation to social research. The specific context for its introduction was the distinction between quantitative and qualitative research as different research strategies. However, the decision to adopt one or the other strategy will not get you far along the road of doing a piece of research. Two other key decisions will have to be made (along with a host of tactical decisions about the way in which the research will be carried out and the data analysed). These decisions concern choices about *research design* and

research method. On the face of it, these two terms would seem to mean the same thing, but it is crucial to draw a distinction between them (see Boxes 2.1 and 2.2).

Research methods can be and are associated with different kinds of research design. The latter represents a structure that guides the execution of a research method and the analysis of the subsequent data. The two terms are often confused. For example, one of the research designs to be covered in this chapter—the case study—is very often referred to as a *method*. As we will see, a case study entails the

> ### Box 2.1 ⚡ *What is a research design?*
>
> A *research design* provides a framework for the collection and analysis of data. A choice of research design reflects decisions about the priority being given to a range of dimensions of the research process. These include the importance attached to:
>
> - expressing causal connections between variables;
> - generalizing to larger groups of individuals than those actually forming part of the investigation;
> - understanding behaviour and the meaning of that behaviour in its specific social context;
> - having a temporal (i.e. over time) appreciation of social phenomena and their interconnections.

> ### Box 2.2 ⚡ *What is a research method?*
>
> A research method is simply a technique for collecting data. It can involve a specific instrument, such as a self-completion questionnaire or a structured interview schedule, or participant observation whereby the researcher listens to and watches others.

detailed exploration of a specific case, which could be a community, organization, or person. But, once a case has been selected, a research method or research methods are needed to collect data. Simply selecting an organization and deciding to study it intensively are not going to provide data. Do you observe? Do you conduct interviews? Do you exam-

ine documents? Do you administer questionnaires? You may in fact use any or all of these research methods, but the crucial point is that deciding to choose a case study approach will not in its own right provide you with data.

In this chapter, five different research designs will be examined: experimental design and its variants, including quasi-experiments; cross-sectional or social survey design; longitudinal design; case study design; and comparative design. However, before embarking on the nature of and differences between these designs, it is useful to consider some recurring issues in social research that cut across some or all of these designs.

Criteria in social research

Three of the most prominent criteria for the evaluation of social research are *reliability*, *replication*, and *validity*. Both of these terms will be treated in much greater detail in later chapters, but in the meantime a fairly basic treatment of them can be helpful.

Reliability

Reliability is concerned with the question of whether the results of a study are repeatable. The term is commonly used in relation to the question of whether the measures that are devised for concepts in the social sciences (such as poverty, racial preju-

dice, deskilling, religious orthodoxy) are consistent. In Chapter 3, we will be looking at the idea of reliability in greater detail, in particular the different ways in which it can be conceptualized. Reliability is particularly at issue in connection with quantitative research. The quantitative researcher is likely to be concerned with the question of whether a measure is stable or not. After all, if we found that IQ tests, which were designed as measures of intelligence, were found to fluctuate, so that people's IQ scores were often wildly different when administered on two or more occasions, we would be concerned about it as a measure. We would consider it an unreliable measure—we could not have faith in its consistency.

Replication

The idea of reliability is very close to another criterion of research—*replication* and more especially *replicability*. It sometimes happens that researchers choose to replicate the findings of others. There may be a host of different reasons for doing so, such as a feeling that the original results do not match other evidence that is relevant to the domain in question. In order for replication to take place, a study must be capable of replication—it must be replic*able*. This is a very obvious point: if a researcher does not spell out his or her procedures in great detail, replication is impossible. Similarly, in order for us to assess the reliability of a measure of a concept, the procedures that constitute that measure must be replicable by someone else.

Validity

A further and in many ways the most important criterion of research is *validity*. Validity is concerned with the integrity of the conclusions that are generated from a piece of research. Like reliability, we will be examining the idea of validity in greater detail in later chapters, but in the meantime it is important to be aware of the main types of validity that are typically distinguished:

- *Measurement validity.* This criterion applies primarily to quantitative research and to the search for measures of social scientific concepts. Measurement validity is also often referred to as *construct validity*. Essentially, it is to do with the question of whether a measure that is devised of a concept really does reflect the concept that it is supposed to be denoting. Does the IQ test really measure variations in intelligence? If we take the study reported in Box 1.5 (p. 9), there are three concepts that needed to be measured in order to test the hypotheses: national religiosity, religious orthodoxy, and family religious orientation. The question then is: do the measures really represent the concepts they are supposed to be tapping? If they do not, the study's findings will be questionable. It should be appreciated that measurement validity

is related to reliability: if a measure of a concept is unstable in that it fluctuates and hence is unreliable, it simply cannot be providing a valid measure of the concept in question. In other words, the assessment of measurement validity presupposes that a measure is reliable.

- *Internal validity.* This form of validity relates mainly to the issue of causality, which will be dealt with in greater detail in Chapter 3. Internal validity is concerned with the question of whether a conclusion that incorporates a causal relationship between two or more variables holds water. If we suggest that *x* causes *y*, can we be sure that it is *x* that is responsible for variation in *y* and not something else that is producing an apparent causal relationship? In the study examined in Box 1.5, the authors were quoted as concluding that 'the religious environment of a nation has a major impact on the beliefs of its citizens' (Kelley and De Graaf 1997: 654). Internal validity raises the question: can we be sure that national religiosity really does cause variation in religious orientation and that this apparent causal relationship is genuine and not produced by something else? In discussing issues of causality, it is common to refer to the factor that has a causal impact as the *independent variable* and the effect as the *dependent variable* (see Box 2.3). In the case of Kelley and De Graaf's research, the 'religious environment of a nation' was an independent variable and religious beliefs were the dependent variable. Thus, internal validity raises the question: how confident can we be that the independent variable really is at least in part responsible for the variation that has been identified in the dependent variable?

- *External validity.* This issue is concerned with the question of whether the results of a study can be generalized beyond the specific research context. In Sullivan's (1996) research that was referred to in Box 1.3 (p. 7), data were collected from 380 heterosexual couples. Can her findings about 'emotion work' be generalized beyond these 380 couples? In other words, if the research was not externally valid, it would apply to the 380 couples

---

Box 2.3 ⋛⟨ʌ⟩⋚ *What is a variable?*

A variable is simply an attribute on which cases vary. 'Cases' can obviously be people, but they can also include things such as households, cities, organizations, schools, and nations. If an attribute does not vary, it is a *constant*. If all manufacturing organizations had the same ratio of male to female managers, this attribute of such organizations would be a constant and not a variable. Constants are rarely of interest to social researchers. It is common to distinguish between different types of variable. The most basic distinction is between *independent variables* and *dependent variables*. The former are deemed to have a causal influence on the latter.

---

and to no other couples. If it was externally valid, we would expect it to apply more generally to heterosexual couples. It is in this context that the issue of how people are selected to participate in research becomes crucial. This is one of the main reasons why quantitative researchers are so keen to generate representative samples (see Chapter 4).

- *Ecological validity.* This criterion is concerned with the question of whether social scientific findings are applicable to people's everyday, natural social settings. As Cicourel (1982: 15) has put it: 'Do our instruments capture the daily life conditions, opinions, values, attitudes, and knowledge base of those we study as expressed in their natural habitat?' This criterion is concerned with the question of whether social research sometimes produces findings that may be technically valid but have little to do with what happens in people's everyday lives. If research findings are ecologically *in*valid, they are in a sense *artefacts* of the social scientist's arsenal of data collection and analytic tools. The more the social scientist intervenes in natural settings or creates unnatural ones, such as a laboratory or even a special room to carry out interviews, the more likely it is that findings will be ecologically invalid. The conclusions deriving from a study using questionnaires may have measurement validity and a reasonable level of internal validity, and it may be externally valid, in the sense that the findings can be generalized to other samples confronted by the same questionnaire, but the unnaturalness of the fact of having to answer a questionnaire may mean that the findings have limited ecological validity.

Relationship with research strategy

One feature that is striking about most of the discussion so far is that it seems to be geared mainly to quantitative rather than to qualitative research. Both reliability and measurement validity are essentially concerned with the adequacy of measures, which are most obviously a concern in quantitative research. Internal validity is concerned with the soundness of findings that specify a causal connection, an issue that is most commonly of concern to quantitative researchers. External validity *may* be relevant to qualitative research, but the whole question of representativeness of research subjects with which the issue is concerned has a more obvious application to the realm of quantitative research with its preoccupation with sampling procedures that maximize the opportunity for generating a representative sample. The issue of ecological validity relates to the naturalness of the research approach and seems to have considerable relevance to both qualitative and quantitative research.

Some writers have sought to apply the concepts of reliability and validity to the practice of qualitative research (e.g. LeCompte and Goetz 1982; Kirk and Miller 1986; Peräkylä 1997), but others argue that the grounding of these ideas in quantitative research renders them inapplicable to or inappropriate for qualitative research. Writers like Kirk and Miller (1986) have applied concepts of validity and reliability to qualitative research but have changed the sense in which the terms are used very slightly. Some qualitative researchers sometimes propose that the studies they produce should be judged or evaluated according to different criteria from those used in relation to quantitative research. Lincoln and Guba (1985) propose that alternative terms and ways of assessing qualitative research are required. For example, they propose *trustworthiness* as a criterion of how good a qualitative study is. Each aspect of trustworthiness has a parallel with the previous quantitative research criteria.

- *Credibility*, which parallels internal validity—i.e. how believable are the findings?

- *Transferability*, which parallels external validity— i.e. do the findings apply to other contexts?

- *Dependability*, which parallels reliability—i.e. are the findings likely to apply at other times?

- *Confirmability*, which parallels objectivity—i.e. has the investigator allowed his or her values to intrude to a high degree?

These criteria will be returned to in Chapter 13.

M. Hammersley (1992a) occupies a kind of middle position here in that, while he proposes validity as an important criterion (in the sense that an empirical account must be plausible and credible and should take into account the amount and kind of evidence used in relation to an account), he also proposes *relevance* as a criterion. Relevance is taken to be assessed from the vantage point of the importance of a topic within its substantive field or the contribution it makes to the literature on that field. The issues in these different views have to do with the different objectives that many qualitative researchers argue are distinctive about their craft. The distinctive features of qualitative research will be examined in later chapters.

However, it should also be borne in mind that one of the criteria previously cited—ecological validity— may have been formulated largely in the context of quantitative research, but is in fact a feature in relation to which qualitative research fares rather well. Qualitative research often involves a *naturalistic* stance (see Box 2.4). This means that the researcher seeks to collect data in naturally occurring situations and environments, as opposed to fabricated, artificial ones. This characteristic probably applies particularly well to ethnographic research, in which participant observation is a prominent element of data collection, but it is sometimes suggested that it applies also to the sort of interview approach typically used by qualitative researchers, which is less directive than the kind used in quantitative research (see e.g. Box 1.5, p. 9). We might expect that much qualitative research is stronger than quantitative investigations in terms of ecological validity.

By and large, these issues in social research have been presented because some of them will emerge in the context of the discussion of research designs in the next section, but in a number of ways they also represent background considerations for some of the issues to be examined. They will be returned to later in the book.

Research designs

In this discussion of research designs, five different types will be examined: experimental design; cross-sectional or social survey design; longitudinal design; case study design; and comparative design. Variations on these designs will be examined in their relevant subsections.

Experimental design

True experiments are quite unusual in sociology, but are employed in related areas of enquiry, such as social psychology and organization studies, while researchers in social policy sometimes use them in

Box 2.4 What is naturalism?

Naturalism is an interesting example of a mercifully relatively rare instance of a term that not only has different meanings, but also has meanings that can actually be contradictory! It is possible to identify three different meanings.

- *Naturalism means a commitment to adopting the principles of natural scientific method*. This meaning, which has clear affinities with positivism, implies that naturalistic enquiry entails the use of the natural science model for studying the social world (Keat and Urry 1975: 1–2).

- *Naturalism means being true to the nature of the phenomenon being investigated*. According to Matza, naturalism is 'the philosophical view that strives to remain true to the nature of the phenomenon under study' (1969: 5) and 'claims fidelity to the natural world' (1969: 8). This meaning of the term represents a fusion of elements of an interpretivist epistemology and a constructionist ontology, which were examined in Chapter 1. Naturalism is taken to recognize that people attribute meaning to behaviour and are authors of their social world rather than passive objects.

- *Naturalism is a style of research that seeks to minimize the intrusion of artificial methods of data collection*. This meaning implies that the social world should be as undisturbed as possible when it is being studied (Hammersley and Atkinson 1995: 6).

The second and third meanings overlap considerably, in that it could easily be imagined that, in order to conduct a naturalistic enquiry in the second sense, a research approach that adopted naturalistic principles in the third sense would be required. Both the second and third meanings are incompatible with, and indeed opposed to, the first meaning. Naturalism, in the sense of a tenet of positivism, is invariably viewed by writers drawing on an interpretative epistemology as not 'true' to the social world, precisely because it entails both the application of natural science methods that ignore the capacity of humans to interpret the social world and to be active agents, and artificial methods of data collection.

---

order to assess the impact of new reforms or policies. Why, then, bother to introduce experimental designs at all in the context of a book about social research? The chief reason, quite aside from the fact that they are sometimes employed, is that a true experiment is often used as a yardstick against which non-experimental research is assessed. Experimental research is frequently held up as a touchstone because it engenders considerable confidence in the robustness and trustworthiness of causal findings. In other words, true experiments tend to be very strong in terms of internal validity.

Manipulation

If experiments are so strong in this respect, why then do social researchers not make far greater use of them? The reason is simple: in order to conduct a true experiment, it is necessary to *manipulate* the independent variable in order to determine whether it does in fact have an influence on the dependent variable. Experimental subjects are likely to be allocated to one of two or more experimental groups, each of which represents different types or levels of the independent variable. It is then possible to establish how far differences between the groups are responsible for variations in the level of the dependent variable. Manipulation, then, entails intervening in a situation to determine which of two or more things happens to subjects. However, the vast majority of independent variables with which social researchers are concerned cannot be manipulated. If we are interested in the effects of gender on work experiences, we cannot *manipulate* gender so that some people are made male and others female. If we are interested in the effects of variations in social class on social and political attitudes or on health, we cannot allocate people to different social class groupings. As with the huge majority of such variables, the levels of social engineering that would be required are beyond serious contemplation.

Before moving on to a more complete discussion of experimental design, it is important to introduce a basic distinction between the *laboratory experiment* and the *field experiment*. As its name implies, the laboratory experiment takes place in a laboratory or in a contrived setting, whereas field experiments occur in real-life settings, such as in classrooms and organizations, or as a result of the implementation of reforms or new policies. It is experiments of the latter type that are most likely to touch on areas of interest to social researchers. In order to illustrate the nature of manipulation and the idea of a field experiment, Box 2.5 describes a well-known piece of research.

Classic experimental design

The research in Box 2.5 includes most of the essential features of what is known as the classical experimental design. Two groups are established and it is this that forms the experimental manipulation and therefore the independent variable—in this case, teacher expectations. The spurters form what is known as the *experimental group* or *treatment group* and the other students form a *control group*. The experimental group receives the *experimental treatment*—teacher expectancies—but the control group does not receive an experimental treatment. The dependent variable—student performance—is measured before and after the experimental manipu-

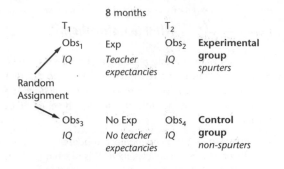

Fig. 2.1 Classical experimental design (*with illustration of the effect of teacher expectancies on IQ*)

lation, so that a before-and-after analysis can be conducted (see Figure 2.1). Moreover, the spurters and the non-spurters were assigned randomly to their respective groups. Because of this use of random assignment to the experimental and control groups, the researchers were able to feel confident that the only difference between the two groups was the fact that teachers expected the spurters to fare better at school than the others. They would have been confident that, if they did establish a difference in performance between the two groups, it was due to the experimental manipulation alone.

Box 2.5 A field experiment

As part of a programme of research into the impact of self-fulfilling prophecies (for example, where someone's beliefs or expectations about someone else influence how the latter behaves), Rosenthal and Jacobson (1968) conducted research into the question of whether teachers' expectations of their students' abilities in fact influence the school performance of the latter. The research was conducted in a lower-class locality in the USA with a high level of children from minority group backgrounds. In the spring of 1964, all of the students completed a test that was portrayed as a means of identifying 'spurters'—that is, students who were likely to excel academically. At the beginning of the following academic year, all of the teachers were notified of the names of the students who had been identified as spurters. In fact, 20 per cent of the schoolchildren had been identified as spurters. However,

the students had actually been administered a conventional IQ test and the so-called spurters had been selected randomly. The test was readministered eight months after the original one. The authors were then able to compare the differences between the spurters and the other students in terms of changes in various measures of academic performance, such as IQ scores, reading ability and intellectual curiosity. Since there was no evidence for there being any difference in ability between the spurters and the rest, any indications that the spurters did in fact differ from their peers could be attributed to the fact that the teachers had been led to expect the former would perform better. The findings show that such differences did in fact exist, but that the differences between the spurters and their peers tended to be concentrated in the first two or three years of schooling.

In order to capture the essence of this design, the following simple notation will be employed:

Obs an **obs**ervation made in relation to the dependent variable; there may well be two or more observations, such as IQ test scores and reading grades before (the *pre-test*) and after (the *post-test*) the experimental manipulation

Exp the **exp**erimental treatment (the independent variable); such as the creation of teacher expectancies. No Exp refers to the absence of an experimental treatment and represents the experience of the control group

T the **t**iming of the observations made in relation to the dependent variable; such as the timing of the administration of an IQ test

Classic experimental design and validity

What is the purpose of the control group? Surely it is what happens to the spurters (the experimental group) that really concerns us? In order for a study to be a true experiment, it must control (in other words, eliminate) the possible effects of rival explanations of a causal finding, such as that teacher expectancies have an impact on student performance. We might then be in a position to take the view that such a study is internally valid. The presence of a control group *and* the random assignment of subjects to the experimental and control groups enable us to eliminate such rival explanations. To see this, consider some of the rival explanations that might occur if there was *no* control group. There would then have been a number of potential threats to internal validity (see Box 2.6). These threats are taken from Campbell (1957) and Cook and Campbell (1979), but not all of the threats to internal validity they refer to are included.

In the case of each of these threats to internal validity, each of which raises the prospect of a rival interpretation of a causal finding, the presence of a control group coupled with random assignment allows us to eliminate these threats. As a result, our confidence in the causal finding, that teacher expectancies influence student performance, is greatly enhanced.

However, simply because research is deemed to be internally valid does not mean that it is beyond reproach or that at least questions cannot be raised about it. When a quantitative research strategy has been employed, the other criteria can be applied to evaluate a study. First, there is the question of measurement validity. In the case of the Rosenthal and Jacobson study, there are potentially two aspects to this. One is the question of whether academic performance has been adequately measured. Measures like reading scores seem to possess *face validity*, in the sense that they appear to exhibit a correspondence with what they are measuring. However, given the controversy surrounding IQ tests and what they measure (Kamin 1974), we might feel somewhat uneasy about how far gains in IQ test scores can be regarded as indicative of academic performance. Similarly, to take another of the authors' measures—intellectual curiosity—how confident can we be that this too is a valid measure of academic performance? Does it really measure what it is supposed to measure? The second question relating to measurement validity is whether the experimental manipulation really worked. In other words, did the random identification of some schoolchildren as spurters adequately create the conditions for the self-fulfilling prophecy to be examined? The procedure very much relies on the teachers being taken in by the procedure, but it is possible that they were not all equally duped. If so, this would contaminate the manipulation.

Secondly, is the research externally valid? This issue is considered in Box 2.7.

Thirdly, are the findings ecologically valid? The fact that the research is a field experiment rather than a laboratory experiment seems to enhance this aspect of the Rosenthal and Jacobson research. Also, the fact that the students and the teachers seem to have had little if any appreciation of the fact that they were in fact participating in an experiment may also have enhanced ecological validity, though this aspect of the research raises enormous *ethical* concerns, since deception seems to have been a significant and probably necessary feature of the investigation. The question of ethical issues is in many ways another dimension of the validity of a study and will be the focus of Chapter 24. The fact

> **Box 2.6 Threats to internal validity (and their application to the Rosenthal and Jacobson (1968) study)**
>
> - *History*. This refers to events other than the manipulation of teacher expectancies that may occur in the environment that may have caused the spurters' scores to rise. The actions of the school head to raise standards in the school may be one such type of event. If there were no control group, we could not be sure whether it was the teachers' expectancies or the head's actions that were producing the increase in spurters' grades. If there is a control group, we are able to say that history would have an effect on the control group subjects too and therefore differences between the experimental and control groups could be attributed to the effect of teacher expectancies alone.
>
> - *Testing*. This threat refers to the possibility that subjects may become more experienced at taking a test or may become sensitized to the aims of the experiment as a result of the pre-test. The presence of a control group, which presumably would also experience the same effect, allows us to discount this possibility if there is a difference between the experimental and control groups.
>
> - *Instrumentation*. This threat refers to the possibility that changes in the way a test is administered could account for an increase (or decrease) in scores between the pre-test and post-test; for example, if slight changes to the test had been introduced. Again, if there is a control group, we can assume that testing would have affected the control group as well.
>
> - *Mortality*. This relates to the problem of attrition in many studies that span a long period of time, in that subjects may leave. School students may leave the area or move to a different school. Since this problem is likely to afflict the control group too, it is possible to establish its significance as a threat relative to the impact and importance of teacher expectancies.
>
> - *Maturation*. Quite simply, people change and the ways in which they change may have implications for the dependent variable. The students identified as spurters may have improved anyway, regardless of the effect of teacher expectancies. Maturation should affect the control group subjects as well. If we did not have a control group, it could be argued that any change in the students' school performance was attributable to the possibility that they would have improved anyway. The control group allows us to discount this possibility.
>
> - *Selection*. If there are differences between the two groups, which would arise if they had been selected by a non-random process, variations between the experimental and control groups could be attributed to pre-existing differences in their membership. However, since a random process of assignment to the experimental and control groups was employed, this possibility can be discounted.
>
> - *Ambiguity about the direction of causal influence*. The very notion of an independent variable and dependent variable presupposes a direction of causality. However, there may be occasions when in a study the temporal sequence is unclear, so that it is not possible to establish which variable affects the other. Since the creation of teacher expectancies preceded the improvements in academic achievement in the earlier years of school, in the Rosenthal and Jacobson study the direction of causal influence is clear.

that Rosenthal and Jacobson made intensive use of various instruments to measure academic performance might be considered a source of concerns about ecological validity, though this is an area in which most if not all quantitative research is likely to be implicated.

A fourth issue that we might want to raise relates to the question of replicability. The authors lay out very clearly the procedures and measures that they employed. If anyone sought to carry out a replication, he or she could obtain further information from them should they need it. Consequently, the research is replicable, although there has not been an exact replication. Clairborn (1969) conducted one of the earliest replications and followed a procedure that was very similar to Rosenthal and Jacobson's. The study was carried out in three middle-class, suburban schools and the timing of the creation of

Box 2.7 **Threats to external validity (and their application to the Rosenthal and Jacobson (1968) study)**

Campbell (1957) and Cook and Campbell (1979) identify five major threats to the external validity and hence generalizability of an investigation.

- *Interaction of selection and treatment.* This threat raises the question: to what social and psychological groups can a finding be generalized? Can it be generalized to a wide variety of individuals who might be differentiated by ethnicity, social class, region, gender and type of personality? In the case of the Rosenthal and Jacobson study, the students were largely from lower social class groups and a large proportion were from ethnic minorities. This might be considered a limitation to the generalizability of the findings.

- *Interaction of setting and treatment.* This threat relates to the issue of how confident we can be that the results of a study can be applied to other settings. In particular, how confident can we be that Rosenthal and Jacobson's findings are generalizable to other schools? There is also the wider issue of how confident we can be that the operation of self-fulfilling prophecies can be discerned in non-educational settings. In fact, Rosenthal and others have been able to demonstrate the role and significance of the self-fulfilling prophecy in a wide variety of different contexts (Rosnow and Rosenthal 1997), though this still does not answer the question of whether the specific findings that were produced can be generalized. One set of grounds for being uneasy about Rosenthal and Jacobson's findings is that they were allowed an inordinate amount of freedom for conducting their investigation. The high level of cooperation from the school authorities was very unusual and may be indicative of the school being somewhat atypical, though whether there is any such thing as a 'typical school' is highly questionable.

- *Interaction of history and treatment.* This threat raises the question of whether the findings can be generalized to the past and to the future. The Rosenthal and Jacobson research was conducted over thirty years ago. How confident can we be that the findings would apply today? Also, their investigation was conducted at a particular juncture in the school academic year. Would the same results have obtained if the research had been conducted at different points in the year?

- *Interaction effects of pre-testing.* As a result of being pre-tested, subjects in an experiment may become sensitized to the experimental treatment. Consequently, the findings may not be generalizable to groups that have *not* been pre-tested, and, of course, in the real world people are rarely pre-tested in this way. The findings may therefore be partly determined by the experimental treatment as such and partly by how pre-test sensitization has influenced the way in which subjects respond to the treatment. This may have occurred in the Rosenthal and Jacobson research, since all students were pre-tested at the end of the previous academic year.

- *Reactive effects of experimental arrangements.* People are frequently, if not invariably, aware of the fact that they are participating in an experiment. Their awareness may influence how they respond to the experimental treatment and therefore affect the generalizability of the findings. Since Rosenthal and Jacobson's subjects do not appear to have been aware of the fact that they were participating in an experiment, this problem is unlikely to have been significant. The issue of *reactivity* and its potentially damaging effects is a recurring theme in relation to many methods of social research.

teacher expectancies was different from that in the original Rosenthal and Jacobson study. Clairborn failed to replicate Rosenthal and Jacobson's findings. This failure to replicate casts doubt on the external validity of the original research and suggests that the first three threats referred to in Box 2.7 may have played an important part in the differences between the two sets of results.

The laboratory experiment

Many experiments in fields like social psychology are laboratory experiments rather than field experiments. One of the main advantages of the former over the latter is that the researcher has far greater influence over the experimental arrangements. For example, it is easier to randomly assign subjects to

Box 2.8 A laboratory experiment

Howell and Frost (1989) were interested in the possibility that charismatic leadership, a term associated with Max Weber's (1947) types of legitimate authority, is a more effective approach to leadership in organizations than other types of leadership. They conducted a laboratory experiment that compared the effectiveness of charismatic leadership as against two other approaches—consideration and structuring. A number of hypotheses were generated, including: 'Individuals working under a charismatic leader will have higher task performance than will individuals working under a considerate leader'

(Howell and Frost 1989: 245). One hundred and forty-four students volunteered for the experiment. Their course grades were enhanced by 3 per cent for agreeing to participate. They were randomly assigned to work under one of the three types of leadership. The work was a simulated business task. All three leadership approaches were performed by two female actresses. In broad conformity with the hypotheses, subjects working under charismatic leaders scored generally higher in terms of measures of task performance than those working under the other leaders, particularly the considerate leader.

different experimental conditions in the laboratory than to do the same in an ongoing, real-life organization. The researcher therefore has a higher level of control and this is likely to enhance the internal validity of the study. It is also likely that laboratory experiments will be more straightforward to replicate because they are less bound up with a certain milieu that is difficult to reproduce.

However, laboratory experiments like the one described in Box 2.8 suffer from a number of limitations. First, the external validity is likely to be difficult to establish. There is the interaction of setting and treatment, since the setting of the laboratory is likely to be unrelated to real world experiences and contexts. Also, there is likely to be an interaction of selection and treatment. In the case of Howell and Frost's (1989) study described in Box 2.8, there are a number of difficulties: the subjects were students who are unlikely to be representative of the general population, so that their responses to the experimental treatment may be distinctive; they were volunteers and it is known that volunteers differ from non-volunteers (Rosnow and Rosenthal 1997: ch. 5); and they were given incentives to participate, which may further demarcate them from others, since not everyone is equally amenable to the blandishments of inducements. There will have been no problem of interaction effects of pre-testing because, like many experiments, there was no pre-testing. However, it is quite feasible that reactive

effects may have been set in motion by the experimental arrangements. Secondly, the ecological validity of the study may be poor because we do not know how well the findings are applicable to the real world and everyday life. However, while the study may lack what is often called *mundane realism*, it may none the less enjoy *experimental realism* (Aronson and Carlsmith 1968). The latter means that the subjects are very involved in the experiment and take it very seriously.

Quasi-experiments

A number of writers have drawn attention to the possibilities offered by *quasi-experiments*—that is, studies that have certain characteristics of experimental designs but that do not fulfil all of the internal validity requirements. A large number of different types of quasi-experiments have been identified (Cook and Campbell 1979) and it is not proposed to cover them here. A particularly interesting form of quasi-experiment occurs in the case of 'natural experiments'. These are 'experiments' in the sense of entailing manipulation of a social setting, but as part of a naturally occurring attempt to alter social arrangements. In such circumstances, it is invariably not possible to randomly assign subjects to experimental and control groups. An example is provided in Box 2.9. The absence of random assignment in the research casts a certain amount of doubt

Box 2.9 A quasi-experiment

Since the mid-1980s, a group of researchers have been collecting medical and psychiatric data on a cohort of over 10,000 British civil servants. The first wave of data collection took place between late 1985 and early 1988 and comprised clinical measurement (for example, blood pressure, ECG, cholesterol) and a self-completion questionnaire that generated data on health, stress, and minor psychiatric symptoms. Further measurements of the same group took place in 1989/90 and 1992/3. The decision in the mid-1980s by the then UK government to transfer many of the executive functions of government to executive agencies operating on a more commercial basis than previously afforded the opportunity to examine the health effects of a major organizational change. Ferrie *et al.* (1998) report the results of their Phase 1 and Phase 3 data. They distinguished between three groups: those

experiencing a change; those anticipating they would be affected by the change; and a 'control group' of those unaffected by the change. The authors found significant adverse health effects among those experiencing and anticipating change compared to the control group, although the extent of the effects of the major organizational change (or its anticipation) varied markedly between men and women. This study uses a quasi-experimental design, in which a control group is compared to two treatment groups. It bears the hallmarks of a classical experimental design but there is no random assignment. Subjects were not randomly assigned to the three groups. Whether they were affected (or anticipated being affected by the changes) depended on decisions deriving from government and civil service policy.

Box 2.10 A natural experiment

The effects of television violence on children is one of the most contested areas of social research and one that frequently causes the media to become especially shrill. St Helena in the South Atlantic provided a fascinating laboratory for the examination of the various claims when television was introduced to the island for the first time in the mid-1990s. The television viewing habits of a large sample of schoolchildren and their behaviour are being monitored and will continue to be monitored for many years to come. The project leader, Tony Charlton, was quoted in *The Times* as saying: 'The argument that watching violent television turns youngsters to violence is not borne out . . . The children have been watching the same amounts of violence, and in many cases the same

programmes, as British children. But they have not gone out and copied what they have seen on TV' (Midgley 1998: 5). A report of the findings in *The Times* in April 1998 found that 'the shared experience of watching television made them less likely to tease each other and to fight, and more likely to enjoy books' (Frean 1998: 7). The findings derive from 900 minutes of video footage of children at play during school breaks, diaries kept by around 300 of the children, and ratings by teachers. The reports of the research in academic journals confirm that there was no evidence to suggest that the introduction of television has led to an increase in anti-social behaviour (e.g. Charlton *et al.* 1998, 1999).

on the study's internal validity, since the groups may not have been equivalent. However, the results of such studies are still compelling, because they are not artificial interventions in social life and because their ecological validity is therefore very strong. Most writers on quasi-experimentation discount natural experiments in which there is no control group or basis for comparison (Cook and Campbell 1979), but occasionally one comes across a single

group natural experiment that is particularly striking (see Box 2.10). Experimental designs and more especially quasi-experimental designs have been particularly prominent in *evaluation research* studies (see Box 2.11).

Significance of experimental design

As was stated at the outset, the chief reason for introducing the experiment as a research design is

Box 2.11 ⌇⟨᷁⟩⌇ *What is evaluation research?*

Evaluation research, as its name implies, is concerned with the evaluation of such occurrences as social and organizational programmes or interventions. The essential question that is typically asked by such studies is: has the intervention (e.g. a new policy initiative or an organizational change) achieved its anticipated goals? A typical design may have one group that is exposed to the treatment, that is the new initiative, and a control group that is not. Since it is often not feasible or ethical to randomly assign research participants to the two groups, such studies are usually quasi-experimental. The use of the principles of experimental design are fairly entrenched in evaluation research, but other approaches have emerged in recent years. Approaches to evaluation based on qualitative research have emerged. While there are differences of opinion about how qualitative evaluation should be carried out, the different views typically coalesce around a recognition of the importance of an in-depth understanding of the context in which an intervention occurs and the diverse viewpoints of the stakeholders (Greene 1994, 2000). Pawson and Tilley (1997) advocate an approach that draws on the principles of *critical realism* (see Box 1.8, p. 13) and which sees the outcome of an intervention as the result of generative mechanisms and the contexts of those mechanisms. A focus of the former element entails examining the causal factors that inhibit or promote change when an intervention occurs. Pawson and Tilley's approach is supportive of the use of both quantitative and qualitative research methods.

because it is frequently considered to be a yardstick against which quantitative research is judged. This occurs largely because of the fact that a true experiment will allow doubts about internal validity to be allayed and reflects the considerable emphasis placed on the determination of causality in quantitative research. As we will see in the next section, cross-sectional designs of the kind associated with social survey research are frequently regarded as limited, because of the problems of unambiguously imputing causality when using such designs.

Logic of comparison

However, before exploring such issues, it is important to draw attention to an important general lesson that an examination of experiments teaches us. A central feature of any experiment is the fact that it entails a *comparison*: at the very least it entails a comparison of results obtained by an experimental group with those engendered by a control group. In the case of the Howell and Frost (1989) experiment in Box 2.8 there is no control group: the research entails a comparison of the effects of three different forms of leadership. The advantage of carrying out any kind of comparison like this is that we understand the phenomenon that we are interested in better when we compare it with something else that is similar to it. The case for arguing that charismatic leadership is an effective, performance-enhancing form of leadership is much more persuasive when we view it in relation to other forms of leadership. Thus, while the specific considerations concerning experimental design are typically associated with quantitative research, the potential of comparison in social research represents a more general lesson that transcends matters of both research strategy and research design. In other words, while the experimental design is typically associated with a quantitative research strategy, the specific logic of comparison provides lessons of broad applicability and relevance. This issue is given more specific attention below in relation to the comparative design.

Cross-sectional design

The cross-sectional design is often called a social survey design, but the idea of the social survey is so closely connected in most people's minds with questionnaires and structured interviewing that the more generic sounding term *cross-sectional design* is preferable. While the research methods associated with social surveys are certainly frequently employed within the context of cross-sectional research, so too are many other research methods, including structured observation, content analysis, official statistics, and diaries. All of these research methods will be covered in later chapters, but in the meantime the basic structure of the cross-sectional design will be outlined.

The cross-sectional design is defined in Box 2.12. A number of elements of this definition have been emphasized.

- *More than one case*. Researchers employing a cross-sectional design are interested in variation. That variation can be in respect of people, families, organizations, nation states, or whatever. Variation can be established only when more than one case is being examined. Usually, researchers employing this design will select a lot more than two cases for a variety of reasons: they are more likely to encounter variation in all of the variables in which they are interested; they can make finer distinctions between cases; and the requirements of sampling procedure are likely to necessitate larger numbers (see Chapter 4).

- *At a single point in time*. In cross-sectional design research, data on the variables of interest are collected more or less simultaneously. When an individual completes a questionnaire, which may contain fifty or more variables, the answers are supplied at essentially the same time. This contrasts with an experimental design. Thus, in the classical experimental design, someone in the experimental group is pre-tested, then exposed to the experimental treatment, and then post-tested.

Days, weeks, months, or even years may separate the different phases. In the case of the Rosenthal and Jacobson (1968) study, eight months separated the pre- and post-testing of the schoolchildren in the study.

- *Quantitative or quantifiable data*. In order to establish variation between cases (and then to examine associations between variables—see next point), it is necessary to have a systematic and standardized method for gauging variation. One of the most important advantages of quantification is that it provides the researcher with a consistent benchmark. The advantages of quantification and of measurement will be addressed in greater detail in Chapter 3.

- *Patterns of association*. With a cross-sectional design it is only possible to examine relationships between variables. There is no time ordering to the variables, because the data on them are collected more or less simultaneously, and the researcher does not (invariably because he or she cannot) manipulate any of the variables. This creates the problem referred to in Box 2.6 as 'ambiguity about the direction of causal influence'. If the researcher discovers a relationship between two variables, he or she cannot be certain whether this denotes a causal relationship, because the features of an experimental design are not present. All that can be said is the variables are related. This is not to say that it is not possible to draw causal inferences from research based on a cross-sectional design. As will be shown in Chapter 11, there are a number of ways in which the researcher is able to draw certain inferences about causality, but these inferences rarely have the credibility of causal findings deriving from an experimental design. As a result, cross-sectional research invariably lacks the internal validity that one finds in most experimental research (see the examples in Boxes 2.13 and 2.14).

In this book, the term 'social survey' will be reserved for research that employs a cross-sectional research design and in which data are collected by questionnaire or by structured interview (see Box 2.15). This will allow me to retain the conventional

---

Box 2.12 **What is a cross-sectional research design?**

A cross-sectional design entails the collection of data on *more than one case* (usually quite a lot more than one) and at *a single point in time* in order to collect a body of *quantitative* or *quantifiable data* in connection with two or more variables (usually many more than two), which are then examined to detect *patterns of association*.

Box 2.13 Cross-sectional design and internal validity: An example based on the Health and Lifestyle Survey

Blaxter (1990) reports some of the findings of a large-scale cross-sectional study in which data were collected by three methods: a structured interview; physiological data on each respondent carried out by a nurse; and a self-administered questionnaire. Data were collected from a *random sample* of around 9,000 individuals. At one point Blaxter shows that there is a relationship between whether a person smokes and his or her diet. But how are we to interpret this relationship? Blaxter is quite properly cautious and does not infer any kind of causal relationship between the two. On the basis of the data, we cannot conclude whether smoking causes diet or whether diet causes smoking or whether the association between the two is actually an artefact of a third variable, such as a commitment or indifference to a 'healthy' lifestyle. There is, therefore, an ambiguity about the direction of causal influence.

Box 2.14 Direction of causality: Is sex good for you?

An article in the *Guardian*'s Health section (Houghton 1998) reviewed evidence about whether sex is good for you. At one point, the author refers to a study of men that seems to suggest that sex does bring health benefits, but she also has to acknowledge the problem of the direction of cause and effect:

A study of 1,000 men in Caerphilly found that those who had two or more orgasms a week halved their mortality risk compared with those who had orgasms less than once a month. But while the authors concluded that sex seems to have a protective effect on men's health, it is always possible that the association is the other way around—people who are ill are less likely to have sex in the first place.   (Houghton 1998: 14)

---

understanding of what a social survey is while recognizing that the cross-sectional research design has a wider relevance—that is, one that is not necessarily associated with the collection of data by questionnaire or by structured interview.

Reliability, replicability, and validity

How does cross-sectional research measure up in terms of the previously outlined criteria for evaluating quantitative research: reliability, replicability, and validity?

• The issues of reliability and measurement validity are primarily matters relating to the quality of the measures that are employed to tap the concepts in which the researcher is interested, rather than matters to do with a research design. In order to address questions of the quality of measures, some of the issues outlined in Chapter 3 would have to be considered.

• Replicability is likely to be present in most cross-sectional research to the degree that the researcher spells out procedures for: selecting respondents; designing measures of concepts; administration of research instruments (such as structured interview or self-administered questionnaire); and the

---

Box 2.15 What is social survey research?

Social survey research comprises a cross-sectional design in relation to which data are collected predominantly by questionnaire or by structured interview on *more than one case* (usually quite a lot more than one) and at *a single point in time* in order to collect a body of *quantitative* or *quantifiable data* in connection with two or more variables (usually many more than two), which are then examined to detect *patterns of association*.

analysis of data. Most quantitative research based on cross-sectional research designs specifies such procedures to a large degree.

- Internal validity is typically weak. As has just been suggested above, it is difficult to establish causal direction from the resulting data. Cross-sectional research designs produce associations rather than findings from which causal inferences can be unambiguously made. However, procedures for making causal inferences from cross-sectional data will be referred to in Chapter 11, though most researchers feel that the resulting causal findings rarely have the internal validity of those deriving from experimental designs.

- External validity is strong when, as in the case of research like Blaxter's (1990) study of Health and Lifestyles, the sample from which data are collected has been randomly selected. When non-random methods of sampling are employed, external validity becomes questionable. Sampling issues will be specifically addressed in Chapter 4.

- Since much cross-sectional research makes a great deal of use of research instruments, such as self-administered questionnaires and structured observation schedules, ecological validity may be jeopardized because the very instruments disrupt the 'natural habitat' as Cicourel (1982) put it (see quotation on p. 31).

Non-manipulable variables

As was noted at the beginning of the section on Experimental Design, in much if not most social research it is not possible to manipulate the variables in which we are interested. This is why most quantitative social research employs a cross-sectional research design rather than an experimental one. If we wanted internally valid findings in connection with the smoking–diet relationship investigated by Blaxter (1990) (see Box 2.12), we would need to manipulate one of the variables. For example, if we believed that smoking influences diet (perhaps because smoking is an expensive habit, which may affect people's ability to afford certain kinds of food), we might envisage an experiment in which we took the following steps:

- select a random sample of members of the public who do not smoke;

- establish their current dietary habits;

- randomly assign them to one of three experimental treatments: heavy smokers, moderate smokers, and non-smokers (who act as a control group); and

- after a certain amount of time establish their dietary habits.

Such a research design is almost laughable, because practical and ethical considerations are bound to render it unworkable. We would have to turn some people into smokers and in view of the evidence of the harmful effects of smoking, this would be profoundly unethical. Also, in view of the evidence about the effects of smoking, it is extremely unlikely that we would find people who would be prepared to allow themselves to be turned into smokers. We might offer incentives for them to become smokers but that might invalidate any findings about the effects on diet if we believe that economic considerations play an important role in relation to the effects of smoking on diet. This research is essentially unworkable.

Moreover, some of the variables in which social scientists are interested, and which are often viewed as potentially significant independent variables, simply cannot be manipulated, other than by extreme measures. To more or less all intents and purposes, our ethnicity, age, gender, and social backgrounds are 'givens' that are not really amenable to the kind of manipulation that is necessary for a true experimental design. A man might be able to present himself through dress and make-up as a woman to investigate the impact of gender on job opportunities, as Dustin Hoffman's character did in the film *Tootsie*, but it is unlikely that we would find a sufficient number of men to participate in a meaningful experiment to allow such an issue to be investigated (although Box 2.16 provides interesting cases of the manipulation of seemingly non-manipulable variables). Moreover, it could be reasonably argued that even if we could bring this research design to fruition, the researcher would be examining the effects of only the external signs of

Box 2.16 **Manipulating a non-manipulable variable: Body weight**

Elizia Volkman, an academic, was interested in the ways in which people respond to 'overweight' as against 'normal weight' people. She could have compared the accounts of people of different body weights through interviews or even observed responses to them. Instead, she conducted a personal experiment because she gorged herself so that she filled her 5ft 2in frame to 15 stone. She then gauged reactions to her as she gradually slimmed down again. Apparently, the effects of being fat were not as negative as might be anticipated, because she claims that she 'had the most unbelievably good-looking man chat her up' (Wilkinson and Whitworth 1998: 3)

Box 2.17 **Manipulating a non-manipulable variable: Ethnicity**

In the 1950s, John Howard Griffin (1961) blackened his face and visible parts of his body and travelled around the American South as a person of colour. He behaved appropriately by keeping his eyes averted to show due deference to whites. He was treated as a black man in a number of ways, such as by having to use water fountains designated for 'coloreds'. Griffin's aim was to experience what it was like being a black person in a period and region of racial segregation.

gender and would be neglecting its more subjective and experiential aspects. Similarly, while the case of a white man presenting himself as a black man in Box 2.17 is interesting, it is doubtful whether a brief sojourn as a person of colour could adequately capture the experience of being black in the American South. Such an experience is formed by many years of personal experience and the knowledge that it will be an ongoing experience. Thus, although the cases described in Boxes 2.16 and 2.17 provide interesting cases of manipulating apparently non-manipulable variables—body size and ethnicity—it is doubtful whether they could meaningfully be applied to an experimental context, not least because it is doubtful whether sufficient numbers of people could be found to endure the discomforts and inconvenience.

On the other hand, the very fact that we can regard certain variables as givens provides us with a clue as to how we can make causal inferences in cross-sectional research. Many of the variables in which we are interested can be *assumed* to be temporally prior to other variables. For example, we can assume that, if we find a relationship between ethnic status and alcohol consumption, that the former is more likely to be the independent variable because it

is temporally prior to alcohol consumption. In other words, while we cannot manipulate ethnic status, we can draw causal inferences from cross-sectional data.

Structure of the cross-sectional design

The cross-sectional research design is not easy to depict in terms of the notation previously introduced, but Figure 2.2 captures its main features, except that in this case Obs simply represents an observation made in relation to a variable.

Figure 2.2 implies that a cross-sectional design comprises the collection of data on a series of variables (Obs_1 Obs_2 Obs_3 Obs_4 Obs_5 . . . Obs_n) at a single point in time, T_1. The effect is to create what Marsh (1982) referred to as a 'rectangle' of data that comprises variables Obs_1 to Obs_n and cases $case_1$ to $case_n$, as in Figure 2.3. For each case (which may be a person, household, city, nation, etc.) data are available for each of the variables, Obs_1 to Obs_n, all of

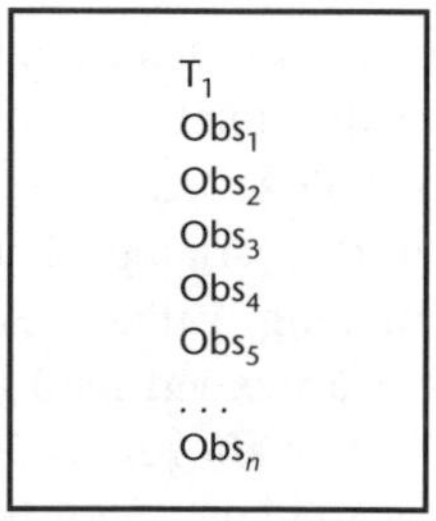

T_1
Obs_1
Obs_2
Obs_3
Obs_4
Obs_5
. . .
Obs_n

Fig. 2.2 A cross-sectional design

	Obs$_1$	Obs$_2$	Obs$_3$	Obs$_4$	$\cdots$	Obs$_n$
Case$_1$						
Case$_2$						
Case$_3$						
Case$_4$						
Case$_5$						
$\cdots$						
Case$_n$						

Fig. 2.3 The data rectangle in cross-sectional research

which will have been collected at T$_1$. Each cell in the matrix will have data in it.

Cross-sectional design and research strategy

This discussion of the cross-sectional design has placed it firmly in the context of quantitative research. Also, the evaluation of the design drew on criteria associated with the quantitative research strategy. It should also be noted, however, that qualitative research often entails a form of cross-sectional design. A fairly typical form of such research is when the researcher employs unstructured interviewing or semi-structured interviewing with a number of people. Box 2.18 provides an illustration of such a study.

While emphatically within the qualitative research tradition, the study described in Box 2.18 bears many research design similarities with cross-sectional studies within a quantitative research tradition, like Blaxter (1990). Moreover, it is a very popular mode of qualitative research. The research was not preoccupied with such criteria of quantitative research as internal and external validity, replicability, measurement validity, and so on. In fact, it could be argued that the conversational interview style made the study more ecologically valid than research using more formal instruments of data collection. It is also striking that the study was concerned with the factors that influence food selection, like vegetarianism. The very notion of an 'influence' carries a strong connotation of causality, suggesting that qualitative researchers are interested in the investigation of causes and effects, albeit not in the context of the language of variables that so pervades quantitative research. Also, the emphasis was much more on elucidating the *experience* of something like vegetarianism than is often the case with quantitative research. However, the chief point in providing the illustration is that it bears many similarities to the cross-sectional design in quantitative research. It entailed the interviewing of quite a large number of people and at a single point in time. Just as with many quantitative studies using a cross-sectional design, the examination of early influences on people's past and current behaviour is based on their retrospective accounts of factors that influenced them in the past.

Longitudinal design(s)

The longitudinal design represents a distinct form of research design. Because of the time and cost involved, it is a relatively little-used design in social

---

Box 2.18 Qualitative research within a cross-sectional design

Beardsworth and Keil (1992) carried out a study of the dietary beliefs and practices of vegetarians. They write that their intention was to contribute 'to the analysis of the cultural and sociological factors which influence patterns of food selection and avoidance. The specific focus is on contemporary vegetarianism, a complex of inter-related beliefs, attitudes and practices . . .' (1992: 253).

The authors carried out 'relatively unstructured interviews', which were 'guided by an inventory of issues' with seventy-six vegetarians and vegans in the East Midlands (1992: 261). Respondents were identified through a *snowball sampling* approach. The interviews were taped and transcribed, yielding a large corpus of qualitative data.

research, so it is not proposed to allocate a great deal of space to it. In the form in which it is typically found in social science subjects such as sociology, social policy, and human geography, it is usually an extension of social survey research based on self-administered questionnaire or structured interview research within a cross-sectional design. Consequently, in terms of reliability, replication, and validity, the longitudinal design is little different from cross-sectional research. However, a longitudinal design can allow some insight into the time order of variables and therefore may be more able to allow causal inferences to be made.

With a longitudinal design a sample is surveyed and is surveyed again on at least one further occasion. It is common to distinguish two types of longitudinal design: the *panel study* and the *cohort study*. With the former type, a sample, often a randomly selected national one, is the focus of data collection on at least two (and often more) occasions. Data may

---

Box 2.20 **The National Child Development Study**

The National Child Development Study (NCDS) is based on all 17,000 children born in Great Britain in the week of 3–9 March 1958. The study was initially motivated by a concern over levels of perinatal mortality, but the data collected reflect a much wider range of issues than this focus implies. Data were collected on the children and their families at age 7. In fact, the study was not originally planned as a longitudinal study. The children and their families have been followed up at ages 11, 16, 23, and 33. Data are collected in relation to a number of areas, including: physical and mental health; family; parenting; occupation and income; and housing and environment.

For further information, see Fox and Fogelman (1990); Hodges (1998); and

http://www.mimas.ac.uk/surveys/ncds

Box 2.19 **The British Household Panel Study**

The British Household Panel Study (BHPS) began in 1991 when a national representative sample of 10,264 individuals in 5,538 households were interviewed for the first time in connection with six main areas of interest:

- household organization;
- labour market behaviour;
- income and wealth;
- housing;
- health; and
- socio-economic values.

Panel members are interviewed annually. An early report of BHPS findings examined voting intentions in the first two waves of data collection (Brynin 1994). The report was able to show that voting intentions are more unstable than is often thought, so that the notion of people identifying with a political party is rendered somewhat problematic.

For further information see:

http://www.iser.essex.ac.uk/bhps

---

be collected from different types of case within a panel study framework: people, households, organizations, schools, and so on. An illustration of this kind of study is the British Household Panel Study (BHPS) (see Box 2.19).

The cohort study selects either an entire cohort of people or a randomly selected sample of them as the focus of data collection. The cohort is made up of people who share a certain characteristic, such as all being born in the same week or having a certain experience, such as being unemployed or getting married on a certain day or in the same week. The National Child Development Study is an example of a cohort study (see Box 2.20). At the end of 1999, the Economic and Social Research Council in the UK anounced a new cohort study—the ESRC Millennium Cohort—which was to collect data on around 15,000 children born in the new millennium (mid-2000 to mid-2001). The first phase of data collection was scheduled to begin around six months after the birth of the sampled children. Further details were available at the time of writing at:

http://www.esrc.ac.uk/millcoh.htm

Panel and cohort studies share similar features. They have a similar design structure: Figure 2.4 portrays this structure and implies that data are collected in at least two waves on the same variables on the same people. They are both concerned with illuminating social change and improving the understanding of causal influences over time. The latter means that longitudinal designs are somewhat better able to deal with the problem of 'ambiguity about the direction of causal influence' that plagues cross-sectional designs. Because certain potentially independent variables can be identified at T_1, the researcher is in a better position to infer that purported effects that are identified at T_2 or later have occurred *after* the independent variables. This does not deal with the entire problem about the ambiguity of causal influence, but it at least addresses the problem of knowing which variable came first. In all other respects, the points made above about cross-sectional designs are the same as those for longitudinal designs.

Panel and cohort studies share similar problems. First, there is the problem of sample attrition through death, moving, and so on, and through subjects choosing to withdraw at later stages of the research. Menard (1991) cites the case of a study of adolescent drug use in the USA in which 55 per cent of subjects were lost over an eight-year period. However, attrition rates are by no means always as high as this. In 1981, the National Child Development Study managed to secure data from 12,537 members of the original 17,414 cohort, which is quite an achievement bearing in mind that twenty-three years would have elapsed since the birth of the children. In 1991, data were elicited from 11,407. The problem with attrition is largely that those who leave the study may differ in some important respects from those who remain, so that the latter do not form a representative group. Secondly, there are few guidelines as to when is the best juncture to conduct further waves of data collection. Thirdly, it is often suggested that many longitudinal studies are poorly thought out and that they result in the collection of large amounts of data with little apparent planning. Fourthly, there is evidence that a *panel conditioning* effect can occur whereby continued participation in a longitudinal study affects how respondents behave. Menard (1991) refers to a study of family caregiving in which 52 per cent of respondents indicated that they responded differently to providing care for relatives as a result of their participation in the research.

Case study design

The basic case study entails the detailed and intensive analysis of a single case. As Stake (1995) observes, case study research is concerned with the complexity and particular nature of the case in question. Some of the best-known studies in sociology are based on this kind of design. They include research on:

- a single community, such as Whyte's (1955) study of Cornerville in Boston, Gans's (1962) study of the East End of Boston, and M. Stacey's (1960) research on Banbury;

- a single school, such as studies by Ball (1981) and by Burgess (1983) on Beachside Comprehensive and Bishop McGregor respectively;

- a single family, like Lewis's (1961) study of the Sánchez family;

- a single organization, such as studies of a factory by writers such as Burawoy (1979), Pollert (1981), and Cavendish (1982), or of management in organizations like Pettigrew's (1985) work on Imperial Chemical Industries (ICI), or of pilferage in a single location like a bakery (Ditton 1977), or of a single police service (Holdaway 1983; see Box 2.21);

T_1	$\cdots$	T_n
Obs_1		Obs_1
Obs_2		Obs_2
Obs_3		Obs_3
Obs_4		Obs_4
Obs_5		Obs_5
$\cdots$		$\cdots$
Obs_n		Obs_n

Fig. 2.4 The longitudinal design

- a person, like the famous study of Stanley, the 'jack-roller' (Shaw 1930); such studies are characterized as using the life history or biographical approach; and

- a single event, such as the Cuban Missile Crisis (Allison 1971), a vicious rape attack (Winkler 1995), the events surrounding the media reporting of a specific issue area (Deacon, Fenton, and Bryman 1999), and the Balinese cockfight (Geertz 1973b).

What is a case?

The most common use of the term associates the case study with a location, such as a community or organization. The emphasis tends to be upon an intensive examination of the setting. There is a tendency to associate case studies with qualitative research, but such an identification is not appropriate. It is certainly true that exponents of the case study design often favour qualitative methods, such as participant observation and unstructured interviewing, because these methods are viewed as particularly helpful in the generation of an intensive, detailed examination of a case. However, case studies are frequently sites for the employment of *both* quantitative and qualitative research, an approach that will receive attention in Chapter 23. Indeed, in some instances, when an investigation is based exclusively upon quantitative research, it can be dif-

ficult to determine whether it is better described as a case study or as a cross-sectional research design. The same point can often be made about case studies based upon qualitative research.

As an illustration of the difficulties of writing about case studies, consider the study described in Box 2.22. Ostensibly, it is similar to Beardsworth and Keil's (1992) study of vegetarians in that it is a piece of qualitative research within a cross-sectional design framework (see Box 2.18). However, it has been described as providing 'case-study evidence' by Davies *et al.* (1994: 157), presumably on the grounds

---

Box 2.21 A case study

Holdaway (1982, 1983) was a police officer who was also conducting doctoral research on his own police service, which was located in a city. His main research method was ethnography, whereby he was a participant observer who observed interaction, listened to conversations, examined documents, and wrote up his impressions and experiences in field notes. Holdaway's superiors did not know that he was conducting research on his own force, so that he was a covert researcher. This is a controversial method on ethical grounds (see Chapters 13 and 24). Holdaway's research provides insights into the nature of police work and the occupational culture with which officers surround themselves.

Box 2.22 Qualitative research within a cross-sectional design, or is it a case study?

McKee and Bell examined forty-five couples in a single location (Kidderminster in the West Midlands) in order to examine 'the impact of male unemployment on family and marital relations' (1985: 387). They describe their research instrument as an 'unstructured, conversational interview style'. In most cases, husbands and wives were interviewed jointly. The interviews were very non-directive, allowing the couples considerable freedom to answer in their own terms and time. Their research focused on the range of problems faced by unemployed families, the processes by which they cope,

and the variations in their experiences. Thus, the focus was very much on the experience of unemployment, from the perspective of the couples. The authors show, for example, that the impact of husbands' unemployment on their wives is often far greater than is usually appreciated, since research often takes the unemployed person as the main hub of the enquiry. Couples often reported changes to the domestic division of labour, which in turn raised questions for them about images of masculinity and identity.

that the fieldwork was undertaken in a single location. I would prefer to reserve the term 'case study' for those instances where the 'case' is the focus of interest in its own right. The study in Box 2.22 is no more a case study of Kidderminster than Beardsworth and Keil's (1992) research is based on a case study of the East Midlands. McKee and Bell's (1985) research is concerned with the experience of unemployment among the forty-five couples whom they interviewed. It is not concerned with Kidderminster as such. The town provides a kind of backdrop to the findings rather than a focus of interest in its own right.

Similarly, Powell and Butterfield (1997) present a quantitative analysis of promotion decisions in a US government department. They were concerned to investigate how far race had an impact on promotions within the department. The researchers found that race did not have a direct effect on promotion, but it did have an indirect effect. This occurred because race had an impact on two variables—whether the applicant was employed in the hiring department and the number of years of work experience—which in turn affected promotion. The impact of race on these two variables was such that people of colour were disadvantaged with respect to promotion. Once again, we see here a study that has the hallmarks of both a cross-sectional design and a case study, but this time the research strategy was a quantitative one. As with the McKee and Bell (1985) research, it seems better to describe it as employing a cross-sectional design rather than a case study, because the case itself is not the apparent object of interest: it is little more than a location that forms a backdrop to the findings. Similarly, I would tend to argue that the study of redundant steelworkers by Westergaard *et al.* (1989) is a case study of the effects of redundancy in which a quantitative research strategy has been employed with clear indications of a cross-sectional design. With a case study, the case is an object of interest in its own right and the researcher aims to provide an in-depth elucidation of it. Unless a distinction of this or some other kind is drawn, it becomes impossible to distinguish the case study as a special research design, because almost any kind of research can be

construed as a case study: research based on a national, random sample of the population of Great Britain would have to be considered a case study of Great Britain! However, it also needs to be appreciated that, when specific research illustrations are examined, they can exhibit features of more than one research design. What distinguishes a case study is that the researcher is usually concerned to elucidate the unique features of the case. This is known as an *idiographic* approach. Research designs like the cross-sectional design are known as *nomothetic* in that they are concerned with generating statements that apply regardless of time and place.

With experimental and cross-sectional designs, the typical orientation to the relationship between theory and research is a deductive one. The research design and the collection of data are guided by specific research questions that derive from theoretical concerns. However, when a qualitative research strategy is employed within a cross-sectional design, as in Beardsworth and Keil's (1992) research, the approach tends to be inductive. In other words, whether a cross-sectional design is inductive or deductive tends to be affected by whether a quantitative or a qualitative research strategy is employed. The same point can be made of case study research. When the predominant research strategy is qualitative, a case study tends to take an inductive approach to the relationship between theory and research; if a predominantly quantitative strategy is taken, it tends to be deductive.

Reliability, replicability, and validity

The question of how well the case study fares in the context of the research design criteria cited early on in this chapter—measurement validity, internal validity, external validity, ecological validity, reliability, and replicability—depends in large part on how far the researcher feels that these are appropriate for the evaluation of case study research. Some writers on case study research, like Yin (1984), consider that they are appropriate criteria and suggest ways in which case study research can be developed to enhance its ability to meet the criteria; for others, like Stake (1995), they are barely mentioned if at all. Writers on case study research whose point of orientation lies primarily with a qualitative research strategy tend to play down or ignore the salience of these factors, whereas those writers who have been strongly influenced by the quantitative research strategy tend to depict them as more significant.

However, one question on which a great deal of discussion has centred concerns the *external validity* or *generalizability* of case study research. How can a single case possibly be representative so that it might yield findings that can be applied more generally to other cases? For example, how could the findings from Holdaway's (1982, 1983) research, referred to in Box 2.21, be generalizable to all police services in Great Britain? The answer, of course, is that they cannot. It is important to appreciate that case study researchers do not delude themselves that it is possible to identify typical cases that can be used to represent a certain class of objects, whether it is factories, mass media reporting, police services, or communities. In other words, they do *not* think that a case study is a sample of one.

Types of case

Following on from the issue of external validity, it is useful to consider a distinction between different types of case that is sometimes made by writers. Yin (1984) distinguishes three types.

- The *critical case*. Here the researcher has a clearly specified hypothesis, and a case is chosen on the grounds that it will allow a better understanding of the circumstances in which the hypothesis will and will not hold. The study by Festinger *et al.* (1956) of a religious cult whose members believed that the end of the world was about to happen is an example. The fact that the event did not happen by the appointed day allowed the researchers to test the authors' propositions about how people respond to thwarted expectations.

- The *unique case*. The unique or *extreme* case is, as Yin observes, a common focus in clinical studies.

For example, some years ago the *Sunday Times Magazine* carried a lead article about Erich Fuchs, an American who seems incapable of catching AIDS (C. Thompson 1996). He has been injected with the virus on a number of occasions, but his body rejects it. He is clearly not representative but a special case who, the authors of the article suggest, may hold some keys to a cure. He is not literally unique, because a small number of similar individuals have been identified, but he warrants being considered a unique case because of the unusual nature of his resistance to the virus. Closer to the social sciences, Margaret Mead's (1928) well-known study of growing up in Samoa seems to have been motivated by her belief that the country represented a unique case. She argued that, unlike most other societies, Samoan youth do not suffer a period of anxiety and stress in adolescence. The factors associated with this relatively trouble-free period in their lives were of interest to her, since they might contain lessons for Western youth. Fielding (1982) conducted research on the extreme right-wing organization, the National Front. While the National Front was not unique on the British political scene, it was extremely prominent at the time of his research and was beginning to become an electoral force. As such, it held an intrinsic interest that made it essentially unique.

- The *revelatory case*. The basis for the revelatory case exists 'when an investigator has an opportunity to observe and analyse a phenomenon previously inaccessible to scientific investigation' (Yin 1984: 44). As examples, Yin cites Whyte's (1955) study of Cornerville, and Liebow's (1967) research on unemployed blacks. While the idea of the revelatory case is interesting, it seems unnecessary to restrict it solely to situations in which something has not previously been studied. Much qualitative case study research that is carried out with a predominantly inductive approach to theory treats single case studies as broadly 'revelatory'.

Exponents of case study research counter suggestions that the evidence they present is limited because it has restricted external validity by arguing that it is not the purpose of this research design to generalize to other cases or to populations beyond the case. This position is very different from that taken by practitioners of social survey research. Social survey researchers are invariably concerned to be able to generalize their findings to larger populations and frequently use random sampling to enhance the representativeness of the samples on which they conduct their investigations and therefore the external validity of their findings. Case study researchers argue strenuously that this is not the purpose of their craft.

Case study as intensive analysis

Instead, case study researchers tend to argue that they aim to generate an intensive examination of a single case, in relation to which they then engage in a theoretical analysis. The central issue of concern is the quality of the theoretical reasoning in which the case study researcher engages. How well do the data support the theoretical arguments that are generated? Is the theoretical analysis incisive? For example, does it demonstrate connections between different conceptual ideas that are developed out of the data? The crucial question is not whether the findings can be generalized to a wider universe, but how well the researcher generates theory out of the findings (Mitchell 1983; Yin 1984). Such a view places case study research firmly in the inductive tradition of the relationship between theory and research. However, a case study design is not necessarily associated with an inductive approach, as can be seen in the research by Adler and Adler (1985), which was referred to in Chapter 1. Thus, case studies can be associated with both theory generation and theory testing.

Longitudinal research and the case study

Case study research frequently includes a longitudinal element. The researcher is often a participant of an organization or member of a community for many months or years. Alternatively, he or she may conduct interviews with individuals over a lengthy period. Moreover, the researcher may be able to inject an additional longitudinal element by analysing archival information and by retrospective interviewing. Box 2.23 provides an illustration of such research.

Another way in which a longitudinal element occurs is when a case that has been studied is returned to at a later stage. A particularly interesting instance of this is Middletown, a pseudonym for a town in the American Midwest that was originally studied by Lynd and Lynd in 1924–5 (Lynd and Lynd 1929) and was restudied to discern trends and changes in 1935 (Lynd and Lynd 1937). In 1977, the community was restudied yet again (Bahr *et al.* 1983), using the same research instruments but with minor changes. Burgess (1987) was similarly concerned with continuity and change at the comprehensive school he had studied in the early 1970s (Burgess 1983) when he returned to study it ten years later. However, as he observes, it is difficult for the researcher to establish how far change is the result of real differences over the two time periods or of other factors, such as different people at the school, different educational issues between the two time periods, and the possible influence of the initial study itself.

Comparative design

It is worth distinguishing one further kind of design: comparative design. Put simply, this design entails the study using more or less identical

---

Box 2.23 A case study of ICI

Pettigrew (1985) conducted research into the use of organizational development expertise at Imperial Chemical Industries (ICI). The fieldwork was conducted between 1975 and 1983. He carried out 'long semistructured interviews' in 1975–7 and again in 1980–2. During the period of the fieldwork he also had fairly regular contact with members of the organization. He writes: 'The continuous real-time data collection was enriched by retrospective interviewing and archival analysis . . .' (1985: 40).

methods of two contrasting cases. It embodies the logic of comparison in that it implies that we can understand social phenomena better when they are compared in relation to two or more meaningfully contrasting cases or situations. The comparative design may be realized in the context of either quantitative or qualitative research. Within the former, the data collection strategy will take the form outlined in Figure 2.5. This figure implies that there are at least two cases (which may be organizations, nations, communities, police forces, etc.) and that data are collected from each usually within a cross-sectional design format.

One of the more obvious forms of such research is in cross-cultural or cross-national research. In a useful definition, Hantrais (1996) has suggested that such research occurs

when individuals or teams set out to examine particular issues or phenomena in two or more countries with the express intention of comparing their manifestations in different socio-cultural settings (institutions, customs, traditions, value systems, life styles, language, thought patterns), using the same research instruments either to carry out secondary analysis of national data or to conduct new empirical work. The aim may be to seek explanations for similarities and differences or to gain a greater awareness and a deeper understanding of social reality in different national contexts.

The research by Kelley and De Graaf (1997),

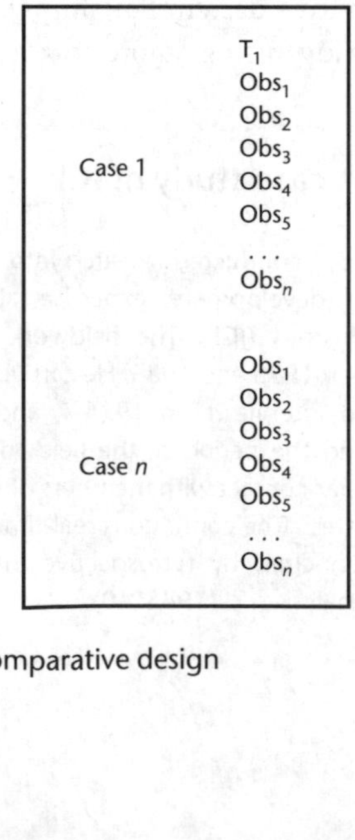

Fig. 2.5 A comparative design

referred to in Box 1.5 (see p. 9), is an illustration of cross-cultural research that entails a secondary analysis of social survey evidence collected in fifteen nations. A further illustration is Gallie's (1978) research on the impact of advanced automation on comparable samples of industrial workers in both England and France. Cross-cultural research is not without problems such as: managing and gaining the funding for such research (see Box 2.24); ensuring, when existing data, such as official statistics or survey evidence, are submitted to a secondary analysis, that the data are comparable in terms of categories and data-collection methods; and ensuring, when new data are being collected, that the need to translate data-collection instruments (for example, interview schedules) does not undermine genuine comparability. This last problem raises the further difficulty that, even when translation is carried out competently, there is still the potential problem of an insensitivity to specific national and cultural contexts. On the other hand, cross-cultural research helps to reduce the risk of failing to appreciate that social science findings are often, if not invariably, culturally specific.

Comparative research should not be treated as solely concerned with comparisons between nations. The logic of comparison can be applied to a variety of situations. The Social Change and Economic Life Initiative, referred to in Box 3.1 (p. 64), entailed identical studies (mainly involving social survey research) in six contrasting labour markets, which were chosen to reflect different patterns of economic change in the early to mid-1980s and in the then recent past. By choosing meaningful contrasts, the significance of the different patterns for a variety of experiences of both employers and employees could be portrayed. Such designs are not without problems: the differences that are observed between the contrasting cases may not be due exclusively to the distinguishing features of the cases. Thus, some caution is necessary when explaining contrasts between cases in terms of differences between them.

In terms of issues of reliability, validity, replicability, and generalizability, the comparative study is no different from the cross-sectional design. The comparative design is essentially two or more cross-

Box 2.24 Managing cross-cultural research

As its name implies, cross-cultural research entails the collection and/or analysis of data from two or more nations. Possible models for the conduct of cross-cultural research are as follows.

1. A researcher, perhaps in conjunction with a research team, collects data in a number of countries. Gallie's (1978) research on the impact of advanced automation on industrial workers is an illustration of this model in that he took comparable samples of industrial workers from two oil refineries in both England and France.

2. A central organization coordinates a portion of the work of national organizations. The article by Kelley and De Graaf (1997) that is cited in this chapter provides an example of this model.

3. The secondary analysis is carried out of data that are comparable, but where the coordination of their collection is limited or non-existent. This kind of cross-cultural analysis might occur if researchers seek to ask survey questions in their own country that have been asked in another country. The ensuing data may then be analysed cross-culturally. A further form of this model is through the secondary analysis of officially collected data, such as unemployment statistics. Wall's (1989) analysis of the living arrangements of the elderly in eighteen European countries is an example of such research. The research uncovered considerable diversity in terms of such factors as whether the elderly lived alone and whether they were in institutional care. However, this approach is beset with problems associated with the deficiencies of many forms of official statistics (see Chapter 10) and problems of cross-national variations in official definitions and collection procedures.

4. Teams of researchers in participating nations are recruited by a person or body that coordinates the programme. Each researcher or group of researchers has the responsibility of conducting the investigation in his/her/their own country. The work is co-ordinated in order to ensure comparability of research questions, survey questions, and procedures for administering the research instruments (e.g. Kohn et al. 1990). This model differs from (2) above in that it usually entails a specific focus on certain research questions.

---

sectional studies carried out at more or less the same point in time.

The comparative design can also be applied in relation to a qualitative research strategy. When this occurs, it takes the form of a multiple-case study (see Box 2.25). In recent years, a number of writers have argued for a greater use of case study research that entails the investigation of more than one case. Indeed, in certain social science fields, like organization studies, this has become a common research design in its own right. Essentially, a multiple-case (or multi-case) study occurs whenever the number of cases examined exceeds one. The main argument in favour of the multiple-case study is that it improves theory building. By comparing two or more cases, the researcher is in a better position to establish the circumstances in which a theory will or will not hold (Yin 1984, Eisenhardt 1989). Moreover, the comparison may itself suggest concepts that are relevant to an emerging theory.

Box 2.25 describes one approach to selecting cases for a multiple-case study. In this illustration, cases were selected on the basis of their representing extreme types—namely, successful and unsuccessful firms, and their operation in certain commercial sectors. With a case selection approach such as this, the findings that are common to the firms can be just as interesting and important as those that differentiate them.

However, not all writers are convinced about the merits of multiple-case study research. Dyer and Wilkins (1991), for example, argue that a multiple-case study approach tends to mean that the researcher pays less attention to the specific context and more to the ways in which the cases can be contrasted. Moreover, the need to forge comparisons tends to mean that the researcher needs to develop an explicit focus at the outset, whereas it may be advantageous to adopt a more open-ended approach in many instances. These concerns about retaining contextual insight and a rather more unstructured research approach are very much associated with the goals of the qualitative research strategy (see Chapter 13).

The key to the comparative design is its ability to allow the distinguishing characteristics of two or more cases to act as a springboard for theoretical reflections about contrasting findings. It is something of a hybrid, in that in quantitative research it is frequently an extension of a cross-sectional design and in qualitative research it is frequently an extension of a case study design. It even exhibits certain features that are similar to experiments and quasi-experiments, which also rely on the capacity to forge a comparison.

Box 2.25 A multiple-case study

In their study of the factors that contribute to competitive success among large British companies, Pettigrew and Whipp (1991) adopted a multiple-case study approach. They examined eight companies, which were made up of a successful and an unsuccessful company in each of four commercial sectors (automobile manufacturing; merchant banking; life assurance; and book publishing). By strategically choosing companies in this way, they could establish the common and differentiating factors that lay behind the successful management of change.

Bringing research strategy and research design together

Finally, we can bring together the two research strategies covered in Chapter 1 with the research designs outlined in this chapter. Table 2.1 shows the typical form associated with each combination of research strategy and research design and a number of examples that either have been encountered so far or will be covered in later chapters. Table 2.1 refers also to research methods that will be encountered in later chapters, but which have not been referred to so far. The Glossary will give you a quick reference to terms used that are not yet familiar to you.

The distinctions are not always perfect. In particular, in some qualitative research it is not obvious whether a study is an example of a longitudinal design or a case study design. Life history studies, research that concentrates on a specific issue over time (e.g. Deacon, Fenton, and Bryman 1999), and ethnography in which the researcher charts change in a single case are examples of studies that cross the two types. Such studies are perhaps better conceptualized as longitudinal case studies rather than as belonging to one category of research design or another. A further point to note is that there is no typical form in the qualitative research strategy/ experimental research design cell. Qualitative research in the context of true experiments is very unusual. However, as noted in the table, Bryman (1988a) refers to a qualitative study by Hall and Guthrie (1981), which employed a quasi-experimental design.

Table 2.1 Research strategy and research design

Research design	Research strategy	
	Quantitative	Qualitative
Experimental	*Typical form*. Most researchers using an experimental design employ quantitative comparisons between experimental and control groups with regard to the dependent variable. *Examples*. Boxes 2.5, 2.8.	No typical form. However, Bryman (1988*a*; 151–2) notes a study in which qualitative data on schoolchildren were collected within a quasi-experimental research design.
Cross-sectional	*Typical form*. Social survey research or structured observation on a sample at a single point in time. Content analysis on a sample of documents. *Examples*. Boxes 2.13, 4.2, 4.6, 8.7, 9.2, 9.3.	*Typical form*. Qualitative interviews or focus groups at a single point in time. Qualitative content analysis of a set of documents relating to a single period. *Examples*. Boxes 2.18, 2.22, 15.2, 15.9, 15.10, 17.5, 18.1, 18.2, 18.5, 18.6.
Longitudinal	*Typical form*. Social survey research on a sample on more than one occasion, as in panel and cohort studies. Content analysis of documents relating to different time periods. *Examples*. Boxes 2.19, 2.20.	*Typical form*. Ethnographic research over a long period, qualitative interviewing on more than one occasion, or qualitative content analysis of documents relating to different time periods. Such research warrants being dubbed longitudinal when there is a concern to map change. *Examples*. Boxes 2.23, 13.6, 14.12.
		$\updownarrow$
Case study	*Typical form*. Social survey research on a single case with a view to revealing important features about its nature. *Examples*. The choice by Goldthorpe *et al.* (1968) of Luton as a site for testing the thesis of *embourgeoisement*; the study of Westergaard *et al.* (1989) of the effects of redundancy at a Sheffield steel plant (Box 3.3).	*Typical form*. The intensive study by ethnography or qualitative interviewing of a single case, which may be an organization, life, family, or community. *Examples*. Boxes 1.10, 2.21, 14.2, 14.5, 14.7, 15.4, 17.6.
Comparative	*Typical form*. Social survey research in which there is a direct comparison between two or more cases, as in cross-cultural research. *Examples*. Box 1.5; Gallie (1978); Box 3.1.	*Typical form*. Ethnographic or qualitative interview research on two or more cases. *Examples*. Boxes 2.25, 13.8, 14.4.

Key points

- There is an important distinction between a research method and a research design.

- It is necessary to become thoroughly familiar with the meaning of the technical terms used as criteria for evaluating research: reliability; validity; replicability; and the types of validity (measurement, internal, external, ecological).

- It is also necessary to be familiar with the differences between the five major research designs covered: experimental; cross-sectional; longitudinal; case study; and comparative. In this context, it is important to realize that the term 'experiment', which is often used somewhat loosely, in everyday speech has a specific technical meaning.

- There are various potential threats to validity in non-experimental research.

- Although the case study is often thought to be a single type of research design, it in fact has several forms. It is also important to be aware of the key issues concerned with the nature of case study evidence in relation to issues like external validity (generalizability).

Revision questions

- In terms of the definitions used in this book, what are the chief differences between each of the following: a research method; a research strategy; and a research design?

Criteria in social research

- What are the differences between reliability and validity and why are these important criteria for the evaluation of social research?

- Outline the meaning of each of the following: measurement validity; internal validity; external validity; and ecological validity.

- Why have some qualitative researchers sought to devise alternative criteria from reliability and validity when assessing the quality of investigations?

- Why have some qualitative researchers *not* sought to devise alternative criteria from reliability and validity when assessing the quality of investigations?

Research designs

- What are the main research designs that have been outlined in this chapter?

- A researcher reasons that people who read broadsheet newspapers are likely to be more knowledgeable about personal finance than readers of tabloid newspapers. He interviews 100 people about the newspapers they read and their level of financial knowledge. Sixty-five people read tabloids and thirty-five read broadsheets. He finds that the broadsheet readers are on average considerably more knowledgeable about personal finance than tabloid readers. He concludes that reading broadsheets enhances levels of knowledge of personal finance. Assess his reasoning.

Experimental design

- 'The main importance of the experimental design for the social researcher is that it represents a model of how to infer causal connections between variables.' Discuss.

- Following on from the last question, if it is so useful and important, why is it not used more?

- What is a quasi-experiment?

Cross-sectional design

- What is meant by a cross-sectional research design?
- In what ways does the social survey exemplify the cross-sectional research design?
- Assess the degree to which the survey researcher can achieve internally valid findings.
- To what extent is the survey design exclusive to quantitative research?

Longitudinal design(s)

- Why might a longitudinal research design be superior to a cross-sectional one?
- What are the main differences between panel and cohort designs in longitudinal research?

Case study design

- What is a case study?
- Is case study research exclusive to qualitative research?
- What are some of the principles by which cases might be selected?

Comparative design

- What are the chief strengths of a comparative research design?
- Why might comparative research yield important insights?

Part Two

Part Two of this book is concerned with quantitative research. Chapter 3 sets the scene by exploring the main features of this research strategy. Chapter 4 discusses the ways in which we sample people on whom we carry out research. Chapter 5 focuses on the structured interview, which is one of the main methods of data collection in quantitative research and in survey research in particular. Chapter 6 is concerned with another prominent method of gathering data through survey research—questionnaires that people complete themselves. Chapter 7 provides guidelines on how to ask questions for structured interviews and questionnaires. Chapter 8 discusses structured observation, a method that provides a systematic approach to the observation of people. Chapter 9 addresses content analysis, which is a distinctive and systematic approach to the analysis of a wide variety of documents. Chapter 10 discusses the possibility of using in your own research data collected by other researchers or official statistics. Chapter 11 presents some of the main tools you will need to conduct quantitative data analysis. Chapter 12 shows you how to use computer software in the form of SPSS—a very widely used package of programs—to implement the techniques learned in Chapter 11.

These chapters will provide you with the essential tools for doing quantitative research. They will take you from the very general issues to do with the generic features of quantitative research to the very practical issues of conducting surveys and analysing your own data.

3 The nature of quantitative research

Reader's guide

This chapter is concerned with the characteristics of quantitative research, an approach that has been the dominant strategy for conducting social research. Its influence has waned slightly since the mid-1970s, when qualitative research became increasingly influential. However, it continues to exert a powerful influence in many quarters. The emphasis in this chapter is very much on what quantitative research typically entails, though at a later point in the chapter the ways in which there are frequently departures from this ideal type are outlined. This chapter explores:

- the main steps of quantitative research that are presented as a linear succession of stages;
- the importance of concepts in quantitative research and the ways in which measures may be devised for concepts; this discussion includes a discussion of the important idea of an *indicator*, which is devised as a way of measuring a concept for which there is no direct measure;
- the procedures for checking the reliability and validity of the measurement process;
- the main preoccupations of quantitative research, which are described in terms of four features: measurement; causality; generalization; and replication;
- some criticisms that are frequently levelled at quantitative research.

Introduction

In Chapter 1, quantitative research was outlined as a distinctive research strategy. In very broad terms, it was described as entailing the collection of numerical data and as exhibiting a view of the relationship between theory and research as deductive, a predilection for a natural science approach (and of positivism in particular), and as having an objectivist conception of social reality. A number of other features of quantitative research were outlined, but in this chapter we will be examining the strategy in much more detail.

It should be abundantly clear by now that the description of the research strategy as 'quantitative research' should not be taken to mean that quantification of aspects of social life is all that distinguishes it from a qualitative research strategy. The very fact that it has a distinctive epistemological and ontological position suggests that there is a good deal more to it than the mere presence of numbers. In this chapter, the main steps in quantitative research will be outlined. We will also examine some of the principal preoccupations of the strategy and how certain issues of concern among practitioners are addressed, like the concerns about measurement validity.

The main steps in quantitative research

Figure 3.1 outlines the main steps in quantitative research. This is very much an ideal-typical account of the process: it is probably never or rarely found in this pure form, but it represents a useful starting point for getting to grips with the main ingredients of the approach and the links between them. Research is rarely as linear and as straightforward as the figure implies, but its aim is to do no more than capture the main steps and to provide a rough indication of their interconnections.

Some of the chief steps have been covered in the first two chapters. The fact that we start off with theory signifies that a broadly deductive approach to the relationship between theory and research is taken. It is common for outlines of the main steps of quantitative research to suggest that a hypothesis is deduced from the theory and is tested. This notion has been incorporated into Figure 3.1. However, a great deal of quantitative research does not entail the specification of a hypothesis and instead theory acts loosely as a set of concerns in relation to which the social researcher collects data. The

specification of hypotheses to be tested is particularly likely to be found in experimental research. Other research designs sometimes entail the testing of hypotheses. In Chapter 1, a cross-sectional design using social survey research instruments that was used as an example (see Box 1.5, p. 9) involved hypothesis testing. However, as a rule, we tend to find that step 2 is more likely to be found in experimental research.

The next step entails the selection of a research design, a topic that was explored in Chapter 2. As we have seen, the selection of research design has implications for a variety of issues, such as the external validity of findings and researchers' ability to impute causality to their findings. Step 4 entails devising measures of the concepts in which the researcher is interested. This process is often referred to as *operationalization*, a term that originally derives from physics to refer to the operations by which a concept (such as temperature or velocity) is measured (Bridgman 1927). Aspects of this issue will be explored below in this chapter.

The next two steps entail the selection of a research site or sites and then the selection of subjects/respondents. (Experimental researchers tend to call the people on whom they conduct research 'subjects', whereas social survey researchers typically call them 'respondents'.) Thus, in social survey research an investigator must first be concerned to establish an appropriate setting for his or her research. A number of decisions may be involved. The well-known *Affluent Worker* research undertaken by Goldthorpe *et al.* (1968: 2–5) involved two decisions about a research site or setting. First, the researchers needed a community that would be appropriate for the testing of the 'embourgeoisement' thesis (the idea that affluent workers were becoming more middle class in their attitudes and lifestyles). As a result of this consideration, Luton was selected. Secondly, in order to come up with a sample of 'affluent workers' (Step 6), it was decided that people working for three

1. Theory
↓
2. Hypothesis
↓
3. Research design
↓
4. Devise measures of concepts
↓
5. Select research site(s)
↓
6. Select research subjects/respondents
↓
7. Administer research instruments/collect data
↓
8. Process data
↓
9. Analyse data
↓
10. Findings/conclusions
↓
11. Write up findings/conclusions

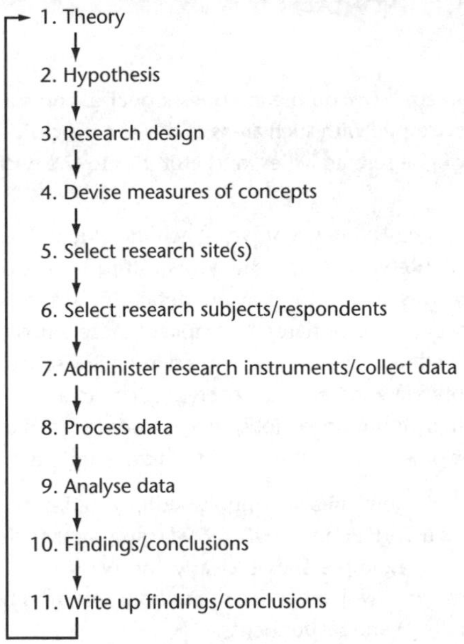

Fig. 3.1 The process of quantitative research

of Luton's leading employers should be interviewed. Moreover, the researchers wanted the firms selected to cover a range of production technologies, because of evidence at that time that technologies had implications for workers' attitudes and behaviour. As a result of these considerations, the three firms were selected. Industrial workers were then sampled, also in terms of selected criteria that were to do with the researchers' interests in embourgeoisement and in the implications of technology for work attitudes and behaviour. Box 3.1 provides a much more recent example of research that involved similar deliberations about selecting research sites and sampling respondents. In experimental research, these two steps are likely to include the assignment of subjects into control and treatment groups.

Step 7 involves the administration of the research instruments. In experimental research, this is likely to entail pre-testing subjects, manipulating the independent variable for the experimental group and post-testing respondents. In cross-sectional research using social survey research

instruments, it will involve interviewing the sample members by structured interview schedule or distributing a self-completion questionnaire. In research using structured observation, this step will mean an observer (or possibly more than one) watching the setting and the behaviour of people and then assigning categories to each element of behaviour.

Step 8 simply refers to the fact that, once information has been collected, it must be transformed into 'data'. In the context of quantitative research, this is likely to mean that it must be prepared so that it can be quantified. With some information this can be done in a relatively straightforward way—for example, for information relating to such things as people's ages, incomes, number of years spent at school, and so on. For other variables, quantification will entail *coding* the information—that is, transforming it into numbers to facilitate the quantitative analysis of the data, particularly if the analysis is going to be carried out by computer. Codes act as tags that are placed on data about people to allow the information to be processed by the computer. This

---

Box 3.1 Selecting research sites and sampling respondents: The Social Change and Economic Life Initiative

The Social Change and Economic Life Initiative (SCELI) involved research in six labour markets: Aberdeen, Coventry, Kirkaldy, Northampton, Rochdale, and Swindon. These labour markets were chosen to reflect contrasting patterns of economic change in the early to mid-1980s and in the then recent past. Within each locality, three main surveys were carried out.

- *The Work Attitudes/Histories Survey*. Across the four localities a random sample of 6,111 individuals was interviewed using a structured interview schedule. Each interview comprised questions about the individual's work history and about a range of attitudes.

- *The Household and Community Survey*. A further survey was conducted on roughly one-third of those interviewed for the Work Attitudes/Histories Survey. Respondents and their partners were interviewed by structured interview schedule and each person also

completed a self-completion questionnaire. This survey was concerned with such areas as the domestic division of labour, leisure activities, and attitudes to the welfare state.

- *The Baseline Employers Survey*. Each individual in each locality interviewed for the Work Attitudes/Histories Survey was asked to provide details of his or her employer (if appropriate). A sample of these employers was then interviewed by structured interview schedule. The interview schedules covered such areas as the gender distribution of jobs, the introduction of new technologies, and relationships with trade unions.

The bulk of the results was published in a series of volumes, including Penn *et al.* (1994) and A. M. Scott (1994). This example shows clearly the ways in which researchers are involved in decisions about selecting both research site(s) and respondents.

consideration leads into Step 9—the analysis of the data. In this step, the researcher is concerned to use a number of techniques of quantitative data analysis to reduce the amount of data collected, to test for relationships between variables, to develop ways of presenting the results of the analysis to others, and so on.

On the basis of the analysis of the data, the researcher must interpret the results of the analysis. It is at this stage that the 'findings' will emerge. The researcher will consider the connections between the findings that emerge out of Step 8 and the various preoccupations that acted as the impetus of the research. If there is a hypothesis, is it supported? What are the implications of the findings for the theoretical ideas that formed the background to the research?

Then the research must be written up. It cannot take on significance beyond satisfying the researcher's personal curiosity until it enters the public domain in some way by being written up as a paper to be read at a conference or as a report to the agency that funded the research or as a book or journal article for academic social researchers. In writing up the findings and conclusions, the researcher is doing more than simply relaying what has been found to others: readers must be convinced that the research conclusions are important and that the findings are robust. Thus, a significant part of the research process entails convincing others of the significance and validity of one's findings.

Once the findings have been published they become part of the stock of knowledge (or 'theory' in the loose sense of the word) in their domain. Thus, there is a feedback loop from Step 11 back up to Step 1. The presence of both an element of deductivism (Step 2) and inductivism (the feedback loop) is indicative of the positivist foundations of quantitative research. Similarly, the emphasis on the translation of concepts into measures (Step 4) is symptomatic of the principle of phenomenalism (see Box 1.7, p. 12) that is also a feature of positivism. It is to this important phase of translating concepts into measures that we now turn. As we will see, certain considerations follow on from the stress placed on measurement in quantitative research. By and large, these considerations are to do with the validity and reliability of the measures devised by social scientists. These considerations will figure prominently in the following discussion.

Concepts and their measurement

What is a concept?

Concepts are the building blocks of theory and represent the points around which social research is conducted. Just think of the numerous concepts that have already been mentioned in relation to research examples cited so far in this book:

structure, agency, social class, job search method, deskilling, emotional satisfaction, religious orthodoxy, religious orientation, preservation of self, informal social control, negotiated order, culture, academic achievement, teacher expectations, charismatic leadership, healthy lifestyle, conversion.

Each represents a label that we give to elements of the social world that seem to have common features and that strike us as significant. As Bulmer succinctly puts it, concepts 'are categories for the organisation of ideas and observations' (1984: 43). One item mentioned in Chapter 2 but omitted from the list of concepts above is IQ. It has been omitted because it is not a concept! It is a *measure* of a concept—namely, intelligence. This is a rare case of a social scientific measure that has become so well known that the measure and the concept are almost as synonymous as temperature and the centigrade or Fahrenheit scales, or as length and the metric scale. The concept of intelligence has arisen as a result of noticing that some people are very clever, some are quite clever, and still others are not at all bright. These variations in what we have come to call the concept of 'intelligence' seem important, because we might try to construct theories to explain these variations. We may try to incorporate the concept of intelligence into theories to explain variations in things like occupational or educational performance. Similarly, with something like social mobility, we notice that some people improve their socio-economic position relative to their parents, others stay roughly the same, and others are downwardly mobile. Out of such considerations, the concept of social mobility is reached.

If a concept is to be employed in quantitative research, it will have to be measured. Once they are measured, concepts can be in the form of independent or dependent variables. In other words, concepts may provide an explanation of a certain aspect of the social world, or they may stand for things we want to explain. A concept like social mobility may be used in either capacity: as a possible explanation of certain attitudes (are there differences between the downwardly mobile and others in terms of their political dispositions or social attitudes?) or as something to be explained (what are the causes of variation in social mobility?). Equally, we might be interested in evidence of changes in amounts of social mobility over time or in variations between comparable nations in levels of social mobility. As we start to investigate such issues, we are likely to formulate theories to help us understand why, for example, rates of social mobility vary between countries or over time. This will in turn generate new concepts, as we try to tackle the explanation of variation in rates.

Why measure?

There are three main reasons for the preoccupation with measurement in quantitative research.

- Measurement allows us to delineate *fine differences* between people in terms of the characteristic in question. This is very useful, since, although we can often distinguish between people in terms of extreme categories, finer distinctions are much more difficult to recognize. We can detect clear variations in levels of job satisfaction—people who

love their jobs and people who hate their jobs—but small differences are much more difficult to detect.

- Measurement gives us a *consistent device* or yardstick for making such distinctions. A measurement device provides a consistent instrument for gauging differences. This consistency relates to two things: our ability to be consistent over time and our ability to be consistent with other researchers. In other words, a measure should be something that is influenced neither by the timing of its administration nor by the person who administers it. Obviously, saying that the measure is not influenced by timing is not meant to indicate that measurement readings do not change: they are bound to be influenced by the process of social change. What it means is that the measure should generate consistent results, other than those that occur as a result of natural changes. Whether a measure actually possesses this quality has to do with the issue of *reliability*, which was introduced in Chapter 2 and which will be examined again below.

- Measurement provides the basis for *more precise estimates of the degree of relationship between concepts* (for example, through correlation analysis, which will be examined in Chapter 11). Thus, if we measure both job satisfaction and the things with which it might be related, such as stress-related illness, we will be able to produce more precise estimates of how closely they are related than if we had not proceeded in this way.

Indicators

In order to provide a measure of a concept (often referred to as an *operational definition*, a term deriving from the idea of operationalization), it is necessary to have an indicator or indicators that will stand for the concept (see Box 3.2). There are a number of ways in which indicators can be devised:

- through a question (or series of questions) that is part of a structured interview schedule or self-completion questionnaire. The question(s) could

---

Box 3.2 ⚡ *What is an indicator?*

It is worth making two distinctions here. First, there is a distinction between an *indicator* and a *measure*. The latter can be taken to refer to things that can be relatively unambiguously counted, such as personal income, household income, age, number of children, number of years spent at school. Measures in other words are quantities. If we are interested in some of the causes of variation in personal income, the latter can be quantified in a reasonably direct way. We use indicators to tap concepts that are less directly quantifiable. If we are interested in the causes of variation in job satisfaction, we will need indicators that will stand for the concept. These indicators will allow job satisfaction to be measured and we can treat the resulting quantitative information as if it were a measure. An indicator, then, is something that is devised or already exists and that is employed *as though it were a measure of a concept*. It is viewed as an indirect measure of a concept, like job satisfaction. An IQ test is a further example, in that it is a battery of indicators of the concept intelligence. We see here a second distinction between *direct* and *indirect* indicators of concepts. Indicators may be direct or indirect in their relationship to the concepts for which they stand. Thus, an indicator of marital status has a much more direct relationship to its concept than an indicator (or set of indicators) relating to job satisfaction. Sets of attitudes always need to be measured by batteries of indirect indicators. So too do many forms of behaviour. When indicators are used that are not true quantities, they will need to be coded to be turned into quantities. Directness and indirectness are not qualities inherent to an indicator: data from a survey question on amount earned per month may be a direct measure of personal income, but, if we treat it as an indicator of social class, it becomes an indirect measure. The issue of indirectness raises the question of where an indirect measure comes from—that is, how does a researcher devise an indicator of something like job satisfaction. Usually, it is based on common-sense understandings of the forms the concept takes or on anecdotal or qualitative evidence relating to that concept.

---

be concerned with the respondents' report of an attitude (e.g. job satisfaction) or their social situation (e.g. poverty) or a report of their behaviour (e.g. leisure pursuits);

- through the recording of individuals' behaviour using a structured observation schedule (e.g. pupil behaviour in a classroom);

- through official statistics, such as the use of Home Office crime statistics to measure criminal behaviour;

- through an examination of mass media content through content analysis, for example, to determine changes in the salience of an issue, such as AIDS, in the mass media (Beharrell 1993).

Indicators, then, can be derived from a wide variety of different sources and methods. Very often the researcher has to consider whether one indicator of a concept will be sufficient. This consideration is frequently a focus for social survey researchers. Rather than have just a single indicator of a concept, the researcher may feel that it may be preferable to ask a number of questions in the course of a structured interview or a self-completion questionnaire that tap a certain concept (see Boxes 3.3 and 3.4).

Using multiple-indicator measures

What are the advantages of using a multiple-indicator measure of a concept? The main reason for their use is a recognition that there are potential problems with a reliance on just a single indicator:

- It is possible that a single indicator will incorrectly classify many individuals. This may be due to the wording of the question or it may be a product of misunderstanding. But if there are a number of indicators, if people are misclassified through a particular question, it will be possible to offset its effects.

- One indicator may capture only a portion of the underlying concept or be too general. A single question may need to be of an excessively high level of generality and so may not reflect the true state of affairs for the people replying to it. Alternatively, a question may cover only one aspect of

Box 3.3 A multiple-indicator measure of a concept

The research on the effects of redundancy by Westergaard *et al.* (1989), which was referred to in Chapters 1 and 2, was conducted by structured interview with 378 steel workers who had been made redundant. One of the authors' interests was whether their respondents' commitment to work varied according to whether they were still unemployed at the time of the interview or had found work or had retired. In order to measure commitment to employment, the authors gave their respondents ten statements and asked them to indicate their level of agreement or disagreement on a seven-point scale running from 'Yes, I strongly agree' to 'No, I strongly disagree'. There was a middle point on the scale that allowed for a neutral response. This approach to investigating a cluster of attitudes is known as a *Likert scale*, though in many cases researchers use a five-point rather than seven-point scale for responses. The ten statements were as follows:

- Work is necessary, but rarely enjoyable.

- Having a job is not very important to me.

- I regard time spent at work as time taken away from the things I want to do.

- Having a job is/was only important to me because it brings in money.

- Even if I won a great deal of money on the pools I'd carry on working.

- If unemployment benefit were really high I would still prefer to work.

- I would hate being on the dole.

- I would soon get bored if I did not go out to work.

- The most important things that have happened to me involved work.

- Any feelings I've had in the past of achieving something worthwhile have usually come through things I've done at work.

In fact, the authors found that their respondents' replies did not differ a great deal in terms of whether they had found work since being made redundant or were still unemployed or had taken retirement.

Box 3.4 A multiple-indicator measure of another concept

In Kelley and De Graaf's (1997) research on religious beliefs, two of the main concepts in which they were interested—national religiosity and family religious orientation—were each measured by a single indicator (see Box 1.5, p. 9). However, religious orthodoxy was measured by four survey questions, answers to which were aggregated for each respondent to form a 'score' for that person. Answers to each of the four questions were given a score and then aggregated to form a religious belief score. The four questions were as follows:

- Please indicate which statement below comes closest to expressing what you believe about God:

  - I don't believe in God.
  - I don't know whether there is a God and I don't believe there is any way to find out.
  - I don't believe in a personal God, but I do believe in a higher power of some kind.
  - I find myself believing in God some of the time, but not at others.
  - While I have doubts, I feel that I do believe in God.

  - I know God really exists and I have no doubts about it.

- Which best describes your beliefs about God?

  - I don't believe in God and I never have.
  - I don't believe in God, but I used to.
  - I believe in God now, but I didn't used to.
  - I believe in God now and I always have.

- How close do you feel to God most of the time?

  - Don't believe in God.
  - Not close at all.
  - Not very close.
  - Somewhat close.
  - Extremely close.

- There is a God who concerns Himself with every human being, personally.

  - Strongly agree.
  - Agree.
  - Neither agree nor disagree.
  - Disagree.
  - Strongly disagree.

the concept in question. For example, if you were interested in job satisfaction, would it be sufficient to ask people how satisfied they were with their pay? Almost certainly not, because most people would argue that there is more to job satisfaction than just satisfaction with pay. A single indicator such as this would be missing out on such things as satisfaction with conditions, with the work itself, and with other aspects of the work environment. By asking a number of questions the researcher can get access to a wider range of aspects of the concept.

- You can make much finer distinctions. Taking the Westergaard *et al.* (1989) measure as an example (see Box 3.3), if we just took one of the indicators as a measure, we would only be able to array people on a scale of 0 to 6, assuming that answers indicating no commitment were assigned 0 and answers indicating a very high level of commitment were assigned 6 and the five other points being scored 1, 2, 3, 4, and 5. However, with a multiple-indicator measure of ten indicators the range is 0 (10×0) to 60 (10×6).

Dimensions of concepts

One elaboration of the general approach to measurement is to consider the possibility that the concept in which you are interested comprises different dimensions. This view is particularly associated with

Lazarsfeld (1958). The idea behind this approach is that, when the researcher is seeking to develop a measure of a concept, the different aspects or components of that concept should be considered. This specification of the dimensions of a concept would be undertaken with reference to theory and research associated with that concept. Examples of this kind of approach can be discerned in Seeman's (1959) delineation of five dimensions of alienation (powerlessness, meaninglessness, normlessness, isolation, and self-estrangement). Bryman and Cramer (2001) demonstrate the operation of this approach with reference to the concept of 'professionalism'. The idea is that people scoring high on one dimension may not necessarily score high on other dimensions, so that for each respondent you end up with a multidimensional 'profile'. Box 3.5 demonstrates the use of dimensions in connection with the concept of 'deskilling' in the sociology of work.

However, in much if not most quantitative research, there is a tendency to rely on a single indicator of concepts. For many purposes this is quite adequate. It would be a mistake to believe that investigations that use a single indicator of core concepts are somehow deficient. In any case, some studies, like Kelley and De Graaf (1997, see Box 3.4), employ both single- and multiple-indicator measures of concepts. What *is* crucial is whether measures are reliable and whether they are valid representations of the concepts they are supposed to be tapping. It is to this issue that we now turn.

Box 3.5 Specifying dimensions of a concept: The case of deskilling

This example is taken from social survey research primarily concerned with social class in Britain by Marshall *et al.* (1988). The research was based on structured interviews with a national, random sample of individuals. One of the researchers' areas of interest was Braverman's (1974) deskilling thesis (see Box 1.2, p. 7). Based on a reading of the literature on this topic at the time, the authors argued that two important components or *dimensions* of deskilling on which they were able to shed light were 'skill as complexity and skill as freedom', which 'are central to the thesis that work is being proletarianized through the

deskilling of tasks' (Marshall *et al.*, 1988: 116). 'Skill as complexity' was measured by a single interview question asking respondents whether their current jobs required more, less, or about the same amount of skill as when they first started. 'Skill as freedom' was measured by seven indicators that were treated separately and not aggregated. The questions entailed asking respondents about such things as whether they were able to reduce the pace of their work or to initiate new tasks in their work. Neither dimension comprised measures that offered significant support for the deskilling thesis.

Reliability and validity

Although the terms *reliability* and *validity* seem to be almost like synonyms, they have quite different meanings in relation to the evaluation of measures of concepts, as was seen in Chapter 2.

Reliability

As Box 3.6 suggests, reliability is fundamentally concerned with issues of consistency of measures. There are at least three different meanings of the term. These are outlined in Box 3.6 and elaborated upon below.

Stability

The most obvious way of testing for the stability of a measure is the *test–retest* method. This involves administering a test or measure on one occasion and then readministering it to the same sample on another occasion, i.e.

T_1 T_2
Obs_1 Obs_2

We should expect to find a high correlation between Obs_1 and Obs_2. Correlation is a measure of the strength of the relationship between two variables. This topic will be covered in Chapter 11 in the context of a discussion about quantitative data analysis. Let us imagine that we develop a multiple-indicator measure that is supposed to tap a concept that we might call 'designerism' (a preference for buying goods and especially clothing with 'designer' labels). We would administer the measure to a sample of respondents and readminister it some time later. If the correlation is low, the measure would appear to be unstable, implying that respondents' answers cannot be relied upon.

However, there are a number of problems with this approach to evaluating reliability. Respondents' answers at T_1 may influence how they reply at T_2. This may result in greater consistency between Obs_1 and Obs_2 than is in fact the case. Secondly, events may intervene between T_1 and T_2 that influence the degree of consistency. For example, if a long span of time is involved, changes in the economy or in respondents' personal financial circumstances could influence their views about and predilection for designer goods. There are no obvious solutions to these problems, other than by introducing a

---

Box 3.6   *What is reliability?*

Reliability refers to the consistency of a measure of a concept. The following are three prominent factors involved when considering whether a measure is reliable:

- *Stability.* This consideration entails asking whether a measure is stable over time, so that we can be confident that the results relating to that measure for a sample of respondents do not fluctuate. This means that, if we administer a measure to a group and then readminister it, there will be little variation over time in the results obtained.

- *Internal reliability.* The key issue is whether the indicators that make up the scale or index are consistent—in other words, whether respondents' scores on any one indicator tend to be related to their scores on the other indicators.

- *Inter-observer consistency.* When a great deal of subjective judgement is involved in such activities as the recording of observations or the translation of data into categories and where more than one 'observer' is involved in such activities, there is the possibility that there is a lack of consistency in their decisions. This can arise in a number of contexts, for example: in content analysis where decisions have to be made about how to categorize media items; when answers to open-ended questions have to be categorized; or in structured observation when observers have to decide how to classify subjects' behaviour.

complex research design and so turning the investigation of reliability into a major project in its own right. Perhaps for these reasons, many if not most reports of research findings do not appear to carry out tests of stability. Indeed, longitudinal research is often undertaken precisely in order to identify social change and its correlates.

Internal reliability

This meaning of reliability applies to multiple-indicator measures like those examined in Boxes 3.3 and 3.4. When you have a multiple-item measure in which each respondent's answers to each question are aggregated to form an overall score, the possibility is raised that the indicators do not relate to the same thing; in other words, they lack coherence. We need to be sure that all our designerism indicators are related to each other. If they are not, some of the items may actually be unrelated to designerism and therefore indicative of something else.

One way of testing internal reliability is the *split-half* method. We can take the commitment to work measure developed by Westergaard *et al.* (1989) as an example (see Box 3.3). The ten indicators would be divided into two halves with five in each group. The indicators would be allocated on a random or an odd–even basis. The degree of correlation between scores on two halves would then be calculated. In other words, the aim would be to establish whether respondents scoring high on one of the two groups also scored high on the other group of indicators.

The calculation of the correlation will yield a figure, known as a coefficient, that varies between 0 (no correlation and therefore no internal consistency) to 1 (perfect correlation and therefore complete internal consistency). It is usually expected that a result of 0.8 and above implies an acceptable level of internal reliability. Do not worry if the figures appear somewhat opaque. The meaning of correlation will be explored in much greater detail later on. The chief point to carry away with you at this stage is that the correlation establishes how closely respondents' scores on the two groups of indicators are related.

Nowadays, most researchers use a test of internal reliability known as *Cronbach's alpha* (see Box 3.7). Its use has grown as a result of its incorporation into computer software for quantitative data analysis.

Inter-observer consistency

The idea of inter-observer consistency is briefly outlined in Box 3.6. The issues involved are rather too advanced to be dealt with at this stage and will be briefly touched on in later chapters. Cramer (1998: ch. 14) provides a very detailed treatment of the issues and appropriate techniques.

Validity

As noted in Chapter 2, the issue of measurement validity has to do with whether a measure of a

---

Box 3.7 ⌖ *What is Cronbach's alpha?*

To a very large extent we are leaping ahead too much here, but it is important to appreciate the basic features of what this widely used test means. Cronbach's alpha is a commonly used test of internal reliability. It essentially calculates the average of all possible split-half reliability coefficients. A computed alpha coefficient will vary between 1 (denoting perfect internal reliability) and 0 (denoting no internal reliability). The figure 0.80 is typically employed as a rule of thumb to denote an acceptable level of internal reliability, though many writers accept a slightly lower figure. In the case of the commitment to work scale devised by Westergaard *et al.*, alpha was 0.70, which they refer to as 'a satisfactory level' (1989: 93). In the case of Kelley and De Graaf's (1997) measure of religious orthodoxy, which comprised four indicators, alpha was 0.93. The alpha levels varied between 0.79 and 0.95 for each of the fifteen national samples that make up the data (see Boxes 1.5 (p. 9) and 3.4 for more information about this research).

Box 3.8   *What is validity?*

Validity refers to the issue of whether an indicator (or set of indicators) that is devised to gauge a concept really measures that concept. Several ways of establishing validity are explored in the text: face validity; concurrent validity; predictive validity; construct validity; and convergent validity. Here the term is being used as a shorthand for what was referred to as *measurement validity* in Chapter 2. Validity should therefore be distinguished from the other terms introduced in Chapter 2: internal validity; external validity; and ecological validity.

---

concept really measures that concept (see Box 3.8). When people argue about whether a person's IQ score really measures or reflects that person's level of intelligence, they are raising questions about the measurement validity of the IQ test in relation to the concept of intelligence. Similarly, one often hears people say that they do not believe that the Retail Price Index really reflects inflation and the rise in the cost of living. Again, a query is being raised in such comments about measurement validity. And whenever students or lecturers debate whether formal examinations provide an accurate measure of academic ability, they too are raising questions about measurement validity.

Writers on measurement validity distinguish between a number of different types of validity. These types really reflect different ways of gauging the validity of a measure of a concept. These different types of validity will now be outlined.

Face validity

At the very minimum, a researcher who develops a new measure should establish that it has *face validity*—that is, that the measure apparently reflects the content of the concept in question. Face validity might be established by asking other people whether the measure seems to be getting at the concept that is the focus of attention. In other words, people, possibly those with experience or expertise in a field, might be asked to act as judges to determine whether

on the face of it the measure seems to reflect the concept concerned. Face validity is, therefore, an essentially intuitive process.

Concurrent validity

The researcher might seek also to gauge the *concurrent validity* of the measure. Here the researcher employs a *criterion* on which cases (for example, people) are known to differ and that is relevant to the concept in question. A new measure of job satisfaction can serve as an example. A criterion might be absenteeism, because some people are more often absent from work (other than through illness) than others. In order to establish the concurrent validity of a measure of job satisfaction, we might see how far people who are satisfied with their jobs are less likely than those who are not satisfied to be *absent* from work. If a lack of correspondence was found, such as there being no difference in levels of job satisfaction among frequent absentees, doubt might be cast on whether our measure is really addressing job satisfaction.

Predictive validity

Another possible test for the validity of a new measure is *predictive validity*, whereby the researcher uses a *future* criterion measure, rather than a contemporary one, as in the case of concurrent validity. With predictive validity, the researcher would take future levels of absenteeism as the criterion against which the validity of a new measure of job satisfaction would be examined. The difference from concurrent validity is that a future rather than a simultaneous criterion measure is employed.

Construct validity

Some writers advocate that the researcher should also estimate the *construct validity* of a measure. Here, the researcher is encouraged to deduce hypotheses from a theory that is relevant to the concept. For example, drawing upon ideas about the impact of technology on the experience of work, the researcher might anticipate that people who are satisfied with their jobs are less likely to work on routine jobs; those who are not satisfied are more likely to work on routine jobs. Accordingly, we could investigate this theoretical deduction by examining the relationship between job satisfaction and job routine. However, some caution is required in interpreting the absence of a relationship between job satisfaction and job routine in this example. First, either the theory or the deduction that is made from it might be misguided. Secondly, the measure of job routine could be an invalid measure of that concept.

Convergent validity

In the view of some methodologists, the validity of a measure ought to be gauged by comparing it to measures of the same concept developed through other methods. For example, if we develop a questionnaire measure of how much time managers spend on various activities (such as attending meetings, touring their organization, informal discussions, and so on), we might examine its validity by tracking a number of managers and using a structured observation schedule to record how much time is spent in various activities and their frequency.

An interesting instance of convergent *in*validity is described in Box 3.9. In the example cited in Box 3.9, the British Crime Survey (BCS) was consciously devised to provide an alternative measure of levels of crime so that it would act as a check on the official statistics. The two sets of data are collected in quite different ways: the official crime statistics are collected as part of the bureaucratic processing of offenders in the course of the activities of members of the British criminal justice system, whereas the BCS entails the collection of data by interview from a national sample of possible victims of crime. In the case reported in Box 3.9 a lack of convergent validity was found. However, the problem with the convergent approach to testing validity is that it is not possible to establish very easily which of the two measures represents the more accurate picture. The BCS is not entirely flawless in its approach to the measurement of crime levels, and, in any case, the 'true' picture with regard to the volume of crime at any one time is an almost entirely metaphysical notion (Reiner 2000). While the authors of the news item were able to draw on bits of anecdotal evidence to support their thesis that the figures were being massaged and this together with the BCS evidence

---

Box 3.9 A case of convergent *in*validity: Home Office crime statistics

An article in the *Sunday Times* (Burrell and Leppard 1994) proclaimed the government's claims about the fall in crime a sham. The opening paragraph put the point as follows:

The government's much heralded fall in crime is a myth. Hundreds of thousands of serious crimes have been quietly dropped from police records as senior officers massage their statistics to meet new Home Office targets. . . . Crime experts say at least 220,000 crimes, including burglary, assault, theft and car crimes, vanished from official statistics last year as a result of police manipulation of the figures.

What gave the 'crime experts' and the reporters the confidence to assert that the much-trumpeted fall in crime was a myth because the figures on which the claim was made had been massaged? The answer is that data from the British Crime Survey (BCS) had 'recently reported that actual crime rose faster over the past two years than during the 1980s'. The BCS was carried out in 1982, 1984,

1988, and 1992, and has been carried out on a biennial basis since 1992. In each case, a large, randomly selected sample of individuals is questioned by structured interview. It is not based on a panel research design, because the survey does not interview the same people with each wave of data collection. The BCS is an example of what is known as a 'victimization survey'. With this kind of survey, a sample of a population is questioned about its experiences as victims of crime. The idea is that unreported crime and other crime that does not show up in the official statistics will be revealed. The categories of crime used in the survey are meant to reflect those reported in the official statistics (Coleman and Moynihan 1996: 83–6). The 1994 survey found that there had been a marked increase in most categories of crime. Since the *Sunday Times* article, there have been several other newspaper exposés of the fiddling of crime figures by the police (Reiner 2000).

casts doubt on the official statistics, it would be a mistake to hold that the survey evidence necessarily represents a definitive and therefore unambiguously valid measure.

Reflections on reliability and validity

There are, then, a number of different ways of investigating the merit of measures that are devised to represent social scientific concepts. However, the discussion of reliability and validity is potentially misleading, because it would be wrong to think that all new measures of concepts are submitted to the rigours described above. In fact, most typically, measurement is undertaken within a stance that Cicourel (1964) described as 'measurement by fiat'. By the term 'fiat', Cicourel was referring not to a well-known Italian car manufacturer but to the notion of 'decree'. He meant that most measures are simply asserted. Fairly straightforward, but minimal steps may be taken to ensure that a measure is reliable and/or valid, such as testing for internal

reliability when a multiple-indicator measure has been devised and examining face validity. But in many, if not the majority of cases in which a concept is measured, no further testing takes place. This point will be further elaborated below.

It should also be borne in mind that, although reliability and validity are analytically distinguishable, they are related because validity presumes reliability. This means that, if your measure is not reliable, it cannot be valid. This point can be made with respect to each of the three criteria of reliability that have been discussed. If the measure is not stable over time, it simply cannot be providing a valid measure. The measure could not be tapping the concept it is supposed to be related to if the measure fluctuated. If the measure fluctuates, it may be measuring different things on different occasions. If a measure lacks internal reliability, it means that a multiple-indicator measure is actually measuring two or more different things. Therefore, the measure cannot be valid. Finally, if there is a lack of inter-observer consistency, it means that observers cannot agree on the meaning of what they are observing, which in turn means that a valid measure cannot be in operation.

The main preoccupations of quantitative researchers

Both quantitative and qualitative research can be viewed as exhibiting a set of distinctive but contrasting preoccupations. These preoccupations reflect epistemologically grounded beliefs about what constitutes acceptable knowledge. In this section, four distinctive preoccupations that can be discerned in quantitative research will be outlined and examined: measurement, causality, generalization, and replication.

Measurement

The most obvious preoccupation is with measurement, a feature that is scarcely surprising in the light

of much of the discussion in the present chapter so far. From the position of quantitative research, measurement carries a number of advantages that were previously outlined. It is not surprising, therefore, that issues of reliability and validity are a concern for quantitative researchers, though this is not always manifested in research practice.

Causality

There is a very strong concern in most quantitative research with explanation. Quantitative researchers are rarely concerned merely to describe how things are, but are keen to say why things are the way they are. This emphasis is also often taken to be a feature of the ways in which the natural sciences proceed. Thus, researchers are often not only interested in a phenomenon like racial prejudice as something to be described, for example, in terms of how much prejudice exists in a certain group of individuals, or what proportion of people in a sample are highly prejudiced and what proportion are largely lacking in prejudice. Rather, they are likely to want to explain it, which means examining its causes. The researcher may seek to explain racial prejudice in terms of personal characteristics (such as levels of authoritarianism) or in terms of social characteristics (such as education, or social mobility experiences). In reports of research you will often come across the idea of 'independent' and 'dependent' variables, which reflect the tendency to think in terms of causes and effects. Racial prejudice might be regarded as the dependent variable, which is to be explained, and authoritarianism as an independent variable, and which therefore has a causal influence upon prejudice.

When an experimental design is being employed, the independent variable is the variable which is manipulated. There is little ambiguity about the direction of causal influence (see Box 2.6, p. 36). However, with cross-sectional designs of the kind used in most social survey research, there is ambiguity about the direction of causal influence in that data concerning variables are simultaneously collected. Therefore, we cannot say that an independent variable precedes the dependent one. To refer to independent and dependent variables in the context of cross-sectional designs, we must *infer* that one causes the other, as in the example concerning authoritarianism and racial prejudice in the previous paragraph. We must draw on common sense or theoretical ideas to infer the likely temporal precedence of variables. However, there is always the risk that the inference will be wrong (see Box 22.5, p. 455, for an example of this possibility).

The concern about causality is reflected in the preoccupation with internal validity that was referred to in Chapter 2. There it was noted that a criterion of good quantitative research is frequently the extent to which there is confidence in the researcher's causal inferences. Research that exhibits the characteristics of an experimental design is often more highly valued than cross-sectional research, because of the greater confidence that can be enjoyed in the causal findings associated with the former. For their part, quantitative researchers who employ cross-sectional designs are invariably concerned to develop techniques that will allow causal inferences to be made. Moreover, the rise of longitudinal research like the British Household Panel Study almost certainly reflects a desire on the part of quantitative researchers to improve their ability to generate findings that permit a causal interpretation.

Generalization

In quantitative research the researcher is usually concerned to be able to say that his or her findings can be generalized beyond the confines of the particular context in which the research was conducted. Thus, if a study of racial prejudice is carried out by a questionnaire with a number of people who answer the questions, we often want to say that the results can apply to individuals other than those who responded in the study. This concern reveals itself in social survey research in the attention that is often given to the question of how one can create a representative sample. Given that it is rarely feasible to send questionnaires to or interview whole populations (such as all members of a town, or the whole population of a country, or all members of an organization), we have to sample. However, we will want the sample to be as representative as possible in order to be able to say that the results are not unique to the particular group upon whom the research was conducted; in other words, we want to be able to generalize the findings beyond the cases (for example, the people) that make up the sample. The preoccupation with generalization can be viewed as an attempt to develop the lawlike findings of the natural sciences.

Probability sampling, which will be explored in Chapter 4, is the main way in which researchers seek to generate a representative sample. This procedure largely eliminates bias from the selection of a sample by using a process of random selection. The use of a random selection process does not guarantee a representative sample, because, as will be seen in Chapter 4, there are factors that operate over and above the selection system used that can jeopardize the representativeness of a sample. A related consideration here is this: even if we did have a representative sample, what would it be representative *of*. The simple answer is that it will be representative of the population from which it was selected. This is certainly the answer that sampling theory gives us. Strictly speaking, we cannot generalize beyond that population. This means that, if the members of the population from which a sample is taken are all inhabitants of a town, city, or region, or are all members of an organization, we can only generalize to the inhabitants or members of the town, city, region, or organization. But it is very tempting to see the findings as having a more pervasive applicability, so that, even if the sample was selected from a large city like Birmingham, the findings are relevant to all similar cities. We should not make inferences beyond the population from which the sample was selected, but researchers frequently do so. The concern to be able to generalize is often so deeply ingrained that the limits to the generalizability of findings are frequently forgotten or sidestepped.

The concern with generalizability or external validity is particularly strong among quantitative researchers using cross-sectional and longitudinal designs. There is a concern about generalizability among experimental research, as the discussion of external validity in Chapter 2 suggested, but users of this research design usually give greater attention to internal validity issues.

Replication

The natural sciences are often depicted as wishing to reduce to a bare minimum the contaminating influence of the scientist's biases and values. The results of a piece of research should be unaffected by the researcher's special characteristics or expectations or whatever. If biases and lack of objectivity were pervasive, the claims of the natural sciences to provide a definitive picture of the world would be seriously undermined. As a check upon the influence of these potentially damaging problems, scientists may seek to replicate, that is to reproduce, each other's experiments. If there was a failure to replicate, so that a scientist's findings repeatedly could not be reproduced, serious questions would be raised about the validity of his or her findings. Consequently, scientists often attempt to be highly explicit about their procedures so that an experiment is capable of replication. Likewise, quantitative researchers in the social sciences often regard replication, or more precisely the ability to replicate, as an important ingredient of their activity. It is easy to see why: the possibility of a lack of objectivity and of the intrusion of the researcher's values would appear to be much greater when examining the social world than when the natural scientist investigates the natural order. Consequently, it is often regarded as important that the researcher spells out clearly his or her procedures so that they can be replicated by others, even if the research does not end up being replicated.

Whether research is in practice replicated is another matter. Replication is not a high-status activity in the natural and social sciences, because it is often regarded as a pedestrian and uninspiring pursuit. Moreover, standard replications do not form the basis for attractive articles, so far as many academic journal editors are concerned. Consequently, replications of research appear in print far less frequently than might be supposed. A further reason for the low incidence of published replications is that it is difficult to ensure in social science research that the conditions in a replication are precisely the same as those that pertained in an original study. So long as there is some ambiguity about the degree to which the conditions relating to a replication are the same as those in the initial study, any differences in findings may be attibutable to the design of the replication rather than to some deficiency in the original study. Nonetheless, it is often regarded as crucial that the methods taken in generating a set of findings are made explicit, so that it is *possible* to replicate a piece of research. Thus, it is replic*ability* that is often regarded as an important quality of quantitative research.

The critique of quantitative research

Over the years, quantitative research along with its epistemological and ontological foundations has been the focus of a great deal of criticism, particularly from exponents and spokespersons of qualitative research. To a very large extent, it is difficult to distinguish between different kinds of criticism when reflecting on the different critical points that have been proffered. These include: criticisms of quantitative research in general as a research strategy; criticisms of the epistemological and ontological foundations of quantitative research; and criticisms of specific methods and research designs with which quantitative research is associated.

Criticisms of quantitative research

To give a flavour of the critique of quantitative research, four criticisms will be covered briefly.

* *Quantitative researchers fail to distinguish people and social institutions from 'the world of nature'*. The phrase 'the world of nature' is from the writings of Schutz and the specific quotation from which it has been taken can be found on p. 14. Schutz and other phenomenologists charge social scientists who employ a natural science model with treating the social world as if it were no different from the natural order. In so doing, they draw attention to one of positivism's central tenets—namely, that the principles of the scientific method can and should be applied to all phenomena that are the focus of investigation. As Schutz argues, this tactic is essentially to imply that this means turning a blind eye to the differences between the social and natural world. More particularly, as was observed in Chapter 1, it therefore means ignoring and riding roughshod over the fact that people interpret the world around them, whereas this capacity for self-reflection cannot be found among the objects of the natural sciences ('molecules, atoms, and electrons', as Schutz put it).
* *The measurement process possesses an artificial and spurious sense of precision and accuracy*. There are a number of aspects to this criticism. For one thing, it has been argued that the connection between the measures developed by social scientists and the concepts they are supposed to be revealing is assumed rather than real; hence, Cicourel's (1964) notion of 'measurement by fiat'. Testing for validity in the manner described in the previous section cannot really address this problem, because the very tests themselves entail measurement by fiat. A further way in which the measurement process is regarded by writers like Cicourel as flawed is that it presumes that when, for example, members of a sample respond to a question on a questionnaire (which is itself taken to be an indicator of a concept), they interpret the key terms in the question similarly. For many writers, sample members simply do not interpret such terms similarly. An often used reaction to this problem is to use questions with fixed-choice answers, but this approach merely provides 'a solution to the problem of meaning by simply ignoring it' (Cicourel 1964: 108).
* *The reliance on instruments and procedures hinders the connection between research and everyday life*. This issue relates to the question of ecological validity that was raised in Chapter 2. Many methods of quantitative research rely heavily on administering research instruments to subjects (such as structured interviews and self-completion questionnaires) or on controlling situations to determine their effects (such as in experiments). However, as Cicourel (1982) asks, how do we know if survey respondents have the requisite knowledge to answer a question or whether they are similar in their sense of the topic being important to them in their everyday lives? Thus, if respondents answer a set of questions designed to measure racial prejudice, can we be sure that they are equally aware of what it is and its manifestations and can we be sure that it is of equal concern to them in the ways in which it connects with everyday

life? One can go ever further and ask how well their answers relate to their everyday lives. People may answer a question designed to measure racial prejudice, but respondents' actual behaviour may be at variance with their answers (LaPiere 1934).

- *The analysis of relationships between variables creates a static view of social life that is independent of people's lives.* Blumer argued that studies that aim to bring out the relationships between variables omit 'the process of interpretation or definition that goes in human groups' (1956: 685). This means that we do not know how what appears to be a relationship between two or more variables has been produced by the people to whom it applies. This criticism incorporates the first and third criticisms that have been referred to—that the meaning of events to individuals is ignored and that we do not know how such findings connect to everyday contexts—but adds a further element—namely, that it creates a sense of a static social world that is separate from the individuals who make it up. In other words, quantitative research is seen as carrying an objectivist ontology that reifies the social world.

We can see in these criticisms the application of a set of concerns associated with a qualitative research strategy that reveals the combination of an interpretivist epistemological orientation (an emphasis on meaning from the individual's point of view) and a constructionist ontology (an emphasis on viewing the social world as the product of individuals rather than as something beyond them). The criticisms may appear very damning, but, as we will see in Chapter 13, quantitative researchers have a powerful battery of criticisms of qualitative research in their arsenal as well!

Is it always like this?

One of the problems with characterizing any research strategy, research design, or research method is that to a certain extent one is always outlining an ideal-typical approach. In other words, one tends to create something that represents that strategy, design, or method, but that may not be reflected in its entirety in research practice. This gap between the ideal type and actual practice can arise as a result of at least two major considerations. First, it arises because those of us who write about and teach research methods cannot cover every eventuality that can arise in the process of social research, so that we tend to provide accounts of the research process that draw upon common features. Thus, a model of the process of quantitative research, such as that provided in Figure 3.1, should be thought of as a general *tendency* rather than as a definitive description of all quantitative research. A second reason why the gap can arise is that, to a very large extent when writing about and teaching research methods, we are essentially providing an account of *good practice*. The fact of the matter is that these practices are often not followed in the published research that students are likely to encounter in the substantive courses that they will be taking. This failure to follow the procedures associated with good practice is not necessarily due to incompetence on the part of social researchers (though in some cases it can be!), but is much more likely to be associated with matters of time, cost, and feasibility—in other words, the pragmatic concerns that cannot be avoided when one does social research.

Reverse operationism

As an example of the first source of the gap between the ideal type and actual research practice we can take the case of something that I have referred to as 'reverse operationism' (Bryman, 1988a: 28). The model of the process of quantitative research in Box 3.1 implies that concepts are specified and measures are then provided for them. As we have noted, this means that indicators must be devised. This is the basis of the idea of 'operationism' or 'operationalism', a term that derives from physics (Bridgman 1927), and that implies a deductive view of how research should proceed. However, this view of research neglects the fact that measurement can entail much more of an inductive element than Box 3.1 implies. Sometimes, measures are developed that in turn lead to conceptualization. One way in which this can occur is when a statistical technique known as *factor analysis* is employed. In order to measure the concept of 'charismatic leadership', a term that owes a great deal to Weber's (1947) notion of charismatic authority, Conger and Kanungo (1998) generated twenty-five items to provide a multiple-item measure of the concept. These items derived from their reading of existing theory and research on the subject, particularly in connection with charismatic leadership in organizations. When the items were administered to a sample of respondents and the results were factor analysed, it was found that the items bunched around six factors, each of which to all intents and purposes represents a dimension of the concept of charismatic leadership:

- strategic vision and articulation behaviour;
- sensitivity to the environment;
- unconventional behaviour;
- personal risk;
- sensitivity to organizational members' needs;
- action orientation away from the maintenance of the status quo.

The point to note is that these six dimensions were not specified at the outset: the link between conceptualization and measurement was an inductive one. Nor is this an unusual situation so far as research is concerned (Bryman 1988*a*: 26–8).

Reliability and validity testing

The second reason why the gap between the ideal type and actual research practice can arise is because researchers do not follow some of the recommended practices. A classic case of this tendency is that, while, as in the present chapter, much time and effort are expended on the articulation of the ways in which the reliability and validity of measures should be determined, a great deal of the time these procedures are not followed. There is evidence from analyses of published quantitative research in organization studies (Podsakoff and Dalton 1987), a field that draws extensively on ideas and methods used in the social sciences, that writers rarely report tests of the stability of their measures and even more rarely report evidence of validity (only 3 per cent of articles

provided information about measurement validity). A large proportion of articles used Cronbach's alpha, but, since this device is relevant only to multiple-item measures, because it gauges internal consistency, the stability and validity of many measures that are employed in the field of organization studies are unknown. This is not to say that this research is necessarily *un*stable and *in*valid, but that we simply do not know. The reasons why the procedures for determining stability and validity are rarely used are almost certainly the cost and time that are likely to be involved. Researchers tend to be concerned with substantive issues and are less than enthusiastic about engaging in the kind of development work that would be required for a thoroughgoing determination of measurement quality. However, what this means is that Cicourel's (1964) previously cited remark about much measurement in sociology being 'measurement by fiat' has considerable weight.

The remarks on the lack of assessment of the quality of measurement should not be taken as a justification for readers to neglect this phase in their work. My aim is merely to draw attention to some of the ways in which practices described in this book are not always followed and to suggest some reasons why they are not followed.

Sampling

A similar point can be made in relation to sampling, which will be covered in the next chapter. As we will see, good practice is strongly associated with *random* or *probability sampling*. However, quite a lot of research is based on non-probability samples—that is, samples that have not been selected in terms of the principles of probability sampling to be discussed in Chapter 4. Sometimes the use of non-probability samples will be due to the impossibility or extreme difficulty of obtaining probability samples. Yet another reason is that the time and cost involved in securing a probability sample are too great relative to the level of resources available. And yet a third reason is that sometimes the opportunity to study a certain group presents itself and represents too good an opportunity to miss. Again, such considerations should not be viewed as a justification and hence a set of reasons for ignoring the principles of sampling to be examined in the next chapter, not least because not following the principles of probability sampling carries implications for the kind of statistical analysis that can be employed (see Chapter 11). Instead, my purpose as before is to draw attention to the ways in which gaps between recommendations about good practice and actual research practice can arise.

Key points

- Quantitative research can be characterized as a linear series of steps moving from theory to conclusions, but the process described in Figure 3.1 is an ideal type from which there are many departures.

- The measurement process in quantitative research entails the search for indicators.

- Establishing the reliability and validity of measures is important for assessing their quality.

- Quantitative research can be characterized as exhibiting certain preoccupations, the most central of which are: measurement; causality; generalization; and replication.

- Quantitative research has been subjected to many criticisms by qualitative researchers. These criticisms tend to revolve around the view that a natural science model is inappropriate for studying the social world.

Revision questions

The main steps in quantitative research

- What are the main steps in quantitative research?
- To what extent do the main steps follow a strict sequence?
- Do the steps suggest a deductive or inductive approach to the relationship between theory and research?

Concepts and their measurement

- Why is measurement important for the quantitative researcher?
- What is the difference between a measure and an indicator?
- Why might multiple-indicator approaches to the measurement of concepts be preferable to those that rely on a single indicator?

Reliability and validity

- What are the main ways of thinking about the reliability of the measurement process? Is one form of reliability the most important?

- 'Whereas validity presupposes reliability, reliability does not presuppose validity'. Discuss.

- What are the main criteria for evaluating measurement validity?

The main preoccupations of quantitative researchers

- Outline the main preoccupations of quantitative researchers. What reasons can you give for their prominence?

- Why might replication be an important preoccupation among quantitative researchers, in spite of the tendency for replications in social research to be fairly rare?

The critique of quantitative research

- 'The crucial problem with quantitative research is the failure of its practitioners to address adequately the issue of meaning.' Discuss.

- How central is the adoption by quantitative researchers of a natural science model of conducting research to the critique by qualitative researchers of quantitative research?

4 Sampling

Reader's guide

This chapter and the three that follow it are very much concerned with principles and practices associated with social survey research. Sampling principles are not exclusively concerned with survey research; for example, they are relevant to the selection of documents for content analysis (see Chapter 8). However, in this chapter the emphasis will be on sampling in connection with the selection of people who would be asked questions by interview or questionnaire. The chapter explores:

- the related ideas of generalization (also known as external validity) and of a representative sample; the latter allows the researcher to generalize findings from a sample to a population;

- the idea of a *probability sample*—that is, one in which a random selection process has been employed;

- the main types of probability sample: the simple random sample; the systematic sample; the stratified random sample; and the multi-stage cluster sample;

- the main issues involved in deciding on sample size;

- different types of non-probability sample, including quota sampling, which is widely used in market research and opinion polls;

- potential sources of error in survey research.

Introduction

I imagine that many of the readers of this book will be university or college students. At some point in your stay at your university (I will use this term from now on to include colleges) you may have wondered about the attitudes of your fellow students to various matters, or about their behaviour in certain areas, or something about their backgrounds. If you were to decide to examine any or all of these three areas, you might consider conducting structured interviews or sending out questionnaires in order to find out about their behaviour, attitudes, and backgrounds. You will, of course, have to consider how best to design your interviews or questionnaires, and the issues that are involved in the decisions that need to be made about designing these research instruments and administering them will be the focus of Chapters 5–7. However, before getting to that point you are likely to be confronted with a problem. Let us say that your university is quite large and has around 9,000 students. It is extremely unlikely that you will have the time and resources to conduct a survey of all these students. It is unlikely that you would be able to send questionnaires to all 9,000 and even more unlikely that you would be able to interview all

of them, since conducting survey research by interview is considerably more expensive and time consuming, all things being equal, than by mail questionnaire (see Chapter 6). It is almost certain that you will need to *sample* students from the total population of students in your university.

The need to sample is one that is almost invariably encountered in quantitative research. In this chapter, I will be almost entirely concerned with matters relating to sampling in relation to social survey research involving data collection by structured interview or questionnaire. Other methods of quantitative research involve sampling considerations, as will be seen in Chapters 8 and 9, when we will examine structured observation and content analysis respectively. The principles of sampling involved are more or less identical in connection with these other methods, but frequently other considerations come to the fore as well.

But will any old sample suffice? Would it be sufficient to locate yourself in a central position on your campus (if it has one) and then interview the students who come past you and whom you are in a position to interview? Alternatively, would it be sufficient to go around your student union asking people to be interviewed? Or again to send questionnaires to everyone on your course?

The answer, of course, depends on whether you want to be able to *generalize* your findings to the entire student body in your university. If you do, it is unlikely that any of the three sampling strategies proposed in the previous paragraph would provide you with a *representative sample* of all students in your university. In order to be able to generalize your findings from your sample to the population from which it was selected, the sample must be representative. See Box 4.1 for an explanation of key terms concerning sampling.

Why might the strategies for sampling students previously outlined be unlikely to produce a representative sample? There are various reasons, of which the following stand out.

- The first two approaches depend heavily upon the availability of students during the time or times that you search them out. Not all students are likely to be equally available at that time, so the sample will not reflect these students.

- They also depend on the students going to the locations. Not all students will necessarily pass the point where you locate yourself or go to the student union, or they may vary hugely in the

---

Box 4.1 **Basic terms and concepts in sampling**

- *Population*—basically, the universe of units from which the sample is to be selected. The term 'units' is employed because it is not necessarily people who are being sampled—the researcher may want to sample from a universe of nations, cities, regions, schools, firms, etc. Finch and Hayes (1994), for example, based part of their research upon a random sample of wills. Their population, therefore, was a population of wills. Thus, 'population' has a much broader meaning than the everyday use of the term, whereby it tends to be associated with a nation's entire population.

- *Sample*—the segment of the population that is selected for investigation. It is a subset of the population. The method of selection may be based on a probability or a non-probability approach (see below).

- *Sampling frame*—the listing of all units in the population from which the sample will be selected.

- *Representative sample*—a sample that reflects the population accurately so that it is a microcosm of the population.

- *Probability sample*—a sample that has been selected using random selection so that each unit in the population has a known chance of being selected. It is generally assumed that a *representative sample* is more likely to be the outcome when this method of selection from the population is employed. The aim of probability sampling is to keep *sampling error* (see below) to a minimum.

- *Non-probability sample*—a sample that has not been

selected using a random selection method. Essentially, this implies that some units in the population are more likely to be selected than others.

- *Sampling error*—the difference between a sample and the population from which it is selected, even though a probability sample has been selected.

- *Non-sampling error*—differences between the population and the sample that arise either from deficiencies in the sampling approach, such as an inadequate sampling frame or *non-response* (see below), or from such problems as poor question wording, poor interviewing, or flawed processing of data.

- *Non-response*—a source of non-sampling error that is particularly likely to happen when individuals are being sampled. It occurs whenever some members of the sample refuse to cooperate, cannot be contacted, or for some reason cannot supply the required data (for example, because of mental incapacity).

- *Census*—the enumeration of an entire population. Thus, if data are collected in relation to all units in a population, rather than in relation to a sample of units of that population, the data are treated as census data. The phrase '*the* census' typically refers to the complete enumeration of all members of the population of a nation state—that is, a national census. This form of enumeration occurs once every ten years in the UK. However, in a statistical context, like the term *population*, the idea of a census has a broader meaning than this.

frequency with which they do so. Their movements are likely to reflect such things as where their halls of residence or accommodation are situated, or where their departments are located, or their social habits. Again, to rely on these locations would mean missing out on students who do not frequent them.

- It is possible, not to say likely, that your decisions about which people to approach will be influenced by your judgements about how friendly or cooperative the people concerned are likely to be or by how comfortable you feel about interviewing students of the same (or opposite) gender to yourself, as well as by many other factors.

- The problem with the third strategy is that students on your course by definition take the same subject as each other and therefore will not be representative of all students in the university.

In other words, in the case of all of the three sampling approaches, your decisions about whom to sample are influenced too much by personal judgements, by prospective respondents' availability, or by your implicit criteria for inclusion. Such limitations mean that, in the language of survey sampling, your sample will be *biased*. A biased sample is one that does not represent the population from which the sample was selected. As far as possible, bias should be removed from the selection of your sample. In fact, it is incredibly difficult to remove bias altogether and to derive a truly representative sample. What needs to be done is to ensure that steps are taken to keep bias to an absolute minimum.

Three sources of bias can be identified (see Box 4.1 for an explanation of key terms).

- *If a non-probability or non-random sampling method is used.* By using a probability or random sampling method for selecting a sample, human intervention in the selection of sample members is eliminated and each member of the population therefore has an equal chance of being selected. The procedure for using the probability sampling method is described below.

- *If the sampling frame is inadequate.* If the sampling frame is not comprehensive or is inaccurate or suffers from some other kind of similar deficiency, the sample that is derived cannot represent the population, even if a random/probability sampling method is employed.

- *If some sample members refuse to participate or cannot be contacted—in other words, if there is non-response.* The problem with non-response is that those who agree to participate may differ in various ways from those who do not agree to participate. Some of the differences may be significant to the research question or questions. If the data are available, it may be possible to check how far, when there is non-response, the resulting sample differs from the population. It is often possible to do this in terms of characteristics such as gender or age, or, in the case of something like a sample of university students, whether the sample's characteristics reflect the entire sample in terms of faculty membership. However, it is usually impossible to determine whether differences exist between the population and the sample after non-response in terms of 'deeper' factors, such as attitudes or patterns of behaviour.

Sampling error

In order to appreciate the significance of sampling error for achieving a representative sample, consider Figures 4.1–4.5. Imagine we have a population of 200 people and we want a sample of 50. Imagine as well that one of the variables of concern to us is whether people watch soap operas and that the population is equally divided between those who do and those who do not. This split is represented by the vertical line that divides the population into two halves (Figure 4.1). If the sample is representative we would expect our sample of 50 to be equally split in terms of this variable (Figure 4.2). If there is a small amount of sampling error, so that we have one person too many who does not watch soap operas and one too few

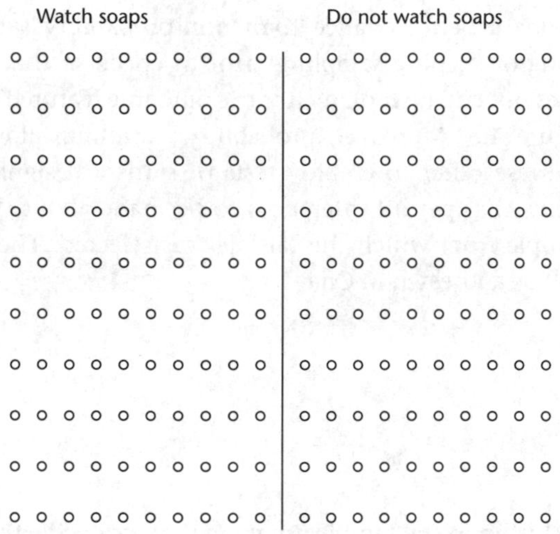

Fig. 4.1 Watching soap operas in a population of 200

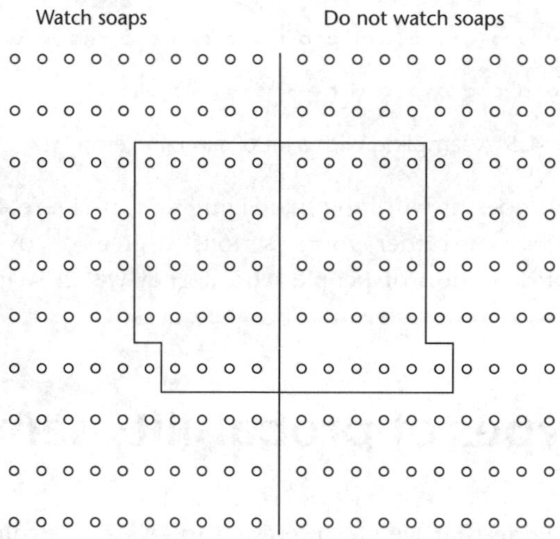

Fig. 4.3 A sample with very little sampling error

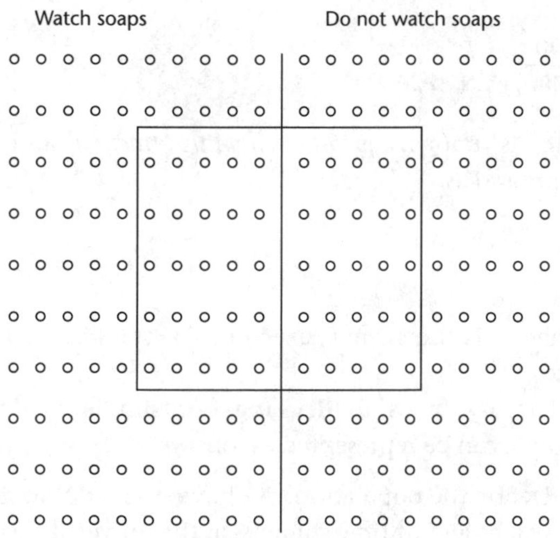

Fig. 4.2 A sample with no sampling error

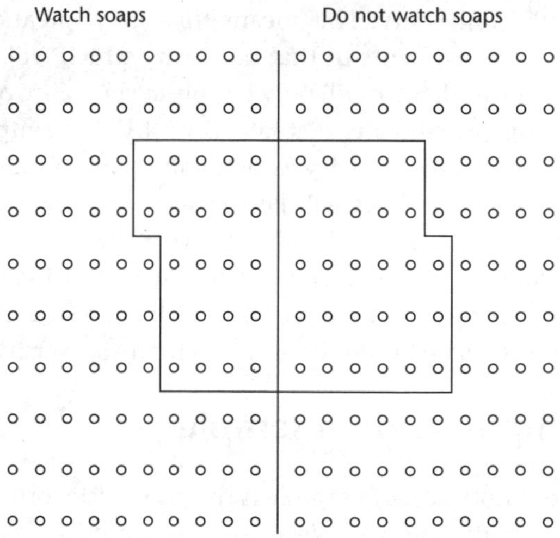

Fig. 4.4 A sample with some sampling error

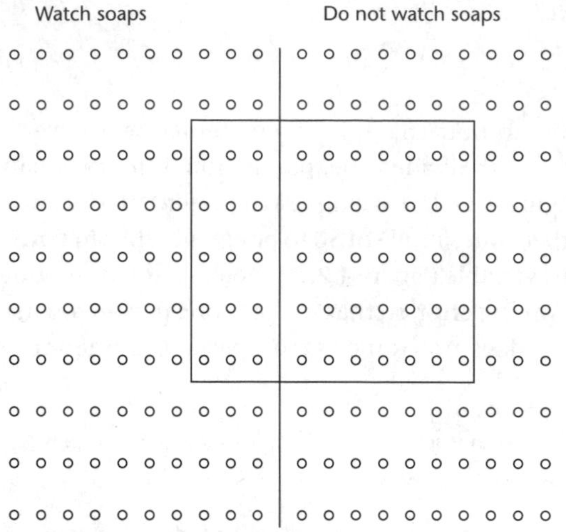

| Watch soaps | Do not watch soaps |

o o o o o o o o o o | o o o o o o o o o o

o o o o o o o o o o | o o o o o o o o o o

o o o o o o o | o o o | o o o o o o o | o o o

o o o o o o o | o o o | o o o o o o o | o o o

o o o o o o o | o o o | o o o o o o o | o o o

o o o o o o o | o o o | o o o o o o o | o o o

o o o o o o o | o o o | o o o o o o o | o o o

o o o o o o o o o o | o o o o o o o o o o

o o o o o o o o o o | o o o o o o o o o o

o o o o o o o o o o | o o o o o o o o o o

Fig. 4.5 A sampling with a lot of sampling error

who does, it will look like Figure 4.3. In Figure 4.4 we see a rather more serious degree of over-representation of people who do not watch soaps.

This time there are three too many who do not watch them and three too few who do. In Figure 4.5 we have a very serious over-representation of people who do not watch soaps, because there are 35 people in the sample who do not watch them, which is much larger than the 25 who should be in the sample.

It is important to appreciate that, as suggested above, probability sampling does not and cannot eliminate sampling error. Even with a well-crafted probability sample, a degree of sampling error is likely to creep in. However, probability sampling stands a better chance than non-probability sampling of keeping sampling error in check so that it does not end up looking like the outcome featured in Figure 4.5. Moreover, probability sampling allows the researcher to employ tests of statistical significance that permit inferences to be made about the sample from which the sample was selected. These will be addressed in Chapter 11.

Types of probability sample

Imagine that we are interested in levels of alcohol consumption among university students and the variables that relate to variation in levels of drinking. We might decide to conduct our research in a single nearby university. This means that our population will be all students in that university which will in turn mean that we will only be able to generalize our findings to students of that university. We simply cannot assume that levels of alcohol consumption and their correlates will be the same in other universities. We might decide that we only want our research to be conducted on full-time students, so that part-time students are omitted. Imagine too that there are 9, 000 full-time students in the university.

Simple random sample

The simple random sample is the most basic form of probability sample. With random sampling, each unit of the population has an equal probability of inclusion in the sample. Imagine that we decide that we have enough money to interview 450 students at the university. This means that the probability of inclusion in the sample is

$$\frac{450}{9,000}, \text{i.e. 1 in 20}$$

This is known as the *sampling fraction* and is expressed as

$$\frac{n}{N}$$

where n is the sample size and N is the population size.

The key steps in devising our simple random sample can be represented as follows:

1. Define the population. We have decided that this will be all full-time students at the university. This is our N and in this case is 9,000.

2. Select or devise a comprehensive sampling frame. It is likely that the university will have an office that keeps records of all students and that this will enable us to exclude those who do not meet our criteria for inclusion—i.e. part-time students.

3. Decide your sample size (*n*). We have decided that this will be 450.

4. List all the students in the population and assign them consecutive numbers from 1 to *N*. In our case, this will be 1 to 9,000.

5. Using a table of random numbers, or a computer program that can generate random numbers, select *n* (450) different random numbers that lie between 1 and *N* (9,000).

6. The students to which the *n* (450) random numbers refer constitute the sample.

Two points are striking about this process. First, there is almost no opportunity for human bias to manifest itself. Students would not be selected on such subjective criteria as whether they looked friendly and approachable. The selection of whom to interview is entirely mechanical. Secondly, the process is not dependent on the students' availability. They do not have to be walking in the interviewer's proximity to be included in the sample. The process of selection is done without their knowledge. It is not until they are contacted by an interviewer that they know that they are part of a social survey.

Step 5 mentions the possible use of a table of random numbers. These can be found in the appendices of many statistics books. The tables are made up of columns of five-digit numbers, such as:

09188
90045
73189
75768
54016

08358
28306
53840
91757
89415

The first thing to notice is that, since these are five-digit numbers and the maximum number that we can sample from is 9,000, which is a four-digit number, none of the random numbers seems appropriate, except for 09188 and 08358, although the former is larger than the largest possible number. The answer is that we should take just four digits in each number. Let us take the last four digits. This would yield the following:

9188
0045
3189
5768
4016

8358
8306
3840
1757
9415

However, two of the resulting numbers—9188 and 9415—exceed 9000. We cannot have a student with either of these numbers assigned to him or her. The solution is simple: we ignore these numbers. This means that the student who has been assigned the number 45 will be the first to be included in the sample; the student who has been assigned the number 3189 will be next; the student who has been assigned the number 5768 will be next; and so on.

An alternative but very similar strategy to the one that has been described is to write (or get someone to write for you) a simple computer program that will select *n* random numbers (in our case 450) that lie between 1 and *N* (in our case 9,000). As with using a table of random numbers, you may be faced with the possibility of some random numbers turning up more than once. Since you will want to interview the person to whom those recurring random numbers refer on only one occasion, you will want to ignore any random number that recurs. This procedure results in a sample known as a simple random sample *without replacement*. More or less all simple random samples will be of this kind in the context of social research and so the qualifier 'without replacement' is invariably omitted.

Systematic sample

A variation on the simple random sample is the systematic sample. With this kind of sample, you select units directly from the sampling frame—that is, without resorting to a table of random numbers.

We know that we are to select 1 student in 20. With a systematic sample, we would make a random start between 1 and 20 inclusive, possibly by using the last two digits in a table of random numbers. If we did this with the ten random numbers above, the first relevant one would be 54016, since it is the first one where the last two digits yield a number of 20 or below, in this case, 16. This means that the sixteenth student on our sampling frame is the first to be in our sample. Thereafter, we take every twentieth student on the list. So the sequence will go:

16, 36, 56, 76, 96, 116, etc.

This approach obviates the need to assign numbers to students' names and then to look up names of the students whose numbers have been drawn by the random selection process. It is important to ensure, however, that there is no inherent ordering of the sampling frame, since this may bias the resulting sample. If there is some ordering to the list, the best solution is to rearrange it.

Stratified random sampling

In our imaginary study of university students, one of the features that we might want our sample to exhibit is a proportional representation of the different faculties to which students are attached. It might be that the kind of discipline a student is studying is viewed as relevant to a wide range of attitudinal features that are relevant to the study of drinking. Generating a simple random sample or a systematic sample *might* yield such a representation, so that the proportion of humanities students in the sample is the same as that in the student population and so on. Thus, if there are 1, 800 students in the humanities faculty, using our sampling fraction of 1 in 20, we would expect to have 90 students in our sample from this faculty. However, because of sampling

error, it is unlikely that this will occur and that there will be a difference, so that there may be, say, 85 or 93 from this faculty.

Because it is almost certain that the university will include in its records the faculty in which students are based, or indeed may have separate sampling frames for each faculty, it will be possible to ensure that students are accurately represented in terms of their faculty membership. In the language of sampling, this means stratifying the population by a criterion (in this case, faculty membership) and selecting either a simple random sample or a systematic sample from each of the resulting strata. In the present example, if there are five faculties we would have five strata, with the numbers in each stratum being one-twentieth of the total for each faculty, as in Table 4.1, which also shows a hypothetical outcome of using a simple random sample, which results in a distribution of students across faculties that does not mirror the population all that well.

The advantage of stratified sampling in a case like this is clear: it ensures that the resulting sample will be distributed in the same way as the population in terms of the stratifying criterion. If you use a simple random or systematic sampling approach, you *may* end up with a distribution like that of the stratified sample, but it is unlikely. Two points are relevant here. First, you can conduct stratified sampling sensibly only when it is relatively easy to identify and allocate units to strata. If it is not possible or it would be very difficult to do so, stratified sampling will not

Table 4.1 The advantages of stratified sampling

Faculty	Population	Stratified sample	Possible simple random or systematic sample
Humanities	1,800	90	85
Social sciences	1,200	60	70
Pure sciences	2,000	100	120
Applied sciences	1,800	90	84
Engineering	2,200	110	91
TOTAL	9,000	450	450

be feasible. Secondly, you can use more than one stratifying criterion. Thus, it may be that you would want to stratify by both faculty and gender or faculty and whether students are undergraduates or postgraduates. If it is feasible to identify students in terms of these stratifying criteria, it is possible to use pairs of criteria or several criteria (such as faculty membership plus gender plus undergraduate/postgraduate).

Stratified sampling is really feasible only when the relevant information is available. In other words, when data are available that allow the ready identification of members of the population in terms of the stratifying criterion (or criteria), it is sensible to employ this sampling method. But it is unlikely to be economical if the identification of population members for stratification purposes entails a great deal of work because there is no available listing in terms of strata.

Multi-stage cluster sampling

In the example we have been dealing with, students to be interviewed are located in a single university. Interviewers will have to arrange their interviews with the sampled students, but, because they are all close together (even in a split-site university), they will not be involved in a lot of travel. However, imagine that we wanted a *national* sample of students. It is likely that interviewers would have to travel the length and breadth of the UK to interview the sampled students. This would add a great deal to the time and cost of doing the research. This kind of problem occurs whenever the aim is to interview a sample that is to be drawn from a widely dispersed population, such as a national population, or a large region, or even a large city.

One way in which it is possible to deal with this potential problem is to employ *cluster sampling*. With cluster sampling, the primary sampling unit (the first stage of the sampling procedure) is not the units of the population to be sampled but groupings of those units. It is the latter groupings or aggregations of population units that are known as *clusters*. Imagine that we want a nationally representative sample of

5,000 students. Using simple random or systematic sampling would yield a widely dispersed sample, which would result in a great deal of travel for interviewers. One solution might be to sample universities and then students from each of the sampled universities. A probability sampling method would need to be employed at each stage. Thus, we might randomly sample ten universities from the entire population of universities, thus yielding ten clusters, and we would then interview 500 randomly selected students at each of the ten universities.

Now imagine that the result of sampling ten universities gives the following list:

- Glasgow Caledonian
- Edinburgh
- Teesside
- Sheffield
- University College, Swansea
- Leeds Metropolitan
- University of Ulster
- University College, London
- Southampton
- Loughborough

This list is fine, but interviewers could still be involved in a great deal of travel, since the ten universities are quite a long way from each other. North American and Australian readers who examine this last comment by looking at a map of the United Kingdom may view the universities as in fact very close to each other!

One solution is likely to be to group all UK universities by standard region (see Box 4.2 for an example of this kind of approach) and to randomly sample two standard regions. Five universities might then be sampled from each of the two lists of universities and then 500 students from each of the ten universities. Thus, there are separate stages:

- group UK universities by standard region and sample two regions;
- sample five universities from each of the two regions;
- sample 500 students from each of the ten universities.

Box 4.2 An example of a multi-stage cluster sample

For their study of social class in modern Britain, Marshall *et al*. designed a sample 'to achieve 2,000 interviews with a random selection of men aged 16–64 and women aged 16–59 who were not in full-time education' (1988: 288).

- *Sampling parliamentary constituencies*
  - Parliamentary constituencies were ordered by standard region (there are eleven).
  - Constituencies were allocated to one of three population density bands within standard regions.
  - These subgroups were then reordered by political party voted to represent the constituency at the previous general election.
  - These subgroups were then listed in ascending order of percentage in owner-occupation.

- 100 parliamentary constituencies were then sampled.

Thus, parliamentary constituencies were stratified in terms of four variables: standard region; population density; political party voted for in last election; and percentage of owner-occupation.

- *Sampling polling districts*
  - Two polling districts were chosen from each sampled constituency.

- *Sampling individuals*
  - Nineteen addresses from each sampled polling district were systematically sampled.
  - One person at each address was chosen according to a number of pre-defined rules.

In a sense, cluster sampling is always a multi-stage approach, because one always samples clusters first and then something else—either further clusters or population units—is sampled.

Many examples of multi-stage cluster sampling entail stratification. We might, for example, want to stratify universities in terms of whether they are 'old' or 'new' universities—that is, those that received their charters after the 1991 White Paper for Higher Education, *Higher Education: A New Framework*. In each of the two regions, we would group universities along the old/new university criterion and then select two or three universities from each of the two strata per region.

Box 4.2 provides an example of a multi-stage cluster sample. It entailed three stages: the sampling of parliamentary constituencies, the sampling of polling districts, and the sampling of individuals. In a

way, there are four stages, because addresses are sampled from polling districts and then individuals are sampled from each address. However, Marshall *et al.* (1988) present their sampling strategy as involving just three stages. Parliamentary constituencies were stratified by four criteria: standard region, population density, voting behaviour, and owner-occupation.

The advantage of multi-stage cluster sampling should be clear by now: it allows interviewers to be far more concentrated than would be the case if a simple random or stratified sample were selected. The advantages of stratification can be capitalized upon because the clusters can be stratified in terms of strata. However, even when a very rigorous sampling strategy is employed, sampling error cannot be avoided, as the example in Box 4.3 shows.

The qualities of a probability sample

The reason why probability sampling is such an important procedure in social survey research is that it is possible to make inferences from information about a random sample to the population from

which it was selected. In other words, we can generalize findings derived from a sample to the population. This is not to say that we treat the population data and the sample data as the same. If we take the

---

Box 4.3 **The 1992 British Crime Survey**

The British Crime Survey (BCS) is a regular survey, funded by the Home Office, of a national sample drawn from the populations of England and Wales. The survey has been carried out on eight occasions: 1982, 1984, 1988, 1992, 1994, 1996, 1998, and 2000. In each instance, over 10,000 people were interviewed. The main object of the survey is to glean information on respondents' experiences of being victims of crime. There is also a self-report component in which a selection of the sample are interviewed on their attitudes to crime and to report on crimes they have committed. Prior to 1992, the BCS used the electoral register as a sampling frame. Relying on a register of the electorate as a sampling frame is not without problems in spite of appearing robust: it omits any persons who are not registered, a problem that was exacerbated by the Community Charge (poll tax), which resulted in a significant amount of non-registration, as some people sought to avoid detection in order not to have to pay the tax. In 1992, the Postcode Address File was employed as a sampling frame and has been used since then. Its main advantage over the electoral register as a sampling frame is that it is updated more frequently. It is not perfect, because the homeless will not be accessible through it. The sample itself is a stratified multi-stage cluster sample. The sampling procedure produced 13,117 residential addresses. Like most surveys, there was some non-response, with 23.3 per cent of the 13,117 addresses not resulting in a 'valid' interview. Just under half of these cases were the result of an outright refusal. In spite of the fact that the BCS is a rigorously selected and very large sample, an examination of the 1992 survey by Elliott and Ellingworth (1997) shows that there is some sampling error. By comparing the distribution of survey respondents with the 1991 census, they show that certain social groups are somewhat under-represented, most notably: owner-occupiers, households in which no car is owned, and male unemployed. However, Elliott and Ellingworth show that, as the level of property crime in postcode address sectors increases, so too does the response rate (see Box 4.4). In other words, people who live in high crime areas tend to be less likely to agree to be interviewed. How far this tendency affects the BCS data is difficult to determine, but the significance of this brief example is that, even when a sample of this quality is selected, the existence of sampling and non-sampling error cannot be discounted. The potential for a larger spread of errors when levels of sampling rigour fall short of a sample like that selected for the BCS is, therefore, considerable.

---

example of the level of alcohol consumption in our sample of 450 students, which we will treat as the number of units of alcohol consumed in the previous seven days, we will know that the mean number of units consumed by the sample ($\bar{x}$) can be used to estimate the population mean (μ) but with known margins of error. The mean, or more properly the arithmetic mean, is the simple average.

In order to address this point it is necessary to use some basic statistical ideas. These are presented in Box 4.4 and can be skipped if just a broad idea of sampling procedures is required.

Sample size

As someone who is known as a teacher of research methods and a writer of books in this area, I often get asked questions about methodological issues. One question that is asked almost more than any other relates to the size of the sample—'how large should my sample be?' or 'is my sample large enough?' The decision about sample size is not a straightforward one: it depends on a number of considerations and there is no one definitive answer. This is frequently a source of great disappointment to those who pose such questions. Moreover, most of the time decisions about sample size are affected by considerations of time and cost. Therefore, invariably decisions about sample size represent a compromise between the

Box 4.4 Generalizing from a random sample to the population

Let us say that the sample mean is 9.7 units of alcohol consumed (the average amount of alcohol consumed in the previous seven days in the sample). A crucial consideration here is: how confident can we be that the mean level of alcohol consumption of 9.7 units is likely to be found in the population, even when probability sampling has been employed? If we take an infinite number of samples from a population, the sample estimates of the mean of the variable under consideration will vary in relation to the population mean. This variation will take the form of a bell-shaped curve known as a *normal distribution* (see Figure 4.6). The shape of the distribution implies that there is a clustering of sample means at or around the population mean. Half the sample means will be at or below the population mean; the other half will be at or above the population mean. As we move to the left (at or lower than the population mean) or the right (at or higher than the population mean), the curve tails off, implying fewer and fewer samples generating means that depart considerably from the population mean. The variation of sample means around the population mean is the *sampling error* and is measured using a statistic known as the *standard error of the mean*. This is an estimate of the amount that a sample mean is likely to differ from the population mean.

This consideration is important because sampling theory tells us that 68 per cent of all sample means will lie between + or − one standard error from the population mean and that 95 per cent of all sample means will lie between + or − 1.96 standard errors from the population mean. It is this second calculation that is crucial, because it is at least implicitly employed by survey researchers when they report their statistical findings. They typically employ 1.96 standard errors as the crucial criterion in how confident they can be in their findings. Essentially, the criterion implies that you can be 95 per cent certain that the population mean lies within + or − 1.96 sampling errors from the sample mean.

If a sample has been selected according to probability sampling principles, we know that we can be 95 per cent certain that the population mean will lie between the sample mean plus or minus 1.96 multiplied by the standard error of the mean. This is known as the *confidence interval*. If the mean level of alcohol consumption in the previous seven days in our sample of 450 students is 9.7 units and the standard error of the mean is 1.3, we can be 95 per cent certain that the population mean will lie between

$$9.7 + (1.96 \times 1.3)$$

and

$$9.7 - (1.96 \times 1.3)$$

i.e. between 12.248 and 7.152.

If the standard error was smaller, the range of possible values of the population mean would be narrower; if the standard error was larger, the range of possible values of the population mean would be wider.

If a stratified sample is selected, the standard error of the mean will be smaller because the variation between strata is essentially eliminated because the population will be accurately represented in the sample in terms of the stratification criterion or criteria employed. This consideration demonstrates the way in which stratification injects an extra increment of precision into the probability sampling process, since a possible source of sampling error is eliminated.

By contrast, a cluster sample without stratification exhibits a larger standard error of the mean than a comparable simple random sample. This occurs because a possible source of variability between students (i.e. membership of one university rather than another, which may affect levels of alcohol consumption) is disregarded. If, for example, some universities had a culture of heavy drinking in which a large number of students participated, and if these universities were not selected because of the procedure for selecting clusters, an important source of variability would have been omitted. It also implies that the sample mean would be on the low side, but that is another matter.

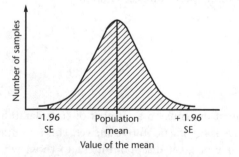

Notes: 95 per cent of sample means will lie within the shaded area. SE = standard error of the mean.

Fig. 4.6 The distribution of sample means

constraints of time and cost, the need for precision, and a variety of further considerations that will now be addressed.

Absolute and relative sample size

One of the most basic considerations, and one that is possibly the most surprising, is that, contrary to what you might have expected, it is the *absolute* size of a sample that is important not its *relative* size. This means that a national probability sample of 1,000 individuals in the UK has as much validity as a national probability sample of 1,000 individuals in the USA, even though the latter has a much larger population. It also means that increasing the size of a sample increases the precision of a sample. This means that the 95 per cent confidence interval referred to in Box 4.4 narrows. However, a large sample cannot *guarantee* precision so that it is probably better to say that increasing the size of a sample increases the *likely* precision of a sample. This means that, as sample size increases, sampling error decreases. Therefore, an important component of any decision about sample size should be how much sampling error one is prepared to tolerate. The less sampling error one is prepared to tolerate, the larger a sample will need to be. Fowler (1993) warns against a simple acceptance of this criterion. He argues that in practice researchers do not base their decisions about sample size on a single estimate of a variable. Most survey research is concerned to generate a host of estimates—that is, of the variables that make up the research instrument that is administered. He also observes that it is not normal for survey researchers to be in a position to specify in advance 'a desired level of precision' (Fowler 1993: 34). Moreover, since sampling error will be only one component of any error entailed in an estimate, the notion of using a desired level of precision as a factor in a decision about sample size is not realistic. Instead, to the extent that this notion does enter into decisions about sample size, it usually does so in a general rather than a calculated way.

Time and cost

Time and cost considerations become very relevant in this context. In the previous paragraph it is clearly being suggested that the larger the sample size the greater the precision (because the amount of sampling error will be less). However, by and large up to a sample size of around 1,000, the gains in precision are noticeable as the sample size climbs from low figures of 50, 100, 150, and so on upwards. After a certain point, often in the region of 1,000, the sharp increases in precision become less pronounced, and, although it does not plateau, there is a slowing down in the extent to which precision increases (and hence the extent to which the sample error of the mean declines). Considerations of sampling size are likely to be profoundly affected by matters of time and cost at such a juncture, since striving for smaller and smaller increments of precision becomes an increasingly uneconomic proposition.

Non-response

However, considerations about sampling error do not end here. The problem of *non-response* should be borne in mind. Most sample surveys attract a certain amount of non-response. Thus, it is likely that only some of our sample will agree to participate in the research. If it is our aim to ensure as far as possible that 450 students are interviewed and if we think that there may be a 20 per cent rate of non-response, it may be advisable to sample 540–50 individuals, on the grounds that approximately ninety will be non-respondents.

The issue of non-response, and in particular of refusal to participate, is of particular significance, because it has been suggested by some researchers that response rates to social surveys (see Box 4.5) are declining in many countries. This implies that there is a growing tendency towards people refusing to participate in social survey research. In 1973, an article in the American magazine *Business Week* carried an article ominously entitled 'The Public Clams up on Survey Takers'. The magazine asked survey companies about their experiences and found

Box 4.5   What is a response rate?

The notion of a response rate is a common one in social survey research. When a social survey is conducted, whether by structured interview or by self-completion questionnaire, it is invariably the case that some people who are in the sample refuse to participate. The response rate is, therefore, the percentage of a sample that does in fact agree to participate. However, the calculation of a response rate is a little more complicated than this. First, not everyone who replies will be included: if a large number of questions are not answered by a respondent or if there are clear indications that he or she has not taken the interview or questionnaire seriously, it is better to employ only the number of *usable* interviews or questionnaires as the numerator. Similarly, it also tends to occur that not everyone in a sample turns out to be a suitable or appropriate respondent or can be contacted. Thus the response rate is calculated as follows:

$$\frac{\text{number of usable questionnaires}}{\text{total sample} - \text{unsuitable or uncontactable}} \times 100$$
$$\text{members of the sample}$$

considerable concern about declining response rates. Similarly, in Britain, a report from a working party on the Market Research Society's Research and Development Committee in 1975 pointed to similar concerns among market research companies. However, an analysis of this issue by T. W. Smith (1995) suggests that, contrary to popular belief, there is no consistent evidence of such a decline. Moreover, Smith shows that it is difficult to disentangle general trends in response rates from such variables as the subject matter of the research, the type of respondent, and the level of effort expended on improving the number of respondents to individual surveys. The strategies that can improve responses to survey instruments such as structured interviews and mail questionnaires will be examined in Chapter 5.

Heterogeneity of the population

Yet another consideration is the homogeneity and heterogeneity of the population from which the sample is to be taken. When a sample is very heterogeneous, like a sample of a whole country or city, the population is likely to be highly varied. When it is relatively homogeneous, such as a population of students or of members of an occupation, the amount of variation is less. The implication of this is that, the greater the heterogeneity of a population, the larger a sample will need to be.

Kind of analysis

Finally, researchers should bear in mind the *kind of analysis* they intend to undertake. A case in point here is the contingency table. A contingency table shows the relationship between two variables in tabular form. It shows how variation in one variable relates to variation in another variable. To understand this point, consider the basic structure of a table in the study by Marshall *et al.* (1988) of social class in Britain (see Box 4.2). The table is based on the 589 cohabiting couples (1,178 people) in which both partners are employed in paid work. The authors aim to show in the table how far couples are of the same or a different social class in terms of Goldthorpe's seven-category scheme for classifying social class. The result is a table in which, because each variable comprises seven categories, there are forty-nine 'cells' in the table (i.e. 7 × 7). In order for there to be an adequate number of cases in each cell, a fairly large sample was required. Imagine that Marshall *et al.* had conducted a survey on a much smaller sample in which they ended up with just 150 couples. If the same kind of analysis as Marshall *et al.* carried out was conducted, it would be found that these 150 couples would be very dispersed across the forty-nine cells of the table. It is likely that many of the cells would be empty or would have very small numbers in them, which would make it difficult to make inferences about what the table showed. In fact, quite a lot of the cells in the actual table in

Marshall *et al.* have very small numbers in them (eight cells contain 1 or 0). This problem would have been even more pronounced if they had ended up with a much smaller sample of couples. Consequently, considerations of sample size should be sensitive to the kinds of analysis that will be subsequently required, such as the issue of the number of cells in a table. In a case such as this, a larger sample will be necessitated by the nature of the analysis to be conducted as well as the nature of the variables in question.

Types of non-probability sampling

The term *non-probability sampling* is essentially an umbrella term to capture all forms of sampling that are not conducted according to the canons of probability sampling outlined above. It is not surprising, therefore, that the term covers a wide range of different types of sampling strategy, at least one of which—the quota sample—is claimed by some practitioners to be almost as good as a probability sample. In this section we will cover three main types of non-probability sample: the convenience sample; the snowball sample; and the quota sample.

Convenience sampling

A convenience sample is one that is simply available to the researcher by virtue of its accessibility. Imagine that a researcher, who teaches education at a university, is interested in the kinds of features that teachers look for in their headmasters. The researcher might administer a questionnaire to several classes of students, all of whom are teachers taking a part-time master's degree in education. The chances are that the researcher will receive all or almost all of the questionnaires back, so that there will be a good response rate. The findings may prove quite interesting, but the problem with such a sampling strategy is that it is impossible to generalize the findings, because we do not know of what population this sample is representative. They are simply a group of teachers who are available to the researcher. They are almost certainly not representative of teachers as a whole—the very fact they are taking this degree programme marks them off as different from teachers in general.

This is not to suggest that convenience samples should never be used. Let us say that our lecturer/researcher is developing a battery of questions that are designed to measure the leadership preferences of teachers. It is highly desirable to pilot such a research instrument before using it in an investigation, and administering it to a group who are not a part of the main study may be a legitimate way of carrying out some preliminary analysis of such issues as whether respondents tend to answer in identical ways to a question, or whether one question is often omitted when teachers respond to it. In other words, for this kind of purpose, a convenience sample may be acceptable though not ideal. A second kind of context in which it may be at least fairly acceptable to use a convenience sample is when the chance presents itself to gather data from a convenience sample and it represents too good an opportunity to miss. The data will not allow definitive findings to be generated, because of the problem of generalization, but it could provide a springboard for further research or allow links to be forged with existing findings in an area.

It also perhaps ought to be recognized that convenience sampling probably plays a more prominent role than is sometimes supposed. Certainly, in the field of organization studies it has been noted that convenience samples are very common and indeed are more prominent than are samples based on probability sampling (Bryman 1989*a*: 113–14). Social research is also frequently based on convenience sampling. Boxes 4.6 and 4.7 contain examples of the use of convenience samples in social research. Probability sampling involves a lot of preparation so that it is frequently avoided because of the difficulty and costs involved.

Box 4.6 A convenience sample

Lucas (1997) describes a study of university students that was undertaken to find out about the extent and kinds of part-time employment among the students. Data were collected in spring 1995 from students in five of the seven faculties at Manchester Metropolitan University, where the author of the report is a lecturer. The specific degree programmes chosen were first degrees in: chemistry, combined studies, electrical engineering, history, hotel and catering management, illustration, law, psychology, and social science. Self-completion questionnaires were given out to students in the first, final, and either second or third years of their degrees (depending on whether the course lasted three or four years). The choice of subjects was designed to maximize the amount of variety in the type of degree programme and to provide similar numbers of males and females (since one gender frequently predominates in particular degree programmes). The questionnaire 'was issued, completed and collected at the end of class contact time by one of the researchers, or by a member of teaching staff' (Lucas 1997: 600–1). These procedures represent a very good attempt to generate a varied sample. It is a convenience sample, because the choice of degree programmes was selected purposively rather than randomly and because absentees from classes were unavailable to answer the questionnaires. On the other hand, because of the way questionnaires were administered, there was a very high rate of response among those students to whom the questionnaires were administered. An interesting question is whether absence from classes might be connected in some way to part-time working; in other words, might absence be due to students working at the time of the class or to students perhaps being too tired to go to the class because of their part-time work?

Box 4.7 Another convenience sample

Miller *et al.* (1998) were interested in theories concerning the role of shopping in relation to the construction of identity in modern society. Since many discussions of this issue have connected with shopping centres (malls), they undertook a study that combined quantitative and qualitative research methods in order to explore the views of shoppers at two London shopping centres: Brent Cross and Wood Green. One phase of the research entailed structured interviews with shoppers exiting the centres. The interviews were conducted mainly during the week in June and July 1994. Shoppers were chiefly questioned as they left the main exits, though some questioning at minor exits also took place. The authors tell us: 'We did not attempt to secure a quota [see below] or random sample but asked every person who passed by, and who did not obviously look in the other direction or change their path, to complete a questionnaire' (Miller *et al.* 1998: 55). Such a sampling strategy produces a convenience sample because only people who are visiting the centre and who are therefore self-selected by virtue of their happening to choose to shop at these times could be interviewed.

Snowball sampling

In certain respects, snowball sampling is a form of convenience sample, but it is worth distinguishing because it has attracted quite a lot of attention over the years. With this approach to sampling, the researcher makes initial contact with a small group of people who are relevant to the research topic and then uses these to establish contacts with others. I used an approach like this to create a sample of British visitors to Disney theme parks (Bryman 1999).

Box 4.8 describes the generation of a snowball sample of marijuana users for what is often regarded as a classic study of drug use.

Becker's comment on this method of creating a snowball sample is interesting: 'The sample is, of course, in no sense "random"; it would not be possible to draw a random sample, since no one knows the nature of the universe from which it would have to be drawn' (Becker 1963: 46). What Becker is essentially saying here (and the same point applies to my study of Disney theme park visitors) is that there is

Box 4.8 A snowball sample: Becker's study of marijuana users

In an article first published in 1953, Becker (1963) reports on how he generated a sample of marijuana users. He writes:

I conducted fifty interviews with marihuana users. I had been a professional dance musician for some years when I conducted this study and my first interviews were with people I had met in the music business. I asked them to put me in contact with other users who would be willing to discuss their experiences with me. . . . Although in the end half of the fifty interviews were conducted with musicians, the other half covered a wide range of people, including laborers, machinists, and people in the professions. (Becker 1963: 45–6)

no accessible sampling frame for the population from which the sample is to be taken and that the difficulty of creating such a sampling frame means that such an approach is the only feasible one. Moreover, even if one could create a sampling frame of marijuana users or of British visitors to Disney theme parks, it would almost certainly be inaccurate straight away, because this is a shifting population. People will constantly be becoming and ceasing to be marijuana users, while new theme park visitors are arriving all the time.

The problem with snowball sampling is that it is very unlikely that the sample will be representative of the population, though, as I have just suggested, the very notion of a population may be problematic in some circumstances. However, by and large, snowball sampling is used not within a quantitative research strategy, but within a qualitative one: both Becker's and my study were carried out within a qualitative research framework. Concerns about external validity and the ability to generalize do not loom as large within a qualitative research strategy as they do in a quantitative research one (see Chapters 3 and 13). In qualitative research, the orientation to sampling is more likely to be guided by a preference for *theoretical sampling* than with the kind of statistical sampling that has been the focus of this chapter (see Box 14.8, p. 302). There is a much better 'fit'

between snowball sampling and the theoretical sampling strategy of qualitative research than with the statistical sampling approach of quantitative research. This is not to suggest that snowball sampling is entirely irrelevant to quantitative research: when the researcher needs to focus upon or to reflect relationships between people, tracing connections through snowball sampling may be a better approach than conventional probability sampling (Coleman 1958).

Quota sampling

Quota sampling is comparatively rarely employed in academic social research, but is used intensively in commercial research, such as market research and political opinion polling. The aim of quota sampling is to produce a sample that reflects a population in terms of the relative proportions of people in different categories, such as gender, ethnicity, age groups, socio-economic groups, and region of residence, and in combinations of these categories. However, unlike a stratified sample, the sampling of individuals is not carried out randomly, since the final selection of people is left up to the interviewer. Information about the stratification of the UK population or about certain regions can be obtained from sources like the Census and from surveys based on probability samples such as the General Household Survey, British Social Attitudes, and the British Household Panel Study.

Once the categories and the number of people to be interviewed within each category (known as *quotas*) have been decided upon, it is then the job of interviewers to select people who fit these categories. The quotas will typically be interrelated. In a manner similar to stratified sampling, the population may be divided into strata in terms of, for example, gender, social class, age, and ethnicity. Census data might be used to identify the number of people who should be in each subgroup. The numbers to be interviewed in each subgroup will reflect the population. Each interviewer will probably seek out individuals who fit several subgroup quotas. Accordingly, an interviewer may know that among the various subgroups of people he or she must find, and interview, five Asian, 25–34-year-old, lower-middle-class females in the area in which the interviewer has been asked to work (say, the Wirral). The interviewer usually asks people who are available to him or her about their characteristics (though gender will presumably be self-evident) in order to determine their suitability for a particular subgroup. Once a subgroup quota (or a combination of subgroup quotas) has been achieved, the interviewer will no longer be concerned to locate individuals for that subgroup.

The choice of respondents is left to the interviewer, subject to the requirement of all quotas being filled, usually within a certain time period. Those of you who have ever been approached on the street by a person toting a clipboard and interview schedule and have been asked about your age, occupation, and so on, before being asked a series of questions about a product or whatever, have almost certainly encountered an interviewer with a quota sample to fill. Sometimes, he or she will decide not to interview you because you do not meet the criteria required to fill a quota. This may be due to a quota already having been filled or to the criteria for exclusion meaning that a person with a certain characteristic you possess is not required.

A number of criticisms are frequently levelled at quota samples.

- Because the choice of respondent is left to the interviewer, the proponents of probability sampling argue that a quota sample cannot be representative. It may accurately reflect the population in terms of superficial characteristics, as defined by the quotas. However, in their choice of people to approach, interviewers may be unduly influenced by their perceptions of how friendly people are or by whether the people make eye contact with the interviewer (unlike most of us who look at the ground and shuffle past as quickly as possible because we do not want to be bothered in our leisure time).

- People who are in an interviewer's vicinity at the times he or she conducts interviews, and are therefore available to be approached, may not be typical. There is a risk, for example, that people in full-time paid work may be under-represented and that those who are included in the sample are not typical.

- The interviewer is likely to make judgements about certain characteristics in deciding whether to approach a person, in particular, judgements about age. Those judgements will sometimes be incorrect—for example, when someone who is eligible to be interviewed, because a quota which he or she fits is unfilled, is not approached because the interviewer makes an incorrect judgement (for example, that the person is older than he or she looks). In such a case, a possible element of bias is being introduced.

- It has also been argued that the widespread use of social class as a quota control can introduce difficulties, because of the problem of ensuring that interviewees are properly assigned to class groupings (Moser and Kalton 1971).

- It is not permissible to calculate a standard error of the mean from a quota sample, because the non-random method of selection makes it impossible to calculate the range of possible values of a population.

All of this makes the quota sample look a poor bet and there is no doubt that it is not favoured by academic social researchers. It does have some arguments in its favour, however.

- It is undoubtedly cheaper and quicker than an interview survey on a comparable probability sample. For example, interviewers do not have to spend a lot of time travelling between interviews.

- Interviewers do not have to keep calling back on people who were not available at the time they were first approached.

- Because calling back is not required, a quota sample is easier to manage. It is not necessary to keep track of people who need to be recontacted or to keep track of refusals. Refusals occur, of course, but it is not necessary (and indeed it is not possible) to keep a record of which respondents declined to participate.

- When speed is of the essence, a quota sample is invaluable when compared to the more cumbersome probability sample. Newspapers frequently need to know how a national sample of voters feel about a certain topic or how they intend to vote at that time. Alternatively, if there is a sudden major news event, such as the death of Princess Diana, the news media may seek a more or less instant picture of the nation's views or responses. Again, a quota sample will be much faster.

- As with convenience sampling, it is useful for conducting development work on new measures or on research instruments. It can also be usefully employed in relation to exploratory work from which new theoretical ideas might be generated.

- Although the standard error of the mean should not be computed for a quota sample, it frequently is. As Moser and Kalton (1971) observe, some writers argue that the use of a non-random method in quota sampling should not act as a barrier to such a computation because its significance as a source of error is small when compared to other errors that may arise in surveys (see Figure 4.7). However, they go on to argue that at least with random sampling the researcher can calculate the amount of sampling error and does not have to be concerned about its potential impact.

There is some evidence to suggest that, when compared to random samples, quota samples often result in biases. They under-represent people in lower social strata, people who work in the private sector and manufacturing, and people at the extremes of income, and they over-represent women in households with children and people from larger households (Marsh and Scarbrough 1990; Butcher 1994). On the other hand, it has to be acknowledged that probability samples are often biased too—for example, it is often suggested that they under-represent men and those in employment (Marsh and Scarbrough 1990; Butcher 1994).

Limits to generalization

One point that is often not fully appreciated is that, even when a sample has been selected using probability sampling, any findings can be generalized only to the population from which that sample was taken. This is an obvious point, but it is easy to think that findings from a study have some kind of broader applicability. If we take our imaginary study of alcohol consumption among students at a university, any findings could be generalized only to that university. In other words, you should be very cautious about generalizing to students at other universities. There are many factors that may imply that the level of alcohol consumption is higher (or lower) than among university students as a whole. There may be a higher (or lower) concentration of pubs in the university's vicinity, there may be more (or fewer) bars on the campus, there may be more (or less) of a culture of drinking at this university, or the university may recruit a higher (or lower) proportion of students with disposable income. There may be many other factors too. Similarly, we should be cautious of overgeneralizing in terms of locality. Lunt and Livingstone's study of consumption habits was based on a postal questionnaire sent to '241 people living in or around Oxford during September 1989' (1992: 173). While the authors' findings represent a fascinating insight into modern consumption patterns, we should be cautious about assuming that they can be generalized beyond the confines of Oxford and its environs.

There could even be a further limit to generalization that is implied by the Lunt and Livingstone (1992) sample. They write that the research was conducted in September 1989. One issue that is rarely discussed in this context and that is almost impossible to assess is whether there is a time limit on the findings that are generated. Quite aside from the fact that we need to appreciate that the findings cannot (or at least should not) be generalized beyond the Oxford area, is there a point at which we have to say, 'well, those findings applied to the Oxford area then but things have changed and we can no longer assume that they apply to that or any other locality'? We are, after all, used to thinking that things have changed when there has been some kind of prominent change. To take a simple example: no one would be prepared to assume that the findings of a study in 1980 of university students' budgeting and personal finance habits would apply to students in the early twenty-first century. Quite aside from changes that might have occurred naturally, the erosion and virtual dismantling of the student grant system has changed the ways students finance their education, including perhaps a greater reliance on part-time work (Lucas 1997), a greater reliance on parents, and use of loans. But, even when there is no definable or recognizable source of relevant change of this kind, there is none the less the possibility (or even likelihood) that findings are temporally specific. Such an issue is impossible to resolve without further research (Bryman 1989*b*).

Error in survey research

We can think of 'error', a term that has been employed on a number of occasions, as being made up of four main factors (Figure 4.7).

- *Sampling error*. See Box 4.1 for a definition. This kind of error arises because it is extremely unlikely that one will end up with a truly representative sample, even when probability sampling is employed.
- We can distinguish what might be thought of as *sampling-related error*. This is error that is subsumed under the category *non-sampling error* (see Box 4.1) but that arises from activities or events that are related to the sampling process and that are connected with the issue of generalizability or external validity of findings. Examples are an inaccurate sampling frame and non-response.
- There is also error that is connected with the implementation of the research process. We might call this *data collection error*. This source of error includes such factors as: poor question wording in self-completion questionnaires or structured interviews; poor interviewing techniques; and flaws in the administration of research instruments.
- Finally, there is *data processing error*. This arises from faulty management of data, in particular, errors in the *coding* of answers.

The third and fourth sources of error relate to factors that are not associated with sampling and instead relate much more closely to concerns about the validity of measurement, which was addressed in Chapter 3. However, the kinds of steps that need to be taken to keep these sources of error to a minimum in the context of social survey research will be addressed in the next three chapters.

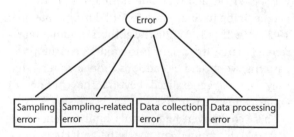

Fig. 4.7 Four sources of error in social survey research

Key points

- Probability sampling is a mechanism for reducing bias in the selection of samples.

- Ensure you become familiar with key technical terms in the literature on sampling such as: representative sample; random sample; non-response; population; sampling error; etc.

- Randomly selected samples are important because they permit generalizations to the population and because they have certain known qualities.

- Sampling error decreases as sample size increases.

- Quota samples can provide reasonable alternatives to random samples, but they suffer from some deficiencies.

- Convenience samples may provide interesting data, but it is crucial to be aware of their limitations in terms of generalizability.

- Sampling and sampling-related error are just two sources of error in social survey research.

Revision questions

- What do each of the following terms mean: population; probability sampling; non-probability sampling; sampling frame; representative sample; and sampling and non-sampling error?
- What are the goals of sampling?
- What are the main areas of potential bias in sampling?

Sampling error

- What is the significance of sampling error for achieving a representative sample?

Types of probability sample

- What is probability sampling and why is it important?
- What are the main types of probability sample?
- How far does a stratified random sample offer greater precision than a simple random or systematic sample?
- If you were conducting an interview survey of around 500 people in Manchester, what type of probability sample would you choose and why?
- A researcher positions herself on a street corner and asks 1 person in 5 who walks by to be interviewed: She continues doing this until she has a sample of 250. How likely is she to achieve a representative sample?

The qualities of a probability sample

- A researcher is interested in levels of job satisfaction among manual workers in a firm that is undergoing change. The firm has 1,200 manual workers. The researcher selects a simple random sample of 10 per cent of the population. He measures job satisfaction on a Likert scale comprising ten items. A high level of satisfaction is scored 5 and a low level is scored 1. The mean job satisfaction score is 34.3. The standard error of the mean is 8.57. What is the 95 per cent confidence interval?

Sample size

- What factors would you take into account in deciding how large your sample should be when devising a probability sample?
- What is non-response and why is it important to the question of whether you will end up with a representative sample?

Types of non-probability sample

- Are non-probability samples useless?
- In what circumstances might you employ snowball sampling?
- 'Quota samples are not true random samples, but in terms of generating a representative sample there is little difference between them, and this accounts for their widespread use in market research and opinion polling.' Discuss.

Limits to generalization

- 'The problem of generalization to a population is not just to do with the matter of getting a representative sample.' Discuss.

Error in survey research

- 'Non-sampling error, as its name implies, is concerned with sources of error that are not part of the sampling process.' Discuss.

5 Structured interviewing

Reader's guide

The structured interview is one of a variety of forms of research interview, but it is the one that is most commonly employed in survey research. The goal of the structured interview is for the interviewing of respondents to be standardized so that differences between interviews in any research project are minimized. As a result, there are many guidelines about how structured interviewing should be carried out so that variation in the conduct of interviews is small. The chapter explores:

- the reasons why the structured interview is a prominent research method in survey research; this issue entails a consideration of the importance of standardization to the process of measurement;

- the different contexts of interviewing, such as the use of more than one interviewer and whether the administration of the interview is in person or by telephone;

- various prerequisites of structured interviewing, including: establishing rapport with the interviewee; asking questions as they appear on the interview schedule; recording exactly what is said by interviewees; ensuring there are clear instructions on the interview schedule concerning question sequencing and the recording of answers; and keeping to the question order as it appears on the schedule;

- problems with structured interviewing, including: the influence of the interviewer on respondents and the possibility of systematic bias in answers (known as *response sets*); the feminist critique of structured interview, which raises a distinctive cluster of problems with the method, is also examined.

Introduction

The interview is a common occurrence in social life, because there are many different forms of interview. There are job interviews, media interviews, social work interviews, police interviews, appraisal interviews. And then there are research interviews, which represent the kind of interview that will be covered in this and other chapters (such as Chapters 15 and 16). These different kinds of interview share some common features, such as the eliciting of information by the interviewer from the interviewee and the operation of rules of varying degrees of formality or explicitness concerning the conduct of the interview.

In the social research interview, the aim is for the interviewer to elicit from the interviewee or *respondent*, as he or she is frequently called in survey research, all manner of information: interviewees' own behaviour or that of others, attitudes, norms, beliefs, and values. There are many different types or styles of research interview, but the kind that is primarily employed in survey research is the structured interview, which is the focus of this chapter. Other kinds of interview will be briefly mentioned in this chapter but will be discussed in greater detail in later chapters.

The structured interview

The research interview is a prominent data-collection strategy in both quantitative and qualitative research. The social survey is probably the chief context within which social researchers employ the structured interview (see Box 5.1) in connection with quantitative research and it is this form of the interview that will be emphasized in this chapter. The reason why survey researchers typically prefer this kind of interview is that it promotes standardization of *both* the asking of questions *and* the recording of answers. This feature has two closely related virtues from the perspective of quantitative research.

Reducing error due to interviewer variability

The standardization of both the asking of questions and the recording of answers means that, if it is properly executed, variation in people's replies will be due to 'true' or 'real' variation and not due to the interview context. To take a simple illustration, when we ask a question that is supposed to be an indicator of a concept, we want to keep error to a minimum, an issue that was touched on at the end of Chapter 4. We can think of the answers to a question as constituting the values that a variable takes. These values, of course, exhibit variation. This could be the question on alcohol consumption among students that was a focus of Chapter 1 at certain points. Students will vary in the number of alcohol units they consume (see Figure 5.1). However, some respondents may be inaccurately classified in terms of the variable. There are a number of possible reasons for this (see Box 5.2).

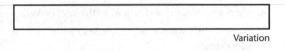

Variation

Fig. 5.1 A variable

Most variables will contain an element of error, so that it is helpful to think of variation as made up of two components: true variation and error. In other words:

variation = true variation + variation due to error.

The aim is to keep the error component to a minimum (see Figure 5.2), since error has an adverse effect on the validity of a measure. If the error component is quite high (see Figure 5.3), validity will be jeopardized. The significance for error of standardization in the structured interview is that two sources of variation due to error—the second and fifth in Box 5.2—are likely to be less pronounced, since the opportunity for variation in interviewer behaviour in these two areas (asking questions and recording answers) is reduced.

The significance of standardization and of thereby reducing interviewer variability is this: assuming

---

Box 5.1   *What is a structured interview?*

A structured interview, sometimes called a *standardized interview*, entails the administration of an interview schedule by an interviewer. The aim is for all interviewees to be given exactly the same context of questioning. This means that each respondent receives exactly the same interview stimulus as any other. The goal of this style of interviewing is to ensure that interviewees' replies can be aggregated and this can be achieved reliably only if those replies are in response to identical cues. Interviewers are supposed to read out questions exactly and in the same order as they are printed on the schedule. Questions are usually very specific and very often offer the interviewee a fixed range of answers (this type of question is often called *closed, closed ended, pre-coded,* or *fixed choice*). The structured interview is the typical form of interview in social survey research.

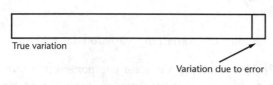

True variation

Variation due to error

Fig. 5.2 A variable with little error

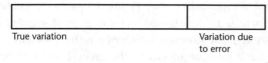

True variation

Variation due to error

Fig. 5.3 A variable with considerable error

that there is no problem with an interview question due to such things as confusing terms or ambiguity (an issue that will be examined in Chapter 7), we want to be able to say as far as possible that the variation that we find is connected with true variation between interviewees and not to variation in the way a question was asked or the answers recorded in the course of the administration of a survey by structured interview. Variability can occur in either of two ways. First, *intra-interviewer variability*, whereby an interviewer is not consistent in the way he or she asks questions and/or records answers. Secondly, when there is more than one interviewer, there may be *inter-interviewer variability*, whereby interviewers are not consistent with each other in the ways they ask questions and/or record answers. Needless to say,

these two sources of variability are not mutually exclusive; they can coexist, compounding the problem even further. In view of the significance of standardization, it is hardly surprising that some writers prefer to call the structured interview a *standardized interview* (e.g. Oppenheim 1992) or *standardized survey interview* (e.g. Fowler and Mangione 1990).

Accuracy and ease of data processing

Like self-completion questionnaires, most structured interviews contain mainly questions that are variously referred to as *closed, closed ended, pre-coded,* or *fixed choice*. This issue will be covered in detail in Chapter 7. However, this type of question has considerable relevance to the current discussion. With the closed question, the respondent is given a limited choice of possible answers. In other words, the interviewer provides respondents with two or more possible answers and asks them to select which one or ones apply. Ideally, this procedure will simply entail the interviewer placing a tick in a box by the answer(s) selected by a respondent or circling the selected answer or using a similar procedure. The advantage of this practice is that the potential for interviewer variability is reduced: there is no problem of whether the interviewer writes down everything that the respondent says or of misinterpretation of the reply given. If an *open* or *open-ended* question is asked, the interviewer may not write down everything said, may embellish what is said, or may misinterpret what is said.

However, the advantages of this type of question in the context of survey research go further than this, as we will see in Chapter 7. One advantage that is particularly significant in the context of the present discussion is that closed questions greatly facilitate the processing of data. When an open question is asked, the answers need to be sifted and *coded* in order for the data to be analysed quantitatively. Not only is this a laborious procedure, particularly if there is a large number of open questions and/or of respondents; it also introduces the potential for another source of error, which is the sixth in Box 5.2:

it is quite likely that error will be introduced as a result of variability in the coding of answers. When open questions are asked, the interviewer is supposed to write down as much of what is said as possible. Answers can, therefore, be in the form of several sentences. These answers have to be examined and then categorized, so that each person's answer can be aggregated with other respondents' answers to a certain question. A number will then be allocated to each category of answer so that the answers can then be entered into a computer database and analysed quantitatively. This general process is known as coding and will be examined in greater detail in Chapter 7.

Coding introduces yet another source of error. First, if the rules for assigning answers to categories, collectively known as the *coding frame*, are flawed, the variation that is observed will not reflect the true variation in interviewees' replies. Secondly, there may be variability in the ways in which answers are categorized. As with interviewing, there can be two sources: *intra-coder variability*, whereby the coder varies over time in the way in which the rules for assigning answers to categories are implemented, and *inter-coder variability*, whereby coders differ from each other in the way in which the rules for assigning answers to categories are implemented. If either (or both) source(s) of variability occur, at least part of the variation in interviewees' replies will not reflect true variation and instead will be caused by error.

The closed question sidesteps this problem neatly, because respondents' allocate *themselves* to categories. The coding process is then a simple matter of attaching a different number to each category of answer and of entering the numbers into a computer database. It is not surprising, therefore, that this type of question is often referred to as pre-coded, because decisions about the coding of answers are typically undertaken as part of the design of the schedule— that is, before any respondents have actually been asked questions. There is very little opportunity for

interviewers or coders to vary in the recording or the coding of answers. Of course, if some respondents misunderstand any terms in the alternative answers with which they are presented, or if the answers do not adequately cover the appropriate range of possibilities, the question will not provide a valid measure. However, that is a separate issue and one that will be returned to in Chapter 7. The chief point to register about closed questions for the moment is that, when compared to open questions, they reduce one potential source of error *and* are much easier to process for quantitative data analysis.

Other types of interview

The structured interview is by no means the only type of interview, but it is certainly the main type that is likely to be encountered in survey research and in quantitative research generally. Unfortunately, a host of different terms have been employed by writers on research methodology to distinguish the diverse forms of research interview. Box 5.3 represents an attempt to capture some of the major terms and types.

All of the forms of interview outlined in Box 5.3, with the exception of the *structured interview* and the *standardized interview*, are primarily used in connection with qualitative research and it is in that context that they will be encountered again later in this book. They are rarely used in connection with quantitative research, and survey research in particular, because the absence of standardization in the asking of questions and recording of answers makes respondents' replies difficult to aggregate and to process. This is not to say that they have no role at all. For example, as we will see in Chapter 7, the unstructured interview can have a useful role in relation to developing the fixed-choice alternatives with which respondents are provided in the kind of closed question that is typical of the structured interview.

Box 5.3 Major types of interview

- *Structured interview*. See Box 5.1.

- *Standardized interview*. See Box 5.1.

- *Semi-structured interview*. This is a term that covers a wide range of instances. It typically refers to a context in which the interviewer has a series of questions that are in the general form of an interview schedule but is able to vary the sequence of questions. The questions are frequently somewhat more general in their frame of reference from that typically found in a structured interview schedule. Also, the interviewer usually has some latitude to ask further questions in response to what are seen as significant replies.

- *Unstructured interview*. The interviewer typically has only a list of topics or issues, often called an *interview guide* or *aide mémoire*, that are typically covered. The style of questioning is usually informal. The phrasing and sequencing of questions will vary from interview to interview.

- *Intensive interview*. This term is employed by Lofland and Lofland (1995) as an alternative term to the *unstructured interview*. Spradley (1979) uses the term *ethnographic interview* to describe a form of interview that is also more or less synonymous with the *unstructured interview*.

- *Qualitative interview*. For some writers, this term seems to denote an *unstructured interview* (e.g. Mason 1996), but more frequently it is a general term that embraces interviews of both the semi-structured and un-structured kind (e.g. Rubin and Rubin 1995).

- *In-depth interview*. Like the term *qualitative interview*, this one sometimes refers to an *unstructured interview* but more often refers to both semi-structured and unstructured interviewing.

- *Focused interview*. This is a term devised by Merton *et al.* (1956) to refer to an interview using predominantly open questions to ask interviewees questions about a specific situation or event that is relevant to them and of interest to the researcher.

- *Focus group*. This is the same as the *focused interview* but interviewees discuss the specific issue in groups. See Box 16.2 (p. 337) for a more detailed definition.

- *Group interview*. Some writers see this term as syn-onymous with the *focus group*, but a distinction may be made between the latter and a situation in which members of a group discuss a variety of matters that may be only partially related.

- *Oral history interview*. This is an *unstructured* or *semi-structured interview* in which the respondent is asked to recall events from his or her past and to reflect on them (see also Box 15.4, p. 316). There is usually a cluster of fairly specific research concerns to do with a particular epoch or event, so there is some resemblance to a *focused interview*.

- *Life history interview*. This is similar to the *oral history interview*, but the aim of this type of *unstructured interview* is to glean information on the entire biography of each respondent (see also Box 15.4, p. 316).

Interview contexts

In an archetypal interview, an interviewer stands or sits in front of the respondent asking the latter a series of questions and writing down the answers. However, there are several possible departures from it, although this archetype is the most usual context for an interview.

More than one interviewee

In the case of group interviews or focus groups, there is more than one, and usually quite a few more than one, respondent or interviewee. Nor is this the only context in which more than one person is inter-viewed. McKee and Bell (1985), for example, inter-viewed couples in their study of the impact of male unemployment, while, in my research on visitors to

Disney theme parks, not just couples but often their children took part in the interview as well (Bryman 1999). However, it is very unusual for structured interviews to be used in connection with this kind of questioning. In survey research, it is almost always a specific individual who is the object of questioning. Indeed, in survey interviews it is very advisable to discourage as far as possible the presence and intrusion of others during the course of the interview. Investigations in which more than one person is being interviewed tend to be exercises in qualitative research, though this is not always the case: Pahl's (1990) study of patterns of control of money among couples employed structured interviewing of couples and of husbands and wives separately.

More than one interviewer

This is a very unusual situation in social research, because of the considerable cost that is involved in dispatching two (or indeed more than two) people to interview someone. Bechhofer *et al.* (1984) describe research in which two people interviewed individuals in a wide range of occupations. However, while their approach achieved a number of benefits for them, their interviewing style was of the unstructured kind that is typically employed in qualitative research, and they argue that the presence of a second interviewer is unlikely to achieve any added value in the context of structured interviewing.

In person or by telephone?

A third way in which the archetype may not be realized is that interviews may be conducted by telephone rather than face to face. While telephone interviewing is quite common in fields like market research, it is still far more common to read reports of studies based on personal interviews in academic social research, but see Box 5.4 for an interesting example.

There are several advantages of telephone over personal interviews.

- On a like-for-like basis, they are far cheaper and also quicker to administer. This arises because, for personal interviews, interviewers have to spend a great deal of time and money travelling between respondents. This factor will be even more pronounced when a sample is geographically dispersed, a problem that is only partially mitigated for personal interview surveys by strategies like cluster sampling. Of course, telephone interviews take time and hired interviewers have to be paid, but the cost of conducting a telephone interview will still be lower than a comparable personal one.

- The telephone interview is easier to supervise than the personal interview. This is a particular advantage when there are several interviewers, since it becomes easier to check on interviewers' transgressions in the asking of questions, such as rephrasing questions or the inappropriate use of probes by the interviewer.

Box 5.4 A telephone survey of the unemployed in Sweden

Nordenmark and Strandh (1999) report the findings of an interesting study of mental well-being among the unemployed in Sweden. Early in 1996, a national random sample of 3,500 was drawn from a register of all unemployed persons that is maintained by the Swedish Labour Market Board. A telephone survey was conducted with members of the sample. The response rate was 74 per cent. The interview schedule included questions on such issues as: 'mental well-being, the economy, work involvement, belief in the future, wage demands and job search behaviour' (Nordenmark and Strandh 1999: 585). Nearly two years later, those who had participated were reinterviewed by telephone with very similar questions. This is, therefore, an example of a *panel study*. The authors inform us that only part (around 6 per cent) of the response rate was due to a refusal to participate; the remainder was due to problems of contacting respondents.

- Telephone interviewing has a further advantage which is to do with evidence (which is not as clear-cut as one might want) which suggests that in personal interviews, respondents replies are sometimes affected by characteristics of the interviewer (for example, class, ethnicity) and indeed by his or her mere presence (implying that the interviewees may reply in ways they feel will be deemed desirable by interviewers). The remoteness of the interviewer in telephone interviewing removes this potential source of bias to a significant extent. The interviewer's personal characteristics cannot be seen and the fact that he/she is not physically present may offset the likelihood of respondents' answers being affected by the interviewer.

Telephone interviewing suffers from certain limitations when compared to the personal interview.

- People who do not own or who are not contactable by telephone obviously cannot be interviewed by telephone. Since this characteristic is most likely to be a feature of poorer households, the potential for sampling bias exists. Also, many people choose to be ex-directory—that is, they have taken action for their telephone numbers not to appear in a telephone directory. Again, these people cannot be interviewed by telephone. One likely solution to this last difficulty is *random digit dialling*. With this technique, the computer randomly selects telephone numbers within a predefined geographical area. Not only is this a random process that conforms to the rules about probability sampling examined in Chapter 4, it also stands a chance of getting at ex-directory households, though it cannot, of course, gain access to those without a telephone at all. The question of whether response rates (see Box 4.5, p. 96), are lower with surveys by telephone interview than with surveys by personal interview is unclear, in that there is little or no consistent evidence on this question, though Frey and Oishi (1995) believe that the latter achieve slightly lower rates.

- Telephone interviewers cannot engage in observation. This means that they are not in a position to respond to signs of puzzlement or unease on the faces of respondents when they are asked a question. In a personal interview, the interviewer may respond to such signs by restating the question or attempting to clarify the meaning of the question, though this has to be handled in a standardized way as far as possible. A further issue relating to the inability of the interviewer to observe is that, sometimes, interviewers may be asked to collect subsidiary information in connection with their visits (for example, whether a house is dilapidated). Such information cannot be collected when telephone interviews are employed.

- It is frequently the case that specific individuals in households or firms are the targets of an interview. In other words, simply anybody will not do. This requirement is likely to arise from the specifications of the population to be sampled, which mean that people in a certain role or position or with particular characteristics are to be interviewed. It is probably more difficult to ascertain by telephone interview whether the correct person is replying.

- The telephone interviewer cannot readily employ visual aids such as show cards (see below) from which respondents might be asked to select their replies or to use diagrams or photographs.

Computer-assisted interviewing

In recent years, increasing use has been made of computers in the interviewing process. A large percentage of telephone interviews is conducted with the aid of personal computers, but the reason for their growing use has been that the portability and affordability of 'laptop' computers provide greater opportunity for them to be used in connection with personal interviews. With computer-assisted interviewing, the questions that comprise an interview schedule appear on the screen. As interviewers ask each question, they 'key in' the appropriate reply using a mouse and proceed to the next question. Moreover, this process has the great advantage that, when *filter questions* (see Box 5.6 below) are asked, so that certain answers may be skipped as a result of a person's reply, the computer can be programmed to 'jump' to the next relevant question. This removes the possibility of interviewers inadvertently asking inappropriate questions or failing to ask ones that should be asked. If the interviewer is out in the field all day, he or she can either take a disk with the saved data to the research office or send the data down a telephone line with the aid of a modem. It is possible that technophobic respondents may be a bit alarmed by their use, but, by and large, the use of computer-assisted interviewing seems destined to grow. My only personal experience with this technique was as a respondent in a market research survey: the laptop started to beep part of the way through the interview because the battery was about to expire and needed to be replaced with a back-up. An incident such as this could be disruptive to the flow of an interview and be alarming for technophobic respondents.

Conducting interviews

Issues concerning the conduct of interviews are examined here in a very general way. In addition to the matters considered here, there is clearly the important issue of how to word the interview questions themselves. This area will be explored in Chapter 7, since many of the rules of question-asking relate to self-completion questionnaire techniques like mail questionnaires as well as to structured interviews. One further general point to make here is that the advice concerning the conduct of interviews provided in this chapter relates to structured interviews. The framework for conducting the kinds of interviewing conducted in qualitative research (such as, unstructured and semi-structured interviewing and focus groups) will be handled in later chapters.

Know the schedule

Before interviewing anybody, an interviewer should be fully conversant with the schedule. Even if you are the only person conducting interviews, make sure you know it inside out. Interviewing can be stressful for interviewers and it is possible that under duress standard interview procedures like filter questions (see Box 5.6 below) can cause interviewers to get flustered and miss questions out or ask the wrong questions. If two or more interviewers are involved, they need to be fully trained to know what is required of them and to know their way around the schedule. Training is especially important in order to reduce the likelihood of interviewer variability in the asking of questions, which is a source of error.

Introducing the research

Prospective respondents have to be provided with a credible rationale for the research in which they are being asked to participate and for giving up their valuable time. This aspect of conducting interview research is of particular significance at a time when response rates to social survey research appear to be declining, though, as noted in Chapter 4, the evidence on this issue is the focus of some disagreement. The introductory rationale may be either spoken by the interviewer or written down. In many cases, respondents may be presented with both modes. It comes in spoken form in such situations as when interviewers make contact with respondents on the street or when they 'cold call' respondents in their homes in person or by telephone. A written rationale will be required to alert respondents that someone will be contacting them in person or on the telephone to request an interview. Respondents will frequently encounter both forms—for example, when they are sent a letter and then ask the interviewer who turns up to interview them what the research is all about. It is important for the two accounts to be consistent, as this could be a test!

Introductions to research should typically contain the bits of information outlined in Box 5.5. Since interviewers represent the interface between the

---

Box 5.5 Topics and issues to include in an introductory statement

There are several issues to include in an introductory statement to a prospective interviewee. The following list comprises the principal considerations.

- Make clear the identity of the person who is contacting the respondent.

- Identify the auspices under which the research is being conducted—for example, a university, a market research agency.

- Mention any research funder, or, if you are a student doing an undergraduate or postgraduate dissertation or doing research for a thesis, make this clear.

- Indicate what the research is about in broad terms and why it is important, and give an indication of the kind of information to be collected.

- Indicate why the respondent has been selected—e.g. selected by a random process.

- Provide reassurance about the confidentiality of any information provided.

- Make it clear that participation is voluntary.

- Reassure the respondent that he or she will not be identified or be identifiable in any way. This can usually be achieved by pointing out that data are anonymized when they are entered into the computer and that analysis will be conducted at an aggregate level.

- Provide the respondent with the opportunity to ask any questions—e.g. provide a contact telephone number if the introduction is in the form of a written statement, or if in person simply ask if the respondent has any questions.

These suggestions are also relevant to the covering letter that accompanies mail questionnaires, except that researchers using this method need to remember to include a stamped-addressed envelope!

---

research and the respondent, they have an important role in maximizing the response rate for the survey. In addition to the advice given in Box 5.5, the following points should be borne in mind.

- Interviewers should be prepared to keep calling back if interviewees are out or unavailable. This will require taking into account people's likely work and leisure habits—for example, there is no point in calling at home on people who work during the day. In addition, people living alone may be reluctant to answer the door when it is dark because of fear of crime.

- Be self-assured in that you may get a better response if you presume that people will agree to be interviewed rather than that they will refuse.

- Reassure people that you are not a salesperson. Because of the tactics of certain organizations whose representatives say they are doing market or social research, many people have become very suspicious of people saying they would just like to ask you a few questions.

- Dress in a way that will be acceptable to a wide spectrum of people.

- Make it clear that you will be happy to find a time to suit the respondent.

Rapport

It is frequently suggested that it is important for the interviewer to achieve *rapport* with the respondent. This means that very quickly a relationship must be established that encourages the respondent to want (or at least be prepared) to participate in and persist with the interview. Unless an element of rapport can be established, some respondents may initially agree to be interviewed but then decide to terminate their participation because of the length of time the interview is taking or perhaps because of the nature of the questions being asked. While this injunction essentially invites the interviewer to be friendly with respondents and to put them at ease, it is important that this quality is not stretched too far. Too much rapport may result in the interview going on too long and the respondent suddenly deciding that too much time is being spent on the activity. Also, the mood of friendliness may result in the respondent answering questions in a way that is designed to please the interviewer. The achievement of rapport between interviewer and respondent is therefore a delicate balancing act. Moreover, it is probably somewhat easier to achieve in the context of the face to face interview rather than the telephone interview, since in the latter the interviewer is unable to offer obvious visual cues of friendliness like smiling or maintaining good eye contact, which is also frequently regarded as conducive to gaining and maintaining rapport.

Asking questions

It was earlier suggested that one of the aims of the structured interview is to ensure that each respondent is asked exactly the same questions. Recall that in Box 5.2 it was pointed out that variation in the ways a question is asked is a potential source of error in survey research. The structured interview is meant to reduce the likelihood of this occurring, but it cannot guarantee that this will not occur, because there is always the possibility that interviewers will embellish or otherwise change a question when it is asked. There is considerable evidence that this occurs, even among centres of social research that have a solid reputation for being rigorous in following correct methodological protocol (Bradburn and Sudman 1979). The problem with such variation in the asking of questions was outlined above: it is likely to engender variation in replies that does not reflect 'true' variation—in other words, error. Consequently, it is important for interviewers to appreciate the importance of keeping exactly to the wording of the questions they are charged with asking.

You might say: 'does it really matter?' In other words, surely small variations to wording cannot make a significant difference to people's replies? While the impact of variation in wording obviously differs from context to context and is in any case difficult to quantify exactly, experiments in question-wording suggest that even small variations in wording can exert an impact on replies (Schuman and Presser 1981). Three experiments in England conducted by Social and Community Planning

Research concluded that a considerable number of interview questions is affected by interviewer variability. The researchers estimated that, for about two-thirds of the questions that were considered, interviewers contributed to less than 2 per cent of the total variation in each question (M. Collins 1997). On the face of it, this is a small amount of error, but the researchers regarded it as a cause for concern.

The key point to emerge, then, is the importance of getting across to interviewers the importance of asking questions as they are written. There are many reasons why interviewers may vary question-wording, such as reluctance to ask certain questions, perhaps because of embarrassment (M. Collins 1997), but the general admonition to keep to the wording of the question needs to be constantly reinforced when interviewers are being trained. It also needs to be borne in mind for your own research.

Recording answers

An identical warning for identical reasons can be registered in connection with the recording of answers by interviewers, who should write down respondents' replies as exactly as possible. Not to do so can result in interviewers distorting respondents' answers and hence introducing error. Such errors are less likely to occur when the interviewer has merely to allocate respondents' replies to a category, as in a closed question. This process can require a certain amount of interpretation on the part of the interviewer, but the error that is introduced is far less than when answers to open questions are being written down (Fowler and Mangione 1990).

Clear instructions

In addition to instructions about the asking of questions and the recording of answers, interviewers need instructions about their progress through an interview schedule. An example of the kind of context in which this is likely to occur is in relation to *filter questions*. Filter questions require the interviewer to ask questions of some respondents but not others. For example, the question

For which political party did you vote at the last general election?

presumes that the respondent did in fact vote. This option can be reflected in the fixed-choice answers that are provided, so that one of these is a 'did-not-vote' alternative. However, a better solution is not to presume anything about voting behaviour but to ask respondents whether they voted in the last general election and then to filter out those who did not vote. The foregoing question about the political party voted for can then be asked of those who did in fact vote. Similarly, in a study of meals, there is no point in asking vegetarians lots of questions about eating meat. It will probably work out best to filter vegetarians out and then possibly ask them a separate series of questions. Box 5.6 provides a simple example in connection with an imaginary study of alcohol consumption. The chief point to register about this example is that it requires clear instructions for the interviewer. If such instructions are not provided, there is the risk that either respondents

will be asked inappropriate questions (which can be irritating for them) or the interviewer will inadvertently fail to ask a question (which results in missing information).

Question order

In addition to warning interviewers about the importance of not varying the asking of questions and the recording of answers, they should be alerted to the importance of keeping to the order of asking questions. For one thing, varying the question order can result in certain questions being accidentally omitted, because the interviewer may forget to ask those that have been leapfrogged during the interview. Also, variation in question order may have an impact on replies: if some respondents have been previously asked a question that they should have been asked whereas others have not, a source of variability in the asking of questions will have been introduced and therefore a potential source of error.

Quite a lot of research has been carried out on the general question of question order, but few if any consistent effects on people's responses that derive

---

Box 5.6 Instructions for interviewers in the use of a filter question

1. Have you consumed any alcoholic drinks in the last twelve months?

     Yes ____

     No ____

     (if **No** proceed to quesion 4)

2. (*To be asked if interviewee replied* Yes *to question 1*)
   Which of the following alcoholic drinks do you consume most frequently?
   (Ask respondent to choose the category that he or she drinks most frequently and tick one category only.)

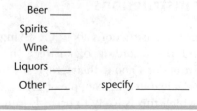

     Beer ____

     Spirits ____

     Wine ____

     Liquors ____

     Other ____   specify _____

3. How frequently do you consume alcoholic drinks?
   (Ask interviewee to choose the category that comes closest to his or her current practice.)

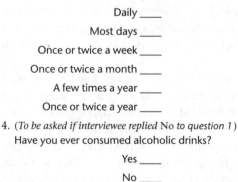

     Daily ____

     Most days ____

     Once or twice a week ____

     Once or twice a month ____

     A few times a year ____

     Once or twice a year ____

4. (*To be asked if interviewee replied* No *to question 1*)
   Have you ever consumed alcoholic drinks?

     Yes ____

     No ____

from asking questions at different points in a question-naire or interview schedule have been unveiled. Different effects have been demonstrated on various occasions. A study in the USA found that people were less likely to say that their taxes were too high when they had been previously asked whether government spending ought to be increased in a number of areas (Schuman and Presser 1981: 32). Apparently, some people perceived an inconsistency between wanting more spending and lower taxes, and adjusted their answers accordingly. Research on crime victimization in the USA suggests that earlier questions may affect the salience of later issues (Schuman and Presser 1981: 45). Respondents were asked whether they had been victims of crime in the preceding twelve months. Some respondents had been previously asked a series of questions about their attitudes to crime, whereas others had not. Those who had been asked about their attitudes reported considerably more crime than those who had not been asked. However, it is difficult to draw general lessons from such research, at least in part because experiments in question order do not always reveal clear-cut effects of varying the order in which questions are asked, even in cases where effects might legitimately have been expected. There are two general lessons.

- Within a survey, question order should not be varied (unless, of course, question order is the subject of the study!).

- Researchers should be sensitive to the possible implications of the effect of asking questions on answers to subsequent questions.

The following rules about question order are sometimes proposed.

- Early questions should be directly related to the topic of the research, about which the respondent has been informed. This removes the possibility that the respondent will be wondering at an early stage in the interview why he or she is being asked apparently irrelevant questions. This injunction means that personal questions about age, social background, and so on should *not* be asked at the beginning of an interview.

- As far as possible, questions that are more likely to be salient to respondents should be asked early in the interview schedule, so that their interest and attention are more likely to be secured. This suggestion may conflict with the previous one, in that questions specifically on the research topic may not be obviously salient to respondents, but it implies that as far as possible questions relating to the research topic that are more likely to grab their attention should be asked at or close to the start of the interview.

- Potentially embarrassing questions or ones that may be a source of anxiety should be left till later. In fact, research should be designed to ensure that as far as possible respondents are not discomfited, but it has to be acknowledged that with certain topics this effect may be unavoidable.

- With a long schedule or questionnaire, questions should be grouped into sections, since this allows a better flow than skipping from one topic to another.

- Within each group of questions, general questions should precede specific ones. Box 5.7 provides an illustration of such a sequence, which follows the recommendations of Gallup (1947, cited in Foddy 1993: 61–2). The example is concerned to demonstrate how the approach might operate in connection with building society demutualization, the process whereby several British mutual building societies turned themselves into banks and hence into public companies quoted on the Stock Exchange. The question order sequence is designed with a number of features in mind. It is designed to establish people's levels of knowledge of demutualization before asking questions about it and to distinguish those who feel strongly about it from those who do not. According to Foddy (1993), the second question is always open ended, so that respondents' frames of references can be established with respect to the topic at hand. However, it seems likely that, if sufficient pilot research has been carried out, a closed question could be envisaged, a point that applies equally to question 4.

- A further aspect of the rule that general questions should precede specific ones is that it has been argued that, when a specific question comes before

---

Box 5.7 A sequence of questions on the topic of building society demutualization

1. Have you heard of demutualization?

        Yes ____   No ____

2. What are your views about demutualization?

3. Do you favour or not favour demutualization?

      Favour ____   Not favour ____

4. Why do you favour (not favour) demutualization?

5. How strongly do you feel about this?

             Very strongly ____
            Fairly strongly ____
      Not at all strongly ____

---

a general one, the aspect of the general question that is covered by the specific one is discounted in the minds of respondents because they feel they have already covered it. Thus, if a question about how people feel about the amount they are paid precedes a general question about job satisfaction, there are grounds for thinking that respondents will discount the issue of pay when responding about job satisfaction.

- During the course of an interview, it sometimes happens that a respondent provides an answer to a question that is to be asked later in the interview. Because of the possibility of a question order effect, when the interviewer arrives at the question that appears already to have been answered, it should be repeated.

However, question order effects remain one of the more frustrating areas of structured interview and questionnaire design, because of the inconsistent evidence that is found and because it is difficult to formulate generalizations or rules from the evidence that does point to their operation. An interesting discussion about question order took place some years ago in connection with the study of social class and is discussed in Box 5.8.

Probing

Probing is a highly problematic area for researchers employing a structured interview method. It frequently happens in interviews that respondents need help with their answers. One obvious case is where it is evident that they do not understand the question—they may either ask for further information or it is clear from what they say that they are struggling to understand the question or to provide an adequate answer. The second kind of situation the interviewer faces is when the respondent does not provide a sufficiently complete answer and has to be probed for more information. The problem in either situation is obvious: the interviewer's intervention may influence the respondent and the nature of interviewers' interventions may differ. A potential source of variability in respondents' replies that does not reflect 'true' variation is introduced—that is, error.

Some general tactics with regard to probes are as follows.

- If further information is required, usually in the context of an open-ended question, standardized probes can be employed, such as 'Could you say a little more about that?' or 'Are there any other reasons why you think that?' or simply 'mmmm . . .?'.

- If the problem is that when presented with a closed question the respondent replies in a way that does not allow the interviewee to select one of the pre-designed answers, the interviewer should repeat the fixed-choice alternatives and make it apparent that the answer needs to be chosen from the ones that have been provided.

- If the interviewer needs to know about something that requires quantification, such as the number of visits to building societies in the last four weeks or

---

Box 5.8 A debate about question order

An interesting case of the issue of question order becoming a focus of controversy is provided by the research on social class by Marshall *et al.* (1988), which is referred to in more detail in Boxes 4.2 (p. 92) and 5.11. In a critique of the book, Saunders (1989) argued that it reveals what he calls 'socialist preconceptions', implying that values overtly intruded into the research (see Figure 1.2, p. 22). Saunders argues that one way in which this was revealed was the sheer weight of questions about social class prior to respondents being asked about the groups to which they saw themselves as belonging. Saunders wrote:

A glance at their questionnaire reveals that respondents were bombarded with questions about class right from the start of the interview. Following no fewer than 28 detailed questions about the class system, respondents were then asked if they thought they belonged to any social class and whether there was, by any chance, any other grouping they identified with apart from their class. Not surprisingly, most agreed that they did belong to one class or another . . . and that they could not think of any other identity . . . Armed with their 'findings', the authors then conclude that we are all class-oriented after all and that other identities are far less important. (Saunders 1989: 4)

Two of the book's authors replied with a spirited rebuttal. They reply that

the question about class was preceded by 30 substantive items. Six of these have no obvious relationship to the issue of social identities; for example, they elicit perceptions of Britain's economic performance . . . No less than 17 . . . were specifically designed to make interviewees see the world in terms *other than* those of social class. They invited people to think of themselves as consumers . . . as voters . . . as members of ethnic or gender groupings; as employees . . . in short, as everything but members of an identifiable social class. Interviewees were also asked whether there were 'any important conflicts in Britain today' before the word social class was ever mentioned. Then, and only then, were they quizzed about their perception of Britain as a specifically class society. (Marshall and Rose 1989: 5)

This is an interesting debate because it raises the issue of the role of values and bias in social research and also because it relates to the issue of question order while demonstrating the difficulty of being definitive about the issue. For example, while Marshall and Rose's reply is convincing, it might be that it is the *relative number* of questions about social class preceding questions of identity that may have been influential and to which Saunders alludes. Nonetheless, the debate usefully demonstrates the difficulty of producing conclusive evidence about question order effects.

---

the number of building societies in which the respondent has accounts, but the respondent resists this by answering in general terms ('quite often' or 'I usually go to the building society every week'), the interviewer needs to persist with securing a number from the respondent. This will usually entail repeating the question. The interviewer should not try to second guess a figure on the basis of the respondent's reply and then suggest that figure to him or her, since the latter may be unwilling to demur from the interviewer's suggested figure.

Prompting

Prompting occurs when the interviewer suggests a possible answer to a question to the respondent. The key prerequisite here is that all respondents receive the same prompts. All closed questions entail standardized prompting, because the respondent is provided with a list of possible answers from which to choose. An unacceptable approach to prompting would be to ask an open question and to suggest possible answers only to some respondents, such as those who appear to be struggling to think of an appropriate reply.

During the course of a face-to-face interview, there are several circumstances in which it will be better for the interviewer to use 'show cards' rather than rely on reading out a series of fixed-choice alternatives. Show cards (sometimes called 'flash cards') display all the answers from which the respondent is to choose and are handed to the respondent at different points of the interview. Three kinds of context in which it might be preferable to employ show cards rather than to read out the entire set of possible answers are as follows:

Box 5.9 A show card

Card 6

Strongly agree

Agree

Undecided

Disagree

Strongly disagree

- When there is a very long list of possible answers. For example, respondents may be asked which daily newspaper they each read most frequently. To read out a list of newspapers would be tedious and it is probably better to hand the respondent a list of newspapers from which to choose.

- Sometimes, during the course of interviews, respondents are presented with a group of questions to which the same possible answers are attached. An example of this approach is Likert scaling, which is an approach to attitude measurement. A typical strategy entails providing respondents with a series of statements and asking them how far they agree or disagree with the statements (see Chapter 3). These are often referred to as *items* rather than as *questions*, since strictly speaking the respondent is not being asked a question. An example was provided in Box 3.3 (p. 68). It would be excruciatingly dull to read out all seven possible answers ten times. Also, it may be expecting too much of respondents to read out the answers once and then require them to keep the possible answers in their heads for the entire batch of questions to which they apply. A show card that can be used for the entire batch and to which respondents can constantly refer is an obvious solution. As was mentioned in Box 3.3 (p. 68),

most Likert scales of this kind comprise five levels of agreement/disagreement and it is this more conventional approach that is illustrated in the show card in Box 5.9.

- Some people are not keen to divulge personal details such as their age or their income. One way of neutralizing the impact of such questioning is to present respondents with age or income bands with a letter or number attached to each band. They can then be asked to say which letter applies to them (see Box 5.10). This procedure will obviously not be appropriate if the research requires *exact* ages or incomes. It may be extendable to sensitive areas such as number of sexual partners or sexual practices for the same kinds of reason.

Leaving the interview

Do not forget common courtesies like thanking respondents for giving up their time. But the period immediately after the interview is one in which some care is necessary in that sometimes respondents try to engage the interviewer in a discussion about the purpose of the interview. Interviewers should resist elaboration beyond their standard statement, because respondents may communicate

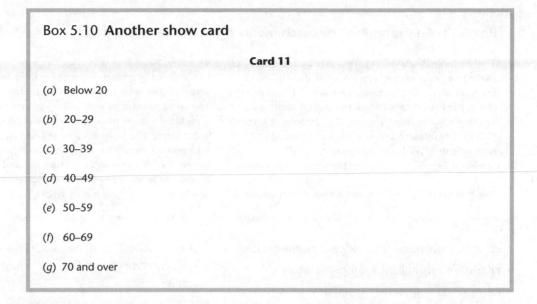

Box 5.10 **Another show card**

Card 11

(a) Below 20

(b) 20–29

(c) 30–39

(d) 40–49

(e) 50–59

(f) 60–69

(g) 70 and over

what they are told to others, which may bias the findings.

Training and supervision

On several occasions, reference has been made to the need for interviewers to be trained. The standard texts on survey research and on interviewing practice tend to be replete with advice on how best to train interviewers. Such advice is typically directed at contexts in which a researcher hires an interviewer to conduct a large amount or even all of the interviews. It also has considerable importance in research in which several interviewers (who may be either collaborators or hired interviewers) are involved in a study, since the risk of interviewer variability in the asking of questions needs to be avoided.

For many readers of this book who are planning to do research, such situations are unlikely to be relevant because they will be 'lone' researchers. You may be doing an undergraduate dissertation, or an exercise for a research methods course, or you may be a postgraduate conducting research for a Master's dissertation or for a thesis. Most people in such a situation will not have the luxury of being able to hire a researcher to do any interviewing (though you may be able to find someone to help you a little). When interviewing on your own, you must in a sense train yourself to follow the procedures and advice provided above. This is a very different situation from a large research institute or market research agency, which relies on an army of hired interviewers who carry out the interviews. Whenever people other than the lead researcher are involved in interviewing, they will need training and supervision in the following areas:

- contacting prospective respondents and providing an introduction to the study;
- reading out questions as written and following instructions in the interview schedule (for example, in connection with filter questions);
- appropriate styles of probing;
- recording exactly what is said;
- maintaining an interview style that does not bias respondents' answers.

Fowler (1993) cites evidence that suggests that training of less than one full day rarely creates good interviewers.

Supervision of interviewers in relation to these issues can be achieved by:

Box 5.11 An example of research involving multiple interviewers

This example is taken from the study by Marshall *et al.* (1988), a team of sociologists from the University of Essex, of social class in modern Britain. The interviewing was carried out by a leading independent social research institute, Social and Community Planning Research (SCPR). The research aimed to achieve a sample of 2,000 respondents (1,770 was the number actually achieved; see Box 4.2 (p. 92) for details of the sampling procedure):

One hundred and twenty-three interviewers were employed on

the survey. Six full-time briefing sessions were held, all of which were attended by a member of the Essex team, and interviewers were also given a full set of written instructions. The first three interviews conducted by each interviewer were subjected to an immediate thorough checking in order that critical comments, where appropriate, could be conveyed. During the course of fieldwork the work of interviewers was subject to personal recall. Ten per cent of issued addresses were re-issued for recall . . . In addition, 36 interviewers were accompanied in the field by supervisors . . .   (Marshall *et al.* 1988: 291)

- checking individual interviewers' response rates;
- tape-recording at least a sample of interviews;
- examining completed schedules to determine whether any questions are being left out or if they are being completed properly;
- call-backs on a sample of respondents (usually around 10 per cent) to determine whether they were interviewed and to ask about interviewers' conduct.

Box 5.11 provides an example of some of the ingredients of research involving multiple interviewers.

Problems with structured interviewing

While the structured interview is a commonly used method of social research, certain problems associated with it have been identified over the years. These problems are not necessarily unique to the structured interview, in that they can sometimes be attributed to kindred methods, such as the self-completion questionnaire in survey research or even semi-structured interviewing in qualitative research. However, it is common for the structured interview to be a seen as a focus for the identification of certain limitations that are briefly examined below.

Characteristics of interviewers

There is evidence that interviewers' attributes can have an impact on respondents' replies, but, unfortunately, the literature on this issue does not lend itself to definitive generalizations. In large part, this ambiguity in the broader implications of experiments relating to the effects of interviewer characteristics is due to several problems, such as: the problem of disentangling the effects of interviewers' different attributes from each other ('race', gender, socio-economic status); the interaction between the characteristics of interviewers and the characteristics of respondents; and the interaction between any effects observed and the topic of the interview. Nonetheless, there is undoubtedly some evidence that effects due to characteristics of interviewers can be discerned.

The ethnicity of interviewers is one area that has attracted some attention. Schuman and Presser (1981) cite a study that asked respondents to nominate two or three of their favourite actors or entertainers. Respondents were much more likely to mention black actors or entertainers when interviewed by black interviewers than when interviewed by white ones. Schuman and Converse (1971) interviewed 619 black Detroiters shortly after Martin Luther King's assassination in 1968. The researchers found significant differences between black and white interviewers in around one-quarter of the questions asked.

Although this proportion is quite disturbing, the fact that the majority of questions appear to have been largely unaffected does not give rise to a great deal of confidence that a consistent biasing factor is being uncovered. Similarly inconclusive findings tend to occur in relation to experiments with other sets of characteristics of interviewers. These remarks are not meant to play down the potential significance of interviewers' characteristics for measurement error, but to draw attention to the limitations of drawing conclusive inferences about the evidence. All that needs to be registered at this juncture is that almost certainly the characteristics of interviewers do have an impact on respondents' replies but that the extent and nature of the impact are not clear and are likely to vary from context to context.

Response sets

Some writers have suggested that the structured interview is particularly prone to the operation among respondents of what Webb *et al.* call 'response sets', which they define as 'irrelevant but lawful sources of variance' (Webb *et al.* 1966: 19). This form of response bias is especially relevant to multiple-indicator measures (see Chapter 3), where respondents reply to a battery of related questions or items, of the kind found in a Likert scale (see Box 3.3, p. 68). The idea of a response set implies that people respond to the series of questions in a consistent way but one that is irrelevant to the concept being measured. Two of the most prominent types of response set are known as the 'acquiescence' (also known as 'yeasaying' and 'naysaying' effect) and the 'social desirability' effect.

Acquiescence

Acquiescence refers to a tendency for some people consistently to agree or disagree with a set of questions or items. Imagine a respondent who replied with agreement to all the items in Box 3.3 (p. 68). The problem is that agreement with some of the items implies a low level of commitment to work (items 1–4), whereas agreement with others implies a high level of commitment to work (items 5–10). One of the reasons why researchers who employ this kind of multiple-item measure use wordings that imply opposite stances (that is, some items implying a high level of commitment and others implying a low level of commitment to work) is to weed out those respondents who appear to be replying within the framework of an acquiescence response set.

Social desirability

The social desirability effect refers to evidence that some respondents' answers to questions are related to their perception of the social desirability of those answers. An answer that is perceived to be socially desirable is more likely to be endorsed than one that is not. This phenomenon has been demonstrated in studies on mental health using psychiatric inventories. These inventories are meant to be concerned not with chronic mental illness but with minor neuroses and anxieties. Research in New York by Dohrenwend (1966) noted that Puerto Ricans tended to score much higher on the inventory that he administered than other ethnic groups. He found that this tendency was not due to a higher level of mental illness in this ethnic group, but to the effect of social desirability in respondents' answers. Puerto Ricans were much less likely than the other ethnic groups to perceive the items in the inventory as undesirable. This meant that what the researcher had found was a link not between ethnicity and mental health, but between ethnicity and perceptions of the social desirability of mental health inventory items. Later research suggested that variation in the social desirability of mental illness symptoms was related to the perceived prevalence of those symptoms among the respondent's friends and acquaintances (Phillips 1973). The presence of social desirability effects has been demonstrated in other settings (e.g. Arnold and Feldman 1981).

In so far as these forms of response error go undetected, they represent sources of error in the measurement of concepts. However, while some writers have proposed outright condemnation of social research on the basis of evidence of response sets (e.g. Phillips 1973), it is important not to get carried away with such findings. We cannot be sure how prevalent these effects are, and to some extent awareness of them has led to measures to limit their impact on data (for example, by weeding out cases obviously affected by them) or by instructing interviewers to limit the possible impact of the social desirability effect by not becoming overly friendly with respondents and by not being judgemental about their replies.

The problem of meaning

A critique of survey interview data and findings gleaned from similar techniques was developed by social scientists influenced by phenomenological and other interpretivist ideas of the kinds touched on in Chapter 1 (Cicourel 1964, 1982; Filmer *et al.* 1972; Briggs 1986; Mishler 1986). This critique revolves around what is often referred to in a shorthand way as the 'problem of meaning'. The kernel of the argument is that when humans communicate they do so in a way that not only draws on commonly held meanings but also simultaneously creates meanings. 'Meaning' in this sense is something that is worked at and achieved—it is not simply pregiven. Allusions to the problem of meaning in structured interviewing draw attention to the notion that survey researchers presume that interviewer and respondent share the same meanings of terms employed in the interview questions and answers. In fact, the problem of meaning implies that the possibility that interviewer and respondent may not be sharing the same meaning systems and hence imply different things in their use of words is simply sidestepped in structured interview research. The problem of meaning is resolved by ignoring it.

The feminist critique

The feminist critique of structured interviewing is difficult to disentangle from the critique launched against quantitative research in general, which was briefly outlined in Chapter 1. However, for many feminist social researchers the structured interview symbolized more readily than other methods the limitations of quantitative research, partly because of its prevalence but also partly because of its nature. By 'its nature' is meant the fact that the structured interview epitomizes the asymmetrical relationship between researcher and subject that is seen as an ingredient of quantitative research: the researcher extracts information from the research subject and gives nothing in return. For example, standard textbook advice of the kind provided in this chapter implies that *rapport* is useful to the interviewer but he or she should guard against becoming too familiar. This means that questions asked by respondents (for example, about the research or about the topic of the research) should be politely but firmly rebuffed on the grounds that too much familiarity should be avoided and because the respondents' subsequent answers may be biased.

This is perfectly valid and appropriate advice from the vantage point of the canons of structured interviewing with its quest for standardization and for valid and reliable data. However, from the perspective of feminism, when women interview women a wedge is hammered between them that, in conjunction with the implication of a hierarchical relationship between the interviewer and respondent, is incompatible with its values. An impression of exploitation is created, but exploitation of women is precisely what feminist social science seeks to fight against. Oakley (1981) found in her research on childbirth that she was frequently asked questions by her respondents. It was these questions that typified the problems of being a feminist interviewing women.

The dilemma of a feminist interviewer interviewing women could be summarised by considering the practical application of some of the strategies recommended in the textbooks for meeting interviewees' questions. For example, these advise that such questions as 'Which hole does the baby come out of?' 'Does an epidural ever para-lyse women?' and 'Why is it dangerous to leave a small baby alone in the house?' should be met with such responses from the interviewer as 'I guess I haven't thought enough about it to give a good answer right now,' or 'a head-shaking gesture which suggests "that's a hard one"' (Goode and Hatt [1952: 198]). (Oakley, 1981: 48)

Oakley's point is clear: to act according to the canons of textbook practice would be irresponsible for a feminist in such a situation. It was this kind of critique of structured interviewing and indeed of quantitative research in general that ushered in a period in which a great many feminist social researchers found qualitative research more compatible with their goals and norms. In terms of interviewing, this trend resulted in a preference for forms of interviewing such as unstructured and semi-structured interviewing and focus groups. These will be the focus of later chapters. However, as noted in Chapter 1, there has been some softening of attitudes towards the role of quantitative research among feminist researchers, although there is still a tendency for qualitative research to remain the preferred research strategy.

Key points

- The structured interview is a research instrument that is used to standardize the asking and often the recording of answers in order to keep interviewer-related error to a minimum.

- It can be administered in person or over the telephone.

- It is important to keep to the wording and order of questions when conducting social survey research by structured interview.

- While there is some evidence that interviewers' characteristics can influence respondents' replies, the findings of experiments on this issue are somewhat equivocal.

- Response sets can be damaging to data derived from structured interviews and steps need to be taken to identify respondents exhibiting them.

- The structured interview symbolizes the characteristics of quantitative research that feminist researchers find distasteful: in particular, the lack of reciprocity and the taint of exploitation.

Revision questions

The structured interview

- Why is it important in interviewing for survey research to keep interviewer variability to a minimum?

- How successful is the structured interview in reducing interviewer variability?

- Why might a survey researcher prefer to use a structured rather than an unstructured interview approach for gathering data?
- Why do structured interview schedules typically include mainly closed questions?

Interview contexts

- Are there any circumstances in which it might be preferable to conduct structured interviews with more than one interviewer?
- 'Given the lower cost of telephone interviews as against personal interviews, the former are generally preferable.' Discuss.

Conducting interviews

- Prepare an opening statement for a study of manual workers in a firm, in which access has already been achieved.
- To what extent is rapport an important ingredient of structured interviewing?
- How strong is the evidence that question order can significantly affect answers?
- How strong is the evidence that interviewers' characteristics can significantly affect answers?
- What is the difference between probing and prompting? How important are they and what dangers are lurking with their use?

Problems with structured interviewing

- What are response sets and why are they potentially important?
- What are the main issues that lie behind the critique of structured interviewing by feminist researchers?

6

Self-completion questionnaires

Reader's guide

Questionnaires that are completed by respondents themselves are one of the main instruments for gathering data using a social survey design, along with the structured interview that was covered in the previous chapter. Probably the most common form is the mail or postal questionnaire. The term *self-completion questionnaire* is often used because it is somewhat more inclusive than *mail questionnaire*. This chapter explores:

- the advantages and disadvantages of the questionnaire in comparison to the structured interview;
- how to address the potential problem of poor response rates, which is often a feature of the mail questionnaire;
- how questionnaires should be designed in order to make answering easier for respondents and less prone to error;
- the use of diaries as a form of self-completion questionnaire.

Introduction

In a very real sense, the bulk of the previous chapter was about questionnaires. The structured interview is in many, if not most, respects a questionnaire that is administered by an interviewer. However, there is a tendency, which borders on a convention, to reserve the term 'questionnaire' for contexts in which a battery of usually closed questions is completed by respondents themselves.

Self-completion questionnaire or mail questionnaire?

The *self-completion questionnaire* is sometimes referred to as a *self-administered questionnaire*. The former term will be followed in this book. With a self-completion questionnaire, respondents answer questions by completing the questionnaire themselves. As a method, the self-completion question-naire can come in several different forms. Probably the most prominent of these forms is the *mail* or *postal questionnaire*, whereby, as its name implies, a questionnaire is sent through the mail to the respondent. The latter, following completion of the instrument, is usually asked to return it by post; an alternative form of return is when respondents are requested to deposit their completed questionnaires in a certain location, such as a box in a school common room or in a supervisor's office in a firm. The self-completion questionnaire also covers forms of administration, such as when a researcher hands out questionnaires to all students in a class and collects them back after they have been completed. 'Self-completion questionnaire' is, therefore, a more inclusive term than 'mail questionnaire', though it is probably true to say that the latter is the most prominent form of the self-completion questionnaire.

In the discussion that follows, when points apply to more or less all forms of self-completion questionnaire, this term will be employed. When points apply specifically or exclusively to questionnaires sent through the post, the term 'mail questionnaire' will be used.

Evaluating the self-completion questionnaire in relation to the structured interview

In many ways, the self-completion questionnaire and the structured interview are very similar methods of social research. The obvious difference between them is that, with the self-completion questionnaire, there is no interviewer to ask the questions; instead, respondents must read each question themselves and answer the questions themselves. Beyond this obvious, but central, difference, they are remarkably similar. However, because there is no interviewer in the administration of the self-completion questionnaire, the research instrument has to be especially easy to follow and its questions have to be particularly easy to answer. After all, respondents cannot be trained in the way interviewers can be; nor do they know their ways around a research instrument in the way a 'lone researcher' might.

As a result, self-completion questionnaires, as compared to structured interviews, tend to:

- have fewer open questions, since closed ones tend to be easier to answer;
- have easy-to-follow designs to minimize the risk that the respondent will fail to follow filter questions or will inadvertently omit a question;
- be shorter to reduce the risk of 'respondent fatigue', since it is manifestly easier for a respondent who becomes tired of answering questions in a long questionnaire to consign it to a waste paper bin than to terminate an interview.

Advantages of the self-completion questionnaire over the structured interview

Cheaper to administer

Interviewing can be expensive. The cheapness of the self-completion questionnaire is especially advantageous if you have a sample that is geographically widely dispersed. When this is the case, a mail questionnaire will be much cheaper, because of the time and cost of travel for interviewers. This advantage is obviously less pronounced in connection with telephone interviews, because of the lower costs of telephone charges relative to travel and time spent travelling. But, even in comparison to telephone interviewing, the mail questionnaire enjoys cost advantages.

Quicker to administer

Self-completion questionnaires can be sent out through the mail or otherwise distributed in very large quantities at the same time. A thousand questionnaires can be sent out through the mail in one batch, but, even with a team of interviewers, it would take a long time to conduct personal interviews with a sample of that size. However, it is important to bear in mind that the questionnaires do not all come back immediately and that they may take several weeks to be returned. Also, there is invariably a need to send out follow-up letters and/or questionnaires to those who fail to return them initially, an issue that will be returned to below.

Absence of interviewer effects

It was noted in Chapter 5 that various studies have demonstrated that characteristics of interviewers (and respondents) may affect the answers that people give. While the findings from this research are somewhat equivocal in their implications, it has been suggested that such characteristics as ethnicity, gender, and the social background of interviewers may combine to bias the answers that respondents provide. Obviously, since there is no interviewer present when a self-completion questionnaire is being completed, interviewer effects are eliminated. However, this advantage probably has to be regarded fairly cautiously, since few consistent patterns have emerged over the years from research to suggest what kinds of interviewer characteristics bias answers. Probably of greater importance to the presence of an interviewer is the tendency for people to be more likely to exhibit social desirability bias when an interviewer is present. Research by Sudman and Bradburn (1982) suggests that mail questionnaires work better than personal interviews when a question carries the possibility of such bias. There is also a tendency for respondents to under-report activities that induce anxiety or about which they are sensitive. Research summarized by Tourangeau and Smith (1996) strongly suggests that respondents tend to report more drug use and alcohol consumption and a higher number of sexual partners and of abortions in self-completion questionnaires than in structured interviews.

No interviewer variability

Self-completion questionnaires do not suffer from the problem of interviewers asking questions in a different order or in different ways.

Convenience for respondents

Self-completion questionnaires are more convenient for respondents, because they can complete a questionnaire when they want and at the speed that they want to go.

Disadvantages of the self-completion questionnaire in comparison to the structured interview

Cannot prompt

There is no one present to help respondents if they are having difficulty answering a question. It is always important to ensure that the questions that are asked are clear and unambiguous, but this is especially so with the self-completion questionnaire, since there is no interviewer to help respondents with questions they find difficult to understand and hence to answer. Also, great attention must be paid to ensure that the questionnaire is easy to complete; otherwise questions will be inadvertently omitted if instructions are unclear.

Cannot probe

There is no opportunity to probe respondents to elaborate an answer. Probing can be very important when open-ended questions are being asked. Interviewers are often trained to get more from respondents. However, this problem largely applies to open questions, which are not used a great deal in self-completion questionnaire research.

Cannot ask many questions that are not salient to respondents

Respondents are more likely than in interviews to become tired of answering questions that are not very salient to them, and which they are likely to perceive as boring. Because of the risk of a questionnaire being consigned to a waste paper bin, it is important to avoid including many non-salient questions in a self-completion questionnaire. However, this point suggests that, when a research issue *is* salient to the respondent, a high response rate is feasible (Altschuld and Lower 1984). This means that, when questions are salient, the self-completion questionnaire may be a good choice for researchers, especially when the much lower cost is borne in mind.

Difficulty of asking other kinds of question

In addition to the problem of asking many questions that are not salient to respondents, as previously suggested, it is also important to avoid asking more than a very small number of open questions (because respondents frequently do not want to write a lot). Questions with complex structures, such as filters, should be avoided as far as possible (because respondents often find them difficult to follow).

Questionnaire can be read as a whole

Respondents are able to read the whole questionnaire before answering the first question. When this occurs, none of the questions asked is truly independent of the others. It also means that you cannot be sure that questions have been answered in the correct order. It also means that the problems of question order effects, of the kind discussed in Chapter 5, may occur.

Do not know who answers

With mail questionnaires, you can never be sure whether the right person has answered the questionnaire. If a questionnaire is sent to a certain person in a household, it may be that someone else in that household completes the questionnaire. It is also impossible to have any control over the intrusion of non-respondents (such as other members of a household) in the asking of questions. Similarly, if a questionnaire is sent to a manager in a firm, the task may simply be delegated to someone else. This advantage of the structured interview over the mail questionnaire does not apply when the former is administered by telephone, since the same problem applies.

Cannot collect additional data

With an interview, interviewers might be asked to collect snippets of information about the home, school, firm, or whatever. This is not going to be possible in connection with a mail questionnaire, but if self-completion questionnaires are handed out in a school or firm, it is more feasible to collect such additional data.

Difficult to ask a lot of questions

As signalled above, because of the possibility of 'respondent fatigue', long questionnaires are rarely feasible. They may even result in a greater tendency for questionnaires not to be answered in the first place, since they can be offputting.

Not appropriate for some kinds of respondent

Respondents whose literacy is limited or whose facility with English is restricted will not be able to answer the questionnaire. The second of these difficulties cannot be entirely overcome when interviews are being employed, but the difficulties are likely to be greater with mail questionnaires.

Greater risk of missing data

Partially answered questionnaires are more likely, because of a lack of prompting or supervision, than is possible in interviews. It is also easier for respondents actively to decide not to answer a question when on their own than when being asked by an interviewer. For example, questions that appear boring or irrelevant to the respondent may be especially likely to be skipped. If questions are not answered, this creates a problem of *missing data* for the variables that are created.

Lower response rates

One of the most damaging limitations is that surveys by mail questionnaire typically result in lower response rates (see Box 4.5, p. 96) than comparable interview-based studies. The significance of a response rate is that, unless it can be proven that those who do not participate do not differ from those that do, there is likely to be the risk of bias. In other words, if, as is likely, there are differences between participants and refusals, it is probable that the findings relating to the sample will be affected. If a response rate is low, it seems likely that the risk of bias in the findings will be greater.

The problem of low response rates seems to apply particularly to mail questionnaires. Box 4.6 (p. 98) describes a survey by self-completion questionnaire that was answered by all students to whom it was administered; the only non-respondents were those who were absent from the lecture. When a self-completion questionnaire is employed in this kind of context, it seems less vulnerable to the problem of a low response rate.

Mangione (1995: 60–1) has provided the following classification of bands of response rate to mail questionnaires:

Over 85%	excellent
70–85%	very good
60–70%	acceptable
50–60%	barely acceptable
Below 50%	not acceptable

Box 6.1 reports a study that achieved an 'excellent' response rate.

Steps to improve response rates to mail questionnaires

Because of the tendency for mail questionnaire surveys to generate lower response rates than comparable structured interview surveys (and the implications this has for the validity of findings), a great deal of thought and research has gone into ways of improving survey response. The following steps are frequently suggested.

• Write a good covering letter explaining the reasons for the research, why it is important, and why the recipient has been selected; mention sponsorship if any, and provide guarantees of confidentiality. The advice provided in Box 5.5 (p. 114) in connection with the kind of letter that might go out in advance of a respondent being asked to be interviewed can be followed to good effect.

• Mail questionnaires should always be accompanied by a stamped addressed envelope or, at the very least, return postage.

• Follow up individuals who do not reply at first, possibly with two or three further mailings. The importance of reminders cannot be overstated—they do work. My preferred approach has been to send out a reminder letter to non-respondents two weeks after the initial mailing, reasserting the nature and aims of the survey with the suggestion that, if the questionnaire has been lost, to contact a research officer or me. Then, two weeks after that all further non-respondents should be sent another letter along with a further copy of the questionnaire. These reminders have a demonstrable effect on the response rate. Some writers argue for further mailings of reminder letters to non-respondents. If a response rate is worryingly low, such further mailings would certainly be desirable.

• Unsurprisingly, shorter questionnaires tend to achieve better response rates than longer ones. However, this is not a clear-cut principle, because it is difficult to specify when a questionnaire becomes 'too long'. Also, the evidence suggests

---

Box 6.1 A monetary incentive

Lunt and Livingstone (1992) conducted a postal questionnaire survey into a variety of issues relating to the notion of consumerism. They were particularly interested in people's attitudes to money. In September 1989 they sent out 241 questionnaires to people living in or around Oxford. Each person was paid 'a nominal £2 for their time' (1992: 173). The questionnaire was long (twenty pages) and took between one and one-and-a-half hours to complete. In spite of its length, 219 returned the questionnaire, making a response rate of 91 per cent.

that the effect of the length of questionnaires on response rates cannot be separated very easily from the salience of the topic(s) of the research for respondents and from the nature of the sample. Respondents may be highly tolerant of questionnaires that contain many questions on topics that interest them.

- Clear instructions and an attractive layout improve mail questionnaire response rates. Dillman (1983), as part of what he calls the Total Design Method (TDM) for mail questionnaire research, recommends lower case for questions and upper case for closed-ended answers.

- Do not allow the questionnaire to appear unnecessarily bulky. Dillman (1983) recommends a booklet format for the questionnaire and using the photocopier to reduce the size of the questionnaire to fit the booklet format. This approach also gives the impression of a more professional approach.

- As with structured interviewing (see Chapter 5), begin with questions which are more likely to be of interest to the respondent. This advice is linked to the issue of salience (see above) but has particular significance in the context of research that may have limited salience for the respondent.

- There is some controversy about how significant for response rates it is to personalize covering letters, by including the respondent's name and address (Baumgartner and Heberlein 1984). However, one of the features of the TDM approach advocated by Dillman (1983) is that these details are supplied on covering letters and each is individually signed.

- I am inclined to the view that in general mail questionnaires should comprise as few open questions as possible, since people are often deterred by the prospect of having to write a lot. In fact, many writers on the subject recommend that open questions are used as little as possible in self-completion questionnaires.

- Providing monetary incentives increases the response rate. These are more effective if the money comes with the questionnaire rather than if it is promised once the questionnaire has been returned. Apparently, respondents typically do not cynically take the money and discard the questionnaire! The evidence also suggests that quite small amounts of money have a positive impact on the response rate, but that larger amounts do not necessarily improve the response rate any further.

Designing the self-completion questionnaire

Do not cramp the presentation

Because of the well-known problem of low response rates to the mail questionnaire in particular, it is sometimes considered preferable to make the instrument appear as short as possible in order for it to be less likely to deter prospective respondents from answering. However, this is almost always a mistake. As Dillman (1983) observes, an attractive layout is likely to enhance response rates, whereas the kinds of tactics that are sometimes employed to make a questionnaire appear shorter than it really

is—such as reducing margins and the space between questions—make it look cramped and thereby unattractive. Also, if questions are too close together, there is a risk of a tendency for them to be inadvertently omitted.

This is not to say that you should be ridiculously liberal in your use of space, as this does not necessarily provide for an attractive format either and may run the risk of making the questionnaire look bulky. As with so many other issues in social research, a steady course needs to be steered between possible extremes.

Clear presentation

Far more important than making a self-completion questionnaire appear shorter than is the case is to make sure that it has a layout that is easy on the eye, as Dillman emphasizes, and that it facilitates the answering of all questions that are relevant to the respondent. Dillman's recommendation of lower case for questions and upper case for closed answers is an example of one consideration, but at the very least a variety of print styles (e.g. different fonts, print sizes, bold, italics, and capitals) can enhance the appearance *but must be used in a consistent manner*. This last point means that you should ensure that you use one style for general instructions, one for headings, perhaps one for specific instructions (like, Go to question 7), one for questions, and one for closed-ended answers. Mixing print styles, so that one style is sometimes used for both general instructions and questions, can be very confusing for respondents.

Vertical or horizontal closed answers?

Bearing in mind that most questions in a self-completion questionnaire are likely to be of the closed kind, one consideration is whether to arrange the fixed answers vertically or horizontally. Very often, the nature of the answers will dictate a vertical arrangement because of their sheer length. Many writers prefer a vertical format whenever possible, because, in some cases where either arrangement is feasible, confusion can arise when a horizontal one is employed (Sudman and Bradburn 1982). Consider the following:

What do you think of the Prime Minister's performance in his job since he took office? (*Please tick the appropriate response*)

Very ____ Good ____ Fair ____ Poor ____ Very ____
good   poor

There is a risk that if the questionnaire is being answered in haste, the required tick will be placed in the wrong space—for example, indicating Good

when Fair was the intended response. Also, a vertical format more clearly distinguishes questions from answers. To some extent, these potential problems can be obviated through the judicious use of spacing and print variation, but they represent significant considerations. A further reason why vertical alignments can be superior is that they are probably easier to code, especially when pre-codes appear on the questionnaire. Very often, self-completion questionnaires are arranged so that to the right of each question are two columns: one for the column in which data relating to the question will appear in a data matrix; the other for all the pre-codes. The latter allows the appropriate code to be assigned to a respondent's answer by circling it for later entry into the computer. Thus, the choice would be between the formats presented in Boxes 6.2*a* and 6.2*b*. In the second case, not only is there less ambiguity about where a tick is to be placed; the task of coding is easier. However, when there is to be a battery of questions with identical answer formats, as in a Likert scale, a vertical format will take up too much space. One way of dealing with this kind of questioning is to use abbreviations with an accompanying explanation. An example can be found in Box 6.3. The four items presented in Box 6.3 are taken from an eighteen-item Likert scale designed to measure job satisfaction (Brayfield and Rothe 1951).

Identifying response sets in a Likert scale

One of the advantages of using closed questions is that they can be pre-coded, thus turning the processing of data for computer analysis into a fairly simple task (see Chapter 7 for more on this). However, some thought has to go into the scoring of the items of the kind presented in Box 6.3. We might for example score question 23 as follows:

Strongly agree = 5
Agree = 4
Undecided = 3
Disagree = 2
Strongly disagree = 1

Accordingly, a high score for the item (5 or 4) indicates satisfaction with the job and a low score (1 or 2)

Box 6.2a Closed question with a horizontal format

What do you think of the Prime Minister's performance in his job since he took office?

(*Please tick the appropriate response*)

Very good ____ Good ____ Fair ____ Poor ____ Very poor ____   27   5 4 3 2 1

Box 6.2b Closed question with a vertical format

What do you think of the Prime Minister's performance in his job since he took office?

(*Please tick the appropriate response*)   27

Very good ____   5

Good   ____   4

Fair   ____   3

Poor   ____   2

Very poor ____   1

Box 6.3 Formatting a Likert scale

In the next set of questions, you are presented with a statement. You are being asked to indicate your level of agreement or disagreement with each statement by indicating whether you: Strongly Agree (SA), Agree (A), are Undecided (U), Disagree (D), or Strongly Disagree (SD).

Please indicate your level of agreement by circling the appropriate response.

23. My job is like a hobby to me.

    SA   A   U   D   SD

24. My job is usually interesting enough to keep me from getting bored.
    SA   A   U   D   SD

25. It seems that my friends are more interested in their jobs.
    SA   A   U   D   SD

26. I enjoy my work more than my leisure time.
    SA   A   U   D   SD

indicates low job satisfaction. The same applies to question 24. However, when we come to question 25, the picture is different. Here, agreement indicates a *lack* of job satisfaction. It is disagreement that is indicative of job satisfaction. We would have to reverse the coding of this item, so that:

Strongly agree = 1
Agree = 2
Undecided = 3
Disagree = 4
Strongly disagree = 5

The point of including such items is to identify people who exhibit response sets, like acquiescence (see Chapter 5). If someone were to agree with all eighteen items, when some of them indicated *lack* of job satisfaction, it is likely that the respondent is affected by a response set and the answers are unlikely to provide a valid assessment of job satisfaction for that person.

Clear instructions about how to respond

Always be clear about how you want respondents to indicate their replies when answering closed questions. Are they supposed to place a tick by or circle or underline the appropriate answer, or are they supposed to delete inappropriate answers? Also, in many cases it is feasible for the respondent to choose more than one answer—is this acceptable to you? If it is not, you should indicate this in your instructions, for example:

(Please choose the ONE answer that best represents your views by placing a tick in the appropriate box)

If you do not make this clear and if some respondents choose more than one answer, you will have to treat their replies as if they had not answered. This possibility increases the risk of missing data from some respondents.

If it is acceptable to you for more than one category to be chosen you need to make this clear, for example:

(Please choose all answers that represent your views by placing a tick in the appropriate boxes)

It is a common error for such instructions to be omitted and for respondents either to be unsure about how to reply or to make inappropriate selections.

Keep question and answers together

This is a simple and obvious, though often transgressed, requirement—namely, that you should never split a question so that it appears on two separate pages. A common error is to have some space left at the bottom of a page into which the question can be slotted but for the closed answers to appear on the next page. Doing so carries the risk of the respondent forgetting to answer the question or providing an answer in the wrong group of closed answers (a problem that is especially likely when a series of questions with a common answer format is being used, as with a Likert scale).

Diaries as a form of self-completion questionnaire

When the researcher is specifically interested in precise estimates of different kinds of behaviour, the diary warrants serious consideration, though it is still a relatively underused method. Unfortunately, the term 'diary' has somewhat different meanings in social research (see Box 6.4). It is the first of the three meanings—what H. Elliott (1997) calls the *researcher-driven diary*—which is the focus of attention here, especially in the context of its use in relation to quantitative research. When employed in this way,

Box 6.4 **The diary in social research**

There are three major ways in which the term 'diary' has been employed in the context of social research.

- *The diary as a method of data collection.* Here the researcher devises a structure for the diary and then asks a sample of diarists to complete the instruments so that they record what they do more or less contemporaneously with their activities. H. Elliott (1997) refers to this kind of use of the diary as *researcher-driven diaries*. Such diaries can be employed for the collection of data within the context of both quantitative and qualitative research. Sometimes, the collection of data in this manner is supplemented by a personal interview in which the diarist is asked questions about such things as what he or she meant by certain remarks. This *diary-interview*, as it is often referred to (Zimmerman and Wieder 1977), is usually employed when diarists record their behaviour in prose form rather than simply indicating the amount of time spent on different kinds of activity.

- *The diary as a document.* The diary in this context is written spontaneously by the diarist and not at the behest of a researcher. Diaries in this sense are often used by historians but have some potential for social researchers working on issues that are of social scientific significance. As Scott (1990) observes, the diary in this sense often shades into autobiography. Diaries as documents will be further addressed in Chapter 18.

- *The diary as a log of the researcher's activities.* Researchers sometimes keep a record of what they do at different stages as an *aide mémoire*. For example, the famous social anthropologist Malinowski (1967) kept an infamous log of his activities ('infamous' because it revealed his distaste for the people he studied and his inappropriate involvement with females). This kind of diary often shades into the writing of field notes by ethnographers, about which more is written in Chapter 14.

the researcher-driven diary functions in a similar way to the self-completion questionnaire. Equally, it could be said that the researcher-driven diary is an alternative method of data collection to observation. It can be thought of as the equivalent of structured observation (see Chapter 8) in the context of research questions that are framed in terms of quantitative research, or of ethnography (see Chapter 14) in the context of research questions in terms of qualitative research.

Corti (1993) distinguishes between 'structured diaries' and 'free text diaries'. Either may be employed by quantitative researchers. The research on the domestic division of labour by Sullivan (1996) is an illustration of the structured kind of diary (see Box 1.3, p. 7). The diary has the general appearance of a questionnaire with largely closed questions. The kind of diary employed in this research is often referred to as a 'time-use' diary, in that it is designed so that diarists can record more or less contemporaneously the amount of time engaged in certain activities, such as food preparation, childcare, selfcare, eating, and so on. Estimates of the amount

of time spent in different activities are often regarded as more accurate, because the events are less subject to memory problems or to the tendency to round up or down. However, it is more intrusive than answering a questionnaire and it could be argued that it causes changes in behaviour. Sullivan also asked couples to record in the diary the amount of enjoyment they derived from the different activities. This information was also recorded simultaneously and was answered on a five-point scale, like a Likert scale.

An example of a free-text diary is provided by Coxon's (1994) sexual diary, which was developed because of worries about the vagueness of answers to questions about sexual activity used in questionnaires and also because of the lack of context to replies. Coxon employed the diary method to study the ways in which gay men are responding to the risks of HIV/AIDS. One of several advantages of the diary method for this research was that it provided information on the time sequencing of events (for example, which practice followed which). This kind of information is much more difficult to glean from questionnaires. The diary method allowed Coxon to collect a variety of information from the written prose relating to sexual activity over a week. The method allowed the following kinds of information to be recorded and coded:

- nature of each item of sexual activity (e.g. anal intercourse, oral sex);
- details of the participants;
- whether the diarist was active or passive in the activity;
- whether the diarist or his partner achieved orgasm;
- whether drugs accompanied the practice;
- whether lubricants were used;
- what activities—sexual or otherwise—preceded each item of sexual activity;
- whether any other aids were employed;
- the location of the activity.

Using free-text recording of behaviour carries the same kinds of problem as those associated with coding answers to structured interview open questions—namely, the time-consuming nature of the exercise and the increased risks associated with the coding of answers. However, the free-text approach is less likely to be problematic when, as in the case of Coxon's (1994) research, diarists can be instructed about what is required and when the kinds of behaviour of interest are specific. It would be much more difficult to code free-text entries relating to a more general arena of types of behaviour of the kind studied by Sullivan (1996).

Corti (1993) recommends that the person preparing the diary should

- provide explicit instructions for diarists;
- be clear about the time periods within which behaviour is to be recorded—i.e. day, twenty-four hours, week;
- provide a model of a completed section of a diary;
- provide checklists of 'items, events or behaviour' that can jog people's memory—but the list should not become too daunting in length or complexity;
- include fixed blocks of time or columns showing when the designated activities start and finish (for

diaries of the kind used by Sullivan (1996), which show how people budget their time).

Advantages and disadvantages of the diary as a method of data collection

The two studies that have been used to illustrate the use of diaries also suggest its potential advantages.

- When fairly precise estimates of the frequency and/or amount of time spent in different forms of behaviour are required, the diary may provide more valid and reliable data than questionnaire data.
- When information about the sequencing of different types of behaviour is required, it is likely to perform better than questionnaires or interviews.
- The first two advantages could be used to suggest that structured observation would be just as feasible, but structured observation is probably less appropriate for producing data on behaviour that is personally sensitive, such as sexual behaviour. Moreover, although data on such behaviour can be collected by structured interview, it is likely that respondents will be less willing to divulge details of the kind revealed in Coxon's (1994) research. If such information were collected by questionnaire, there is greater risk of recall and rounding problems (see the first point in this list).

On the other hand, diaries may suffer from the following problems.

- They tend to be more expensive than personal interviews (because of the costs associated with recruiting diarists and of checking that diaries are being properly completed).
- Diaries can suffer from a process of attrition, as people decide they have had enough of the task of completing a diary.
- This last point raises the possibility that diarists become less diligent over time about their record keeping.
- There is sometimes failure to record details

sufficiently quickly, so that memory recall problems set in.

However, diary researchers such as Coxon and Sullivan argue that the resulting data are more accurate than the equivalent data based on interviews or questionnaires.

Key points

- Many of the recommendations relating to the self-completion questionnaire apply equally or almost equally to the structured interview, as has been mentioned on several occasions.

- Closed questions tend to be used in survey research rather than open ones. Coding is a particular problem when dealing with answers to open questions.

- Structured interviews and self-completion questionnaires both have their respective advantages and disadvantages, but a particular problem with questionnaires sent by mail is that they frequently produce a low response rate. However, steps can be taken to boost response rates for mail questionnaires.

- Presentation of closed questions and the general layout constitute important considerations for the self-completion questionnaire.

- The researcher-driven diary was also introduced as a possible alternative to using questionnaires and interviews when the research questions are very specifically concerned with aspects of people's behaviour.

Revision questions

Self-completion questionnaire or mail questionnaire?

- Are the self-completion questionnaire and the mail questionnaire the same thing?

Evaluating the self-completion questionnaire in relation to the structured interview

- 'The low response rates frequently achieved in research with mail questionnaires mean that the structured interview is invariably a more suitable choice.' Discuss.
- What steps can be taken to boost mail questionnaire response rates?

Designing the self-completion questionnaire

- Why are self-completion questionnaires usually made up mainly of closed questions?
- Why might a vertical format for presenting closed questions be preferable to a horizontal format?

Diaries as a form of self-completion questionnaire

- What are the main kinds of diary used in the collection of social science data?
- Are there any circumstances when the diary approach might be preferable to the use of a self-completion questionnaire?

7 Asking questions

Reader's guide

This chapter is concerned with the considerations that are involved in asking questions that are used in structured interview and questionnaires of the kinds discussed in the two previous chapters. As such, it continues the focus upon social survey research that began with Chapter 4. The chapter explores:

- the issues involved in deciding whether or when to use open or closed questions;
- the different kinds of question that can be asked in structured interviews and questionnaires;
- rules to bear in mind when designing questions;
- vignette questions in which respondents are presented with a scenario and are asked to reflect on the scenario;
- the importance of piloting questions;
- the possibility of using questions that have been used in previous survey research.

Introduction

To many people, how to ask questions represents the crux of considerations surrounding the use of social survey instruments such as the structured interview or the self-completion questionnaire. As the previous two chapters have sought to suggest, there is much more to the design and administration of such research instruments than how best to phrase questions. However, there is no doubt that the issue of how questions should be asked is a crucial concern for the survey researcher and it is not surprising that this aspect of designing survey instruments has been a major focus of attention over the years and preoccupies many practising researchers.

Open or closed questions?

One of the most significant considerations for many researchers is whether to ask a question in an open or closed format. This distinction was first introduced in Chapter 5. The issue of whether to ask a question in an open or closed format is relevant to the design of both structured interview and self-administered questionnaire research.

With an open question respondents are asked a question and can reply however they wish. With a closed question they are presented with a set of fixed alternatives from which they have to choose an appropriate answer. All of the questions in Box 5.6 (p. 116) are of the closed kind. So too are the Likert-scale items in Boxes 3.3 and 6.3 (pp. 68, 135); these form a particular kind of closed question. What, then, are some of the advantages and limitations of these two types of question format?

Open questions

Open questions present both advantages and disadvantages to the survey researcher, though, as the following discussion suggests, the problems associated with the processing of answers to open questions tend to mean that closed questions are more likely to be used.

Advantages

Although survey researchers typically prefer to use closed questions, open questions do have certain advantages over closed ones, as outlined in the list below.

- Respondents can answer in their own terms. They are not forced to answer in the same terms as those foisted on them by the closed answers.

- They allow unusual responses to be derived. Replies that the survey researcher may not have contemplated (and that would therefore not form the basis for fixed-choice alternatives) are possible.

- The questions do not suggest certain kinds of answer to respondents. Therefore, respondents' levels of knowledge and understanding of issues can be tapped. The salience of issues for respondents can also be explored.

- They are useful for exploring new areas or ones in which the researcher has limited knowledge.

- They are useful for generating fixed-choice format answers. This is a point that will be returned to below.

Disadvantages

However, open questions present problems for the survey researcher, as the following list reveals.

- They are time-consuming for interviewers to administer. Interviewees are likely to talk for longer than is usually the case with a comparable closed question.

- Answers have to be 'coded'. This is very time-consuming. For each open question it entails reading through answers, deriving themes that can be employed to form the basis for codes, and then going through the answers again so that the answers can be coded for entry into a computer spreadsheet. The process is essentially identical to that involved in *content analysis* and is sometimes called *post-coding* to distinguish it from *pre-coding*, whereby the researcher designs a coding frame in advance of administering a survey instrument and often includes the pre-codes in the questionnaire (as in Box 7.3). However, in addition to being time-consuming, post-coding can be an unreliable process, because it can introduce the possibility of variability in the coding of answers and therefore of measurement error (and hence lack of validity). This is a form of data-processing error (see Figure 4.7, p. 102). Boxes 7.1 and 7.2 deal with aspects of the coding of open questions.

- They require greater effort from respondents. Respondents are likely to talk for longer than would be the case for a comparable closed question, or, in the case of a self-completion questionnaire, would need to write for much longer. Therefore, it is often suggested that open questions have limited utility in the context of self-completion questionnaires. Because of the greater effort involved, many prospective respondents are likely to be put off by the prospect of having to write extensively, which may exacerbate the problem of low response rates with mail questionnaires in particular (see Chapter 6).

- There is the possibility in research based on structured interviews of variability between interviewers in the recording of answers. This possibility is likely to arise as a result of the difficulty of writing down verbatim what respondents say to interviewers. The obvious solution is to employ a tape recorder. However, it is not always practicable to employ one, for example, in a noisy environment. Also, the transcription of answers to tape-recorded open questions is immensely time-consuming and adds additional costs to a survey. The problem of transcription is one continually faced by qualitative researchers using semi-structured and unstructured interviews (see Chapter 15).

Box 7.1 Coding an open question

Coding an open question usually entails reading and rereading transcripts of respondents' replies and formulating distinct themes in their replies. A *coding frame* then needs to be designed that identifies the types of answer associated with each question and their respective codes (i.e. numbers). A coding schedule may also be necessary to keep a record of rules to be followed in the identification of certain kinds of answer in terms of a theme. The numbers allocated to each answer can then be used in the computer processing of the data.

Charles and Kerr (1988) conducted interviews concerning the consumption of food in the home with 200 British women. Their interviews were of the semi-structured kind (see Box 5.3, p. 110), so that the questions were open-ended. Charles and Kerr were working within a qualitative research strategy, but, for several of the questions that they asked, they found it helpful to quantify respondents' answers. Thus, while the bulk of the presentation of their findings is in the form of passages from interview transcripts, which is the conventional way of presenting such findings in qualitative research (see Chapter 15), some of their findings were far more redolent of the kind typically encountered in quantitative research. As the authors say: 'The material that we have is . . . qualitative, as we included many open-ended questions which gave the women the chance to talk freely, and quantitative, as the sample was large enough to produce useful statistical data' (Charles and Kerr 1988: 7).

One of their analyses is a contingency table (see Chapter 11 below), which shows the relationship between social class of male partner and responsibility for meal preparation. The latter variable was coded so that five categories of responsibility were generated: self prepares all meals; self mainly, partner sometimes; either or both (50/50); self mainly with help from partner and/or children sometimes; and other. Men in classes I and II were more likely to participate than in the other social classes. Another table shows the relationship between class and the occasions that alcohol is drunk at home. The latter variable comprised the following categories: Christmas and special occasions; Christmas, special occasions and when having company; at other times but not frequently; once a week or more; never drink at home; and other. These categories were generated after the data had been collected and essentially entailed a process of discerning likely categories and then systematically coding each respondent's answer to determine how it should be coded in terms of such considerations as responsibility for preparing meals or the occasions when alcohol is consumed in the home.

Box 7.2 Coding a very open question

Foddy (1993) reports the results of an exercise in which he asked a small sample of his students 'Your father's occupation is (was) . . .' and requested three details: nature of business; size of business; and whether owner or employee. In answer to the size of business issue, the replies were particularly variable in kind, including: 'big', 'small', 'very large', '3,000 acres', 'family', 'multinational', '200 people', and 'Phillips'. The problem here is obvious: you simply cannot compare and therefore aggregate people's replies. In a sense, the problem is only partly to do with the difficulty of coding an open question. It is also due to a lack of specificity in the question. If, instead, Foddy had asked 'How many employees are (were) there in your father's organization?', a more comparable set of answers should have been forthcoming. Whether his students would have known this information is, of course, yet another issue. However, the exercise does illustrate the potential problems of asking an open question, particularly one like this that lacks a clear reference point for gauging size.

Closed questions

The advantages and disadvantages of closed questions are in many respects implied in some of the considerations relating to open questions.

Advantages

Closed questions offer the following advantages to researchers.

- It is easy to process answers. For example, the respondent in a self-completion questionnaire or the interviewer using a structured interview schedule will place a tick or circle an answer for the appropriate response. The appropriate code can then be almost mechanically derived from the selected answer, since the pre-codes are placed to the side of the fixed-choice answers. See Box 7.3 for an example based on Box 6.2b (p. 135).

- Closed questions enhance the comparability of answers. With post-coding there is always a problem of knowing how far respondents' answers that receive a certain code are genuinely comparable. As previously noted, the assignment of codes to people's answers may be unreliable (see the sixth point in Box 5.2, p. 108). Checks are necessary to ensure that there is a good deal of agreement between coders and that coders do not change their coding conventions over time. Closed questions essentially circumvent this problem.

- Closed questions may clarify the meaning of a question for respondents. Sometimes, respondents may not be clear about what a question is getting at and the availability of answers may help to clarify the situation for them.

- Closed questions are easy for interviewers and/or respondents to complete. Precisely because interviewers and respondents are not expected to write extensively and instead have to place ticks or circle answers, closed questions are easier and quicker to complete.

- In interviews, closed questions reduce the possibility of variability in the recording of answers in structured interviewing. As noted in Chapter 5, if interviewers do not write down exactly what respondents say to them when answering questions, a source of bias and hence of invalidity is in prospect. Closed questions reduce this possibility, though there is still the potential problem that interviewers may have to *interpret* what is said to them in order to assign answers to a category.

Disadvantages

However, closed questions exhibit certain disadvantages.

- There is a loss of spontaneity in respondents' answers. There is always the possibility that they might come up with interesting replies that are not covered by the fixed answers that are provided. One solution to this possible problem is to ensure that an open question is used to generate the

---

Box 7.3 Processing a closed question

What do you think of the Prime Minister's performance in his job since he took office?

(*Please tick the appropriate response*)   27

Very good ____   5

Good   ✓   ④

Fair   ____   3

Poor   ____   2

Very poor ____   1

categories (see Box 7.4). Also, there may be a good case for including a possible response category of 'Other' and to allow respondents to indicate what they mean by this category.

- It can be difficult to make forced-choice answers mutually exclusive. The fixed answers that respondents are provided should not overlap. If they do overlap, they will not know which one to choose and so will arbitrarily select one or the other or alternatively may tick both answers. If a respondent were to tick two or more answers when one is required it would mean that you would have to treat the respondent's answer as missing data, since you would not know which of the ticked answers represented the true one. One of the most frequently encountered forms of this problem can be seen in the following age bands:

18–30
30–40
40–50
50–60
60 and over

In which band would a 40-year-old position him- or herself?

- It is difficult to make forced-choice answers exhaustive. All possible answers should really be catered for, although in practice this may be difficult to achieve, since this rule may result in excessively long lists of possible answers. Again, a category of 'Other' may be desirable to provide a wide range of answers.

- There may be variation among respondents in the interpretation of forced-choice answers. There is always a problem when asking a question that certain terms may be interpreted differently by respondents. If this is the case, then validity will be jeopardized. The presence of forced-choice answers can exacerbate this possible problem, because there may be variation in the understanding of key terms in the answers.

- Closed questions may be irritating to respondents when they are not able to find a category that they feel applies to them.

- In interviews, a large number of closed questions may make it difficult to establish rapport, because the respondent and interviewer are less likely to engage with each other in a conversation. The interview is more likely to have an impersonal feel to it. However, given the fact that the extent to which rapport is a desirable attribute of structured interviewing is somewhat difficult to determine (see Chapter 5), this is not necessarily too much of a problem.

Types of questions

It is worth bearing in mind that, when you are employing a structured interview or self-completion questionnaire, you will probably be asking several different types of question. There are various ways of classifying these, but here are some prominent types of question:

- *Personal factual questions*. These are questions that ask the respondent to provide *personal information*, such as age, occupation, marital status, income, and so on. This kind of question also includes questions about *behaviour*. Such factual questions may have to rely on the respondents' memories, as when they are asked about such things as frequency of church attendance, how often they visit the cinema, or when they last ate out in a restaurant.

- *Factual questions about others*. Like the previous type, this one asks for personal information about others, sometimes in combination with the respondent. An example of such a question would be one about household income, which would require respondents to consider their own incomes in conjunction with those of their partners. Charles and Kerr's (1988) question about

Box 7.4 A comparison of results for a closed and an open question

Schuman and Presser (1981) conducted an experiment to determine how far responses to closed questions can be improved by asking the questions first as open questions and then developing categories of reply from respondents' answers. They asked a question about what people look for in work in both open and closed format. Different samples were used. They found considerable disparities between the two sets of answers (40 per cent of the open format categories were not capable of being subsumed by the closed format answers). They then revised the closed categories to reflect the answers they had received from people's open-ended answers. They readministered the open question and the revised closed question to two large samples of Americans. The question and the answers they received are as follows.

This next question is on the subject of work. People look for different things in a job. Which one of the following five things do you most prefer in a job? [closed question]. What would you most prefer in a job? [open question]

Closed format		Open format	
Answer	%	Answer	%
Work that pays well	13.2	Pay	16.7
Work that gives a feeling of accomplishment	31.0	Feeling of accomplishment	14.5
Work where there is not too much supervision and you make most decisions yourself	11.7	Control of work	4.6
Work that is pleasant and people are nice to work with	19.8	Pleasant work	14.5
Work that is steady + little chance of being laid off	20.3	Security	7.6
	96% of sample		57.9% of sample
		Opportunity for promotion	1.0
		Short hours/lots of free time	1.6
		Working conditions	3.1
		Benefits	2.3
		Satisfaction/liking a job	15.6
Other/DK/NA	4.0	Other responses	18.3

With the revised form for the closed question, Schuman and Presser were able to find a much higher proportion of the sample whose answers to the open question corresponded to the closed one. They argue that the new closed question was superior to its predecessor and is also superior to the open question. However, it is still disconcerting that only 58 per cent of respondents answering the open question could be subsumed under the same categories as those answering the closed one. Also, the distributions are somewhat different: for example, twice as many respondents answer in terms of a feeling of accomplishment with the closed format than with the open one. Nonetheless, the experiment demonstrates the desirability of generating forced-choice answers from open questions.

who is involved in meal preparation (see Box 7.1) is one that asked wives what they and their husbands do when preparing meals. Indeed, a criticism of such research is precisely that it relies on the possibly distorted views of respondents concerning their own and others' behaviour (Beardsworth and Keil 1997). Like personal factual questions, an element of reliance on memory recall is likely to be present.

- *Informant factual questions*. Sometimes, we place people who are interviewed or who complete a questionnaire in the position of informants rather than as respondents answering questions about themselves. This kind of question can also be found in such contexts as when people are asked about such things as the size of the firm for which they work, who owns it, whether it employs certain technologies, and whether it has certain specialist functions. Such questions are essentially about characteristics of an entity of which they have knowledge, in this case, a firm. However, informant factual questions may also be concerned with behaviour: the Charles and Kerr (1988) questions are examples of this kind, in that the person being asked the question is being asked to reply about behaviour in terms of the household or family.

- *Questions about attitudes*. Questions about attitudes are very common in both structured interview and self-completion questionnaire research. The Likert scale is one of the most frequently encountered formats for measuring attitudes.

- *Questions about beliefs*. Respondents are frequently asked about their beliefs, possibly religious and political beliefs. Another form of asking questions about beliefs is when respondents are asked whether they believe that certain matters are true or false—for example, a question asking whether the respondent believes the UK is better off as a result of being a member of the European Community. Or a survey about crime might ask respondents to indicate whether they believe that the incidence of certain crimes is increasing.

- *Questions about normative standards and values*. Respondents may be asked to indicate what principles of behaviour influence them or they hold dear. The elicitation of such norms of behaviour is likely to have considerable overlap with questions about attitudes and beliefs, since norms and values can be construed as having elements of both.

- *Questions about knowledge*. Questions can sometimes be employed to 'test' respondents' knowledge in an area. For example, a study of drinking and driving might ask a respondent to indicate the legal limit for alcohol in the blood. It might also ask about the number of units of alcohol in certain drinks.

Most structured interview schedules and self-completion questionnaires will comprise more than one, and often several, of these types of question. It is important to bear in mind the distinction between different types of question. There are a number of reasons for this.

- It is useful to keep the distinctions in mind because they force you to clarify in your own mind what you are asking about, albeit in rather general terms.

- It will help to guard against asking questions in an inappropriate format. For example, a Likert scale is entirely unsuitable for asking factual questions about behaviour.

- When building scales like a Likert scale, it is best not to mix different types of question. For example, attitudes and beliefs sound similar and you may be tempted to use the same format for mixing questions about them. However, it is best not to do this and instead to have separate scales for attitudes and beliefs. If you mix them, the questions cannot really be measuring the same thing, so that measurement validity is threatened.

Rules for designing questions

Over the years, numerous rules (and rules of thumb) have been devised in connection with the dos and don'ts of asking questions. In spite of this, it is one of the easiest areas for making mistakes. There are three simple rules of thumb as a starting point; beyond that the rules specified below act as a means of avoiding further pitfalls.

General rules of thumb

Always bear in mind your research questions

The questions that you will ask in your self-completion questionnaire or structured interview should always be geared to answering your research questions. This first rule of thumb has at least two implications. First, it means that you should make sure that you ask questions that relate to your research questions. Ensure, in other words, that the questionnaire questions you ask will allow your research questions to be addressed. You will definitely not want to find out at a late stage that you forgot to include some crucial questions. Secondly, it means that there is little point in asking questions that do not relate to your research questions. It is also not fair to waste your respondents' time answering questions that are of little value.

What do you want to know?

Rule of thumb number two is decide exactly what it is you want to know. Consider the seemingly harmless question.

Do you have a car?

What is it that the question is seeking to tap? Is it car ownership? If it is car ownership, the question is inadequate, largely because of the ambiguity of the word 'have'. The question can be interpreted as: per-sonally owning a car; having access to a car in a household; and 'having' a company car or a car for business use. Thus, an answer of 'yes' may or may not be indicative of car ownership. If you want to know whether your respondent owns a car, ask him or her directly about this matter. Similarly, there is nothing wrong with the question

How many children do you have?

However, if what you are trying to address is the standard of living of a person or household, the crucial issue is how many are living at home.

How would *you* answer it?

Rule of thumb number three is put yourself in the position of the respondent. Ask yourself the question and try to work out how you would reply. If you do this, there is at least the possibility that the ambiguity that is inherent in the 'Do you have a car?' question will manifest itself and its inability to tap car ownership would become apparent. Let us say as well that there is a follow-up question to the previous one:

Have you driven the car this week?

Again, this looks harmless, but if you put yourself in the role of a respondent, it will be apparent that the phrase 'this week' is vague. Does it mean the last seven days or does it mean the week in which the questioning takes place, which will, of course, be affected by such things as whether the question is being asked on a Monday or a Friday? In part, this issue arises because the question designer has not decided what the question is about. Equally, however, a moment's reflection in which you put yourself in the position of the respondent might reveal the difficulty of answering this question.

Taking account of these rules of thumb and the following rules about asking questions may help you to avoid the more obvious pitfalls.

Specific rules when designing questions

Avoid ambiguous terms in questions

Avoid terms such as 'often' and 'regularly' as measures of frequency. They are very ambiguous, because respondents will operate with different frames of reference when employing them. Sometimes, their use is unavoidable, but when there is an alternative that allows actual frequency to be measured, this will nearly always be preferable. So, a question like

How often do you usually visit the cinema?

Very often	____
Quite often	____
Not very often	____
Not at all	____

suffers from the problem that, with the exception of 'not at all', the terms in the response categories are ambiguous. Instead, try to ask about actual frequency, such as:

How frequently do you usually visit the cinema? *(Please tick whichever category comes closest to the number of times you visit the cinema.)*

More than once a week	____
Once a week	____
2 or 3 times a month	____
Once a month	____
A few times a year	____
Once a year	____
Less than once a year	____

Alternatively, you might simply ask respondents about the number of times they have visited the cinema in the previous four weeks.

Words like 'family' are also ambiguous, because people will have different notions of who makes up their family. As previously noted, words like 'have' can also be sources of ambiguity.

It is also important to bear in mind that certain common words, such as 'dinner' and 'book', mean different things to different people. For some, dinner is a midday snack, whereas for others it is a substantial evening meal. Similarly, some people refer to magazines or to catalogues and brochures as books,

whereas others work with a more restricted definition. In such cases, it will be necessary to define what you mean by such terms.

Avoid long questions

It is commonly believed that long questions are undesirable. In a structured interview the interviewee can lose the thread of the question and in a self-completion questionnaire the respondent may be tempted to omit such questions or to skim them and therefore not give them sufficient attention. However, Sudman and Bradburn (1982) have suggested that this advice applies better to attitude questions than to ones that ask about behaviour. They argue that, when the focus is on behaviour, longer questions have certain positive features in interviews—for example: they are more likely to provide memory cues and they facilitate recall because of the time taken to complete the question. However, by and large, the general advice to keep questions short is the main piece of advice to be followed.

Avoid double-barrelled questions

Double-barrelled questions are ones that in fact ask about two things. The problem with this kind of question is that it leaves respondents unsure about how best to respond. Take the question

How satisfied are you with pay and conditions in your job?

The problem here is obvious: the respondent may be satisfied with one but not the other. Not only will the respondent be unclear about how to reply, but any answer that is given is unlikely to be a good reflection of the level of satisfaction with pay *and* conditions. Similarly,

How frequently does your husband help with cooking and cleaning?

suffers from the same problem. A husband may provide extensive help with cooking but be totally uninvolved in cleaning, so that any stipulation of frequency of help is going to be ambiguous and to create uncertainty for respondents.

The same rule applies to fixed-choice answers. In Box 7.4, one of Schuman and Presser's (1981) answers is

Work that is pleasant and people are nice to work with.

While there is likely to be a symmetry between the two ideas in this answer—pleasant work and nice people—there is no *necessary* correspondence between them. Pleasant work may be important for someone, but he or she may be relatively indifferent to the issue of how pleasant their co-workers are. A further instance of a double-barrelled question is provided in Box 7.5.

Avoid very general questions

It is easy to ask a very general question when in fact what is wanted is a response to a specific issue. The problem with questions that are very general is that they lack a frame of reference. Thus,

How satisfied are you with your job?

seems harmless but it lacks specificity. Does it refer to pay, conditions, the nature of the work, or all of these? If there is the possibility of such diverse interpretations, respondents are likely to vary in their interpretations too, and this will be a source of error. My favourite general question comes from Karl Marx's *Enquête Ouvrière*, a questionnaire that was sent to 25,000 French socialists and others (though there is apparently no record of any being returned). The final (one-hundredth) question reads:

What is the general, physical, intellectual, and moral condition of men and women employed in your trade? (Bottomore and Rubel 1963: 218)

Avoid leading questions

Leading or loaded questions are ones that appear to lead the respondent in a particular direction. Questions of the kind 'Do you agree with the view that . . .?' fall into this class of question. The obvious problem with such a question is that it is suggesting a particular reply to respondents, although invariably they do have the ability to rebut any implied answer. However, it is the fact that they might feel pushed in a certain direction that is undesirable. Such a question as

Would you agree to cutting taxes further even though welfare provision for the most needy sections of the population might be reduced?

is likely to make it difficult for some people to answer in terms of fiscal probity. But once again, Marx is the source of a favourite leading question:

If you are paid piece rates, is the quality of the article made a pretext for fraudulent deductions from wages? (Bottomore and Rubel 1963: 215)

Avoid questions that are actually asking two questions

The double-barrelled question is a clear instance of the transgression of this rule, but in addition there is the case of a question like:

Which political party did you vote for at the last general election?

What if the respondent did not vote? It is better to ask two separate questions:

Did you vote at the last general election?
Yes ____
No ____
If YES, which political party did you vote for?

Another way in which more than one question can be asked is with a question like:

How effective have your different job search strategies been?
Very effective ____
Fairly effective ____
Not very effective ____
Not at all effective ____

The obvious difficulty is that, if the respondent has used more than one job search strategy, his or her estimation of effectiveness will vary for each strategy. A mechanism is needed for assessing the success of each strategy rather than forcing respondents to average out their sense of how successful the various strategies were.

Avoid questions that include negatives

The problem with questions with 'not' or similar formulations in them is that it is easy for the respondent to miss the word out when completing a self-completion questionnaire or to miss it when being interviewed. If this occurs, a respondent is likely to answer in the opposite way from the one intended. There are occasions when it is impossible to avoid negatives, but a question like the following should be avoided as far as possible:

Do you agree with the view that students should not have to take out loans to finance higher education?

Instead, the question should be asked in a positive format. Questions with double negatives should be totally avoided, because it is difficult to know how to respond to them. Oppenheim (1966) gives the following as an example of this kind of question:

Would you rather not use a non-medicated shampoo?

It is quite difficult to establish what an answer of 'yes' or 'no' would actually mean in response to this question.

One context in which it is difficult to avoid using questions with negatives is when designing Likert scale items. Since you are likely to want to identify respondents who exhibit response sets and will therefore want to reverse the direction of your question asking (see Chapter 6), the use of negatives will be difficult to avoid.

Avoid technical terms

Use simple, plain language and avoid jargon. Do not ask a question like

Do you sometimes feel alienated from work?

The problem here is that many respondents will not know what is meant by 'alienated', and furthermore are likely to have different views of what it means, even if it is a remotely meaningful term to them.

Consider the following question:

The influence of the TUC on national politics has declined in recent years.

Strongly ___ Agree ___ Undecided ___ Disagree ___ Strongly ___
agree   disagree

The use of acronyms like TUC can be a problem, because some people may be unfamiliar with what they stand for.

Does the respondent have the requisite knowledge?

There is little point in asking respondents lots of questions about matters of which they have no knowledge. It is very doubtful whether meaningful data about computer use could be extracted from respondents who have never used or come into direct contact with one.

Make sure that there is a symmetry between a closed question and its answers

A common mistake is for a question and its answers to be out of phase with each other. Box 7.5 describes such an instance.

Memory problems

Do not rely too much on stretching people's memories to the extent that the answers for many of them are likely to be inaccurate. It would be nice to have accurate replies to a question about the number of times respondents have visited the cinema in the previous twelve months, but it is highly unlikely that most will in fact recall events accurately over such a long space of time (other perhaps than those who have not gone at all or only once or twice in the preceding twelve months). It was for this reason that, in the similar question referred to above, the time frame was predominantly just one month.

Box 7.5 Matching question and answers in closed questions (and some double-barrelled questions too)

While this book was being prepared, I was reading a novel whose publisher had inserted a feedback questionnaire within its pages. At one point in the questionnaire, there was a series of Likert-style items regarding the book's quality. In each case, the respondent is asked to indicate whether the attribute being asked about is: poor; acceptable; average; good; or excellent. However, in each case, the items are presented as questions, for example:

Was the writing elegant, seamless, imaginative?

The problem here is that an answer to this question is 'yes' or 'no'. At most, we might have gradations of yes and no, such as: definitely; to a large extent; to some extent; not at all. However, 'poor' or 'excellent' cannot be answers to this question. The problem is that the questions should have been presented as statements, such as:

Please indicate the quality of the book in terms of each of the following criteria:

The elegance of the writing:

Poor ___   Acceptable ___   Average ___   Good ___   Excellent ___

Of course, I have changed the sense slightly here, because, as it was stated, a further problem with the question is that it is a double-barrelled question. In fact, it is 'treble-barrelled', because it actually asks about three attributes of the writing in one. The reader's views about the three qualities may vary. A similar question asked:

Did the plot offer conflict, twists, and a resolution?

Again, not only does the question imply a 'yes' or 'no', it actually asks about three attributes. How would you answer if you had different views about each of the three criteria?

It might be argued that the issue is a nit-picking one: someone reading the question obviously knows that he or she is being asked to rate the quality of the book in terms of each attribute. The problem is that we simply do not know what the impact might be of a disjunction between question and answer, so you may as well get the connection between question and answers right (and do not ask double- or treble-barrelled questions either!).

Vignette questions

A form of asking mainly closed questions that has been used in connection with the examination of people's normative standards is the vignette technique. The technique essentially comprises presenting respondents with one or more scenarios and then asking them how they would respond when confronted with the circumstances of that scenario. Box 7.6 describes a vignette that was employed in the context of a study of family obligations in Britain. The aim was to elicit respondents' normative judgements about how family members should respond to relatives who are in need and indeed *who* should do the responding.

The vignette is designed to tease out respondents' norms concerning family obligations in respect of several factors: the nature of the care (whether long or short term and whether it should entail direct involvement or just the provision of resources); the significance of geographical propinquity; the dilemma of paid work and care; and the gender component of who should give up a job if that was deemed the appropriate course of action. There is a gradual increase in the specificity of the situation facing Jim and Margaret and therefore the respondent. Initially, we are not aware of whether Jim and Margaret are prepared to move; then we know they are; and then we learn they do in fact decide to move, which leads to the question of whether one of them should become a full-time carer.

Many aspects of the issues being tapped by the series of questions could be accessed through attitude items, such as

When a working couple decide that one of them should care for parents, the wife should be the one to give up her job.

Strongly ___ Agree ___ Undecided ___ Disagree ___ Strongly ___
agree   disagree

The advantage of the vignette over such an attitude question is that it anchors the choice in a situation and as such reduces the possibility of an unreflective reply. Finch (1987) also argues that, when the subject matter is a sensitive area (in this case, dealing with family relationships), there is the possibility that the questions may be seen as threatening by respondents. Respondents may feel that they are being judged by their replies. Finch argues that the fact that the questions are about other people (and imaginary ones at that) permits a certain amount of distance between the questioning and the respondent and results in a less threatening context. However, it is hard to believe that respondents will not feel that their replies will at least in part be seen as reflecting on them, even if the questions are not about them as such.

One obvious requirement of the vignette technique is that the scenarios must be believable, so that considerable effort needs to go into the construction of credible situations. Finch points to some further considerations in relation to this style of questioning. It is more or less impossible to establish how far assumptions are being made about the characters in the scenario (such as their ethnicity) and what the significance of those assumptions might be for the validity and comparability of people's replies. It is also difficult to establish how far people's answers reflect their own normative views or indeed how they themselves would act when confronted with the kinds of choices revealed in the scenarios. However, in spite of these reservations, the vignette technique warrants serious consideration when the research focus is concerned with an area that lends itself to this style of questioning.

Box 7.6 A vignette to establish family obligations

Jim and Margaret Robinson are a married couple in their early forties. Jim's parents, who live several hundred miles away, have had a serious car accident and they need long term daily care and help. Jim is their only son. He and his wife both work for the Electricity Board and they could both get transfers so they could work near his parents.

CARD E

(a) From the card, what should Jim and Margaret do?

Move to live near Jim's parents
Have Jim's parents move to live with them
Give Jim's parents money to help them pay for daily care
Let Jim's parents make their own arrangements
Do something else (SPECIFY)
Don't know

(b) In fact, Jim and Margaret are prepared to move and live near Jim's parents, but teachers at their children's school say that moving might have a bad effect on their children's education. Both children will soon be taking O-levels [predecessors to the current GCSE examinations].

What should Jim and Margaret do? Should they move or should they stay?

Move
Stay

(c) Why do you think they should move/stay?

PROBE FULLY VERBATIM

(d) Jim and Margaret *do* decide to go and live near Jim's parents. A year later Jim's mother dies and his father's condition gets worse so that he needs full-time care.

Should Jim or Margaret give up their jobs to take care of Jim's father?   *IF YES*: Who should give up their job, Jim or Margaret?

Yes, Jim should give up his job
Yes, Margaret should give up her job
No, neither should give up their jobs
Don't know/Depends

Source: Finch (1987: 108)

Piloting and pre-testing questions

It is always desirable, if at all possible, to conduct a pilot study before administering a self-completion questionnaire or structured interview schedule to your sample. In fact, the desirability of piloting such instruments is not solely to do with trying to ensure that survey questions operate well; piloting also has a role in ensuring that the research instrument as a whole functions well. Pilot studies may be particularly crucial in relation to research based on the self-completion questionnaire, since there will not be an interviewer present to clear up any confusion. Also, with interviews, persistent problems may emerge after a few interviews have been carried out and these can then be addressed. However, with self-completion questionnaires, since they are sent or handed out in large numbers, considerable wastage may occur prior to any problems becoming apparent.

Here are some uses of pilot studies in survey research.

- If the main study is going to employ mainly closed questions, open questions can be asked in the pilot to generate the fixed-choice answers. Glock (1988), for example, extols the virtues of conducting qualitative interviews in preparation for a survey for precisely this kind of reason.

- Piloting an interview schedule can provide interviewers with some experience of using it and can infuse them with a greater sense of confidence.

- If everyone (or virtually everyone) who answers a question replies in the same way, the resulting data are unlikely to be of interest because they do not form a variable. A pilot study allows such a question to be identified.

- In interview surveys, it may be possible to identify questions that make respondents feel uncomfortable and to detect any tendency for respondents' interest to be lost at certain junctures.

- Questions that seem not to be understood (more likely to be realized in an interview than in a self-completion questionnaire context) or questions that are often not answered should become apparent. The latter problem of questions being skipped may be due to confusing or threatening phrasing, poorly worded instructions, or confusing positioning in the interview schedule or questionnaire. Whatever the cause might be, such missing data are undesirable and a pilot study may be instrumental in identifying the problem.

- Pilot studies allow the researcher to determine the adequacy of instructions to interviewers, or to respondents completing a self-completion questionnaire.

- It may be possible to consider how well the questions flow and whether it is necessary to move some of them around to improve this feature.

The pilot should not be carried out on people who might have been members of the sample that would be employed in the full study. One reason for this is that, if you are seeking to employ probability sampling, the selecting-out of a number of members of the population or sample may affect the representativeness of any subsequent sample. If possible, it is best to find a small set of respondents who are comparable to members of the population from which the sample for the full study will be taken.

Using existing questions

One final observation regarding the asking of questions is that you should also consider using questions that have been employed by other researchers for at least part of your questionnaire or interview schedule. This may seem like stealing and you would be advised to contact the researchers concerned regarding the use of questions they have devised. However, employing existing questions allows you to use questions that have in a sense been piloted for you. If any reliability and validity testing has taken place, you will know about the measurement qualities of the existing questions you use. A further advantage of using existing questions is that they allow you to draw comparisons with other research. This might allow you to indicate whether change has occurred or whether place makes a difference to findings. At the very least, examining questions used by others might give you some ideas about how best to approach your own questions, even if you decide not to make use of them as they stand.

The process of finding questions has been made a great deal easier by the creation of 'question banks', which act as repositories of questions employed in surveys and elsewhere. A very useful question bank is located at the Centre for Applied Social Surveys and can be found at the following address:

http://www.natcen.ac.uk/cass

The Question Bank includes questions from major surveys. They are presented in the context of the questionnaire in which they appeared and are accompanied by technical details. The search mechanism allows you to search for a particular questionnaire or it allows you to input keywords to find cases of the use of topics in questions. For the latter, select **Quick search . . .** and then enter your keyword as requested.

Key points

- While open questions undoubtedly have certain advantages, closed questions are typically preferable for a survey, because of the ease of asking questions and recording and processing answers.

- This point applies particularly to the self-completion questionnaire.

- Open questions of the kind used in qualitative interviewing have a useful role in relation to the formulation of fixed-choice answers and piloting.

- It is crucial to learn the rules of question-asking to avoid some of the more obvious pitfalls.

- Remember always to put yourself in the position of the respondent when asking questions and to make sure you will generate data appropriate to your research questions.

- Piloting or pre-testing may clear up problems in question formulation.

Revision questions

Open or closed questions?

- What difficulties do open questions present in survey research?
- Why are closed questions frequently preferred to open questions in survey research?
- What are the limitations of closed questions?
- How can closed questions be improved?

Types of question

- What are the main types of question that are likely to be used in a structured interview or self-administered questionnaire?

Rules for designing questions

- What is wrong with each of the following questions?

    What is your annual salary?

    | Below £10,000 | ____ |
    | £10,000–15,000 | ____ |
    | £15,000–20,000 | ____ |
    | £20,000–25,000 | ____ |
    | £25,000–30,000 | ____ |
    | £30,000–35,000 | ____ |
    | £35,000 and over | ____ |

    Do you ever feel alienated from your work?

    | All the time | ____ |
    | Often | ____ |
    | Occasionally | ____ |
    | Never | ____ |

    How satisfied are you with the provision of educational services and social services in your area?

    | Very satisfied | ____ |
    | Fairly satisfied | ____ |
    | Neither satisfied nor dissatisfied | ____ |
    | Fairly dissatisfied | ____ |
    | Very dissatisfied | ____ |

    What is your marital status?

    | Single | ____ |
    | Married | ____ |
    | Divorced | ____ |

Vignette questions

- In what circumstances are vignette questions appropriate?

Piloting and pre-testing questions

- Why is it important to pilot questions?

Using existing questions

- Why might it be useful to use questions devised by others?

8

Structured observation

Reader's guide

Structured observation is a method that is relatively underused in social research. It entails the direct observation of behaviour and the recording of that behaviour in terms of categories that have been devised prior to the start of data collection. This chapter explores:

• the limitations of survey research for the study of behaviour;

- the different forms of observation in social research;
- the potential of structured observation for the study of behaviour;
- how to devise an observation schedule;
- different strategies for observing behaviour in structured observation;
- sampling issues in structured observation research; with this method, the issue of sampling is to do not just with people but also with the sampling of time and contexts;
- issues of reliability and validity in structured observation;
- field stimulations, whereby the researcher actively intervenes in social life and records what happens as a consequence of the intervention, as a form of structured observation;
- some criticisms of structured observation.

Introduction

Structured observation is a method for sytstematically observing the behaviour of individuals in terms of a schedule of categories. It is a technique in which the researcher employs explicitly formulated rules for the observation and recording of behaviour. One of its main advantages is that it allows behaviour to be observed directly, unlike in survey research, which only allows behaviour to be inferred. In survey research, respondents frequently report their behaviour, but there are good reasons for thinking that such reports may not be entirely accurate. Structured observation constitutes a possible solution in that it entails the direct observation of behaviour.

Problems with social survey research on social behaviour

Chapters 5 through 7 have dealt with several different aspects of survey research. In the course of outlining procedures associated with the social survey, certain problems with the techniques with which it is typically associated have been identified. To some extent the deficiencies associated with the survey are recognized by practitioners, who have developed ways of dealing with them or at least of offsetting their impact to some degree. When social survey techniques such as the structured interview or the self-completion questionnaire are employed in connection with the study of respondents' *behaviour*, certain characteristic difficulties are encountered, some of which have been touched on in earlier chapters. Box 8.1 identifies some of the difficulties entailed in using survey methods to research behaviour. The list is by no means exhaustive but it does capture some of the main elements.

Box 8.1 Problems with using social survey research to investigate behaviour

- *Problem of meaning*. People may vary in their interpretations of key terms in a question (see Box 8.2).

- *Problem of omission*. When answering the question, respondents may inadvertently omit key terms in the question (see Box 8.2).

- *Problem of memory*. They may misremember aspects of the occurrence of certain forms of behaviour.

- *Social desirability effect*. They may exhibit a tendency towards replying in ways that are meant to be consistent with their perceptions of the desirability of certain kinds of answer.

- *Question threat*. Some questions may appear threatening and result in a failure to provide an honest reply.

- *Interviewer characteristics*. Aspects of the interviewer may influence the answers provided.

- *Gap between stated and actual behaviour*. How people say they are likely to behave and how they actually behave may be inconsistent (see Box 8.3).

Box 8.2 Accurate reporting of behaviour and the problems of meaning and omission

Belson (1981) has conducted detailed studies of how people interpret questions designed to gauge attitudes and behaviour. One question concerned with the latter was embedded in a structured interview schedule administered to fifty-nine British adults and went as follows:

When you turn on your television in the evening, do you generally go on viewing till the end of the evening or do you just watch one or two programmes? (Belson 1981: 59)

Intensive interviews carried out after the structured interviews had been carried out revealed that no respondents interpreted the question totally correctly. Twenty-five respondents arrived at incorrect interpretations; the rest were broadly correct but in varying degrees. A common problem was that the question was designed to refer to when the respondents themselves turned the television on. This was correctly interpreted by thirty-eight respondents, but fifteen interpreted the question to mean when the set is switched on—that is, not necessarily by the respondent (problem of meaning). Nine respondents appeared not to have taken any notice of the phrase 'when you turn on your television' (problem of omission). Similarly, ten failed to consider 'till the end of the evening' in their answers, while 'generally' spawned several interpretations. We see here problems of omission and meaning respectively.

So why not observe behaviour?

An obvious solution to the problems identified is to observe people's behaviour directly rather than to rely on research instruments like questionnaires to elicit such information. In this chapter, I am going to outline a method called *structured observation* (see Box 8.4), also often called *systematic observation*.

Much like the interview (see Box 5.3, p. 110), there are many different forms of observation approach in social research. Box 8.5 outlines some major ways of conducting observation studies in social research.

It has been implied that structured observation can be viewed as an alternative to social survey methods of research. After all, in view of the various problems identified in Box 8.1, it would seem an obvious solution to observe people instead. However, structured observation has not attracted a large following and instead tends to be in use in certain specific research areas, such as the behaviour of school teachers and pupils and interaction between them.

Box 8.3 Gap between stated and actual behaviour

This is one of the most infamous cases of problems of the gap between what people say they do (or are likely to do) and their actual behaviour. Questionnaires tap people's attitudes and reports of their behaviour, but one might legitimately question how well these relate to actual behaviour. A study of racial prejudice conducted many years ago by LaPiere (1934) illustrates this issue. He spent two years travelling with a young Chinese student and his wife to determine if they were refused entry at hotels and restaurants. They twice crossed the USA. Of 66 hotels they were refused entry once; of 184 restaurants and diners, none refused entry. LaPiere sought to eliminate himself as a possible contaminating influence by ensuring that he was not involved in gaining access to the various establishments and indeed seems to have sought to load the dice slightly in favour of being turned away:

Whenever possible I let my Chinese friend negotiate for accommodation . . . or sent them into a restaurant ahead of me. In this way I attempted to 'factor' myself out. We sometimes patronized high-class establishments after a hard and dusty day on the road and stopped at inferior auto camps when in our most presentable condition.   (LaPiere 1934: 232)

LaPiere then allowed six months to elapse and sent questionnaires to the hotels and restaurants they had visited. One of the questions asked: 'Will you accept members of the Chinese race as guests in your establishment?' Of the establishments that replied, 92 per cent of restaurants said no; and 91 per cent of hotels said no. LaPiere's simple though striking study clearly illustrates the gap that may exist between reports of behaviour and actual behaviour. It should also be noted that the question asked is somewhat unclear, a feature that is not usually remarked upon in connection with this widely cited study. 'Will you . . .?' can be interpreted as asking the respondent to project into the future or to state the establishment's policy. Quite why the more obvious formulation of 'Do you . . .?' was not used is not clear, though it is unlikely that this point has a significant bearing on the findings and their implications for survey research.

Box 8.4 *What is structured observation?*

Structured observation, often also called *systematic observation*, is a technique in which the researcher employs explicitly formulated rules for the observation and recording of behaviour. The rules inform observers about what they should look for and how they should record behaviour. Each person who is part of the research (we will call these people 'participants') is observed for a predetermined period of time using the same rules. These rules are articulated in what is usually referred to as an *observation schedule*, which bears many similarities to a structured interview schedule with closed questions. The aim of the observation schedule is to ensure that each participant's behaviour is systematically recorded so that it is possible to aggregate the behaviour of all those in the sample in respect of each type of behaviour being recorded. The rules that constitute the observation schedule are as specific as possible in order to direct observers to exactly what aspects of behaviour they are supposed to be looking for. The resulting data resemble questionnaire data considerably, in that the procedure generates information on different aspects of behaviour that can be treated as variables. Moreover, structured observation research is typically underpinned by a cross-sectional research design (see Box 2.12, p. 41, and Figures 2.2 and 2.3, pp. 44, 45).

Central to any structured observation study will be the *observation schedule* or *coding scheme*. This specifies the categories of behaviour that are to be observed and how behaviour should be allocated to those categories. It is best to illustrate what this involves by looking at examples. One of the best-known schedules for the observation of classrooms is Flanders Interaction Analysis Categories (FIAC), devised by Flanders (1970). This scheme was developed in the USA, but has been employed fairly extensively in other countries. An observer watches a classroom during a lesson and every three seconds

Box 8.5 Major types of observation research

- *Structured observation*. See Box 8.4.

- *Systematic observation*. See Box 8.4.

- *Participant observation*. This is one of the best-known methods of research in the social sciences. It is primarily associated with qualitative research and entails the relatively prolonged immersion of the observer in a social setting in which he or she seeks to observe the behaviour of members of that setting (group, organization, community, etc.) and to elicit the meanings they attribute to their environment and behaviour. Participant observers vary considerably in how much they participate in the social settings in which they locate themselves. See Box 14.1 (p. 291) and Chapter 14 generally for a more detailed treatment.

- *Non-participant observation*. This is a term that is used to describe a situation in which the observer observes but does not participate in what is going on in the social setting. Structured observers are usually non-participant in that they are in the social setting being observed but rarely participate in what is happening. The term can also be used in connection with unstructured observation.

- *Unstructured observation*. As its name implies, unstructured observation does not entail the use of an observation schedule for the recording of behaviour. Instead, the aim is to record in as much detail as possible the behaviour of participants with the aim of developing a narrative account of that behaviour. In a sense, most participant observation is unstructured but the term unstructured observation is usually employed in conjunction with non-participant observation.

- *Simple observation* and *contrived observation*. Webb *et al.* (1966) write about forms of observation in which the observer is unobtrusive and is not observed by those being observed. With simple observation, the observer has no influence over the situation being observed; in the case of contrived observation, the observer actively alters the situation to observe the effects of an intervention. These two types of observation are invariably forms of non-participant observation and can entail either structured or unstructured observation.

allocates a category number to the type of activity that takes place in that three-second period. (See Box 8.6 for the different types of activity in the FIAC scheme.) In other words, in each and every minute, the observer will write down twenty numbers, each of which will relate directly to the coding scheme.

From such data a number of features can be derived. For example, it becomes possible to compare teachers' styles in terms of such things as the relative emphasis upon teachers doing the talking and pupils talking. One can also compare teachers in terms of the amounts of silence or confusion that take place in their lessons. It also becomes possible to compare classes in terms of these categories. In fact, we tend to find, using the FIAC scheme, that two-thirds of time in the classroom is made up of talk. Of that talk, two-thirds derives from the teacher. It is helpful in bringing about an understanding of what happens in lessons and can be useful in developing information about which styles seem most effective.

For example, are better exam results achieved by teachers who exhibit a high level of talking relative to that of pupils, or are teachers who allow more pupil talk more effective? The scheme can also be used in teacher training in order to help trainees to become aware of features of their teaching style, and possibly to begin to question its appropriateness.

It is interesting to think about how a scheme like this might be employed in connection with higher education teaching and in particular in tutorials and seminars. In the following imaginary scheme, the focus is on the teacher. The categories might be:

Tutor:
1. asking question addressed to group;
2. asking question addressed to individual;
3. responding to question asked by member of group;
4. responding to comment by member of group;
5. discussing topic;
6. making arrangements;

7. silence.

Students(s):

8. asking question;
9. responding to question from tutor;
10. responding to comment from tutor;
11. responding to question from another student;
12. responding to comment from another student;
13. talking about arrangements.

We might want to code what is happening every five seconds. The coding sheet for a five-minute period in the tutorial might then look like Figure 8.1. We might try to relate the amount of time that the tutor is engaged in particular activities to such things as: number of students in the group; layout of the room; subject discipline; gender of tutor; age of tutor; and so on.

Box 8.6 FIAC categories

Teacher Talk	Response	1. **Accepts feeling** (e.g. accepts and clarifies an attitude or the feeling tone of a pupil)
		2. **Praises or encourages**
		3. **Accepts or uses ideas of pupils**
	Initiation	4. **Asks questions**
		5. **Lecturing**
		6. **Giving direction**
		7. **Criticizing or justifying authority**
Pupil talk		8. **Pupil talk—response**
		9. **Pupil talk—initiation**
Silence		10. **Silence or confusion**

The observation schedule

Devising a schedule for the recording of observations is clearly a crucial step in the structured observation project. The considerations that go into this phase are very similar to those involved in producing a structured interview schedule. The following considerations are worth taking into account.

- A clear focus is necessary. There are two aspects to this point. First, it should be clear to the observer exactly who or what (and possibly both) is to be observed. For example, if people are the focus of attention, the observer needs to know precisely who is to be observed. Also, the observer needs to know which if any aspects of the setting are to be observed and hence recorded. The second sense in which a clear focus is necessary is that the research problem needs to be clearly stated so that the observer knows which of the many things going on in any setting are to be recorded.

- As with the production of a closed question for a structured interview schedule or self-completion questionnaire, the forms taken by any category of behaviour must be both mutually exclusive (i.e.

3	3	3	3	10	10	10	10	10	10	10	10
10	10	10	10	10	10	7	7	7	8	8	8
8	8	8	8	8	8	8	8	11	11	11	11
11	11	11	11	11	11	11	11	11	11	11	11
7	7	7	7	7	4	4	4	4	4	4	1

Fig. 8.1 Coding sheet for imaginary study of university tutors

Note: Each cell represents a five-second interval and each row is one minute.

not overlap) and inclusive. Taking the earlier example of coding behaviour in a university tutorial, we might conceivably run into a problem of the twelve categories not being exhaustive if a student knocks on the tutor's door and quickly asks him or her a question (perhaps about the tutorial topic if the student is from another of the tutor's groups). An observer unfamiliar with the ways of university life might well be unsure about whether this behaviour needs to be coded in terms of the twelve categories or whether the coding should be temporarily suspended. Perhaps the best approach would be to have another category of behaviour to be coded that we might term 'interruption'. It is often desirable for a certain amount of unstructured observation to take place prior to the construction of the observation schedule and for there to be some piloting of it so that possible problems associated with a lack of inclusiveness can be anticipated.

• The recording system must be easy to operate.

Complex systems with large numbers of types of behaviour will be undesirable. Much like interviewers using a structured interview schedule, observers need to be trained, but even so it is easy for an observer to become flustered or confused if faced with too many options.

• One possible problem with some observation schedules is that they sometimes require a certain amount of interpretation on the part of the observer. For example, it might be difficult to distinguish between a student responding to a question raised by another student and discussing the tutorial topic. To the extent that it may be difficult to distinguish the two, a certain amount of interpretation on the part of the observer may be required. If such interpretation is required, there would need to be clear guidelines for the observer and considerable experience would be required (see Box 8.7 for an illustration of a study in which a good deal of interpretation seems to have been necessary).

Strategies for observing behaviour

There are different ways of conceptualizing how behaviour should be recorded.

• We can record in terms of *incidents*. This means waiting for something to happen and then recording what follows from it. Essentially, this is what LaPiere (1934) did (see Box 8.3), in that he waited for the Chinese couple to negotiate entry to each hotel or restaurant and then recorded whether they were allowed entry or not. I remember reading many years ago in a newspaper that someone placed a ladder over a pavement and then observed whether people preferred to go under the ladder or to risk life and limb in the face of oncoming traffic. A considerable number preferred the latter option, confirming the persistence of superstitious beliefs in an apparently secular society. Once again, an incident (someone approaching the ladder) triggered the observation, which Webb

Box 8.7 Observing jobs

Jenkins *et al.* (1975) report the results of an exploratory study employed to measure the nature of jobs. The research focused on several different types of job in a number of different types of organization. An observation schedule was devised to assess the nature of twenty aspects (dimensions) of the jobs in question. Most of the dimensions were measured through more than one indicator, each of which took the form of a question that observers had to answer on a six- or seven-point scale. These were then aggregated for each dimension. While the research has a predominantly psychological slant, many of the twenty dimensions relate to issues that have been raised in the sociology of work by labour process theorists and others (e.g. Braverman 1974). One dimension relates to 'Worker pace control' and comprises three observational indicators such as:

How much control does the employee have in setting the pace of his/her work?

Another dimension was 'Autonomy' which comprised four items, such as:

The job allows the individual to make a lot of decisions on his/her own.

Most of the observers were university students. The procedure for conducting the observations was as follows: 'Each respondent was observed twice for an hour. The observations were scheduled so that the two different observations were separated by at least 2 days, were usually made at different times of the day, and were always made by two different observers' (Jenkins *et al.* 1975: 173).

et al. (1966) would regard as an example of *contrived observation*, because the researchers fabricated the situation. The discussion later in this chapter of *field stimulations* provides further illustrations of this kind of research.

- We can observe and record in terms of short periods of time. In Croll and Moses' (1985) research on children with special educational needs, each child was observed for a few minutes at a time, though each child was observed for two hours in total. A slight variation on this theme can be found in the research reported in Box 2.10, p. 39. Children in St Helena were video-taped over a two-week period during their morning, lunchtime, and afternoon breaks. The tapes were then coded using

the Playgound Behaviour Observation Schedule which is an instrument for recording the occurrence of 23 behaviours (e.g. games; fantasy play; character imitation; anti-social and pro-social behaviour) and their behaviour groupings (i.e. whether the behaviour was undertaken by an individual, a pair, or with 3–5 or 6 or more children). . . . A separate Playgound Behaviour Observation Schedule was completed for each 30-second segment.　(Charlton *et al.* 1998: 7)

- We can observe and record observations for quite

long periods of time. The observer watches and records more or less continuously. The FIAC scheme adopts this strategy. Another example is the study of job characteristics by Jenkins *et al.* (1975), which entailed the observation of each worker on two occasions but for an hour on each occasion (see Box 8.7): 'The observation hour was structured so that the observer spent 10 min becoming oriented to the job, 30 min observing specific job actions, and 20 min rating the job in situ. The observers then typically spent an additional 15 min away from the job completing the observation instrument' (Jenkins *et al.* 1975: 174). This last study is an example of what Martin and Bateson (1986) refer to as 'continuous recording', whereby the observer observes for extended periods, thus allowing the frequency and duration of forms of behaviour to be measured. They contrast this approach with time sampling.

- *Time sampling* is a further approach to the observation of behaviour. An example here would be a study of schools known as the ORACLE (Observational Research and Classroom Learning Evaluation) project (Galton *et al.* 1980). In this research, eight children (four of each gender) in each class in which observation took place were observed for around four minutes but on ten separate occasions. A mechanical device made a noise every twenty-five seconds and on each occasion this occurred the observer made a note of what the teacher or pupils were doing in terms of the observation schedule. The sampling of time periods was random.

Sampling

Just like social survey research, structured observation necessitates decisions about sampling. However, with structured observation, issues surrounding sampling do not revolve solely around how to sample people. Several other sampling issues are involved.

Sampling people

When people are being sampled, considerations very similar to those encountered in Chapter 4 in respect of probability sampling come to the fore. This means that the observer will ideally want to sample on a random basis. In Croll and Moses' (1985) research on children with special educational needs, thirty-four classrooms from a number of different schools were selected for observation. All children were within the same age range. Initially, each teacher was interviewed to determine which children in his or her class were regarded as having special needs. In addition, tests of both reading ability and non-verbal reasoning were administered to children to identify children who appeared to have special needs, but who had not been identified by the teacher. Up to six children with special needs in each class were then randomly sampled as being the focus of structured observation; so too were four children who had not been identified as having special needs—these children acted as a kind of control group. In this way, 280 children were sampled, of whom 151 were identified as having special needs; the other 129 served as control subjects. The teachers did not know exactly which children were being observed. Each child was observed for a few minutes, after which the observer proceeded to the next child to be observed in a predetermined random order. In the end, each child was observed for a total of two hours. This was made up of a large number of short observation periods. Similarly, in the ORACLE research, eight children in each class were sampled randomly for observation (Galton *et al.* 1980). One boy and one girl from both the highest and the lowest achieving groups in each class were randomly sampled along with two boys and two girls from among the moderate achievers. They were then observed in a random order on many occasions. In the study of job characteristics (Box 8.7), the individuals who were observed at work were randomly selected (Jenkins *et al.* 1975).

Sampling in terms of time

As implied by the idea of time sampling (see above), it is often necessary to ensure that if certain individuals are sampled on more than one occasion, they are not always observed at the same time of the day. This means that, if particular individuals are selected randomly for observation on several different occasions for short periods, it is desirable for the observation periods to be randomly selected. For example, it would not be desirable for a certain pupil in a school classroom always to be observed at the end of the day. He or she may be tired and this will give a false impression of that pupil's behaviour.

Further sampling considerations

The sampling procedures mentioned so far conform to probability sampling principles, because it is feasible to construct a sampling frame for individuals. However, this is not always possible for different kinds of reason. Studies in public areas, like the research on superstition mentioned above, do not permit random sampling, because we cannot very easily construct a sampling frame of people walking along a street. Similarly, it is not feasible to construct a sampling frame of interactions. Reiss (1976), for example, has written about the difficulty of developing a random sample of encounters between police officers and the public. The problem with doing structured observation research on such a topic is that it does not lend itself to the specification of a sampling frame and therefore the researcher's ability to generate a probability sample is curtailed.

As suggested in Chapter 4, considerations relating to probability sampling derive largely from concerns surrounding the external validity of findings. Such concerns are not necessarily totally addressed by resorting to probability sampling, however. For example, if a structured observation study is conducted over a relatively short span of time, issues of the representativeness of findings are likely to arise. If the research was conducted in schools, observations conducted towards the end of the school year, when examinations are likely to loom large in the thinking of both teachers and students, may affect the results obtained compared to observations at a different point in the academic year. Consequently, consideration has to be given to the question of the timing of observation. This potential problem was dealt with in the ORACLE research by ensuring that teachers and each target pupil were observed on six occasions during each of the three school terms. Furthermore, how are the sites in which structured observation is to take place selected? Can we presume that they are themselves representative?

Clearly, a random sampling procedure for the selection of schools may assuage any worries in this connection. However, in view of the difficulty of securing access to settings such as schools and business organizations, it is likely that the organizations to which access is secured may not be representative of the population of appropriate ones.

A further set of distinctions between types of sampling in structured observation have been drawn by Martin and Bateson (1986) between:

- 'ad libitium sampling', whereby the observer records whatever is happening at the time;

- 'focal sampling', in which a specific individual is observed for a set period of time; the observer records all examples of whatever forms of behaviour are of interest in terms of a schedule;

- 'scan sampling', whereby an entire group of individuals is scanned at regular intervals and the behaviour of all of them is recorded at that time. This sampling strategy allows only one or two types of behaviour to be observed and recorded; and

- 'behaviour sampling', whereby an entire group is watched and the observer records who was involved in a particular kind of behaviour.

Most structured observation research seems to employ the first two types: Flanders's FIAC scheme is an example of *ad libitium* sampling; the research by Croll and Moses (1985), Galton *et al.* (1980), Jenkins *et al.* (1975), and the research by Buckle and Farrington (1994) cited in Box 8.8 are illustrations of focal sampling.

Issues of reliability and validity

One writer has concluded that, when compared to interviews and questionnaires, structured observation 'Provides (*a*) more reliable information about events; (*b*) greater precision regarding their timing, duration, and frequency; (*c*) greater accuracy in the time ordering of variables; and (*d*) more accurate and

economical reconstructions of large-scale social episodes' (McCall 1984: 277). This is a very strong endorsement for structured observation, but, as McCall notes, there are several issues of reliability and validity that confront practitioners of the method. Some of these issues are similar to those

---

Box 8.8 A study of shoplifting

Buckle and Farrington (1994) report the results of a replication of an earlier study of shoplifting in a department store in Peterborough (Buckle and Farrington 1984). The replication was conducted in a similar store in Bedford. Customers were selected at random as they entered the store and followed by two observers until they left. The observers recorded such details as: cost of items bought; gender, race, and estimated age; and behaviour. In Peterborough, 486 people formed the basis of the sample and in Bedford it was 502. Nine people shoplifted in Peterborough and six in Bedford. Somewhat surprisingly, shoplifters were more likely to be male and either under 25 (in Peterborough) or over 55 (in Bedford). Most shoplifters also purchased goods. Most shoplifting was of small items of relatively little monetary value. The sampling and observation strategies entailed random sampling of people followed by continuous recording for a short or long period depending on how long the person remained in the store.

---

faced by researchers when seeking to develop measures in social research in general (see Chapter 3) and by social survey research in particular. However, certain concerns are specific to structured observation.

Reliability

Practitioners of structured observation have been concerned with the degree of inter-observer consistency. Essentially, this issue entails considering the degree to which two or more observers of the same behaviour agree in terms of their coding of that behaviour on the observation schedule—that is, *inter-observer consistency*. The chief mechanism for assessing this component of reliability is a statistic called *Kappa* (see Box 8.9; *this box can be ignored if you feel unsure about addressing more complex statistical issues at this stage*).

A second consideration in relation to reliability is the degree of consistency of the application of the observation schedule over time—that is, *intra-observer consistency*. This is clearly a difficult notion, because of the capacity for and often necessity for people to behave in different ways on different occasions and in different contexts. Assessing the consistency of observation ratings across all possibilities is clearly a difficult undertaking. The procedures for assessing this aspect of reliability are broadly similar to those applied to the issue of inter-observer consistency. The Jenkins *et al.* (1975) research addressed the issue of inter-observer consistency over time and found that the measures fared even worse in this respect.

It is clearly not an easy matter to achieve reliability in structured observation. This is a point of some significance in view of the fact that validity presupposes reliability (see Chapter 3). Reliability may be difficult to achieve on occasions, because of the effects of such factors as observer fatigue and lapses in attention. However, this point should not be exaggerated, because the ORACLE researchers were able to achieve high levels of reliability for many of their measures, and indeed two critics of structured observation have written that 'there is no doubt that observers can be trained to use complex coding schedules with considerable reliability' (Delamont and Hamilton 1984: 32). (Using the Scott coefficient referred to in Box 8.9, it was found that the average inter-observer reliability level across the different components of pupil behaviour was 0.90.) The high levels of reliability may be due to the factors that are intrinsic to the school classroom and to the fact that there is a long tradition of structured observation research in schools, so that a fund of experience has been accumulated in this domain.

Validity

Measurement validity relates to the question of whether a measure is measuring what it is supposed to measure. The validity of any measure will be affected by:

Box 8.9 Cohen's kappa

Cohen's kappa is a measure of the degree of agreement over the coding of items by two people. As such, it could be applied to the coding of any textual information, as in the content analysis of newspaper articles or of answers to open interview questions, as well as to the coding of observation. Much like Cronbach's alpha (see Box 3.7, p. 71) you will end up with a coefficient that will vary between 0 and 1. The closer the coefficient is to 1, the higher the agreement and the better the inter-observer consistency. A coefficient of 0.75 or above is considered very good; between 0.6 and 0.75, it is considered good; and between 0.4 and 0.6, it is regarded as fair. The meaning of kappa is that it measures the degree of agreement between observers beyond that which would occur by chance. Croll (1986) refers to a very similar statistic, the Scott coefficient of agreement, which can be interpreted in an identical way.

The values of kappa in the study of job characteristics referred to in Box 8.7 were mainly in the 'fair' category. The two items referred to in Box 8.7 achieved kappa values of 0.43 and 0.54 respectively (Jenkins *et al.* 1975). These are not very encouraging and suggest that the coding of job characteristics was not very reliable.

- whether the measure reflects the concept it has been designed to measure (see Chapter 3), and
- error that arises from the implementation of the measure in the research process (see Chapter 5).

The first of these issues simply means that in structured observation it is necessary to attend to the same kinds of issues concerning the checking of validity (assessing face validity, concurrent validity, and so on) that are encountered in research based on interviews and questionnaires. The second aspect of validity—error in implementation—relates to two matters in particular.

- Is the observation instrument administered as it is supposed to be? This is the equivalent of ensuring that interviewers using a structured interview schedule follow the research instrument and its instructions exactly as they are supposed to. If there is variability between observers or over time, the measure will be unreliable and therefore cannot be valid. Ensuring that observers have as complete an understanding as possible of how the observation schedule should be implemented is therefore crucial.

- Do people change their behaviour because they know they are being observed? This is an instance of what is known as the 'reactive effect' (Box 8.10). After all, if people adjust the way they behave because they know they are being observed (perhaps because they want to be viewed in a favourable way by the observer), their behaviour would have to be considered atypical. As a result, we could hardly regard the results of structured observation research as indicative of what happens in reality. As McCall (1984) notes, there is evidence that a reactive effect occurs in structured observation, but that by and large research participants become accustomed to being observed, so that the researcher essentially becomes less intrusive the longer he or she is present. Moreover, it should be borne in mind that frequently people's awareness of the observer's presence is offset by other factors. For example, teachers and students have many tasks to accomplish that reflect the demands of the classroom, so that the observer's ability to make a big impact on behaviour may be curtailed by the requirements of the situation.

Box 8.10 Reactive effect

Webb *et al.* wrote about the 'reactive measurement effect', by which they meant that 'the research subject's knowledge that he is participating in a scholarly search may confound the investigator's data' (1966: 13). They distinguished four components of this effect:

- *The guinea pig effect—awareness of being tested.* Examples of the kind of concern that Webb *et al.* were writing about are such effects as the research participant wanting to create a good impression or feeling prompted to behave in ways (or express attitudes) that would not normally be exhibited.

- *Role selection.* Webb *et al.* argue that participants are often tempted to adopt a particular kind of role in research. An example is that there is a well-known effect in experimental research (but which may have a broader applicability) whereby some individuals seek out cues about the aims of the research and adjust what they say and do in line with their perceptions (which may of course be false) of those aims.

- *Measurement as a change agent.* The very fact of a researcher being in a context in which no researcher is normally present may itself cause things to be different. For example, the fact that there is an observer sitting in the corner of a school classroom means that there is space and a chair being used that otherwise would be unoccupied. This very fact may influence behaviour.

- *Response sets.* This is an issue that primarily relates to questionnaire and interview research and occurs when the respondent replies to a set of questions in a consistent but clearly inappropriate manner. Examples of this kind of effect are measurement problems like the social desirability effect and yeasaying and naysaying (consistently answering yes or no to questions or consistently agreeing or disagreeing with items regardless of the meaning of the question or item).

Reactive effects are likely to occur in any research in which participants know they are the focus of investigation. Webb *et al.* called for greater use of what they call *unobtrusive measures* or *non-reactive methods* that do not entail participants' knowledge of their involvement in research (see Box 10.6, p. 209, for more information).

Field stimulations as a form of structured observation

Salancik (1979) has used the term 'field stimulation' to describe a form of observation research that shares many of structured observation's characteristics. Although he classifies field stimulations as a qualitative method, they are in fact better thought of as operating with a quantitative research strategy, since the researcher typically seeks to quantify the outcomes of his or her interventions. In terms of the classification offered in Box 8.5, it is in fact 'contrived observation'. Part of LaPiere's study (see Box 8.3) was a field stimulation: when he arranged for the Chinese couple to seek entry to the hotels and restaurants in order to observe the effects of their attempts, he was employing a field stimulation. A field stimulation, therefore, is a study in which the researcher directly intervenes in and/or manipulates a natural setting in order to observe what happens as a consequence of that intervention. However, unlike most structured observation, in a field stimulation respondents do not know they are being studied. A famous field stimulation is described in Box 8.11.

Some field stimulations can take the form of an experimental design (see Chapter 2). An example is a study by Daniel (1968) of racial discrimination in Britain in the 1960s. Daniel undertook conventional attitude studies among immigrant groups to establish levels of discrimination. In addition, he developed 'situation tests' to back up his findings. For example, in one set of situation tests he examined discrimination in the area of accommodation.

Box 8.11 A field stimulation

David Rosenhan (1973) was one of eight people who sought to gain entry as patients to mental hospitals in the USA. Some of them—they are referred to as 'pseudo-patients'—sought entry to more than one hospital, so that twelve hospitals were approached. Each pseudo-patient was instructed to say that he or she was hearing voices. All successfully gained entry, in eleven of the twelve cases with a diagnosis of schizophrenia. As soon as they had succeeded in gaining entry, the pseudo-patients were instructed to cease exhibiting any symptoms. In spite of the fact that the pseudo-patients were all 'sane', it took many of them quite a long time to be released. The length of hospitalization varied between 7 and 52 days with a mean of 19 days. In four of the hospitals, pseudo-patients approached psychiatrists and nurses with a request for release, with no member of staff being approached more than once on any day. The pseudo-patients recorded the nature of the response to their requests: 71 per cent of psychiatrists responded by moving on with their heads averted and 88 per cent of nurses did likewise. Rosenhan regards this evidence as indicating that the mental patient becomes powerless and depersonalized. The study has been highly controversial as many psychiatrists have sought to question its implications, while others have raised ethical issues of the kind addressed in Chapter 24 (such as the use of deception).

Sixty advertisements for accommodation to let were selected from a number of regions. Advertisements stipulating 'no coloureds' or 'Europeans only' were deliberately excluded. At the time, it was not illegal for landlords to place such instructions in their advertisements. Each landlord was approached by each of the following: a West Indian; a white Hungarian; and a white Englishman. The applicants were presented with identical sets of characteristics, but they differed in terms of ethnicity. The applicant was requesting accommodation for a married couple with no children. In half of the applications (i.e. 30), the testers adopted 'professional roles'. In these roles they sought more expensive accommodation. In the other half, they adopted manual roles. In 15 of the 60 cases, all 3 applicants got the same information (e.g. let, still vacant). This means that discrimination occurred in the remaining 45 cases (see Table 8.1).

Daniel's research strongly suggests that, because the Hungarian was rarely discriminated against, it is colour rather than being a member of an ethnic minority as such that causes discrimination. Similar studies were conducted in relation to house purchase, employment, and car insurance. Interestingly, the researchers often found that these tests implied that discrimination was *greater* than had been indicated by the attitude surveys, presumably because it is difficult to know if you really have been discriminated against.

While such research provides some quite striking findings and gets around the problem of reactivity by not alerting research participants to the fact that they are being observed, like the pseudo-patient study in Box 8.11, ethical concerns are sometimes raised, such as the use of deception. Moreover, the extent to which an observation schedule can be employed is inevitably limited because excessive use will blow the observer's cover. All that can usually be done is to engage in limited coding, in particular the nature of the effect of the intervention, as in the LaPiere (1934) and Daniel (1968) studies, or to include a limited amount of further observation, as in the Rosenhan (1973) research.

Table 8.1 Daniel's (1968) situation test: The case of accommodation

Reaction to request for accommodation	No
West Indian was told accommodation taken; both other applicants told it was vacant	38
West Indian was asked for higher rent than the others	4
West Indian and Hungarian were told accommodation let	2
West Indian and Hungarian were asked for higher rent	1
All applicants received the same information	15
TOTAL	60

Criticisms of structured observation

Although it is not extensively used in social research, structured observation has been quite controversial. Certain criticisms have been implied in some of the previous discussion of reliability and validity issues, as well as in connection with the issue of generalizability. However, certain other areas of criticism warrant further discussion.

- There is a risk of imposing a potentially inappropriate or irrelevant framework on the setting being observed. This point is similar to the problem of the closed question in questionnaires. This risk is especially great if the setting is one about which little is known. One solution is for the structured observation to be preceded by a period of unstructured observation, so that appropriate variables and categories can be specified.

- Because it concentrates upon directly observable behaviour, structured observation is rarely able to get at intentions behind behaviour. Sometimes, when intentions are of concern, they are imputed by observers. Thus, in the FIAC scheme (see Box 8.6), the category 'teacher praises or encourages' means imputing a motive to something that the teacher says. In the ORACLE research, the observers had to interpret whether a child gazing out of the window was working or not (Galton *et al.* 1980; Delamont and Hamilton 1984). Essentially, the problem is that structured observation does not readily allow the observer to get a grasp of the meaning of behaviour.

- There is a tendency for structured observation to generate lots of bits of data. The problem here can be one of trying to piece them together to produce an overall picture, or one of trying to find general themes that link the fragments of data together. It becomes difficult, in other words, to see a bigger picture that lies behind the segments of behaviour that structured observation typically uncovers. It has been suggested, for example, that the tendency for structured observation studies of managers at work to find little evidence of planning in their everyday work (e.g. Mintzberg 1973) is due to

the tendency for the method to fragment a manager's activities into discrete parts. As a result, something like planning, which may be an element in many managerial activities, becomes obscured from view (Snyder and Glueck 1980).

- It is often suggested that structured observation neglects the context within which behaviour takes place. Delamont and Hamilton (1984), for example, note in connection with the ORACLE research that it was found that teachers' styles were related to their ages. However, they argue that such a finding can really be understood only 'if data are gathered on teacher careers and life histories of a kind eschewed by ORACLE' (1984: 9). Of course, were such data collected, this criticism would have little weight, but the tendency of structured observation researchers to concentrate on overt behaviour tends to engender this kind of criticism.

On the other hand . . .

It is clear from the previous section that there are undeniable limitations to structured observation. However, it also has to be remembered that, when overt behaviour is the focus of analysis and perhaps issues of meaning are less salient, structured observation is almost certainly more accurate and effective than getting people to report on their behaviour though questionnaires. It may also be that structured observation is a method that works best when accompanied by other methods. Since it can rarely provide reasons for observed patterns of behaviour, if it is accompanied by another method that can probe reasons, it is of greater utility. Delamont (1976) in her research in a school found FIAC to be useful as a means of exploring differences in teaching style between teachers. However, she was able to get at some of the reasons for the quantitative differences that she discerned only because she had carried out some participant observation and semi-structured interviewing (two of the main methods of qualitative research) in various school classes. For example, she compared two Latin teachers who were similar in certain respects but differed in terms of 'the proportion of questioning to lecturing in their speech' (Delamont 1976: 108). These differences in teaching style reflected contrasting views about teaching and differences in personal demeanour.

In laboratory experiments in fields like social psychology, observation with varying degrees of structure is quite commonplace, but in social research structured observation has not been frequently used. Perhaps one major reason is that, although interviews and questionnaires are limited in terms of their capacity to tap behaviour accurately, as noted above, they do offer the opportunity to reveal information about both behaviour *and* attitudes and social backgrounds. In other words, they are more flexible and offer the prospect of being able to uncover a variety of correlates of behaviour (albeit reported behaviour), such as social background factors. They can also ask questions about attitudes and investigate explanations that people proffer for their behaviour. As a result, researchers using questionnaires are able to gain information about some factors that may lie behind the patterns of behaviour they uncover. Also, not all forms of behaviour are liable to be accessible to structured observation and it is likely that social survey research or researcher-driven diaries (see Box 6.4, p. 137) are the only likely means of gaining access to them. However, greater use of structured observation may result in greater facility with the method so that reliable measures of the kind developed in areas like education might emerge.

Key points

- Structured observation is an approach to the study of behaviour that is an alternative to survey-based measures.

- It comprises explicit rules for the recording of behaviour.

- Structured observation has tended to be used in relation to a rather narrow range of forms of behaviour, such as that occurring in schools.

- It shares with social survey research many common problems concerning reliability, validity, and generalizability.

- Reactive effects have to be taken into account but should not be exaggerated.

- Field stimulations represent a form of structured observation but suffer from difficulties concerning ethics.

- Problems with structured observation revolve around the difficulty of imputing meaning and ensuring that a relevant framework for recording behaviour is being employed.

Revision questions

Problems with social survey research on social behaviour

- What are the chief limitations of survey research with regard to the study of behaviour?

So why not observe behaviour?

- What are the chief characteristics of structured observation?
- To what extent does it provide a superior approach to the study of behaviour than questionnaires or structured interviews?

The observation schedule

- What is an observation schedule?
- 'An observation schedule is much like a self-completion questionnaire or structured interview except that it does not entail asking questions.' Discuss.
- Devise an observation schedule of your own for observing an area of social interaction in which you are regularly involved. Ask people with whom you normally interact in those situations how well they think it fits what goes on. Have you missed anything out?

Strategies for observing behaviour

- What are the main ways in which behaviour can be recorded in structured observation?

Sampling

- Identify some of the main sampling strategies in structured observation.

Issues of reliability and validity

- How far do considerations of reliability and validity in structured observation mirror those encountered in relation to the asking of questions in structured interviews and self-completion questionnaires.
- What is the reactive effect and why might it be important in relation to structured observation research?

Field stimulations as a form of structured observation

- What are field stimulations and what ethical concerns are posed by them?

Criticisms of structured observation

- 'The chief problem with structured observation is that it does not allow us access to the intentions that lie behind behaviour.' Discuss.
- How far do you agree with the view that structured observation works best when used in conjunction with other research methods?

9 Content analysis

Reader's guide

Content analysis is an approach to the analysis of documents and texts (which may be printed or visual) that seeks to quantify content in terms of predetermined categories and in a systematic and replicable manner. It is a very flexible method that can be applied to a variety of different media. In a sense, it is not a research method in that it is an approach to the analysis of documents and texts rather than a means of generating data. However, it is usually treated as a research method because of its distinctive approach to analysis. This chapter explores:

- the kinds of research question to which content analysis is suited;
- how to approach the sampling of documents to be analysed;
- what kinds of features of documents or texts are counted;
- how to go about *coding*, which is probably the central and most distinctive stage of doing a content analysis;
- the advantages and disadvantages of content analysis.

Introduction

Imagine that you are interested in the amount and nature of the interest shown by the mass media, such as newspapers, in a major news item such as AIDS or mad cow disease (BSE). You might ask such questions as:

- When did news items on this topic first begin to appear?
- Which newspapers were fastest in generating an interest in the topic?
- Which newspapers have shown the greatest interest in the topic?
- At what point did media interest begin to wane?
- Have journalists' stances on the topic changed, for example, in terms of pro- versus anti-science or pro- versus anti-government.

If you want to know the answers to research questions such as these, you are likely to need to use content analysis to answer them.

Probably the best-known definition of content analysis is as follows:

Content analysis is a research technique for the objective, systematic and quantitative description of the manifest content of communication.   (Berelson 1952: 18)

Another well-known and apparently similar definition is:

Content analysis is any technique for making inferences by objectively and systematically identifying specified characteristics of messages.   (Holsti 1969: 14)

It is striking that both of these definitions contain a reference to two qualities: objectivity and being systematic. The former quality means that, as with something like an observation schedule (Chapter 8), rules are clearly specified in advance for the assignment of the raw material (such as newspaper stories) to categories. Objectivity in this sense resides in the fact that there is transparency in the procedures for assigning the raw material to categories so that the analyst's personal biases intrude as little as possible in the process. The content analyst is simply applying the rules in question. The quality of being systematic means that the application of the rules is done in a consistent manner so that bias is again suppressed. As a result of these two qualities, anyone could employ the rules and (hopefully) come up with the same results. The process of analysis is one that means that the results are not an extension of the analyst and his or her personal biases. The rules in question may, of course, reflect the researcher's interests and concerns and therefore these might be a product of subjective bias, but the key point is that, once formulated, the rules can be (or should be capable of being) applied without the intrusion of bias.

Berelson's definition also makes reference to 'quantitative description'. Content analysis is firmly rooted in the quantitative research strategy in that the aim is to produce quantitative accounts of the raw material in terms of the categories specified by the rules. The feature of quantification adds to the general sense of the systematic and objective application of neutral rules, so that it becomes possible to say with some certainty and in a systematic way that, for example, during a certain period in which it was potentially at the forefront of media attention, *The Times* and other broadsheet newspapers carried far more coverage of AIDS/HIV than tabloid news papers, with the interesting exception of the *Sun* (Beharrell 1993).

Two other elements in Berelson's definition are striking especially when juxtaposed against Holsti's. First, Berelson refers to 'manifest content'. This means that content analysis is concerned with uncovering the apparent content of the item in question: what it is clearly about. Holsti makes no such reference, alluding only to 'specified characteristics'. The latter essentially opens the door to conducting an analysis in terms of what we might term 'latent content'—that is, with meanings that lie beneath the superficial indicators of content. Uncovering such latent content means interpreting meanings that lie beneath the surface, such as whether the impression is given that the author construes the AIDS/HIV issue as one solely of concern in relation to the gay community and its sexual practices or as having a broader set of implications that would include heterosexuals. A related distinction is sometimes made between an emphasis on the text (in particular, counting certain words) and an emphasis on themes within the text, which entails searching for certain ideas within the text (Beardsworth 1980).

A second element in Berelson's definition not found in Holsti's is the reference to 'communication'. Berelson's (1952) book was concerned with communication research, a field that has been especially concerned with newspapers, television, and other mass media. Holsti refers somewhat more generally to 'messages', which raises the prospect of a quite wide applicability of content analysis beyond the specific boundaries of the mass media and mass communications. Content analysis becomes applicable to many different forms of unstructured information, such as transcripts of semi- and unstructured interviews (e.g. Bryman, Stephens, and A Campo 1996) and even qualitative case studies of organizations (e.g. Hodson 1996). Nor is it necessary for the medium being analysed to be in a printed form. Research has been conducted on:

- the visual images (as well as the text) of women's and men's magazines to examine the degree to which messages about bodily appearance are gendered (Malkin *et al.* 1999);
- gender roles in animated cartoons (Thompson and Zerbinos 1995);
- radio and television news programmes (see Box 9.2 for an example).

However, there is little doubt that the main use of content analysis has been in the examination of printed texts and documents and of mass media items in particular. In this regard, content analysis is one of a number of approaches to the examination of texts that have been developed over the years (see Box 9.1).

What are the research questions?

As with most quantitative research, it is necessary to specify the research questions precisely, as these will guide both the selection of the media to be content analysed and the coding schedule. If the research questions are not clearly articulated, there is a risk that inappropriate media will be analysed or that the coding schedule will miss out key dimensions. Most content analysis is likely to entail several research questions. The research referred to in Box 9.2 was concerned with 'the reporting of social science research in the British mass media'. In itself this is not very specific and hardly directs you to a clear specification of the media to be examined or the development of a coding schedule. However, like most researchers, Fenton *et al.* (1998) had certain specific research questions in mind, such as:

- How much social science research is reported?

> ## Box 9.1 :◯: *What is content analysis?*
>
> - *Content analysis.* An approach to the analysis of documents and texts that seeks to quantify content in terms of predetermined categories and in a systematic and replicable manner.
>
> Content analysis can be usefully contrasted with two other approaches to the analysis of the content of communication:
>
> - *Semiotics.* The study/science of signs. An approach to the analysis of documents and other phenomena which emphasizes the importance of seeking out the deeper meaning of those phenomena. A semiotic approach is concerned to uncover the processes of meaning production and how signs are designed to have an effect upon actual and prospective consumers of those signs. This approach will be explored in Chapter 18.
>
> - *Ethnographic content analysis.* A term employed by Altheide (1996) to refer to an approach to documents that emphasizes the role of the investigator in the construction of the meaning of and in texts. It is sometimes also referred to as *qualitative content analysis*. As with most approaches that are described as ethnographic, there is an emphasis on allowing categories to emerge out of data and on recognizing the significance for understanding meaning in the context in which an item being analysed (and the categories derived from it) appeared. This approach will be explored in Chapter 18.
>
> When the term 'content analysis' is employed in this chapter, it will be referring to quantitative content analysis—that is, the first of the three forms of analysis referred to in this list and which is the kind of analysis to which Berelson (1952) and Holsti (1969) refer.

- Do certain mass media report a disproportionate amount of social science research?

- In what locations does social science research tend to get reported (for example, special features rather than general news items)?

- Do some topics receive greater attention than others?

- Are certain social science disciplines favoured by the mass media?

- Do the mass media tend to report research conducted by particular methods?

- What tends to prompt the reporting of social science research?

- Are researchers of a particular status (for example, professors) or from certain institutions (for example, prestigious universities) more likely to receive coverage than others?

Such questions seem to revolve around the questions of: *who* (gets reported); *what* (gets reported); *where* (does the issue get reported); *location* (of coverage within the items analysed); *how much* (gets reported); and *why* (does the issue get reported).

As with much content analysis, the researchers were just as interested in omissions in coverage as in what *does* get reported. For example, details about the status of the researcher(s) and about research methods were frequently omitted. Such omissions are in themselves potentially interesting, as they may reveal what is and is not important to reporters and their editors.

Another kind of issue that is frequently encountered in content analysis is one that was not a concern for the researchers looking at the reporting of social science research:

How far does the amount of coverage of the issue change over time?

This kind of research question or problem is particularly asked by researchers who are keen to note trends in coverage to demonstrate ebbs and flows in media interest. An example of this kind of research is a study by Miller and Reilly (1995) of British newspaper coverage of 'food scares'. They show how newspaper coverage of the salmonella in eggs scare was the focus of a massive amount of coverage of salmonella over a period of around twenty days in December 1988 following the statements of a British Government minister and the ensuing controversy. However, in the eleven months prior to that salmonella had rarely been in the news and in the

Box 9.2 An illustration of content analysis: Social science research in the British mass media

Fenton *et al.* (1998) conducted a study using content analysis of the amount and nature of the reporting of social science research in the British mass media. A sample of eighty-one days of media coverage between 26 May 1994 and 31 March 1995 was taken. The authors state that: 'Any media item that mentioned original research conducted by a social scientist or social scientific institution, whether domestic or foreign, was coded, along with any times in which a social scientist (as identified by the item) commented on social issues' (Fenton *et al.* 1998: 24). The media monitored comprised:

- 12 national newspapers—6 broadsheet and 6 tabloid newspapers; five of the 12 newspapers were Sunday papers;
- 4 local newspapers—1 costed and 1 free newspaper from both Nottingham and Manchester;
- 5 magazines—2 weekly women's publications, 2 monthly women's publications and 1 monthly men's publication;
- 13 national and local television news programmes covering all four terrestrial television channels broadcasting at the time;
- 6 weekly investigative journalism/social reportage television programmes;
- 5 weekly/daily television talk shows/magazine programmes;
- any prime time *ad hoc* television programmes deemed relevant;

- national radio news on both Radio 4 and Radio 5 Live;
- 9 national Radio 4 investigative journalism/social reportage/studio talk shows and magazine programmes;
- local radio news in two regions: BBC Radio Nottingham and BBC GMR;
- local radio current affairs on BBC GMR Talkback.

The researchers uncovered 466 cases of research being reported. A further 126 news items were coded in which social scientists acted as pundits. The researchers included the cases of 'punditry' in many of their analyses, because the number of items in which social science research featured in news items was considerably smaller than they had envisaged.

Each news item was coded in terms of a number of features, such as:

- the source of the item (for example, which newspaper or television programme);
- the topic of the research;
- the social science discipline referred to in the news item;
- when no social science discipline was referred to, the 'inferred discipline';
- the professional status of the researcher;
- the main research method employed.

subsequent twelve months the amount of coverage was sharply lower than it had been in December 1988. It petered out further over the next four years. However, this decline in coverage occurred in spite of public health evidence that the incidence of salmonella poisoning was increasing. Similarly, Beharrell (1993) has charted for the period 1988–1991 the changes in the amount of UK newspaper coverage of AIDS/HIV issues.

Selecting a sample

There are several phases in the selection of a sample for content analysis. Because it is a method that can be applied to many different kinds of document, the case of applying it to the mass media will be explored here. However, the basic principles have a broader relevance to a wide range of applications of content analysis.

Sampling media

Many studies of the mass media entail the specification of a research problem in the form of 'the representation of X in the mass media'. The 'X' may be trade unions, food scares, crime, drink driving, or social science research. But which mass media might one choose to focus upon? Will it be newspapers or television or radio or magazines, or whatever? And, if newspapers, will it be all newspapers or tabloids or broadsheets? And, if both tabloids and broadsheets, will it be all of them and will it include Sunday papers? If it will be a sample of newspapers, including Sunday ones, will these be national or local or both? And will it include free newspapers? And if newspapers, will all news items be candidates for analysis—for example, would feature articles and letters to the editor be included?

The research reported in Box 9.2 chose to cover a very wide variety of mass media, which is just as well since the authors were not able to locate a very large number of appropriate items (news items covering social science research). More typically, researchers will opt for one or possibly two of the mass media and may sample within that type or types. Beharrell's (1993) study of the reporting and representation of AIDS/HIV in the British mass media concentrated on all national and Sunday national newspapers from November 1988 to August 1991, as a result of which a sample of over 4,000 news items was created.

Sampling dates

Sometimes, the decision about dates is more or less dictated by the occurrence of a phenomenon. For example, the representation of NATO bombing raids in Serbia in 1999 will have been dictated by the inception of the raids. One could hardly examine the issue prior to the raids, though there may be an important consideration in deciding at what point the content analysis should cease, since discussions about the raids could continue for some time after the cessation of formal hostilities and may entail a reappraisal as a result of subsequent events.

With a research question that entails an ongoing general phenomenon, such as the representation of social science research or crime, the matter of dates is more open. The principles of probability sampling outlined in Chapter 4 can readily be adapted for sampling dates. For example, generating a systematic sample of dates by randomly selecting one day of the week and then selecting every nth day thereafter. Alternatively, Monday newspapers could provide the first set of newspapers for inclusion, followed by Tuesday the following week, Wednesday the week after, and so on.

One important factor is whether the focus will be on an issue that entails keeping track of representation as it happens, in which case the researcher may begin at any time and the key decision becomes when to stop, or whether it is necessary to go backwards in time to select media from one or more time periods in the past. For example, if Jagger (1998) had wanted to examine whether there had been a marked change in the ways in which men and women represent themselves in dating advertisements (see Box 9.3), she would obviously have needed to examine the columns of earlier years. She might have taken comparable samples from ten and twenty years earlier and perhaps even beyond. Warde (1997) was interested in changes in the representation of food (what should be eaten and how it should be eaten) in the food columns of women's magazines. He writes:

> ## Box 9.3 Finding love
>
> Jaqqer (1998) reports a content analysis of 1,094 dating advertisements in two Scottish newspapers and two newspapers with a general readership throughout Britain. The sample of advertisements was chosen over two four-week periods: March 1996 and May 1996. Three research questions drove the study.
>
> - What is 'the relative significance of resources and lifestyle choices as identity markers and desirable attributes for men and women' (1998: 799)?
>
> - How far do men and women vary in the degree to which they market themselves and describe their preferred (or ideal) partners in terms of the body?
>
> - How far are 'traditional stereotypes of masculinity and femininity . . . still in operation' (1998: 799)?
>
> Jagger particularly noted the tendency for a considerable percentage of the advertisers to market themselves in terms of their lifestyle choices, a tendency that was not substantially affected by gender. She also found that women were far more likely than men to stress the importance of economic and other resources for their preferred partners. There was also a somewhat greater propensity for women to market themselves in terms of physical appearance. However, men were just as likely to market themselves as 'slim', suggesting that certain norms of bodily shape may no longer be exclusive to one gender. Jagger also found that men frequently market themselves in 'feminine' terms and women in 'masculine' terms—a rather surprising finding. More generally, her results point to the significance of the body in identity construction in modern society for both men and women.

My primary sources were the five most widely read women's weekly magazines and the five most widely read monthly magazines in each of two twelve-month periods in 1967–8 and 1991–2. The magazines were sampled at the mid-point of the months of November, February, May and August in each year, in order to control for seasonal variation in the contents of food columns. . . . From the selected magazines I drew a systematic sample of recipes. This produced 114 recipes in the earlier year, 124 in the later period[,] which, given their random selection, should be sufficient to make some generalizations about recipes and any changes over time.   (Warde 1997: 44–5)

Three points stand out in this passage. First, there is the concern, which has just been alluded to, with being able to establish change by tracking back in time to earlier issues of the mass medium being analysed. Secondly, Warde wanted to ensure that the magazines were selected from four different points in each of the two twelve-month periods in order to ensure that seasonal factors did not overly influence the findings. If he had selected magazines just from November, there might have been a preoccupation with Christmas fare, while findings from magazines from a summer month might have been affected by the greater availability of certain foods, such as particular fruit. A decision was made to cover the four seasons in order to reduce the impact of such factors. Thirdly, there is a clear concern to enhance the representativeness of the recipes and therefore the generalizability of the findings by using a probability sampling method in that a systematic sample was arrived at (see Chapter 4).

What is to be counted?

Obviously, decisions about what should be counted in the course of a content analysis are bound to be profoundly affected by the nature of the research questions under consideration. Content analysis offers the prospect of different kinds of 'units of analysis' being considered. The following kinds of units of analysis are frequently encountered and can be used as guides to the kinds of objects that might be the focus of attention. However, what you would actually *want* or *need* to count will be significantly dictated by your research question.

Significant actors

Particularly in the context of mass media news reporting, the main figures in any news item and their characteristics are often important items to code. These considerations are likely to result in such persons as the following being recorded in the course of a content analysis.

- What kind of person has produced the item (e.g. general or specialist news reporter)?
- Who is or are the main focus of the item (e.g. politician, expert, government spokesperson, or representative of an organization)?
- Who provides alternative voices (e.g. politician, expert, government spokesperson, representative of an organization, or person in the street)?
- What was the context for the item (e.g. interview, release of a report, or an event such as an outbreak of hostilities or a minister's visit to a hospital)?

In the case of the content analysis of the reporting of social science research in the mass media (see Box 9.2), the significant actors included:

- the author of the item (e.g. type of correspondent);
- the type of item (e.g. in the case of the press, whether the research was reported in a general article, feature article, or some other context);
- the details of the researcher who was most prominent in the item (e.g. personal details, status, and whether he or she was acting as a researcher or pundit in the context of the item);
- what prompted the item (e.g. launch of a report, new research initiative, or a conference);
- the details of the main (if any) commentators on the research;
- any other actors.

The chief objective in recording such details is to map the main protagonists in news reporting in an area and to begin to reveal some of the mechanics involved in the production of information for public consumption.

Words

While it may seem a dull activity, the counting of the frequency with which certain words occur is sometimes undertaken in content analysis. However, the use of some words rather than others can often be of some significance, because it can reveal the predilection for sensationalizing certain events. For example, Dunning *et al.* (1988) have noted a tendency for the British press in the late 1960s to sensationalize the reporting of disturbances at football matches. The use of such emotive words as 'hooligan' and 'lout', along with inferences about 'war', are clearly significant. Alternative, less dramatic terms could have been used. Instead, the florid accounts of violence at football matches may have created the kind of 'moral panic' that Cohen (1973) has written about. While Dunning *et al.* did not conduct a content analysis of such news reporting, their analysis points to the potential significance of the choice of certain words and the neglect of others. Jagger's (1998) study of dating advertisements (see Box 9.3) counted such words as 'slim' and 'non-smoker' to uncover some of the characteristics deemed desirable.

A variation on the search for the occurrence of certain words is the examination of key words in the context of other words. Hansen (1995) provides an interesting example in a study of the reporting of BSE (mad cow disease) in the *Today* newspaper. He found that news items in which BSE appeared often included other prominent words, such as 'beef', 'food', 'meat', 'pounds [£]', 'Government', and 'ban'. The frequency with which such words accompanied 'mad', 'cow' and 'disease' led Hansen to infer that 'there is a clear indication ... that the coverage focuses on: (1) the danger which the disease poses for a key component of the British diet, (2) on costs, and (3) on what the government is doing or should be doing about it' (Hansen, 1995: 159). The examination of such key accompanying words can then be a springboard for a more thematic analysis (see next section). Hansen notes that the frequent occurrence of certain words suggests certain types of 'discourse'. For example, he identifies a discourse concerned with the *transmission* of BSE (such words as: infected, catch, spread, etc.) and a discourse emphasizing risk and threat (such words as: safe, risk, fears, danger, etc.). The growing availability of the printed news media in electronic form, such as CD-ROM, greatly facilitates the search for and counting of key words in this kind of context.

Subjects and themes

Frequently in a content analysis the researcher will want to code text in terms of certain subjects and themes. Essentially, what is being sought is a categorization of the phenomenon or phenomena of interest. For example, in the case of the content analysis of the reporting of social science research in the British mass media, Fenton *et al.* (1998) were concerned to classify the main social science discipline that formed the backcloth to the research being reported (Box 9.2). This entailed a classification into one of seven types: sociology, social policy, economics, psychology, business and management, political science, and interdisciplinary. Research drawing on other social science disciplines was not included in the study. Another topic was the methodology of the research being reported, which resulted in research being classified in terms of such categories as: survey/mail questionnaire; interview; ethnography; and, of course, content analysis.

However, while such categorizations are often relatively straightforward, when the process of coding is thematic, a more interpretative approach needs to be taken. At this point, the analyst is searching not just for manifest content but latent content as well. It becomes necessary to probe beneath the surface in order to ask deeper questions about what is happening. In the research on social science research in the mass media (see Box 9.2), each reported study was classified in terms of the subject area of the research (Fenton *et al.* 1998). Sixty-two categories were employed and were grouped into seven main areas: UK and overseas economy; UK and overseas government politics and policy; social integration and control; health; demographics; social analysis—general; and lifestyles. Another example of having to interpret derives from the researchers' examination of what they refer to as the 'inferred discipline' involved in a reported piece of research. This issue arose because, in many cases (nearly 60 per cent of all news items in which social science research was reported), no social science discipline was mentioned in the news report, so that it was necessary to infer which discipline was involved.

Dispositions

A further level of interpretation is likely to be entailed when the researcher seeks to demonstrate a disposition in the texts being analysed. For example, it may be that the researcher wants to establish whether journalists, in the reporting of an issue in the news media, are favourably inclined or hostile towards an aspect of it, such as their stances on the government's handling of a food scare crisis. In the case of the study by Fenton *et al.* (1998; see Box 9.2) of the reporting of social science research, each item was coded in terms of whether the editorial commentary on the research was positive, negative, or merely descriptive. In many cases, it was necessary to infer whether the editorial commentary was implicitly positive or negative if there were no manifest indications of such value positions. Such an analysis entails establishing whether a judgemental stance can be discerned in the items being coded and what the nature of the judgements is.

Another way in which dispositions may be revealed in content analysis is through the coding of ideologies, beliefs, or principles. Jagger (1998) coded dating advertisements in terms of whether gendered stereotypical categories of masculinity and femininity were employed when advertisers were describing themselves (see Box 9.3). She came up with the surprising finding that women were more likely than men to advertise themselves in terms of a masculine stereotype, whilst men were more likely to advertise themselves in terms of a feminine stereotype.

Coding

As much of the foregoing discussion has implied, coding is a crucial stage in the process of doing a content analysis. There are two main elements to a content analysis coding scheme: designing a coding schedule and designing a coding manual. To illustrate its use, imagine a student interested in crime reporting in a local newspaper. The student chooses to focus on the reporting of crime subject to court proceedings. To simplify the issue we will just have the following variables.

1. nature of the offence;
2. gender of perpetrator;
3. social class of perpetrator;
4. age of perpetrator;
5. gender of victim;
6. social class of victim;
7. age of victim;
8. depiction of victim;
9. position of news item.

Content analysts would normally be interested in a much larger number of variables than this, but a simple illustration like this can be helpful for getting across the operation of a coding schedule and a coding manual. Also, it is quite likely that the student would want to record the item so that the details of more than one offender and more than one victim are included. In other words, very often a crime will entail multiple perpetrators and/or victims, so that the details of each of the key figures (age, gender, occupation, depiction of victim) would need to be recorded. However, to keep the illustration simple, just one perpetrator and victim is assumed.

Coding schedule

The coding schedule is a form onto which all the data relating to an item being coded will be entered. Figure 9.1 provides an example of a coding schedule. The schedule is very much a simplification in order to facilitate the discussion of the principles of coding in content analysis and of the construction of a coding schedule in particular.

Each of the columns in Figure 9.1 is a dimension that is being coded. The column headings indicate the dimension to be coded. The rows with numbers are the column numbers. The blank cells on the coding form are the places in which codes are written in. One form would be used for each media item that was coded. The codes can then be transferred to a computer data file for analysis with a software package like SPSS (see Chapter 12).

Coding manual

On the face of it, the coding schedule in Figure 9.1 seems very bare and does not appear to provide much information about what is to be done or where. This is where the coding manual comes in. The coding manual is a statement of instructions to coders that also includes all the possible categories for each dimension being coded. It provides: a list of all the dimensions; the different categories subsumed under each dimension; the numbers (i.e. *codes*) that correspond to each category; and guidance on what each dimension is concerned with and any factors that should be taken into account in deciding how to allocate any particular code to each

Case number		Day		Month		Nature of offence I	Gender of perpetrator	Occupation of perpetrator	Age of perpetrator	Gender of victim	Occupation of victim	Age of victim	Dipiction of victim	Nature of offence II	Position of news item
1	2	3	4	5	6	7	8	9	10	11	12	13	14	15	16	17	18	19	20	21	22	23

Fig. 9.1 Coding schedule

Nature of offence I
1. Violence against the person
2. Sexual offences
3. Robbery
4. Burglary in a dwelling
5. Burglary other than in a dwelling
6. Theft from a person
7. Theft of pedal cycle
8. Theft from shops
9. Theft from vehicle
10. Theft of motor vehicle
11. Vehicle interference and tampering
12. Other theft and handling stolen goods
13. Fraud and forgery
14. Criminal damage
15. Drug offences
16. Other notifiable offences

Gender of perpetrator
1. Male
2. Female
3. Unknown

Occupation of perpetrator
1. I Higher grade professionals, administrators, and officials; managers in large establishments; large proprietors
2. II Lower-grade professionals, administrators, and officials; higher-grade technicians; managers in small business and industrial establishments; supervisors of nonmanual employees
3. IIIa Routine nonmanual employees in administration and commerce
4. IIIb Personal service workers
5. IVa Small proprietors, artisans, etc., with employees
6. IVb Small proprietors, artisans, etc., without employees

7. IVc Farmers and smallholders; self-employed fishermen
8. V Lower-grade technicians, supervisors of manual workers
9. VI Skilled manual workers
10. VIIa Semi-skilled and unskilled manual workers (not in agriculture)
11. VIIb Agricultural workers
12. Unemployed
13. Retired
14. Housewife
15. Other
16. Unknown

Age of perpetrator
Record age (0 if unknown)

Gender of victim
1. Male
2. Female
3. Unknown

Occupation of victim
Same as for occupation of perpetrator

Age of victim
Record age (0 if unknown)

Depiction of victim
1. Victim responsible for crime
2. Victim partly responsible for crime
3. Victim not at all responsible for crime
4. Not applicable

Nature of offence II (code if second offence mentioned in relation to the same incident; code 0 if no second offence)
Same as for Nature of offence I

Position of news item
1. Front page
2. Inside
3. Back page

Figure 9.2 Coding manual

dimension. Figure 9.2 provides the coding manual that might correspond to the coding schedule in Figure 9.1. A coding manual includes all the dimensions that would be employed in the coding process, indications of the guidance for coders, and the kinds of lists of categories that were created for each dimension.

The coding manual includes the occupation of both the perpetrator and the victim. It uses Goldthorpe's social class categorization and is based on the summary by Marshall *et al.* (1988: 22). To this scheme have been added three further categories that might be used in newspapers: unemployed; retired; and housewife. There is also a category of 'other'. The offences are categorized in terms of those used by the police in recording crimes notified to them according to Home Office rules. Much finer distinctions could be used, but, since the student may not be planning to examine a large sample of news items, broader categories might be preferable. They have the further advantage of being comparable to the Home Office data. Recorded crime statistics have been criticized for their reliability and validity (see Chapter 10) but the comparison between such data and the reporting of crime in local newspapers would be potentially illuminating.

The coding schedule and manual permit two offences to be recorded when an incident entails more than one offence. If there are more than two, the student has to make a judgement concerning the most significant offence. The student should also treat as the first offence the main one mentioned in the article.

The coding manual is crucial because it provides coders with complete listings of all categories for each dimension they are coding and guidance about how to interpret the dimensions. It is on the basis of these lists and guidance that a coding schedule of the kind presented in Figure 9.1 will be completed. Even if you are a lone researcher, such as a student conducting a content analysis for a dissertation or thesis, it is important to spend a lot of time providing yourself with instructions about how to code. While you may not face the problem of inter-coder reliability, the issue of intra-coder reliability is still significant for you (see below).

We might encounter a news item that presents a so-called road rage incident. Two male motorists—one described as a retired schoolteacher aged 68, the other a 26-year-old assembly-line worker at a local factory—get into an argument and the latter

punches the retired man, causing him to fall and hit his head on the ground, resulting in concussion. The item is reported on 24 November on page 4 of the newspaper. No other offence is involved in the incident—for example, the perpetrator does not deliberately harm the victim's vehicle as part of the road rage attack. The student uses a zero when there is no information to suggest a second offence.

The coding of the incident would then appear as in Figure 9.3 and the data would be entered into a computer program like SPSS as follows:

077 24 11 01 1 10 26 1 13 68 3 00 2

Each newspaper report of a crime would create a row of data with an identical structure.

Potential pitfalls in devising coding schemes

There are several potential dangers in devising a content analysis coding scheme and they are very similar to the kinds of consideration that are involved in the design of structured interview and structured observation schedules.

- *Discrete dimensions*. Make sure that your dimensions are entirely separate; in other words, there should be no conceptual or empirical overlap between them. For example, in the research presented in Box 9.2, it is necessary to be clear about the difference between discipline and topic of the research even though they have a similar ring.

- *Mutually exclusive categories*. Make sure that there is no overlap in the categories supplied for each dimension. If the categories are not mutually exclusive, coders will be unsure about how to code each item.

Case number		Day		Month		Nature of offence I		Gen- der of perpe- trator	Social class of perpetra- tor		Age of perpetra- tor		Gen- der of victim	Social class of victim		Age of victim		Dipic- tion of victim	Nature of offence II		Pos- ition of news item
0	7	7	2	4	1	1	0	1	1	1	0	2	6	1	1	3	6	8	3	0	0	2
1	2	3	4	5	6	7	8	9	10	11	12	13	14	15	16	17	18	19	20	21	22	23

Fig. 9.3 A completed coding schedule

- *Exhaustive.* For each dimension, all possible categories should be available to coders.

- *Clear instructions.* Coders should be clear about how to interpret what each dimension is about and what factors to take into account when assigning codes to each category. Sometimes, these will have to be very elaborate. Coders should have little or no discretion in how to allocate codes to units of analysis.

- *Be clear about the unit of analysis.* For example, in the study of social science research in the mass media (see Box 9.2), the authors found it necessary to operate with a clear distinction between the media item and the social science research being reported. Thus some of the data recorded were to do with the media item; other data recorded were to do with the research being referred to. The researchers content analysed up to three social science research profiles per media item, because often the media reporting of research referred to more than one investigation. Similarly, in the imaginary study of the media reporting of crime in the local press, more than one offence per media item can be recorded. You need to be clear about the distinction between the media item (for example, a newspaper article) and the topic being coded (an offence). In practice, a

researcher is interested in both but needs to keep the distinction in mind.

In order to be able to enhance the quality of a coding scheme, it is highly advisable to pilot early versions of the scheme. Piloting will help to identify difficulties in applying the coding scheme, such as uncertainty about which category to employ when considering a certain dimension or discovering that no code was available to cover a particular case. Piloting will also help to identify any evidence that one category of a dimension tends to subsume an extremely large percentage of items. If this occurs, it may be necessary to consider breaking that category down so that it allows greater discrimination between the items being analysed.

The reliability of coding is a further potential area of concern. Coding must be done in a consistent manner. As with structured observation, coding must be consistent between coders (*inter-coder reliability*) and each coder must be consistent over time (*intra-coder reliability*). An important part of piloting the coding scheme will be testing for consistency between coders and, if time permits, intra-coder reliability. The process of gauging reliability is more or less identical to that briefly covered in the context of structured observation in Box 8.9 (p. 170).

Advantages of content analysis

Content analysis has several advantages, which are outlined below.

- Content analysis is a very transparent research method. The coding scheme and the sampling procedures can be clearly set out so that replications and follow-up studies are feasible. It is this transparency that often causes content analysis to be referred to as an objective method of analysis.

- It can allow a certain amount of longitudinal analysis with relative ease. Several of the studies referred to above allow the researcher to track

changes in frequency over time (Beharrell 1993; Miller and Reilly 1995; Warde 1997). For example, Warde's (1997) research entailed an analysis of women's magazines over two different time periods. Similarly, changes in emphasis in crime reporting in newspapers over two very different periods can be examined.

- Content analysis is often referred to favourably as an *unobtrusive method*, a term devised by Webb *et al.* (1966) to refer to a method that does not entail participants in a study having to take the researcher into account (see Box 10.6, p. 209). It is therefore a *non-reactive method* (see Box 8.10, p. 171). However, this point has to be treated with a little caution. It is certainly the case that, when the focus of a content analysis is upon things such as newspaper articles or television programmes, there is no reactive effect. Newspaper articles are obviously not written in the knowledge that a content analysis may one day be carried out on them. On the other hand, if the content analysis is being conducted on documents such as interview transcripts or ethnographies (e.g. Hodson 1996), while the process of content analysis does not itself introduce a reactive effect, the documents may have at least partly been influenced by such an effect.

• It is a highly flexible method. It can be applied to a wide variety of different kinds of unstructured information. While content analysis is primarily associated with the analysis of mass media outputs, it has a much broader applicability than this. Box 9.4 presents an illustration of a rather unusual but none the less interesting application of content analysis.

• Content analysis can allow information to be generated about social groups that are difficult to gain access to. For example, most of our knowledge of the social backgrounds of elite groups, such as senior clergy, company directors, and top military personnel, derives from content analyses of such publications as *Who's Who* and *Burke's Peerage* (Bryman 1974).

Box 9.4 A content analysis of qualitative research on the workplace

Hodson reports the results of a content analysis of 'book-length ethnographic studies based on sustained periods of direct observation' (1996: 724). The idea of ethnography will be explored in detail in Chapter 14. As a method, ethnography entails a long period of participant observation in order to understand the culture of a social group. Hodson's content analysis concentrated on ethnographic studies of workplaces that had been published in book form (that is, published articles were excluded because they rarely included sufficient detail). Thousands of case studies were assessed for possible inclusion in the sample, but in the end 86 ethnographies were selected, which meant that 106 cases were analysed (several published ethnographies were of more than one case). The sample was made up of studies from different countries and included some well-known British ones (Beynon 1975; Nichols and Beynon 1977; Pollert 1981; Cavendish 1982). Each case was coded in terms of one of five types of workplace organization (craft, direct supervision, assembly line, bureaucratic, and worker participation). This was the independent variable. Various dependent variables and 'control' variables (variables deemed to have an impact on the relationships between independent and dependent variables) were also coded. Here are two of the variables and their codes:

Job satisfaction
1 = very low; 2 = moderately low; 3 = average; 4 = high; 5 = very high

Autonomy
1 = none (the workers' tasks are completely determined by others, by machinery or by organizational rules); 2 = little (workers occasionally have the chance to select among procedures or priorities); 3 = average (regular opportunities to select procedures or set priorities within definite limits); 4 = high (significant latitude in determining procedures and setting priorities); 5 = very high (significant interpretation is needed to reach broadly specified goals). (Hodson 1996: 728)

Hodson's findings suggest that some pessimistic accounts of worker participation schemes (for example, that they do not genuinely permit participation and do not necessarily have a beneficial impact on the worker) are incomplete. A more detailed treatment of this research can be found in Hodson (1999).

Disadvantages of content analysis

Like all research techniques, content analysis suffers from certain limitations, which are described below.

- A content analysis can only be as good as the documents on which the practitioner works. J. Scott (1990) recommends assessing documents in terms of such criteria as: authenticity (that the document is what it purports to be); credibility (whether there are grounds for thinking that the contents of the document have been or are distorted in some way); and representativeness (whether the documents examined are representative of all possible relevant documents, as if certain kinds of document are unavailable or no longer exist generalizability will be jeopardized). These kinds of consideration will be especially important to bear in mind when a content analysis is being conducted on documents like letters. These issues will be explored in further detail in Chapter 18.

- It is almost impossible to devise coding manuals that do not entail some interpretation on the part of coders. Coders must draw upon their everyday knowledge as participants in a common culture in order to be able to code the material with which they are confronted (Cicourel 1964; Garfinkel 1967). To the extent that this occurs, it is questionable whether it is justifiable to assume a correspondence of interpretation between the persons responsible for producing the documents being analysed and the coders (Beardsworth 1980).

- Particular problems are likely to arise when the aim is to impute latent rather than manifest content. In searching for traditional markers of masculinity and femininity (Box 9.3) or inferring a social science discipline (Box 9.4), the potential for invalid inference being made is magnified.

- It is difficult to ascertain the answers to 'why?' questions through content analysis. For example, Jagger found that 'the body of their partner, its attractiveness, shape and size, was of less importance to advertisers when in the buying mode

[advertising for a partner]' (1998: 807) than when in the selling mode (marketing oneself) (see Box 9.3). Why? And finding that this was true of both men and women is, as Jagger suggests, even more surprising. But again, why? We can speculate, but our suggested answers can usually only be speculations. Similarly, Fenton *et al.* (1998) found that sociology was only the fourth most common discipline to be referred to when social science research was being reported (see Box 9.2). However, Fenton *et al.* also inferred subject disciplines when they were not referred to explicitly by journalists. Sociology was by far the most frequent *inferred* discipline. Again, while this is an interesting finding, the reasons for it can only be speculated about (Fenton *et al.* 1998). Sometimes, users of content analysis have been able to shed some light on 'why?' questions raised by their investigations by conducting additional data collection exercises. Such exercises might include qualitative content analysis (e.g. Glasgow University Media Group 1976) and/or interviews with journalists and others (e.g. Fenton *et al.* 1998).

- Content analytic studies are sometimes accused of being atheoretical. It is easy to see why an atheoretical approach might arise. The emphasis placed in content analysis on measurement can easily and unwittingly result in an accent being placed on what is measurable rather than what is theoretically significant or important. However, content analysis is not necessarily atheoretical. Jagger (1998) placed her findings on dating advertisements in the context of current ideas about consumerism and the body. Fenton *et al.* (1998) conducted their content analysis within an overall approach that stressed the importance of studying the mass communication process from inception to reception and the importance of power and contestation within that process. Hodson's (1996) content analysis of workplace ethnographies was underpinned by theoretical ideas deriving from the work of influential writers such as Blauner (1964) and Edwards (1979) concerning development in modes of workplace organization and their impacts on workers' experiences.

Key points

- Content analysis is very much located within the quantitative research tradition of emphasizing measurement and the specification of clear rules that exhibit reliability.

- While traditionally associated with the analysis of mass media content, it is in fact a very flexible method that can be applied to a wide range of phenomena.

- It is crucial to be clear about your research questions in order to be certain about your units of analysis and what exactly is to be analysed.

- You also need to be clear about *what* is to be counted.

- The *coding schedule* and *coding manual* are crucial stages in the preparation for a content analysis.

- Content analysis becomes particularly controversial when it is used to seek out latent meaning and themes.

Revision questions

- To what kinds of documents and media can content analysis be applied?
- What is the difference between manifest and latent content? What are the implications of the distinction for content analysis?

What are the research questions?

- Why are precise research questions especially crucial in content analysis?
- With what general kinds of research questions is content analysis concerned?

Selecting a sample

- What special sampling issues does content analysis pose?

What is to be counted?

- What kinds of things might be counted in the course of doing a content analysis?
- To what extent do you need to infer latent content when you go beyond counting words?

Coding

- Why is coding so crucial in content analysis?
- What is the difference between a coding schedule and a coding manual?
- What potential pitfalls need to be guarded against when devising coding schedules and manuals?

Advantages of content analysis

- 'One of the most significant virtues of content analysis is its immense flexibility in that it can be applied to a wide variety of documents.' Discuss.

Disadvantages of content analysis

- To what extent does the need for coders to interpret meaning undermine content analysis?
- How far are content analysis studies atheoretical?

10 Secondary analysis and official statistics

Reader's guide

This chapter explores the possibilities associated with the analysis of data that have been collected by others. There are two main types discussed in this chapter:

- the secondary analysis of data collected by other researchers;
- the secondary analysis of official statistics—that is, statistics collected by government departments in the course of their work or specifically for statistical purposes.

This chapter explores:

- the advantages and disadvantages of carrying out secondary analysis of data collected by other researchers, particularly in view of many data sets being based on large, high-quality investigations that are invariably beyond the means of students;
- how to obtain such data sets;
- the potential of official statistics in terms of their reliability and validity;
- the growing recognition in recent years of the potential of official statistics after a period of neglect as a result of criticisms levelled at them;

- the notion that official statistics are a form of *unobtrusive method*—that is, a method that is not prone to a reaction on the part of those being studied to the fact that they are research participants.

Introduction

Many of the techniques we have covered so far—survey research by questionnaire or structured interview, structured observation, and content analysis—can be extremely time consuming and expensive to conduct. Students in particular may have neither the time nor the financial resources to conduct very extensive research. Yet we know that large amounts of quantitative data are collected by social scientists and others. Moreover, many organizations, most notably government departments and their various representatives, collect data that are presented in statistical form and that may be usable by social scientists. Would it not be a good idea to analyse such data rather than collect new data? It would have the additional advantage for the long-suffering public that they would not be bothered by interviewers and by questionnaires popping through their letter boxes.

This is where *secondary analysis* comes in. Secondary analysis offers this kind of opportunity. Box 10.1 contains a brief definition of secondary analysis and raises one or two basic points about what it involves. As the opening paragraph suggests, we will in this chapter be concerned with two kinds of issue:

- the secondary analysis of data that have been collected by other researchers;
- the secondary analysis of data that have been collected by various institutions in the course of their business.

One prominent form of such data is official statistics concerned with areas of social life such as crime, unemployment, and strikes. The use of such official statistics for social research has been controversial, and aspects of the ensuing debate will be addressed below.

Box 10.1 ⌇(☀)⌇ *What is secondary analysis?*

Secondary analysis is the analysis of data by researchers who will probably not have been involved in the collection of those data for purposes that in all likelihood were not envisaged by those responsible for the data collection. Secondary analysis may entail the analysis of either quantitative data (Dale *et al*. 1988) or qualitative data (Corti *et al*. 1995), but it is with the former that we will be concerned in this chapter. To some extent, it is difficult to know where primary and secondary analysis start and

finish. If a researcher is involved in the collection of survey interview data and analyses some of the data, resulting in some publications, but then some time later decides to rework the data, it is not entirely clear how far the latter is primary or secondary analysis. Typically, secondary analysis entails the analysis of data that others have collected, but, as this simple scenario suggests, this need not necessarily be the case.

Other researchers' data

There are several reasons why secondary analysis should be considered a serious alternative to collecting new data. These advantages of secondary analysis have been covered by Dale *et al.* (1988), from which I have borrowed most of the following observations. In considering the various advantages of secondary analysis, I have in mind the particular needs of the lone student conducting a small research project as an undergraduate or a more substantial piece of work as a postgraduate. However, this emphasis should definitely not be taken to imply that secondary analysis is really appropriate or relevant only to students. Quite the contrary: secondary analysis should be considered by all social research, and, indeed, the Economic and Social Research Council (ESRC) requires applicants for research grants who are proposing to collect new data to demonstrate that relevant data are not already available in the Data Archive (see below). My reason for emphasizing the prospects of secondary analysis for students is simply based on my personal experience that they tend to assume that any research they carry out has to entail the collection of primary data.

Advantages of secondary analysis

Secondary analysis offers numerous benefits to students carrying out a research project. These are outlined below.

- *Cost and time.* As noted at the outset, secondary analysis offers the prospect of having access to good quality data for a tiny fraction of the resources involved in carrying out a data collection exercise yourself. Numerous data sets are available from the Data Archive, which is housed at the University of Essex in Colchester. You do not even have to go to Colchester yourself to search for data. The Archive publishes a regular *Bulletin*, which provides information about new acquisitions. Back copies are readily available from most academic libraries. The Archive has a very good Internet website, which can be searched in a variety of ways, such as keywords (see below).

- *High quality data.* Many of the data sets that are employed most frequently for secondary analysis are of extremely high quality. By this I mean several things. First, the sampling procedures have been rigorous, in most cases resulting in samples that are as close to being representative as one is likely to achieve. While the organizations responsible for these studies suffer the same problems of survey non-response as anybody else, well-established procedures are usually in place for following up non-respondents and thereby keeping this problem to a minimum. Secondly, the samples are often national samples or at least cover a wide variety of regions of Great Britain or the UK. The degree of geographical spread and the sample size of such data sets are invariably attained only in research that attracts quite substantial resources. It is certainly inconceivable that student projects could even get close to the coverage that such data sets attain. Thirdly, many data sets have been generated by highly experienced researchers and, in the case of some of the large data sets, like the General Household Survey (GHS—see Box 10.2), the British Social Attitudes survey, and the British Household Panel Study (BHPS), the data have been gathered by social research organizations that have developed structures and control procedures to check on the quality of the emerging data.

- *Opportunity for longitudinal analysis.* Partly linked to the last point is the fact that secondary analysis can offer the opportunity for longitudinal research, which, as noted in Chapter 2, is rather rare in the social sciences because of the time and cost involved. Sometimes, as with the BHPS, a panel design has been employed and it is possible to chart trends and connections over time. Such data are sometimes analysed cross-sectionally, but there are obviously opportunities for longitudinal

> **Box 10.2 The labour force participation of women in mid-life: An example of secondary analysis**
>
> Ginn and Arber (1995) were interested in the reasons behind the declining labour force participation of married women in the fifteen or so years before they reach the pensionable age. In order to explore some of the factors behind this tendency, the General Household Surveys for 1988, 1989, and 1990 were 'pooled' to provide a sample of over 11,000 women aged 40–64 and living in private households in Britain. The authors were especially interested in the relative importance of women's personal characteristics (such as their age, health, and class) and the characteristics of their households (whether husband is employed and if so his income and class, number of children). Ginn and Arber found that, for women in their forties, household characteristics were more significant than personal ones, but in their fifties the latter were more important. One of the most significant 'household' variables for women of all mid-life ages was whether their partners were employed; if partners were not in paid employment, women also tended not to be in employment. While the analysis clearly demonstrates the role of certain variables, the authors also note the significance of not having information on certain issues: 'The correlation between partners' non-employment may be due to several factors, which cannot be distinguished with this data; husbands and wives may synchronise their retirement in order to avoid the wife being employed when the husband is at home, or their joint non-employment may reflect the local labour market conditions faced by couples' (Ginn and Arber 1995: 90).

analysis as well. Also, with data sets such as the GHS and the British Social Attitudes survey, where similar data are collected over time, usually because certain interview questions are recycled each year, trends (such as shifting opinions or changes in behaviour) can be identified over time. With such data sets, respondents differ from year to year, so that causal inferences over time cannot be readily established, but nonetheless it is still possible to gauge trends. See Box 10.3 for an example of the creative use of secondary data for a longitudinal analysis.

- *Subgroup analysis*. When large samples are the source of data (as in the GHS and BHPS), there is the opportunity to study what can often be quite sizeable subgroups. Very often, in order to study specialized categories of individuals, small localized studies are the only feasible way forward because of costs. Large data sets can frequently yield quite large nationally representative samples. For example, Arber and Gilbert (1989) used the 1980 GHS to isolate a sample of over 4,500 elderly people living in private households. In 1980, respondents aged 65 and over were asked various questions about their ability to perform certain tasks. This information was used to com-

pile a disability index. Levels of disability could then be related to patterns of caring for the elderly. As Arber and Gilbert observe: 'The large sample size, high response rate (82 per cent) and representative nature of the sample size make the GHS a valuable data source to complement, extend and systematically test findings and theoretical ideas derived from small, qualitative and localised studies' (Arber and Gilbert 1989: 75). While the data did not address the elderly in institutional care, it nonetheless provides a valuable source of high-quality data on the elderly. It is easy to see how a wide range of different subgroups could be identified for similar kinds of analysis. Box 10.2 provides a further example of subgroup analysis based on the GHS (married women over 40).

- *Opportunity for cross-cultural analysis*. Cross-cultural research has considerable appeal at a time when social scientists are more attuned to the processes associated with globalization and to cultural differences. It is easy to forget that many findings should not be taken to apply to countries other than that in which the research was conducted. However, cross-cultural research presents barriers to the social scientist. There are obvious barriers to do with the cost and practical difficulties of doing research in a different country, especially when language and cultural differences are likely to be significant. The secondary analysis of comparable data from two or more countries provides one possible model for conducting cross-cultural research. In order for a cross-cultural analysis to be conducted, some coordination is necessary so that the questions asked are comparable. The research on religiosity described in Boxes 1.5 and 3.4 (pp. 9, 68) by Kelley and De Graaf (1997) provides an example of such coordination. The authors describe the process as follows:

Data are from the 1991 'Religion' module of the International Social Survey Programme (ISSP), an international consortium composed primarily of academic survey organizations . . . Each year, the ISSP creates a module containing exactly the same questions, answer categories, and sequencing for all countries surveyed. . . . The samples are all large, representative national samples of adults. The most common procedure is to hold face-to-face interviews with a stratified random sample . . . followed by a leave-behind self-completion questionnaire containing the ISSP module . . .   (Kelley and De Graaf 1997: 642)

Kelley and De Graaf's results were based upon a secondary analysis of the data from the fifteen nations involved in the research.

- *More time for data analysis.* Precisely because data collection is time consuming, the analysis of data is often squeezed. It is easy to perceive the data collection as the difficult phase and to take the view that the analysis of data is relatively straightforward. This is not the case. Working out what to make of your data is no easy matter and requires considerable thought and often a preparedness to consider learning about unfamiliar techniques of data analysis. While secondary analysis invariably entails a lot of data management—partly so that you can get to know the data and partly so that you can get it into a form that you need (see below)—and this phase should not be underestimated—the fact that you are freed from having to collect fresh data means that your approach to the analysis of data can be more

> **Box 10.3 Health and the labour market: an example of secondary analysis**
>
> In Box 2.13 (p. 42), the Health and Lifestyle Survey (HALS) was used as an illustration. The original research was conducted in 1984–5 and, in 1991–2, 5,352 of those who were still alive were re-interviewed. This second wave of data collection means that the two sets of data can be analysed as a panel study (see Chapter 2). Bellaby and Bellaby (1999) conducted a secondary analysis of these two sets of data to shed light on debates in recent years concerning the effects of unemployment on health. The authors write that the survey 'has not, to our knowledge, so far been used for the purpose to which we are putting it' (1999: 467). The authors' findings suggest that '*high levels* of unemployment exert an adverse effect on the relative chances of poor health, whether subjective or objective, across a national population of working age' (Bellaby and Bellaby 1999: 479).

considered than perhaps it might otherwise have been.

- *Reanalysis may offer new interpretations.* It is easy to take the view that, once a set of data has been analysed, the data have in some sense been drained of further insight. What, in other words, could possibly be gained by going over the same data that someone else has analysed? In fact, data can be analysed in so many different ways that it is very unusual for the range of possible analyses to be exhausted. Several possibilities can be envisaged. A secondary analyst may decide to consider the impact of a certain variable on the relationships between variables of interest. Such a possibility may not have been envisaged by the initial researchers. Secondly, the arrival of new theoretical ideas may suggest analyses that could not have been conceived of by the original researchers. In other words, the arrival of such new theoretical directions may prompt a reconsideration of the relevance of the data. Thirdly, an alternative method of quantitative data analysis may be employed and offer the prospect of a rather different interpretation of the data. Fourthly (and related to the last point), new methods of quantitative data analysis are continuously emerging. Disciplines such as statistics and econometrics are continually developing new techniques of analysis, whilst some techniques are developed within the social sciences themselves. As awareness of such techniques spreads, and their potential relevance is recognized, researchers become interested in applying them to new data sets.

- *The wider obligations of the social researcher.* For all types of social research, research participants give up some of their time, usually for no reward. It is not unreasonable that the public should expect that the data that they participate in generating should be mined to its fullest extent. However, much social research is chronically under-analysed. Primary researchers may feel they want to analyse only data relating to central research questions or lose interest as a new set of research questions interpose themselves into their imagination. Making data available for secondary analysis enhances the possibility that fuller use will be made of data.

Limitations of secondary analysis

The foregoing list of benefits of secondary analysis sounds almost too good to be true. In fact, there are not very many limitations but the following warrant some attention.

- *Lack of familiarity with data.* When you collect your own data, when the data set is generated, it is hardly surprising that you are very familiar with the structure and contours of your data. However, with data collected by others, a period of familiarization is necessary. You have to get to grips with the range of variables, the ways in which the variables have been coded, and various aspects of the organization of the data. The period of familiarization can be quite substantial with large complex data sets and should not be underestimated.

- *Complexity of the data.* Some of the best-known data sets that are employed for secondary analysis, such as the GHS, are very large in the sense of having large numbers of both respondents and variables. Sometimes, the sheer volume of data can present problems with the management of the information at hand, and, again, a period of acclimatization may be required. Also, some of the most prominent data sets that have been employed for secondary analysis are known as *hierarchical* data sets, such as the GHS and the BHPS. The difficulty here is that the data are collected and presented at the level of both the household and the individual, as well as other levels. The secondary analyst must decide which level of analysis is going to be employed. If the decision is to analyse individual-level data, the individual-level data must then be extracted from the data set. Different data will apply to each level. Thus, at the household level, the GHS provides data on such variables as number of cars and consumer durables, while, at the individual level, data on income and employment can be found. Dale (1987) was interested in life cycle stages and employed household level data from the 1979 GHS to develop a typology of life cycle stages, which included fourteen categories, and various correlates of the various categories, such as net disposable household income.

- *No control over data quality.* The point has been made on several occasions that secondary analysis offers the opportunity for students and others to examine data of far higher quality than they could collect themselves. However, this point applies mainly to data sets such as the GHS (see Box 10.2), the BHPS (see Box 2.19, p. 46), the BCS (see Box 3.9, p. 73), the NCDS (see Box 2.20, p. 46), the Social Change in Economic Life Initiative (see Box 3.1, p. 64), and the British Social Attitudes survey (see Box 1.5, p. 9). While the quality of data should never be taken for granted, in the case of such data sets it is reasonably assured, though that is not to say that they will necessarily meet all of a prospective secondary analyst's needs, since data may not have been collected on an aspect of a topic that would have been of considerable interest. With other data sets, somewhat more caution may be necessary in connection with data quality, although certain fundamental checks on quality are usually made by archives in which data are deposited.

- *Absence of key variables.* Because secondary analysis entails the analysis of data collected by others for their own purposes, it may be that one or more key variables may not be present (see Box 10.2 for an example). You may, for example, want to examine whether a relationship between two variables holds even when one or more *other* variables are taken into account. Such an analysis is known as *multivariate analysis*, an area that will be touched on in the next chapter. The inability to examine the significance or otherwise of a theoretically important variable can be frustrating and can arise when, for example, a theoretical approach that has emerged since the collection of the data suggests its importance. Obviously, when researchers

collect primary data themselves, the prospect of this happening should be less pronounced.

Accessing the Data Archive

The Data Archive at the University of Essex is likely to be your main source of quantitative data for secondary analysis, although it may be that some of your lecturers will have data sets that they are prepared to put at your disposal. The Data Archive publishes a regular *Bulletin*, which includes information about many data sets that are deposited in it. To find out whether the Archive contains data on a topic in which you are interested, you could examine back copies of the *Bulletin*, which are likely to be in your institution's library. However, a better route is to examine the Archive's online catalogue, BIRON.

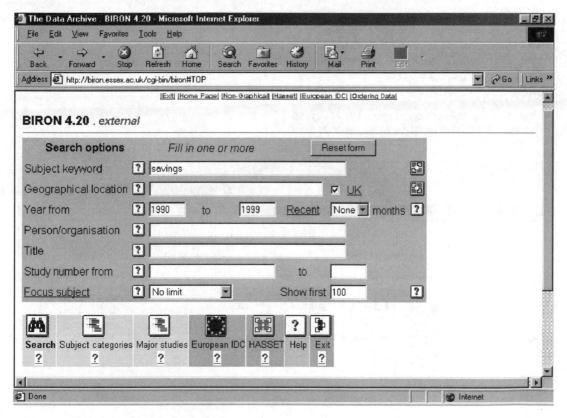

Plate 10.1 Searching the BIRON catalogue

Access to this catalogue can be obtained by going to the Archive's home page at:

http://biron.essex.ac.uk/cgi-bin/biron

This will bring up the BIRON catalogue (see Plate 10.1). I asked for any studies with the keyword 'savings' with the UK as the Geographical Location and between 1990 and 1999. I clicked on the search button (the one with a pair of binoculars). This resulted in 88 studies being found. I selected Project Number 3704, the Family and Working Lives Survey, 1994–1995 and requested a Complete Study Description (see Plate 10.2). The information provided gave a description of the study, along with a variety of particulars: sponsors; sampling details; method of data collection; main topics of the survey; and information about publications deriving from the study. It also informs you whether there are special conditions relating to access. With the one I

specified, I was told that there are special conditions and that further details are available from the Archive, but that the conditions normally entail signing an undertaking form. To order the study, I would need to go back to the home page and select **Ordering Data**. You will need to find out if there is an administrative charge for receiving the data, but it is likely that if you are a student at or a member of staff in a UK institution of higher education, there will be no charge. There is a charge for documentation. Information about charges and access can be found at the **Ordering Data** page.

Information about searching for qualitative data for the purpose of conducting a secondary analysis can be found in Chapter 19. Qualitative data can be searched for through Qualidata, which, like the Data Archive, is located at the University of Essex, but, unlike the Archive, is not in itself a repository of data.

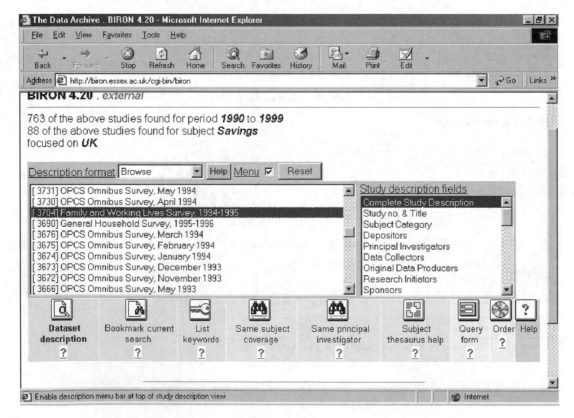

Plate 10.2 Choosing a study

Table 10.1 Large data sets suitable for secondary analysis

Title	Data set details	Topics covered
General Household Survey (GHS)	Annual interviews since 1971 with members aged over 16 in over 8,000 randomly sampled households.	Has tended to cover standard issues such as education and health that are asked each year, plus additional items that vary annually. Huge variety of questions relating to social behaviour and attitudes.
Family Expenditure Survey (FES)	Annual interviews since 1950s with members of around 7,000 households who keep diary records of expenditure and income over two-week period.	Family expenditure and income.
Labour Force Survey (LFS)	Biennial interviews, 1973–83, annual interviews, 1984–91, comprising a quarterly survey of around 15,000 addresses per quarter and an additional survey in March–May; since 1991, quarterly survey of around 60,000 addresses.	Covers hours worked, job search methods, training, and personal details, such as nationality and gender.
British Household Panel Study (BHPS)	Began in 1991 and conducted annually by interview and questionnaire with a national representative sample of 10,264 individuals in 5,538 households.	Household organization; labour market behaviour; income and wealth; housing; health; and socio-economic values.
British Crime Survey (BCS)	Irregular survey of randomly selected sample of people questioned by structured interview. The 2000 BCS interviewed around 23,000 people. Began in 1982 and since then carried out in 1984, 1988, and 1992. Biennially since 1992.	Experience of and attitudes to crime; fear of crime; risk of crime.
National Food Survey (NFS)	First set up in 1940, entails interviews with representative sample of around 8,000 households. Diary records for one week.	Nature of household; food shopping; meals.
Workplace Employee Relations Survey (WERS)	This survey has been carried out in 1980, 1984, 1990, and 1998. Workplaces of ten or more employees are sampled, and interviews carried out with managers, worker representatives, and employees.	Wide range of areas covered, including: pay determination; recruitment and training; equal opportunities; workplace change; work attitudes; management organization; and employee representation.
British Social Attitudes survey	More or less annual survey since 1983 of representative sample aged 18 and over by interview and questionnaire.	Covers wide range of areas of social attitudes and behaviour. Some areas are core ones asked annually; others are irregularly asked.
National Child Development Study (NCDS)	Irregular but ongoing study of all 17,000 children born in Great Britain in the week of 3–9 March 1958. Since 1981 comprises interview and questionnaire.	Areas covered include: physical and mental health; family; parenting; occupation and income; and housing and environment.
Expenditure and Food Survey (EFS)	A new survey, scheduled to begin in April 2001, that will combine and replace the FES and NFS.	Will address areas formerly covered by FES and NFS.
ONS Omnibus Survey	A regular commercial survey by interview since 1990 of just under 2,000 people.	Covers core each year of questions about respondents plus modules (asked for participating organizations) on topics that change annually concerning, e.g. food safety, eating behaviour, personal finance, sports participation.

A website that has been designed to increase the use of secondary analysis and that provides a variety of hyper-links to useful sites is:

http://tramss.data-archive.ac.uk

Table 10.1 lists several large data sets that are accessible to students and would repay further investigation in terms of their potential use in the context of research questions in which you might be interested. Further information about these data sets can be found via the BIRON catalogue and at the following site:

http://www.mimas.ac.uk/surveys

Official statistics

The use and analysis of official statistics for purposes of social research has been a very controversial area for many years. Agencies of the state, in the course of their business, are required to keep a running record of their areas of activity. When these records are aggregated, they form the official statistics in an area of activity. Thus, in Great Britain, the police compile data that form the crime rate (also known as 'notifiable crimes recorded by the police') and the Employment Service collects data that form the basis for the level of unemployment (also known as the 'claimant count'). These are just two, as it happens high-profile, sets of statistics that can be subsumed under the general category of 'official statistics'. Such statistics are frequently the cause of headlines in the mass media—for example, if there has been a sharp increase in the level of recorded crime or unemployment. But they would also seem to offer considerable potential for social researchers.

We could imagine such official statistics offering the social researcher certain advantages over some other forms of quantitative data, such as data based on surveys.

- The data have already been collected. Therefore, as with other kinds of secondary analysis of data (see above), considerable time and expense may be saved. Also, the data may not be based on samples, so that a complete picture can be obtained.

- Since the people who are the source of the data are not being asked questions that are part of a research project, the problem of *reactivity* will be much less pronounced than when data are collected by interview or questionnaire.

- There is the prospect of analysing the data both cross-sectionally and longitudinally. When analysing the data cross-sectionally, we could examine crime rates (and indeed the incidence of specific crimes) in terms of such standard variables as social class, income, ethnicity, age, gender, and region. Such analyses allow us to search for the factors that are associated with crime or unemployment. Also, we can analyse the data over time. Precisely because the data are compiled over many years, it is possible to chart trends over time and perhaps to relate these to wider social changes.

- There is the prospect as well of cross-cultural analysis, since the official statistics from different nation states can be compared for a specific area of activity. After all, a sociological classic of the stature of Durkheim's *Suicide* (Durkheim 1952) was the result of a comparative analysis of official statistics on suicide in several countries.

However, readers who recall Box 3.9 (p. 73) will already be on their guard. The official statistics concerned with an area of social life like crime can be very misleading, because they record only those individuals who are processed by the agencies that have the responsibility for compiling the statistics. Crime and other forms of deviance have been a particular focus of attention and concern among critics of the use of official statistics. Figure 10.1 illustrates

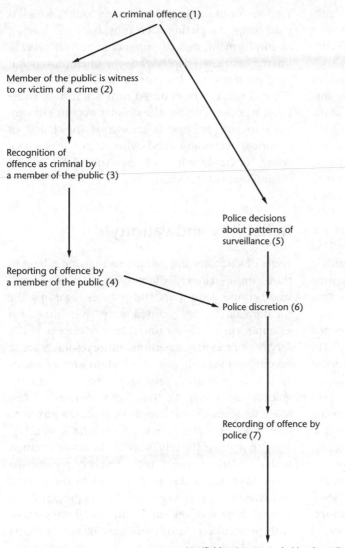

A criminal offence (1)

Member of the public is witness
to or victim of a crime (2)

Recognition of
offence as criminal by
a member of the public (3)

Police decisions
about patterns of
surveillance (5)

Reporting of offence by
a member of the public (4)

Police discretion (6)

Recording of offence by
police (7)

Notifiable crimes recorded by the police
'the crime rate' (8)

Fig. 10.1 The social construction of
crime statistics—eight steps

Source: adapted from a figure in Beardsworth
et al. (n.d.)

in connection with crime and the crime rate the kinds of factor that can lead to concern.

If we take a criminal offence as the starting point (step 1), we can consider the factors that might or might not result in its becoming part of the crime rate. An offence might become a candidate for inclusion in the crime rate as a result of either of two events (it might be that others can be envisaged but these two represent major possibilities). First, the crime may be seen by a member of the public or a member of the public may be a victim of a crime (step 2). However, a crime has to be recognized as such before it will be reported to the police (step 3). Even if it is recognized as a criminal offence, the member of the public (even if he or she is a victim) may choose not to bring the crime to the notice of the police. This means that, if a criminal act goes unnoticed, or is noticed but not recognized as criminal, or is noticed and recognized as criminal but not reported to the police, it will not enter the official statistics. Step 4 is the reporting of the crime to the police. Even then the crime may not be entered into the crime statistics, because the police have considerable discretion about whether to proceed with a conviction and may choose to let the person off with a warning (step 6). They may be influenced by such factors as the severity of the crime, the perpetrator's previous record, the perpetrator's demeanour or suggestions of contrition, or their volume of work at the time.

Alternatively, a crime may be observed by the police as a result of their patterns of surveillance, which is a product of decisions about how best to deploy police officers (step 5). Once again, the crime may not become part of the crime rate because of the operation of police discretion. Thereafter, once the police exercise discretion in such a way as to lead them to seek a prosecution (step 6), the offence is recorded (step 7) and it becomes a 'notifiable crime recorded by the police' and as such part of the crime rate (step 8).

What are the implications of this process for the crime rate and for criminal statistics generally? For one thing, it means that a substantial amount of crime undoubtedly goes unrecorded as a result of: not coming to the attention of members of the public; not being recognised as criminal; not being reported; decisions regarding police surveillance that may result in some crimes being given lower priority; and the operation of police discretion. This undercurrent of unrecorded crime is frequently referred to as 'the dark figure' (Coleman and Moynihan 1996). Nor can crime be regarded as alone in this connection. Suicide statistics almost certainly fail to record many potential cases for inclusion and may even include a small number that are not in fact suicides (as a result of problems of deciding whether the 'victim' was involved in an accident or intended to commit suicide). It is extremely difficult to determine whether someone is the victim of suicide when there is no suicide note. Moreover, those responsible for concluding whether a death is a suicide or not may come under considerable pressure not to record it as such, possibly because of feelings of potential stigma or because of religious taboos concerning suicide. To push the point even further, the deficiencies of official statistics do not just relate to areas of deviant behaviour such as crime and suicide. For example, the 'claimant count', which is used to gain a picture each month of the level of unemployment, may misrepresent the 'real' level of unemployment: people who are unemployed but who do not claim benefits or whose claim is disallowed will not be counted in the statistics, while those who form part of the claimant count but who work in part of what is known as the 'black' or 'informal' economy (and who therefore are not really unemployed) *will* be included in the unemployment statistics.

Reliability and validity

Issues of reliability and validity seem to loom large in these considerations. Reliability seems to be jeopardized because definitions and policies regarding the phenomena to be counted vary over time. For example, the UK Government Home Office or police service policies may mean that more resources are to be put into surveillance of a certain area of crime, such as drugs or drink-driving. Moreover, as part of a crackdown, it may be that police officers are less likely to operate their discretion in such a way as to result in perpetrators being let off with a warning. The problem for the reliability of the crime statistics is that variations over time in levels of a particular crime may not be due to variations in the level of transgression but to variations in the propensity to expend resources on surveillance and to proceed with prosecution. Also, there may be changes over time in the definitions of crime or in the propensity of victims to proceed with a complaint. Such changes will clearly affect the degree to which fluctuations in the rate of occurrence of certain crimes reflect 'real' fluctuations in the incidence of those crimes or other factors (that is, variations over time in surveillance, operation of discretion, definition, propensity to report, and other factors). A further factor that can impair the reliability of crime statistics is 'fiddling' by police officers (see Boxes 3.9, p. 73, and 10.4). To the extent that such factors operate, the reliability of the crime data will be adversely affected and, as a result, validity will be similarly impaired.

Box 10.4 Fiddling the crime figures

An article in *The Times* (Leake 1998) reported that there was growing evidence that senior police officers frequently massage the crime statistics for their forces. The author argued that many officers deliberately 'lose' crimes in order to make their detection rates look better. As a result, crime rates are often lower than they should be. The article cites the following methods of suppressing crimes:

- classifying multiple burglaries—for example, in a block of flats in one day—as a single incident;
- cataloguing multiple credit card or cheque card frauds as a single offence;

- excluding common assaults, when people are not seriously injured, from the figures for violent crime;
- excluding drug offences where people admit to offending but are only cautioned.

These methods of reducing the crime rate will adversely affect reliability, because it is not possible to compare the figures over different time periods because of variations over time in the propensity to massage the data. Validity will be similarly affected, in part because measurement validity presupposes reliability (see Chapter 3) and also because the figures cannot be regarded as providing a picture of the true level of crime.

Also, the problems with official statistics extend to the examination of the variables with which the crime rate is associated. For example, it might be assumed that, if an examination of regional differences demonstrates that the crime rate varies by the chief ethnic or social class composition of area, this implies that ethnic status and social class are themselves related to crime. There are two problems with drawing such an inference. First, there is an analytic difficulty known as *the ecological fallacy* (see Box 10.5). Secondly, even if we could ignore the problem of the ecological fallacy (which we cannot, of course), we would still be faced with an issue that is related to the matter of validity. Variations between ethnic groups or social classes may be a product of factors other than variations between ethnic groups and social classes in their propensity to commit crimes. Instead, the variations may be due to such factors as: variations in the likelihood of members of the public reporting a crime when the perpetrator is of one ethnic group or class rather than others; variations in the surveillance activities of the police so that areas with a high concentration of members of one ethnic group or class rather than others are more likely to be the focus of activity; variations between ethnic groups or social classes in the propensity of police officers to exercise discretion; and problems for the police of learning about and investigating certain

crimes that are themselves related to ethnicity or class (for example, white-collar crime). Similarly, as Douglas (1967) observes in connection with suicide statistics, it is quite likely that variations between ethnic and religious groups in suicide rates may be a product at least in part of variations in the predilection of the families of suicide victims to put pressure on official figures like coroners not to treat a death as a suicide.

Box 10.5 What is the ecological fallacy?

The ecological fallacy is the error of assuming that inferences about individuals can be made from findings relating to aggregate data. Coleman and Moynihan (1996) provide the example of the relationship between ethnicity and crime. They observe that findings showing a higher incidence of crime in regions with high concentrations of ethnic minorities have been used to imply that members of such minority groups are more likely to commit crimes. However, research on this issue in the 1960s suggested that in fact members of ethnic minority groups were less likely to offend. The fallacy can arise for several reasons—for example, it may not be the members of the minority groups who are responsible for the high levels of offending.

Condemning and resurrecting official statistics

In the 1960s, in particular, there was a torrent of criticism of various kinds of official statistics, especially those connected with crime and deviance. The various criticisms previously outlined were very much to the fore. In fact, so entrenched was the belief in many quarters that official statistics were of dubious value to social researchers that the view took root that they were virtually worthless. Instead, it was recommended that social researchers should turn their attention to the investigation of the organizational processes that lead to the various deficiencies identified by the various writers. In the words of the writers of one influential article, rates of crime and other forms of deviance 'can be viewed as indices of organizational processes rather than as indices of certain forms of behavior' (Kitsuse and Cicourel 1963: 137). The effect of this view was to consign official statistics to the sidelines of social research so that they became an object of research interest rather than a potential source of data, although research based on official statistics continued in certain quarters. It would also be wrong to think that the critique formulated by writers such as Kitsuse and Cicourel (1963) and Douglas (1967) was the sole reason for the neglect of official statistics during this period. The fact that official statistics, because they are a sideline for many state agencies, are invariably not tailored to the needs of social researchers can be considered a further limitation. In other words, it may be that the definitions of apparently similar or identical terms (such as unemployment or socio-economic class) employed by those responsible for compiling official statistics may not be commensurate with the definitions employed by social researchers.

An important article by Bulmer (1980) questioned the relative neglect of official statistics by British sociologists in particular and represented a turning point in the views of many researchers towards this source of data (Levitas and Guy 1996). For one thing, Bulmer argued that the critique of official statistics had largely revolved around the elabor-ation of criticisms surrounding statistics relating to crime and deviance. He observes that these are subject to special well-known problems and it would be wrong to generalize these problems to the full range of official statistics. Many official statistics may be flawed in certain respects, but the flaws are not necessarily as pronounced as those to do with crime and deviance. Moreover, the flaws in many of the official statistics not concerned with crime and deviance are probably no worse than the errors that occur in much measurement deriving from methods like social surveys based on questionnaires and structured interviews. Indeed, some forms of official statistics are probably very accurate by almost any set of criteria, such as statistics relating to births, marriages, and deaths.

Bulmer also argues that, so far as some of the key variables in social research are concerned, the distance between the definitions employed by the compilers of official statistics and those employed by social researchers is not as great as is sometimes supposed. However, he notes that the case of social class is somewhat different. The development of the Registrar General's classification of social class groupings seems to have taken little notice of the schemes devised by sociologists, such as the influential Hall–Jones and Hope–Goldthorpe approaches. However, Bulmer notes that the Registrar General's classification nonetheless helpfully brings out clear divergences of socio-economic position between the groupings it comprises and is frequently employed by social researchers to make precisely this point. Bulmer points to the fact that data deriving from official statistics that show pronounced social class differences in mortality are extremely important and of considerable significance to medical and other sociologists. The data are not without problems and detractors, but there is a considerable willingness to use the statistics. The same applies to Inland Revenue data based on estate duties that have been employed to examine wealth distribution.

A further criticism of the rejection of various forms of official statistics is that it seems to imply that quantitative data compiled by social researchers are somehow error free or at least superior. However, as we have seen in previous chapters, while social researchers do their best to reduce the amount of error in their measurement of key concepts (such as through the standardization of the asking of questions and the recording of answers in survey research), it is not the case that the various measures that are derived are free of error. All social measurement is prone to error; what is crucial is taking steps to keep that error to a minimum. Therefore, to reject official statistics because they contain errors is misleading if in fact all measurement in social research contains errors. The problem here is that some

---

Box 10.6 What are unobtrusive measures?

An unobtrusive measure is 'any method of observation that directly removes the observer from the set of interactions or events being studied' (Denzin 1970). Webb *et al*. (1966) distinguished four main types.

1. *Physical traces*. These are the 'signs left behind by a group' and include such things as graffiti and trash.

2. *Archive materials*. This category includes statistics collected by governmental and non-governmental organizations, diaries, the mass media, and historical records.

3. *Simple observation*. This refers to 'situations in which the observer has no control over the behavior or sign in question, and plays an unobserved, passive, and nonintrusive role in the research situation' (Webb *et al*. 1966: 112).

4. *Contrived observation*. This is the same as simple observation, but the observer either actively varies the setting in some way (but without jeopardizing the unobtrusive quality of the observation) or employs hidden hardware to record observations, such as video cameras.

Official statistics would be subsumed under Category 2, as would content analysis of media content of the kind described in Chapter 9. However, a content analysis like that described in Box 9.4 (p. 190) would not be considered an example of an unobtrusive measure, because the material being content analysed (workplace ethnographies) derives from studies in which the data were generated in an obtrusive fashion. Structured observation of the kind covered in Chapter 8 will typically not fall into Categories 3 and 4 because the observer is usually known to those being observed. The study by Rosenhan (1973) described in Box 8.11 (p. 172) is an illustration of contrived observation, because the pseudo-patients were not known to be researchers and they actively varied the situation by their own behaviour. The Daniel (1968) study described in Table 8.1 (p. 172) is also an example of contrived observation, because the 'actors' were not known to be researchers and by applying for rented accommodation they were actively varying the situation.

It is important to realise that Webb *et al*. were not intending that unobtrusive methods should supplant conventional methods. Instead, they argued that the problem they were identifying was the almost exclusive reliance upon methods that were likely to be affected by reactivity. Webb *et al*. argued for greater 'triangulation' (see Box 13.4, p. 274) in social research, whereby conventional (reactive) and unobtrusive (non-reactive) methods would be employed in conjunction. For example, they wrote that they were providing an inventory of unobtrusive methods 'because they demonstrate ways in which the investigator may shore up reactive infirmities of the interview and questionnaire' (Webb *et al*. 1966: 174).

It is worth noting that unobtrusive methods or measures encapsulate at least two kinds of ways of thinking about the process of capturing data. First, many so-called unobtrusive measures are in fact *sources* of data, such as graffiti, diaries, media articles, and official statistics. Such sources require analysis in order to be rendered interesting to a social scientific audience. Secondly, it includes *methods* of data collection, such as simple and contrived observation. While the data generated by such methods of data collection also require analysis, the data have to be produced by the methods. The data are not simply out there awaiting analysis in the way in which diaries or newspaper articles are (although, of course, a great deal of detective work is often necessary to unearth such sources). This means that neither of the terms 'unobtrusive methods' or 'unobtrusive measures' captures the variety of forms terribly well. A further disadvantage of the term 'unobtrusive measure' is that it seems to imply a connection to quantitative research alone, whereas certain approaches employed by qualitative researchers may qualify as unobtrusive methods.

official statistics are particularly prone to error, such as those relating to crime and deviance.

However, even here some caution is necessary. While data deriving from the British Crime Survey (BCS) may be employed to show that only a proportion of all crimes are notified to the police (see Box 3.9, p. 73), it would be wrong to conclude that the survey is an error-free yardstick. Coleman and Moynihan (1996) point to several measurement errors that are likely to afflict the BCS. For example, there is evidence to suggest that the BCS results in an over estimation of serious incidents through a process known as 'forward telescoping'. This means that serious incidents that are outside the recall period of twelve months (the period about which respondents are questioned) are erroneously considered to have occurred during that period. In other words, people have a tendency to believe that serious crimes of which they have been victims, but that occurred more than twelve months previously, actually occurred during the recall period. Coleman and Moynihan (1996) also point to errors arising from factors such as concealment in the course of interviewing. For example, there is some evidence to suggest that women are more likely to report sexual offences and domestic violence to the police (step 4 in Figure 10.1) than to a survey interviewer. In other words, dismissing official statistics on crime on the basis of survey evidence of the kind generated by the BCS is not without problems because it is not free of error itself.

It is clear that, following Bulmer's (1980) statement of the issue, the wholesale rejection of official statistics by many social researchers has been tempered. While there is widespread recognition and acknowledgement that problems remain with certain forms of official statistics (in particular those relating to crime and deviance), each set of statistics has to be evaluated for the purposes of social research on its own merits.

Official statistics as a form of unobtrusive method

One of the most compelling and frequently cited cases for the continued use of official statistics is that they can be considered a form of unobtrusive measure, although nowadays many writers prefer to use the term 'unobtrusive method' (Lee 2000). This term is derived from the notion of 'unobtrusive measure' coined by Webb *et al.* (1966). In a highly influential book, Webb *et al.* argued that social researchers are excessively reliant on measures of social phenomena deriving from methods of data collection that are

---

Box 10.7 Using *un*official statistics? The case of New York taxi cab drivers

Following his informal observation on the behaviour of New York taxi drivers (cabbies), Camerer (1997) was interested in testing two different theories about the relationship between the number of hours a cabby works and average hourly earnings. One theory—the law of supply—predicted that cabbies would want to work more when their average hourly earnings would be high (for example, during bad weather or on working days when more business people are around) rather than when they are low. The second theory—daily income targeting—suggests that cabbies set themselves an income target for the day and once that target is attained they stop work for the day. On good days (when hourly wages are higher) this theory simply means they will stop earlier. Camerer obtained taximeter readings from the New York Taxi and Limousine Commission. The data allowed 3,000 observations of cabbies' behaviour for 1988, 1990, and 1994. Tips are not recorded, so a guess had to be made about likely levels in this area. The data provided unequivocal support for the daily income targeting theory. However, further analysis revealed a difference between newer and more experienced drivers: the former behaved very much in line with income targeting theory; the more experienced drivers were much more varied and their overall levels of behaviour were closer to the law of supply theory, though not entirely in conformity with it. Overall, if cabbies obeyed the law of supply, their mean incomes would rise by around 15 per cent.

prone to *reactivity* (see Boxes 2.7 and 8.10 (pp. 37, 171), where this idea is introduced). This means that, whenever people know that they are participating in a study (which is invariably the case with methods of data collection such as structured interviewing, self-administered questionnaire, and structured observation), a component of their replies or behaviour is likely to be influenced by their knowledge that they are being investigated. In other words, their answers to questions or the behaviour they exhibit may be untypical.

Official statistics fit fairly squarely in the second of the four types of unobtrusive measures outlined in Box 10.6. As noted in the box, this second grouping covers a very wide range of sources of data which includes statistics generated by organizations that are not agencies of the state. This is a useful reminder that potentially interesting statistical data are frequently compiled by a wide range of organizations. An interesting use of such data is described in Box 10.7.

However, social researchers do not make a great deal of use of such data and it is not irrelevant that the author referred to in the research presented in Box 10.7 is an economist. There may be greater potential for searching out and mining statistical data produced by organizations that are relatively independent of the state.

Key points

- Secondary analysis of existing data offers the prospect of being able to explore research questions of interest to you without having to go through the process of collecting the data yourself.

- Very often, secondary analysis offers the opportunity of being able to employ high-quality data sets that are based on large reasonably representative samples.

- Secondary analysis presents few disadvantages.

- The analysis of official statistics may be thought of as a special form of secondary analysis but one that is more controversial because of the unease about the reliability and validity of certain types of official data, especially those relating to crime and deviance.

- The problems associated with official data relating to crime and deviance should not be generalized to all official statistics. Many forms of official statistics are much less prone to the kinds of errors that are detectable in relation to crime and deviance data, but there remains the possible problem of divergences of definition between compilers of such data and social researchers.

- Official statistics represent a form of unobtrusive method and enjoy certain advantages (especially lack of reactivity) because of that.

Revision questions

- What is secondary analysis?

Other researchers' data

- Outline the main advantages and limitations of secondary analysis of other researchers' data.
- Examine recent issues of one of the British sociology journals, like *Sociology*. Locate an article that uses secondary analysis. How well do the advantages and limitations you outlined fit with this article?
- Does the possibility of conducting a secondary analysis only apply to quantitative data produced by other researchers?

Official statistics

- Why have many social researchers been sceptical about the use of official statistics for research purposes?
- How justified is their scepticism?
- What reliability and validity issues do official statistics pose?
- What are unobtrusive methods or measures? What is the chief advantage of such methods?

11 Quantitative data analysis

Reader's guide

In this chapter, some of the basic, but nonetheless most frequently used, methods for analysing quantitative data analysis will be presented. In order to illustrate the use of the methods of data analysis, a small imaginary set of data based on attendance at a gym is used. It is the kind of small research project that would be feasible for most students doing undergraduate research projects for a dissertation or similar exercise.

The chapter explores:

- the importance of *not* leaving considerations of how you will analyse your quantitative data until after you have collected all your data; you should be aware of the ways in which you would like to analyse your data from the earliest stage of your research;
- the distinctions between the different kinds of variable that can be generated in quantitative research; knowing how to distinguish types of variables is crucial so that you appreciate which methods of analysis can be applied when you examine variables and relationships between them.
- methods for analysing a single variable at a time (*univariate analysis*);
- methods for analysing relationships between variables (*bivariate analysis*);
- the analysis of relationships between three variables (*multivariate analysis*).

Introduction

In this chapter, some very basic techniques for analysing quantitative data will be examined. In the next chapter, the ways in which these techniques can be implemented using sophisticated computer software (SPSS for Windows) will be introduced. The formulae that underpin the techniques to be discussed will not be presented, since the necessary calculations can easily be carried out by using SPSS for Windows. Two chapters cannot do justice to these topics and readers are advised to move as soon as possible on to books that provide more detailed and advanced treatments (e.g. Bryman and Cramer 2001).

Before beginning this exposition of techniques, I would like to give you advance warning of one of the biggest mistakes that people make about quantitative data analysis:

I don't have to concern myself with how I'm going to analyse my survey data until after I've collected my data.

I'll leave thinking about it till then, because it doesn't impinge on how I collect my data.

This is a common error that arises because quantitative data analysis looks like a distinct phase that occurs after the data have been collected (see for example Figure 3.1, p. 63, in which the analysis of quantitative data is depicted as a late step—number 9—in quantitative research). Quantitative data analysis is indeed something that occurs typically at a late stage in the overall process and is also a distinct stage.

However, that does not mean that you should not be considering how you will analyse your data until then. In fact, you should be fully aware of what techniques you will apply at a fairly early stage—for example, when you are designing your questionnaire, observation schedule, coding frame, or whatever. The two main reasons for this are as follows.

- You cannot apply just any technique to any

variable. Techniques have to be appropriately matched to the types of variables that you have created through your research. This means that you must be fully conversant with the ways in which different types of variable are classified.

- The size and nature of your sample are likely to impose limitations on the kinds of techniques you

can use (see the discussion in Chapter 4, p. 96, of the issue of 'Kind of analysis').

In other words, you need to be aware that decisions that you make at quite an early stage in the research process, such as the kinds of data you collect and the size of your sample, will have implications for the sorts of analysis that you will be able to conduct.

A small research project

The discussion of quantitative data analysis will be based upon an imaginary piece of research carried out by an undergraduate for a dissertation. The student in question is interested in the area of leisure in modern society and in particular, because of her own enthusiasm for leisure clubs and gyms, with the ways in which such venues are used and people's reasons for joining them. She has a hunch that they may be indicative of a 'civilizing process' and uses this theory as a framework for her findings (Rojek 1995: 50–6). The student is also interested in issues relating to gender and body image and suspects that men and women will differ in their reasons for going to a gym and the kinds of activities in which they engage in the gym.

She secures the agreement of a gym close to her home to contact a sample of its members by post. The gym has 1,200 members and she decides to take a simple random sample of 10 per cent of the membership (i.e. 120 members). She sends out postal questionnaires to members of the sample with a covering letter testifying to the gym's support of her research. One thing she wants to know is how much time people spend on each of the three main classes of activity in the gym: cardiovascular equipment, weights equipment, and exercises. She defines each of these carefully in the covering letter and asks members of the sample to keep a note of how long they spend on each of the three activities on their next visit. They are then requested to return the questionnaires to her in a pre-paid reply envelope. She ends up with a sample of 90 questionnaires—a response rate of 75 per cent.

Part of the questionnaire is presented in Box 11.1. The entire questionnaire runs to four pages. Twelve of the questions are provided in Box 11.1. Many of the questions (1, 3, 4, 5, 6, 7, 8, and 9) are pre-coded and the student simply has to circle the code to the far right of the question under the column 'code'. With the remainder of the questions, specific figures are requested and she simply transfers the relevant figure to the code column. An example of a questionnaire that has been completed by a respondent and coded by the student is presented in Box 11.2.

Missing data

The data for all 90 respondents are presented in Box 11.3. Each of the twelve questions is known for the time being as a variable number (var00001, etc.). Each variable number corresponds to the question number in Box 11.1 (i.e. var00001 is question 1, var00002 is question 2, etc.). An important issue arises in the management of data as to how to handle 'missing data'. Missing data arise when respondents fail to reply to a question—either by accident or because they do not want to answer the question. Thus, respondent 24 has failed to answer question 2, which is concerned with age. This has been coded as a zero (0) and it will be important to ensure that the computer software is notified of this fact, since it needs to be taken into account during the analysis. Also, question 9 has a large number of zeros, because many people did not answer it, because they have

Box 11.1 Part of a questionnaire used in research on use of a gym

Questionnaire

	Col	Code
1. Are you male or female (please tick)?		
Male _____ Female _____	1	1 2

2. How old are you?

	Col	Code
_____ years	2	

3. Which of the following best describes your *main* reason for going to the gym? (please tick *one* only)

	Col	Code
Relaxation _____	3	1
Maintain or improve fitness _____		2
Lose weight _____		3
Meet others _____		4
Build strength _____		5
Other (please specify) _____		6

4. When you go to the gym, how often do you use the cardiovascular equipment (jogger, step machine, bike, rower)? (please tick)

	Col	Code
Always _____	4	1
Usually _____		2
Rarely _____		3
Never _____		4

5. When you go to the gym, how often do you use the weights machines (including free weights)? (please tick)

	Col	Code
Always _____	5	1
Usually _____		2
Rarely _____		3
Never _____		4

6. How frequently do you usually go to the gym? (please tick)

	Col	Code
Every day _____	6	1
4–6 days a week _____		2
2 or 3 days a week _____		3
Once a week _____		4
2 or 3 times a month _____		5
Once a month _____		6
Less than once a month _____		7

7. Are you usually accompanied when you go to the gym or do you usually go on your own? (please tick *one* only)

	Col	Code
On my own _____	7	1
With a friend _____		2
With a partner/spouse _____		3

8. Do you have sources of regular exercise other than the gym?

   Yes ____   No ____   8   1 2

   *If you have answered **No** to this question, please proceed to question 10*

9. If you have replied **Yes** to question 9, please indicate the *main* source of regular exercise in the last six months from this list. (please tick *one* only)

Sport	_____	9	1
Cycling on the road	_____		2
Jogging	_____		3
Long walks	_____		4
Other (please specify)	_____		5

10. During your last visit to the gym, how many minutes did you spend on the cardiovascular equipment (jogger, step machine, bike, rower)?

    ____ minutes   10

11. During your last visit to the gym, how many minutes did you spend on the weights machines (including free weights)?

    ____ minutes   11

12. During your last visit to the gym, how many minutes did you spend on other activities (e.g. stretching exercises)?

    ____ minutes   12

been filtered out by the previous question (i.e. they do not have other sources of regular exercise). These have also been coded as zero to denote missing data, though strictly speaking their failure to reply is more indicative of the question not being applicable to them. Note also, that there are zeros for var00010, var00011, and var00012. However, these do *not* denote missing data but that the respondent spends zero minutes on the activity in question. Everyone has answered questions 10, 11, and 12, so there are in fact no missing data for these variables. If there had been missing data, it would be necessary to code missing data with a number that could not also be a true figure. For example, nobody has spent 99 minutes on these activities, so this might be an appropriate number as it is easy to remember and could not be read by the computer as anything other than missing data.

Types of variable

One of the things that might strike you when you look at the questions is that the kinds of information that you receive varies by question. Some of the questions call for answers in terms of real numbers: questions 2, 10, 11, and 12. Questions 1 and 8 yield either/or answers and are therefore in the form of dichotomies. The rest of the questions take the form of lists of categories, but there are differences

Box 11.2　A completed and processed questionnaire

Questionnaire

	Col	Code

1. Are you male or female (please tick)?

   Male ✓　　Female ____　　　　　　　　　　　1　　　　①2

2. How old are you?

   __21__ years　　　　　　　　　　　　　　　　　2　　　　21

3. Which of the following best describes your *main* reason for going to the gym?
   (please tick *one* only)

		Col	Code
Relaxation	____	3	1
Maintain or improve fitness	✓		②
Lose weight	____		3
Meet others	____		4
Build strength	____		5
Other (please specify)	____		6

4. When you go to the gym, how often do you use the cardiovascular equipment (jogger, step
   machine, bike, rower)? (please tick)

		Col	Code
Always	✓	4	①
Usually	____		2
Rarely	____		3
Never	____		4

5. When you go to the gym, how often do you use the weights machines (including free
   weights)? (please tick)

		Col	Code
Always	✓	5	①
Usually	____		2
Rarely	____		3
Never	____		4

6. How frequently do you usually go to the gym? (please tick)

		Col	Code
Every day	____	6	1
4–6 days a week	____		2
2 or 3 days a week	✓		③
Once a week	____		4
2 or 3 times a month	____		5
Once a month	____		6
Less than once a month	____		7

7. Are you usually accompanied when you go to the gym or do you usually go on your own?
   (please tick *one* only)

		Col	Code
On my own	✓	7	①
With a friend	____		2
With a partner/spouse	____		3

8. Do you have sources of regular exercise other than the gym?

Yes ___   No ✓   8   1 ②

*If you have answered **No** to this question, please proceed to question 10*

9. If you have replied **Yes** to question 9, please indicate the *main* source of regular exercise in the last six months from this list. (please tick *one* only)

◯

Sport	_____	9	1
Cycling on the road	_____		2
Jogging	_____		3
Long walks	_____		4
Other (please specify)	_____		5

10. During your last visit to the gym, how many minutes did you spend on the cardiovascular equipment (jogger, step machine, bike, rower)?

33 minutes   10   33

11. During your last visit to the gym, how many minutes did you spend on the weights machines (including free weights)?

17 minutes   11   17

12. During your last visit to the gym, how many minutes did you spend on other activities (e.g. stretching exercises)?

5 minutes   12   S

between these too. Some of the questions are in terms of answers that are rank ordered: questions 4, 5, and 6. Thus we can say in the case of question 6 that the category 'every day' implies greater frequency than '4–6 days a week', which in turn implies greater frequency than '2 or 3 days a week', and so on. However, in the case of questions 3, 7, and 9, the categories are *not* capable of being rank ordered. We cannot say in the case of question 3 that 'relaxation' is more of something than 'maintain or improve fitness' or 'lose weight'.

These considerations lead to a classification of the different types of variable that are generated in the course of research. The four main types are:

• *Interval/ratio variables.* These are variables where the distances between the categories are identical across the range of categories. In the case of variables var00010 to var00011, the distance between the categories is one minute. Thus, a person may spend 32 minutes on cardiovascular equipment, which is one minute more than someone who spends 31 minutes on this equipment. That difference is the same as the difference between someone who spends 8 minutes and another who spends 9 minutes on the equipment. This is the highest level of measurement and a very wide range of techniques of analysis can be applied to interval/ratio variables. There is, in fact, a distinction between interval and ratio variables, in that the latter are interval variables with a fixed zero point. However, since most ratio variables exhibit this quality in the social sciences (e.g. income, age), they are not being distinguished here.

• *Ordinal variables.* These are variables whose categories can be rank ordered (as in the case of interval/ratio variables) but the distances between the categories are not equal across the range. Thus, in the case of question 6, the difference between the category 'every day' and '4–6 days a week' is

Box 11.3 Gym survey data

var00001	var00002	var00003	var00004	var00005	var00006	var00007	var00008	var00009	var00010	var00011	var00012
1	21	2	1	1	3	1	2	0	33	17	5
2	44	1	3	1	4	3	1	2	10	23	10
2	19	3	1	2	2	1	1	1	27	18	12
2	27	3	2	1	2	1	2	0	30	17	3
1	57	2	1	3	2	3	1	4	22	0	15
2	27	3	1	1	3	1	1	3	34	17	0
1	39	5	2	1	5	1	1	5	17	48	10
2	36	3	1	2	2	2	1	1	25	18	7
1	37	2	1	1	3	1	2	0	34	15	0
2	51	2	2	2	4	3	2	0	16	18	11
1	24	5	2	1	3	1	1	1	0	42	16
2	29	2	1	2	3	1	2	0	34	22	12
1	20	5	1	1	2	1	2	0	22	31	7
1	22	2	1	3	4	2	1	3	37	14	12
2	46	3	1	1	5	2	2	0	26	9	4
2	41	3	1	2	2	3	1	4	22	7	10
1	25	5	1	1	3	1	1	1	21	29	4
2	46	3	1	2	4	2	1	4	18	8	11
1	30	3	1	1	5	1	2	0	23	9	6
1	25	5	2	1	3	1	1	1	23	19	0
2	24	2	1	1	3	2	1	2	20	7	6
2	39	1	2	3	5	1	2	0	17	0	9
1	44	3	1	1	3	2	1	2	22	8	5
1	0	1	2	2	4	2	1	4	15	10	4
2	18	3	1	2	3	1	2	1	18	7	10
1	41	3	1	1	3	1	2	0	34	10	4
2	38	2	1	2	5	3	1	2	24	14	10
1	25	2	1	1	2	1	2	0	48	22	7
1	41	5	2	1	3	1	1	2	17	27	0
2	30	3	1	1	2	2	2	0	32	13	10
2	29	3	1	3	2	1	2	0	31	0	7
2	42	1	2	2	4	2	1	4	17	14	6
1	31	2	1	1	2	1	2	0	49	21	2
2	25	3	1	1	2	3	2	0	30	17	15
1	46	3	1	1	3	1	1	3	32	10	5
1	24	5	2	1	4	1	1	2	0	36	11
2	34	3	1	1	3	2	1	4	27	14	12
2	50	2	1	2	2	3	2	0	28	8	6
1	28	5	1	1	3	2	1	1	26	22	8
2	30	3	1	1	2	1	1	4	21	9	12
1	27	2	1	1	2	1	1	3	64	15	8
2	27	2	1	2	4	2	1	4	22	10	7
1	36	5	1	1	3	2	2	0	21	24	0
2	43	3	1	1	4	1	2	0	25	13	8
1	34	2	1	1	3	2	1	1	45	15	6
2	27	3	1	1	2	1	1	4	33	10	9
2	38	2	1	3	4	2	2	0	23	0	16
1	28	2	1	1	3	3	1	2	38	13	5

1	44	5	1	1	2	1	2	0	27	19	7
2	31	3	1	2	3	2	2	0	32	11	5
2	23	2	1	1	4	2	1	1	33	18	8
1	45	3	1	1	3	1	1	?	26	10	7
2	34	3	1	2	2	3	2	0	36	8	12
1	27	3	1	1	2	3	1	3	42	13	6
2	40	3	1	1	2	2	1	4	26	9	10
2	24	2	1	1	2	1	1	2	22	10	9
1	37	2	1	1	5	2	2	0	21	11	0
1	22	5	1	1	4	1	1	1	23	17	6
2	31	3	1	2	3	1	1	4	40	16	12
1	37	2	1	1	2	3	2	0	54	12	3
2	33	1	2	2	4	2	2	0	17	10	5
1	23	5	1	1	3	1	1	1	41	27	8
1	28	3	1	1	3	3	2	0	27	11	8
2	29	2	1	2	5	2	1	2	24	9	9
2	43	3	1	1	2	1	2	0	36	17	12
1	28	5	1	1	3	1	1	1	22	15	4
1	48	2	1	1	5	1	1	4	25	11	7
2	32	2	2	2	4	2	2	0	27	13	11
1	28	5	1	1	2	2	2	0	15	23	7
2	23	2	1	1	5	1	1	4	14	11	5
2	43	2	1	2	5	1	2	0	18	7	3
1	28	2	1	1	4	3	1	2	34	18	8
2	23	3	1	1	2	1	2	0	37	17	17
2	36	1	2	2	4	2	1	4	18	12	4
1	50	2	1	1	3	1	1	2	28	14	3
1	37	3	1	1	2	2	2	0	26	14	9
2	41	3	1	1	2	1	1	4	24	11	4
1	26	5	2	1	5	1	1	1	23	19	8
2	28	3	1	1	4	1	2	0	27	12	4
2	35	2	1	1	3	1	1	1	28	14	0
1	28	5	1	1	2	1	1	2	20	24	12
2	36	2	1	1	3	2	2	0	26	9	14
2	29	3	1	1	4	1	1	4	23	13	4
1	34	1	2	2	4	2	1	0	24	12	3
1	53	2	1	1	3	3	1	1	32	17	6
2	30	3	1	1	4	1	2	0	24	10	9
1	43	2	1	1	2	1	1	2	24	14	10
2	26	5	2	1	4	1	1	1	16	23	7
2	44	1	1	1	4	2	2	0	27	18	6
1	45	1	2	2	3	3	2	0	20	14	5

not the same as the difference between '4–6 days a week' and '2 or 3 days a week', and so on. Nonetheless, we can say that 'every day' is more frequent than '4–6 days a week', which is more frequent than '2 or 3 days a week', etc. You should also bear in mind that, if you subsequently group an interval/ratio variable like var00002, which refers to people's ages, into categories (e.g. 20 and under; 21–30; 31–40; 41–50; 51 and over), you are transforming it into an ordinal variable.

• *Nominal variables*. These variables, also known as *categorical variables*, comprise categories that cannot be rank ordered. As noted previously, we cannot say in the case of question 3 that 'relaxation'

Table 11.1 Types of variable

Type	Description	Examples in gym study	Variable Name in SPSS (see Chapter 12)
Interval/ratio	Variables where the distances between the categories are identical across the range	var00002 var00010 var00011 var00012	age cardmins weimins othmins
Ordinal	Variables whose categories can be rank ordered but the distances between the categories are not equal across the range	var00004 var00005 var00006	carduse weiuse frequent
Nominal	Variables whose categories cannot be rank ordered; also known as *categorical*	var00003 var00007 var00009	reasons accomp exercise
Dichotomous	Variables containing data that have only two categories	var00001 var00008	gender othsourc

is more of something than 'maintain or improve fitness' or 'lose weight'.

- *Dichotomous variables.* These variables contain data that have only two categories (e.g. gender). Their position in relation to the other types is slightly ambiguous, as they have only one interval. They therefore can be considered as having attributes of the other three types of variable. They look as though they are nominal variables, but because they have only one interval they are sometimes treated as ordinal variables. However, it is probably safest to treat them for most purposes as if they were ordinary nominal variables.

The four main types of variable and illustrations of them from the gym survey are provided in Table 11.1.

Multiple-indicator (or multiple-item) measures of concepts, like Likert scales (see Box 3.3, p. 68), produce strictly speaking ordinal variables. However, many writers argue that they can be treated as though they produce interval/ratio variables, because of the relatively large number of categories they generate. For a brief discussion of this issue, see Bryman and Cramer, who distinguish between 'true' interval/ratio variables and those produced by multiple-indicator measures (2001: 58–9).

Figure 11.1 provides guidance about how to identify variables of each type.

Univariate analysis

Univariate analysis refers to the analysis of one variable at a time. In this section, the commonest approaches will be outlined.

Frequency tables

A frequency table provides the number of people and the percentage belonging to each of the categories for the variable in question. It can be used in relation to all of the different types of variable. An example of a frequency table is provided for var00003 in Table 11.2. Notice that nobody chose two of the possible choices of answer—'meet others' and 'other'—so these are not included in the table. The table shows, for example, that 33 members of the sample go the gym to lose weight and that they represent 37 per cent (percentages are often rounded up and down in frequency tables) of the entire sample.

If an interval/ratio variable (like people's ages) is to

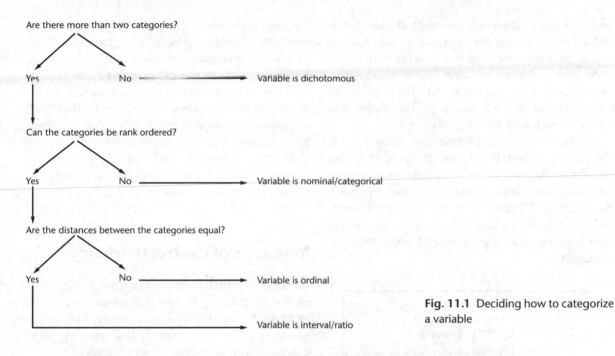

Fig. 11.1 Deciding how to categorize a variable

Table 11.2 Frequency table showing reasons for visiting the gym

Reason	n	per cent
Relaxation	9	10
Maintain or improve fitness	31	34
Lose weight	33	37
Build strength	17	19
TOTAL	90	100

Table 11.3 Frequency table showing ages of gym members

Age	n	per cent
20 and under	3	3
21–30	39	44
31–40	23	26
41–50	21	24
51 and over	3	3
TOTAL	89	100

be presented in a frequency table format, it is invariably the case that the categories will need to be grouped. When grouping in this way, take care to ensure that the categories you create do not overlap (for example, like this: 20–30, 30–40, 40–50, etc.). An example of a frequency table for an interval/ratio variable is shown in Table 11.3, which provides a frequency table for var00002, which is concerned with the ages of those visiting the gym. If we do not group people in terms of age ranges, there would be thirty-four different categories, which is too many to take in. By creating five categories, the distribution of ages is easier to comprehend. Notice that the

sample totals 89 and that the percentages are based on a total of 89 rather than 90. This is because this variable contains one missing value (respondent 24).

Diagrams

Diagrams are among the most frequently used methods of displaying quantitative data. Their chief advantage is that they are relatively easy to interpret and understand. If you are working with nominal or ordinal variables, the *bar chart* and the *pie chart* are two of the easiest methods to use. A bar chart of the same data presented in Table 11.2 is presented in Figure 11.2. Each bar represents the number of people falling in each category. This figure was produced with SPSS for Windows.

Another way of displaying the same data is through a pie chart, like the one in Figure 11.3. This also shows the relative size of the different categories but brings out as well the size of each slice relative to the total sample. The percentage that each slice represents of the whole sample is also given in this diagram, which was also produced with SPSS for Windows.

If you are displaying an interval/ratio variable, like var00002, a *histogram* is likely to be employed. Figure 11.4, which was also generated by SPSS for Windows, uses the same data and categories as Table 11.3. As with the bar chart, the bars represent the relative size of each of the age bands. However, note that, with the histogram, there is no space between the bars, whereas there is a space between the bars of a bar chart. Histograms are produced for interval/ratio variables, whereas bar charts are produced for nominal and ordinal variables.

Measures of central tendency

Measures of central tendency encapsulate in one figure a value that is typical for a distribution of values. In effect, we are seeking out an average for a distribution, but, in quantitative data analysis, three different forms of average are recognized.

- *Arithmetic mean.* This is the average as we understand it in everyday use—that is, we sum all the values in a distribution and then divide by the number of values. Thus, the arithmetic mean (or more simply the *mean*) for var00002 is 33.6, meaning that the average age of gym visitors is nearly 34 years of age. The mean should be employed only in relation to interval/ratio variables, though it is

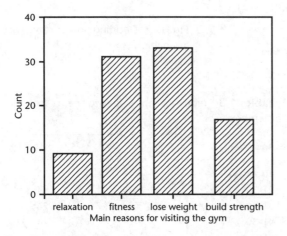

Fig. 11.2 Bar chart showing main reasons for visiting the gym (SPSS output)

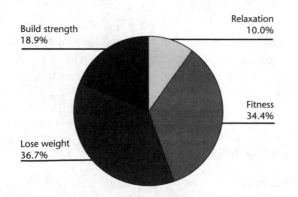

Fig. 11.3 Pie chart showing main reasons for visiting the gym (SPSS output)

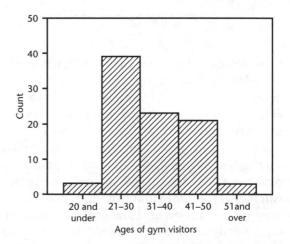

Fig. 11.4 Histogram showing the ages of gym visitors (SPSS output)

not uncommon to see it being used for ordinal variables as well.

- *Median*. This is the mid-point in a distribution of values. Whereas the mean is vulnerable to *outliers* (extreme values at either end of the distribution), which will exert considerable upwards or downwards pressure on the mean, by taking the mid-point of a distribution the median is not affected in this way. The median is derived by arraying all the values in a distribution from the smallest to the largest and then finding the middle point. If there is an even number of values, the median is calculated by taking the mean of the two middle numbers of the distribution. In the case of var00002, the median is 31. This is slightly lower than the mean in part because some considerably older members (especially respondents 5 and 10) inflate the mean slightly. The median can be employed in relation to both interval/ratio and ordinal variables.
- *Mode*. This is the value that occurs most frequently in a distribution. The mode for var00002 is 28. The mode can be employed in relation to all types of variable.

Measures of dispersion

The amount of variation in a sample can be just as interesting as providing estimates of the typical value of a distribution. For one thing, it becomes possible to draw contrasts between comparable distributions of values. For example, is there more or less variability in the amount of time spent on cardiovascular equipment as compared to weights machines?

The most obvious way of measuring dispersion is by the *range*. This is simply the difference between the maximum and the minimum value in a distribution of values associated with an interval/ratio variable. We find that the range for the two types of equipment is 64 minutes for the cardiovascular equipment and 48 minutes for the weights machines. This suggests that there is more variability in the amount of time spent on the former. However, like the mean, the range is influenced by outliers, such as respondent 60 in the case of var00010.

Another measure of dispersion is the *standard deviation*, which is essentially the average amount of variation around the mean. Although the calculation is somewhat more complicated than this, the standard deviation is calculated by taking the difference between each value in a distribution and the mean and then dividing the total of the differences by the number of values. The standard deviation for var00010 is 9.9 minutes and for var00011 it is 8 minutes. Thus, not only is the average amount of time spent on the cardiovascular equipment higher than for the weights equipment, the standard deviation is greater too. The standard deviation is also affected by outliers, but, unlike the range, their impact is offset by dividing by the number of values in the distribution.

Bivariate analysis

Bivariate analysis is concerned with the analysis of two variables at a time in order to uncover whether the two variables are related. Exploring relationships between variables means searching for evidence that the variation in one variable coincides with variation in another variable. A variety of techniques are available for examining relationships, but their use depends on the nature of the two variables being analysed. Figure 11.5 attempts to portray the main types of bivariate analysis according to the types of variable involved.

	Nominal	Ordinal	Interval/ratio	Dichotomous
Nominal	Contingency table + chi-square (χ^2) + Cramér's V	Contingency table + chi-square (χ^2) + Cramér's V	Contingency table + chi-square (χ^2) + Cramér's V. If the interval/ratio variable can be identified as the dependent variable, compare means + eta	Contingency table + chi-square (χ^2) + Cramér's V
Ordinal	Contingency table + chi-square (χ^2) + Cramér's V	Spearman's rho (ρ)	Spearman's rho (ρ)	Spearman's rho (ρ)
Interval/ratio	Contingency table + chi-square (χ^2) + Cramér's V. If the interval/ratio variable can be identified as the dependent variable, compare means + eta	Spearman's rho (ρ)	Pearson's r	Spearman's rho (ρ)
Dichotomous	Contingency table + chi-square (χ^2) + Cramér's V	Spearman's rho (ρ)	Spearman's rho (ρ)	phi (φ)

Fig. 11.5 Methods of bivariate analysis

Relationships not causality

An important point to bear in mind about all of the methods for analysing relationships between variables is that it is precisely *relationships* that they uncover. As was noted in Chapter 2 in relation to cross-sectional designs (see p. 41), this means that you cannot infer that one variable causes another. Indeed, there are cases when what appears to be a causal influence working in one direction actually works in the other way. An interesting example of this problem of causal direction will be presented much later in the book in Chapter 22. The example shows that Sutton and Rafaeli (1988) expected to find a relationship between the display of positive emotions (for example, smiling, or friendliness on

the part of checkout staff) in retail outlets and sales in those outlets. In other words, the display of positive emotions was deemed to have a causal influence on levels of retail sales. In fact, the relationship was found to be the other way round: levels of retail sales exerted a causal influence on the display of emotions (see Box 22.5, p. 455, for further details).

Sometimes, we may feel confident that we can infer a causal direction when a relationship between two variables is discerned—for example, if we find that age and voting behaviour are related. It is impossible for the way people vote to influence their age, so, if we do find the two variables to be related, we can infer with complete confidence that age is the independent variable. It is not uncommon for researchers, when analysing their data, to draw inferences about causal direction based on their assumptions about the likely causal direction among related variables, as Sutton and Rafaeli (1988) did in their study. Although such inferences may be based on sound reasoning, they can only be inferences and there is the possibility that the real pattern of causal direction is the opposite of that which is anticipated.

Contingency tables

Contingency tables are probably the most flexible of all methods of analysing relationships in that they can be employed in relation to any pair of variables, though they are not the most efficient method for some pairs, which is the reason why the method is not recommended in all of the cells in Figure 11.5. A contingency table is like a frequency table but it allows two variables to be simultaneously analysed so that relationships between the two variables can be examined. It is normal for contingency tables to include percentages, since these make the tables easier to interpret. Table 11.4 examines the relationship between two variables from the gym survey: gender and reasons for visiting the gym. The percentages are *column percentages*—that is, they calculate the number in each cell as a percentage of the total number in that column. Thus, to take the top left hand cell, the

Table 11.4 Contingency table showing the relationship between gender and reasons for visiting the gym

Reasons	Gender			
	Male		Female	
	No.	%	No.	%
Relaxation	3	7	6	13
Fitness	15	36	16	33
Lose weight	8	19	25	52
Build strength	16	38	1	2
TOTAL	42		48	

Note: $\chi^2 = 22.726\ p < 0.0001$.

3 men who go to the gym for relaxation are 7 per cent of all 42 men in the sample. Users of contingency tables often present the presumed independent variable (if one can in fact be presumed) as the column variable and the presumed dependent variable as the rows variable. In this case, we are presuming that gender influences reasons for going to the gym. In fact, we know that going to the gym cannot influence gender. In such circumstances, it is column rather than row percentages that will be required.

Contingency tables are generated so that patterns of association can be searched for. In this case, we can see clear gender differences in reasons for visiting the gym. As our student anticipated, females are much more likely than men to go to the gym to lose weight. They are also somewhat more likely to go the gym for relaxation. By contrast, men are much more likely to go to the gym to build strength. There is little difference between the two genders in terms of fitness as a reason.

Pearson's *r*

Pearson's *r* is a method for examining relationships between interval/ratio variables. The chief features of this method are as follows:

- the coefficient will almost certainly lie between 0 (zero or no relationship between the two variables) and 1 (a perfect relationship)—this indicates the *strength* of a relationship;
- the closer the coefficient is to 1, the stronger the relationship; the closer it is to zero, the weaker the relationship;
- the coefficient will be either positive or negative— this indicates the *direction* of a relationship.

To illustrate these features consider Box 11.4, which gives imaginary data for five variables, and the scatter diagrams in Figures 11.6–11.9, which look at the relationship between pairs of interval/ratio variables. The scatter diagram for variables 1 and 2 is presented in Figure 11.6 and shows a perfect positive relationship, which would have a Pearson's *r* correlation of +1. This means that, as one variable increases, the other variable increases by the same

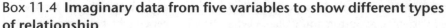

Box 11.4 **Imaginary data from five variables to show different types of relationship**

Variables 1	2	3	4	5
1	10	50	7	9
2	12	45	13	23
3	14	40	18	7
4	16	35	14	15
5	18	30	16	6
6	20	25	23	22
7	22	20	19	12
8	24	15	24	8
9	26	10	22	18
10	28	5	24	10

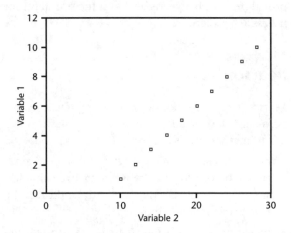

Fig. 11.6 Scatter diagram showing a perfect positive relationship

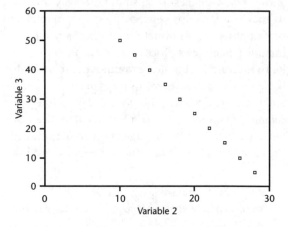

Fig. 11.7 Scatter diagram showing a perfect negative relationship

amount and that no other variable is related to either of them. If the correlation was below 1, it would mean that variable 1 is related to at least one other variable as well as variable 2.

The scatter diagram for variables 2 and 3 (Figure 11.7) shows a perfect negative relationship, which would have a Pearson's *r* correlation of –1. This means that, as one variable increases, the other variable decreases and that no other variable is related to either of them.

If there was no or virtually no correlation between

the variables, there would be no apparent pattern to the markers in the scatter diagram. This is the case with the relationship between variables 2 and 5. The correlation is virtually zero at –0.041. This means that the variation in each variable is associated with other variables than the ones present in this analysis. Figure 11.8 shows the appropriate scatter diagram.

If a relationship is strong, a clear patterning to the variables will be evident. This is the case with variables 2 and 4, whose scatter diagram appears in Figure 11.9. There is clearly a positive relationship and

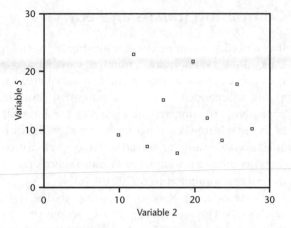

Fig. 11.8 Scatter diagram showing two variables that are not related

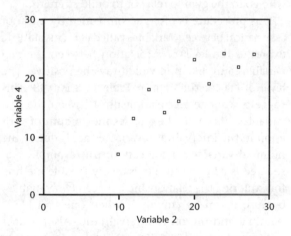

Fig. 11.9 Scatter diagram showing a strong positive relationship

in fact the Pearson's *r* value is +0.88 (usually, positive correlations are presented without the + sign). This means that the variation in the two variables is very closely connected, but that there is some influence of other variables in the extent to which they vary.

Going back to the gym survey, we find that the correlation between age (var00002) and the amount of time spent on weights equipment (var00011) is −0.27, implying a weak negative relationship. This suggests that there is a tendency such that, the older a person is, the less likely he or she is to spend much time on such equipment, but that other variables clearly influence the amount of time spent on this activity.

In order to be able to use Pearson's *r*, the relationship between the two variables must be broadly *linear*—that is, when plotted on a scatter diagram, the values of the two variables approximate to a straight line (even though they may be scattered as in Figure 11.9) and do not curve. Therefore, plotting a scatter diagram before using Pearson's *r* is important, in order to determine that the nature of the relationship between a pair of variables does not violate the assumptions being made when this method of correlation is employed.

If you square a value of Pearson's *r*, you can derive a further useful statistic—namely the *coefficient of determination*, which expresses how much of the variation in one variable is due to the other variable. Thus, if *r* is −0.27, r^2 is 0.0729. We can then express this as a percentage by multiplying r^2 by 100. The product of this exercise is 7 per cent. This means that just 7 per cent of the variation in the use of cardiovascular equipment is accounted for by age. The coefficient of determination is a useful adjunct to the interpretation of correlation information.

Spearman's rho

Spearman's rho, which is often represented with the Greek letter ρ, is designed for the use of pairs of ordinal variables, but is also used, as suggested by Figure 11.5, when one variable is ordinal and the other is interval/ratio. It is exactly the same as Pearson's *r* in terms of the outcome of calculating it, in that the computed value of rho will be either positive or negative and will vary between 0 and 1. If we look at the gym study, there are three ordinal variables: var00004, var00005, and var00006 (see Table 11.1). If we use Spearman's rho to calculate the correlation between the first two variables, we find that the correlation between var00004 and var00005— frequency of use of the cardiovascular and weights equipment—is low at 0.2. A slightly stronger relationship is found between var00006 (frequency of going to the gym) and var00010 (amount of time spent on the cardiovascular equipment) which is 0.4. Note that the latter variable is an interval/ratio variable. When confronted with a situation in which we want to calculate the correlation between an ordinal and an interval/ratio variable, we cannot use Pearson's r, because both variables must be at the interval/ratio level of measurement. Instead, we must use Spearman's rho (see Figure 11.5).

Phi and Cramér's V

Phi (φ) and Cramér's V are two closely related statistics. The phi coefficient is used for the analysis of the relationship between two dichotomous variables. Like Pearson's r, it results in a computed statistic that varies between 0 and + or −1. The correlation between var00001 (gender) and var00008 (other sources of regular exercise) is 0.24, implying that males are somewhat more likely than females to have other sources of regular exercise, though the relationship is weak.

Cramér's V uses a similar formula to phi and can be employed with nominal variables (see Figure 11.5). However, this statistic can take on only a positive value, so that it can give an indication only of the strength of the relationship between two variables, not of the direction. The value of Cramér's V associated with the analysis presented in Table 11.4 is 0.50. This suggests a moderate relationship between the two variables. Cramér's V is usually reported along with a contingency table and a chi-square test (see below). It is not normally presented on its own.

Comparing means and eta

If you need to examine the relationship between an interval/ratio variable and a nominal variable, and if the latter can be relatively unambiguously identified as the independent variable, a potentially fruitful approach is to compare the means of the interval/ratio variable for each subgroup of the nominal variable. As an example, consider Table 11.5, which presents the mean number of minutes spent on cardiovascular equipment (var00010) for each of the four categories of reasons for going to the gym (var00003). The means suggest that people who go to the gym for fitness or to lose weight spend considerably more time on this equipment than people who go to the gym to relax or to build strength.

This procedure is often accompanied by a test of association between variables called *eta*. This statistic expresses the level of association between the two variables and, like phi, will always be positive. The level of eta for the data in Table 11.5 is 0.48. This suggests a moderate relationship between the two variables. Eta-squared expresses the amount of variation in the interval/ratio variable that is due to the nominal variable. In the case of this example, eta-squared is 22 per cent. Eta is a very flexible method for exploring the relationship between two variables, because it can be employed when one variable is nominal and the other interval/ratio. Also, it does not make the assumption that the relationship between variables is linear.

Table 11.5 Comparing subgroup means: time spent on cardiovascular equipment by reasons for going to the gym

Time	Reasons				
	Relaxation	Fitness	Lose weight	Build strength	Total
Mean number of minutes spent on cardiovascular equipment	18.33	30.55	28.36	19.65	26.47
n	9	31	33	17	90

Multivariate analysis

Mutivariate analysis entails the simultaneous analysis of three or more variables. This is quite an advanced topic and it is recommended that readers examine a textbook on quantitative data analysis for an exposition of techniques (e.g. Bryman and Cramer 2001). There are three main contexts within which multivariate analysis might be employed.

Could the relationship be spurious?

In order for a relationship between two variables to be established, not only must there be evidence that there is a relationship but the relationship must be shown to be *non-spurious*. A spurious relationship exists when there appears to be a relationship between two variables, but the relationship is not real: it is being produced because each variable is itself related to a third variable. For example, if we find a relationship between income and voting behaviour, we might ask: could the relationship be an artefact of age (see Figure 11.10)? The older one is, the more likely one is to earn more, whilst age is known to influence voting behaviour. If age were found to be producing the apparent relationship between income and voting behaviour, we would conclude that the relationship is spurious. An interesting possible case of a spurious relationship was highlighted in a very short report in *The Times* (1 October 1999: 2) of some medical findings. The article noted that there is evidence to suggest that women on hormone replacement therapy (HRT) have lower levels of heart disease than those not on this form of therapy. The article cites Swedish findings that suggest that the relationship may be due to the fact that women who choose to start the therapy are 'thinner, richer and healthier' than those who do not. These background factors would seem to affect both the likelihood of taking HRT *and* the likelihood of getting heart disease.

Could there be an intervening variable?

Let us say that we do not find that the relationship is spurious, we might ask *why* there is a relationship between income and voting. One possibility is that people of different incomes vary in their political attitudes, which in turn has implications for their voting behaviour. Political attitudes would then be an *intervening variable*:

income → political attitudes → voting behaviour.

An intervening variable allows us to answer questions about the bivariate relationship between variables. It suggests that the relationship between the two variables is not a direct one, since the impact of income on voting behaviour is viewed as occurring via political attitudes.

Could a third variable moderate the relationship?

We might ask a question like: does the relationship between two variables hold for men but not for women? If it does, the relationship is said to be moderated by gender. We might ask in the gym study, for example, whether the relationship between age and whether visitors have other sources of regular exercise (var00008) is moderated by gender. This would imply that, if we find a pattern relating age to other sources of exercise, that pattern will vary by gender. Table 11.6 shows the relationship between age and other sources of exercise. In this table, age has been

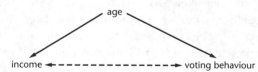

Fig. 11.10 A spurious relationship

Table 11.6 Contingency table showing the relationship between age and whether gym visitors have other sources of regular exercise (percentages)

Other source of exercise	Age		
	30 and under	31–40	41 and over
Other source	64	43	58
No other source	36	57	42
n	42	23	24

Table 11.7 Contingency table showing the relationship between age and whether gym visitors have other sources of regular exercise for males and females (percentages)

Other source of exercise	Gender					
	Male			Female		
	30 and under	31–40	41 and over	30 and under	31–40	41 and over
Other source	70	33	75	59	50	42
No other source	30	67	25	41	50	58
n	20	9	12	22	14	12

broken down into just three age bands to make the table easier to read. The table suggests that the 31–40 age group are less likely to have other sources of regular exercise than the 30 and under and 41 and over age groups. However, Table 11.7, which breaks the relationship down by gender, suggests that the pattern for males and females is somewhat different. Among males, the pattern shown in Table 11.6 is very pronounced, but for females the likelihood of having other sources of exercise declines with age. It would seem that the relationship between age and other sources of exercise is moderated by age. This example illustrates the way in which contingency tables can be employed for multivariate analysis. However, there is a wide variety of other techniques (Bryman and Cramer 2001: ch. 10).

Statistical significance

One difficulty with working on data deriving from a sample is that there is often the lingering worry that, even though you have employed a probability sampling procedure (as in the gym survey), your findings will not be generalizable to the population from which the sample was drawn. As we saw in Chapter 4, there is always the possibility that *sampling error* (difference between the population and the sample that you have selected) has occurred, even when probability sampling procedures have been followed. If this happens, the sample will be unrepresentative of the wider population and therefore any findings will be invalid. To make matters worse, there is no feasible way of finding out

---

Box 11.5 ⌖ *What is a test of statistical significance?*

A test of statistical significance allows the analyst to estimate how confident he or she can be that the results deriving from a study based on a randomly selected sample are generalizable to the population from which the sample was drawn. When examining statistical significance in relation to the relationship between two variables, it also tells us about the risk of concluding that there is in fact a relationship in the population when there is no such relationship in the population. If an analysis reveals a statistically significant finding, this does not mean that that finding is intrinsically significant or important. The word 'significant' seems to imply importance. However, statistical significance is solely concerned with the confidence researchers can have in their findings. It does not mean that a statistically significant finding is substantively significant.

---

whether they do in fact apply to the population! What you can do is to provide an indication of how confident you can be in your findings. This is where statistical significance and the various tests of statistical significance come in.

We need to know how confident we can be that our findings can be generalized to the population from which that sample was selected. Since we cannot be absolutely certain that a finding based on a sample will also be found in the population, we need a technique that allows us to establish how confident we can be that the finding exists in the population and what risk we are taking in inferring that the finding exists in the population. These two elements—confidence and risk—lie at the heart of tests of statistical significance (see Box 11.5). However, it is important to appreciate that tests of statistical significance can be employed only in relation to samples that have been drawn using probability sampling.

In Chapter 4 (see Box 4.4, p. 94), in the context of the discussion of the standard error of the mean, we began to get an appreciation of the ideas behind statistical significance. For example, we know that the mean age of the gym sample is 33.6. Using the concept of the standard error of the mean, we can calculate that we can be 95 per cent confident that the population mean lies between 31.72 and 35.47. This suggests that we can determine in broad outline the degree of confidence that we can have in a sample mean.

In the rest of this section, we will look at the tests that are available for determining the degree of confidence we can have in our findings when we explore relationships between variables. All of the tests have a common structure.

- *Set up a null hypothesis.* This stipulates that two variables are not related in the population—for example, that there is *no* relationship between gender and visiting the gym in the population from which the sample was selected.

- *Establish the level of statistical significance that you find acceptable.* This is essentially a measure of the degree of risk that you might reject the null hypothesis (implying that there *is* a relationship in the population) when you should support it (implying that there is no relationship in the population). Levels of statistical significance are expressed as probability levels—that is, the probability of rejecting the null hypothesis when you should be confirming it. See Box 11.6 on this issue. The convention among most social researchers is that the maximum level of statistical significance that is acceptable is $p < 0.05$, which implies that there are fewer than five chances in 100 that you could have a sample that shows a relationship when there is not one in the population.

- *Determine the statistical significance of your findings* (i.e. use a statistical test like chi-square).

- If your findings are statistically significant at the 0.05 level—so that the risk of getting a relationship as strong as the one you have found, when there is *no* relationship in the population, is no higher than 5 in 100—you would *reject* the null hypothesis. Therefore, you are implying that the results are unlikely to have occurred by *chance*.

There are in fact two types of error that can be

Box 11.6 ⋛⃝⋚ *What is the level of statistical significance?*

The level of statistical significance is the level of risk that you are prepared to take that you are inferring that there is a relationship between two variables in the population from which the sample was taken when in fact no such relationship exists. The maximum level of risk that is conventionally taken in the social sciences is to say that there are up to 5 chances in 100 that we might be falsely concluding that there is a relationship when there is not one in the population from which the sample was taken. This means that, if we drew 100 samples, we are recognizing that as many as 5 of them might exhibit a relationship when there is not one in the population. Our sample might be one of those five, but the risk is fairly small. This significance level is denoted by $p < 0.05$ (p means *probability*). If we accepted a significance level of $p < 0.1$, we would be accepting the possibility that as many as 10 in 100 samples might show a relationship where none exists in the population. In this case, there is a greater risk than

with $p < 0.05$ that we might have a sample that implies a relationship when there is not one in the population, since the probability of our having such a sample is greater when the risk is 1 in 10 (10 out of 100 when $p < 0.1$) than when the risk is 1 in 20 (5 out of 100 when $p < 0.05$). Therefore, we would have greater confidence when the risk of falsely inferring that there is a relationship between 2 variables is 1 in 20, as against 1 in 10. But, if you want a more stringent test, perhaps because you are worried about the use that might be made of your results, you might choose the $p < 0.01$ level. This means that you are prepared to accept as your level of risk a probability of only 1 in 100 that the results could have arisen by chance (that is, due to sampling error). Therefore, if the results, following administration of a test, show that the results are statistically significant at the $p < 0.05$ level, but *not* the $p < 0.01$ level, you would have to confirm the null hypothesis.

made when inferring statistical significance. These errors are known as Type I and Type II errors (see Figure 11.11). A Type I error occurs when you reject the null hypothesis when it should in fact be confirmed. This means that your results have arisen by chance and you are falsely concluding that there is a relationship in the population when there is not one. Using a $p < 0.05$ level of significance means that we are more likely to make a Type I error than when using a $p < 0.01$ level of significance. This is because with 0.01 there is less chance of falsely rejecting the null hypothesis. However, in doing so, you increase the chance of making a Type II error (accepting the

null hypothesis when you should reject it). This is because you are more likely to confirm the null hypothesis when the significance level is 0.01 (1 in 100) than when it is 0.05 (1 in 20).

The chi-square test

The chi-square (χ^2) test is applied to contingency tables like Table 11.4. It allows us to establish how confident we can be that there is a relationship between the two variables in the population. The test works by calculating for each cell in the table an expected frequency or value—that is, one that would occur on the basis of chance alone. The chi-square value, which in Table 11.4 is 22.726, is calculated by calculating the differences between the actual and expected values for each cell in the table and then summing those differences (it is slightly more complicated than this, but the details need not concern us here). The chi-square value means nothing on its own and can be meaningfully interpreted only in relation to its associated level of statistical significance, which in this case is $p < 0.0001$. This means that there is only one chance in 10,000 of rejecting

	Error	
	Type I (risk of rejecting the null hypothesis when it should be confirmed)	**Type II** (risk of confirming the null hypothesis when it should be rejected)
p level 0.05	Greater risk	Lower risk
0.01	Lower risk	Greater risk

Fig. 11.11 Type I and Type II errors

the null hypothesis (that is, inferring that there *is* a relationship in the population when there is no such relationship in the population). You could be extremely confident that there is a relationship between gender and reasons for visiting the gym among all gym members, since the chance that you have obtained a sample that shows a relationship when there is no relationship among all gym members is 1 in 10, 000.

Whether a chi-square value achieves statistical significance depends not just on its magnitude but also on the number of categories of the two variables being analysed. This latter issue is governed by what is known as the 'degrees of freedom' associated with the table. The number of degrees of freedom is governed by the simple formula:

Number of degrees of freedom =
(number of columns – 1)(number of rows – 1)

In the case of Table 11.5, this will be $(2 – 1)(4 – 1)$, that is, 3. In other words, the chi-square value that is arrived at is affected by the size of the table, and this is taken into account when deciding whether the chi-square value is statistically significant or not.

Correlation and statistical significance

Examining the statistical significance of a computed correlation coefficient, which is based on a randomly selected sample, provides information about the likelihood that the coefficient will be found in the population from which the sample was taken. Thus, if we find a correlation of –0.62, what is the likelihood that a relationship of at least that size exists in the population? This tells us whether the relationship could have arisen by chance.

If the correlation coefficient r is –0.62 and the significance level is $p < 0.05$, we can reject the null hypothesis that there is no relationship in the population. We can infer that there are only five chances in 100 that a correlation of at least –0.62 could have arisen by chance alone. You *could* have one of the five samples in 100 that shows a relationship when there is not one in the population, but the degree of

risk is reasonably small. If, say, it was found that $r =$ –0.62 and $p < 0.1$, there could be as many as ten chances in 100 that there is no correlation in the population. This would *not* be an acceptable level of risk for most purposes. It would mean that in as many as one sample in 10 we might find a correlation of –0.62 or above when there is not a correlation in the population. If $r = –0.62$ and $p < 0.001$, there is only one chance in 1, 000 that no correlation exists in the population. There would be a very low level of risk if you inferred that the correlation had not arisen by chance.

Whether a correlation coefficient is statistically significant or not will be affected by two factors:

- the size of the computed coefficient, and
- the size of the sample.

This second factor may appear surprising. Basically, the larger a sample, the more likely it is that a computed correlation coefficient will be found to be statistically significant. Thus, even though the correlation between age and the amount of time spent on weights machines in the gym survey was found to be just –0.27, which is a fairly weak relationship, it is statistically significant at the $p < 0.01$ level. This means that there is only one chance in 100 that there is no relationship in the population. Because the question of whether a correlation coefficient is statistically significant depends so much on the sample size, it is important to realize that you should always examine *both* the correlation coefficient *and* the significance level. You should not examine one at the expense of the other.

This treatment of correlation and statistical significance applies to both Pearson's r and Spearman's rho. A similar interpretation can also be applied to phi and Cramér's V.

Comparing means and statistical significance

A test of statistical significance can also be applied to the comparison of means that was carried out in Table 11.5. This procedure entails treating the total amount of variation in the dependent variable—amount of time spent on cardiovascular equipment—as made up of two types: variation *within* the four subgroups that make up the independent variable and variation *between* them. The latter is often called the *explained variance* and the former as the *error variance*. A test of statistical significance for the comparison of means entails relating the two types of variance to form what is known as the *F* statistic. This statistic expresses the amount of explained variance in relation to the amount of error variance. In the case of the data in Table 11.5, the resulting *F* statistic is statistically significant at the $p < 0.001$ level. This finding suggests that there is only one chance in 1,000 that there is no relationship between the two variables among all gym members.

Key points

- You need to think about your data analysis *before* you begin designing your research instruments.

- Techniques of data analysis are applicable to some types of variable and not others. You need to know the difference between nominal, ordinal, interval/ratio, and dichotomous variables.

- You need to think about the kinds of data you are collecting and the implications your decisions will have for the sorts of techniques you will be able to employ.

- Become familiar with computer software like SPSS before you begin designing your research instruments, because it is advisable to be aware at an early stage of difficulties you might have in presenting your data in SPSS.

- Make sure you are thoroughly familiar with the techniques introduced in this chapter and when you can and cannot use them.

- The basic message, then, is *not* to leave these considerations until your data have been collected, tempting though it may be.

- Do not confuse statistical significance with substantive significance.

Revision questions

- At what stage should you begin to think about the kinds of data analysis you need to conduct?
- What are missing data and why do they arise?

Types of variable

- Make sure you are thoroughly familiar with the differences between the four types of variable outlined in this chapter: interval/ratio; ordinal; nominal; and dichotomous.

- Why is it important to be able to distinguish between the four types of variable?
- Imagine the kinds of answers you would receive if you administered the following four questions in an interview survey. What kind of variable would each question generate: dichotomous; nominal; ordinal; or interval/ratio?

  1. Do you enjoy going shopping?

     Yes ____

     No ____

  2. How many times have you shopped in the last month? Please write in the number of occasions below.

     ____

  3. For which kinds of items do you most enjoy shopping? Please tick one only.

     Clothes (including shoes)   ____

     Food   ____

     Things for the house   ____

     Presents   ____

     Entertainment (CDs, videos, etc.) ____

  4. How important is it to you to buy clothes with designer labels?

     Very important   ____

     Fairly important   ____

     Not very important   ____

     Not at all important ____

Univariate analysis

- What is an outlier and why might one have an adverse effect on the mean and the range?
- In conjunction with which measure of central tendency would you expect to report the standard deviation: the mean; the median; or the mode?

Bivariate analysis

- Can you infer causality from bivariate analysis?
- Why are percentages crucial when presenting contingency tables?
- In what circumstances would you use each of the following: Pearson's r; Spearman's rho; phi; Cramér's V; eta.

Multivariate analysis

- What is a spurious relationship?
- What is an intervening variable?
- What does it mean to say that a relationship is moderated?

Statistical significance

- What does statistical significance mean and how does it differ from substantive significance?

- What is a significance level?
- What does the chi-square text achieve?
- What does it mean to say that a correlation of 0.42 is statistically significant at $p < 0.05$?

12 Using SPSS for Windows

Reader's guide

In order to implement the techniques that you learned in Chapter 11, you would need to do either of two things: learn the underlying formula for each technique and apply your data to it, or use computer software to analyse your data. The latter is the approach chosen in this book for two main reasons.

- It is closer to the way in which quantitative data analysis is carried out in real research nowadays.

- It helps to equip you with a useful transferable skill.

You will be learning SPSS for Windows, which is the most widely used package of computer software for doing this kind of analysis. It is relatively straightforward to use. We will be continuing to refer to the techniques introduced in Chapter 11 and will continue to use the gym survey as an example.

This chapter largely operates in parallel to Chapter 11, so that you can see the links between the techniques learned there and the use of SPSS to implement them.

Introduction

This chapter aims to provide a familiarity with some basic aspects of SPSS for Windows, which is possibly the most widely used computer software for the analysis of quantitative data for social scientists. SPSS, which originally was short for Statistical Package for the Social Sciences, has been in existence since the mid-1960s and over the years has undergone many revisions, particularly since the arrival of personal computers. The version that was used in preparing this section was Release 10. From this point on, when referring to SPSS for Windows in the text, it will be called simply SPSS. The gym survey used in Chapter 11 will be employed to illustrate SPSS operations and methods of analysis. The aim

here is to introduce ways of using SPSS to implement the methods of analysis discussed in Chapter 11.

SPSS operations will be presented in **bold**, for example, **Variable Name:** and **Analyze**. Names given to variables in the course of using SPSS will also be presented in **bold italics**, e.g. **gender** and **reasons**. Labels given to values or to variables are also in bold but in a different font, e.g. **reasons for visiting** and **male**. Box 12.1 presents a list of basic operations in SPPS. One further element in the presentation is that a right-pointing arrow—**→** —will be used to denote 'click once with the left-hand button of your mouse'. This action is employed to make selections and similar activities.

Getting started in SPSS

Beginning SPSS

To start SPSS, double click on the **spsswin** icon on your computer screen. If there is no icon, **→** the **Start** button in the bottom left-hand corner of your screen. From the menu of programs, **→ SPSS for Windows**. A follow-on menu will appear, from which you should select **SPSS 10.0 for Windows**. When SPSS loads, you *may* be faced with an opening dialog box with the title 'What do you want to do?' and a list of

options. Many users prefer to disable this opening box. It is not important in relation to the following exposition, so **→ Cancel**. You will then be faced with the **SPSS Data Editor**. This is made up of two components: **Data View** and **Variable View**. In the following discussion, these two screens are referred to as the **Data Viewer** and the **Variable Viewer**. You move between these two viewers by selecting the appropriate tab at the bottom of the screen. The **Data Viewer** is in the form of a spreadsheet grid into which you

Box 12.1 Basic operations in SPSS for Windows

- The **SPSS Data Editor**. This is the sphere of SPSS into which data are entered and subsequently edited and defined. It is made up of two screens: the **Data Viewer** and the **Variable Viewer**. You move between these two viewers by selecting the appropriate tab at the bottom of the screen.

- The **Data Viewer**. This is the spreadsheet into which your data are entered. When you start up SPSS, the **Data Viewer** will be facing you.

- The **Variable Viewer**. This is another spreadsheet, but this one displays information about each of the variables and allows you to change that information. It is the platform from which you provide for each variable such information as: the variable name; a variable label; and value labels (see below).

- The **Output**. When you perform an analysis or produce a diagram (called a 'chart' in SPSS), your output will be deposited here. The **Output Viewer** superimposes itself over the **Data Editor** after an analysis has been performed or a chart generated.

- A **Variable Name**. This is the name that you give to a variable, e.g. *gender*. The name must be no more than eight characters. Until you give a variable a name, it will be referred to as *var00001*, etc. When the variable has been given a name, it will appear in the column for that variable in the **Data View** window. It is generated from the **Variable Viewer**.

- A **Variable Label**. This is a label that you can give to a variable but which is not restricted to eight characters. Spaces can be used, e.g. **reasons for visiting**. The Label will appear in any output you generate. It is generated from the **Variable Viewer**.

- A **Value Label**. This is a label that you can attach to a code that has been used when entering data for all types of variables other than interval/ratio variables. Thus, for var00001, we would attach the label **male** to 1 and **female** to 2. When you generate output, such as a frequency table or chart, the labels for each value will be presented. This makes the interpretation of output easier. It is generated from the **Variable Viewer**.

- **Missing Values...**. When you do not have data for a particular variable when entering data for a case, you must specify how you are denoting missing values for that variable. Missing values are generated from the **Variable Viewer**.

- **Recode**. A procedure that allows codes or numbers to be changed. It is especially helpful when you need to combine groups of people—for example, when producing age bands.

- **Compute...**. A procedure that allows you to combine two or more variables to form a new variable.

- **Analyze**. This is the point on the menu bar above the **Data Editor** from which you choose (via a drop-down menu) which method of analysis you want to select. Note that, whenever an item on a menu appears with a right-pointing arrowhead after it, this means that, if you select that option, a further menu will follow on.

- **Graphs**. This is the point on the menu bar above the **Data Editor** from which you choose (via a drop-down menu) which chart you want to select.

- **Chart Editor**. When you produce a graph, you can edit it with the **Chart Editor**. To activate this editor, double-click anywhere in the graph. A small chart editor window will appear and your main graph will appear opaque until you exit the Editor. From the Editor, you can make various changes and enhancements to your graph.

---

enter your data. The columns represent *variables*—in other words, information about characteristics of each person in the gym study sample. Until data are entered, each column simply has **var** as its heading. The rows represent *cases*, which can be people (as in the example you will be working through) or any unit of analysis. Each block in the grid is referred to as a 'cell'. Note also that when the data are in the SPSS spreadsheet, they will look different, for example, 1 will be 1.00.

Entering data in the Data Viewer

To input the data into the **Data Viewer**, make sure that the top left-hand cell in the grid is highlighted (Plate 12.1). If it is not highlighted, simply click once in

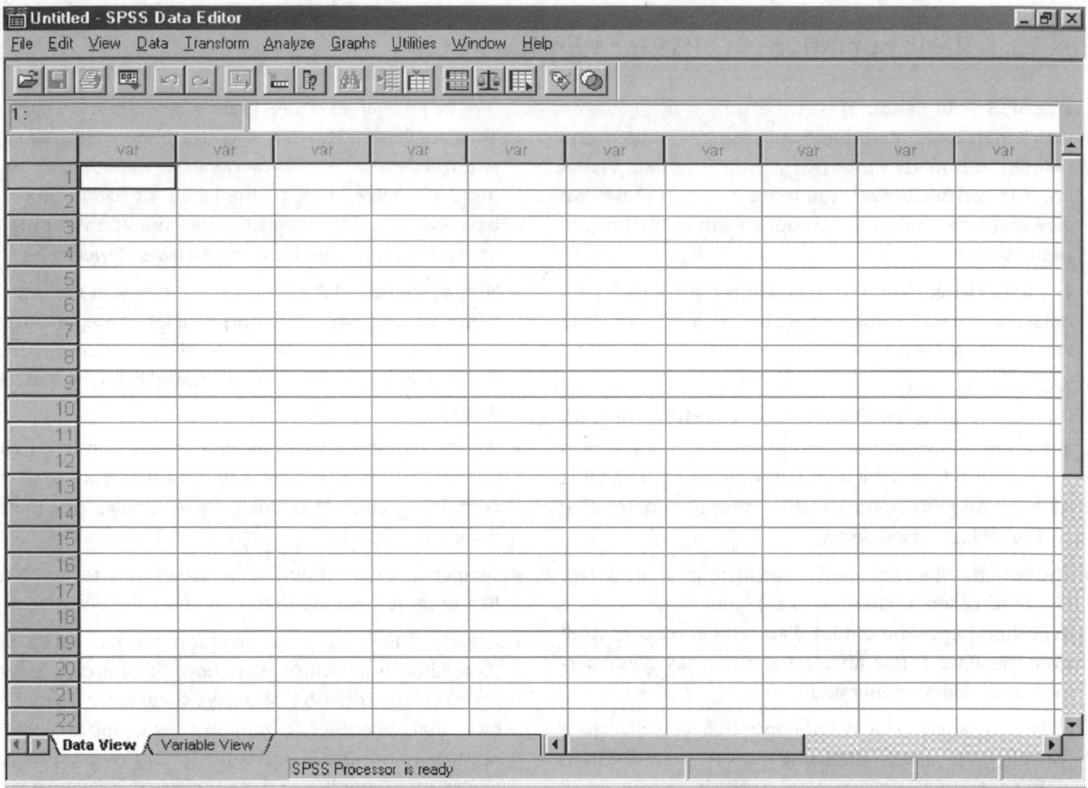

Plate 12.1 The SPSS for Windows **Data Viewer**

that cell. Then, type the appropriate figure for that cell—that is, 1. This number goes directly into that cell and into the box beneath the toolbar. As an alternative to using the mouse, many people find it easier to use the arrow keys on their keyboard to move from cell to cell. If you make a mistake at any point, simply click once in the cell in question, type in the correct value, and click once more in that cell. When you have finished, you should end up in the bottom right-hand cell of what will be a perfect rectangle of data. Plate 12.2 shows the **Data Viewer** with the data from the gym survey entered (though only part of the set of data is visible, in that only the first twenty-two respondents and ten of the twelve variables are visible). The first row of data contains the coded answers from the completed questionnaire in Box 11.2 (pp. 218–19).

In order to proceed further, you will find that SPSS works in the following typical sequence for defining variables and analysing your data.

1. You make a selection from the menu bar at the top of the screen, e.g. → **Analyze**.

2. From the menu that will appear, make a selection, e.g. → **Descriptive Statistics**.

3. This will bring up a *dialog box* into which you will usually inform SPSS of what you are trying to do—e.g. which variables are to be analysed.

4. Very often, you then need to convey further information and to do this you have to → a button that will bring up what is called, following Bryman and Cramer (2001), a *sub-dialog box*.

5. You then provide the information in the sub-dialog box and then go back to the dialog box. Sometimes, you will need to bring up a further

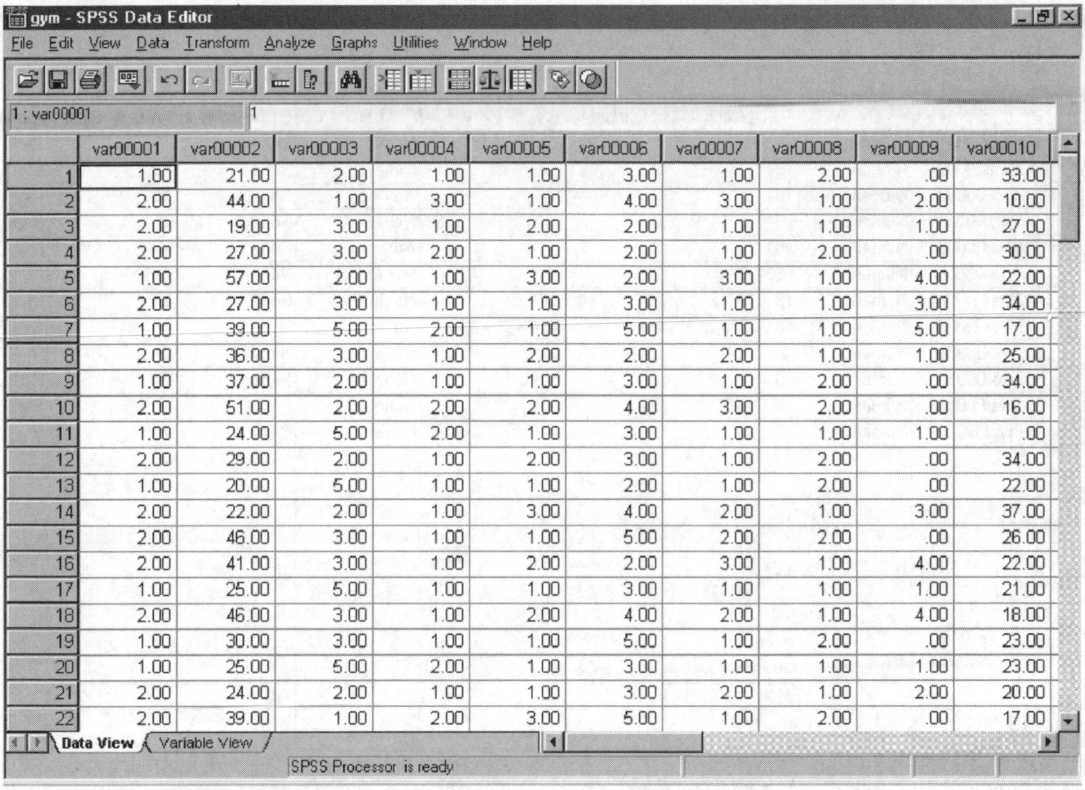

	var00001	var00002	var00003	var00004	var00005	var00006	var00007	var00008	var00009	var00010
1	1.00	21.00	2.00	1.00	1.00	3.00	1.00	2.00	.00	33.00
2	2.00	44.00	1.00	3.00	1.00	4.00	3.00	1.00	2.00	10.00
3	2.00	19.00	3.00	1.00	2.00	2.00	1.00	1.00	1.00	27.00
4	2.00	27.00	3.00	2.00	1.00	2.00	1.00	2.00	.00	30.00
5	1.00	57.00	2.00	1.00	3.00	2.00	3.00	1.00	4.00	22.00
6	2.00	27.00	3.00	1.00	1.00	3.00	1.00	1.00	3.00	34.00
7	1.00	39.00	5.00	2.00	1.00	5.00	1.00	1.00	5.00	17.00
8	2.00	36.00	3.00	1.00	2.00	2.00	2.00	1.00	1.00	25.00
9	1.00	37.00	2.00	1.00	1.00	3.00	1.00	2.00	.00	34.00
10	2.00	51.00	2.00	2.00	2.00	4.00	3.00	2.00	.00	16.00
11	1.00	24.00	5.00	2.00	1.00	3.00	1.00	1.00	1.00	.00
12	2.00	29.00	2.00	1.00	2.00	3.00	1.00	2.00	.00	34.00
13	1.00	20.00	5.00	1.00	1.00	2.00	1.00	2.00	.00	22.00
14	2.00	22.00	2.00	1.00	3.00	4.00	2.00	1.00	3.00	37.00
15	2.00	46.00	3.00	1.00	1.00	5.00	2.00	2.00	.00	26.00
16	2.00	41.00	3.00	1.00	2.00	2.00	3.00	1.00	4.00	22.00
17	1.00	25.00	5.00	1.00	1.00	3.00	1.00	1.00	1.00	21.00
18	2.00	46.00	3.00	1.00	2.00	4.00	2.00	1.00	4.00	18.00
19	1.00	30.00	3.00	1.00	1.00	5.00	1.00	2.00	.00	23.00
20	1.00	25.00	5.00	2.00	1.00	3.00	1.00	1.00	1.00	23.00
21	2.00	24.00	2.00	1.00	1.00	3.00	2.00	1.00	2.00	20.00
22	2.00	39.00	1.00	2.00	3.00	5.00	1.00	2.00	.00	17.00

Plate 12.2 The **Data Viewer** with 'gym study' data entered

sub-dialog box and then go back to the dialog box.

When you have finished going through the entire procedure, ➔ **OK**. The toolbar beneath the menu bar allows shortcut access to certain SPSS operations.

Defining variables: variable names, missing values, variable labels, and value labels

Once you have finished entering your data, you need to define your variables. The following steps will allow you to do this:

1. ➔ the **Variable View** tab at the bottom of the **Data Viewer** (opens the **Variable Viewer** shown in Plate 12.3).
2. To provide a variable name, click on the current variable name (e.g. **var00003**) and type the name of the name you want to give it (e.g. ***reasons***). Remember that this name must be no more than eight characters and you can*not* use spaces.
3. You can then give your variable a more detailed name, known in SPSS as a variable label. To do this, ➔ cell in the **Label** column relating to the variable for which you want to supply a variable label. Then, simply type in the variable label (i.e. **reasons for visiting**).
4. Then you will need to provide 'value labels' for variables that have been given codes. The procedure generally applies to variables that are not interval/ratio variables. The latter, which are numeric variables, do not need to be coded (unless you are grouping them in some way). To assign value labels, ➔ in the **Values** column

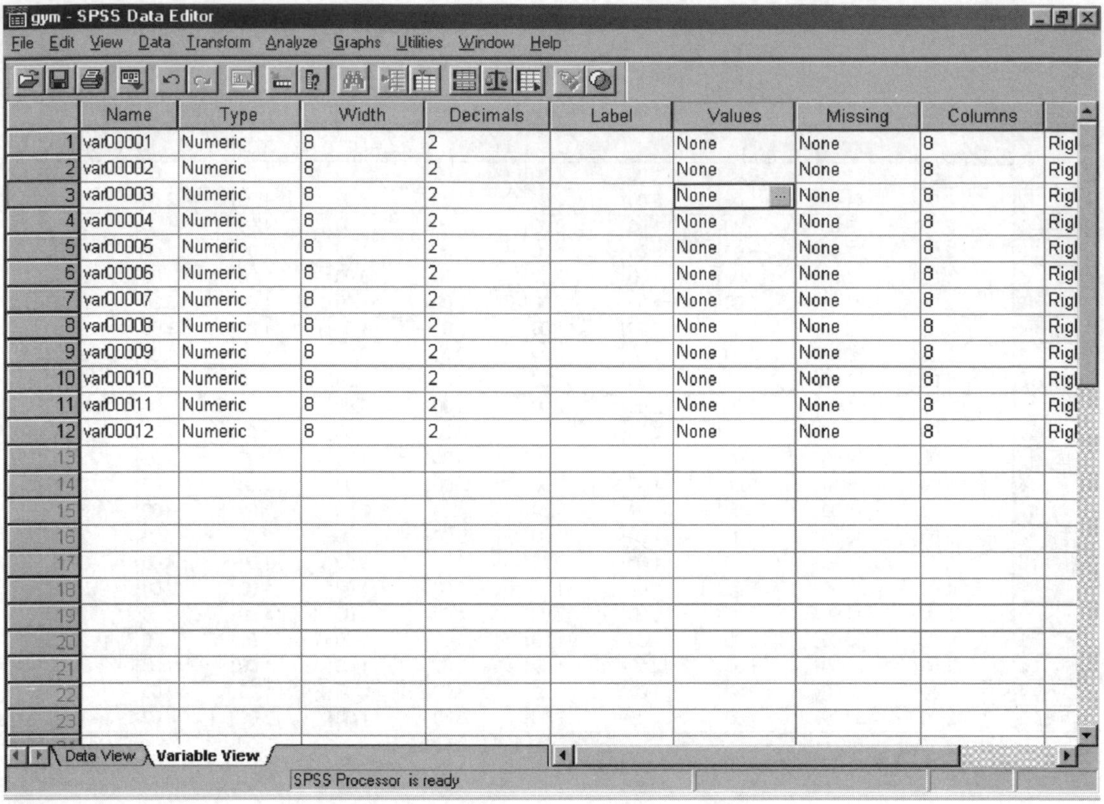

Plate 12.3 The **Variable Viewer**

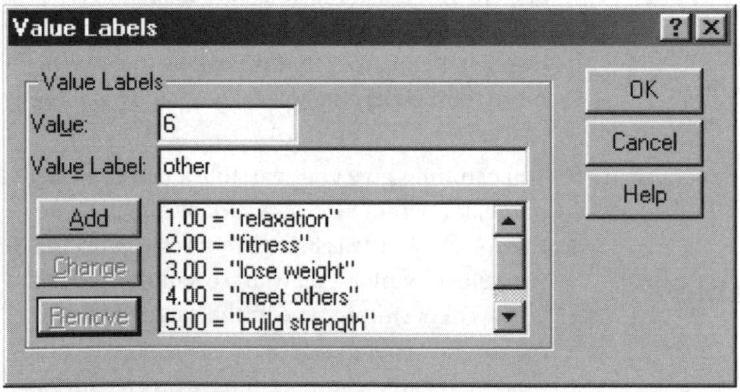

Plate 12.4 The **Value Labels** dialog box

relating to the variable you are working on. A small button with three dots on it will appear. → the button. The **Value Labels** dialog box will appear (Plate 12.4). → the box to the right of **Value** and begin to define the value labels. To do this,

enter the value (e.g. **1**) in the area to the right of **Value** and then the value label (e.g. **relaxation**) in the area to the right of **Value Label**. Then → **Add**. Do this for each value. When you have finished → **OK**

5. You will then need to inform SPSS of the value that you have nominated for each variable to indicate a missing value. In the case of *reasons*, the value is 0 (zero). To assign the missing value, → the cell for this variable in the **Missing** column. Again, → the button that will appear with three dots on it. This will generate the **Missing Values** dialog box (Plate 12.5). In the **Missing Values** dialog box, enter the missing value (**0**) below **Discrete missing value:** and then → **OK**

In order to simplify the following presentation, *reasons* will be the only variable for which a variable label will be defined.

Recoding variables

Sometimes you need to recode variables—for example, when you want to group people. You would need to do this in order to produce a table like Table 11.3 (p. 223) for an interval/ratio variable like **var00002**, which we will give the variable name *age*. SPSS offers two choices: you can recode *age* so that it will be changed in the **Data Viewer**, or you can keep *age* as it is and create a new variable. This latter option is desirable whenever you want to preserve the variable in question as well as create a new one. Since we may want to carry out analyses involving *age* as an interval/ratio variable, we will recode it so that a new variable, which we will call *agegp*, for **age** groups, will be created. The aim of the following

operations is to create a new variable—*agegp*—which will comprise five age bands, as in Table 11.3.

1. → **Transform** → **Recode** → **Into Different Variables** [opens **Recode into Different Variables** dialog box shown in Plate 12.6]

2. → *age* → ▶button [puts **age** in **Numeric Variable->Output Variable:** box] → box beneath **Output Variable Name:** and type *agegp* → **Change** [puts *agegp* in the **Numeric Variable->Output Variable:** box] → **Old and New Values...** → [opens **Recode into Different Variables: Old and New Values** sub-dialog box shown in Plate 12.7]

3. → the circle by **System- or user-missing** and by **System-missing** under **New Value**, if you have missing values for a variable, which is the case for this variable

4. → circle by **Range: Lowest Through** and type **20** in the box → box by **Value** in **New Value** and type **1** → **Add** [the new value will appear in the **Old-- >New:** box]

5. → first box by **Range:** and type **21** and in box after **through** type **30** → box by **Value** in **New Value** and type **2** → **Add**

6. → first box by **Range:** and type **31** and in box after **through** type **40** → box by **Value** in **New Value** and type **3** → **Add**

7. → first box by **Range:** and type **41** and in box after **through** type **50** → box by **Value** in **New Value** and type **4** → **Add**

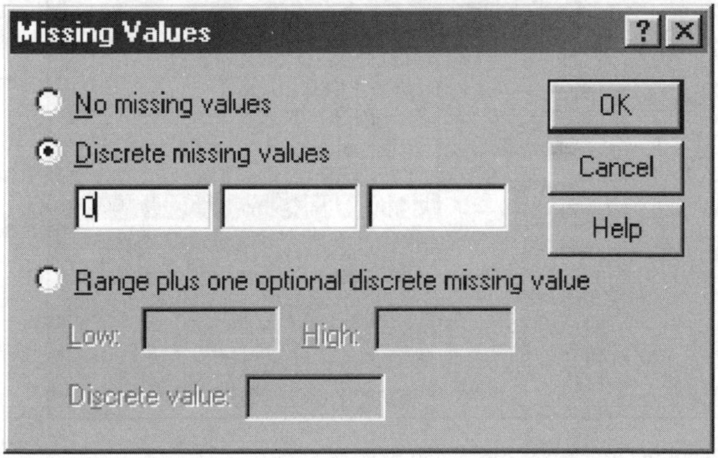

Plate 12.5 The **Missing Values** dialog box

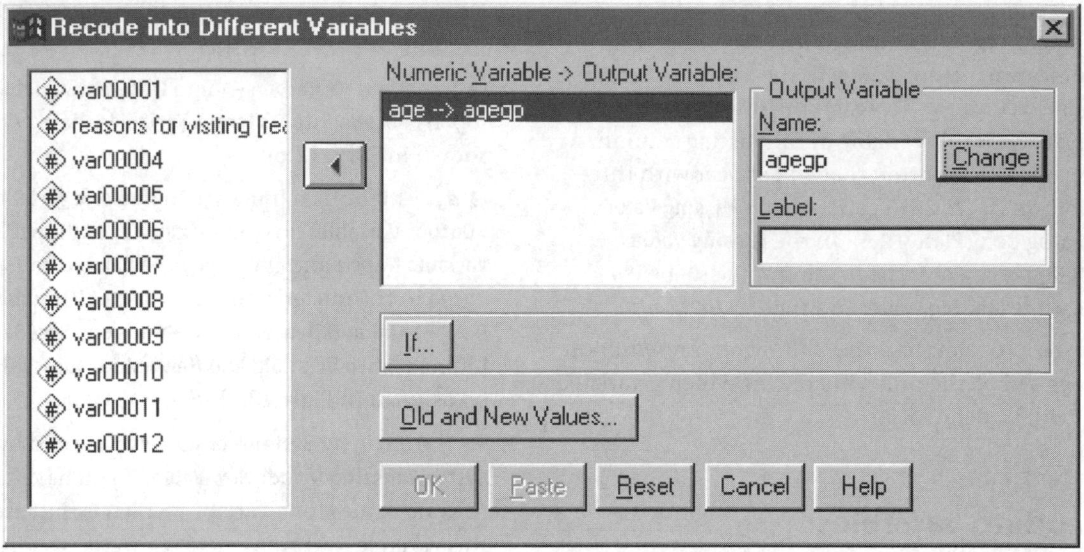

Plate 12.6 The **Recode into Different Variables** dialog box

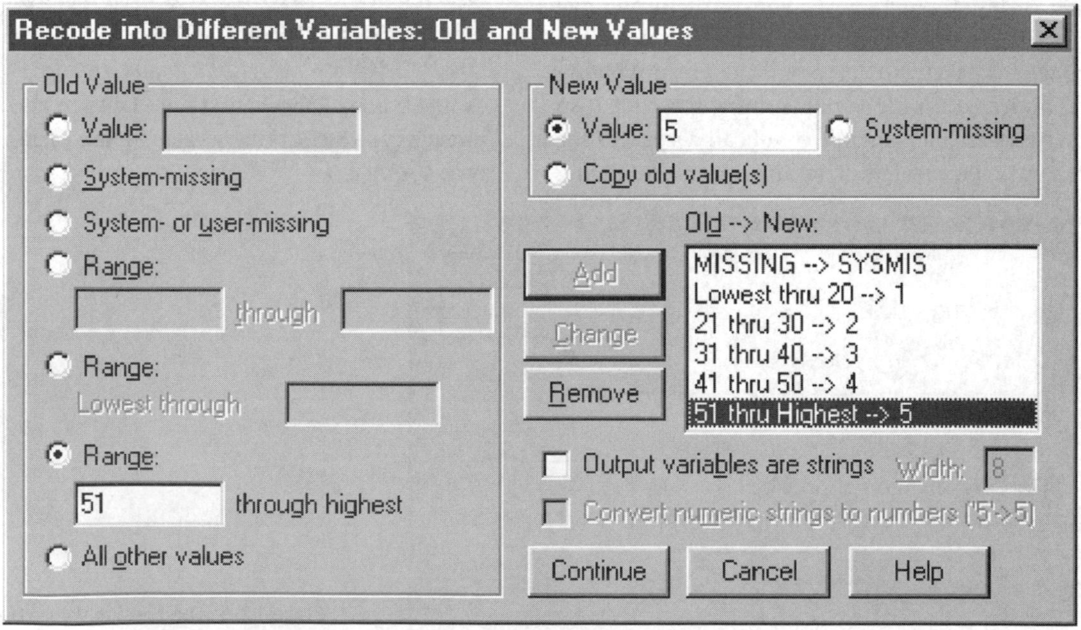

Plate 12.7 The **Recode into Different Variables: Old and New Values** sub-dialog box

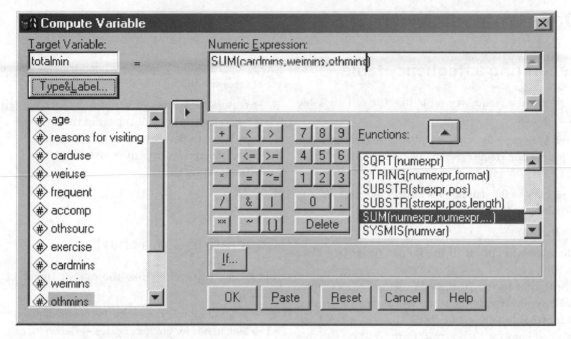

Plate 12.8 The **Compute Variable** dialog box

8. → circle by **Range: through highest** and type **51** in the box → box by **Value** in **New Value** and type **5** → **Add** → **Continue** [closes the **Recode into Different Variables: Old and New Values** sub-dialog box shown in Plate 12.7 and returns you to the **Recode into Different Variables** shown in Plate 12.6]

9. → **OK**

The new variable *agegp* will be created and will appear in the **Data Viewer**. You would then need to generate **value labels** for the five age bands and possibly a **variable label** using the approach described above.

Computing a new variable

A person's total amount of time spent in the gym is made up of three variables: *cardmins*, *weimins*, and *othmins*. If we add these up, we should arrive at the total number of minutes spent on activities in the gym. In so doing, we will create a new variable *totalmin*. To do this, this procedure should be followed:

1. → **Transform** → **Compute...** [opens the **Compute Variable** dialog box shown in Plate 12.8]

2. under **Target Variable:** type *totalmin*

3. select **SUM[numexpr,numexpr,...]** from the list underneath **Functions:** and click on the button with an upward-pointing arrowhead to send it into the box underneath **Numeric Expression:**

4. from the list of variables at the left, → *cardmins* → ►button [puts *cardmins* in box after **SUM**]; → *weimins* → ►button [puts *weimins* in box after **,cardmins**]; → *othmins* → ►button [puts *othmins* in box after **,weimins**]

5. → **OK**

The new variable *totalmin* will be created and will appear in the **Data Editor**.

Now at last, we can begin to analyse the data!

Data analysis with SPSS

Generating a frequency table

To produce a frequency table like the one in Table 11.2 (p. 223):

1. → **Analyze** → **Descriptive Statistics** → **Frequencies...** [opens the **Frequencies** dialog box shown in Plate 12.9]

2. → **reasons for visiting** → ▶button [puts **reasons for visiting** in **Variable[s]:** box]

3. → **OK**

The table will appear in the **Output Viewer** (see Plate 12.10).

Note that in the **Frequencies** dialog box, variables that have been assigned labels will appear in terms of their variable labels, but those that have not been assigned labels will appear in terms of their variable names. This is a feature of all dialog boxes produced via **Analyze** and **Graphs** (see below).

Generating a bar chart

To produce a bar chart like the one in Figure 11.2 (p. 224):

1. → **Graphs** → **Bar...** [opens **Bar Charts** dialog box]

2. → **Simple** → **Summaries for groups of cases** → **Define**

→ [opens **Define Simple Bar: Summaries for Groups of Cases** sub-dialog box shown in Plate 12.11]

3. → **reasons for visiting** → ▶button by **Category Axis** [**reasons for visiting** will appear in the box] → **N of cases** beneath **Bars Represent** [*if* this has not already been selected, otherwise continue without doing this]

4. → **OK**

Generating a pie chart

To produce a pie chart like the one in Figure 11.3 (p. 224):

1. → **Graphs** → **Pie...** [opens the **Pie Charts** dialog box] → **Summaries for groups of cases** → **Define** [opens the **Define Pie: Summaries for Groups of Cases** sub-dialog box]

2. → **reasons for visiting** → ▶button by **Define slices by** [**reasons for visiting** will appear in the box] → **N of cases** beneath **Slices Represent:** [if this has *not* already been selected, otherwise continue without doing this]

3. → **OK**

In order to include percentages, as in Figure 11.3 (p. 224), *double-click* anywhere in the chart in order

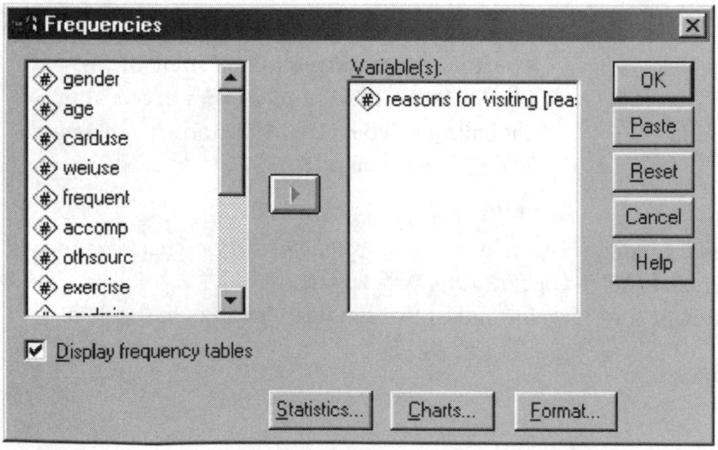

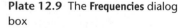

Plate 12.9 The **Frequencies** dialog box

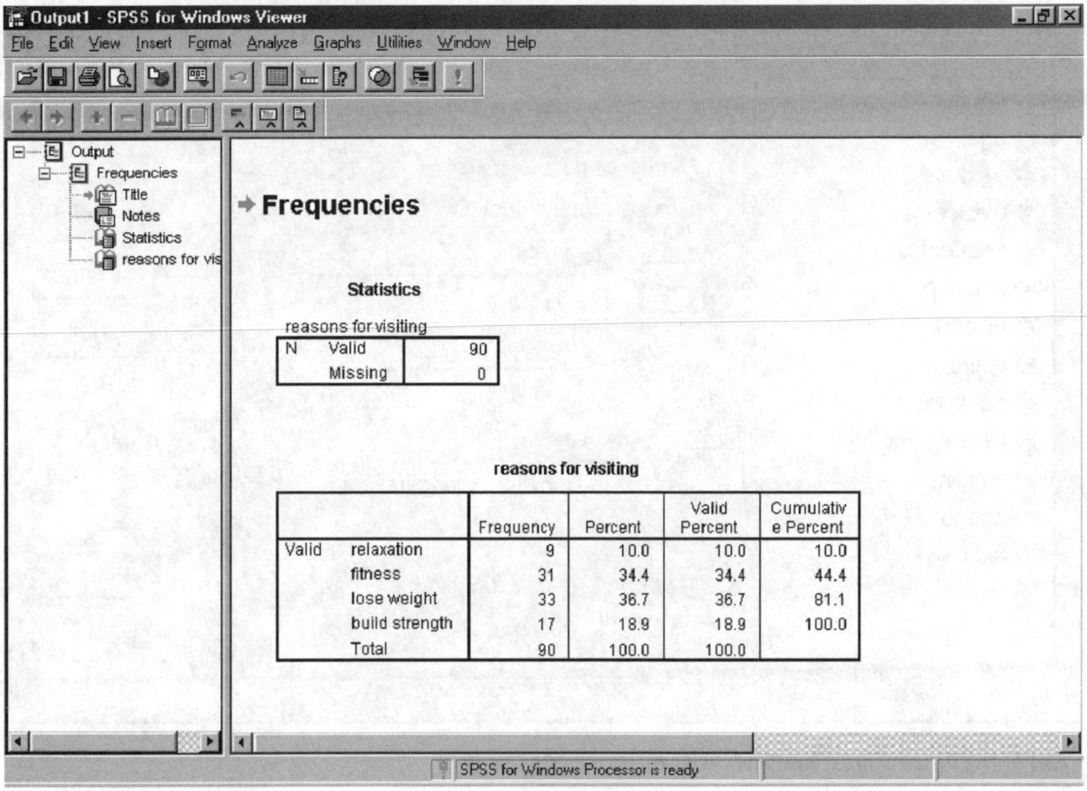

```
Output1 - SPSS for Windows Viewer                              _ | 🗗 | X
File  Edit  View  Insert  Format  Analyze  Graphs  Utilities  Window  Help
```

→ Frequencies

Statistics

reasons for visiting

N	Valid	90
	Missing	0

reasons for visiting

		Frequency	Percent	Valid Percent	Cumulativ e Percent
Valid	relaxation	9	10.0	10.0	10.0
	fitness	31	34.4	34.4	44.4
	lose weight	33	36.7	36.7	81.1
	build strength	17	18.9	18.9	100.0
	Total	90	100.0	100.0	

SPSS for Windows Processor is ready

Plate 12.10 The **Output Viewer**

to bring up the **Chart Editor**. The chart will appear in the **Chart Editor** and the main figure will become opaque. Then **→ Chart** and then **→ Options...** and then place a tick by **Percents** [there should also be a tick by **Text**].

Your chart will be in colour, but, if you only have access to a monochrome printer, you can change your pie chart into patterns, which allows the slices to be clearer. At the end of the next section, there is a description of how to do this.

Generating a histogram

Producing a histogram like the one in Figure 11.4 (p. 224) is somewhat more complicated. The standard procedure for generating a histogram is **→ Graphs → Histogram** and then selecting the relevant variable.

This procedure will generate a very good histogram but SPSS will define the age bands. If you want to define the bars yourself, you should follow the steps for the one produced for Figure 11.4, which involved following the steps entailed in generating a bar chart:

1. **→ Graphs → Bar...** [opens **Bar Charts** dialog box]

2. **→ Simple → Summaries for groups of cases → Define →** [opens **Define Simple Bar: Summaries for Groups of Cases** sub-dialog box shown in Plate 12.11]

3. **→** *agegp* **→ ►**button by **Category Axis** [*agegp* will appear in the box] **→ N of cases** beneath **Bars Represent** [*if* this has not already been selected, otherwise continue without doing this] **→ OK**

4. after the bar chart appears in the **SPSS for Windows** viewer, double-click anywhere in the body of the figure; this will bring up the **SPSS for Windows Chart**

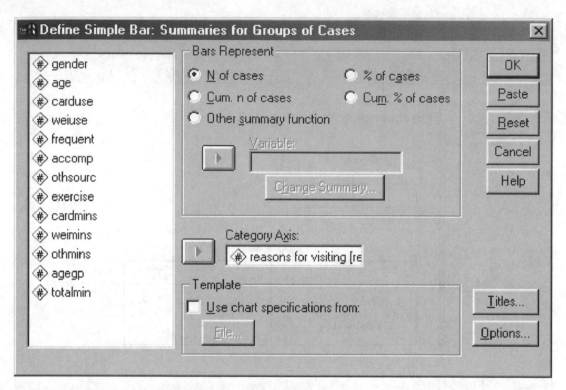

Plate 12.11 The **Define Simple Bar: Summaries for Groups of Cases**

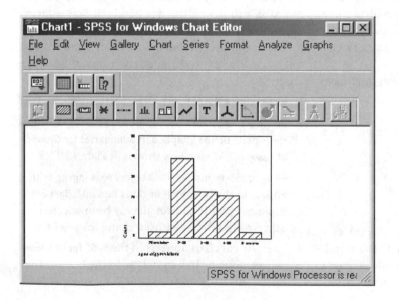

Plate 12.12 The **Chart Editor**

Editor shown in Plate 12.12 → **Chart** → **Bar Spacing...** [opens the **Bar Spacing** sub-dialog box]

5. in the small box to the right of **Inter-Bar Spacing** replace the figure in the box with **0** → **OK** [closes the **Bar Spacing** sub-dialog box and returns you to the **SPSS for Windows Chart Editor** shown in Plate 12.12]

6. → **File** → **Close**

A new bar chart will appear in the **SPSS for Windows Chart Editor**, which will be the same as the one produced in Figure 11.4 (p. 224). This procedure essentially entails producing a bar chart but with the spaces between bars removed so that a histogram is generated. This procedure allows you to define your own bars.

When the **SPSS for Windows Chart Editor** is open, all figures can be edited, so that, for example, colours can be changed or patterns inserted. This can be very useful if you do not have access to a colour printer. Figures 11.2, 11.3, and 11.4 (p. 224) were produced by changing the bars or slices to white and then introducing patterns. When in the **SPSS for Windows Chart Editor**, you can experiment by → **Format** and then selecting from the choices there. This procedure applies to all charts.

Generating the arithmetic mean, median, standard deviation, and range

To produce the mean, median, standard deviation and the range for an interval/ratio variable like *age*, the following steps should be followed:

1. → **Analyze** → **Descriptive Statistics** → **Explore...** [opens the **Explore** dialog box]

2. → *age* → ▶button to the left of **Dependent List:** [puts *age* in the **Dependent List:** box] → **Statistics** under **Display** → **OK**

The output will also include the 95 per cent confidence interval for the mean, which is based on the standard error of the mean. The output can be found in Table 12.1.

Generating a contingency table, chi-square, and Cramér's *V*

In order to generate a contingency table, like that in Table 11.4 (p. 227), along with a chi-square test and Cramér's *V*, the following procedure should be followed:

1. → **Analyze** → **Descriptive Statistics** → **Crosstabs...** [opens the **Crosstabs** dialog box shown in Plate 12.13]

2. → **reasons for visiting** → ▶button by **Row[s]** [**reasons for visiting** will appear in the **Row[s]:** box] → *gender* → ▶button by **Column[s]:** [*gender* will appear in the **Column[s]:** box] → **Cells** [opens **Crosstabs: Cell Display** sub-dialog box shown in Plate 12.14]

3. Make sure **Observed** in the **Counts** box has been selected. Make sure **Column** under **Percentages** has been selected. If either of these has not been selected, simply click at the relevant point. → **Continue** [closes **Crosstabs: Cell Display** sub-dialog box and returns you to the **Crosstabs** dialog box shown in Plate 12.13]

4. → **Statistics...** [opens the **Crosstabs: Statistics** sub-dialog box shown in Plate 12.15]

5. → **Chi-square** → **Phi and Cramér's V** → **Continue** [closes **Crosstabs: Statistics** sub-dialog box and returns you to the **Crosstabs** dialog box shown in Plate 12.13]

6. → **OK**

The resulting output can be found in Table 12.2.

If you have a table with two dichotomous variables, you would use the same sequence of steps to produce phi.

Generating Pearson's *r* and Spearman's rho

To produce Pearson's *r* in order to find the correlations between *age*, **cardmins**, and **weimins**, follow these steps:

1. → **Analyze** → **Correlate** → **Bivariate...** [opens **Bivariate Correlations** dialog box shown in Plate 12.16]

Table 12.1 Explore output for *age* (SPSS output)

Explore

Case Processing Summary

	Cases					
	Valid		Missing		Total	
	N	Percent	N	Percent	N	Percent
AGE	89	98.9%	1	1.1%	90	100.0%

Descriptives

			Statistic	Std. Error
AGE	Mean		33.5955	.9420
	95% Confidence	Lower bound	31.7235	
	Interval for mean	Upper bound	35.4675	
	5% Trimmed mean		33.3159	
	Median		31.0000	
	Variance		78.971	
	Std. Deviation		8.8866	
	Minimum		18.00	
	Maximum		57.00	
	Range		39.00	
	Interquartile Range		14.0000	
	Skewness		.446	.255
	Kurtosis		−.645	.506

2. → *age* → ▶button → *cardmins* → ▶button → *weimins* → ▶button [*age*, *cardmins*, and *weimins* should now be in the **Variables:** box] → **Pearso̲n** [*if not already selected*] → **OK**

The resulting output is in Table 12.3.

To produce correlations with Spearman's rho, follow the same procedure but instead of selecting **Pearson**, you should → **Spearman** instead.

Generating scatter diagrams

Scatter diagrams, known as *scatterplots* in SPSS, are produced in the following way. Let us say that we want to plot the relationship between *age* and *cardmins*. There is a convention that, if one variable can be identified as likely to be the independent variable, it should be placed on the *x* axis, that is, the horizontal axis. Since *age* is bound to be the independent variable, we would follow these steps:

1. → **G̲raphs** → **S̲catter...** [opens the **Scatter Plot** dialog box]

2. → **Simple** [usually this has been automatically selected] → **Define** [opens the **Simple Scatterplot** sub-dialog box shown in Plate 12.17]

3. → *cardmins* → ▶button by **Y̲ Axis:** → *age* → ▶button by **X̲ Axis:** → **OK**

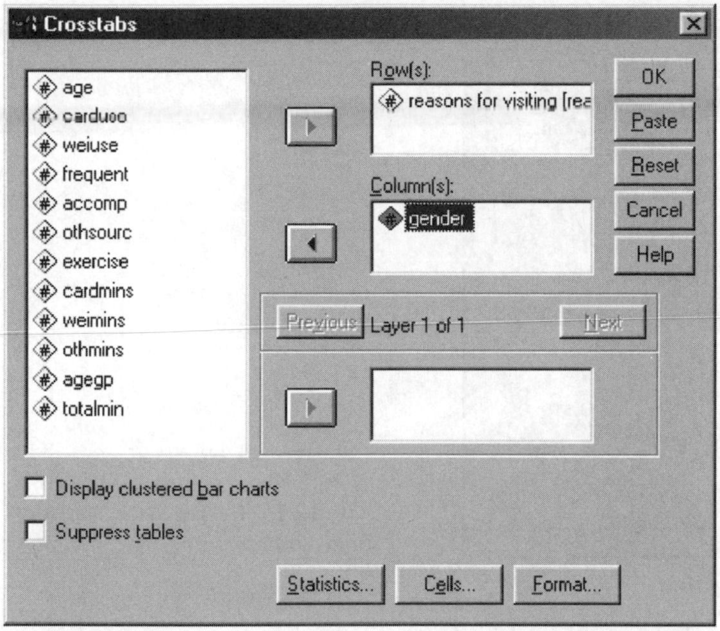

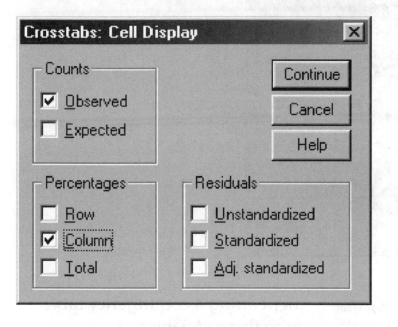

Plate 12.13 The **Crosstabs** dialog box

Plate 12.14 The **Crosstabs: Cell Display** sub-dialog box

The scatter diagram can then be edited by bringing up the **SPSS for Windows Chart Editor**. For example, the type and size of the markers can be changed by clicking anywhere in the chart in the **Chart Editor** and then → **Format** and then → **Marker...**.

Comparing means and eta

To produce a table like Table 11.5 (p. 230), these steps should be followed:

1. → **Analyze** → **Compare Means** → **Means...** [opens the **Means** dialog box shown in Plate 12.18]

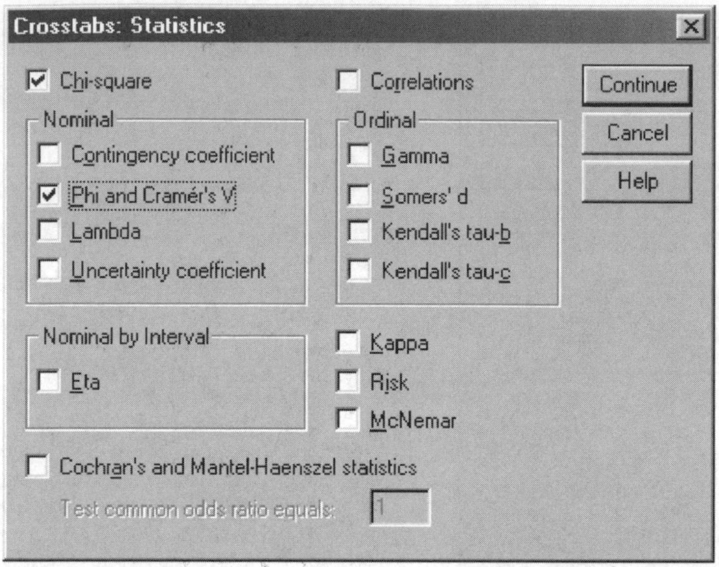

Crosstabs: Statistics

☑ Chi-square   ☐ Correlations

Nominal
☐ Contingency coefficient
☑ Phi and Cramér's V
☐ Lambda
☐ Uncertainty coefficient

Ordinal
☐ Gamma
☐ Somers' d
☐ Kendall's tau-b
☐ Kendall's tau-c

Nominal by Interval
☐ Eta

☐ Kappa
☐ Risk
☐ McNemar

☐ Cochran's and Mantel-Haenszel statistics
  Test common odds ratio equals: [1]

Continue
Cancel
Help

Plate 12.15 The **Crosstabs: Statistics** sub-dialog box

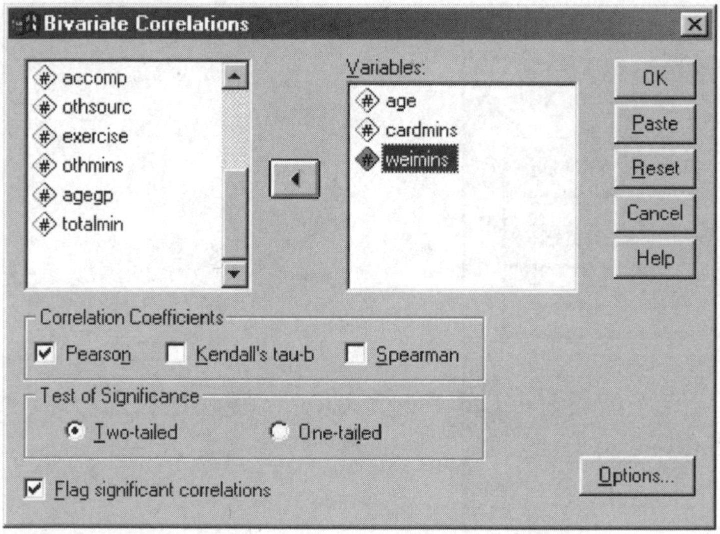

Bivariate Correlations

accomp
othsourc
exercise
othmins
agegp
totalmin

Variables:
age
cardmins
iweimins

OK
Paste
Reset
Cancel
Help

Correlation Coefficients
☑ Pearson   ☐ Kendall's tau-b   ☐ Spearman

Test of Significance
◉ Two-tailed   ○ One-tailed

☑ Flag significant correlations   Options...

Plate 12.16 The **Bivariate Correlations** dialog box

2. → *cardmins* → ►button to the left of **Dependent List:** → **reasons for visiting** → ►button to the left of **Independent List:** → **Options** [opens the **Means: Options** sub-dialog box]

3. → **Anova table and eta** underneath **Statistics for First Layer** → **Continue** [closes the **Means: Options** sub-dialog box and returns you to the **Means** dialog box shown in Plate 12.18] → **OK**

Generating a contingency table with three variables

To create a table like that in Table 11.7 (p. 232), you would need to follow these steps:

1. → **Analyze** → **Descriptive Statistics** → **Crosstabs...** [opens the **Crosstabs** dialog box shown in Plate 12.13]

Table 12.2 Contingency table for **reasons for visiting** by *age* (SPSS output)

Crosstabs

Case Processing Summary

	Cases					
	Valid		Missing		Total	
	N	Percent	N	Percent	N	Percent
reasons for visiting * GENDER	90	100.0%	0	.0%	90	100.0%

reasons for visiting * GENDER Crosstabulation

			GENDER		
			1.00	2.00	Total
reasons for visiting	relaxation	Count	3	6	9
		% within GENDER	7.1%	12.5%	10.0%
	fitness	Count	15	16	31
		% within GENDER	35.7%	33.3%	34.4%
	lose weight	Count	8	25	33
		% within GENDER	19.0%	52.1%	36.7%
	build strength	Count	16	1	17
		% within GENDER	38.1%	2.1%	18.9%
Total		Count	42	48	90
		% within GENDER	100.0%	100.0%	100.0%

Chi-Square Tests

	Value	df	Asymp. Sig. (2-sided)
Pearson Chi-Square	22.726[a]	3	.000
Likelihood Ratio	25.805	3	.000
Linear-by-Linear Association	9.716	1	.002
N of Valid Cases	90		

[a.] 2 cells (25.0%) have expected count less than 5. The minimum expected count is 4.20.

Symmetric Measures

		Value	Approx. Sig.
Nominal by Nominal	Phi	.503	.000
	Cramer's V	.503	.000
N of Valid Cases		90	

[a.] Not assuming the null hypothesis.

[b.] Using the asymptotic standard error assuming the null hypotheses.

Table 12.3 Correlations output for *age*, *weimins*, and *cardmins* (SPSS output)

Correlations

Correlations

		AGE	WEIMINS	CARDMINS
AGE	Pearson Correlation	1.000	−.273**	−.109
	Sig. (2-tailed)	.	.010	.311
	N	89	89	89
WEIMINS	Pearson Correlation	−.273**	1.000	−.161
	Sig. (2-tailed)	.010	.	.130
	N	89	90	90
CARDMINS	Pearson Correlation	−.109	−.161	1.000
	Sig. (2-tailed)	.311	.130	.
	N	89	90	90

** Correlation is significant at the 0.01 level (2-tailed).

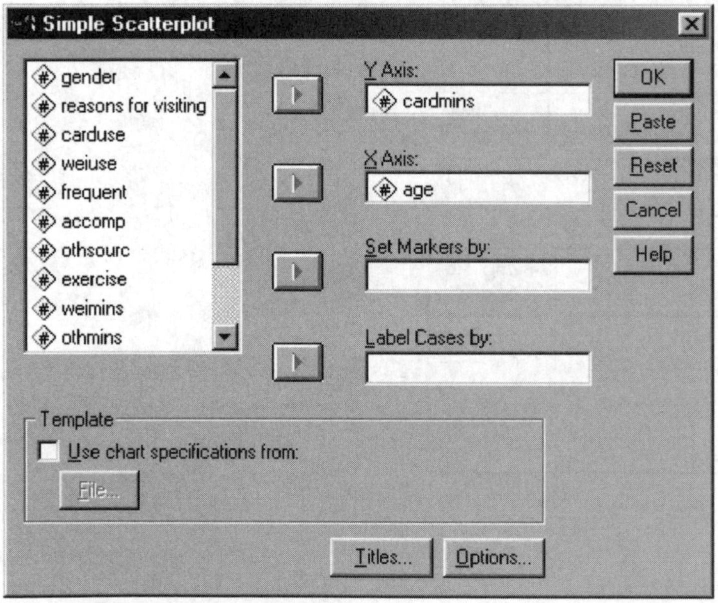

Plate 12.17 The **Simple Scatterplot** sub-dialog box

2. → *othsourc* → ►button by **R̲ow[s]** [*othsourc* will appear in the **R̲ow[s]:** box]

3. → *age3* [this is the name I gave when I created a new variable with *age* recoded into three categories] → ►button by **C̲olumn[s]:** [*age3* will appear in the **C̲olumn[s]:** box] → *gender* → ►

beneath **Pre̲vious** [*gender* will appear in the box underneath **Layer 1 of 1**]→ **C̲ells** [opens **Crosstabs: Cell Display** sub-dialog box shown in Plate 12.14]

4. Make sure **O̲bserved** in the **Counts** box has been selected. Make sure **Column** under **Percentages** has been selected. If either of these has not been

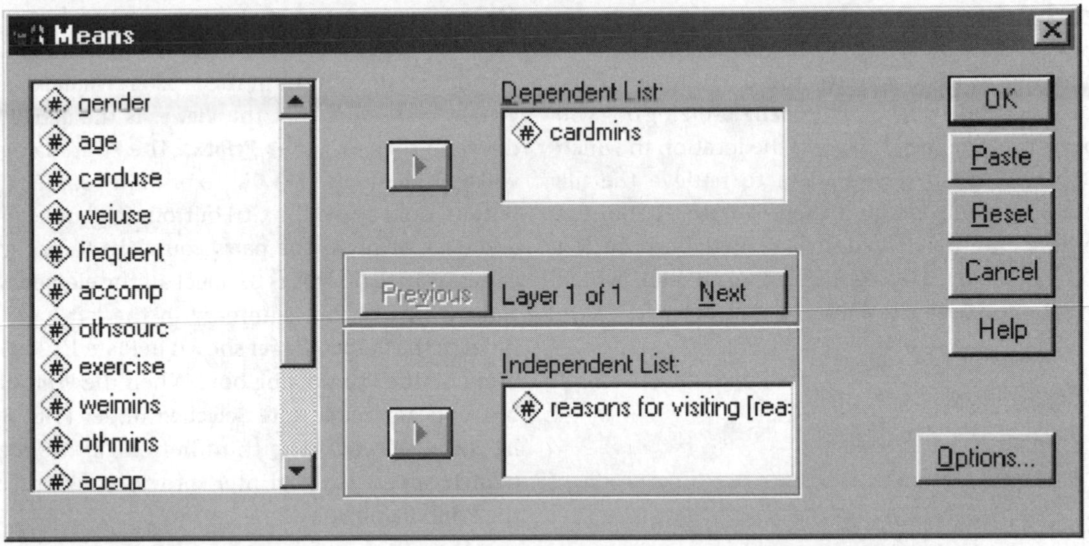

Plate 12.18 The **Means** dialog box

selected, simply click at the relevant point. →
Continue [closes **Crosstabs: Cell Display** sub-dialog
box and returns you to the **Crosstabs** dialog box
shown in Plate 12.13]

5. → **OK**

The resulting table will look somewhat different
from Table 11.7 (p. 232) in that *gender* will appear as
a row rather than as a column variable.

Further operations in SPSS

Saving your data

You will need to save your data for future use. To do
this, make sure that the **Data Editor** is the active window. Then,

→ **File** → **Save As...**

The **Save Data As** dialog box will then appear. You will
need to provide a name for your data, which will be
placed after **File name:**. I called the file 'gym study'.
You also need to decide where you are going to save
the data—for example, onto a floppy disk. To select
the destination drive, → the downward pointing
arrow to the right of the box by **Save in**. Then choose

the drive to which you want to save your data. Then
→ **Save**.

Remember that this procedure saves your data *and*
any other work you have done on your data—for
example, value labels and recoded variables. If you
subsequently use the data again and do more work
on your data, such as creating a new variable, you
will need to save the data again or the new work will
be lost. SPSS will give you a choice of renaming your
data, in which case you will have two files of data
(one with the original data and one with any
changes), or keeping the same name, in which case
the file will be changed and the existing name
retained.

Retrieving your data

When you want to retrieve the data file you have created, → **File** → **Open...**. The **Open File** dialog box will appear. You then need to go to the location in which you have deposited your data to retrieve the file containing your data and then → **Open**. A shortcut alternative to this procedure is to → the first button on the toolbar (it looks like an open file), which brings up the **Open File** dialog box.

Printing output

To print all the output in the **SPSS for Windows Output Viewer**, make sure that the **Viewer** is the active window and then → **File** → **Print...**. The **Print** dialog box will appear and then → **OK**. To print just some of your output, hold down the Ctrl button on your keyboard and click once on the parts you want to print. The easiest way to do this is to select all the elements you want in the output summary in the left-hand segment of the **Output Viewer** shown in Plate 12.10. Then bring up the **Print** dialog box. When the **Print** dialog box appears, make sure **Selection** under **Print Range** has been selected. The third button on the toolbar (which appears as a printer) provides a shortcut to the **Print** dialog box.

Overview

The aim of this chapter has been to introduce the ways in which SPSS can be employed to implement the techniques learned in Chapter 11. Learning new software requires some perseverance and at times the work put in does not seem to be worth the learning process. But it is worth it. It would take you far longer to perform calculations on a sample of around 100 than to learn the software. If you find yourself moving into much more advanced techniques, the time saved is even more substantial, particularly with large samples. One final point is to remind you of the desirability of becoming familiar with SPSS *before* you begin designing your research instruments, because it is advisable to be aware of difficulties you might have in presenting your data in SPSS at an early stage.

Revision questions

Getting started in SPSS

- Outline the differences between: variable names, variable labels, and value labels.
- In what circumstances might you want to recode a variable?
- In what circumstances might you want to create a new variable?

Data analysis with SPSS

Using the gym survey data, create:

- a frequency table for *exercise*;
- a bar chart and pie chart for *exercise* and compare their usefulness;
- a histogram for *cardmins*;
- measures of central tendency and dispersion for *cardmins*;
- a contingency table and chi-square test for *exercise* and *gender*;
- Pearson's *r* for *age* and *cardmins*;
- Spearman's rho for *carduse* and *weiuse;*
- a scatter diagram for *age* and *cardmins*;
- a comparing means analysis for *totalmin* and **reasons for visiting**.

Part Three

Part Three of this book is concerned with qualitative research. Chapter 13 sets the scene by exploring the main features of this research strategy. Chapter 14 deals with ethnography and participant observation, which are among the main ways of collecting qualitative data. Chapter 15 is concerned with the kind of interviewing that is carried out in qualitative research. Chapter 16 addresses the focus group method, which is an increasingly popular technique that allows groups of people to be interviewed. Chapter 17 explores two approaches to the study of language in social research: conversation analysis and discourse analysis. Chapter 18 explores the types of documents with which qualitative researchers tend to be concerned and approaches to examining them. Chapter 19 examines different approaches to qualitative data analysis and offers advice on how it can be carried out. Chapter 20 shows you how to use computer software in the form of NVivo to conduct the kind of analysis discussed in Chapter 19.

These chapters will provide you with the essential tools for doing qualitative research. They will take you from the very general issues to do with the generic features of qualitative research to the very practical issues of conducting your own observational studies or interviews and analysing your own data.

13 The nature of qualitative research

Reader's guide

Qualitative research is a research strategy that usually emphasizes words rather than quantification in the collection and analysis of data. As a research strategy it is inductivist, constructionist, and interpretivist, but qualitative researchers do not always subscribe to all three of these features. This chapter is concerned with outlining the main features of qualitative research, which has become an increasingly popular approach to social research. The chapter explores:

- the main steps in qualitative research; delineating the sequence of stages in qualitative research is more controversial than with quantitative research, because it exhibits somewhat less codification of the research process;

- the relationship between theory and research;

- the nature of concepts in qualitative research and their differences from concepts in quantitative research;

- how far reliability and validity are appropriate criteria for qualitative researchers and whether alternative criteria that are more tailored to the research strategy are necessary;

- the main preoccupations of qualitative researchers; five areas are identified in terms of an emphasis on: seeing through the eyes of research participants; description and context; process; flexibility and lack of structure; and concepts and theory as outcomes of the research process;

- some common criticisms of qualitative research;

- the main contrasts between qualitative and quantitative research;

- the stance of feminist researchers on qualitative research.

Introduction

We began Chapter 3 by noting that *quantitative* research had been outlined in Chapter 1 as a distinctive research strategy. Much the same kind of general point can be registered in relation to *qualitative* research. In Chapter 1 it was suggested that qualitative research differs from quantitative research in several ways. Most obviously, qualitative research tends to be concerned with words rather than numbers, but three further features were particularly noteworthy:

- an inductive view of the relationship between theory and research, whereby the former is generated out of the latter;

- an epistemological position described as interpretivist, meaning that, in contrast to the adoption of a natural scientific model in quantitative research, the stress is on the understanding of the social world through an examination of the interpretation of that world by its participants; and

- an ontological position described as constructionist, which implies that social properties are outcomes of the interactions between individuals, rather than phenomena 'out there' and separate from those involved in its construction.

As Bryman and Burgess (1999) observe, although

there has been a proliferation of writings on qualitative research since the 1970s, stipulating what it is and is not as a distinct research strategy is by no means straightforward. They propose three reasons for this state of affairs.

- As a term 'qualitative research' is sometimes taken to imply an approach to social research in which quantitative data are not collected or generated. Many writers on qualitative research are critical of such a rendition of qualitative research, because (as we will see) the distinctiveness of qualitative research does not reside solely in the absence of numbers.

- Writers like Gubrium and Holstein (1997) have suggested that several different traditions in qualitative research can be identified (see Box 13.1).

- Sometimes, qualitative research is discussed in terms of the ways in which it differs from quantitative research. A potential problem with this tactic is that it means that qualitative research ends up being addressed in terms of what quantitative research is *not*.

Silverman (1993) has been particularly critical of accounts of qualitative research that do not acknowledge the variety of forms that the research strategy can assume. In other words, writers like Silverman are critical of attempts to specify the nature of qualitative research as a general approach. However, unless we can talk to a certain degree about the nature of qualitative research, it is difficult to see how it is possible to refer to qualitative research as a distinctive research strategy. In much the same way that in Chapter 3 it was recognized that quantitative researchers employ different research designs, in writing about the characteristics of qualitative research we will need to be sensitive to the different orientations of qualitative researchers. Without at least a sense of what is common to a set of many if not most studies that might be described as qualitative, the very notion of qualitative research would be rendered problematic. Yet it is clear that, for many social scientists, it is a helpful and meaningful category that can be seen in a variety of ways. Examples are: the arrival of specialist journals, such as *Qualitative Sociology* and *Qualitative Inquiry*; texts on qualitative research (e.g. Silverman 1993, 2000; Seale 1999); a huge *Handbook of Qualitative Research* (Denzin and Lincoln 1994, 2000); and a series of books on different facets of qualitative research (the Sage Qualitative Research Methods Series).

Several reasons might be proposed for the unease among some writers concerning the specification of the nature of qualitative research. Two reasons might

---

Box 13.1 Four traditions of qualitative research

Gubrium and Holstein (1997) suggest four traditions of qualitative research.

- *Naturalism*—seeks to understand social reality in its own terms; 'as it really is'; provides rich descriptions of people and interaction in natural settings.

- *Ethnomethodology*—seeks to understand how social order is created through talk and interaction; has a naturalistic orientation.

- *Emotionalism*—exhibits a concern with subjectivity and gaining access to 'inside' experience; concern with the inner reality of humans.

- *Postmodernism*—there is an emphasis on 'method talk'; sensitive to the different ways social reality can be constructed.

We encountered the term *naturalism* in Box 2.4 (p. 33). The use of the term here is more or less the same as the second meaning referred to in Box 2.4. The naturalist tradition has probably been the most common one over the years. The second tradition will be encountered in Chapter 17 when we will be looking at an approach to the collection of qualitative data known as *conversation analysis*. The more recent postmodern standpoint will be addressed in Chapter 23. The third tradition— emotionalism—has not become the focus of a significant stream of research and will not be emphasized in this book. However, the mere presence of these four contrasting traditions points to the difficulty of creating a definitive account of what qualitative research is and is not.

be regarded as having particular importance. First, qualitative research subsumes several diverse research methods that differ from each other considerably. The following are the main research methods associated with qualitative research.

- *Ethnography/participant observation.* While some caution is advisable in treating ethnography and participant observation as synonyms, in many respects they refer to similar if not identical approaches to data collection in which the researcher is immersed in a social setting for some time in order to observe and listen with a view to gaining an appreciation of the culture of a social group. It has been employed in such social research classics as Whyte's (1955) study of street corner life in a slum community and Gans's (1962) research on a similar group in the throes of urban redevelopment.

- *Qualitative interviewing.* This is a very broad term to describe a wide range of interviewing styles (see Box 5.3, p. 110, for an introduction). Moreover, qualitative researchers employing ethnography or participant observation typically engage in a substantial amount of qualitative interviewing.

- Focus groups (see Box 5.3, p. 110).

- Language-based approaches to the collection of qualitative data, such as discourse and conversation analysis.

- The collection and qualitative analysis of texts and documents.

Each of these approaches to data collection will be examined in Part Three. The picture with regard to the very different methods and sources that comprise qualitative research is made somewhat more complex by the fact that a multi-method approach is frequently employed. As noted above, researchers employing ethnography or participant observation frequently conduct qualitative interviews. However,

they also often collect and analyse texts and documents as well. Thus, there is considerable variability in the collection of data among studies that are typically deemed to be qualitative. Of course, quantitative research also subsumes several different methods of data collection (these were covered in Part Two), but the inclusion of methods concerned with the analysis of language as a form of qualitative research implies somewhat greater variability.

A second reason why there is some resistance to a delineation of the nature of qualitative research is that the connection between theory and research is somewhat more ambiguous than in quantitative research. With the latter research strategy, theoretical issues drive the formulation of a research question, which in turn drives the collection and analysis of data. Findings then feed back into the relevant theory. This is rather a caricature, because what counts as 'theory' is sometimes little more than the research literature relating to a certain issue or area. In qualitative research, theory is supposed to be an outcome of an investigation rather than something that precedes it. However, some writers, like Silverman (1993: 24), have argued that such a depiction of qualitative research is 'out of tune with the greater sophistication of contemporary field research design, born out of accumulated knowledge of interaction and greater concern with issues of reliability and validity'. This is particularly the case with conversation analysis, an approach to the study of language that will be examined in Chapter 17. However, qualitative research is more usually regarded as denoting an approach in which theory and categorization emerge out of the collection and analysis of data. The more general point being made is that such a difference within qualitative research may account for the unease about depicting the research strategy in terms of a set of stages.

The main steps in qualitative research

The sequence outlined in Figure 13.1 provides a representation of how the qualitative research process can be visualized. In order to illustrate the steps, a published study by Foster (1995) of crime in communities will be used. This study was previously encountered in Box 1.10 (p. 16).

- *Step 1. General research question(s).* The starting point for Foster's (1995) study of crime in communities, particularly ones that contain predominantly public housing, is the high levels of crime in poorer areas. To the extent that it is a focus of attention, it is frequently assumed that communities with high levels of crime tend to have low levels of social control. But Foster argues that we know very little about how informal social control operates in such communities and what its significance for crime is. She also notes that council estates are frequently presumed to be crime prone but that there is little evidence on 'the diversity in experience and attitudes of residents

within individual estates' (Foster 1995: 563). It would be easy to presume that, to the extent that council estates are prone to high crime levels, they exhibit low levels of social control. Thus Foster formulates a general set of concerns revolving around council estates and their crime-proneness and the possible role and dynamics of social control in the process. She also notes that some writers have suggested that the propensity to crime in council estates may be in part attributed to flaws in the design of the estates.

- *Step 2. Selecting relevant site(s) and subjects.* The research was conducted on a London council estate (with the fictitious name 'Riverside'), which had a high level of crime and which exhibited the kinds of housing features that are frequently associated with a propensity to crime. Relevant research participants, such as residents, were identified.

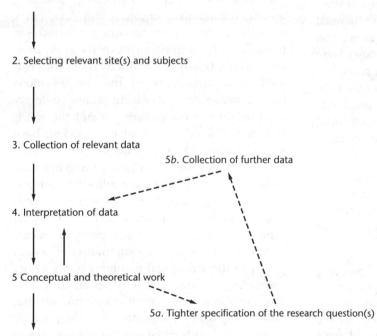

Fig. 13.1 An outline of the main steps of qualitative research

- *Step 3. Collection of relevant data.* Foster describes her research as 'ethnographic'. She spent eighteen months 'getting involved in as many aspects of life there as possible from attending tenant meetings, the mothers and toddlers group, and activities for young people, to socializing with some of the residents in the local pub' (Foster 1995: 566). Foster also tells us that 'extended interviews' were conducted with forty-five residents of Riverside (and another London estate, but the majority were from Riverside) and twenty-five 'officials', such as police and housing officers. Foster's account of her research methods suggests that she is likely to have generated two types of data: fieldwork notes based on her ethnographic observation of life in the community and detailed notes (and most probably transcripts) of interviews undertaken.

- *Step 4. Interpretation of data.* One of the key findings to emerge from the data is that, in spite of the fact that Riverside has a high crime rate, it is not perceived as a problem in this regard by Riverside residents. For example, she quotes from an interview with an elderly tenant: 'They used to say that they couldn't let the flats [apartments] here . . . but I mean as far as muggings or anything like that you don't hear of nothing like that even now' (Foster, 1995: 568). Instead, housing problems loomed larger in the minds of residents than crime. She also found that 'hidden economy' crimes were prevalent on the estate and that much crime was tolerated by residents. She also observes that, contrary to expectations about estates like Riverside, there was clear evidence of informal social control mechanisms at work, such as shaming practices.

- *Step 5. Conceptual and theoretical work.* No new concepts seem to emerge from Foster's research, but her findings enable her to tie together some of the elements outlined above under Step 1. For example, she writes:

Crime then need not be damaging *per se* providing other factors cushion its impact. On Riverside these included support networks in which tenants felt that someone was watching out for their properties and provided links with people to whom they could turn if they were in trouble. Consequently while generalized fears about crime remained prevalent, familiarity and support went some way to reducing the potential for hostile encounters.   (Foster 1995: 580)

It is this step, coupled with the interpretation of data, that forms the study's findings.

- *Steps 5a. Tighter specification of the research question(s),* and 5b. *Collection of further data.* There is no specific evidence from Foster's account that she followed a process in which she collected further data after she had built up early interpretations of her data. When this occurs, as it sometimes does in research within a grounded theory framework, there can be an interplay between interpretation and theorizing, on the one hand, and data collection, on the other. Such a strategy is frequently referred to as an *iterative* one. She does write at one point that some residents and officials were interviewed twice and in some cases even three times in the course of her research. This raises the possibility that she was re-interviewing certain individuals in the light of her emerging ideas about her data, but this can only be a speculation.

- *Step 6. Writing up findings/conclusions.* There is no real difference between the significance of writing up in quantitative research and qualitative research, so that exactly the same points made in relation to step 11 in Figure 3.1 (p. 63) apply here. An audience has to be convinced about the credibility and significance of the interpretations offered. Researchers are not and cannot be simply conduits for the things they see and the words they hear. The salience of what researchers have seen and heard has to be impressed on the audience. Foster does this by making clear to her audience that her findings have implications for policies regarding estates and crime and for our understanding of the links between housing, community, and crime. A key point to emerge from her work, which she emphasizes at several points in the article and hammers home in her concluding section, is that being an insider to Riverside allowed her to see that a community that may be regarded by outsiders as having a high propensity towards crime should not be presumed to be seen in this way by members of that community.

Two particularly distinctive aspects of the sequence of steps in qualitative research are the highly related issues of the links between theory and concepts with research data. It is to these issues that we now turn.

Theory and research

Most qualitative researchers when writing about their craft emphasize a preference for treating theory as something that emerges out of the collection and analysis of data. As will be seen in Chapter 19, practitioners of grounded theory—a frequently cited approach to the analysis of qualitative data— especially stress the importance of allowing theoretical ideas to emerge out of one's data. But some qualitative researchers argue that qualitative data can and should have an important role in relation to the *testing* of theories as well. Silverman (1993), in particular, has argued that in more recent times qualitative researchers have become increasingly interested in the testing of theories and that this is a reflection of the growing maturity of the strategy. Certainly, there is no reason why qualitative research cannot be employed in order to test theories that are specified in advance of data collection. In any case, much qualitative research entails the testing of theories in the course of the research process.

So, in Figure 13.1, the loop back from Step 5*a* 'tighter specification of the research question(s)' to Step 5*b* 'collection of further data' implies that a theoretical position may emerge in the course of research and may spur the collection of further data to test that theory. This kind of oscillation between testing emerging theories and collecting data is a particularly prominent feature of grounded theory. It is presented as a dashed line in Figure 13.1, because it is not as necessary a feature of the process of qualitative research as the other steps.

One key point that is implied by Figure 13.1 is that the typical sequence of steps in qualitative research entails the generation of theories rather than the testing of theories that are specified at the outset. Silverman (1993) is undoubtedly correct that prespecified theories *can be* and sometimes *are* tested with qualitative data, but the generation of theory tends to be the preferred approach.

Concepts in qualitative research

A central feature of Chapter 3 was the discussion of concepts and their measurement. For most qualitative researchers, developing measures of concepts will not be a significant consideration, but concepts are very much part of the landscape in qualitative research. However, the way in which concepts are developed and employed is often rather different from that implied in the quantitative research strategy. Blumer's (1954) distinction between 'definitive' and 'sensitizing' concepts captures aspects of the different ways in which concepts are thought about.

Blumer (1954) argued stridently against the use of definitive concepts in social research. The idea of definitive concepts is typified by the way in which, in quantitative research, a concept, once developed, becomes fixed through the elaboration of indicators. For Blumer, such an approach entailed the application of a straitjacket on the social world, because the concept in question comes to be seen exclusively in terms of the indicators that have been developed for it. Fine nuances in the form that the concept can assume or alternative ways of viewing the concept and its manifestations are sidelined. In other words, definitive concepts are excessively concerned with what is common to the phenomena that the concept is supposed to subsume rather than variety. Instead, Blumer recommended that social researchers should recognize that the concepts they use are sensitizing concepts in that they provide 'a general sense of reference and guidance in approaching empirical instances' (1954: 7). For Blumer, then, concepts should be employed in such a way that they give a very general sense of what to look for and act as a means for uncovering the variety of forms that the phenomena to which they refer can assume. In providing a critique of definitive concepts, it is clear that Blumer had in mind the concept-indicator model described in Chapter 3. In other words, his views entailed in large part a critique of quantitative research and a programmatic statement that would form a springboard for an alternative approach that

nowadays we would recognize as qualitative research.

Blumer's distinction is not without its problems. It is not at all clear how far a very general formulation of a concept can be regarded as a useful guide to empirical enquiry. If it is too general, it will simply fail to provide a useful starting point because its guidelines are too broad; if too narrow, it is likely to repeat some of the difficulties Blumer identified in relation to definitive concepts. However, his general view of concepts has attracted some support, because his preference for not imposing preordained schemes on the social world chimes with that of many qualitative researchers. As the example in Box 13.2 suggests, the researcher frequently starts out with a broad outline of a concept, which is revised and narrowed during the course of data collection. For subsequent researchers, the concept may be taken up and revised as it is employed in connection with different social contexts or in relation to somewhat different research questions.

Reliability and validity in qualitative research

In Chapters 2 and 3 it was noted that reliability and validity are important criteria in establishing and assessing the quality of research for the quantitative researcher. However, there has been some discussion among qualitative researchers concerning their relevance for qualitative research. Moreover, even writers who do take the view that the criteria are relevant have considered the possibility that the meanings of the terms need to be altered. For example, the issue of measurement validity almost by definition seems to carry connotations of measurement. Since measurement is not a major preoccupation among qualitative researchers, the issue of validity would seem to have little bearing on such studies. As foreshadowed briefly in Chapter 2, a number of different stances have been taken by qualitative researchers in relation to these issues.

Adapting reliability and validity for qualitative research

One stance is to assimilate reliability and validity into qualitative research with little change of meaning other than playing down the salience of measurement issues. Mason, for example, in her book on qualitative research, argues that reliability, validity and generalizability (which is the main component of external validity—see Chapter 2) 'are different kinds of measures of the quality, rigour and wider potential of research, which are achieved according to certain methodological and disciplinary conventions and principles' (1996: 21). She sticks very close to the meaning that these criteria have in quantitative research, where they have been largely developed. Thus, validity refers to whether 'you are observing, identifying, or "measuring" what you say

---

Box 13.2 The emergence of a concept in qualitative research: The case of emotional labour

Hochschild's (1983) idea of emotional labour—labour that 'requires one to induce or suppress feelings in order to sustain the outward countenance that produces the proper state of mind in others' (1983: 7)—has become a very influential concept in the sociology of work and in the developing area of the sociology of emotions. Somewhat ironically for a predominantly qualitative study, Hochschild's initial conceptualization appears to have emerged from a questionnaire she distributed to 261 university students. Within the questionnaire were two requests: 'Describe a real situation that was important to you in which you experienced a deep emotion' and 'Describe as fully and concretely as possible a real situation that was important to you in which you either changed the situation to fit your feelings or changed your feelings to fit the situation' (1983: 13). Thus, although a self-completion questionnaire was employed, the resulting data were qualitative. The data were analysed in terms of the idea of emotion *work*, which is the same as emotional labour but occurs in a private context. Emotional labour is essentially emotion work that is performed as part of one's paid employment. In order to develop the idea of emotional labour, Hochschild looked to the world of work. The main occupation she studied was the flight attendant. Several sources of data on emotional labour among flight attendants were employed. She gained access to Delta Airlines, a large American airline, and in the course of her investigations she:

- watched sessions for training attendants and had many conversations with both trainees and experienced attendants during the sessions;

- interviewed various personnel, such as managers in various sections, and advertising agents;

- examined Delta advertisements spanning thirty years;

- observed the flight attendant recruitment process at Pan American Airways, since she had not been allowed to do this at Delta;

- conducted 'open-ended interviews lasting three to five hours each with thirty flight attendants in the San Francisco Bay Area' (1983: 15).

As a contrasting occupational group that is nonetheless also involved in emotional labour, she also interviewed five debt collectors. In her book, she explores such topics as the human costs of emotional labour and the issue of gender in relation to it. It is clear that Hochschild's concept of emotional labour began as a somewhat imprecise idea that emerged out of a concern with emotion work and that was gradually developed in order to address its wider significance. The concept has been picked up by other qualitative researchers in the sociology of work. For example, Leidner (1993) has explored through ethnographic studies of a McDonald's restaurant and an insurance company the ways in which organizations seek to 'routinize' the display of emotional labour.

---

you are' (1996: 24). LeCompte and Goetz (1982) and Kirk and Miller (1986) also write about reliability and validity in relation to qualitative research but invest the terms with a somewhat different meaning from Mason. LeCompte and Goetz write about the following.

- *External reliability*, by which they mean the degree to which a study can be replicated. This is a difficult criterion to meet in qualitative research, since, as LeCompte and Goetz recognize, it is impossible to 'freeze' a social setting and the circumstances of an initial study to make it replicable in the sense in which the term is usually employed (see Chapter 3). However, they suggest several strategies that can be introduced in order to approach the requirements of external reliability. For example, they suggest that a qualitative researcher replicating ethnographic research needs to adopt a similar social role to that adopted by the original researcher. Otherwise what a researcher conducting a replication sees and hears will not be comparable to the original research.

- *Internal reliability*, by which they mean whether, when there is more than one observer, members of the research team agree about what they see and hear. This is a similar notion to *inter-observer consistency* (see Box 3.6, p. 70).

- *Internal validity*, by which they mean whether there is a good match between researchers' observations and the theoretical ideas they develop.

LeCompte and Goetz argue that internal validity tends to be a strength of qualitative research, particularly ethnographic research, because the prolonged participation in the social life of a group over a long period of time allows the researcher to ensure a high level of congruence between concepts and observations.

- *External validity*, which refers to the degree to which findings can be generalized across social settings. LeCompte and Goetz argue that unlike internal validity, external validity represents a problem for qualitative researchers because of their tendency to employ case studies and small samples.

As this brief treatment suggests, qualitative researchers have tended to employ the terms reliability and validity in very similar ways to quantitative researchers when seeking to develop criteria for assessing research.

Alternative criteria for evaluating qualitative research

However, a second position in relation to reliability and validity in qualitative research can be discerned. Some writers have suggested that qualitative studies should be judged or evaluated according to quite different criteria from those used by quantitative researchers. Lincoln and Guba (1985) and Guba and Lincoln (1994) propose that it is necessary to specify terms and ways of establishing and assessing the quality of qualitative research that provide an alternative to reliability and validity. They propose two primary criteria for assessing a qualitative study: *trustworthiness* and *authenticity*.

Trustworthiness is made up of four criteria, each of which has an equivalent criterion in quantitative research:

- *credibility*, which parallels internal validity;
- *transferability*, which parallels external validity;
- *dependability*, which parallels reliability;
- *confirmability*, which parallels objectivity.

A major reason for Guba and Lincoln's unease about the simple application of reliability and validity standards to qualitative research is that the criteria presuppose that a single absolute account of social reality is feasible. In other words, they are critical of the view (described in Chapter 1 as *realist*) that there are absolute truths about the social world that it is the job of the social scientist to reveal. Instead, they argue that there can be more than one and possibly several accounts.

Credibility

The significance of this stress on multiple accounts of social reality is especially evident in the trustworthiness criterion of *credibility*. After all, if there can be several possible accounts of an aspect of social reality, it is the feasibility or credibility of the account that a researcher arrives at that is going to determine its acceptability to others. The establishment of the credibility of findings entails both ensuring that research is carried out according to the canons of good practice *and* submitting research findings to the members of the social world who were studied for confirmation that the investigator has correctly understood that social world. This latter technique is often referred to as *respondent validation* or *member validation* (see Box 13.3). Another technique they recommend is *triangulation* (see Box 13.4).

Transferability

Because qualitative research typically entails the intensive study of a small group, or of individuals sharing certain characteristics (that is, depth rather than the breadth that is a preoccupation in quantitative research), qualitative findings tend to be oriented to the contextual uniqueness and significance of the aspect of the social world being studied. As Guba and Lincoln put it, whether findings 'hold in some other context, or even in the same context at some other time, is an empirical issue' (Lincoln and Guba 1985: 316). Instead, qualitative researchers are encouraged to produce what Geertz (1973a) calls *thick description*—that is, rich accounts of the details of a culture. Guba and Lincoln argue that a thick description provides others with what they refer to

Box 13.3 ⌇☀⌇ *What is respondent validation?*

Respondent validation, which is also sometimes called *member validation*, is a process whereby a researcher provides the people on whom he or she has conducted research with an account of his or her findings. The aim of the exercise is to seek corroboration or otherwise of the account that the researcher has arrived at. Respondent validation has been particularly popular among qualitative researchers, because they frequently want to ensure that there is a good correspondence between their findings and the perspectives and experiences of their research participants. The form that respondent validation can assume varies. There are several different forms of respondent validation.

- The researcher provides each research participant with an account of what he or she has said to the researcher in an interview and conversations or of what the researcher observed by watching that person in the course of an observational study. For example, Bloor (1978, 1997) reports that he carried out observations of ear, nose, and throat (ENT) consultants concerning their approaches to making decisions about the assessment of patients. He submitted a report to each consultant on his or her practices.

- The researcher feeds back to a group of people or an organization his or her impressions and findings in relation to that group or organization. Bloor (1997) says that, for his research on therapeutic communities, he conducted group discussions (which were taped) with community members to gauge reactions to draft research reports.

- The researcher feeds back to a group of people or an organization some of his or her writings that are based on a study of that group or organization (e.g. articles, book chapters). Ball (1984) asked teachers in a school in which he had conducted ethnographic research to comment on draft articles and chapters, and similarly Willis (1977) asked the young working-class males who

were the focus of his ethnography to comment on draft chapters, as did Skeggs (1994) for her parallel study of young working-class women (see Box 14.12, p. 308, for further details).

In each case, the goal is to seek confirmation that the researcher's findings and impressions are congruent with the views of those on whom the research was conducted and to seek out areas in which there is a lack of correspondence and the reasons for it. However, the idea is not without practical difficulties.

- Respondent validation may occasion defensive reactions on the part of research participants and even censorship.

- Bloor (1997: 45) observes that, because some approaches to enquiry may result in research participants developing relationships with the researcher of 'fondness and mutual regard', there may be a reluctance to be critical.

- It is highly questionable whether research participants can validate a researcher's analysis, since this entails inferences being made for an audience of social science peers. This means that, even though the first two methods of respondent validation may receive a corroborative response, the researcher still has to make a further leap, through the development of concepts and theories, in providing a social science frame for the resulting publications. If the third method of respondent validation is employed, it is unlikely that the social scientific analyses will be meaningful to research participants. Hobbs (1993) fed back some of his writings on entrepreneurship in London's East End to his informants and it is clear that they made little sense of what he had written. Similarly, Skeggs (1994: 86) reports: '"Can't understand a bloody word it says" was the most common response' (see Box 14.12, p. 308, for further details of this study).

---

as a database for making judgements about the possible transferability of findings to other milieux.

Dependability

As a parallel to reliability in quantitative research, Guba and Lincoln propose the idea of dependability and argue that, to establish the merit of research in

terms of this criterion of trustworthiness, researchers should adopt an 'auditing' approach. This entails ensuring that complete records are kept of all phases of the research process—problem formulation, selection of research participants, fieldwork notes, interview transcripts, data analysis decisions, and so on—in an accessible manner. Peers would then act as

Box 13.4 ⌁ *What is triangulation?*

Triangulation entails using more than one method or source of data in the study of social phenomena. The term has been employed somewhat more broadly by Denzin (1970: 310) to refer to an approach that uses 'multiple observers, theoretical perspectives, sources of data, and methodologies', but the emphasis has tended to be on methods of investigation and sources of data. One of the reasons for the advocacy by Webb *et al.* (1966) of greater use of unobtrusive methods was their potential in relation to a strategy of triangulation (see Box 10.6, p. 209). Triangulation can operate within and across research strategies. It was originally conceptualized by Webb *et al.* (1966) as an approach to the development of measures of concepts, whereby more than one method would be employed in the development of measures, resulting in greater confidence in findings. As such, triangulation was very much associated with a quantitative research

strategy. However, triangulation can also take place within a qualitative research strategy. In fact, ethnographers often check out their observations with interview questions to determine whether they might have misunderstood what they had seen. Bloor (1997) reports that he tackled the process of death certification in a Scottish city in two ways: interviews with clinicians with a responsibility for certifying causes of deaths, and asking the same people to complete dummy death certificates based on case summaries he had prepared. Increasingly, triangulation is also being used to refer to a process of cross-checking findings deriving from both quantitative and qualitative research (Deacon *et al.* 1998). Triangulation represents just one way in which it may be useful to think about the integration of these two research strategies and is covered in Chapter 22.

auditors, possibly during the course of the research and certainly at the end to establish how far proper procedures are being and have been followed. This would include assessing the degree to which theoretical inferences can be justified. Auditing has not become a popular approach to enhancing the dependability of qualitative research. A rare example is a study of behaviour at an American 'swap meet', where second-hand goods are bought and sold (Belk *et al.* 1988). A team of three researchers collected data over four days through observation, interviews, photography, and video-recording. The researchers conducted several trustworthiness tests, such as respondent validation and triangulation. But, in addition, they submitted their draft manuscript and entire data set to three peers, whose task 'was to criticize the project for lack of sufficient data for drawing its conclusions if they saw such a void' (Belk *et al.* 1988: 456). The study highlights some problems associated with the auditing idea. One is that it is very demanding for the auditors, bearing in mind that qualitative research frequently generates extremely large data sets, and it may be that this is a major reason why it has not become a pervasive approach to validation.

Confirmability

Confirmability is concerned with ensuring that, while recognizing that complete objectivity is impossible in social research, the researcher can be shown to have acted in good faith; in other words, it should be apparent that he or she has not overtly allowed personal values or theoretical inclinations manifestly to sway the conduct of the research and findings deriving from it. Guba and Lincoln propose that establishing confirmability should be one of the objectives of auditors.

Authenticity

In addition to these four trustworthiness criteria, Guba and Lincoln suggest criteria of *authenticity*. These criteria raise a wider set of issues concerning the wider political impact of research. These are the criteria.

- *Fairness*. Does the research fairly represent different viewpoints among members of the social setting?

- *Ontological authenticity*. Does the research help members to arrive at a better understanding of their social milieu?

- *Educative authenticity*. Does the research help members to appreciate better the perspectives of other members of their social setting?

- *Catalytic authenticity*. Has the research acted as an impetus to members to engage in action to change their circumstances?

- *Tactical authenticity*. Has the research empowered members to take the steps necessary for engaging in action?

The authenticity criteria are thought provoking but have not been influential, and their emphasis on the wider impact of research is controversial. They have certain points of affinity with *action research* (see Box 13.5), which by and large has not been a popular form of social research, though it has had some impact in areas like organization studies. The emphasis on practical outcomes differentiates it from most social research.

However, the main point of discussing Guba and Lincoln's ideas is that they differ from writers like LeCompte and Goetz in seeking criteria for evaluating qualitative research that represent a departure from those employed by quantitative researchers.

Between the criteria of quantitative research and alternative criteria in evaluating qualitative research

M. Hammersley (1992*a*) lies midway between the two positions. He proposes that validity is an important criterion but reformulates it somewhat. For Hammersley, validity means that an empirical account must be plausible and credible and should take into account the amount and kind of evidence used in relation to an account. In proposing this criterion, Hammersley shares with realism (see Box 1.8, p. 13) the notion that there is an external social reality that can be accessed by the researcher. However, he simultaneously shares with the critics of the empirical realist position the rejection of the notion that such access is direct and in particular that the researcher can act as a mirror on the social world, reflecting its image back to an audience. Instead, the researcher is always engaged in representations or constructions of that world. The plausibility and credibility of a researcher's 'truth claims' then become the main considerations in evaluating qualitative research.

Hammersley also suggests *relevance* as an important criterion of qualitative research. Relevance is

---

Box 13.5 💡 *What is action research?*

There is no single type of action research, but broadly it can be defined as an approach in which the action researcher and a client collaborate in the diagnosis of a problem and in the development of a solution based on the diagnosis. The collection of data is likely to be involved in the formulation of the diagnosis of a problem and in the evaluation of a problem. In action research, the investigator becomes part of the field of study. Action research can involve the collection of both quantitative and qualitative data. A. Kelly (1985) describes an action research project that was concerned with the problem of encouraging girls in school to become more interested in science and technology. The researchers collected both quantitative and qualitative data on pupils' views on

science subjects and fed these back to teachers in the schools involved in the research. The research team collaborated with the teachers on formulating interventions in each school that were designed to improve girls' interest and then examined the impact of these interventions.

Action research should not be confused with *evaluation research* (Box 2.11, p. 40) which usually denotes the study of the impact of an intervention, such as a new social policy or a new innovation in organizations. The research referred to in Box 13.8 was conducted broadly with an evaluation research frame of reference in that it was concerned to evaluate the impact of the introduction of performance appraisal in British universities.

taken to be assessed from the vantage point of the importance of a topic within its substantive field or the contribution it makes to the literature on that field. Hammersley also discusses the question of whether the concerns of practitioners (that is, people who are part of the social setting being investigated and who are likely to have a vested interest in the research question and the implications of findings deriving from it) might be an aspect of considerations of relevance. In this way, his approach touches on the kinds of consideration that are addressed by Guba and Lincoln's authenticity criteria (Lincoln and Guba 1985; Guba and Lincoln 1994). However, he recognizes that the kinds of research questions and findings that might be of interest to practitioners and researchers are likely to be somewhat different. As Hammersley notes, practitioners are likely to be interested in research that helps them to understand or address problems with which they are confronted. These may not be (and perhaps are unlikely to be) at the forefront of a researcher's set of preoccupations. However, there may be occasions when researchers can combine the two and may even be able to use this capability as a means of securing access to organizations in which they wish to conduct research (see Chapter 14 for a further discussion of access issues).

Overview of the issue of criteria

There is a recognition—albeit to varying degrees—that a simple application of the quantitative researcher's criteria of reliability and validity to qualitative research is not desirable, but writers vary in the degree to which they propose a complete overhaul of those criteria. Nor do the three positions outlined above represent the full range of possible stances on this issue (M. Hammersley 1992a; Seale 1999). To a large extent, the differences between the three positions reflect divergences in the degree to which a realist position is broadly accepted or rejected. Writers on qualitative research who apply the ideas of reliability and validity with little if any adaptation broadly position themselves as realists—that is, as saying that social reality can be captured by qualitative researchers through their concepts and theories. Lincoln and Guba reject this view, arguing instead that qualitative researchers' concepts and theories are representations and that there may, therefore, be other equally credible representations of the same phenomena. Hammersley's position occupies a middle ground in terms of the axis, with realism at one end and anti-realism at the other, in that, while acknowledging the existence of social phenomena that are part of an external reality, he disavows any suggestion that it is possible to reproduce that reality for the audiences of social scientific endeavour. Most qualitative researchers nowadays probably operate around the midpoint on this realism axis, though without necessarily endorsing Hammersley's views. Typically, they treat their accounts as one of a number of possible representations rather than as definitive versions of social reality. They also bolster those accounts through some of the strategies advocated by Lincoln and Guba, such as thick descriptions, respondent validation exercises, and triangulation.

The main preoccupations of qualitative researchers

As was noted in Chapter 3, quantitative and qualitative research can be viewed as exhibiting a set of distinctive but contrasting preoccupations. These preoccupations reflect epistemologically grounded beliefs about what constitutes acceptable knowledge. In Chapter 1, it was suggested that at the level of epistemology, whereas quantitative research is profoundly influenced by natural science approach of what should count as acceptable knowledge, qualitative researchers are more influenced by *interpretivism* (see Box 1.9, p. 13). This position can itself be viewed as the product of the confluence of three related stances: Weber's notion of *Verstehen*; symbolic interactionism; and phenomenology. In this section, five distinctive preoccupations among qualitative researchers will be outlined and examined.

Seeing through the eyes of the people being studied

An underlying premiss of many qualitative researchers is that the subject matter of the social sciences (that is, people and their social world) does differ from the subject matter of the natural sciences. A key difference is that the objects of analysis of the natural sciences (atoms, molecules, gases, chemicals, metals, and so on) cannot attribute meaning to events and to their environment. However, people *do*. This argument is especially evident in the work of Schutz and can particularly be seen in the passage quoted on page 14, where Schutz draws attention to the fact that, unlike the objects of the natural sciences, the objects of the social sciences—people—are capable of attributing meaning to their environment. Consequently, many qualitative researchers have suggested that a methodology is required for studying people that reflects these differences between people and the objects of the natural sciences. As a result, many qualitative researchers express a commitment to viewing events and the social world through the eyes of the people that they study. The social world must be interpreted from the perspective of the people being studied, rather than as though those subjects were incapable of their own reflections on the social world. The epistemology underlying qualitative research has been expressed by the authors of one widely read text as involving two central tenets: '(1) . . . face-to-face interaction is the fullest condition of participating in the mind of another human being, and (2) . . . you must participate in the mind of another human being (in sociological terms, "take the role of the other") to acquire social knowledge' (Lofland and Lofland 1995: 16).

It is not surprising, therefore, that many researchers make claims in their reports of their investigations about having sought to take the views of the people they studied as the point of departure. This tendency reveals itself in frequent references to empathy and seeing through others' eyes. Here are some examples.

- Fielding (1982) carried out research on members of the National Front, a British extreme right-wing political party. In spite of his feelings of revulsion for the racist doctrine, he sought to examine the party's position 'as a moral posture and its members' interpretations were to be illuminated by an empathetic immersion in their world. In the process of "telling it like it was for them", I could reproduce an account from which outsiders could understand the ideology's persuasiveness to people so placed' (Fielding, 1982: 83).

- Armstrong (1993) carried out ethnographic research on football hooliganism through participant observation with Sheffield United supporters. He describes his work as located in '*Verstehende* sociology—trying to think oneself into the situations of the people one is interested in . . . in this case the "Hooligan". This approach involves recognizing social and historical phenomena as beyond any single or simple identifying cause and attempting to make sense from the social actors' viewpoint' (Armstrong 1993: 5–6).

- Like Armstrong, A. Taylor (1993), in relation to her ethnographic study of female injecting drug users, draws attention to the influence of Weber's idea of *Verstehen* on her research. The significance of the idea for her was that it meant that 'in order to understand social actions we must grasp the meaning that actors attach to their actions' (A. Taylor 1993: 7). She also acknowledges the influence of symbolic interactionism on her position.

This predilection for seeing through the eyes of the people studied in the course of qualitative research is often accompanied by the closely related goal of seeking to probe beneath surface appearances. After all, by taking the position of the people you are studying, the prospect is raised that they might view things differently from what an outsider with little direct contact might have expected. This stance reveals itself in:

- Foster's (1995) research on a high crime

community, which was not perceived as such by its inhabitants;

- Skeggs's (1994: 74) study of young working-class women, showing that they were not 'ideological dupes of both social class and femininity';

- A. Taylor's (1993: 8) study of intravenous female drug users, showing the people she studied are not 'pathetic, inadequate individuals' but 'rational, active people making decisions based on the contingencies of both their drug using careers and their roles and status in society';

- Armstrong's (1993: 11) quest in his research on football hooliganism to 'see beyond mere appearances' and his finding that, contrary to the popular view, hooligans are not a highly organized group led by a clearly identifiable group of ringleaders.

The empathetic stance of seeking to see through the eyes of one's research participants is very much in tune with interpretivism and demonstrates well the epistemological links with phenomenology, symbolic interactionism, and *Verstehen*. However, it is not without practical problems. For example: the risk of 'going native' and losing sight of what you are studying (see Box 14.6, p. 300); the problem of how far the researcher should go, such as the potential problem of participating in illegal or dangerous activities, which could be a risk in research like that engaged in by Taylor and Armstrong; and the possibility that the researcher will be able to see through the eyes of only some of the people who form part of a social scene but not others, such as only people of the same gender. These and other practical difficulties will be addressed in the chapters that follow.

Description and the emphasis on context

Qualitative researchers are much more inclined than quantitative researchers to provide a great deal of descriptive detail when reporting the fruits of their research. This is not to say that they are exclusively concerned with description. They *are* concerned

with explanation, and indeed the extent to which qualitative researchers ask 'why?' questions is frequently understated. For example, Skeggs (1997) has written that her first question for her research on young working-class women was 'why do women, who are clearly not just victims of some ideological conspiracy, consent to a system of class and gender oppression which appears to offer few rewards and little benefit?' (Skeggs 1997: 22; see Box 14.12, p. 308, for further details of this study).

Many qualitative studies provide a detailed account of what goes on in the setting being investigated. Very often qualitative studies seem to be full of apparently trivial details. However, these details are frequently important for the qualitative researcher, because of their significance for their subjects and also because the details provide an account of the context within which people's behaviour takes place. It was with this point in mind that Geertz (1973a) recommended the provision of thick descriptions of social settings, events, and often individuals. As a result of this emphasis on description, qualitative studies are often full of detailed information about the social worlds being examined. On the surface, some of this detail may appear irrelevant, and, indeed, there is a risk of the researcher becoming too embroiled in descriptive detail. Lofland and Lofland (1995: 164–5), for example, warn against the sin of what they call 'descriptive excess' in qualitative research, whereby the amount of detail overwhelms or inhibits the analysis of data.

One of the main reasons why qualitative researchers are keen to provide considerable descriptive detail is that they typically emphasize the importance of the contextual understanding of social behaviour. This means that behaviour, values, or whatever must be understood in context. This recommendation means that we cannot understand the behaviour of members of a social group other than in terms of the specific environment in which they operate. In this way, behaviour that may appear odd or irrational can make perfect sense when we understand the particular context within which that behaviour takes place. The emphasis on context in qualitative research goes back to many of the classic studies in social anthropology, which often demonstrated how a particular practice, such as the magical ritual that may accompany the sowing of seeds, made little sense unless we understand the belief systems of that society. One of the chief reasons for the emphasis on descriptive detail is that it is often precisely this detail that provides the mapping of context in terms of which behaviour is understood. The propensity for description can also be interpreted as a manifestation of the naturalism that pervades much qualitative research (see Box 2.4, p. 33, and Box 13.1), because it places a premium on detailed, rich descriptions of social settings.

Emphasis on process

Qualitative research tends to view social life in terms of processes. This tendency reveals itself in a number of different ways. One of the main ways is that there is often a concern to show how events and patterns unfold over time. As a result, qualitative evidence often conveys a strong sense of change and flux. As Pettigrew (1997: 338) usefully puts it, process is 'a sequence of individual and collective events, actions, and activities unfolding over time in context'. Qualitative research that is based in ethnographic methods is particularly associated with this emphasis on process (although, ironically, British

social anthropology, which is often associated with the early development of ethnographic research, is sometimes thought of as presenting a static picture of social reality by virtue of its association with functionalism). It is the element of participant observation that is a key feature of ethnography that is especially instrumental in generating this feature. Ethnographers are typically immersed in a social setting for a long time—frequently years. Consequently, they are able to observe the ways in which events develop over time or the ways in which the different elements of a social system (values, beliefs, behaviour, and so on) interconnect. Such findings can inject a sense of process by seeing social life in terms of streams of interdependent events and elements (see Box 13.6 for an example).

This is not to say, however, that ethnographers are the only qualitative researchers who inject a sense of process into our understanding of social life. It can also be achieved through semi-structured and unstructured interviewing, by asking participants to reflect on the processes leading up to or following on from an event. McKee and Bell (1985: 388; see also Box 2.22, p. 48), for example, show, through the use of a 'largely unstructured, conversational interview style' with forty-five couples in which the man was unemployed, the accommodations that are made over time by both husbands and wives to the fact of male unemployment. The various

---

Box 13.6 Process in (strike) action

Waddington (1994) describes his experiences associated with his participant observation of a strike at the Ansells brewery in Birmingham in the 1980s. As a participant observer, he was involved in 'attending picket lines, mass meetings and planning discussions, and accompanying the strikers on flying picketing and intelligence gathering manœuvres' (1994: 113). In addition to observation, he carried out informal interviews and linked these data to other sources, such as 'material deriving from newspaper archives, company and trade union documents, letters and richly detailed minutes of trade union–management meetings' (1994: 115). As a result, he was able to show 'how the contemporary beliefs, values and attitudes of

the workforce, and the mutual feelings of animosity and distrust between employees and management, were shaped by a sequence of historical events stretching back over 20 years' (1994: 115). We can see in this example the development of a sense of process in three ways: through observation of the strike over its entirety, so that developments and interconnections between events could be brought out; through connecting these events with historical and other data, so that the links between the strike and previous and other events and actions could be outlined; and through the sketching of the context (in the form of the past, as well as current beliefs and values) and its links with behaviour during the strike.

accommodations are not an immediate effect of unemployment but are gradual and incremental responses over time. The life history approach is an example of a form of qualitative research. One of the best-known studies of this kind is Lewis's (1961) study of a poor Mexican family. Lewis carried out extended taped interviews with the family members to reconstruct their life histories. For his study of disasters in the UK, and in particular of the fire at a holiday leisure complex on the Isle of Man, Turner (1994) employed published documents to arrive at a reconstruction of the events leading up to the fire and a theoretical understanding of those events. Thus, the emphasis on process in qualitative research can be seen in the use of quite different approaches to data collection.

Flexibility and lack of structure

Many qualitative researchers are disdainful of approaches to research that entail the imposition of predetermined formats on the social world. This position is largely to do with the preference for seeing through the eyes of the people being studied. After all, if a structured method of data collection is employed, since this is bound to be the product of an investigator's ruminations about the object of enquiry, certain decisions must have been made about what he or she expects to find and about the nature of the social reality that is to be encountered. Therefore, the researcher is limited in the degree to which he or she can genuinely adopt the world view of the people being studied. Consequently, most qualitative researchers prefer a research orientation that entails as little prior contamination of the social world as possible. To do otherwise risks imposing an inappropriate frame of reference on people. Keeping structure to a minimum is supposed to enhance the opportunity of genuinely revealing the perspectives of the people you are studying. Also, in the process, aspects of people's social world that are particularly important to them, but that might not even have crossed the mind of a researcher unacquainted with it, are more likely to be forthcoming. As a result, qualitative research tends to be a strategy that tries

not to delimit areas of enquiry too much and to ask fairly general rather than specific research questions (see Figure 13.1).

Because of the preference for an unstructured approach to the collection of data, qualitative researchers adopt methods of research that do not require the investigator to develop highly specific research questions in advance and therefore to devise instruments specifically for those questions to be answered. Ethnography, with its emphasis on participant observation, is particularly well suited to this orientation. It allows researchers to submerge themselves in a social setting with a fairly general research focus in mind and gradually to formulate a narrower emphasis by making as many observations of that setting as possible. They can then formulate more specific research questions out of their collected data. Similarly, interviewing is an extremely prominent method in the qualitative researcher's armoury, but it is not of the kind we encountered in the course of most of Chapter 5—namely, the structured interview. Instead, qualitative researchers prefer less structured approaches to interviewing, as we will see in Chapter 15. Blumer's (1954) argument for sensitizing rather than definitive concepts (that is, the kind employed by quantitative researchers) is symptomatic of the preference for a more open-ended, and hence less structured, approach.

An advantage of the unstructured nature of most qualitative enquiry (that is, in addition to the prospect of gaining access to people's world views) is that it offers the prospect of flexibility. The researcher can change direction in the course of his or her investigation much more easily than in quantitative research, which tends to have a built-in momentum once the data collection is under way: if you send out hundreds of mail questionnaires and realize after you have started to get some back that there is an issue that you would have liked to investigate, you are not going to find it easy to retrieve the situation. Structured interviewing and structured observation can involve some flexibility, but the requirement to make interviews as comparable as possible for survey investigations limits the extent to which this can happen. See Box 13.7 for an illustration of the ways in which the unstructured data collection style of qualitative research can be used to suggest alternative avenues of enquiry or ways of thinking about the phenomenon being investigated.

Concepts and theory grounded in data

This issue has already been addressed in much of the exposition of qualitative research above. For qualitative researchers, concepts and theories are usually inductively arrived at from the data that are collected (see Boxes 13.2 and 13.8).

Box 13.7 Flexibility in action

In the course of a study of young people with learning difficulties using qualitative interviews, C. A. Davies (1999) reports that she found that on many occasions her interviewees mentioned food in the course of conversations. Initially, she followed these conversations up largely in order to establish rapport with these young people. However, she gradually came to realize that in fact food was of considerable significance for her research, because it represented a lens through which her participants viewed their anxieties about the ways people attempted to control them. Food was also a focus for their strategies of resistance to control.

Box 13.8 Emerging concepts

In the late 1980s and early 1990s, most UK universities were in the throes of introducing staff appraisal schemes for both academic and academic-related staff. Staff appraisal is employed to review the appraisee's performance and activities over a period of usually one or two years. Along with some colleagues, I undertook an evaluation of staff appraisal schemes in four universities (Bryman *et al.* 1994). The research entailed the collection of both quantitative and qualitative data within the framework of a comparative research design. The qualitative data were derived from large numbers of interviews with appraisers, appraisees, senior managers, and many others. In the course of conducting the interviews and analysing the subsequent data we became increasingly aware of a cynicism among many of the people we interviewed. This attitude revealed itself in several ways, such as: a view that appraisal had been introduced just to pacify the government; a belief that nothing happened of any significance in the aftermath of an appraisal meeting;

the view that it was not benefiting universities; and a suggestion that many participants to the appraisal process were just going through the motions. As one of the interviewees said in relation to this last feature: 'It's like going through the motions of it [appraisal]. It's just get it over with and signed and dated and filed and that's the end of it' (quoted in Bryman *et al.* 1994: 180).

On the basis of these findings it was suggested that the attitudes towards appraisal and the behaviour of those involved in appraisal were characterized by *procedural compliance*, which was defined as 'a response to an organizational innovation in which the technical requirements of the innovation . . . are broadly adhered to, but where there are substantial reservations about its efficacy and only partial commitment to it, so that there is a tendency for the procedures associated with the innovation to be adhered to with less than a total commitment to its aims' (1994: 178).

The critique of qualitative research

In a similar way to the criticisms that have been levelled at quantitative research mainly by qualitative researchers, a parallel critique has been built up of qualitative research. Some of the more common ones follow.

Qualitative research is too subjective

Quantitative researchers sometimes criticize qualitative research as being too impressionistic and subjective. By these criticisms they usually mean that qualitative findings rely too much on the researcher's often unsystematic views about what is significant and important, and also upon the close personal relationships that the researcher frequently strikes up with the people studied. Precisely because qualitative research often begins in a relatively open-ended way and entails a gradual narrowing-down of research questions or problems, the consumer of the writings deriving from the research is given few clues as to why one area was the chosen area upon which attention was focused rather than another. By contrast, quantitative researchers point to the tendency for the problem formulation stage in their work to be more explicitly stated in terms of such matters as the existing literature on that topic and key theoretical ideas.

Difficult to replicate

Quantitative researchers also often argue that these tendencies are even more of a problem because of the difficulty of replicating a qualitative study, although replication in the social sciences is by no means a straightforward matter regardless of this particular issue (see Chapter 3). Precisely because it is unstructured and often reliant upon the qualitative researcher's ingenuity, it is almost impossible to conduct a true replication, since there are hardly any

standard procedures to be followed. In qualitative research, the investigator him- or herself is the main instrument of data collection, so that what is observed and heard and also what the researcher decides to concentrate upon is very much a product of his or her predilections. There are several possible components of this criticism: what qualitative researchers (especially perhaps in ethnography) choose to focus upon while in the field is a product of what strikes them as significant, whereas other researchers are likely to empathize with other issues; the responses of participants (people being observed or interviewed) to qualitative researchers is likely to be affected by the characteristics of the researcher (personality, age, gender, and so on); and because of the unstructured nature of qualitative data, interpretation will be profoundly influenced by the subjective leanings of a researcher. Because of such factors it is difficult—not to say impossible—to replicate qualitative findings. The difficulties ethnographers experience when they revisit grounds previously trodden by another researcher (often referred to as a 'restudy') do not inspire confidence in the replicability of qualitative research (Bryman 1994).

Problems of generalization

It is often suggested that the scope of the findings of qualitative investigations is restricted. When participant observation is used or when unstructured interviews are conducted with a small number of individuals in a certain organization or locality, they argue that it is impossible to know how the findings can be generalized to other settings. How can just one or two cases be representative of all cases? In other words, can we really treat Holdaway's (1982) research on the police in Sheffield as representative of all police forces, or Armstrong's (1998) research on Sheffield United supporters as representative of all football supporters, or Waddington's (1994) study of a strike as generalizable to all lengthy strikes? In the case of research based on interviews rather than participation, can we treat interviewees who have not been selected through a probability procedure or even quota sampling as representative? Are A. Taylor's (1993) female intravenous drug users typical of all members of that category or are Skeggs's (1994; see Box 14.12, p. 308) young working-class women typical?

The answer in all these cases is, of course, emphatically 'no'. A case study is not a sample of one drawn from a known population. Similarly, the people who are interviewed in qualitative research are not meant to be representative of a population and indeed, in some cases, like female intravenous drug users, we may find it more or less impossible to enumerate the population in any precise manner. Instead, the findings of qualitative research are to generalize to theory rather than to populations. It is 'the cogency of the theoretical reasoning' (Mitchell 1983: 207), rather than statistical criteria, that is decisive in considering the generalizability of the findings of qualitative research. In other words, it is the quality of the theoretical inferences that are made out of qualitative data that is crucial to the assessment of generalization.

These three criticisms reflect many of the preoccupations of quantitative research that were discussed in Chapter 3. A further criticism that is often made of qualitative research, but that is perhaps less influenced by quantitative research criteria, is the suggestion that qualitative research frequently lacks transparency in how the research was conducted.

Lack of transparency

It is sometimes difficult to establish from qualitative research what the researcher actually *did* and how he or she arrived at the study's conclusions. For example, qualitative research reports are sometimes unclear about such matters as how people were chosen for observation or interview. This deficiency contrasts sharply with the sometimes laborious accounts of sampling procedures in reports of quantitative research. However, it does not seem plausible to suggest that outlining in some detail the ways in which research participants are selected constitutes the application of quantitative research criteria. Readers have a right to know how far research participants were selected to correspond to a wide range of people. Also, the process of qualitative data analysis is frequently unclear (Bryman and Burgess 1994*a*). It is often not obvious how the analysis was conducted—in other words what the researcher was actually doing when the data were analysed and therefore how the study's conclusions were arrived at. To a large extent, these areas of a lack of transparency are increasingly being addressed by qualitative researchers.

Is it always like this?

This was a heading that was employed in Chapter 3 in relation to quantitative research, but it is perhaps less easy to answer in relation to qualitative research. To a large extent, this is because qualitative research is less codified than quantitative research—that is, it is less influenced by strict guidelines and directions about how to go about data collection and analysis. As a result, and this may be noticed by readers of the chapters that follow this one, accounts of qualitative research are frequently less prescriptive in tone than those encountered in relation to quantitative research. Instead, they often exhibit more of a descriptive tenor, outlining the different ways qualitative researchers have gone about research or suggesting alternative ways of conducting research or analysis based on the writer's own experiences or those of others. To a large extent, this picture is changing, in that there is a growing number of books that seek to make clear-cut recommendations about how qualitative research should be carried out.

However, if we look at some of the preoccupations

of qualitative research that were described above, we can see certain ways in which there are departures from the practices that are implied by these preoccupations. One of the main departures is that qualitative research is sometimes a lot more focused than is implied by the suggestion that the researcher begins with general research questions and narrows it down so that theory and concepts are arrived at during and after the data collection. There is no *necessary* reason why qualitative research cannot be employed to investigate a specific research problem. For example, Hammersley *et al.* (1985) describe a study that was designed to explore the impact of external assessments on schools. More specifically, they wanted to examine the contention, which was based on other studies of schools, that 'external examinations lead to lecturing and note-taking on the part of secondary-school teachers and instrumental attitudes among their pupils' (Hammersley *et al.* 1985: 58). This contention was examined through a comparison of two schools that varied considerably in the emphasis they placed on examinations. This study exhibits a comparative research design (see Chapter 2), with its accent on a comparison of two cases. A related way in which qualitative research differs from the standard model is in connection with the notion of a lack of structure in approaches to collecting and analysing data. As will be seen in Chapter 17, techniques like conversation analysis entail the application of a highly codified method for analysing talk. Moreover, the growing use of computer-assisted qualitative data analysis software (CAQDAS), which will be the subject of Chapter 20, is leading to greater transparency in the procedures used for analysing qualitative data. This greater transparency may lead to more codification in qualitative data analysis than has previously been the case.

Some contrasts between quantitative and qualitative research

Several writers have explored the contrasts between quantitative and qualitative research by devising tables that allow the differences to be brought out (e.g. Halfpenny 1979; Bryman 1988; Hammersley 1992b). Table 13.1 attempts to draw out the chief contrasting features:

- *Numbers vs. Words.* Quantitative researchers are often portrayed as preoccupied with applying measurement procedures to social life, while qualitative researchers are seen as using words in the presentation of analyses of society.
- *Point of view of researcher vs. Point of view of participants.* In quantitative research, the investigator is in the driving seat. The set of concerns that he or she brings to an investigation structures the investigation. In qualitative research, the perspective of those being studied—what they see as important and significant—provides the point of orientation.

- *Researcher is distant vs. Researcher is close.* In quantitative research, researchers are uninvolved with their subjects and in some cases, as in research based on mail questionnaires or on hired interviewers, may have no contact with them at all. Sometimes, this lack of a relationship with the subjects of an investigation is regarded as desirable by quantitative researchers, because they feel that their objectivity might be compromised if they become too involved with the people they study. The qualitative researcher seeks close involvement with the people being investigated, so that he or she can genuinely understand the world through their eyes.
- *Theory and concepts tested in research vs. Theory and concepts emergent from data.* Quantitative researchers typically bring a set of concepts to bear on the research instruments being employed, so that theoretical work precedes the collection of

Table 13.1 Some common contrasts between quantitative and qualitative research

Quantitative	Qualitative
Numbers	Words
Point of view of researcher	Points of view of participants
Researcher distant	Researcher close
Theory testing	Theory emergent
Static	Process
Structured	Unstructured
Generalization	Contextual understanding
Hard, reliable data	Rich, deep data
Macro	Micro
Behaviour	Meaning
Artificial settings	Natural settings

data, whereas in qualitative research concepts and theoretical elaboration emerge out of data collection.

- *Static vs. Process.* Quantitative research is frequently depicted as presenting a static image of social reality with its emphasis on relationships between variables. Change and connections between events over time tend not to surface, other than in a mechanistic fashion. Qualitative research is often depicted as attuned to the unfolding of events over time and to the interconnections between the actions of participants of social settings.

- *Structured vs. Unstructured.* Quantitative research is typically highly structured so that the investigator is able to examine the precise concepts and issues that are the focus of the study; in qualitative research the approach is invariably unstructured,

so that the possibility of getting at actors' meanings and of concepts emerging out of data collection is enhanced.

- *Generalization vs. Contextual understanding.* Whereas quantitative researchers want their findings to be generalizable to the relevant population, the qualitative researcher seeks an understanding of behaviour, values, beliefs, and so on in terms of the context in which the research is conducted.

- *Hard, reliable data vs. Rich, deep data.* Quantitative data are often depicted as 'hard' in the sense of being robust and unambiguous, owing to the precision offered by measurement. Qualitative researchers claim, by contrast, that their contextual approach and their often prolonged involvement in a setting engender rich data.

- *Macro vs. Micro.* Quantitative researchers are often depicted as involved in uncovering large-scale social trends and connections between variables, whereas qualitative researchers are seen as concerned with small-scale aspects of social reality, such as interaction.

- *Behaviour vs. Meaning.* It is sometimes suggested that the quantitative researcher is concerned with people's behaviour and the qualitative researcher with the meaning of action.

- *Artificial settings vs. Natural settings.* Whereas quantitative researchers conduct research in a contrived context, qualitative researchers investigate people in natural environments.

However, as we will see in Chapter 21, while these contrasts depict reasonably well the differences between quantitative and qualitative research, they should not be viewed as constituting hard and fast distinctions.

Feminism and qualitative research

A further dimension that could have been included in the previous section is that, in the view of some writers, qualitative research is associated with a feminist sensitivity, and that, by implication, quantitative research is viewed by many feminists as incompatible with feminism. This issue was briefly signposted in Chapter 1. The link between feminism and qualitative research is by no means a cut-and-dried issue, in that, although it became something of an orthodoxy among some writers, it has not found favour with all feminists. Indeed, there are signs at the time of writing that views on the issue are changing.

The notion that there is an affinity between feminism and qualitative research has at least two main components to it: a view that quantitative research is inherently incompatible with feminism, and a view that qualitative research provides greater opportunity for a feminist sensitivity to come to the fore. Quantitative research is frequently viewed as incompatible with feminism for the following reasons.

- According to Mies (1993), quantitative research suppresses the voices of women either by ignoring them or by submerging them in a torrent of facts and statistics.

- The criteria of valid knowledge associated with quantitative research are ones that turn women, when they are the focus of research, into objects. This means that women are again subjected to exploitation, in that knowledge and experience are extracted from them with nothing in return, even when the research is conducted by women (Mies 1993).

- The emphasis on controlling variables further exacerbates this last problem, and indeed the very idea of control is viewed as a masculine approach.

- The use of predetermined categories in quantitative research results in an emphasis on what is already known and consequently in 'the silencing of women's own voices' (Maynard 1998: 18).

- The criteria of valid knowledge associated with quantitative research also mean that women are to be researched in a value-neutral way, when in fact the goals of feminist research should be to conduct research specifically *for* women.

By contrast, qualitative research was viewed by many feminists as either more compatible with feminism's central tenets or as more capable of being adapted to those tenets. Thus, in contrast to quantitative research, qualitative research allows

- women's voices to be heard;

- exploitation to be reduced by giving as well as receiving in the course of fieldwork;

- women *not* to be treated as objects to be controlled by the researcher's technical procedures; and

- the emancipatory goals of feminism to be realized.

How qualitative research achieves these goals will be addressed particularly in relation to the next three chapters, since the issues and arguments vary somewhat from one method to the other. In fact, the issue of qualitative research as providing the opportunity for a feminist approach has somewhat different aspects when looking at ethnography, qualitative interviewing, and focus groups—the topics of the next three chapters. However, it also ought to be recognized that there has been a softening of attitude among some feminist writers towards quantitative research in recent years. Examples of this softening are as follows.

- There is a recognition that many of the worst excesses of discrimination against women might not have come to light so clearly were it not for the collection and analysis of statistics revealing discrimination (Maynard 1994; Oakley 1998). The very presence of factual evidence of this kind has allowed the case for equal opportunities legislation to be made much more sharply, although, needless to say, there is much more that still needs to be done in this field.

- As Jayaratne and Stewart (1991) and Maynard (1994, 1998) have pointed out, at the very least it is difficult to see why feminist research that combines quantitative and qualitative research would be incompatible with the feminist cause.

- There has also been a recognition of the fact that qualitative research is not *ipso facto* feminist in orientation. If, for example, ethnography, which is covered in the next chapter, provided for a feminist sensitivity, we would expect subjects like social anthropology, which have been virtually founded on the approach, to be almost inherently feminist, which is patently not the case (Reinharz 1992: 47–8). If this is so, the question of appropriate approaches to feminist research would seem to reside in the *application* of methods rather than something that is inherent in them. Consequently, some writers have preferred to write about *feminist research practice* rather than about *feminist methods* (Maynard 1998: 128).

These issues will be returned to in the next three chapters.

Key points

- There is disagreement over what precisely qualitative research is.

- Qualitative research does not lend itself to the delineation of a clear set of linear steps.

- It tends to be a more open-ended research strategy than is typically the case with quantitative research.

- Theories and concepts are viewed as outcomes of the research process.

- There is considerable unease about the simple application of the reliability and validity criteria associated with quantitative research to qualitative research. Indeed, some writers prefer to use alternative criteria that have parallels with reliability and validity.

- Most qualitative researchers reveal a preference for seeing through the eyes of research participants.

- Several writers have depicted qualitative research as having a far greater affinity with a feminist standpoint than quantitative research can exhibit.

Revision questions

- What are some of the difficulties with providing a general account of the nature of qualitative research?
- Outline some of the traditions of qualitative research.
- What are some of the main research methods associated with qualitative research?

The main steps in qualitative research

- Does a research question in qualitative research have the same significance and characteristics as in quantitative research?

Theory and research

- Is the approach to theory in qualitative research inductive or deductive?

Concepts in qualitative research

- What is the difference between definitive and sensitizing concepts?

Reliability and validity in qualitative research

- How have some writers adapted the notions of reliability and validity to qualitative research?
- Why have some writers sought alternative criteria for the evaluation of qualitative research?
- Evaluate Lincoln and Guba's criteria.
- What is respondent validation?
- What is triangulation?

The main preoccupations of qualitative researchers

- Outline the main preoccupations of qualitative researchers.
- How do these preoccupations differ from those of quantitative researchers, which were considered in Chapter 3?

The critique of qualitative research

- What are some of the main criticisms that are frequently levelled at qualitative research?
- To what extent do these criticisms reflect the preoccupations of quantitative research?

Is it always like this?

- Can qualitative research be employed in relation to hypothesis testing?

Some contrasts between quantitative and qualitative research

- 'The difference between quantitative and qualitative research revolves entirely around the concern with numbers in the former and with words in the latter.' How far do you agree with this statement?

Feminism and qualitative research

- Why have many feminist researchers preferred qualitative research?
- Is there no role for quantitative research in relation to feminist research?

14 Ethnography and participant observation

Reader's guide

Ethnography and participant observation entail the extended involvement of the researcher in the social life of those he or she studies. However, the former term is also frequently taken to refer to the written output of that research. The chapter explores:

- the problems of gaining access to different settings and some suggestions about how they might be overcome;

- the issue of whether a covert role is practicable and acceptable;

- the role of key informants for the ethnographer;
- the different kinds of roles that ethnographers can assume in the course of their fieldwork;
- sampling strategies in ethnography, in particular *theoretical sampling*, which is associated with the grounded theory approach to qualitative data analysis, which will be examined in Chapter 19;
- the role of field notes in ethnography and the varieties of forms they can assume;
- bringing ethnography to an end;
- the controversy about the nature of feminist ethnography.

Introduction

Discussions about the merits and limitations of participant observation have been a fairly standard ingredient in textbooks on social research for many years. However, for some time, writers on research methods have increasingly preferred to write about ethnography rather than participant observation. It is difficult to date the point at which this change of terminology (though it is more than just this) occurred, but sometime in the 1970s ethnography began to become the preferred term. Prior to that, ethnography was primarily associated with social anthropological research, whereby the investigator visits a (usually) foreign land, gains access to a group (for example, a tribe or village), spends a considerable amount of time (often many years) with that group with the aim of uncovering its culture, watches and listens to what people say and do, engages people in conversations to probe specific issues of interest, takes copious field notes, and returns home to write up the fruits of his or her labours.

Box 14.1 represents an attempt to deal with some of these issues and to arrive at a working definition of ethnography. The seven bullet points at the end of Box 14.1 that make up the definition of ethnography featured there could be viewed as a simple process of joining a group, watching what goes on, making some notes, and writing it all up. In fact, ethnography is nowhere nearly as straightforward as

this implies. This chapter will outline some of the main decision areas that confront ethnographers, along with some of the many contingencies they face. However, it is not easy to generalize about the ethnographic research process in such a way as to provide definitive recommendations about research practice. As prefigured at the end of the last chapter, the diversity of experiences that confront ethnographers and the variety of ways in which they deal with them does not readily permit clear-cut generalizations. The following comment in a book on ethnography makes this point well:

Every field situation *is* different and initial luck in meeting good informants, being in the right place at the right time and striking the right note in relationships may be just as important as skill in technique. Indeed, many successful episodes in the field do come about through good luck as much as through sophisticated planning, and many unsuccessful episodes are due as much to bad luck as to bad judgement.   (Sarsby 1984: 96)

However, this statement should not be taken to imply that forethought and an awareness of alternative ways of doing things are irrelevant. It is with this kind of issue that the rest of this chapter will be concerned. However, issues to do with the conduct of interviews by ethnographers will be reserved for Chapter 15.

Box 14.1 What are ethnography and participant observation?

Many definitions of ethnography and participant observation are very difficult to distinguish. Both draw attention to the fact that the participant observer/ ethnographer immerses him- or herself in a group for an extended period of time, observing behaviour, listening to what is said in conversations both between others and with the fieldworker, and asking questions. It is possible that the term 'ethnography' is sometimes preferred because 'participant observation' seems to imply just observation, though in practice participant observers do more than simply observe. Typically, participant observers and ethnographers will gather further data through interviews and the collection of documents. It may be, therefore, that the apparent emphasis on observation in the term 'participant observation' has meant that an apparently more inclusive term would be preferable, even though in fact it is generally recognized that the method entails a wide range of methods of data collection and sources. Ethnography is also sometimes taken to refer to a study in which participant observation is the prevalent research method but which also has a specific focus on the culture of the group in which the ethnographer is immersed.

However, the term 'ethnography' has an additional meaning, in that it frequently simultaneously refers to both a method of research of the kind outlined above *and* the written product of that research. Indeed, 'ethnography' frequently denotes both a research process and the written outcome of the research. For example, consider the opening sentences of A. Taylor's (1993) book on female drug users, which was mentioned on several occasions in Chapter 13:

This book provides an account of the lives and experiences of a group of female intravenous drug users in Glasgow. It is based on fifteen months' participant observation of the women in their own setting and on in-depth interviews carried out at the end of the observation period. It is the first full ethnographic account of the lifestyle of female drug users.   (A. Taylor 1993: 1)

It is worth noting the following features

- The book is subtitled *An Ethnography of a Female Injecting Community*. The term 'ethnography' therefore seems to apply both to the method of investigation and to the book itself. This is underlined by the phrase 'the first full ethnographic account'.
- The mention of the main data collection methods as participant observation *and* interviewing suggests that the ethnographic research comprises these two techniques of data collection but that interviewing is viewed as something separate from participant observation. In fact, participant observers frequently conduct interviews in the course of their research.
- The passage draws on several qualitative research motifs encountered in the previous chapter, such as the preference for seeing through the eyes of the people being studied (reference to 'lives and experiences') and a naturalistic stance ('in their own setting').

In this book, ethnography will be taken to mean a research method in which the researcher

- is immersed in a social setting for an extended period of time;
- makes regular observations of the behaviour of members of that setting;
- listens to and engages in conversations;
- interviews informants on issues that are not directly amenable to observation or that the ethnographer is unclear about (or indeed for other possible reasons);
- collects documents about the group;
- develops an understanding of the culture of the group and people's behaviour within the context of that culture;
- and writes up a detailed account of that setting.

Thus, ethnography is being taken to include participant observation and is also taken to encapsulate the notion of ethnography as a written product of ethnographic research.

Access

One of the key and yet most difficult steps in ethnography is gaining access to a social setting that is relevant to the research problem in which you are interested. The way in which access is approached differs along several dimensions, one of which is whether the setting is a relatively open one or a relatively closed one (Bell 1969). Hammersely and Atkinson (1995) make a similar distinction when they refer to 'public' settings as opposed to ones that are not public (see also Lofland and Lofland 1995). Closed, non-public settings are likely to be organizations of various kinds, such as firms, schools, cults, social movements, and so on. The open/public setting is likely to be everything else—that is, research involving communities, gangs, drug users, and so on.

Overt versus covert ethnography

One way to ease the access problem is to assume a *covert* role—in other words, not to disclose the fact that you are a researcher. This strategy obviates the need to negotiate access to organizations or to explain why you want to intrude into people's lives and make them objects of study. As we will see, seeking access is a highly fraught business and the adoption of a covert role removes some of the difficulties. These two distinctions—the open/public versus closed setting and the overt versus covert role—suggest, following Bell (1969), a fourfold distinction in forms of ethnography (see Figure 14.1, which contains for each of the four types examples that have been encountered in earlier chapters or will be mentioned in this one).

Three points should be registered about Figure 14.1. First, the open/public setting versus closed setting distinction is not a hard-and-fast one. Sometimes, gaining access to groups can have a near formal quality, such as having to pacify a gang leader's anxieties about your goals. Also, organizations sometimes create contexts that have a public character, such as the meetings that are arranged for members or prospective recruits by social movements such as religious cults or political movements like the National Front.

Secondly, the overt versus covert distinction is not without problems. For example, while an ethnographer may seek access through an overt route, there may be many people with whom he or she comes into contact who will not be aware of the ethnographer's status as a researcher. P. Atkinson (1981: 135) notes in connection with his research on the training of doctors in a medical school that, although he was 'an "open" observer with regard to the doctors and students', he was 'a "disguised" observer with regard to the patients'. Also, some ethnographers move between the two roles (see Box 14.2).

Another interesting case is provided by Glucksman (1994), who in the 1970s left her academic post to work on a factory assembly line in order to shed light on the reasons why feminism appeared not to be relevant to working-class women. In a sense, she was a covert observer, but her motives for the research were primarily political and she says that, at the time she was undertaking the research, she had no intention of writing the book that subsequently appeared and that was published under a pseudonym (Cavendish 1982). After the book's publication, it was treated as an example of ethnographic research. Was she an overt or a covert observer (or neither or both)? Whichever description applies, this is an interesting case of what might be termed *retrospective ethnography*.

A third point to note about Figure 14.1 is that entries are more numerous in the Types 1 and 2 cells than in the Types 3 and 4 cells. In large part, this reflects the fact that ethnographers are far more likely to be in an overt role than a covert one. There are several reasons for this situation. As Box 14.3 reveals, the reasons for the preference of most ethnographers for an overt role are to do with practical and ethical considerations, but the latter predominate in most researchers' thinking. Because of the ethical problems that beset covert research (and indeed

	Open/public setting	Closed setting
Overt role	*Type 1* • A. Taylor's (1993) study of intravenous drug users • Foster's (1995) study of a high-crime community • Willis's (1977) study of working-class 'lads' • Giulianotti's (1995) research on football hooligans (Box 14.4) • Hobbs's (1988, 1993) research on entrepreneurship in London's East End • Whyte's (1955) classic study of street corner life in a Boston slum area	*Type 2* • Leidner's (1993) studies of a McDonald's outlet and an insurance firm • Coffey's (1999) research in a UK accountancy firm • Burgess's (1983, 1987) research on a Roman Catholic comprehensive school • Barker's (1984) study of Moonies (a religious cult) • Waddington's (1994) study of a prolonged strike (Box 13.6, p. 279)
Covert role	*Type 3* • Patrick's (1973) study of a violent Glasgow gang	*Type 4* • Holdaway's (1982, 1983) study of a police force in which he was already a policeman • Fielding's (1981, 1982) study of the National Front

Figure 14.1 Four forms of ethnography

Note: This figure is a development of a table in Bell (1969).

Box 14.2 An example of the perils of covert observation: The case of field notes in the lavatory

Ditton's (1977) research on 'fiddling' in a bakery provides an interesting case of the practical difficulties of taking notes during covert observation as well as an illustration of an ethnographer who shifted his position from covert to overt observation at least in part because of those difficulties:

Nevertheless, I *was* able to develop personal covert participant–observation skills. Right from the start, I found it impossible to keep everything that I wanted to remember in my head until the end of the working day . . . and so had to take rough notes as I was going along. But I was stuck 'on the line', and had nowhere to retire to privately to jot things down. Eventually, the wheeze of using innocently provided laboratory cubicles occurred to me.

Looking back, all my notes for that third summer were on Bronco toilet paper! Apart from the awkward tendency for pencilled notes to be self-erasing from hard toilet paper . . . my frequent requests for 'time out' after interesting happenings or conversations in the bakehouse and the amount of time I was spending in the lavatory began to get noticed. I had to pacify some genuinely concerned work-mates, give up totally undercover operations, and 'come out' as an observer—albeit in a limited way. I eventually began to scribble notes more openly, but still not in front of people when they were talking. When questioned about this, as I was occasionally, I coyly said that I was writing things down that occurred to me about 'my studies'.   (Ditton 1977: 5)

Box 14.3 The covert role in ethnography

Advantages

- *There is no problem of access.* Adopting a covert role largely gets around the access problem because the researcher does not have to seek permission to gain entry to a social setting or organization.

- *Reactivity is not a problem.* Using a covert role also reduces reactivity (see Boxes 2.7 and 8.10, pp. 37, 131) because participants do not know the person conducting the study is a researcher. Therefore, they are less likely to adjust their behaviour because of the researcher's presence.

Disadvantages

- *The problem of taking notes.* As Ditton (1977; see Box 14.2) discovered, it is difficult and probably in some circumstances impossible to take notes when people do not realize you are conducting research. As we will see below, notes are very important to an ethnographer, and it is too risky to rely exclusively on your memory.

- *The problem of not being able to use other methods.* Ethnography entails the use of several methods, but, if the researcher is in a covert role, it is difficult to steer conversations in a certain direction for fear of detection and it is essentially impossible to engage in interviewing.

- *Anxiety.* The ethnographer is under constant threat of having his or her cover blown. Ethnography is frequently a stressful research method and the worries about detection can add to those anxieties. Moreover, if the ethnographer *is* found out, the whole research project may be jeopardized.

- *Ethical problems.* Covert observation transgresses two important ethical tenets: it does not provide participants with the opportunity for 'informed consent' (whereby they can agree or disagree to participate on the basis of information supplied to them) and it entails deception. It can also be taken to be a violation of the principle of privacy. Also, many writers take the view that, in addition to being potentially damaging to research participants, it can also harm the practice of research, because of fears about social researchers being identified by the public as snoopers or voyeurs if they are found out. Ethical issues are considered in greater detail in Chapter 24.

However

- As the main text points out, in some circumstances the overt/covert distinction may be a matter of degree.

---

some of the practical difficulties), the bulk of the discussion of access issues that follows will focus upon ethnographers seeking to employ an overt role.

Access to closed settings

As Van Maanen and Kolb (1985: 11) observe, 'gaining access to most organizations is not a matter to be taken lightly but one that involves some combination of strategic planning, hard work and dumb luck'. In selecting a particular social setting to act as a case study in which to conduct an ethnographic investigation, the researcher may employ several criteria. These criteria should be determined by the general research area in which he or she is interested. Very often a number of potential cases (and sometimes very many) will be relevant to your research

problem. You may choose a certain case because of its 'fit' with your research questions, but there are no guarantees of success, as Van Maanen and Kolb's remark suggests. Sometimes, sheer perseverance pays off. Leidner (1993) was determined that one of the organizations in which she conducted ethnographic research on the routinization of service work should be McDonald's. She writes:

I knew from the beginning that I wanted one of the case studies to be of McDonald's. The company was a pioneer and exemplar of routinized interaction, and since it was locally based, it seemed like the perfect place to start. McDonald's had other ideas, however, and only after tenacious pestering and persuasion did I overcome corporate employees' polite demurrals, couched in terms of protecting proprietary information and the company's image. (Leidner 1993: 234–5)

This kind of determination is necessary for any instance in which you want to study a specific organization, such as a particular religious sect or social movement. Rejection is likely to require a complete rethink.

However, with many research questions, several potential cases are likely to meet your criteria. Organizational researchers have developed a range of tactics, many of which may seem rather unsystematic in tone, but they are worth drawing attention to.

- Use friends, contacts, colleagues, academics to help you gain access; provided the organization is relevant to your research question, the route should not matter.

- Try to get the support of someone within the organization who will act as your champion. This person may be prepared to vouch for you and the value of your research. Such people are placed in the role of 'sponsors'.

- Usually you will need to get access through top management/senior executives. Even though you may secure a certain level of agreement lower down the hierarchy, you will usually need clearance from them. Such senior people act as 'gatekeepers'.

- Offer something in return (e.g. a report). This strategy carries risks in that it may turn you into a cheap consultant and may invite restrictions on your activities, such as insistence on seeing what you write. However, it helps to create a sense of being *trustworthy*. Some writers on research methodology do not recommend this approach, although, among researchers on formal organizations, it is commonplace.

- Provide a clear explanation of your aims and methods and be prepared to deal with concerns. Suggest a meeting at which you can deal with worries and provide an explanation of what you intend to do in terms that can readily be understood by others.

- Be prepared to negotiate—you will want complete access but it is unlikely you will be given a *carte blanche*.

- Be reasonably honest about the amount of people's time you are likely to take up. This is a question you will almost certainly be asked if you are seeking access to commercial organizations and probably to many not-for-profit ones too.

Access to open/public settings

Gaining access to public settings is beset with problems, many of which are similar in nature to access to closed settings. An example of the difficulties that await the researcher is one of Whyte's (1955) early encounters in the field in his classic case study *Street Corner Society*, when trying to make contacts during his early days in the field in Boston's North End. The following incident occurred in a hotel bar:

I looked around me again and now noticed a threesome: one man and two women. It occurred to me that here was a maldistribution of females which I might be able to rectify. I approached the group and opened with something like this: 'Pardon me. Would you mind if I join you?' There was a moment of silence while the man stared at me. He then offered to throw me downstairs. I assured him that this would not be necessary and demonstrated as much by walking right out of there without any assistance.   (Whyte, 1955: 289)

Sometimes, ethnographers will be able to have their paths smoothed by individuals who act as both sponsor and gatekeeper. In Whyte's case, the role played by 'Doc' has become the stuff of legend and there is a temptation to seek out your Doc when attempting to gain access to a group. Indeed, when Gans (1962) decided to conduct ethnographic research in an area that was adjacent to the part of Boston on which Whyte had carried out his research, he visited Whyte 'to find out how [he] could meet a "Doc"' (Gans 1968: 311).

In seeking to gain access to one group of football hooligans, Giulianotti (1995; see Box 14.4) actively sought out someone who could adopt this role for him, but, in gaining access to a second group, he was able to draw upon existing acquaintances who could ease his entrée into the group. We see here two

Box 14.4 Access to football hooligans

Giulianotti (1995) sought access to two groups of football supporters engaged in hooligan activity: Aberdeen and Hibernian 'casuals', as the particular groups he was interested in termed themselves. Access to the Aberdeen casuals was reasonably smooth in that he was a close friend of three of the forty-seven Aberdeen casuals who had been caught by the police at a notorious match in 1985. He had also gone to school and socialized with many of the first group of casuals to emerge in Aberdeen in the 1982–5 period. He also claims that in terms of 'age, attire, and argot' his personal characteristics were similar to those of the people he was studying. Gradually his contacts with Aberdeen casuals broadened out and eventually he 'began socializing freely with the gang at football matches, travelling to and from matches within the main grouping of the Aberdeen casuals' (Giulianotti 1995: 4). Access to the equivalent Hibernian (Hibs) supporters in Edinburgh was much more difficult for three reasons: absence of prior acquaintanceships; his Aberdonian background and accent; and a high level of negative newspaper publicity about the Hibs casuals at the time he was seeking access, which made the group sensitive to

infiltration and people writing about them. Eventually, he was able to negotiate access to the group by striking what he, following Becker (1970), calls a 'research bargain': he provided the Hibs supporters with answers to questions about the Aberdeen 'casual scene', such as ' "What do Aberdeen say about us?" ' (Giulianotti 1995: 6). This allowed him to establish among the Hibs supporters his reasons for studying the Aberdeen casuals as well. Giulianotti also actively sought out a gatekeeper who could ease his entry into the group. After some abortive attempts, he was finally introduced to someone at a game and this contact allowed his access to further supporters to spread. Giulianotti describes his overall research strategy thus:

The research . . . consists of regularly introducing myself to new research acquaintances; renegotiating association with familiar casuals; talking with them, drinking with them, and going to matches with them; generally participating with them in a variety of social situations; but disengaging myself from preparing for and participating in violence, within and outside of football match contexts.   (Giulianotti 1995: 3)

common methods of gaining access to groups—via gatekeepers and via acquaintances who then act as sponsors. In seeking access to intravenous female drug users, A. Taylor (1993) consciously used a gatekeeper strategy. She contacted a local detached drug worker in the area who introduced her to some local users and accompanied her on her first few research visits. A form of research bargain (see Box 14.4) was set up in that Taylor agreed that the drug worker could refer clients to her if any of his clients said they preferred to discuss issues with a female. Similarly, Hobbs (1988) says that he used his skills as a football coach to gain access to various entrepreneurial networks for his study of London's East End.

'Hanging around' is another common access strategy. As a strategy, it typically entails either loitering in an area until you are noticed or gradually becoming incorporated into or asking to join a group. The second of these was roughly the approach Whyte was taking, which nearly led to an encounter with a staircase. Wolf (1991) employed a hanging-around

strategy in gaining access to outlaw bikers in Canada. On one occasion he met a group of them at a motorcycle shop and expressed an interest in 'hanging around' with them but tried to move too quickly in seeking information about and access to them and was forced to abandon his plans. Eventually, a hanging-around strategy resulted in him being approached by the leader of a biker group (Rebels MC), who acted as his sponsor. In order to bring this off, Wolf ensured that he was properly attired. Attention to dress and demeanour can be a very important consideration when seeking access to either public or closed settings.

As these anecdotes suggest, gaining access to social settings is a crucial first step in ethnographic research, in that, without access, your research plans will be halted in their tracks. It is also fraught with difficulties and in certain cases with danger—for example, when the research is likely to be on groups engaged in violent or criminal activities. Therefore, this discussion of access strategies can be only a starting point in knowing what kinds of approach can be considered.

Ongoing access

But access does not finish when you have made contact and gained an entrée to the group. You still need access to *people*. Simply because you have gained access to an organization does not mean that you will have an easy passage through the organization. Securing access is in many ways an ongoing activity. It is likely to prove a problem in closed contexts like organizations.

- People will have suspicions about you, perhaps seeing you as an instrument of top management (it is very common for members of organizations to believe that researchers are placed there to check up on them).

- They will worry that what they say or do may get back to bosses or to colleagues. Van Maanen (1991) notes from his research on the police that when conducting ethnographic research among officers, you are likely to observe activities that may be deeply discrediting and even illegal. Your credibility among police officers will be determined by your reactions to situations and events that are known to be difficult for individuals.

- If they have these worries, they may go along with your research but in fact sabotage it, engaging in deceptions, misinformation, and not allowing access to 'back regions' (Goffman 1956).

There are three things you can do to smooth the path of ongoing access.

- Play up your credentials—past work and experience; your knowledge of the organization and/or its sector; understanding of their problems.

- Pass tests—be non-judgemental when things are said to you about informal activities or about the organization; make sure information given to you does not get back to others, whether bosses or peers.

- You may need a role—if research involves quite a lot of participant observation, the role will be part

of your position in the organization; otherwise, you will need to construct a 'front', by your dress, by your explanations about what you are doing there, by helping out occasionally with work or offering advice. Be consistent—do not behave ambiguously or inconsistently.

Similar considerations apply to research in public settings.

- Make sure you have thought about ways in which people's suspicions can be allayed. You will need a 'front', as Ditton (1977; Box 14.2) had when referring to 'his studies'. Similarly, Giulianotti (see Box 14.4) simply said that he was doing research on football supporters for a book.

- Be prepared for tests of either competence or credibility. A. Taylor (1993) reports that, at a drop-in centre at which she had been allowed to attend a meeting, 'proper cups' for tea were put out. Afterwards Taylor was told that, if she had crooked her 'wee finger' as the leader of the centre had done, her informant 'would have put [Taylor] down in such a way that you'd never want to speak to us again' (1993: 15).

- Be prepared for changes in circumstances. Both Giulianotti (Box 14.4) and Armstrong (1993) found that sudden newspaper exposés of football hooliganism or evidence of police infiltration can engender worries that you are not what or who you say you are.

Key informants

One aspect of having sponsors or gatekeepers who smooth access for the ethnographer is that they may become *key informants* in the course of the subsequent fieldwork. The ethnographer relies a lot on informants, but certain informants may become particularly important to the research. They often develop an appreciation of the research and direct the ethnographer to situations, events, or people likely to be helpful to the progress of the investigation. Whyte's (1955) study is again an extreme example of this development. Whyte reports Doc as saying to him at one point: 'You tell me what you want to see, and we'll arrange it. When you want some information, I'll ask for it, and you listen. When you want to find out their philosophy of life, I'll start an argument and get it for you. If there's something else you want to get, I'll stage an act for you' (Whyte 1955: 292). Doc was also helpful in warning Whyte that he was asking too many questions, when he told him to 'go easy on that "who," "what," "why," "when," "where" stuff' (1955: 303). Patrick (1973) was able to develop a similarly fruitful relationship with 'Tim' for his study of a violent gang in Glasgow. A. Taylor (1993) says that her period of participant observation was in relation to fifty female drug users and that intensive interviews were carried out with twenty-six women, but that eight of the women were key informants.

Key informants can clearly be of great help to the ethnographer and frequently provide a support that helps with the stress of fieldwork. However, it also needs to be borne in mind that they carry risks in that the ethnographer may develop an undue reliance on the key informant and rather than seeing social reality through the eyes of members of the social setting, the researcher is seeing social reality through the eyes of the key informant.

In addition, the ethnographer will encounter many people who will act as informants. Their accounts may be solicited or unsolicited (Hammersley and Atkinson 1995). Some researchers prefer the latter, because of its greater spontaneity and naturalism. Very often, research participants develop a sense of the kinds of events the ethnographer wants to see or encounters that it would be beneficial to be present at. Armstrong (1993) says that, while

doing research on 'The Blades', a group of supporters of Sheffield United Football Club who were engaged in hooligan activity (see Chapter 13 for other references to this research), he would sometimes get tip-offs:

'We're all gonna' Leeds in a couple o' weeks . . . four coaches, Pond Street, town centre. If you're serious about this study you'll be down there on one of 'em.' I often travelled on the same coach as Ray [an informant]; he would then sit with me at matches and in pubs and point out Blades, giving me background information. Sometimes he would start conversations with Blades about incidents which he knew I wanted to know about and afterwards would ask 'Did you get all that down then?' . . . There was never one particular informant; rather, there were many Blades I could ring up and meet at any time, who were part of the core and would always welcome a beer and a chat about 'It', or tell me who I 'ought to 'ave a word wi''.   (Armstrong, 1993: 24–5).

Such unsolicited sources of information are highly attractive to the ethnographer because of their relative spontaneity, although, as Hammersley and Atkinson (1995: 130–1) observe, they may on occasions be staged for the ethnographer's benefit. Solicited accounts can occur in two ways: by interview (see Chapter 15) or by casual questioning during conversations (though in ethnographic research the boundary between an interview and a conversation is by no means clear-cut, as Burgess (1984) makes clear). When the ethnographer needs specific information concerning an issue that is not amenable to direct observation or that is not cropping up during 'natural' conversations, solicited accounts are likely to be the only way forward.

Roles for ethnographers

Related to the issue of ongoing access (or relationships in the field, as it is sometimes called) is the question of the kind of role the ethnographer adopts in relation to the social setting and its members. Several schemes have been devised by writers on

research methods to describe the various roles that can be and have been adopted by ethnographers.

One of the most widely cited schemes is Gold's (1958) classification of participant observer roles, which can be arrayed on a continuum of degrees of involvement with and detachment from members of the social setting (see Figure 14.2). The four roles are:

- *Complete participant.* According to Gold, the complete participant is a fully functioning member of the social setting and his or her true identity is not known to members. As such, the complete participant is a covert observer, like Fielding (1982) and Holdaway (1982).

- *Participant-as-observer.* This role is the same as the complete participant one, but members of the social setting are aware of the researcher's status as a researcher. The ethnographer is engaged in regular interaction with people and participates in their daily lives. All of the studies referred to in Figure 14.1 as involving an overt role—whether in open/public or closed settings—are of this kind, as was Giulianotti's research (see Box 14.4).

- *Observer-as-participant.* In this role, the researcher is mainly an interviewer. There is some observation but very little of it involves any participation. Many of the studies covered in Chapter 15 are of this type. Ethnographic research on the police is often of this type, since the opportunities for genuine participation are few, because of considera-

tions of legality and interrupting operational policing. Thus, as an observer-as-participant, Norris (1993) has described how in this role he concentrated on gathering two types of data: 'naturally occurring inter-officer talk' and 'detailed descriptions of how officers handled "live" incidents' (1993: 126). See also Box 14.5 for a further illustration.

- *Complete observer.* The researcher does not interact with people. According to Gold, people do not have to take the researcher into account. It can be found in studies using forms of observation that are unobtrusive in character.

Most writers would take the view that, since ethnography entails immersion in a social setting and fairly prolonged involvement, the complete observer role should not be considered as participant observation or ethnography at all, since participation is likely to be more or less entirely missing. Some writers might also question whether research based on the observer-as-participant role can genuinely be regarded as ethnography, but, since it is likely that certain situations are unlikely to be amenable to the immersion that is a key ingredient of the method, it could be argued that to dismiss it totally as an approach to ethnography is rather restrictive. It is significant in this context that Gold referred to the four roles in relation to conducting 'fieldwork', which has the potential for a broader meaning than either participant observation or ethnography.

Each role carries its own advantages and risks. The

Involvement ◄─────────────► Detachment

| Complete participant | Participant-as-observer | Observer-as-participant | Complete observer |

Fig. 14.2 Gold's classification of participant observer roles

---

Box 14.5 An observer-as-participant in the Magic Kingdom

An interesting illustration of research that comes very close to the observer-as-participant role is Raz's (1999) study of Tokyo Disneyland. His main sources of data were: many visits to the theme park, including being part of several official and unofficial tours; interviews with current and former employees; a textual analysis of company guidebooks; and an examination of the reception of the park by visitors through a focus group. Raz's goal was to explore the meeting place of the forces of globalization, in the form of the familiar themes associated with the Disney company, and forces of the 'local', in the form of the distinctive character of Japanese culture. He draws on ideas like 'globalization' in order to develop an understanding of the ways in which the combination of global and local forces is played out and on Hochschild's (1983) concept of 'emotional labour' (see Box 13.2) to develop an appreciation of the world of work for the Disney employee.

Box 14.6 🔆 *What is 'going native'?*

'Going native' refers to a plight that is supposed some-times to afflict ethnographers when they lose their sense of being a researcher and become wrapped up in the world view of the people they are studying. The pro-longed immersion of ethnographers in the lives of the people they study, coupled with the commitment to see-ing the social world through their eyes, lie behind the risk and actuality of going native. Going native is a potential problem for several reasons but especially because the ethnographer can lose sight of his or her position as a

researcher and therefore find it difficult to develop a social scientific angle on the collection and analysis of data. When Hobbs (1988: 6) writes in connection with his fieldwork on entrepreneurship in London's East End that he 'often had to remind himself that [he] was not in a pub to enjoy [himself] but to conduct an academic inquiry, and repeatedly woke up the following morning with an incredible hangover facing the dilemma of whether to bring it up or write it up', he may have been on the brink of going native.

---

issues concerning being a complete participant were covered in Box 14.3. According to Gold, the participant-as-observer role carries the risk of over-identification and hence of 'going native' (see Box 14.6), but offers the opportunity to get close to people. Gold argues that the observer-as-participant role carries the risk of not understanding the social setting and people in it sufficiently and therefore of making incorrect inferences. The complete observer role shares with complete participa-tion the removal of the possible problem of reactivity, but it carries even further risks than the observer-as-participant role of failing to understand situations.

Gans (1968) has devised a classification of partici-pant observer roles, but he views these as roles that will coexist in any project. In other words, the three roles he outlines will be employed at different times in the course of ethnographic research and for differ-ent purposes. The three roles are:

- *total participant*, in which the ethnographer is completely involved in a certain situation and has to resume a researcher stance once the situation has unfolded and then write down notes;
- *researcher-participant*, whereby the ethnographer participates in a situation but is only semi-involved, so that he or she can function fully as a researcher in the course of the situation;
- *total researcher*, which entails observation without involvement in the situation, as in attendance at a public meeting or watching what is going on in

a bar; when in this role, the researcher does not participate in the flow of events.

The advantage of Gans's classification is that, like Gold's, it reflects degrees of involvement and detachment, but has the advantage that it deals only with overt observation and recognizes that ethnographers do not typically adopt a single role throughout their dealings. It is arguably the case that, even if it were possible to adopt a single ethnographic role over the entire course of a pro-ject, it is likely that it would be undesirable, because there would be a lack of flexibility in hand-ling situations and people, and risks of excessive involvement (and hence going native) or detach-ment would loom large. The issue of the kind of role(s) the ethnographer adopts is of considerable significance, because it has implications for field relationships in the various situations that are encountered.

Active or passive?

A further issue that is raised about any situation in which the ethnographer participates is the degree to which he or she should be or can be an active or a passive participant (Van Maanen 1978). Even when the ethnographer is in an observer-as-participant role, there may be contexts in which either participa-tion is unavoidable or a compulsion to join in in a limited way may be felt. For example, Fine's (1996) research on the work of chefs in restaurants was carried out largely by semi-structured interview. In spite of his limited participation, he found himself involved in washing up in the kitchens to help out during busy periods. In many instances, the researcher has no choice. Researchers who do ethnographic research on the police, for example, unless they are covert observers like Holdaway (1982) or take steps to become police officers like Rubinstein (1973), are unlikely to be able to be active participants beyond offering fairly trivial assistance. An example of this can be found in an incident reported in Punch's field notes in connection with his research on the police in Amsterdam: 'Tom wanted to move the cars which were blocking the narrow and busy street in front of the station, and said sternly to the suspect, but with a smile at me behind his back, "You stay here with your hands up and don't try anything because this detective here [pointing at me] is keeping an eye on you". I frowned authoritatively' (Punch 1979: 8). Punch travelled with the officers in their cars but in civilian clothes and employed as a 'front' the role of a plain clothes policeman.

Sometimes, ethnographers may *feel* they have no choice in getting involved, because a failure to participate actively might indicate to members of the social setting a lack of commitment and hence a loss of credibility. This can often lead to dilemmas on the part of ethnographers, especially when the activities in which they actively take part (or might do so) are illegal or dangerous (see Box 14.7). On the other hand, many writers counsel against active participa-

---

Box 14.7 Active ethnography and illegal activity

In the context of his study of entrepreneurship (a euphemism for several kinds of legal and illegal activity) among East Enders in London, Hobbs admits he engaged in illegal activities:

A refusal, or worse still an enquiry concerning the legal status of the 'parcel', would provoke an abrupt conclusion to the relationship. Consequently, I was willing to skirt the boundaries of criminality on several occasions, and I considered it crucial to be willingly involved in 'normal' business transactions, legal or otherwise. I was pursuing an interactive, inductive study of an entrepreneurial culture, and in order to do so I had to display entrepreneurial skills myself. . . . [My] status as an insider meant that I was afforded a great deal of trust by my informants, and I was allowed access to settings, detailed conversations, and information that might not otherwise have been available.   (Hobbs 1988: 7, 15)

---

tion in criminal or dangerous activities (Polsky 1967). Both Armstrong (1993) and Giulianotti (see Box 14.4) refused to participate in fights while doing research into football hooliganism. The latter writes: 'My own rules are that I will not get involved in fighting or become a go-between for the two gangs in organizing fights' (Giulianotti 1995: 10). Indeed, we see here a strong argument against covert research on criminals or those involved in dangerous activities, since it will be much more difficult for someone in such a role not to participate.

Sampling

The sampling of informants in ethnographic research is often a combination of convenience sampling and snowball sampling (see Chapter 4 for an explanation of these terms). Much of the time ethnographers are forced to gather information from whatever sources are available to them. Very often they face opposition or at least indifference to their research and are relieved to glean information or views from whoever is prepared to divulge such details. This seems to have been the essence of Armstrong's (1993: 21) strategy in the context of football hooliganism when he tried to 'locate individuals within the group networks that constituted the Blades'. However, as the lengthy quotation from his work above suggests, he was regularly able to secure from his informants details of others whom it would be useful for him to consult. Similarly, A. Taylor has written in connection with her study of female drug users that her research participants were

eventually obtained by a mix of 'snowballing techniques' . . . and my almost continuous presence in the area. . . . Rather than ask to be introduced or given names of others I could contact, when I met a woman I would spend as much time with her as she would allow, participating in her daily round, and through this come to meet others in her social circle. My continued presence in the area also led other women drug users to approach me when I was alone . . . In addition, the drug worker in the area would mention my presence and interest to women with whom he came in contact and facilitate introductions where possible.   (A. Taylor 1993: 16)

Ethnographers who take on a role that is closer to the observer-as-participant one rely somewhat more on formally asking for names of others who might be relevant and who could be contacted.

Whichever of the two strategies is adopted, the question is raised as to the degree to which either can result in a representative sample of informants. Probability sampling is almost never used in ethnographic research and is even rarely employed in qualitative research based on interviews. In many cases, it is not feasible to conduct a probability sampling exercise because of the constraints of ongoing fieldwork and also because it can be difficult and often impossible to map 'the population' from which a random sample might be taken—that is, to create a sampling frame. Instead, ethnographers

have to ensure that they gain access to as wide a range of individuals relevant to the research question as possible, so that many different perspectives and ranges of activity are the focus of attention.

Theoretical sampling

An alternative strategy is *theoretical sampling* (see Box 14.8), advocated by Glaser and Strauss (1967) and Strauss and Corbin (1998) in the context of an approach to qualitative data analysis they developed known as grounded theory. In Glaser and Strauss's view, because of its reliance on statistical rather than theoretical criteria, probability sampling is not appropriate to qualitative research. Theoretical sampling is meant to be an alternative strategy. As they put it: 'Theoretical sampling is done in order to discover categories and their properties and to suggest the interrelationships into a theory. Statistical sampling is done to obtain accurate evidence on distributions of people among categories to be used in descriptions and verifications' (Glaser and Strauss 1967: 62).

Figure 14.3 outlines the main steps in theoretical sampling. The reference in Box 14.8 to 'places, people, or events' reminds us that, in ethnographic research, it is not just people who are being sampled but also events and contexts as well (see below).

In grounded theory, you carry on collecting data (observing, interviewing, collecting documents)

Box 14.8 What is theoretical sampling?

According to Glaser and Strauss (1967: 45), theoretical sampling 'is the process of data collection for generating theory whereby the analyst jointly collects, codes, and analyzes his data and decides what data to collect next and where to find them, in order to develop his theory as it emerges. The process of data collection is *controlled* by the emerging theory, whether substantive or formal.' This definition conveys a crucial characteristic of theoretical sampling—namely, that it is an ongoing process rather than a distinct and single stage, as it is, for example, in probability sampling. Moreover, it is important to realize

that it is not just people that are the 'objects' of sampling, as can be seen in a more recent definition: 'Data gathering driven by concepts derived from the evolving theory and based on the concept of "making comparisons," whose purpose is to go to places, people, or events that will maximize opportunities to discover variations among concepts and to densify categories in terms of their properties and dimensions' (Strauss and Corbin 1998: 201). For Charmaz (2000: 519), theoretical sampling is a 'defining property of grounded theory' and is concerned with the refinement of ideas, rather than boosting sample size.

Box 14.9 ☼ *What is theoretical saturation?*

The key idea is that you carry on sampling theoretically until a category has been saturated with data. 'This means, until (a) no new or relevant data seem to be emerging regarding a category, (b) the category is well developed in terms of its properties and dimensions demonstrating variation, and (c) the relationships among categories are well established and validated' (Strauss and

Corbin 1998: 212). In the language of grounded theory, a category operates at a somewhat higher level of abstraction than a concept in that it may group together several concepts that have common features denoted by the category. Theoretical sampling refers to the sampling, not just of people, but also of settings and events.

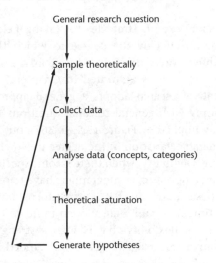

Fig. 14.3 The process of theoretical sampling

until you have achieved *theoretical saturation* (see Box 14.9). This means that: successive interviews/observations have both formed the basis for the creation of a category and confirmed its importance; there is no need to continue with data collection in relation to that category or cluster of categories; instead, the researcher should move on and generate hypotheses out of the categories that are building up and then move on to collecting data in relation to these hypotheses. Proponents of grounded theory argue that there is a great deal of redundancy in statistical sampling. For example, committing yourself to interviewing x per cent of an organization's members may mean that you end up wasting time and resources because you could have confirmed the significance of a concept and/or its connections with other concepts by using a much smaller sample. Instead, grounded theory advocates that you sample

in terms of what is relevant to and meaningful for your theory. The key is to ensure you sample so as to test your emerging theoretical ideas.

The ideas of theoretical sampling and theoretical saturation will be encountered again when grounded theory is examined in greater detail in the context of qualitative data analysis in Chapter 19.

Not just people

As was pointed out in the last section, in ethnographic research sampling is not just about people but also other things. Hammersley and Atkinson (1995) mention time and context as units that need to be considered in the context of sampling. Attending to *time* means that the ethnographer must make sure that people or events are observed at different times of the day and different days of the week. To do otherwise, risks drawing inferences about certain people's behaviour or about events that are valid only for mornings or for weekdays rather than weekends. It is impossible to be an ethnographer all the time for several reasons: need to take time out to write up notes; other commitments (work or domestic); and body imperatives (eating, sleeping, and so on). When the group in question operates a different cycle from the ethnographer's normal regime (such as night shifts in a hospital or going to nightclubs), the requirement to time sample may necessitate a considerable change of habit.

It can also be important to sample in terms of *context*. People's behaviour is influenced by contextual factors so that it is important to ensure that such behaviour is observed in a variety of locations. For example, one of the important features of research on football hooliganism is that, of course, those engaged in such activity are not full-time football hooligans. In order to understand the culture and world-view of football hooligans, writers like Armstrong (1993) and Giulianotti (Box 14.4) had to ensure that they interacted with them not just around the time of football matches, but also in a variety of contexts (pubs, general socializing) which also meant at different times.

Field notes

Because of the frailties of human memory, ethnographers have to take notes based on their observations. These should be fairly detailed summaries of events and behaviour and the researcher's initial reflections on them. The notes need to specify key dimensions of whatever is observed or heard. There are some general principles.

- Write down notes, however brief, as quickly as possible after seeing or hearing something interesting.

- Write up full field notes at the very latest at the end of the day and include such details as location, who is involved, what prompted the exchange or whatever, date and time of the day, etc.

- Nowadays, people may prefer to use a dictaphone to record initial notes, but this may create a problem of needing to transcribe a lot of speech.

- Notes must be vivid and clear—you should not have to ask at a later date 'what did I mean by that?'

- You need to take copious notes, so, if in doubt, write it down. The notes may be of different types (see below).

Obviously, it can be very useful to take your notes down straight away, i.e. as soon as something interesting happens. However, wandering around with a notebook and pencil in hand and scribbling notes down on a continuous basis runs the risk of making people self-conscious. It may be necessary, therefore, to develop strategies of taking small amounts of time out, though hopefully without generating the anxieties Ditton (1977) appears to have occasioned (see Box 14.2).

To some extent, strategies for taking field notes will be affected by the degree to which the ethnographer enters the field with clearly delineated research questions. As noted in Chapter 13, most qualitative research adopts a general approach of beginning with general research questions (as specifically implied by Figure 13.1, p. 267), but there is considerable variation in the degree to which this is the case. Obviously, when there is some specificity to a research question, ethnographers have to orientate their observations to that research focus, but at the same time maintain a fairly open mind so that the element of flexibility that is such a strength of a qualitative research strategy is not eroded. Ditton (Box 14.2) provides an illustration of a very open-ended approach when he writes that his research 'was not set up to answer any empirical questions' (1977: 11). Similarly, in the context of her research on female drug users, A. Taylor (1993: 15) explains that in her early days in the field she tended to listen rather than talk because she 'did not know what questions [she] wanted to ask'. Armstrong (1993: 12) writes in connection with his research on football hooliganism that his research 'began without a focus' and that as a result 'he decided to record everything'. As a result, a typical Saturday 'would result in thirty sides of notes handwritten on A4 paper'. This period of open-endedness usually cannot last long, because there is the temptation to try to record the details of absolutely everything, which can be very trying. Usually the ethnographer will begin to narrow down the focus of his or her research and to match observations to the emerging research focus. This approach is implied by the sequence

> ## Box 14.10 Taking field notes: Encounters with doctors and patients in a medical school training programme
>
> In the context of his research in a medical school, P. Atkinson (1981) provides an account that strongly implies that ethnographers need to be flexible in their note-taking tactics:
>
> I found that my strategies for observation and recording changed naturally as the nature of the social scene changed. Whenever possible I attempted to make rough notes and jottings of some sort whilst I was in the field. Such notes were then amplified and added to later in the day when I returned to the office. The quantity and type of on the spot recording varied across recurrent types of situation. During 'tutorials', when one of the doctors taught the group in a more or less formal manner, or when there was some group discussion . . . then it seemed entirely natural and appropriate to sit among the students with my notebook on my knee and take notes almost continuously. At the other extreme, I clearly did not sit with my notebook and pen whilst I was engaged in casual conversations with students over a cup of coffee. Whereas taking notes is a normal thing to do, taking notes during a coffee break chat is not normal practice. . . . Less clear cut was my approach to the observation and recording of bedside teaching. On the whole I tried to position myself at the back of the student group and make occasional jottings: main items of information on the patients, key technical terms, and brief notes on the shape of the session (e.g. the sequence of topics covered, the students who were called on to perform and so on). (P. Atkinson 1981: 131–2)

suggested by Figure 13.1, p. 267, and can be seen in the account by P. Atkinson (1981; see Box 14.10).

For most ethnographers, the main equipment with which they will need to supply themselves in the course of observation will be a note pad and pen (see e.g. Armstrong 1993: 28, and P. Atkinson in Box 14.10). A dictaphone can be another useful addition to one's hardware, but, as suggested above it is likely to increase radically the amount of transcription and is possibly more obtrusive than writing notes. Most ethnographers report that after a period of time they become less obtrusive to participants in social settings, who become familiar with their presence (e.g. P. Atkinson 1981: 128). Speaking into a dictaphone may rekindle an awareness of the ethnographer's presence. Also, in gatherings it may be difficult to use, because of the impact of extraneous noise. Photography can be an additional source of data and helps to stir the ethnographer's memory, but it is likely that some kinds of research (especially involving crime and deviance) will render the taking of photographs unworkable.

Types of field notes

Some writers have found it useful to classify the types of field notes that are generated in the process of conducting an ethnography. The following classification is based on the similar categories suggested by Lofland and Lofland (1995) and Sanjek (1990):

- *Mental notes*—particularly useful when it is inappropriate to be seen taking notes (for example, during the coffee breaks referred to by Atkinson in Box 14.10).

- *Jotted notes* (also called *Scratch notes*)—very brief notes written down on pieces of paper or in small notebooks to jog one's memory about events that should be written up later. Lofland and Lofland (1995: 90) refer to these as being made up of 'little phrases, quotes, key words, and the like'. They need to be jotted down inconspicuously, preferably out of sight, since detailed note-taking in front of people may make them self-conscious. These are equivalent to the 'rough notes and jottings' that Atkinson refers to in Box 14.10.

- *Full field notes*—as soon as possible make detailed notes, which will be your main data source. They should be written at the end of the day or sooner if possible. Write as promptly and as fully as possible. Write down information about events, people, conversations, etc. Write down initial ideas about interpretation. Record impressions and feelings. When Atkinson in Box 14.10 refers to notes in which he 'amplified and added to' the jottings made during the day, he was producing full field notes. An example of a full field note is provided in Box 14.11.

It is worth adding that field notes are often to do with the ethnographer as well as the social setting being observed. It is frequently in field notes that the ethnographer's presence is evident. We see this in the field note on page 301 from Punch's work on police work in which he confirms his (false) status as a plain clothes officer and in the field note in Box 14.11 when he lends support to letting the cyclist go. Precisely because they record the quotidian as observed and experienced by ethnographers, it is here that they come to the surface. In the finished work—the ethnography in the sense of a written account of a group and its culture—the ethnographer is frequently written out of the picture (Van Maanen 1988). A major difference here is that field notes, except for brief passages like those taken from Punch's work, are invariably for personal consumption (Coffey 1999), whereas the written ethnography is for public consumption and has to be presented as a definitive account of the social setting and culture in question. To keep on allowing the

---

> **Box 14.11 A field note: Police work in Amsterdam**
>
> Punch's (1979) ethnographic research on police work in Amsterdam was briefly mentioned above. One of the ideas he developed was the way in which police officers often cultivated distinctive styles of working. One of them, Anton, was inflexible and therefore disinclined to use his discretion (perhaps because he was new to the work), as the following passage from Punch's field notes suggests:
>
> Once Jan had been sitting inside for a couple of hours doing nothing and was desperate to get out. He was sent out in a car with a newcomer, Anton. The three of us stepped outside the station and immediately saw a young man cycling erratically the wrong way down the Warmoesstraat which is a one-way street. Anton stopped him, smelt his breath, and ordered him to leave the bike and walk home. The man refused and Anton threatened to take him inside and book him for being drunk on a bike [under an article normally applied to car-drivers and almost never used for cyclists]. Jan pleaded with Anton to let the man go so that we could get out on patrol. I also added support to Jan's plea. But Anton was adamant and took the youth inside where the brigadier talked the cyclist into seeing reason and proceeding by foot. (Punch 1979: 110–11)

ethnographer to surface in the text risks conveying a sense of the account as an artifice rather than an authoritative chronicle. This issue will be addressed in further detail in Chapter 23.

The end

Knowing when to stop is not an easy or straightforward matter in ethnography. Because of its unstructured nature and the absence of specific hypotheses to be tested (other than those that might emerge during data collection and analysis), there is a tendency for ethnographic research to lack a sense of an obvious end point. But clearly ethnographic research does come to an end! It may be that there is

an almost natural end to the research, such as in Waddington's study of a strike (see Box 13.6, p. 279), but this is a fairly rare occurrence. Sometimes, the rhythms of the ethnographer's occupational career or personal and family life will necessitate withdrawal from the field or research funding commitments will bring fieldwork to a close. Such factors include: the end of a period of sabbatical leave; the need to write up and submit a doctoral thesis by a certain date; or funding for research drawing to a close. As regards family and personal commitments, for example, A. Taylor (1993) writes that one of the factors that was instrumental in her departure from the field was an illness of her youngest son that lasted many months.

Moreover, ethnographic research can be highly stressful for many reasons: the nature of the topic, which places the fieldworker in stressful situations (as in research on crime); the marginality of the researcher in the social setting and the need constantly to manage a front; and the prolonged absence from one's normal life that is often necessary. The ethnographer may feel that he or she has simply had enough. A further possibility that may start to bring about moves to bring fieldwork to a close is that the ethnographer may begin to feel that the research questions on which he or she has decided to concentrate are answered, so that there are no new data worth generating. The ethnographer may even feel a strong sense of *déjà vu* towards the end of data collection. Altheide (1980: 310) has written that his decision to leave the various news organizations in which he had conducted ethnographic research was often motivated by 'the recurrence of familiar situations and the feeling that little worthwhile was being revealed.' In the language of

grounded theory, all the researcher's categories are thoroughly *saturated*, although Glaser and Strauss's approach would invite you to be certain that there are no new questions to be asked of the area you are investigating, or no new comparisons to be made.

The reasons for bringing ethnographic research to a close can involve a wide range of factors from the personal to matters of research design. Whatever the reason, disengagement has to be *managed*. For one thing, this means that promises must be kept, so that, if you promised a report to an organization as a condition of entry, that promise should not be forgotten. It also means that ethnographers must provide good explanations for their departure. Members of a social setting always know that the researcher is a temporary fixture, but over a long period of time, and especially if there was genuine participation in activities within that setting, people may forget that the ethnographer's presence is finite. The farewells have to be managed and in an orderly fashion. Also, the ethnographer's *ethical* commitments must not be forgotten, such as the need to ensure that persons and settings are anonymized—unless, of course, as sometimes happens, there has been an agreement that the nature of the social setting can be disclosed (as often occurs in the study of religious sects and cults).

Can there be a feminist ethnography?

This heading is in fact the title of a widely cited article by Stacey (1988). It is a rebuttal of the view that there is and/or can be a distinctively feminist ethnography that both draws on the distinctive strengths of ethnography and is informed by feminist tenets of the kind outlined at the end of Chapter 13. Reinharz (1992) sees feminist ethnography as significant in terms of feminism, because

- it documents women's lives and activities, which were previously largely seen as marginal and subsidiary to men's;

- it understands women from their perspective, so that the tendency that 'trivializes females' activities and thoughts, or interprets them from the standpoint of men in the society or of the male researcher' (Reinharz 1992: 52), is militated against; and

- it understands women in context.

However, such commitments and practices go only part of the way. Of great significance to feminist researchers is the question of whether the research allows for a non-exploitative relationship between

---

Box 14.12 **A feminist ethnography**

Skeggs (1997: 1) refers to 'the 83 White working-class women of this longitudinal ethnographic study, set in the North West of England' and writes that it was 'based on research conducted over a total period of 12 years including three years' full-time, in-the-field participant observation. It began when the women enrolled on a "caring" course at a local college and it follows their trajectories through the labour market, education and the family' (Skeggs 1997: 1).

The elements of a distinctively feminist ethnography can be seen in the following comments:

- 'This ethnography was politically motivated to provide space for the articulations and experiences of the marginalized' (Skeggs 1997: 23).

- The 'study was concerned to show how young women's experience of structure (their class and gender positioning) and institutions (education and the

media) framed and informed their responses and how this process informed constructions of their own subjectivity' (Skeggs 1994: 74). This comment, like the previous one, reflects the commitment to documenting women's lives and allowing their experiences to come through, while also pointing to the significance of the understanding of women in context, to which Reinharz (1992) refers.

Skeggs also feels that the relationship with the women was not an exploitative one. For example, she writes that the research enabled the women's 'sense of self-worth' to be 'enhanced by being given the opportunity to be valued, knowledgeable and interesting' (Skeggs 1994: 81). She also claims she was able to 'provide a mouthpiece against injustices' and to listen 'to disclosures of violence, child abuse and sexual harassment' (Skeggs 1994: 81).

---

researcher and researched. One of the main elements of such a strategy is that the ethnographer does not treat the relationship as a one-way process of extracting information from others, but actually provides something in return.

Skeggs's (1994, 1997) account of her ethnographic research on young women, which was briefly mentioned in Chapter 13, represents an attempt to address this issue of a non-exploitative relationship when women conduct ethnographic research on other women (see Box 14.12). Stacey (1988), however, argues, on the basis of her fieldwork experience, that the various situations she encountered as a feminist ethnographer placed her 'in situations of inauthenticity, dissimilitude, and potential, perhaps inevitable betrayal, situations that I now believe are inherent in fieldwork method. For no matter how welcome, even enjoyable the fieldworker's presence may appear to "natives", fieldwork represents an intrusion and intervention into a system of relationships, a system of relationships that the researcher is far freer to leave' (Stacey 1988: 23). Stacey also argues that, when the research is written up, it is the feminist ethnographer's interpretations and judgements that come through and that have authority. Skeggs

responds to this general charge against feminist ethnography by acknowledging in the case of her own study that her academic career was undoubtedly enhanced by the research, but argues that Stacey's views construe women as victims. Instead, she argues

The young women were not prepared to be exploited; just as they were able to resist most things which did not promise economic or cultural reward, they were able to resist me. . . . They enjoyed the research. It provided resources for developing a sense of their self-worth. More importantly, the feminism of the research has provided a framework which they use to explain that their individual problems are part of a wider structure and not their personal fault. (Skeggs 1994: 88).

Similarly, Reinharz (1992: 74–5) argues that, although ethnographic fieldwork relationships may sometimes *seem* manipulative, a clear undercurrent of reciprocity often lies beneath them. The researcher, in other words, may offer help or advice to her research participants, or she may be exhibiting reciprocity by giving a public airing to normally marginalized voices (although the ethnographer is always the mouthpiece for such voices and may be imposing a particular 'spin' on them). Moreover, it seems extreme to abandon feminist ethnography on the grounds that the ethnographer cannot fulfil all possible obligations simultaneously. Indeed, this would be a recipe for the abandonment of all research, feminist or otherwise. What is also crucial is transparency—transparency in the feminist ethnographer's dealings with the women she studies and transparency in the account of the research process, both of which are a great strength in Skeggs's work. Nonetheless, it is clear that the question of whether there is or can be a feminist ethnography is a matter of ongoing debate.

Key points

- Ethnography is a term that refers to both a method and the written product of research based on that method.

- The ethnographer is typically a participant observer who also uses non-observational methods and sources such as interviewing and documents.

- The ethnographer may adopt an overt or covert role, but the latter carries ethical difficulties.

- The method of access to a social setting will depend in part on whether it is a public or closed one.

- Key informants frequently play an important role for the ethnographer but care is needed to ensure that their impact on the direction of research is not excessive.

- There are several different ways of classifying the kinds of role that the ethnographer may assume. These are not necessarily mutually exclusive.

- Sampling considerations differ from those addressed in the context of quantitative research, in that issues of representativeness are emphasized less.

- Field notes are important for prompting the ethnographer's memory.

- Feminist ethnography has become a popular approach to collecting data from a feminist standpoint but there have been debates about whether there really can be a feminist ethnography.

Revision questions

- Is it possible to distinguish ethnography and participant observation?
- How does participant observation differ from structured observation?
- To what extent do participant observation and ethnography rely solely on observation?

Access

- 'Covert ethnography obviates the need to gain access to inaccessible settings and therefore has much to recommend it.' Discuss.
- Examine some articles in British sociology journals in which ethnography and participant observation figure strongly. Was the researcher in an overt or covert role? Was access needed to closed or open settings? How was access achieved?
- Is access to closed settings necessarily more difficult to achieve than to open settings?
- Does the problem of access finish once access to a chosen setting has been achieved?
- What might be the role of key informants in ethnographic research? Is there anything to be concerned about when using them?

Roles for ethnographers

- Compare Gold's and Gans's schemes for classifying participant observer roles.
- What is meant by going native?
- Should ethnographers be active or passive in the settings in which they conduct research?

Sampling

- What is snowball sampling?
- What is theoretical sampling?
- How crucial is the idea of theoretical saturation to theoretical sampling?

Field notes

- Why are field notes important for ethnographers?
- Why is it useful to distinguish between different types of field notes?

The end

- How do you decide when to complete the data collection phase in ethnographic research?

Can there be a feminist ethnography?

- What are the main ingredients of feminist ethnography?
- Assess Stacey's argument about whether feminist ethnography is possible in the light of Skeggs's research or any other ethnographic study that describes itself, or can be seen, as feminist.

15 Interviewing in qualitative research

Reader's guide

This chapter is concerned with the interview in qualitative research. The term *qualitative interview* is often used to capture the different types of interview that are used in qualitative research. Such interviews tend to be far less structured than the kind of interview associated with survey research, which was discussed in Chapter 5 in terms of structured interviewing. This chapter is concerned with individual interviews in qualitative research; the focus group method, which is a form of interview but with several people, is discussed in the next chapter. The two forms of qualitative interviewing discussed in this chapter are unstructured and semi-structured interviewing. The chapter explores:

- the differences between structured interviewing and qualitative interviews;
- the main characteristics of and differences between unstructured and semi-structured interviewing; this entails a recognition that the two terms refer to extremes and that in practice a wide range of interviews with differing degrees of structure lie between the extremes;
- how to devise and use an interview guide for semi-structured interviewing;
- the different kinds of question that can be asked in an interview guide;
- the importance of tape-recording and transcribing qualitative interviews;
- approaches to sampling in studies using qualitative interviews;
- the significance of qualitative interviewing in feminist research;
- the advantages and disadvantages of qualitative interviewing relative to participant observation.

Introduction

The interview is probably the most widely employed method in qualitative research. Of course, as we have seen in Chapter 14, ethnography usually involves a substantial amount of interviewing and this factor undoubtedly contributes to the widespread use of the interview by qualitative researchers. However, it is the flexibility of the interview that makes it so attractive. Since ethnography entails an extended period of participant observation, which is very disruptive for researchers because of the sustained absence(s) required from work and/or family life, research based more or less exclusively on interviews is a highly attractive alternative for the collection of qualitative data. Interviewing, the transcription of interviews, and the analysis of transcripts are all very time-consuming, but they can be more readily accommodated into researchers' personal lives.

In Box 5.3 (p. 110), several different types of interview were briefly outlined. The bulk of the types outlined there—other than the structured interview and the standardized interview—are ones associated with qualitative research. *Focus groups* and *group interviewing* will be examined in the next chapter and the remaining forms of interview associated with qualitative research will at various points be explored in this chapter. However, in spite of the apparent proliferation of terms describing types of interview in qualitative research, the two main types are the *unstructured interview* and the *semi-structured* interview. Researchers sometimes employ the term *qualitative interview* to encapsulate these two types of interview. There is clearly the potential for consider- able confusion here, but the types and definitions offered in Box 5.3, p. 110 are meant to inject a degree of consistency of terminology.

Differences between the structured interview and qualitative research interviews

Qualitative interviewing is usually very different from interviewing in quantitative research in a number of ways.

- The approach tends to be much less structured in qualitative research. In quantitative research, the approach is structured to maximize the reliability and validity of measurement of key concepts. It is also more structured because the researcher has a clearly specified set of research questions that are to be investigated. The structured interview is designed to answer these questions. Instead, in qualitative research, there is an emphasis on greater generality in the formulation of initial research ideas and on interviewees' own perspectives.

- In qualitative interviewing, there is much greater interest in the interviewee's point of view; in quantitative research, the interview reflects the researcher's concerns. This contrast is a direct outcome of the previous one.

- In qualitative interviewing, 'rambling' or going off at tangents is often encouraged—it gives insight into what the interviewee sees as relevant and important; in quantitative research, it is usually regarded as a nuisance and discouraged.

- In qualitative interviewing, interviewers can depart significantly from any schedule or guide that is being used. They can ask new questions that follow up interviewees' replies and can vary the order of questions and even the wording of questions. In quantitative research, none of these things should be done, because they will compromise the standardization of the interview process and hence the reliability and validity of measurement.

- As a result, qualitative interviewing tends to be flexible, responding to the direction in which interviewees take the interview and perhaps adjusting the emphases in the research as a result of significant issues that emerge in the course of interviews (see Box 15.3 for an example). By contrast, structured interviews are typically inflexible, because of the need to standardize the way in which each interviewee is dealt with.

- In qualitative interviewing, the researcher wants rich, detailed answers; in quantitative research the interview is supposed to generate answers that can be coded and processed quickly.

- In qualitative interviewing, the interviewee may be interviewed on more than one and sometimes even several occasions (see Box 15.1 for an example). In quantitative research, unless the research is longitudinal in character, the person will be interviewed on one occasion only.

Box 15.1 Unstructured interviewing

Malbon (1999) describes his interviewing strategy for his research on 'clubbers' in the following way:

Clubbers were usually interviewed twice, with the second interview happening after we had been clubbing together. Both interviews were very much 'conversational' in style and I avoided interview schedules, although all interviews were taped. The first interview was designed to achieve three main goals: to put the clubber at ease while also explaining fully and clearly in what ways I was hoping for help; to begin to sketch in details of the clubbers' clubbing preferences, motivations and histories; and to allow me an opportunity to decide how to approach the night(s) out that I would be spending with the clubber . . .

The second interview provided a forum for what was invariably a more relaxed meeting than the first interview . . . The main content of the second interview consisted of comments, discussion and questions about the club visits we had made together, and the nature of the night out as an experience. In the latter half of these second interviews, discussion occasionally diversified in scope to cover wider aspects of the clubbers' lives: their relationships to work or study, their relationships with friends and loved ones, their hopes and fears for the future and their impressions of a social life beyond and after clubbing. (Malbon 1999: 33)

Unstructured and semi-structured interviewing

However, qualitative interviewing varies a great deal in the approach taken by the interviewer. The two major types were mentioned at the beginning of the chapter.

- The almost totally *unstructured interview*. Here the researcher uses at most an *aide mémoire* as a brief set of prompts to him- or herself to deal with a certain range of topics. There may be just a single question that the interviewer asks and the interviewee is then allowed to respond freely, with the interviewer simply responding to points that seem worthy of being followed up. Unstructured interviewing tends to be very similar in character to a conversation (Burgess 1984). See Box 15.1 for an illustration of an unstructured interview style.

- A *semi-structured interview*. The researcher has a list of questions or fairly specific topics to be covered, often referred to as an *interview guide*, but the interviewee has a great deal of leeway in how to reply. Questions may not follow on exactly in the way outlined on the schedule. Questions that are not included in the guide may be asked as the interviewer picks up on things said by interviewees. But, by and large, all of the questions will be asked and a similar wording will be used from inter-

viewee to interviewee. Boxes 15.2 and 15.3 provide examples of these features.

In both cases, the interview process is *flexible*. Also, the emphasis must be on how the interviewee frames and understands issues and events—that is, what the interviewee views as important in explaining and understanding events, patterns, and forms of behaviour. Thus, Leidner (1993: 238) describes the interviewing she carried out in a McDonald's restaurant as involving a degree of structure, but adds that the interviews also 'allowed room to pursue topics of particular interest to the workers'. Once again, we must remember that qualitative research is *not* quantitative research with the numbers missing. The kinds of interviewing carried out in qualitative research are typical also of *life history* and *oral history* interviewing (see Box 15.4).

The two different types of interview in qualitative research are extremes and there is quite a lot of variability between them (the example in Box 15.2 seems somewhat more structured than that in Box 15.3, for example, though both are illustrative of semi-structured interviewing), but most qualitative interviews are close to one type or the other. In neither case does the interviewer slavishly follow a schedule, as is done in quantitative research

Box 15.2 **Semi-structured interviewing**

Lupton (1996) was interested in investigating people's food preferences and to this end her research entailed thirty-three semi-structured interviews conducted by four female interviewers (of whom she was one) living in Sydney in 1994. She writes:

Interviewees were asked to talk about their favourite and most detested foods; whether they thought there was such a thing as 'masculine' or 'feminine' foods or dishes; which types of foods they considered 'healthy' or 'good for you' and which not; which types of foods they ate to lose weight and which they avoided for

the same reason; memories they recalled about food and eating events from childhood and adulthood; whether they liked to try new foods; which foods they had tasted first as an adult; whether there had been any changes in the types of food they had eaten over their lifetime; whether they associated different types of food with particular times, places or people; whether they ever had any arguments about food with others; whether they themselves cooked and if they enjoyed it; whether they ate certain foods when in certain moods and whether they had any rituals around food.   (Lupton 1996: 156, 158)

Box 15.3 **Flexibility in semi-structured interviewing**

Like Lupton (Box 15.2), Beardsworth and Keil (1992) were interested in food-related issues, and in particular in vegetarianism. They carried out seventy-three 'relatively unstructured interviews' in the East Midlands. They write that the interviews were

guided by an inventory of issues which were to be covered in each session. As the interview programme progressed,

interviewees themselves raised additional or complementary issues, and these form an integral part of the study's findings. In other words, the interview programme was not based upon a set of relatively rigid pre-determined questions and prompts. Rather, the open-ended, discursive nature of the interviews permitted an iterative process of refinement, whereby lines of thought identified by earlier interviewees could be taken up and presented to later interviewees.   (Beardsworth and Keil 1992: 261–2)

interviewing; but in semi-structured interviews the interviewer does follow a script to a certain extent. The choice of whether to veer towards one type rather than the other is likely to be affected by a variety of factors.

- Researchers who are concerned that the use of even the most rudimentary interview guide will not allow genuine access to the world views of members of a social setting or of people sharing common attributes are likely to favour an unstructured interview.

- If the researcher is beginning the investigation with a fairly clear focus, rather than a very general notion of wanting to do research on a topic, it is likely that the interviews will be semi-structured ones, so that the more specific issues can be addressed.

- If more than one person is to carry out the fieldwork, in order to ensure a modicum of com-

parability of interviewing style, it is likely that semi-structured interviewing will be preferred. See Boxes 15.2 and 15.3 for examples.

- If you are doing multiple-case study research, you are likely to find that you will need some structure in order to ensure cross-case comparability. Certainly, all of my qualitative research on different kinds of organization has entailed semi-structured interviewing and it is not a coincidence that this is because most of it has been multiple-case study research (e.g. Bryman *et al.* 1994—see Box 13.8, p. 281; Bryman, Gillingwater and McGuinness 1996).

Preparing an interview guide

The idea of an interview guide is much less specific than the notion of a structured interview schedule. In fact, the term can be employed to refer to the brief

Box 15.4 Life history and oral history interviews

Two special forms of the kind of interview associated with qualitative research are the *life history* and *oral history* interviews. The former is generally associated with the *life history method*, where it is often combined with various kinds of personal documents like diaries, photographs, and letters. This method is often referred to alternatively as the *biographical method*. A life history interview invites the subject to look back in detail across his or her entire life course. It has been depicted as documenting 'the inner experience of individuals, how they interpret, understand, and define the world around them' (Faraday and Plummer 1979: 776). However, the method is very much associated with the life history interview, which is a kind of unstructured interview covering the totality of an individual's life. Thomas and Znaniecki, who are among the pioneers of the approach as a result of their early use of it in relation to Polish immigrants to the USA, regarded it as 'the *perfect* type of sociological material' (quoted in Plummer 1983: 64). Their use, in particular, of a solicited autobiography that was written for them by one Polish peasant is regarded as an exemplification of the method.

However, in spite of Thomas and Znaniecki's endorsement, while there was a trickle of studies using the approach over the years (a table in Plummer (1983) points to twenty-six life histories dating from Thomas and Znaniecki's research in the 1910s and the publication of Plummer's book), it has not been a popular approach. It has tended to suffer because of an erroneous treatment of the life in question as a sample of one and hence of limited generalizability. However, it has certain clear strengths from the point of view of the qualitative researcher: its unambiguous emphasis on the point of view of the life in question and a clear commitment to the processual aspects of social life, showing how events unfold and interrelate in people's lives. The terms *life history* and *life story* are sometimes employed interchangeably, but R. L. Miller (2000: 19) suggests that the latter is an account someone gives about his or her life and that a life history dovetails a life story with other sources, such as diaries and letters (of the kind discussed in Chapter 18).

An example of the life history interview approach is provided by Lewis in the context of his research on the Sánchez family and their experiences of a Mexican slum:

In the course of our interviews I asked hundreds of questions of [the five members of the Sánchez family] . . . While I used a directive approach to the interviews, I encouraged free association, and

I was a good listener. I attempted to cover systematically a wide range of subjects: their earliest memories, their dreams, their hopes, fears, joys, and sufferings; their jobs; their relationship with friends, relatives, employers; their sex life; their concepts of justice, religion, and politics; their knowledge of geography and history; in short, their total world view of the world. Many of my questions stimulated them to express themselves on subjects which they might otherwise never have thought about.   (Lewis 1961: p. xxi)

R. L. Miller (2000) distinguishes between certain aspects of life history inteviews. One distinction has to do with age and life course effects. The former relates to the ageing process, in the sense of biological ageing and its effects and manifestations; life course effects are the patterned features associated with the stages of the life course. He also points to the need to distinguish cohort effects, which are the unique clusters of experiences associated with a specific generation.

R. L. Miller (2000) suggests there has been a resurgence of interest in recent years and Chamberlayne *et al.* (2000) argue that there has been a recent 'turn to biographical methods'. To a large extent, the revival of the approach derives from a growth of interest in the role and significance of agency in social life. The revival is largely associated with the growing use of life story interviews and especially those that are often referred to as *narrative interviews* (see Box 19.8, p. 401). Moreover, the growing use of such interviews has come to be associated less and less with the study of a single life (or indeed just one or two lives) and increasingly with the study of several lives. Squire (2000: 198), for example, conducted narrative interviews with 'thirty-four people infected or affected by HIV, who used HIV support groups for HIV positive people, and for workers, carers and volunteers in the HIV field'. Some were interviewed on more then one occasion.

An *oral history interview* is usually somewhat more specific in tone in that the subject is asked to reflect upon specific events or periods in the past. It too is sometimes combined with other sources, such as documents. The chief problem with the oral history interview (which it shares with the life history interview) is the possibility of bias introduced by memory lapses and distortions (Grele 1998). On the other hand, oral history testimonies have allowed the voices to come through of groups that are typically marginalized in historical research (a point that also applies to life history interviews), either because of their lack of power or because they are typically regarded as unexceptional (Samuel 1976).

list of memory prompts of areas to be covered that is often employed in unstructured interviewing or to the somewhat more structured list of issues to be addressed or questions to be asked in semi-structured interviewing. What is crucial is that the questioning allows interviewers to glean the ways in which research participants view their social world and that there is flexibility in the conduct of the interviews. The latter is as much if not more to do with the conduct of the interview than with the nature of the interview guide as such.

In preparing for qualitative interviews, Lofland and Lofland (1995: 78) suggest asking yourself the question 'Just what about this thing is puzzling me?' This can be applied to each of the research questions you have generated or it may be a mechanism for generating some research questions. They suggest that your puzzlement can be stimulated by various activities: random thoughts in different contexts, which are then written down as quickly as possible; discussions with colleagues, friends, and relatives; and, of course, the existing literature on the topic. The formulation of the research question(s) should not be so specific that alternative avenues of enquiry that might arise during the collection of fieldwork data are closed off. Such premature closure of your research focus would be inconsistent with the process of qualitative research (Figure 13.1, p. 267), with the focus on the world view of the people you will be interviewing, and with the approaches to qualitative data analysis like grounded theory that emphasize the importance of not starting out with too many preconceptions (see Chapter 19). Gradually, an order and structure will begin to emerge in your meanderings around your research question(s) and will form the basis for your interview guide.

You should also consider 'What do I need to know in order to answer each of the research questions I'm interested in?' This means trying to get an appreciation of what the interviewee sees as significant and important in relation to each of your topic areas. Thus, your questioning will need to cover the areas that you need but from the perspective of your interviewees. This means that, even though qualitative research is predominantly unstructured, it is rarely

so unstructured that the researcher cannot at least specify a research focus.

Some basic elements in the preparation of your interview guide will be:

- create a certain amount of order on the topic areas, so that your questions about them flow reasonably well, but be prepared to alter the order of questions during the actual interview;
- formulate interview questions or topics in a way that will help you to answer your research questions (but try not to make them too specific);
- try to use a language that is comprehensible and relevant to the people you are interviewing;
- just as in interviewing in quantitative research, do not ask leading questions;
- remember to ensure that you ask or record 'facesheet' information of a general kind (name, age, gender, etc.) and a specific kind (position in company, number of years unemployed, number of years involved in a group, etc.), because such information is useful for contextualizing people's answers.

There are some practical details to attend to before the interview.

- Make sure you are familiar with the setting in which the interviewee works or lives or engages in the behaviour of interest to you. This will help you to understand what he/she is saying in the interviewee's own terms.
- Get hold of a good tape recorder and microphone. Qualitative researchers nearly always tape-record and then transcribe their interviews. This procedure is important for detailed analysis required in qualitative research and to ensure that the interviewees' answers are captured in their own terms. If you are taking notes, it is easy to lose the phrases and language used. Also, because the interviewer is supposed not to be following a strictly formulated schedule of questions of the kind used in structured interviewing, he or she will need to be responsive to the interviewee's answers so that it is possible to follow them up. A good microphone is highly desirable because many interviews are let down by poor recording.
- Make sure as far as possible that the interview takes

place in a setting that is quiet (so there is no or little outside noise that might affect the quality of the tape recording) and private (so the interviewee does not have to worry about being overheard).

- Prepare yourself for the interview by cultivating as many of the criteria of a quality interviewer suggested by Kvale as possible (Box 15.5).

After the interview, make notes about:

- how the interview went (was interviewee talkative, cooperative, nervous, well-dressed/scruffy, etc.?);
- where the interview took place;
- any other feelings about the interview (did it open up new avenues of interest?);
- the setting (busy/quiet, many/few other people in the vicinity, new/old buildings, use of computers).

These various guidelines suggest the series of steps in formulating questions for an interview guide in qualitative research presented in Figure 15.1.

Kinds of question

The kinds of questions asked in qualitative interviews are highly variable. Kvale (1996) has suggested nine different kinds of question. Most interviews will contain virtually all of them, although interviews that rely on lists of topics are likely to follow a somewhat looser format. Kvale's nine types of question are as follows.

- *Introducing questions*: 'Please tell me about when your interest in X first began?'; 'Have you ever . . .?'; 'Why did you go to . . .?' .
- *Follow-up questions*: getting the interviewee to elaborate his/her answer, such as 'Could you say some more about that?'; 'What do you mean by that . . .?'; even 'Yeeees?'
- *Probing questions*: following up what has been said through direct questioning.
- *Specifying questions*: 'What did you do then?'; 'How did X react to what you said?'
- *Direct questions*: 'Do you find it easy to keep smiling when serving customers?'; 'Are you happy with the way you and your husband decide how money should be spent?' Such questions are perhaps best left until towards the end of the interview, in order not to influence the direction of the interview too much.
- *Indirect questions*: 'What do most people round here

Box 15.5 Kvale's list of qualification criteria of an interviewer (plus two others)

Kvale (1996) has proposed a very useful list of ten criteria of a successful interviewer.

- *Knowledgeable*: is thoroughly familiar with the focus of the interview; pilot interviews of the kind used in survey interviewing can be useful here.
- *Structuring*: gives purpose for interview; rounds it off; asks whether interviewee has questions.
- *Clear*: asks simple, easy, short questions; no jargon.
- *Gentle*: lets people finish; gives them time to think; tolerates pauses.
- *Sensitive*: listens attentively to what is said and how it is said; is empathetic in dealing with the interviewee.
- *Open*: responds to what is important to interviewee and is flexible.
- *Steering*: knows what he/she wants to find out.

- *Critical*: is prepared to challenge what is said, for example, dealing with inconsistencies in interviewees' replies.
- *Remembering*: relates what is said to what has previously been said.
- *Interpreting*: clarifies and extends meanings of interviewees' statements, but without imposing meaning on them.

To Kvale's list I would add the following.

- *Balanced*: does not talk too much, which may make the interviewee passive, and does not talk too little, which may result in the interviewee feeling he or she is not talking along the right lines.
- *Ethically sensitive*: is sensitive to the ethical dimension of interviewing, ensuring the interviewee appreciates what the research is about, its purposes, and that his or her answers will be treated confidentially.

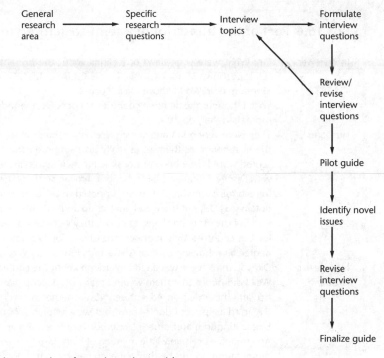

Fig. 15.1 Formulating questions for an interview guide

think of the ways that management treats its staff?', perhaps followed up by 'Is that the way you feel too?', in order to get at the individual's own view.

- *Structuring questions*: 'I would now like to move on to a different topic'.

- *Silence*: allow pauses to signal that you want to give the interviewee the opportunity to reflect and amplify an answer.

- *Interpreting questions*: 'Do you mean that your leadership role has had to change from one of encouraging others to a more directive one?'; 'Is it fair to say that what you are suggesting is that you don't mind being friendly towards customers most of the time, but when they are unpleasant or demanding you find it more difficult?'

As this list suggests, one of the main ingredients of the interview is listening—being very attentive to what the interviewee is saying or even not saying. It means that the interviewer is active without being too intrusive—a difficult balance. But it also means that, just because the interview is being tape-

recorded (the generally recommended practice whenever it is feasible), the interviewer cannot take things easy. In fact, an interviewer must be very attuned and responsive to what the interviewee is saying and doing. This is also important because something like body language may indicate that the interviewee is becoming uneasy or anxious about a line of questioning. An ethically sensitive interviewer will not want to place undue pressure on the person he or she is talking to and will need to be prepared to cut short that line of questioning if it is clearly a source of concern.

Remember as well that in interviews you are going to ask about different kinds of things, such as:

- values—of interviewee, of group, of organization;
- beliefs—of interviewee, of others, of group;
- behaviour—of interviewee, of others;
- formal and informal roles—of interviewee, of others;
- relationships—of interviewee, of others;
- places and locales;
- emotions—particularly of the interviewee, but also possibly of others;

Box 15.6 Part of the transcript of a semi-structured interview

Interviewer	OK. What were your views or feelings about the presentation of different cultures, as shown in, for example, Jungle Cruise or It's a Small World at the Magic Kingdom or in World Showcase at Epcot?
Wife	Well, I thought the different countries at Epcot were wonderful, but I need to say more than that, don't I?
Husband	They were very good and some were better than others, but that was down to the host countries themselves really, as I suppose each of the countries represented would have been responsible for their own part, so that's nothing to do with Disney, I wouldn't have thought. I mean some of the landmarks were hard to recognize for what they were supposed to be, but some were very well done. Britain was OK, but there was only a pub and a Welsh shop there really, whereas some of the other pavilions, as I think they were called, were good ambassadors for the countries they represented. China, for example, had an excellent 360 degree film showing parts of China and I found that very interesting.
Interviewer	Did you think there was anything lacking about the content?
Husband	Well I did notice that there weren't many black people at World Showcase, particularly the American Adventure. Now whether we were there on an unusual day in that respect I don't know, but we saw plenty of black Americans in the Magic Kingdom and other places, but very few if any in that World Showcase. And there was certainly little mention of black history in the American Adventure presentation, so maybe they felt alienated by that, I don't know, but they were noticeable by their absence.
Interviewer	So did you think there were any special emphases?
Husband	Well thinking about it now, because I hadn't really given this any consideration before you started asking about it, but thinking about it now, it was only really representative of the developed world, you know, Britain, America, Japan, world leaders many of them in technology, and there was nothing of the Third World there. Maybe that's their own fault, maybe they were asked to participate and didn't, but now that I think about it, that does come to me. What do you think, love?
Wife	Well, like you, I hadn't thought of it like that before, but I agree with you.

- encounters;
- stories.

Try to vary the questioning in terms of types of question (as suggested by Kvale's nine types, which were outlined above) *and* the types of phenomena you ask about.

Using an interview guide: An example

Box 15.6 is taken from an interview from a study of visitors to Disney theme parks (Bryman 1999). The study was briefly mentioned in Chapter 4 as an example of a snowball sampling procedure. The interviews were concerned to elicit visitors' interpretations of the parks that had been visited. The interview is with a man who was in his sixties and his wife who was two years younger. They had visited Walt Disney World in Orlando, Florida, and were very enthusiastic about their visit.

The sequence begins with the interviewer asking what would be considered a 'direct question' in terms of the list of nine question types suggested by Kvale (1996) and outlined above. The replies are very bland and do little more than reflect the interviewees' positive feelings about their visit to Disney World. The wife acknowledges this when she says 'but I need to say more than that, don't I?' Interviewees frequently know that they are expected to be expansive in their answers. This sequence occurred around halfway through the interview, so the interviewees were primed by then into realizing that more details were expected. There is almost a tinge of embarrassment that the answer has been so brief and unilluminating. The husband's answer is more expansive but not particularly enlightening.

There then follows the first of two important prompts by the interviewer. The husband's reponse is more interesting in that he now begins to answer in terms of the possibility that black people were under-represented in attractions like the American Adventure, which tells the story of America through tableaux and films via a debate between two audio-animatronic figures—Mark Twain and Benjamin Franklin. The second prompt yields further useful reflection, this time carrying the implication that Third World countries are under-represented in World Showcase in the Epcot Centre. The couple are clearly aware that it is the prompting that has made them provide these reflections when they say: 'Well thinking about it now, because I hadn't really given this any consideration before you started asking about it' and 'Well, like you, I hadn't thought of it like that before'. This is the whole point of prompting—to get the interviewee to think more about the topic and to provide the opportunity for a more detailed response. It is not a leading question, since the interviewees were not being asked 'Do you think that the Disney company fails to recognize the significance of Black history (or ignores the Third World) in its presentation of different cultures?' There is no doubt that it is the prompts that elicit the more interesting replies, but that is precisely their role.

Tape recording and transcription

The point has already been made on several occasions that, in qualitative research, the interview is usually tape-recorded and transcribed whenever possible (see Box 15.7). Qualitative researchers are frequently interested not just in *what* people say but also in the *way* that they say it. If this aspect is to be fully woven into an analysis, it is necessary for a complete account of the series of exchanges in

---

Box 15.7 Why should you record and transcribe interviews?

With approaches that entail detailed attention to language, such as conversation analysis and discourse analysis (see Chapter 17), the recording of conversations and interviews is to all intents and purposes mandatory. However, researchers who use qualitative interviews and focus groups (see Chapter 16) also tend to record and then transcribe interviews. Heritage (1984: 238) suggests that the procedure of recording and transcribing interviews has the following advantages:

- it helps to correct the natural limitations of our memories and of the intuitive glosses that we might place on what people say in interviews;

- it allows more thorough examination of what people say;

- it permits repeated examinations of the interviewees' answers;

- it opens up the data to public scrutiny by other researchers, who can evaluate the analysis that is carried out by the original researchers of the data (that is, a secondary analysis);

- it therefore helps to counter accusations that an analysis might have been influenced by a researcher's values or biases;

- it allows the data to be reused in other ways from those intended by the original researcher—for example, in the light of new theoretical ideas or analytic strategies.

However, it has to be recognized that the procedure is very time-consuming. It also requires good equipment, usually in the form of a good-quality tape recorder and microphone but also, if possible, a transcription machine. Transcription also very quickly results in a daunting pile of paper. Also, recording equipment may be offputting for interviewees.

an interview to be available. Also, because the interviewer is supposed to be highly alert to what is being said—following up interesting points made, prompting and probing where necessary, drawing attention to any inconsistencies in the interviewee's answers—it is best if he or she is not distracted by having to concentrate on getting down notes on what is said.

As with just about everything in conducting social research, there is a cost (other than the financial cost of tape recorders and tapes), in that the use of a tape recorder may disconcert respondents, who become self-conscious or alarmed at the prospect of their words being preserved. Most people accede to the request for the interview to be tape-recorded, though it is not uncommon for a small number to refuse (see Box 15.8). When faced with refusal, you should still go ahead with the interview, as it is highly likely that useful information will still be forthcoming. This advice also applies to cases of tape recorder malfunction (again see Box 15.8). Among those who do agree to be tape-recorded, there will be some who will not get over their alarm at being confronted with a microphone. As a result, some interviews may not be as interesting as you might have hoped. In qualitative research, there is often quite a large amount of variation in the amount of time that interviews take. For example, in Chattoe and Gilbert's (1999) study of budgeting in what they call 'retired households', the twenty-six interviews they carried out lasted between thirty minutes and three hours; in the research in Box 15.8, the twenty interviews varied between forty-five minutes and three hours. It should not be assumed that shorter interviews are necessarily inferior to longer ones, but very short ones that are a product of interviewee non-cooperation or anxiety about being tape-recorded are likely to be less useful, though it is not being suggested that this applies to these researchers' shorter interviews. In the extreme, when an interview has produced very little of significance, it may not be worth the time and cost of transcription. Thankfully, such occasions are relatively unusual. If people do agree to be interviewed, they usually do so in a co-operative way and loosen up after initial anxiety about the

> ## Box 15.8 Getting it taped and transcribed: An illustration of two problems
>
> Rafaeli *et al.* (1997) conduct semi-structured interviews with twenty female administrators in a university business school in order to study the significance of dress at the workplace. They write:
>
> Everyone we contacted agreed to participate. Interviews took place in participants' offices or in a school lounge and lasted between 45 minutes and three hours. We recorded and transcribed all but two interviews: 1 participant refused to be taped, and the tape recorder malfunctioned during another interview. For interviews not taped, we recorded detailed notes. We assured all participants that their responses would remain confidential and anonymous and hired an outside contractor to transcribe the interviews. (Rafaeli *et al.* 1997: 14)

microphone. As a result, even short interviews are often quite revealing.

The problem with transcribing interviews is that it is very time consuming. It is best to allow around five to six hours for transcription for every hour of speech. Also, transcription yields vast amounts of paper, which you will need to wade through when analysing the data. Beardsworth and Keil (1992: 262) report that their seventy-three interviews on vegetarianism (see Box 15.3) generated 'several hundred thousand words of transcript material'. It is clear, therefore, that, while transcription has the advantage of keeping intact the interviewee's (and interviewer's) words, it does so by piling up the amount of text to be analysed. It is no wonder that writers like Lofland and Lofland (1995) advise that the analysis of qualitative data is not left until all the interviews have been completed and transcribed. To procrastinate may give the researcher the impression that he or she faces a monumental task. Also, there are good grounds for making analysis an ongoing activity, because it allows the researcher to be more aware of emerging themes that he or she may want to ask about in a more direct way in later interviews (see

Box 15.3 for an example). The preference for ongoing analysis is also very much recommended by proponents of approaches to qualitative data analysis like grounded theory (see Chapter 19).

It is easy to take the view that transcription is a relatively unproblematic translation of the spoken into the written word. However, given the reliance on transcripts in qualitative research based on interviews, the issue should not be taken lightly. Transcribers need to be trained in much the same way that interviewers do. Moreover, even among experienced transcribers errors can creep in. Poland (1995) has provided some fascinating examples of mistakes in transcription that can be the result of many different factors (mishearing, fatigue, carelessness). For example, one transcript contained the following passage:

I think unless we want to become like other countries, where people have, you know, democratic freedoms . . .

But the actual words on the audiotape were:

I think unless we want to become like other countries, where people have no democratic freedoms . . . (Poland 1995: 294)

Steps clearly need to be taken to check on the quality of transcription.

Flexibility in the interview

One further point to bear in mind is that you need to be generally flexible in your approach to interviewing in qualitative research. This advice is not just to do with needing to be responsive to what interviewees say to you and following up interesting points that they make. Such flexibility *is* important and is an important reminder that, with semi-structured interviewing, you should not turn the interview into a kind of structured interview but with open questions. Flexibility is important in such areas as varying the order of questions, following up leads, and clearing up inconsistencies in answers. Flexibility is important in other respects, such as coping with audio-recording equipment breakdown and refusals by interviewees to allow a recording to take place (see Box 15.8). A further element is that interviewers often find that, as soon as they switch off their tape recorders, the interviewee continues to ruminate on the topic of interest and frequently will say more interesting things than in the interview. It is usually not feasible to switch the machine back on again, so try to take some notes either while the person is talking or as soon as possible after the interview. Such 'unsolicited accounts' can often be the source of revealing information or views (Hammersley and Atkinson 1995). This is certainly what Parker found in connection with his research on three British organizations—a National Health Service District Health Authority, a building society, and a manufacturing company—which was based primarily on semi-structured interviews: 'Indeed, some of the most valuable parts of the interview took place after the tape had been switched off, the closing intimacies of the conversation being prefixed with a silent or explicit "well, if you want to know what I really think . . .". Needless to say, a visit to the toilet to write up as much as I could remember followed almost immediately' (Parker 2000: 236).

Sampling

Many, if not most, of the issues raised in connection with sampling in ethnographic research apply more or less equally to sampling in qualitative interviewing. Very often, the lack of transparency that is sometimes a feature of qualitative research (referred to in Chapter 13) is particularly apparent in relation to sampling. It is sometimes more or less impossible to discern from researchers' accounts of their methods either *how* their interviewees were selected or *how many* there were of them. Often, qualitative researchers are clear that their samples are convenience or opportunistic ones, and, on other occasions, the reader suspects that this is the case. For the study referred to in Box 15.2, Lupton (1996) used four interviewers, each of whom interviewed 'personal contacts'. The resort to convenience sampling is usually the product of such factors as the availability of certain individuals who are otherwise difficult to contact, such as homeless people (Wardhaugh 1996), or a belief that, because it aims to generate an in-depth analysis, issues of representativeness are less important in qualitative research than they are in quantitative research. Sometimes, convenience samples may be the result of restrictions placed on the researcher—for example, when members of an organization select interviewees rather than give the researcher a free rein to do so. Snowball sampling is sometimes used to contact groups of people for whom there is no sampling frame. This approach was employed in my study of visitors to Disney theme parks and by Beardsworth and Keil in their study of vegetarians (see Box 15.9).

Sometimes, a probability sampling approach is employed. The research on organizational dress by Rafaeli *et al.* (1997; see Box 15.8) employed such an approach. The authors write: 'First, we identified a

stratified random sample of 20 people from the population of full-time, permanent administrative employees in the organization' (1997: 13–14). The stratifying criteria were administrative section and hierarchical level. A similar kind of sampling strategy occurs when a sample of interviewees is taken (sometimes randomly, sometimes by ensuring a 'spread' in terms of stratifying criteria) from a much larger sample generated for social survey purposes. This approach allows the researcher to sample purposively (if not randomly) and so ensure a wide range of characteristics of interviewees. King (1994) used this approach for a study of general practitioners who had taken part in a survey of GP referrals eighteen months earlier. Similarly, for their study of media representations of social science research, Fenton *et al.* (1998) carried out a mail questionnaire survey of social scientists who had received coverage of their research in the content analysis referred to in Box 9.2 (p. 181). A total of 123 questionnaires were posted and, of those returned, twenty social scientists were selected to be interviewed. The interviews were of a semi-structured kind.

In addition, a theoretical sampling approach might be employed (see Box 14.8 and Figure 14.3, pp. 302, 303). This approach entails sampling interviewees until your categories achieve theoretical saturation (see Box 14.9, p. 303) and selecting further interviewees on the basis of your emerging theoretical focus. The approach is supposed to be an iterative one—that is, one in which there is a movement backwards and forwards between sampling and theoretical reflection, but it may be that the researcher feels that his or her categories achieve theoretical saturation at a relatively early stage. For example, for their research on organization dress, which was referred to in Box 15.8, Rafaeli *et al.* (1997: 14) employed initially a stratified random sampling approach (see above), but then evaluated their data 'after completing interviews with the 20 individuals selected and concluded that, because we had reached theoretical saturation (Glaser and Strauss 1967), no additional interviews were necessary'. A sampling approach that is more in tune with Glaser and Strauss's (1967) idea of theoretical

---

Box 15.9 A snowball sample

For their study of vegetarians, Beardsworth and Keil (see Box 15.3) describe their sampling approach as follows:

The drawing of a simple random sample in order to ensure statistical representativeness is clearly impossible in that it is not feasible to enumerate the total United Kingdom population of self-defined vegetarians. . . . For these reasons it was concluded that the only practicable mode of tracing suitable respondents would be through the use of 'snowball' sampling techniques. Quite clearly, such techniques cannot possibly claim to produce a statistically representative sample, since they rely upon the social contacts between individuals to trace additional respondents. (Beardsworth and Keil 1992: 261)

Through this sampling procedure, they were able to conduct seventy-three interviews.

Box 15.10 Theoretical sampling in a study of family obligations

Finch and Mason's (1990: 26) Family Obligations Project was a study of 'patterns of support, aid and assistance . . . between adult kin' in Manchester. Initially, survey research, using a structured interview, was conducted and yielded nearly 1,000 completed interviews. A sample of these interviewees was then approached to be interviewed by semi-structured interview. The initial sample for this phase of the investigation was selected purposively—that is, with specific target subgroups in mind. These were divorced and/or remarried people and the youngest group at the time of the survey (18–24 years of age). Their rationale for this purposive selection is as follows: 'Since fieldwork was principally to be concerned with understanding the process of negotiation between relatives, we decided that it would be much more useful to focus upon individuals who might currently or recently have been involved in processes of negotiation and renegotiation of family relationships' (1990: 33).

Finch and Mason sampled five at a time from the total of each of these subgroups who were willing to be interviewed again (112 in the divorced/remarried subgroup and 117 young adults). Individuals were sampled using random numbers. In addition, the authors wanted to interview the kin groups of individuals from the initial social survey as providing examples of 'negotiations between relatives over issues concerning financial or material support' (1990: 38). They decided to conduct two further interviews with the focal person in a negotiation over family obligations and one interview with each of that person's relatives. However, the sampling strategy was based on the selection not of individuals as cases but of *situations*. In order to make the data comparable, they searched out individuals and their kin who had been identified in the survey—for example, as having moved back into their parents' home following a divorce. A further element in their sampling strategy was that the authors 'tried to keep an eye on the range of experiences that [they] were studying, and to identify any obvious gaps' (1990: 43). As a result of this ongoing 'stocktaking exercise', as they call it, they identified certain gaps in their data: men, because by and large they were the focus of interviews as part of kin networks rather than initial key informants in their own right; unemployed people, particularly because of high levels at the time of the research; ethnic minorities; social classes I, IV, and V; widows and widowers; and stepchildren and stepgrandparents. As Finch and Mason's experience shows, the process of theoretical sampling is not only one that gives priority to theoretical significance in sampling decisions, but is also one that forces researchers to sharpen their reflections on their findings during the fieldwork process.

sampling is provided by Finch and Mason's (1990) account of their Family Obligations Project (see Box 15.10).

The chief virtue of theoretical sampling is that the emphasis is upon using theoretical reflection on data as the guide to whether more data are needed. It therefore places a premium on theorizing rather than the statistical adequacy of a sample, which may be a limited guide to sample selection in many instances.

Feminist research and interviewing in qualitative research

Unstructured and semi-structured interviewing have become extremely prominent methods of data gathering within a feminist research framework. In part, this is a reflection of the preference for qualitative research among feminist researchers, but it also reflects a view that the kind of interview with which qualitative research is associated allows many of the goals of feminist research to be realized. Indeed, the view has been expressed that, 'Whilst several brave women in the 1980s defended quantitative methods, it is nonetheless still the case that not just qualitative methods, but the in-depth face-to-face interview has become the paradigmatic "feminist method"' (Kelly *et al.* 1994: 34). This comment is enlightening because it implies that it is not simply that qualitative research is seen by many writers and researchers as more consistent with a feminist position than quantitative research, but that specifically qualitative interviewing is seen as especially appropriate. The point that is being made here is not necessarily that such interviewing is somehow more in tune with feminist values than, say, ethnography (especially since it is often an ingredient of ethnographic research). Instead, it could be that the intensive and time-consuming nature of ethnography means that, although it has great potential as an approach to feminist research (see Chapter 14), qualitative interviewing is often preferred because it is usually less invasive in these respects.

However, it is specifically interviewing of the kind conducted in qualitative research that is seen as having potential for a feminist approach, not the structured interview with which social survey research is associated. Why might one type of interview be consistent with a sensitivity to feminism and the other not? In a frequently cited article, Oakley outlines the following points about the standard survey interview.

- It is a one-way process—the interviewer extracts information or views from the interviewee.

- The interviewer offers nothing in return for the extraction of information. For example, interviewers using a structured interview do not offer information or their own views if asked. Indeed, they are typically advised not to do such things because of worries about contaminating their respondents' answers.

- The interviewer–interviewee relationship is a form of hierarchical or power relationship. Interviewers arrogate to themselves the right to ask questions, implicitly placing their interviewees in a position of subservience or inferiority.

- The element of power is also revealed by the fact that the structured interview seeks out information from the perspective of the researcher.

- Because of these points, the standard survey interview is inconsistent with feminism when women interview other women. This view arises because it is seen as indefensible for women to 'use' other women in these ways.

Instead of this framework for conducting interviews, feminist researchers advocate one that establishes

- a high level of rapport between interviewer and interviewee;

- a high degree of reciprocity on the part of the interviewer;

- the perspective of the women being interviewed;

- a non-hierarchical relationship.

In connection with the reciprocity that she advocates, Oakley noted, for example, that, in her research on the transition to motherhood, she was frequently asked questions by her respondents. She argues that it was ethically indefensible for a feminist not to answer when confronted with questions of a certain kind with which she was confronted (see pages 124–5 for an illustration of this point). For Oakley, therefore, the qualitative interview was viewed as a means of resolving the dilemmas that she encountered as a feminist interviewing other women. However, as noted in previous chapters, while this broad adherence to a set of principles for interviewing in feminist research continues, it has been tempered by a greater recognition of the possible value of quantitative research.

An interesting dilemma that is perhaps not so easily resolved is the question of what feminist researchers should do when their own 'understandings and interpretations of women's accounts would either not be shared by some of them [i.e. the research participants], and/or represent a form of challenge or threat to their perceptions, choices and coping strategies' (Kelly *et al.* 1994: 37). It is the first type of situation that will be examined, at least in part, because, while it is of particular significance to feminist researchers, its implications are somewhat broader. It raises the tricky question of how far the commitment of seeing through the eyes of the people you study can and/or should be stretched. Two examples are relevant here. Reinharz (1992:

28–9) cites the case of an American study by Andersen (1981), who interviewed twenty 'corporate wives', who came across as happy with their lot and were supportive of feminism only in relation to employment discrimination. Andersen interpreted their responses to her questions as indicative of 'false consciousness'—in other words, she did not really believe her interviewees. When Andersen wrote an article on her findings, the women wrote a letter rejecting her account, affirming that women can be fulfilled as wives and mothers. A similar situation confronted Millen (1997) when she interviewed thirty-two British female scientists using 'semi-structured, in-depth individual interviewing' (Millen 1997: 4.6). As Millen (1997: 5.6, 5.9) puts it:

There was a tension between my interpretation of their reported experience as sex-based, and the meaning the participants themselves tended to attribute to their experience, since the majority of respondents did not analyse these experiences in terms of patriarchy or sex–gender systems, but considered them to be individualised, or as 'just something that had to be coped with'. . . . From my external, academically privileged vantage point, it is clear that sexism pervades these professions, and that men are assumed from the start by other scientists to be competent scientists of status whilst women have to prove themselves, overcome the barrier of their difference before they are accepted. These women, on the other hand, did not generally view their interactions in terms of gendered social systems. There is therefore a tension between their characterisation of their experience and my interpretation of it . . .

Three interesting issues are thrown up by these two accounts. First, how can such a situation arise? This is an issue that pervades qualitative research that makes claims to reveal social reality as viewed by members of the setting in question. If researchers are genuinely seeing through others' eyes, the 'tension' to which Millen refers should not arise. However, it clearly can and does, and this strongly suggests that qualitative researchers are more affected by their own perspectives and research questions when collecting and analysing data than might be expected from textbook accounts of the research process. Secondly, there is the question of how to handle such a 'tension'—that is, how do you reconcile the two accounts? Andersen's (1981) solution to the tension she encountered was to reinterpret her findings in terms of the conditions that engender the contentment she uncovered. Thirdly, given that feminist research is often concerned with wider political goals of emancipation, a tension between participants' world views and the researcher's position raises moral questions about the appropriateness of imposing an interpretation that is not shared by research participants themselves. Such an imposition could hardly be regarded as consistent with the principle of a non-hierarchical relationship in the interview situation.

Therefore, while qualitative interviewing has become a highly popular research method for feminist researchers because of its malleability into a form that can support the principles of feminism, interesting questions are raised in terms of the relationship between researchers' and participants' accounts. Such questions have a significance generally for the conduct of qualitative research.

Qualitative interviewing versus participant observation

The aim of this section is to compare the merits and limitations of interviewing in qualitative research with those of participant observation. These are probably the two most prominent methods of data collection in qualitative research, so there is some virtue in assessing their strengths, a debate that was first begun many years ago (Becker and Geer 1957*a*, *b*; Trow 1957). In this section, interviewing is being compared to participant observation rather than ethnography, because the latter invariably entails a significant amount of interviewing. So too does participant observation, but in this discussion I will be following the principle that I outlined in Box 14.1 (p. 291)—namely, that the term will be employed to refer to the specifically observational activities in which the participant observer engages. As noted in Box 14.1, the term 'ethnography' is being reserved for the wide range of data collection activities in which ethnographers engage—one of which is participant observation—along with the written account that is a product of those activities.

Advantages of participant observation in comparison to qualitative interviewing

Seeing through others' eyes

As noted in Chapters 1 and 13, this is one of the main tenets of qualitative research, but, on the face of it, the participant observer would seem to be better placed for gaining a foothold on social reality in this way. The researcher's prolonged immersion in a social setting would seem to make him or her better equipped to see as others see. The participant observer is in much closer contact with people for a longer period of time; also, he or she participates in many of the same kinds of activity as the members of the social setting being studied. Research that relies on interviewing alone is likely to entail much more fleeting contacts, though in qualitative research interviews can last many hours and re-interviewing is not unusual.

Learning the native language

Becker and Geer (1957a) argued that the participant observer is in the same position as a social anthropologist visiting a distant land, in that in order to understand a culture the language must be learned. However, it is not simply the formal language that must be understood in the case of the kinds of social

research in which a participant observer in a complex urban society engages. It is also very often the 'argot'—the special uses of words and slang that are important to penetrate that culture. Such an understanding is arrived at through the observation of language use.

The taken for granted

The interview relies primarily on verbal behaviour and as such matters that interviewees take for granted are less likely to surface than in participant observation, where such implicit features in social life are more likely to be revealed as a result of the observer's continued presence and because of the ability to observe behaviour rather than just rely on what is said.

Deviant and hidden activities

Much of what we know about criminal and deviant subcultures has been gleaned from participant observation. These are areas that insiders are likely to be reluctant to talk about in an interview context alone. Understanding is again likely to come through prolonged interaction. Many of the examples in Chapter 14 entailed participant observation of criminal or deviant worlds, such as drug taking, violent gangs, pilferage, illegal commerce, and hooliganism. Ethnographers conducting participant observation are more likely to place themselves in situations in which their continued involvement allows them gradually to infiltrate such social worlds and to insinuate themselves into the lives of people who might be sensitive to outsiders. For similar reasons, participant observers have found that they are able to gain access to areas like patterns of resistance at work or to groups of people who support a deviant ideology, like the National Front.

Sensitivity to context

The participant observer's extensive contact with a social setting allows the context of people's behaviour to be mapped out fully. The participant observation interacts with people in a variety of different situations and possibly roles, so that the links between behaviour and context can be forged.

Encountering the unexpected and flexibility

It may be that, because of the unstructured nature of participant observation, it is more likely to uncover unexpected topics or issues. Except with the most unstructured forms of interview, the interview process is likely to entail some degree of closure as the interview guide is put together, which may blinker the researcher slightly. Also, participant observation may be more flexible because of the tendency for interviewers to instil an element of comparability (and hence a modicum of structure) in their questioning of different people. Ditton's (1977) decision at a very late stage in the data collection process to focus on pilferage in the bakery in which he was a participant observer is an example of this feature.

Naturalistic emphasis

Participant observation has the potential to come closer to a naturalistic emphasis, because the qualitative researcher confronts members of a social setting in their natural environments. Interviewing, because of its nature as a disruption of members' normal flow of events, even when it is at its most informal, is less amenable to this feature. It is unsurprising, therefore, that, when referring to naturalism as a tradition in qualitative research, Gubrium and Holstein (1997; see Box 13.1, p. 265) largely refer to studies in which participant observation was a prominent component (e.g. Whyte 1955).

Advantages of qualitative interviewing in comparison to participant observation

Issues resistant to observation

It is likely that there is a wide range of issues that are simply not amenable to observation, so that asking people about them represents the only viable means of finding out about them within a qualitative

research strategy. For example, consider Beardsworth and Keil's (1992) research on vegetarianism (see Boxes 15.3 and 15.5). It is not really feasible for investigators to insinuate themselves into the lives of vegetarians in order to uncover issues like reasons for their conversion to this eating strategy. For most people, vegetarianism is a matter that surfaces only at certain points, such as meals and shopping. It is not really sensible or feasible to carry out participant observation in relation to something like this, which is clearly highly episodic.

Reconstruction of events

Qualitative research frequently entails the reconstruction of events by asking interviewees to think back over how a certain series of events unfolded in relation to a current situation. Beardsworth and Keil (see Boxes 15.3 and 15.5) employed the symbolic interactionist notion of *career* to gain an understanding of how people came to be vegetarians. Similarly, for their study of the impact of male unemployment McKee and Bell (1985; see Box 2.22, p. 48, and the reference to this work in Chapter 13, pages 279–80) asked husbands and their wives to reconstruct events following unemployment. Yet another example is Pettigrew's (1985) research on Imperial Chemicals Industries (ICI), which entailed interviewing about contemporaneous events but also included 'retrospective interviewing', as Pettigrew calls it (see Box 2.23, p. 51). This reconstruction of events is something that cannot be accomplished through participant observation alone. See Box 15.11 for a further example.

Ethical considerations

There are certain areas that could be observed—albeit indirectly through hidden hardware like a microphone—but would raise ethical considerations. McKeganey and Barnard's (1996; see Box 15.11) research on prostitution furnishes an example of this. One of the areas they were especially interested in was negotiations between prostitutes and their clients over the use of condoms in

Box 15.11 Information through interviews: research on prostitution

McKeganey and Barnard (1996) have discussed their strategies for conducting research into prostitutes and their clients. Their research was based in a red light area in Glasgow. Their approach was largely that of observer-as-participant (see Figure 14.2), in that their research was based primarily on interviews with prostitutes and their clients, as well as some (frequently accidental) observation of interactions and overheard conversations. The interviews they conducted were especially important in gaining information in relation to such areas as: how the prostitutes had moved into this line of work; permitted and prohibited sex acts; links with drug use; experience of violence; and the management of identity. In the following passage, a prostitute reconstructs her movement into prostitution:

I was 14 and I'd run away from home. I ended up down in London where I met a pimp. . . . He'd got me a place to stay, buying me things and everything and I ended up sleeping with him as well. . . . One night we got really drunk and stoned and he brought someone in. . . . [Then] after it happened I thought it was bad, I didn't like it but at least I was getting paid for it. I'd been abused by my granddad when I was 11 and it didn't seem a million miles from that anyway. (1996: 25)

One area of particular concern to McKeganey and Barnard was the spread of HIV/AIDS infection and its implications for prostitutes and their work. This area was specifically addressed in interviews. For example,

I've got a couple of punters who'll say I'll give you so and so if you'll do it without [a condom]. But never, I always use a condom for anal sex, oral sex and even for hand jobs, there's no way I'll let them come anywhere near me. (1996: 66)

You still get the bam-pots [idiots] asking for sex without. I had one the other night—I said, 'where have you been living—on a desert island?' (1996: 66)

the light of the spread of HIV/AIDS infection. It is not inconceivable that such transactions could have been observed with the aid of hidden hardware and it is possible that some prostitutes would have agreed to being wired up for this purpose. However, clients would not have been party to such agreements, so that ethical principles of informed consent and invasion of privacy would have been transgressed (see Box 14.3, p. 294). As a result, the researchers relied on interview accounts of such negotiations or of prostitutes' stances on the matter (see Box 15.11), as well as the views of a small number of clients.

Reactive effects

The question of reactive effects is by no means a straightforward matter. As with structured observation (see Chapter 8), it might be anticipated that the presence of a participant observer would result in reactive effects (see Box 8.10, p. 171). People's knowledge of the fact that they are being observed may make them behave less naturally. However, participant observers, like researchers using structured observation, typically find that people become accustomed to their presence and begin to behave more naturally the longer they are around. Indeed, members of social settings sometimes express surprise when participant observers announce their imminent departure when they are on the verge of disengagement. Interviewers clearly do not suffer from the same kind of problem, but it could be argued that the unnatural character of the interview encounter can also be regarded as a context within which reactive effects may emerge. Participant observation also suffers from the related problem of observers disturbing the very situation being studied, because conversations and interactions will occur in conjunction with the observer that otherwise would not happen. This is by no means an easy issue to resolve and it seems likely that both participant observation and qualitative interviewing set in motion reactive effects but of different kinds.

Less intrusive in people's lives

Participant observation can be very intrusive in people's lives in that the observer is likely to take up a lot more of their time than in an interview. Interviews in qualitative research can sometimes be very long and re-interviewing is not uncommon, but the impact on people's time will probably be less than having to take observers into account on a regular basis, though it is likely that this feature will vary from situation to situation. Participant observation is likely to be especially intrusive in terms of the amount of people's time taken up when it is in organizational settings. In work organizations, there is a risk that the rhythms of work lives will be disrupted.

Longitudinal research easier

One of the advantages of participant observation is that it is inherently longitudinal in character because the observer is present in a social setting for a period of time. As a result, change and connections between events can be observed. However, there are limits to the amount of time that participant observers can devote to being away from their normal routines. Consequently, participant observation does not usually extend much beyond two to three years in duration. When participant observation is being conducted into an area of research that is episodic rather than requiring continued observation, a longer time period may be feasible. Armstrong's (1993) research on football hooliganism, which was referred to several times in Chapters 13 and 14, entailed six years of participant observation, but, since football hooligans are not engaged full-time in this area of activity, the research did not require the researcher's continued absence from his work and other personal commitments. Interviewing can be carried out within a longitudinal research design somewhat more easily because repeat interviews may be easier to organize than repeat visits to participant observers' research settings, though the latter is not impossible (e.g. Burgess 1987, who revisited the comprehensive school in which he had conducted participant observation). Following up interviewees on several occasions is likely to be easier than returning to research sites on a regular basis.

Greater breadth of coverage

In participant observation, the researcher is invariably constrained in his or her interactions and observations to a fairly restricted range of people, incidents, and localities. Participant observation in a large organization, for example, is likely to mean that knowledge of that organization far beyond the confines of the department or section in which the observation is carried out is likely not to be very extensive. Interviewing can allow access to a wider variety of people and situations.

Specific focus

As noted in Chapter 13, qualitative research sometimes begins with a specific focus, and indeed Silverman (1993) has been critical of the notion that it should be regarded as an open-ended form of research. Qualitative interviewing would seem to be better suited to such a situation, since the interview can be directed at that focus and its associated research questions. Thus, the research by my colleagues and myself on the police had a very specific research focus in line with its Home Office funding—namely, conceptions of leadership among police officers (Bryman, Stephens, and A Campo 1996). The bulk of the data gathering was in two police forces and entailed the interviewing of police officers at all levels using a semi-structured interview guide. Because it had such a clear focus, it was more appropriate to conduct the research by interview rather than participant observation, since issues to do with leadership notions may not crop up on a regular basis, which would make observation a very extravagant method of data collection.

Overview

When Becker and Geer (1957a: 28) proclaimed over forty years ago that the 'most complete form of the sociological datum . . . is the form in which the participant observer gathers it', Trow (1957: 33) reprimanded them for making such a universal claim and argued that 'the problem under investigation properly dictates the methods of investigation'. The latter view is very much the one taken in this book. Research methods are appropriate to researching some issues and areas but not others. The discussion of the merits and limitations of participant observation and qualitative interviews is meant simply to draw attention to some of the considerations that might be taken into account if there is a genuine opportunity to use one or the other in a study.

Equally, and to repeat an earlier point, the comparison is a somewhat artificial exercise, because participant observation is usually carried out as part of ethnographic research and as such it is usually accompanied by interviewing as well as other methods. In other words, participant observers frequently buttress their observations with methods of data collection that allow them access to important areas that are not amenable to observation. However, the aim of the comparison was to provide a kind of balance sheet in considering the strengths and limitations of a reliance on either participant observation or qualitative interview alone. Its aim is to draw attention to some of the factors that might be taken into account in deciding how to plan a study and even how to evaluate existing research.

Key points

- Interviewing in qualitative research is typically of the unstructured or semi-structured kind.

- In qualitative research, interviewing may be the sole method in an investigation or may be used as part of an ethnographic study, or indeed in tandem with another qualitative method.

- Qualitative interviewing is meant to be flexible and to seek out the world views of research participants.

- If an interview guide is employed, it should not be too structured in its application and should allow some flexibility in the asking of questions.

- The qualitative interview should be tape-recorded and then transcribed.

- As with ethnographic research, investigations using qualitative interviews tend not to employ random sampling to select participants.

- The qualitative interview has become an extremely popular method of data collection in feminist studies.

- Whether to use participant observation or qualitative interviews depends in large part on their relative suitability to the research questions being addressed. However, it must also be borne in mind that participant observers invariably conduct some interviews in the course of their investigations.

Revision questions

Differences between the structured interview and qualitative research interviews

- How does qualitative interviewing differ from structured interviewing?

Unstructured and semi-structured interviewing

- What are the differences between unstructured and semi-structured interviewing?
- Could semi-structured interviewing stand in the way of flexibility in qualitative research?
- What are the differences between life history and oral history interviews?
- What kinds of consideration need to be borne in mind when preparing an interview guide?
- What kinds of question might be asked in an interview guide?
- What kinds of skill does the interviewer need to develop in qualitative interviewing?
- Why is it important to tape-record and transcribe qualitative interviews?

Sampling

- Compare theoretical sampling and snowball sampling.

Feminist research and interviewing in qualitative research

- Why has the qualitative interview become such a prominent research method for feminist researchers?
- What dilemmas might be posed for feminist researchers using qualitative interviewing?

Qualitative interviewing versus participant observation

- Outline the relative advantages and disadvantages of qualitative interviewing and participant observation.
- Does one method seem more in tune with the preoccupations of qualitative researchers than the other?

16 Focus groups

Reader's guide

The focus group method is an interview with several people on a specific topic or issue. It has been used extensively in market research but has only relatively recently made inroads into social research. This chapter explores:

- the possible reasons for preferring focus group interviews to individual interviews of the kind discussed in the previous chapter;
- how focus groups should be conducted in terms of such features as the need for tape recording, the number and size of groups, how participants can be selected, and how direct the questioning should be;
- the significance of interaction between participants in focus group discussions;
- the suggestion that the focus group method fits particularly well with a feminist research approach;

- some practical difficulties with focus group sessions, such as the possible loss of control over proceedings and the potential for unwanted group effects.

Introduction

We are used to thinking of the interview as something that involves an interviewer and one interviewee. Most textbooks reinforce this perception by concentrating on individual interviews. The focus group technique is a method of interviewing that involves more than one, usually at least four, interviewees. Essentially it is a group interview. Some authors draw a distinction between the focus group and the group interview techniques. Three reasons are sometimes put forward to suggest a distinction.

- Focus groups typically emphasize a specific theme or topic that is explored in depth, whereas group interviews often span very widely.

- Sometimes group interviews are carried out so that the researcher is able to save time and money by carrying out interviews with a number of individuals simultaneously. However, focus groups are not carried out for this reason.

- The focus group practitioner is invariably interested in the ways in which individuals *as members of a group* discuss a certain issue, rather than simply as individuals. In other words, with a focus group the researcher will be interested in such things as how people respond to each other's views and build up a view out of the interaction that takes place within the group.

However, the distinction between the focus group method and the group interview is by no means clear-cut and the two terms are frequently employed interchangeably. Nonetheless, the definition proposed in Box 16.1 provides a starting point.

Most focus group researchers undertake their work within the traditions of qualitative research. This means that they are explicitly concerned to reveal how the group participants view the issues with which they are confronted; therefore the researcher will aim to provide a fairly unstructured setting for the extraction of their views and perspectives. The person who runs the focus groups session is usually called the *moderator* or *facilitator* and he or she will be expected to guide each session but not to be too intrusive.

Another general point about the focus group method is that, while it is gaining in popularity at the moment, it is by no means a new technique. It has been used for many years in market research, where it is employed for such purposes as testing responses to new products and advertising initiatives (see Box 16.2 for an example). In fact there is a large literature within market research to do with the practices that are associated with focus group research and their implementation (e.g. Calder 1977).

Uses of focus groups

What are the uses of the focus group method? In many ways its uses are bound up with the uses of qualitative research in general, but, over and above these, the following points can be registered.

- The original idea for the focus group—the focused interview—was that people who were known to have had a certain experience could be interviewed in a relatively unstructured way about that

Box 16.1 ⌇☼⌇ *What is the focus group method?*

The focus group method is a form of group interview in which: there are several participants (in addition to the moderator/facilitator); there is an emphasis in the questioning on a particular fairly tightly defined topic; and the accent is upon interaction within the group and the joint construction of meaning. As such, the focus group contains elements of two methods: the group interview, in which several people discuss a number of topics; and what has been called a *focused interview*, in which inter-

viewees are selected because they 'are known to have been involved in a particular situation' (Merton *et al.* 1956: 3) and are asked about that involvement. The focused interview may be administered to individuals or to groups. Thus, the focus group method appends to the focused interview the element of interaction within groups as an area of interest and is more focused than the group interview.

Box 16.2 **The real and the unreal thing: Focus groups in market research**

On 23 April 1985 a product was launched that proved to be one of the greatest marketing blunders in business history. On that day, the Coca-Cola company not only launched what it called its New Coke but it removed from sale the old one, on which the massive corporation had been built. New Coke was a flop and the public clamoured for the return of its predecessor, in spite of assurances from the company that people would get used to the new formula and get to like it better. Yet close attention to data drawn from focus group research that the company had commissioned in the lead-up to the launch of New Coke might have prevented the disaster from happening. In 1982 and 1983, focus group research was conducted across the USA. At one point in each session, local consumers were presented with a scenario in which they were told that a new formula for a certain product had been introduced and that the response to it

was very favourable. The participants were then asked how *they* would feel when it came to their town. The response to the prospect of new, improved Budweiser beer and of Hershey chocolate bars being replaced was met with a positive response. However, when the replacement of Coke was being considered, the consumers became vehemently antagonistic to the idea. Taste tests had shown that consumers liked New Coke but they had not been asked how they would feel if traditional Coke was taken off supermarket shelves. The focus groups made it clear how they would feel, but Coca-Cola's chief executive officer was determined to plough ahead and his assistant who liaised with the firm conducting the focus groups chose to follow his boss's lead.

Sources: Pendergrast (1993) and Greising (1998).

experience. The bulk of the discussion by Merton *et al.* (1956) of the notion of the focused interview was in terms of individual interviews, but their book also considered the extension of the method into group interview contexts. Subsequently, the focus group has become a popular method for researchers examining the ways in which people in conjunction with one another construe the general topics in which the researcher is interested. One of the best-known studies using the method in the context of a social scientific topic is Morgan and Spanish's (1985) study of the ways in

which people organize knowledge about health issues. Their special interest was the question of people's knowledge about who has heart attacks and why they have them. Thus, the emphasis was on how focus group participants make sense of the causation of heart attacks in terms of the knowledge they have picked up over the years. However, a major impetus for the growing use of focus groups in social research has been their intensive use in the field of media and cultural studies. The growing emphasis in these fields is on what is known as 'audience reception'—how audiences respond to television and radio programmes, films, newspaper articles, and so on (McGuigan 1992; Fenton *et al.* 1998: ch. 1). An influential study in this context was Morley's (1980) research on *Nationwide*, a British news programme shown in the early evening that was popular in the 1970s. Morley organized focus groups made up of specific categories of people (for example, managers, trade unionists, students) and showed them recordings of the programme. He found that the different groups arrived at somewhat divergent interpretations of the programmes they had watched, implying the meaning does not reside solely in the programmes but also in the ways in which they are watched and interpreted. This research and the increasing attention paid to audience reception set in motion a growth of interest in the use of the focus group method for the study of audience interpretations of cultural and media 'texts'.

- The technique allows the researcher to develop an understanding about *why* people feel the way they do. In a normal individual interview the interviewee is often asked about his or her reasons for holding a particular view, but the focus group approach offers the opportunity of allowing people to probe each other's reasons for holding a certain view. This can be more interesting than the sometimes predictable question-followed-by-answer approach of normal interviews. For one thing, an individual may answer in a certain way during a focus group, but, as he or she listens to others' answers, he or she may want to qualify or modify a view; or alternatively may want to voice agreement to something that he or she probably would not have thought of without the opportunity of hearing the views of others. These possibilities mean that focus groups may also be very helpful in the elicitation of a wide variety of different views in relation to a particular issue.

- In focus groups participants are able to bring to the fore issues in relation to a topic that they deem to be important and significant. This is clearly an aim of individual interviews too, but, because the moderator has to relinquish a certain amount of control to the participants, the issues that concern them can surface. This is clearly an important consideration in the context of qualitative research, since the viewpoints of the people being studied are an important point of departure.

- In conventional one-to-one interviewing, interviewees are rarely challenged; they might say things that are inconsistent with earlier replies or that patently could not be true, but we are often reluctant to point out such deficiencies. In the context of a focus group, individuals will often argue with each other and challenge each other's views. This process of arguing means that the researcher may stand a chance of ending up with more realistic accounts of what people think, because they are forced to think about and possibly revise their views.

- The focus group offers the researcher the opportunity to study the ways in which individuals collectively make sense of a phenomenon and construct meanings around it. It is a central tenet of theoretical positions like symbolic interactionism that the process of coming to terms with (that is, understanding) social phenomena is not undertaken by individuals in isolation from each other. Instead, it is something that occurs in interaction and discussion with others. In this sense, therefore, focus groups reflect the processes through which meaning is constructed in everyday life and to that extent can be regarded as more naturalistic (see Box 2.4, p. 33, on the idea of naturalism) than individual interviews (Wilkinson 1998).

Conducting focus groups

There are a number of practical aspects of the conduct of focus group research that require some discussion.

Tape recording and transcription

As with interviewing for qualitative research, the focus group session will work best if it is tape-recorded and subsequently transcribed. The following reasons are often used to explain this preference.

- One reason is the simple difficulty of writing down not only exactly what people say but also who says it. In an individual interview you might be able to ask the respondent to hold on while you write something down, but to do this in the context of an interview involving several people would be extremely disruptive.

- The researcher will be interested in who expresses views within the group, such as whether certain individuals seem to act as opinion leaders or dominate the discussion. This also means that there is an interest in ranges of opinions within groups; for example, in a session, does most of the range of opinion derive from just one or two people or from most of the people in the group?

- A major reason for conducting focus group research is the fact that it is possible to study the processes whereby meaning is collectively constructed within each session (see above). It would be very difficult to do this by taking notes, because of the need to keep track of *who* says what (see also previous point). If this element is lost, the dynamics of the focus group session would also be lost, and a major rationale for doing focus group interviews rather than individual ones would be undermined.

- Like all qualitative researchers, the focus group practitioner will be interested in not just what people say but *how* they say it, for example, the particular language that they employ. There is

every chance that the nuances of language will be lost if the researcher has to rely on notes.

It should be borne in mind that transcribing focus group sessions is more complicated and hence more time-consuming than transcribing traditional interview recordings. This is because you need to take account of *who* is talking in the session, as well as what is said. This is sometimes difficult, since people's voices are not always easy to distinguish. Also, people sometimes talk over each other, which can make transcription even more difficult. In addition, it is extremely important to ensure that you equip yourself with a very high-quality microphone, which is capable of picking up voices, some of which may be quite faint, from many directions. Focus group transcripts always seem to have more missing bits due to lack of audibility than transcripts from conventional interviews.

How many groups?

How many groups do you need? Table 16.1 provides data on the number of groups and other aspects of the composition of focus groups in several studies based on this method and follows a similar table in Deacon, Pickering, Golding, and Murdock (1999) in taking the view that this is a helpful way of providing basic information on this issue. As Table 16.1 suggests, there is a good deal of variation in the numbers of groups used in the studies referred to, with a range from nine to fifty-two. However, there does seem to be a tendency for the range mainly to be from twelve to fifteen.

Clearly, it is unlikely that just one group will suffice the needs of the researcher, since there is always the possibility that the responses are particular to that one group. Obviously, time and resources will be a factor, but there are strong arguments for saying that too many groups will be a waste of time. Calder (1977) proposes that, when the moderator reaches the point that he or she is able to anticipate fairly

Table 16.1 Composition of groups in focus group research

Authors	Morgan and Spanish (1985)	Schlesinger et al. (1992)	Kitzinger (1993, 1994)	Livingstone and Lunt (1994)	Lupton (1996)	Fenton et al. (1998)	Stirling Media Research Institute (1998)
Area of research	Lay health beliefs concerning heart attacks	The responses of women to watching violence	Audience responses to media messages about AIDS	Audience responses to audience discussion programmes	Responses to controversies concerning diet and health	Audience responses to reporting of social science research	The responses of men to watching violence
Number of groups	9	14	52	12	12	14	15
Size range of groups	4 or 5	5–9	Not specified but appears to be 3 to 9 or 10	4–8	3–5	4–6	3–8
Average (mean) size of groups	4.4	6.6	6.75	5.75	4.1	5	5.9
Stratifying criteria (if any)	None mentioned, but all participants needed to be aged 35–50 and those who had experienced a heart attack were excluded	Experience of violence, Scottish/ English, ethnicity, class	No, but groups made up of specific groups (e.g. civil engineers, retirement club members, male prostitutes)	None mentioned	Gender	Gender, education, occupation (private/ public sector)	Class, Scottish/ English, ethnicity, age, sexual preference
Natural groups?	No, but all participants were mature university students	Some	Yes	No	Yes	Some	No

accurately what the next group is going to say, then there are probably enough groups already. This notion is very similar to the *theoretical saturation* criterion that was briefly introduced in Box 14.9, p. 303. In other words, once your major analytic categories have been saturated, there seems little point in continuing, and so it would be appropriate to bring data collection to a halt. For their study of audience discussion programmes, Livingstone and Lunt (1994: 181; see Table 16.1) used this criterion: 'The number of focus groups was determined by continuing until comments and patterns began to repeat and little new material was generated'. When this point of theoretical saturation is reached, as an

alternative to terminating data collection, there may be a case for moving on to an extension of the issues that have been raised in the focus group sessions that have been carried out.

One factor that may affect the number of groups is whether the researcher feels that the kinds and range of views are likely to be affected by socio-demographic factors such as age, gender, class, and so on. Many focus group researchers like to use stratifying criteria like these to ensure that groups with a wide range of features will be included. If so, a larger number of groups may be required to reflect the criteria. In connection with the research described in Box 16.3, Kitzinger (1994) writes that a large number

---

Box 16.3 Focus group in action: AIDS in the Media Research Project

Focus group research on the representation of AIDS in the mass media was part of a larger project on this topic. The focus groups were concerned with the examination of the ways in which 'media messages are explored by audiences and how understandings of AIDS are constructed. We were interested not solely in what people thought but in *how* they thought and *why* they thought as they did.' (Kitzinger 1994: 104).

Details of the groups are in Table 16.1. Since one goal of the research was to emphasize the role of interaction in the construction of meaning, it was important to provide a platform for enhancing this feature. Accordingly, 'instead of working with isolated individuals, or collec-

tions of individuals drawn together simply for the purposes of the research, we elected to work with pre-existing groups—people who already lived, worked or socialized together' (Kitzinger 1993: 272).

As a result, the groups were made up of such collections of people as a team of civil engineers working on the same site, six members of a retirement club, intravenous drug users, and so on. The sessions themselves are described as having been 'conducted in a relaxed fashion with minimal intervention from the facilitator— at least at first' (Kitzinger 1994: 106). Each session lasted approximately two hours and was tape-recorded.

---

of groups was preferred, not because of concerns about the representativeness of the views gleaned during the sessions, but in order to capture as much diversity in perspectives as possible. However, it may be that high levels of diversity are not anticipated in connection with some topics, in which case a large number of groups could represent an unnecessary expense.

One further point to bear in mind when considering the number of groups is that more groups will increase the complexity of your analysis. For example, Schlesinger *et al*. (1992: 29; see Table 16.1) report that the fourteen tape-recorded sessions they organized produced over 1,400 pages of transcription. This pile of paper was accumulated from discussions in each group of an average of one hour for each of the four screenings of violence that session participants were shown. Although this means that the sessions were longer than is normally the case, it does demonstrate that the amount of data to analyse can be very large, even though a total of fourteen sessions may not sound a lot to someone unfamiliar with the workings of the method.

Size of groups

How large should groups be? Morgan (1998*a*) suggests that the typical group size is six to ten

members, although the numbers in Table 16.1, which admittedly is not randomly selected and is mainly British, suggests that this calculation is slightly high in terms of both the range and the mean. One major problem faced by focus group practitioners is people who agree to participate but who do not turn up on the day. It is almost impossible to control for 'no-shows' other than consciously over-recruiting, a strategy that is sometimes recommended (e.g. Wilkinson 1999*a*: 188).

This point aside (which almost certainly accounts for the figures at the low end of the size ranges in Table 16.1), Morgan (1998*a*) recommends smaller groups when participants are likely to have a lot to say on the research topic. This is likely to occur when participants are very involved in or emotionally preoccupied with the topic. He also suggests smaller groups when topics are controversial or complex and when gleaning participants' personal accounts is a major goal. Morgan recommends larger groups when involvement with a topic is likely to be low or when the researcher wants 'to hear numerous brief suggestions' (1998*a*: 75). However, I am not convinced that larger groups are necessarily superior for topics in which participants have little involvement, since it may be more difficult to stimulate discussion in such a context. Larger groups may make it even more difficult if people are rather diffident about talking about a topic about which they know little or have little experience. A topic like media representations of social science research, which most people are unlikely to have much interest in or even to have thought about, could easily have resulted in a wall of silence in large groups (Fenton *et al.* 1998; see Table 16.1).

Level of moderator involvement

How involved should the moderator/facilitator be? In qualitative research, the aim is to get at the perspectives of those being studied. Consequently, the approach should not be intrusive and structured. Therefore, there is a tendency for researchers to use a fairly small number of very general questions to guide the focus group session. Moreover, there is a further tendency for moderators to allow quite a lot of latitude to participants, so that the discussion can range fairly widely. Obviously, if the discussion goes off at a total tangent it may be necessary to refocus the participants' attention, but even then it may be necessary to be careful, because what may appear to be digressions may in fact reveal something of interest to the group participants. The advantage of allowing a fairly free rein to the discussion is that the researcher stands a better chance of getting access to what individuals see as important or interesting. On the other hand, too much totally irrelevant discussion may prove too unproductive, especially in the commercial environment of market research. It is not surprising, therefore, that, as Wilkinson (1999*a*) observes, some writers on focus groups perceive the possibility that participants come to take over the running of a session from the moderator as a problem and offer advice on how to reassert control (e.g. Krueger 1988).

One way in which the moderator may need to be involved is in responding to specific points that are of potential interest to the research questions but that are not picked up by other participants. In the extract in Box 16.4 from the study of the reception of media representations of social science research from Fenton *et al.* (1998), a group of men who have been in higher education and are in private-sector employment begin to talk about the differences between the natural and the social sciences.

It is interesting to see the way in which a consensus about the social sciences is built up in this discussion with a particular emphasis on the lack of control in social research and on the supposed subjectivity of interpretation when compared to the 'pure' sciences. On other occasions, a little nudge from the moderator may be required when a particularly interesting point is not followed up by other participants. An example of this is provided in Box 16.5 from the same research, but this time the focus group is made up of women in private-sector employment and whose education is up to GCSE level. They are talking about a news item reporting research on victims of crime but that includes a

---

Box 16.4 Extract from a focus group discussion showing no moderator involvement

R1:   Essentially with the pure sciences I get an end result. Whereas with the social sciences it's pretty vague because it's very, very subjective.

R2:   I suppose for me the pure sciences seem to have more control of what they are looking at because they keep control of more. Because with social sciences there are many different aspects that could have an impact and you can't necessarily control them. So it seems more difficult to pin down and therefore to some extent controversial.

R3:   Pure science is more credible because you've got control over test environments, you've got an ability to test and control factually the outcome and then establish relationships between different agents or whatever. I think in social science it's always subject to interpretation. . . . I think if you want to create an easy life and be unaccountable to anybody, to obtain funding and spend your time in a stress-free way then one of the best things to do is to work in funded research and one of the best areas to do it in is in social science.   (Fenton *et al.* 1998: 127)

Box 16.5 Extract from a focus group discussion showing some moderator involvement

R1:   That was easy and interesting.

[Moderator]:   Why interesting? Why easy?

R2:   Because it affects all of us.

R1:   It was actually reading about what had happened to people. It wasn't all facts and figures. I know it was, but it has in the first sentence, where it says 'I

turned the key and experienced a sinking feeling'. You can relate to that straight away. It's how you'd feel.

R3:   She's in a flat and she hears noises—it's something that everyone does. Being on their own and they hear a noise.   (Fenton *et al.* 1998: 129)

---

number of detailed case studies of individual experiences of being a victim.

On this occasion, the moderator's intervention usefully allows the discussion to bring out the kinds of attributes that make for an easy and interesting media item on this topic. In particular, the participants feel that they can appreciate the media representation of social science research when it is something they can relate to and that an important way of doing this is the ability to use people's personal experiences as a lens through which the research can be viewed.

Clearly, the moderator has to straddle two positions: allowing the discussion to flow freely and intervening to bring out especially salient issues, particularly when group participants do not do so. This is not an easy conundrum to resolve and each tactic—intervention and non-intervention—carries risks. The best advice is to err on the side of minimal intervention—other than to start the group on a fresh set of issues—but to intervene when the group is struggling in its discussions or when it has not alighted on something that is said in the course of the session that appears significant for the research topic.

Selecting participants

Who can participate? Anyone for whom the topic is relevant can logically be an appropriate participant. Sometimes, certain topics do not require participants

of a particular kind, so that there is little if any restriction on who might be appropriate. This is a fairly unusual situation and normally some restriction is required. For example, for their research on the organization of knowledge about heart attacks, Morgan and Spanish (1985: 257) recruited people in the 35–50 age range, since they 'would be likely to have more experience with informal discussions of our chosen topic', but they excluded anyone who had had a heart attack or who was uneasy about discussing the topic.

More often, as Table 16.1 suggests and as previously noted, a wide range of people is required but they are organized into separate groups in terms of stratifying criteria, such as age, gender, education, occupation, and having or not having had a certain experience. Participants for each group can then be selected randomly or through some kind of snowball sampling method. The aim is to establish whether there is any systematic variation in the ways in which different groups discuss a matter. For example, in his research on the *Nationwide* news programme, Morley (1980) found that groups of managers interpreted the programmes they were shown in ways that were broadly consistent with the intentions of the programme producers, but that groups of trade unionists derived interpretations that were in opposition to those intentions. Such an inference can be derived only when focus group participation has been organized in terms of such stratifying criteria. Similarly, drawing on findings from their research into the responses of women to viewing violence, Schlesinger *et al.* (1992) derived a similar kind of conclusion. They showed their fourteen groups (see Table 16.1) four items: an episode of *Crimewatch UK* featuring some violence; an episode of *EastEnders* in which violence was incidental; a television drama, *Closing Ranks*, featuring marital violence; and the Hollywood movie *The Accused*, which contains an extremely vivid rape scene. Drawing on their findings concerning the groups' responses to these showings, the authors concluded:

in general, the salience in any particular programme of ethnicity, class, or gender or a lived experience such as violence is greatest for those *most directly involved* and diminishes in importance with social distance. Having a particular experience or a particular background does significantly affect the interpretation of a given text. The four programmes screened are obviously open to various readings. However, on the evidence, *how* they are read is fundamentally affected by various socio-cultural factors and by lived experience.   (Schlesinger *et al.* 1992: 168; emphases in original)

A slight variation on this approach can be seen in Kitzinger's (1994) study of reactions to media representations of AIDS (see Box 16.3 and Table 16.1). Her groups were made up of people in a variety of different situations. Some of these were what she calls 'general population groups' (for example, a team of civil engineers working on the same site) but others were made up of groups that might have a special interest in AIDS (for example, male prostitutes, intravenous drug users). However, the general point is that increasingly focus group practitioners try to discern patterns of variation by putting together groups with particular attributes or clusters of attributes.

A further issue in relation to the selection of group participants is whether to select people who are unknown to each other or to use natural groupings (for example, friends, co-workers, students on the same course). Some researchers prefer to exclude people who know each other on the grounds that pre-existing styles of interaction or status differences may contaminate the session. Not all writers accept this rule of thumb. Some prefer to select natural groups whenever possible. Kitzinger (Box 16.3 and Table 16.1) used groups made up of people who knew each other. The reason was that she wanted the discussions to be as natural as possible and she felt that this quality would be enhanced through the use of members of what she calls 'pre-existing groups'. Holbrook and Jackson (1996; see Box 16.6) report that, for their research on shopping centres, they initially tried to secure participants who did not know each other, but this strategy did not result in anybody coming forward. They then sought out participants from various clubs and social centres in the vicinity of the two North London shopping centres in which they were interested. They argue that, in view of their interest in research questions concerning shopping in relation to the construction of identity and how it relates to people's sense of place, recruiting people who knew each other was a highly appropriate strategy.

However, opting for a strategy of recruiting people entirely from natural groups is not always feasible, because of difficulties of securing participation. Fenton *et al.* (1998: 121), in the context of their research on the representation of social science research (Boxes 16.4 and 16.5 and Table 16.1), report that they preferred to recruit 'naturally occurring groups' but that 'this was not always achievable'. Morgan (1998*a*) suggests that one problem with using natural groups is that people who know each other well are likely to operate with taken-for-granted assumptions that they feel do not need to be brought to the fore. He suggests that, if it is important for the researcher to bring out such assumptions, groups of strangers are likely to work better.

Asking questions

An issue that is close to the question of the degree of involvement on the part of the moderator is the matter of how far there should be a set of questions that must be addressed. This issue is very similar to the considerations about how unstructured an interview should be in qualitative interviewing (see Chapter 15). Some researchers prefer to use just one or two very general questions to stimulate discussion, with

Box 16.6 Asking about shopping

For their research on the linkages between shopping, people's sense of place and locality, and the construction of identity (see Miller *et al*. 1998), Holbrook and Jackson (1996) describe their questioning strategy as follows:

We endeavoured to maintain spontaneity of discussion within the groups and only intervened when it was clear that the conversation was going off track, where there were unproductive silences or where there was continuous repetition of the same issue. Our interventions were mostly in the form of open questions on themes we had prepared beforehand, but we were careful that these questions should naturally fit with the general flow of conversation. The themes that we developed for our focus group discussion were as follows:

- Experiences of Wood Green Shopping City and Brent Cross Shopping Centre
- The differences between shopping on high streets and markets and going to a shopping centre
- Gender differences
- Shopping as pleasure, work or leisure
- Christmas shopping and shopping in sales.
(Holbrook and Jackson 1996: 138)

---

the moderator intervening as necessary along the lines outlined above. For example, in their research on knowledge about heart attacks, Morgan and Spanish (1985) asked participants to discuss just two topics. One topic was 'who has heart attacks and why?; here participants were encouraged to talk about people they knew who had had attacks. The second topic was 'what causes and what prevents heart attacks?' However, other researchers prefer to inject somewhat more structure into the organization of the focus group sessions. An example of this is the research on the viewing of violence by women by Schlesinger *et al*. (1992; see Table 16.1). For example, in relation to the movie *The Accused*, the reactions of the audiences were gleaned through 'guiding questions' under five main headings, the first three of which had several more specific elements.

- Initially, the participants were given the opportunity to discuss the film in terms of such issues as: perceived purpose of the film; gratifications from the film; and realism and storyline.

- The questioning then moved on to reactions to the characters such as: Sarah Tobias (the woman who is raped); the three rapists; the female lawyer; and the male lawyers.

- Participants were then asked about their reactions to scenes, such as: the rape; the female lawyer's

decision to change from not supporting Sarah Tobias's case to supporting it; and the winning of the case.

- Participants were asked about their reactions to the inclusion of the rape scene.

- Finally, they were asked about how they perceived the film's value, in particular whether the fact that it is American made a difference to their reactions.

While the research by Schlesinger *et al*. (1992) clearly contained quite a lot of specific questions to be addressed, the questions themselves were fairly general and were designed to ensure that there was some comparability between the focus group sessions in terms of gauging participants' reactions to each of the four programmes that were shown. Moreover, there was ample opportunity for moderators to react to points made in the course of the sessions. The authors write that 'due allowance was made for specific issues raised within a given group' (1992: 28). Moreover, the initial questions were designed to generate initial reactions in a relatively open-ended way. Such a general approach to questioning, which is fairly common in focus group research, allows the researcher to navigate the channel between, on the one side, addressing the research questions and ensuring comparability between sessions, and, on the other side, allowing participants to raise issues they see as significant and in their own terms.

Clearly, there are somewhat different questioning strategies and approaches to moderating focus group sessions. Most seem to approximate to the one described in Box 16.6, which lies in between the rather open-ended approach employed by Morgan and Spanish (1985) and the somewhat more structured one used by Schlesinger *et al.* (1992). There is probably no one best way and the style of questioning and moderating is likely to be affected by various factors, such as the nature of the research topic (for example, is it one that the researcher already knows a lot about, in which case a modicum of structure is feasible) and levels of interest and/or knowledge among participants in the research (for example, a low level of participant interest may require a somewhat more structured approach). Whichever strategy of questioning is employed, the focus group researcher should generally be prepared to allow at least some discussion that departs from the interview guide, since such debate may provide new and unexpected insights. A more structured approach to questioning might inhibit such spontaneity, but it is unlikely to remove it altogether.

Group interaction in focus group sessions

Kitzinger (1994) has observed that reports of focus group research frequently do not take into account interaction within the group. This is surprising, because it is precisely the operation of social interaction and its forms and impact that would seem to distinguish the focus group session from the individual interview. Yet, as Kitzinger observes, very few publications based on focus group research cite or draw inferences from patterns of interaction within the group. Wilkinson reviewed over 200 studies based on focus groups and published between 1946 and 1996. She concluded: 'Focus group data is most commonly presented as if it were one-to-one interview data, with interactions between group participants rarely reported, let alone analysed' (1998: 112).

In the context of her research on AIDS in the mass media, Kitzinger (1994) drew attention to two types of interaction in focus groups: complementary and argumentative interactions. The former bring out the elements of the social world that provide participants' own frameworks of understanding. The discussion in Box 16.4 brings out the agreement that emerges about the differences between the natural and the social sciences in people's minds. The discussion demonstrates broad agreement between the participants concerning such issues as the lack of control and the subjective nature of interpretation. Such a view is an emergent product of the interaction, with each participant building on the preceding remark. A similar sequence can be discerned in the following passage, which is taken from Morgan and Spanish's (1985) research on heart attack victims:

No. 1: But I think maybe what we're saying here is that there's no one cause of heart attacks, there's no one type of person, there's probably umpteen different types of heart attacks and causes coming from maybe smoking, maybe obesity, maybe stress, maybe design fault, hereditary, overwork, change in life style. Any of these things in themselves could be . . .

No. 2: And when you start putting them in combination [unclear] be speeding up on yourself.

No. 3: Yeah, you may be really magnifying each one of these particular things.

No. 2: Yeah, and depending on how, and in each person that magnification is different. Some people can take a little stress without doing any damage, some people can take a little smoking, a little drinking, a little obesity, without doing any damage. But you take a little of each of these and put them together and you're starting to increase the chances of damage. And any one of these that takes a magnitude leap increases the chances. (Morgan and Spanish 1985: 414)

This sequence from the transcript helpfully brings out the consensus that emerges around the question of who has heart attacks and why. No. 1 summarizes several factors that have been discussed; No. 2 then introduces the possible significance of some of these factors existing in combination; No. 3 agrees about the importance of combinations of factors; and No. 2 summarizes the position of the group on the salience of combinations of factors, raising at the same time the possibility that for each person there are unique combinations of factors that may be responsible for heart attacks.

However, as Kitzinger (1994) suggests, arguments in focus groups can be equally revealing. She suggests that moderators can play an important role in identifying differences of opinion and exploring with participants the factors that may lie behind them. Disagreement can provide participants with the opportunity to revise their opinions or to think more about the reasons why they hold the view that they do. By way of illustration, a passage from Schlesinger *et al.* (1992; see Table 16.1) is presented. The group is made up of English Afro-Caribbean women with no experience of violence. The debate is concerned with the rape scene in *The Accused* and reveals a misgiving that its inclusion may actually be exploiting sexual violence:

Speaker 1: I think . . . that they could've explained it. They could easily leave that rape scene.

Speaker 2: But it's like that other film we watched. You don't realise the full impact, like, the one we were watching, the first one [*Crimewatch*], until you've got the reconstruction.

Speaker 3: Yeah, but I think with that sort of film, it would cause more damage than it would good, I mean, if someone had been raped, would you like to have [to] sit through that again? (Schlesinger *et al.* 1992: 151–2)

The debate then continues to consider the significance of the scene for men:

Speaker 1: But you wouldn't miss anything, would you? What would you? All right, if you didn't watch that particular part, would you miss anything? You could still grasp it couldn't you?

Speaker 2: You could still grasp it but the enormous effect that it's had on us at the moment, it wouldn't be as drastic . . . without those.

Speaker 1: Yeah, but I'm thinking how would men see it? . . .

Speaker 3: That's what I'm saying, how would they view that scene?

Speaker 4: They couldn't believe it either, I mean, they didn't—they didn't think they were doing any wrong.

Speaker 1: Men would sit down and think, 'Well, she asked for it. She was enjoying it and look, the men around enjoyed it.' (Schlesinger *et al.* 1992: 152)

One factor, then, that seems to be behind the unease of some of the women about the inclusion of the vivid rape scene is that it may be enjoyed by men, rather than being found repulsive, and that they would identify with the onlookers in the film. This account has come about because of the discussion that is stimulated by disagreement within the group and allows a rounded account of women's reactions to the scene to be forged. As Kitzinger (1994) argues, drawing attention to patterns of interaction within focus groups allows the researcher to determine how group participants view the issues with which they are confronted in their own terms. The posing of questions by and agreement and disagreement among participants helps to bring out their own stances on these issues. The resolution of disagreements also helps to force participants to express the grounds on which they hold particular views.

The focus group as a feminist method

The use of focus groups by feminist researchers has grown considerably in recent years and Wilkinson (1998, 1999b) has argued that it has great potential in this regard. Three aspects of the method stand out in terms of their compatibility with the ethics and politics of feminism:

- Focus group research is less artificial than many other methods, because, in emphasizing group interaction, which is a normal part of social life, it does not suffer from the problem of gleaning information in an unnatural situation. Moreover, the tendency of many focus group researchers to recruit participants from naturally occurring groups underpins the lower level of artificiality of the method, since people are able to discuss in situations that are quite normal for them. As a result, there is greater opportunity to derive understandings that chime with the 'lived experience' of women. However, not all writers accept the contention that focus groups are more naturalistic than individual interviews. Even when natural groups are used, gathering people to discuss a certain topic (such as a television programme) is not inherently naturalistic, because the social setting is to a significant extent contrived (Morrison 1998: 154–5). Indeed, completing questionnaires or being interviewed may appear more natural, because such instruments are fairly commonplace, whereas being asked to discuss in a group an issue not necessarily of one's choosing is less so.
- Feminist researchers have expressed a preference for methods that avoid *decontextualization*—that is, that successfully study the individual within a social context. The tendency for most methods to treat the individual as a separate entity devoid of a social context is disliked by many feminist researchers who prefer to analyse 'the self as relational or as socially constructed' (Wilkinson 1999b: 229–30). Because the individual is very much part of a group in the focus group method, this tendency towards decontextualization is avoided.
- As we have seen in previous chapters, feminist researchers are suspicious of research methods that are exploitative and create a power relationship between the female researcher and the female respondent. Wilkinson observes that the risk of this occurring is greatly reduced because focus group participants are able to take over much of the direction of the session from the moderator. Indeed, they may even subvert the goals of the session in ways that could be of considerable interest to the moderator. As a result, participants' points of view are much more likely to be revealed than in a traditional interview.

Wilkinson does not argue that focus groups or indeed any method can be described as inherently feminist. Instead, she argues that, because of these three features and when employed with a sensitivity towards feminist concerns, the focus group method has considerable potential as a tool of feminist research.

The kinds of argument put forward regarding the fit between the focus group method and feminist research have been extended to suggest they may have a further role in allowing the voices of highly marginalized groups of women to surface. Madriz (2000: 843) argues that, for a group like lower-socio-economic-class women of colour, focus groups constitute a relatively rare opportunity for them to 'empower themselves by making sense of their experience of vulnerability and subjugation'.

Limitations of focus groups

Focus groups clearly have considerable potential for research questions in which the processes through which meaning is jointly constructed is likely to be of particular interest. Indeed, it may be that, even when this is not a prominent emphasis, the use of the focus group method may be appropriate and even advantageous, since it allows participants' perspectives—an important feature of much qualitative research (see Chapter 13)—to be revealed in ways that are different from individual interviews (for example, through discussion, participants' questions, arguments, and so on). It also offers considerable potential for feminist researchers. What, then, might be its chief limitations?

- The researcher probably has less control over proceedings than with the individual interview. As we have seen, by no means all writers on focus groups perceive this as a disadvantage and indeed feminist researchers often see it as an advantage. However, the question of control raises issues for researchers of how far they can allow a focus group to 'take over' the running of proceedings. There is clearly a delicate balance to be taken into account over how involved moderators should be and how far a set of prompts or questions should influence the conduct of a focus group, as some of the earlier discussions have suggested. What is not clear is the degree to which it is appropriate to surrender control of a focus group to its participants, especially when there is a reasonably explicit set of research questions to be answered, as is commonly the case, for example, in funded research.

- The data are difficult to analyse. A huge amount of data can be very quickly produced. Developing a strategy of analysis that incorporates both themes in what people say and patterns of interaction is not easy. Also, as previously pointed out, focus group recordings are particularly prone to inaudible elements, which affects transcription. However, studies like those of Kitzinger (1994) and Morgan and Spanish (1985) show that the examination of group interaction can be used to show how issues of thematic interest arise in the course of discussion.

- They are difficult to organize. Not only do you have to secure the agreement of people to participate in your study; you also need to persuade them to turn up at a particular time. Small payments, such as book or store tokens, are sometimes made to induce participation, but nonetheless it is common for people not to turn up.

- The recordings are probably more time-consuming to transcribe than equivalent recordings of individual interviews, because of variations in voice pitch and the need to take account of who says what.

- There are possible problems of group effects. This includes the obvious problem of dealing with reticent speakers and with those who hog the stage! In this respect, they are a bit like tutorials. Krueger (1998) suggests in relation to the problem of overly prominent participants that the moderator should make clear to the speaker and other group participants that other people's views are definitely required; for example, he suggests saying something like 'That's one point of view. Does anyone have another point of view?' (1998: 59). As for those who do not speak very much, it is recommended that they are actively encouraged to say something. Also, as the well-known Asch experiments showed, an emerging group view may mean that a perfectly legitimate perspective held by just one individual may be suppressed (Asch 1951). There is also evidence that, as a group comes to share a certain point of view, group members come to think uncritically about it and to develop almost irrational attachments to it (Janis 1982). It is not known how far such group effects have an adverse impact on focus group findings, but it is clear that they cannot be entirely ignored. In this context, it would be interesting to know how far agreement among focus group participants is more frequently encountered than disagreement (I have a hunch that it is), since the effects to which both Asch and Janis referred would lead us to expect more agreement than disagreement in focus group discussions.

- Madriz (2000) proposes that there are circumstances when focus groups may not be appropriate, because of their potential for causing discomfort among participants. When such discomfort might arise, individual interviews are likely to be preferable. Situations in which unease might be occasioned are: when intimate details of private lives need to be revealed; when participants may not be comfortable in each other's presence (for example, bringing together people in a hierarchical relationship to each other); and when participants are likely to disagree profoundly with each other.

Key points

- The focus group is a group interview that is concerned with exploring a certain topic.

- The moderator generally tries to provide a relatively free rein to the discussion. However, there may be contexts in which it is necessary to ask fairly specific questions, especially when cross-group comparability is an issue.

- There is concern with the joint production of meaning.

- Focus group discussions need to be tape-recorded and transcribed.

- There are several issues concerning the recruitment of focus group participants—in particular, whether to use natural groupings and whether to employ stratifying criteria.

- Group interaction is an important component of discussions.

- Some writers view focus groups as well suited to a feminist standpoint.

Revision questions

- Why might it be useful to distinguish between a focus group and a group interview?

Uses of focus groups

- What advantages might the focus group method offer in contrast to an individual qualitative interview?

Conducting focus groups

- How involved should the moderator be?

- Why is it necessary to tape-record and transcribe focus group sessions?

- Are there any circumstances in which it might be a good idea to select participants who know each other?
- What might be the advantages and disadvantages of using an interview guide in focus group sessions?

Group interaction in focus group sessions

- Why might it be important to treat group interaction as an important issue when analysing focus group data?

The focus group as a feminist method

- Evaluate the argument that the focus group can be viewed as a feminist method.
- To what extent are focus groups a naturalistic approach to data collection?

Limitations of focus groups

- Does the potential for the loss of control over proceedings and group effects damage the potential utility of the focus group as a method?
- How far do the greater problems of transcription and difficulty of analysis undermine the potential of focus groups?

17 Language in qualitative research

Reader's guide

This chapter is concerned with two approaches to the examination of language: conversation analysis and discourse analysis. For the practitioners of both approaches language is an object of interest in its own right and not simply a resource through which research participants communicate with researchers. The chapter explores:

• the roots of conversation analysis in ethnomethodology;

- some of its rules and principles;
- the assumptions of discourse analysis;
- some of its analytic strategies;
- points of difference between the two approaches.

Introduction

Language is bound to be of importance for social researchers. It is after all through language that we ask people questions in interviews and through which the questions are answered. Understanding language categories has been an important component of research involving participant observation, because knowing how words are used and the meanings of specific terms in the local vernacular (often called 'argot') is frequently viewed as crucial to an appreciation of how the social world being studied is viewed by its members.

In this chapter, however, two approaches will be examined that treat language as their central focal points. They are called conversation analysis (CA) and discourse analysis (DA). What is crucial about these approaches is that, unlike traditional views of the role of language in social research, they treat language as a topic rather than as a resource (admittedly a clichéd phrase). This means that language is treated as significantly more than as a medium through which the business of social research is conducted (such as asking questions in interviews). It becomes a focus of attention in its own right. While CA and DA do not exhaust the range of possibilities for studying language as a topic, they do represent two of the most prominent approaches. Each has evolved a technical vocabulary and set of techniques. This chapter will outline some of the basic elements of each of them and draw attention to some contrasting features.

Conversation analysis

The roots of CA lie in ethnomethodology, a sociological position developed in the USA under the general tutelage of Harold Garfinkel and Harvey Sacks, though it is the latter with whom CA is most associated. Ethnomethodology takes as its basic focus of attention 'practical, common-sense reasoning' in everyday life and as such is fundamentally concerned with the notion of social life as an accomplishment. Social order is not seen as a pre-existing force constraining individual action, but as something that is worked at and accomplished through interaction. Contrary to what its name implies, ethnomethodology is *not* a research methodology; it is the study of the methods employed in everyday life though which social order is accomplished. As Garfinkel put it in his inimitable style:

in contrast to certain versions of Durkheim that teach that the objective reality of social facts is sociology's fundamental principle, the lesson is taken instead, and used as a study policy, that the objective reality of social facts *as* an ongoing accomplishment of the concerted activities of daily life, with the ordinary, artful ways of that accomplishment being by members known, used, and taken for granted, is, for members doing sociology, a fundamental phenomenon.   (Garfinkel 1967: p. vii)

Two ideas are particularly central to ethnomethodology and find clear expression in CA:

indexicality and reflexivity. The former means that the meaning of an act, which in CA essentially means spoken words or utterances including pauses and sounds, depends upon the context in which it is used. Reflexivity means that spoken words are constitutive of the social world in which they are located; in other words, the principle of reflexivity in ethnomethodology means that talk is not a 'mere' representation of the social world, so that it does much more than just stand for something else. In these ways, ethnomethodology fits fairly squarely with two aspects of qualitative research—the predilection for a contextual understanding of action (see Chapter 13) and an ontological position associated with constructionism (see Chapter 1).

In the years following its initial introduction into sociology, ethnomethodological research split into two camps. One entailed drawing on traditional social research methods, albeit in perhaps a somewhat altered form, and on ethnography in particular (e.g. Cicourel 1968). The other, which is mainly associated with Sacks and his co-workers (e.g. Sacks *et al*. 1974), sought to conduct fine-grained analyses of talk in naturally occurring situations. Moreover, it is not just talk in itself that is the object of interest but talk as it occurs in and through social interaction. CA concerns itself with the organization of such talk in the context of interaction (see Box 17.1). In order to conduct such investigations, a premium was placed on the recording of naturally occurring conversations and their transcription for the purpose of intensive analysis of the sequences of interaction revealed in the subsequent transcripts. As such, CA is a multifaceted approach—part theory, part method of data acquisition, part method of analysis. The predilection for the analysis of talk gleaned from naturally occurring situations suggests that CA chimes with another preoccupation among qualitative researchers—namely, a commitment to naturalism (see Boxes 2.4 and 13.1, pp. 33, 265).

As the definition of CA in Box 17.1 and the preceding discussion suggest, CA takes from ethnomethodology a concern with the production of social order through and in the course of social interaction but takes conversation as the basic form through which that social order is achieved. The element of indexicality is also evident, in that practitioners of CA argue that the meaning of words is contextually grounded, whilst the commitment to reflexivity is revealed in the view that talk is constitutive of the social context in which it occurs.

Conversation analysts have developed a variety of procedures for the study of talk in interaction. Psathas (1995: 1) has described them as 'rigorous, systematic procedures' that can 'provide reproducible results'. Such a framework smacks of the commitment to the codification of procedures that generate valid, reliable, and replicable findings that are a feature of quantitative research. It is not surprising, therefore, that CA is sometimes described as having a positivist orientation. Thus, a cluster of features that are broadly in tune with qualitative research (contextual, naturalistic, studying the social world in its own terms and without prior theoretical commitments) are married to traits that are resonant of quantitative research. However, the emphasis on context in CA is somewhat at variance with the way in which contextual understanding is normally conceptualized in qualitative research. For CA practitioners, context refers to the specific here-and-now context of immediately preceding talk, whereas for most qualitative researchers it has a much wider set of resonances, which has to do with an appreciation of such things as the culture of the group within which action occurs. In other words, action is to be understood in terms of the values,

---

Box 17.1 What is conversation analysis?

Conversation analysis (CA) is the fine-grained analysis of talk as it occurs in interaction in naturally occurring situations. The talk is recorded and transcribed so that the detailed analyses can be carried out. These analyses are concerned with uncovering the underlying structures of talk in interaction and as such with the achievement of order through interaction.

beliefs, and typical modes of behaviour of that group. This is precisely the kind of attribution from which CA practitioners are keen to refrain. It is no wonder, therefore, that writers like Gubrium and Holstein (1997) treat it as a separate tradition within qualitative research (see Box 13.1, p. 265), while Silverman (1993) finds it difficult to fit CA into broad descriptions of the nature of qualitative research.

Assumptions of conversation analysis

Heritage (1984, 1987) has proposed that CA is governed by three basic assumptions:

- *Talk is structured.* Talk comprises invariant patterns—that is, it is structured. Participants are implicitly aware of the rules that underpin these patterns. As a result, conversation analysts eschew attempts to infer the motivations of speakers from what they say or to ascribe their talk to personal characteristics. Such information is unnecessary, since the conversation analyst is oriented to the underlying structures of action, as revealed in talk.

- *Talk is forged contextually.* Action is revealed in talk and as such talk must be analysed in terms of its context. This means that we must seek to understand what someone says in terms of the talk that has preceded it and that therefore talk is viewed as exhibiting patterned sequences.

- *Analysis is grounded in data.* Conversation analysts shun prior theoretical schemes and instead argue that characteristics of talk and of the constitutive nature of social order in each empirical instance must be induced out of data. Heritage (1987: 258) has written: 'it is assumed that social actions work *in detail* and hence that the specific details of interaction cannot simply be ignored as insignificant without damaging the prospects for coherent and effective analyses'. This assumption represents a manifesto for the emphasis on fine-grained details (including length of pauses, prolongation of sounds, and so on) that is the hallmark of CA.

Transcription and attention to detail

As the third of the three assumptions associated with CA indicates, the approach requires the analyst to produce detailed transcripts of natural conversation. Consider the portion of transcript in Box 17.2 that contains some of the basic notational symbols employed in CA.

The transcript in Box 17.2 includes some basic symbols employed by conversation analysts:

We:ll	A colon indicates that the sound that occurs directly before the colon is prolonged. More than one colon means further prolongation (e.g. ::::).
.hh	h's preceded by a dot indicate an intake of breath. If no dot is present, it means breathing out.
(0.8)	A figure in parentheses indicates the length of a period of silence, usually measured in tenths of one second. Thus, (0.8) signals eight-tenths of a second of silence.
<u>you</u> and k<u>n</u>owing	An underline indicates an emphasis in the speaker's talk.
(.)	Indicates a very slight pause.

The attention to detail in the sequence in Box 17.2 is very striking and represents a clear difference from the way in which talk is normally treated by social researchers—for example, in their transcription conventions when analysing qualitative interviews. But what is significant in this sequence of talk?

Silverman (1994) draws two main inferences from the sequence in Box 17.2. First, *P* initially tries to deflect any suggestion that there might be a special reason that she needs a test. As a result, the disclosure that she has been engaging in potentially risky behaviour is delayed. Secondly, *P*'s use of '*you*' depersonalizes her behaviour. Silverman argues that sequences like these show how 'people receiving HIV

Box 17.2 Conversation analysis in action showing a question and answer adjacency pair

Silverman (1994: 72) provides the following extract from a conversation between an HIV counsellor (C) at a clinic and a patient (P):

1 C   Can I just briefly ask why: you thought about having
2   an HIV test done:

3 P   .hh We:ll I mean it's something that you have these
4   I mean that you have to think about these da: ys, and
5   I just uh: m felt (0.8) you- you have had sex with
6   several people and you just don't want to go on (.)
7   not knowing.

---

counselling skilfully manage their talk about delicate topics' (1994: 75). The hesitations are designed by patients to establish that issues like these are not the subject of normal conversation; the rather general replies to questions are meant to indicate that the speaker is not the kind of person who will immediately launch into a discussion about difficult sexual matters with a stranger. Silverman suggests that the notion that the hesitancy and depersonalization on the part of *P* is to do with her embarrassment about talking about sex is 'severely limited' and that instead we find that 'the production and management of delicate topics is skilfully and co-operatively organized between professionals and clients' (1994: 76).

This analysis shows how attention to fine details is an essential ingredient of CA work. Pauses and emphases are not to be regarded as incidental or of little significance in terms of what the speaker is trying to achieve; instead, they are part of 'the specific details of interaction [that] cannot simply be ignored as insignificant', as Heritage put it in the quotation above.

Some basic tools of conversation analysis

The gradual accumulation of detailed analyses of talk in interaction has resulted in a recognition that there are recurring features of the ways in which that talk is organized. These features can be regarded as tools that can be applied to sequences of conversation. The following tools are presented merely to provide a flavour of the ways in which CA proceeds.

Turn-taking

One of the most basic ideas in CA is the notion that one of the ways in which order is achieved in everyday conversation is through turn-taking. This is a particularly important tool of conversation analysis, because it illustrates that talk depends on shared codes. If such codes did not exist, there would not be smooth transitions in conversation. In other words, there must be codes for indicating the ends of utterances.

Hutchby and Wooffitt (1998: 47) summarize this model as indicating that: '(1) turn-taking occurs; (2) one speaker tends to talk at a time; and (3) turns are taken with as little gap or overlap between them as possible'. This is not to say that turn-taking 'errors' do not occur. They manifestly do, as the discussion of *repair mechanisms* below suggests. One of the ways in which turn-taking is revealed is through the examination of *adjacency pairs*, which are the focus of the next section.

Adjacency pairs

The idea of the *adjacency pair* draws attention to the well-attested tendency for some kinds of activity as revealed in talk to involve two linked phases: a question followed by an answer, as in Box 17.2; an invitation followed by a response (accept/ decline); or a greeting followed by a returned greeting. The first phase invariably implies that the other part of the adjacency pair will be forthcoming—for example, that an invitation will be responded to. The second phase is of interest to the conversation analyst not just because it becomes a springboard for a response in its own right but because compliance with the putative normative structure of the pairing indicates an appreciation of how one is supposed to respond to the initial phase. In this way, 'intersubjective understandings' are continuously reinforced (Heritage 1987: 259–60). This is not to imply that the second phase will *always* follow the first; indeed, the response to a failure to comply with the expected response has itself been the focus of attention by conversation analysts.

Preference organization

While it is true to say that the second phase in an adjacency pair is always anticipated, some responses are clearly preferential to others. An example is that, when an invitation or a request is proffered, acceptance does not have to be justified, whereas a refusal does have to be justified. A further example is that, when an attempt to be self-deprecating is provided, it will be met with disagreement rather than agreement. In each case, the former (acceptance, disagreement) is the *preferred response* and the latter (refusal, agreement) is the *dispreferred response*. Therefore, the preference structure is discovered by the conversation analyst through the response to an initial statement.

Speakers' awareness of the preference organization of such pairings has implications for the structure of a conversation. For example, Potter (1996: 59) contrasts a sequence in which an offer is met with a straightforward preferred response of acceptance— 'thank you'—with the sequence in Box 17.3, in which an invitation is declined (the dispreferred response).

Potter argues that this kind of response by *A* is fairly typical of acceptance rejections, which are, of course, dispreferred responses. Potter draws attention to several features that contrast strikingly with the unequivocal 'thank you' associated with the case of acceptance. For example, *A* delays the start of his or her response and fills it with 'hehh'. Also, the rejection is 'softened' by *A* saying that he or she doesn't 'think' he or she can make it and is accompanied by an explanation for failing to provide the

preferred response. Moreover, Potter follows the admonition not to make inferences about speakers' motivations by observing that the notion of a preference structure is a feature of the talk not the motivations of the participants. After all, *A* may actually have preferred to accept the invitation but was prevented from doing so by a prior commitment. The key point is that the participants recognize the preference structure of this kind of adjacency pairing and this affects the form of their response (that is, hesitancy, acknowledgement of the invitation, and providing an explanation) in the case of declining the offer or an unelaborated (or barely elaborated) response in the case of acceptance.

Accounts

A feature of the sequence in Box 17.3 is that from line 7 onwards *A* formulates an account of why it is that the invitation cannot be accepted. As Potter observes, the account does two things: it establishes a reason for declining the invitation and depicts *A* as constrained by circumstances. The important feature to note in the treatment of accounts in CA is that they are analysed in context—that is, the form that they assume is handled as being occasioned by what precedes it (an invitation). Unlike the traditional view of accounts in sociology, a CA view of *A*'s account is to stress the importance of depicting it as allowing the invitation to be construed in a positive

---

Box 17.3 Conversation analysis in action: A dispreferred response

1. *B*:   Uh if you'd care to come over and visit a little while
2.   this morning I'll give you a cup of <u>coffee</u>.
3. *A*:   hehh
4.   Well
5.   that's awfully sweet of you,
6.   I don't think I can make it this morning. hh uhm
7.   I'm running an ad in the paper and-and uh I have to
8.   stay near the phone   (Atkinson and Drew 1979: 58, quoted in Potter 1996: 59)

light even though it cannot be accepted, thereby allowing the relationship between the two parties not to be jeopardized. Moreover, in CA, accounts are not unusual phenomena to be deployed when things go wrong but are intrinsic to talk in a variety of situations. What is also striking about this sequence as an account is that it is in essence simply a description of a state of affairs (having an advertisement in the paper and as a result needing to stay close to the telephone in case there are calls). The factual nature of the account further allows the relationship between the two parties to be unharmed by A's dispreferred response.

Repair mechanisms

Of course, things do go wrong in conversations, as occurs when turn-taking conventions are not followed so that there is overlapping of people talking. Silverman (1993: 132) notes several repair mechanisms, such as:

- when someone starts to speak before someone else has finished, the initial speaker stops talking before completing his or her turn;

- when a turn transfer does not occur at an appropriate point (for example, when someone does not respond to a question), the speaker may speak again, perhaps reinforcing the need for the other person to speak (for example, by reinforcing the question).

The crucial point to note about such repair mechanisms is that they allow the rules of turn-taking to be maintained in spite of the fact that they have been breached.

Overview

This review of CA can only scratch the surface of an approach that has developed a highly sophisticated way of studying talk in interaction. It has sometimes been suggested that it fails to capture body movements, but in recent times the use of video recordings has supplemented its tool kit of methods (e.g. Heath 1997). In recent times, there has been a growing use of CA in connection with the examination of talk in institutional settings such as organizations and mediation sessions.

The insistence of conversation analysts that it is important to locate understanding in terms of sequences of talk, and therefore to avoid making extraneous inferences about the meanings of that talk, marks CA as representing a somewhat different approach from much qualitative research. As we have seen in previous chapters, qualitative researchers often claim (perhaps erroneously from the perspective of CA) that they seek to achieve understanding from the perspective of those being studied. Conversation analysts claim to do this only in so far as that understanding can be revealed in the specific contexts of talk. To import elements that are not specifically grounded in the here and now of what has just been said during a conversation risks the implanting of understanding that is not grounded in participants' own terms (Schegloff 1997).

Two points seem relevant here. First, this is a somewhat limiting stance, in that it means that the attribution of motives and meanings as a result of an in-depth understanding of a culture is illegitimate. While an interpretive understanding of social action carries risks on misunderstanding, an approach that prohibits such speculation is potentially restrictive. Secondly, CA is contextual in that it locates understanding in the sequences of talk. However, for the participants of an exchange, much of their talk is informed by their mutual knowledge of contexts. The analyst is restricted from taking those additional components of the context into account if they are not specifically part of the organization of talk. Again, this admonition seems to restrict the analyst more than is desirable in many circumstances and to consign CA to a range of research questions that are amenable solely to the location of meaning in talk alone. On the other hand, CA reduces the risk about making unwarranted speculations about what is happening in social interaction and has contributed much to our understanding of the accomplishment of social order, which is one of the classic concerns of social theory.

Discourse analysis

Unlike CA, DA is an approach to language that can be applied to forms of communication other than talk. As such, it can be and has been applied to forms like texts, such as newspaper articles, and is in this respect more flexible than CA. Moreover, in DA there is much less of an emphasis on naturally occurring talk, so that talk in research interviews can be a legitimate target for analysis. However, DA should not be treated totally in opposition or contradistinction to CA, since it incorporates insights from it.

Unlike CA, which by and large reveals a uniformity based on an orthodoxy associated with certain classic statements concerning its core practices (e.g. Sacks *et al.* 1974), there are several different approaches that are labelled as DA (Potter 1997). The version to be discussed here is one that has been of special interest to social researchers and is associated with such writers as Potter (1997); Potter and Wetherell 1987, 1994); Billig (1992); and Gilbert and Mulkay (1984). This version of DA (see Box 17.4) has been described as exhibiting two distinctive features at the level of epistemology and ontology (Potter 1997).

- It is *anti-realist*; in other words, it denies that there is an external reality awaiting a definitive portrayal by the researcher and it therefore disavows the notion that any researcher can arrive at a privileged account of the aspect of the social world being investigated. Some discourse analysts, however, adopt a stance that is closer to a realist position, but most seem to be anti-realist in orientation.

- It is *constructionist*; in other words, the emphasis is placed on the versions of reality propounded by members of the social setting being investigated and on the fashioning of that reality through their renditions of it (see Box 1.12, p. 18). More specifically, the constructionist emphasis entails a recognition that discourse entails a selection from many viable renditions and that in the process a particular depiction of reality is built up.

Thus, discourse is not simply a neutral device for imparting meaning. People seek to accomplish things when they talk or when they write; DA is concerned with the strategies they employ in trying to create different kinds of effect. In addition, DA shares with CA a preference for locating contextual understanding in terms of the situational specifics of talk. As Potter (1997: 158) puts it, discourse analysts prefer to avoid making reference in their analyses to what he refers to as 'ethnographic particulars' and argues that instead they prefer 'to see things as things that are worked up, attended to and made relevant in interaction rather than being external determinants'. However, DA practitioners are less wedded to this principle than conversation analysts, in that the former sometimes show a greater preparedness to make reference to 'ethnographic particulars'.

Discourse analysts resist the idea of a codification of their practices and indeed argue that such a codification is probably impossible. Instead, they prefer to see their style of research as an 'analytic mentality' and as such as 'a craft skill, more like bike riding or chicken sexing than following the recipe for a mild chicken rogan josh' (Potter 1997: 147–8). One useful point of departure for DA research that has been suggested by Gill (1996) following Widdicombe (1993) is to treat the way that something is said as being 'a solution to a problem' (Widdicombe 1993: 97, quoted in Gill 1996: 146). She also suggests adopting a posture of 'sceptical reading' (Gill 2000). This means searching for a purpose lurking behind the ways that something is said or presented.

The bulk of the exposition of DA that follows is based on two studies: research on scientists' discourse and the use of numbers in a television programme on cancer. In the case of the former, we will see that attention to scientists' discourse is a solution to problems of how to represent their practices in formal and informal settings; the study of the television programme demonstrates that the examination of discourse reveals how claims about facts can be boosted or undermined through the use of a language of quantification. A further element to be sensitive to is that, as Gill (1996), following Billig (1991), suggests, what is said is always a way of *not* saying something else. In other words, either total silence on a topic, or formulating an argument in a conversation or article in one way rather than in another way, is a crucial component of seeing discourse as a solution to a problem. As we will see, the silences about aspects of their procedures in the scientists' published papers are crucial to conveying a sense of the fixed, neutral nature of their findings; in the case of the television programme, conveying a quantitative argument in one way rather than in another way is crucial to undermining the credibility of claims about success in the treatment of cancer.

Potter and Wetherell (1994) suggest that there are two tendencies within the kind of DA work being discussed in this chapter, although they acknowledge that the distinction is somewhat artificial. One is the identification of 'the general resources that are used to construct discourse and enable the performance of particular actions' (1994: 48–9), which is concerned with identifying *interpretative repertoires*. The other is concerned to identify 'the detailed procedures through which versions are constructed and

made to look factual' (1994: 49). We will now explore these two strands of DA.

Uncovering interpretative repertoires

In order to illustrate the idea of an *interpretative repertoire*, an influential study of scientists by Gilbert and Mulkay (1984) will be employed. This research is outlined in some detail in Box 17.5. Gilbert and Mulkay noticed a distinct difference between the ways in which the scientists presented their work in formal contexts, most notably the scientific paper, and in informal contexts, such as in the interviews with the researchers. Such differences went far beyond rather predictable differences in tone of presentation, in that they also related to such areas as the depiction of the ways in which the findings emerged. For example, Gilbert and Mulkay noted an instance in which a scientific paper portrayed a model as emerging out of the data, whereas in the research interview the rendition is one of reinterpreting the model, which in turn suggested seeing the existing data from a different perspective, which in turn suggested a new series of experiments. Similarly, Gilbert and Mulkay found that the sections of the scientific papers that described the experimental methodology portrayed the procedures in terms that suggested they were neutral operations that were largely independent of the scientist and could be replicated by anyone. In the research interviews, however, the scientists emphasized the operation of practical skills that are the product of experience and developing a 'feel' for experimental work. As one scientist put it:

How could you write it up? It would be like trying to write a description of how to beat an egg. Or like trying to read a book on how to ski. You'd just get the wrong idea altogether. You've got to go and watch it, see it, do it. There's no substitute for it. These are *practical* skills. We all know that practical skills are not well taught by bits of paper.   (quoted in Gilbert and Mulkay 1984: 53)

Gilbert and Mulkay argue that in the formal context of the scientific paper an *empiricist repertoire*

Box 17.5 Discourse analysis in action: The study of interpretative repertoires in scientists' discourse

Gilbert and Mulkay's (1984) research on scientists' discourse is concerned with the field of bioenergetics and in particular with the process whereby scientists working in this area come to understand a mechanism dubbed by them 'oxidative phosphorylation'. The main source of Gilbert and Mulkay's data derives from interviews with thirty-four researchers in this field. The interviews lasted between two-and-a-half and three hours on average. The authors describe the process of analysing the resulting data as follows:

The interviews were tape-recorded and transcribed in full. We then read through the transcripts and copied those pages which included material relating to the topics which interested us. The passages from the interviews concerning each topic were placed together in 'topic files', so that we had convenient access to all the material on, for instance, consensus or diagrams and pictorial representations. We aimed to make each file as inclusive as possible so that no passage which could be read as dealing with a particular topic was omitted from its file. (Gilbert and Mulkay 1984: 19)

In addition, the authors drew on further sources, such as: privately circulated letters written by leading authorities in the field; the main articles in the field; and copies of the chief textbooks in the field.

---

prevailed. This concept was derived from 'the observation that the texts of experimental papers display certain recurrent stylistic, grammatical and lexical features which appear to be coherently related' (1984: 55–6). The empiricist repertoire was revealed in such features as: an emphasis on procedural routines in the conduct of experiments, such that the findings appear as an inevitable, logical outcome; no mention of theoretical commitments on the part of authors; and an impersonal writing style with little or no mention of the authors' role in the production of the findings. By contrast, in the informal milieu of the research interview, a *contingent repertoire* was in operation. In this context, 'scientists presented their actions and beliefs as heavily dependent on speculative insights, prior intellectual commitments, personal characteristics, indescribable skills, social ties and group membership' (1984: 56). In other words, when describing their research within a contingent repertoire, scientists were much less likely to present their findings as the inevitable outcome of their experimental engagement with natural phenomena and were therefore far more likely to recognize their own role in the production of scientific findings. Gilbert and Mulkay then go on to show that, when scientists disagree with the positions of other scientists, they describe their own work within an empiricist repertoire, in which their own findings take on the character of natural inevitability through the following of proper procedure, but that of other scientists within a contingent repertoire, which shows up their competitors' errors as the product of prejudices, theoretical commitments, bias, and so on.

The notion of the interpretative repertoire is interesting because it brings out the idea that belief and action take place within templates that guide and influence the writer or speaker. The two repertoires discussed by Gilbert and Mulkay by no means exhaust the range of possibilities: Potter and Wetherell (1987), for example, suggest that a community repertoire was used in the context of a riot in Bristol in 1980 to cast light on events and beliefs. In the process, the police were cast in the role of *agents provocateurs* rather than as keepers of the peace. What is particularly striking about Gilbert and Mulkay's research, however, is that the two repertoires are employed by scientists but in different contexts (in formal or informal contexts, and whether describing their own or competitors' procedures). In a similar vein, Billig's (1992: 149) research on the ways in which people talk about the royal family suggested that, when referring to the role of newspapers in providing information about its members, two positions were frequently held and deployed on different occasions: 'the papers as the sources of lies and the papers as the source of knowledge'. Such a recognition of the almost simultaneous use of different repertoires brings to the fore the 'dilemmatic' nature of thinking in these and other environments (Billig *et al.* 1988).

Producing facts

As with the exposition of interpretative repertoires in DA, in this section a study will be employed as a lens through which to view the practice of discourse analytic research. On this occasion, the emphasis is upon the resources that are employed in conveying allegedly factual knowledge. The researchers were especially interested in the role of what they call *quantification rhetoric*, by which is meant the ways in which numerical and non-numerical statements are made to support or refute arguments. The interest in this issue lies in part in the importance of quantification in everyday life and in part in the tendency for many social scientists to make use of this strategy themselves (John 1992). The specific focus of the research was upon a study of a television programme shown on Channel 4 in April 1988 and entitled *Cancer: Your Money or Your Life* (Potter *et al.* 1991; Potter and Wetherell 1994). Among other things, the pro-

gramme claimed to show that the huge amounts of money donated by the public to cancer charities are doing little to 'cure' the disease. The details of the materials used in the research and an outline of the process of analysis are provided in Box 17.6. Box 17.7 provides a key part of the transcript for the television programme itself.

In proceeding with an analysis of their data, such as the portions of transcript in Box 17.7, Potter and Wetherell employed several devices.

Using variation as a lever

The authors draw attention to the phrase '1 per cent of a quarter of a million' (see Box 17.7), because it incorporates two quantitative expressions: a relative expression (a percentage) and an absolute frequency (quarter of a million). The change of the register of quantification is important, because it allows the programme makers to make their case about the low cure levels (just 1 per cent) compared with the large number of new cases of cancer. They could have pointed to the absolute number of people who are cured, but the impact would have been less. Also, the 1 per cent is not being contrasted with 243,000 but with quarter of a million. Not only does this citation

---

Box 17.6 Discourse analysis in action: Producing facts through quantification rhetoric

The study of the representation of facts in the television programme *Cancer: Your Money or Your Life* (Potter *et al.* 1991; Potter and Wetherell 1994) used a variety of different sources:

- a video recording of the programme;
- the observations of one of the members of the team making the programme, who acted as a participant observer while it was being made;
- drafts of the script, shooting schedules, and recordings of editing sessions;
- the entire interviews with the various people interviewed for the programme (such as cancer research specialists and heads of charities);
- research interviews with some of the latter people;
- research interviews with some of the people involved in making the programme.

One of the phases of the analysis entailed the 'coding' of the various sources that had been collected. The authors tell us:

We made a list of about a dozen keywords and phrases that related to the sequence—percentage, cure rates, death rates, 1 per cent, etc.—and then ran through each of the interview and interaction files, looking for them with a standard word-processor . . . Whenever we got a 'hit' we would read the surrounding text to see if it had relevance to our target sequence. When it did we would copy it across to an already opened coding file . . . noting the transcript page numbers at the same time. If we were not sure if the sequence was relevant we copied it anyway, for, unlike the sorts of coding that take place in traditional content analysis, the coding is not the analysis itself but a preliminary to make the task of analysis manageable.   (Potter and Wetherell 1994: 52)

A prominent sequence used in the research is provided in Box 17.7.

Box 17.7 Sequence from the study of the television programme *Cancer: Your Money or Your Life*

The following sequence occurred roughly halfway through the programme, following interviews with cancer scientists who cast doubt on whether their research, much of it funded by charities, results in successful treatment:

COMMENTARY: The message from these scientists is clear—exactly like the public—they hope their basic research will lead to cures in the future—although at the moment they can't say how this will happen. In the meantime, their aim is to increase scientific knowledge on a broad front and they're certainly achieving this. But do their results justify them getting so much of the money that has been given to help fight cancer? When faced with this challenge the first thing the charities point to are the small number of cancers which are now effectively curable.

[on screen: DR NIGEL KEMP CANCER RESEARCH CAMPAIGN]

KEMP: The outlook for individuals suffering from a number of types of cancer has been totally revolutionized. I mean for example—children suffering from acute leukaemia—in old days if they lived six months they were lucky—now more than half the children with leukaemia are cured. And the same applies to a number of other cancers—Hodgkin's Disease in young people, testicular tumours in young men, and we all know about Bob Champion's success [Champion was a prominent jockey who contracted testicular cancer, made a much-heralded recovery, won the Grand National, and even had a movie made about him].   (Potter and Wetherell 1994: 52–3)

At this point a table showing the annual incidence of thirty-four types of cancer begins to scroll on the screen. The total incidence is 243,000 and the individual incidences range from placenta (20) to lung (41,400). The three forms of cancer mentioned by Kemp and their levels of incidence are highlighted in yellow: childhood leukaemia (350), testis (1,000), and Hodgkin's Disease (1,400). The programme continues while the table is scrolling.

COMMENTARY: But those three curable types are amongst the rarest cancers—they represent around 1 per cent of a quarter of a million cases of cancers diagnosed each year. Most deaths are caused by a small number of very common cancers.

KEMP: We are well aware of the fact that erm once people develop lung cancer or stomach cancer or cancer of the bowel sometimes—the outlook is very bad and aaa obviously one is frustrated by the sss relatively slow rate of progress on the one hand but equally I think there are a lot of real opportunities and and positive signs that advances can be made—even in the more intractable cancers.   (Potter and Wetherell 1994: 53)

---

allow the figure to grow by 7,000 but also quarter of a million sounds larger.

Reading the detail

Discourse analysts incorporate the CA preference for attention to the details of discourse. For example, Potter and Wetherell suggest that the description of the three 'curable cancers' as 'amongst the rarest cancers' is deployed to imply that these are atypical cancers, so that it is unwise to generalize to all cancers from experiences with them.

Looking for rhetorical detail

Attention to rhetorical detail entails a sensitivity to the ways in which arguments are constructed. Thus, during the editing of the film, the programme makers' discourse suggested they were looking for ways to provide a convincing argument for their case that cancer remains largely intractable in spite of the money spent on it. The programme makers very consciously devised the strategy outlined in the discussion of 'using variation as a lever' of playing down the numerical significance of those cancers that are amenable to treatment. Moreover, Potter *et al.* (1991) point out that one element of their argumentative strategy is to employ a tactic they call a 'preformulation', whereby a possible counter-argument is discounted in the course of presenting an argument, as when the commentary informs us: 'When faced with this challenge the first thing the charities point to are the small number of cancers which are now effectively curable.'

Looking for accountability

Discourse analysts draw on CA practitioners' interest in and approach to accounts. The programme makers were concerned to be accountable for the position they took, and Potter and Wetherell's (1994: 61) transcript of an editing session suggest they were keen to ensure they could defend their inference about the 1 per cent. From the point of view of both CA and DA, the extracts presented in Box 17.7 can and should be regarded as accounts. The editing session notes suggest that it is the credibility of the account that was of concern to the programme makers. For DA practitioners, the search for accountability entails attending to the details through which accounts are constructed.

Cross-referencing discourse studies

Potter and Wetherell suggest that reading other discourse studies is itself an important activity. First, it helps to sharpen the analytic mentality at the heart of DA. Secondly, other studies often provide insights that are suggestive for one's own data. They indicate that they were influenced by a study of market traders by Pinch and Clark (1986). This research showed that a kind of quantification rhetoric was often being used by the traders (though Pinch and Clark did not use this term) in order to convey a sense of value (such as selling a pen with a pencil). It appeared that something similar was occurring when the table was being scrolled whereby the large number of cancers and the long list of types was being contrasted with the small number (three) of curable ones.

Overview

As this discussion of DA has emphasized on several occasions, DA draws on insights from CA. Particularly when analysing strings of talk, DA draws on conversation analytic insights into the ways in which interaction is realized in and through talk in interaction. The CA injunction to focus on the talk itself and the ways in which intersubjective meaning is accomplished in sequences of talk is also incorporated into DA. This is not easy to accomplish, and, when one reads articles based on DA, it sometimes seems as though the practitioners come perilously close to invoking speculations that do not seem to be directly discernible in the sequences being analysed—that is, speculations about 'ethnographic particulars' and hence about motives.

Sometimes, there is a more explicit recognition of the potential contribution of an appreciation of the ethnographic context. Edley and Wetherell (1997) report findings relating to a study conducted within a DA framework. The data were gathered from discussions held in three-person groups with 17–18-year-old boys in a UK school. The focus of the article was upon the construction of masculinity as it emerged in the course of the group discussions. However, one of the authors carried out observations within the school. This ethnographic research 'led to the identification of divisions within friendship groups in the sixth form as a major participant concern connected with formulations of masculinity within the school' (1997: 207). One of the key components of the friendship structure was the division between rugby players and the rest. Edley and Wetherell show that an important component of the construction of masculinity during talk among the non-players is their antipathy towards the rugby players. In other words, they defined their masculinity in contradistinction to the concepts of masculinity associated with the rugby players. However, the key point is that it is clear that the periods of ethnographic observation at least in part informed the discourse analytic interpretation of the sequences of talk that had been recorded. Such research suggests that the proscription concerning the recourse to ethnographic particulars is honoured more by some discourse analysts than others. It is easy to see why: attention to ethnographic details may alert the analyst to nuances and understandings that are not directly entrenched in the flow of discourse.

DA is in certain respects a more flexible approach to language in social research than CA, because it is not solely concerned with the analysis of naturally occurring talk, since practitioners also use various kinds of documents and research interviews in their work. Also, it permits the intrusion of understandings of what is going on that are not spe-cific to the immediacy of previous utterances. It is precisely this to which conversation analysts object, as when Schegloff (1997: 183) writes about DA: 'Dis-course is too often made subservient to contexts not of its participants' making, but of its analysts' insist-ence.' For their part, discourse analysts object to the restriction that this injunction imposes, because it means that conversation analysts 'rarely raise their eyes from the next turn in the conversation, and, further, this is not an entire conversation or sizeable slice of social life but usually a tiny fragment' (Wetherell 1998: 402). Thus, for discourse analysts, phenomena like interpretative repertoires are very much part of the context within which talk occurs, whereas in CA they are inadmissible evidence. But it is here that we see the dilemma for the discourse analyst, for, in seeking to admit a broader sense of context (such as attention to interpretative reper-toires in operation) while wanting to stick close to the conversation analysts' distaste for ethnographic particulars, they are faced with the uncertainty of just how far to go in allowing the inclusion of conversationally extraneous factors.

The anti-realist inclination of many DA prac-titioners has been a source of controversy, because the emphasis on representational practices through discourses sidelines any notion of a pre-existing material reality that can constrain individual agency. Reality becomes little more than that which is constituted in and through discourse. This lack of attention to a material reality that lies behind and underpins discourse has proved too abstracted for some social researchers and theorists. For example, writing from a critical realist position (see Box 1.8, p. 13), Reed (2000) has argued that discourses should be examined in relation to social structures, such as power relationships, that are responsible for the occasioning of those discourses. Attention would additionally be focused on the ways in which discourses then work through existing structures. Discourse is thereby conceived as a 'generative mechanism' rather than as a self-referential sphere in which nothing of significance exists outside it. Reed provides an interesting example of such an alternative view:

Discourses—such as the quantitatively based discourses of financial audit, quality control and risk management— are now seen as the generative mechanisms through which new regulatory regimes 'carried out' by rising expert groups—such as accountants, engineers and scientists—become established and legitimated in mod-ern societies. What they represent is less important than what they do in facilitating a radical re-ordering of pre-existing institutional structures in favour of social groups who benefit from the upward mobility which such innovative regulatory regimes facilitate . . . (Reed 2000: 529)

As this passage suggests, while many DA practi-tioners are anti-realist, an alternative, realist position in relation to discourse is feasible. Such an alterna-tive position is perhaps closer to the classic concerns of the social sciences than an anti-realist stance.

Key points

- Both CA and DA approaches take the position that language is itself a focus of interest and not just a medium through which research participants communicate with researchers.

- CA is a systematic approach to conversation that locates action in talk.

- In CA, talk is deemed to be structured in the sense of following rules.

- Practitioners of CA seek to make inferences about talk that are not grounded in contextual details that are extraneous to talk.

- DA shares many features with CA but there are several different versions of it.

- DA can be applied to a wider variety of phenomena than CA, which is just concerned with naturally occurring talk.

- Discourse is conceived of as a means of conveying meaning.

- DA practitioners display a greater inclination to relate meaning in talk to contextual factors.

Revision questions

- In what ways does the role of language in conversation and discourse analysis differ from that which is typical in most other research methods?

Conversation analysis

- In what ways is CA fundamentally about the production of social order in interaction?
- Why are tape recording and transcription crucial in CA?
- What is meant by each of the following: turn-taking; adjacency pair; preference organization; account; repair mechanism?
- How do the terms in the last question relate to the production of social order?
- Evaluate Schegloff's argument that CA obviates the need to make potentially unwarranted assumptions about participants' motives.

Discourse analysis

- What is the significance of saying that DA is anti-realist and constructionist?
- What is an interpretative repertoire?
- What techniques are available to the discourse analyst when trying to understand the ways in which facts are presented through discourse?
- What are the chief points of difference between CA and DA?

18 Documents as sources of data

Reader's guide

The term 'documents' covers a very wide range of different kinds of source. This chapter aims to reflect that variability by examining a wide range of different documentary sources that have been or can be used in qualitative research. In addition, the chapter touches on approaches to the analysis of such sources. The chapter explores:

- personal documents in both written form (such as diaries and letters) and visual form (such as photographs);

- official documents deriving from the state (such as public inquiries);

- official documents deriving from private sources (such as documents produced by organizations);
- mass media outputs;
- virtual outputs, such as Internet resources;
- the criteria for evaluating each of the above sources;
- how far readers of documents are active or passive consumers of documents;
- three approaches to the analysis of documents: qualitative content analysis; semiotics; and hermeneutics.

Introduction

This chapter will be concerned with a fairly heterogeneous set of sources of data, such as letters, diaries, autobiographies, newspapers, magazines, and photographs. The emphasis is placed on documents that have not been produced at the request of a social researcher—instead, the objects that are the focus of this chapter are simply 'out there' waiting to be assembled and analysed. However, this is not to suggest that the fact that documents are available for the social researcher to work on renders them somehow less time-consuming or easier to deal with than needing to collect primary data. On the contrary, the search for documents relevant to your research can often be a frustrating and highly protracted process. Moreover, once they are collected, considerable interpretative skill is required to ascertain the meaning of the materials that have been uncovered.

Documents of the kind referred to in this chapter are materials that

- can be read (though the term 'read' has to be understood in a somewhat looser fashion than is normally the case when we come to visual materials, like photographs);
- have not been produced specifically for the purpose of social research;
- are preserved so that they become available for analysis; and
- are relevant to the concerns of the social researcher.

Documents have already been encountered in this book, albeit in a variety of contexts or guises. For example, the kinds of source upon which content analysis is often carried out are documents, such as newspaper articles. However, the emphasis in this chapter will be upon the use of documents in qualitative research. A further way in which documents have previously surfaced was in the brief discussion in Box 10.6 (p. 209), which noted that archive materials are one form of unobtrusive measure. Indeed, this points to an often-noted advantage of using documents of the kind discussed in this chapter—namely, they are non-reactive. This means that, because they have not been created specifically for the purposes of social research, the possibility of a reactive effect can be largely discounted as a limitation on the validity of data.

In discussing the different kinds of documents used in the social sciences, J. Scott (1990) has usefully distinguished between personal documents and official documents and has further classified the latter in terms of private as opposed to state documents. These distinctions will be employed in much of the discussion that follows. A further set of important distinctions made by Scott relate to the criteria for assessing the quality of documents. He suggests (J. Scott 1990:6) four criteria.

- *Authenticity*. Is the evidence genuine and of unquestionable origin?
- *Credibility*. Is the evidence free from error and distortion?
- *Representativeness*. Is the evidence typical of its

kind, and, if not, is the extent of its untypicality known?

- *Meaning.* Is the evidence clear and comprehensible?

This is an extremely rigorous set of criteria against which documents might be gauged, and frequent reference to them will be made in the following discussion.

Personal documents

Diaries, letters, and autobiographies

Diaries and letters have been used a great deal by historians but have not been given a great deal of attention by social researchers. The latter have tended to employ these as sources when they have been specifically elicited from their authors. The researcher-driven diary has been used as a method of data collection in both quantitative and qualitative research (see Boxes 1.3 and 6.4, pp. 7, 137). A similar approach can be employed in relation to letters: for example, Ang (1985) placed an advertisement in a Dutch women's magazine asking readers to write to her about their reactions to and feelings about the American television series *Dallas*. She received forty-two letters in response to this advertisement. However, the kinds of diary and letter that are the focus of attention here are ones that have not been solicited by a researcher. Boxes 18.1 and 18.2 provide examples of the use of personal documents in social research in both historical and more contemporary contexts.

It is likely that the potential of letters in historical and social research is or will be fairly limited to a certain time period. As J. Scott (1990) observes, letter writing became a significant activity only after the introduction of an official postal service and in particular after the penny post in 1840. The emergence of the telephone as a prevalent form of communication may have limited the use of letter writing, and it is likely that the emergence of e-mail communication, especially in so far as e-mails are not kept in electronic or printed form, is likely to mean that the role of letters has been declining for some time and

may continue to do so. On the other hand, there is growing interest in e-mails in their own right among social researchers. For example, Sharf (1999) has reported how, while conducting research into rhetoric about breast cancer, she joined a listserv (a managed list of e-mail addresses around a specific theme) on breast cancer and gradually realized that electronic communications had considerable potential for her research.

Whereas letters are a form of communication with other people, diarists invariably write for themselves, but, when written for wider consumption, diaries are difficult to distinguish from another kind of personal document—the autobiography. Like letters and diaries, autobiographies can be written at the behest of the researcher, particularly in connection with life history studies (see Box 15.4, p. 316). When used in relation to the life history or biographical method, letters, diaries, and autobiographies (whether solicited or unsolicited) can either be the primary source of data or may be used as adjuncts to another source of data, such as life history or life story interviews. However, it is with extant (that is, unsolicited) documents that this chapter is primarily concerned.

The widespread distinction between biographies and autobiographies can sometimes break down. Walt Disney provides a case in point. As I have shown, Disney provided, in short articles he authored and in articles written by others, many snippets about his life (Bryman 1995). The first biography of Disney, written by his daughter, Diane Disney Miller (1956), would almost certainly have been fed information by its subject. Moreover, several writers have noted the 'sameness' about subsequent biographies. This feature can be attributed to the tight control by

Box 18.1 Using historical personal documents: The case of Augustus Lamb

Dickinson (1993) provides an interesting account of the use of historical personal documents in the case of Augustus Lamb (1807–36), who was the only child of Lady Caroline Lamb and William Lamb, the second Viscount Melbourne. It is possible that Augustus suffered throughout his short life from epilepsy, though he seems to have suffered from other complaints as well. Dickinson was drawn to him because of her interest in nineteenth-century reactions to people with mental handicaps who were not institutionalized. In fact, Dickinson doubts whether the term 'mental handicap' is applicable to Augustus and suggests the somewhat milder description of having learning difficulties. The chief sources of data are 'letters from family and friends; letters to, about and

(rarely) from Augustus' (1993: 122). These letters were found in collections at the Hertfordshire County Office, the British Museum, and Southampton University Library. Other sources used include: the record of the post-mortem examination of Augustus and extracts from the diary of Augustus's resident tutor and physician for the years 1817–21. Dickinson employs these materials to demonstrate the difficulty of arriving at a definitive portrayal of what Augustus was like. At the same time, she shows the difficulties that people around him experienced in coming to terms with his conditions, in large part because of the difficulty they experienced in finding a vocabulary that was consistent with his high social status.

the Disney Archive, which is itself controlled by the Walt Disney Corporation. It is from the primary materials of this archive (letters, notes of meetings, and so on) that biographies would be fashioned. As a result, while Walt Disney never wrote an autobiography in the conventional meaning of the term, his hand and subsequently that of the company can be seen in the biographies that have been written.

When we evaluate personal documents, the *authenticity* criterion is clearly of considerable importance. Is the purported author of the letter or diary the real author? In the case of autobiographies, this has become a growing problem in recent years as a result of the increasing use of 'ghost' writers by the famous. But the same is potentially true of other documents. For example, in the case of Augustus Lamb (Box 18.1), Dickinson (1993: 126–7) notes that there are 'only three letters existing from Augustus himself (which we cannot be certain were written in Augustus's own hand, since the use of amanuenses was not uncommon)'. This remark raises the question of how far Augustus was in fact the author of the entirety of the letters, especially in the light of his apparent learning difficulties. Turning to the issue of *credibility*, J. Scott (1990) observes that there are at least two major concerns with respect to personal documents: the factual accuracy of reports and

whether they do in fact report the true feelings of the writer. The case of Augustus Lamb, in which clear differences were found in views about him and his condition, suggests that the notion that there might be a definitive factually accurate account is at the very least problematic. Scott recommends a strategy of healthy scepticism regarding the sincerity with which the writer reports his or her true feelings. Famous people may be fully aware that their letters or diaries will be of considerable interest to others and may, therefore, have one eye firmly fixed on the degree to which they really reveal themselves in their writings, or alternatively ensure that they convey a 'front' that they want to project.

Autobiographies have to be treated with similar caution, since they can frequently be exercises in reputation building. In the case of the suicide notes analysed by Jacobs (1967) (see Box 18.2), although the notes themselves were found to be rational and coherent, it is possible that the individuals themselves were in a highly distressed state, so that it is not clear how far their true feelings were being revealed.

Representativeness is clearly a major concern for these materials. Since literacy was far lower in earlier times, letters, diaries, and autobiographies are likely to be the preserve of the literate and by and large the middle class. Moreover, since boys were often more likely to receive an education than girls, the voices of women tend to be under-represented in these documents. Women are also less likely to have had the self-confidence to write diaries and autobiographies. Therefore, such historical documents are likely to be biased in terms of authorship. A further problem is the selective survival of documents like letters. Why do any survive at all and what proportion are damaged, lost, or thrown away? We do not know, for example, how representative the 112 suicide notes analysed by Jacobs (1967; see Box 18.2) are. Quite aside from the fact that only a relatively small percentage of suicide victims leave notes, it may be that they are sometimes destroyed by family members. The question of *meaning* is often rendered problematic by such things as damage to letters and diaries and the use by authors of abbreviations or codes that are difficult to decipher. Also, as J. Scott (1990) observes, letter writers may leave much unsaid in their communications, because they share with their recipients common values and assumptions that are not revealed.

Box 18.2 **Using contemporary personal documents**

Jacobs (1967) analysed 112 suicide notes written by adults and adolescents in the Los Angeles area who had successfully committed suicide. The notes were acquired in the course of a study of attempts by adolescents to commit suicide. The author writes that he was impressed with the 'rational and coherent character' of the notes (1967: 62) and attempts what he describes as a 'phenomenological' analysis of them. This analysis entailed attending to 'the conscious deliberations that take place before the individual is able to consider and execute the act of suicide' (1967: 64). Jacobs found that the notes fell into six groups, such as notes referring to an illness, a category which in turn was of two types: those in which the writers begged forgiveness and those in which they did not.

Visual objects

There is a growing interest in the visual in social research. The photograph is the most obvious manifestation of this trend, in that, rather than being thought of as incidental to the research process, photographs are becoming objects of interest in their own right. Once again, there is a distinction between photographs and other visual objects that are produced as part of fieldwork and those that are extant (which are the focus of attention here). One of the main ways in which photographs may be of interest to social research is in terms of what they reveal about families. As J. Scott (1990) observes, many family photographs are taken as a record of ceremonial occasions (weddings, christenings) and of recurring events such as Christmas, annual holidays, and wearing a new uniform at the start of the new school year. Scott refers to a distinction between three types of home photograph: *idealization*, which is a formal pose—for example, the wedding photograph or a photograph of the family in its finery; *natural portrayal*, which entails capturing actions as they happen, though there may be a contrived component to the photograph; and *demystification*, which entails capturing an image of the subject in an untypical (and often embarrassing) situation. Scott suggests that it is necessary to be aware of these different types in order not to be exclusively concerned with the superficial appearance of the images and so that we can probe beneath that surface. He writes:

There is a great deal that photographs do not tell us about their world. Hirsch [1981: 42] argues, for example, that 'The prim poses and solemn faces which we associate with Victorian photography conceal the reality of child labour, women factory workers, whose long hours often brought about the neglect of their infants, nannies sedating their charges with rum, and mistresses diverting middle class fathers.'   (J. Scott 1990: 195)

As Scott argues, this means not only that the photograph must not be taken at its face value when used as a research source; it is also necessary to have considerable additional knowledge of the social context to probe beneath the surface. In fact, one might

Box 18.3 Photographs of the Magic Kingdom

Sutton (1992) has noted a paradox about people's visits to Disney theme parks. On the one hand, the Magic Kingdom is supposed to be 'the happiest place on Earth' with employees ('cast members') being trained to enhance the experience. However, it is clear that some people do not enjoy themselves while visiting a park. The time spent in queues, in particular, was a gripe for Sutton, as it often is for other visitors ('guests') (Bryman 1995). Nonetheless, people expect their visit to be momentous and therefore take along their cameras (and increasingly camcorders, though Sutton does not make this point).

Sutton argues that photographs distort people's memories of their visit. They take pictures that support their anticipation that the Disney theme parks are happy places, and, when they return home, they 'discard photographs that remind them of unpleasant experiences and keep photographs that remind them of pleasant experiences' (Sutton 1992: 283). In other words, positive feelings are a post-visit reconstruction that are substantially aided by one's photographs. As a result, Sutton argues, the photographs do not provide accurate recollections of a visit but distorted ones.

wonder whether the photograph in such a situation can be of any use to a researcher at all. The researcher does not need the photograph to uncover the ills that formed the underbelly of Victorian society; its only purpose seems to be to suggest that there is a gap between the photographic image and the underlying reality. A similar kind of point is made by Sutton in Box 18.3.

Scott sees the issue of *representativeness* as a particular problem for the analyst of photographs. As he suggests, the photographs that survive the passage of time—for example, in archives—are very unlikely to be representative. They are likely to have been subject to all sorts of hazards, such as damage and selective retention. The example provided in Box 18.3 of photographs of visits to Disney theme parks suggests that the process of discarding photographs may be systematic. The other problem relates to the issue of what is not photographed, as suggested by the quotation by Hirsch, and Sutton's suggestion that unhappy events at Disney theme parks may not be photographed at all. A sensitivity to what is not photographed can reveal the 'mentality' of the person(s) behind the

camera. This is the point that Sutton is making: the absence of photographs depicting less happy experiences at the parks suggests something about how the prospect of a visit to a Disney theme park is viewed and therefore tells us something about the reach of an influential corporation in the culture industry. What is clear is that the question of representativeness is much more fundamental than the issue of what survives, because it points to the way in which the selective survival of photographs may be constitutive of a reality that family members (or others) seek to fashion. As in Sutton's example, that very manufactured reality may then become a focus of interest for the social researcher in its own right.

Moreover, such considerations do not take account of the possibility of active distortion of photographs through tricks and the use of props to create artificial effects. Stalin ensured, for example, that his adversary Leon Trotsky, whom he had exiled and assassinated, was airbrushed out of existence in classic photographs of the Russian Revolution in which he appeared alongside Lenin (B. Hammersley 1999).

Official documents deriving from the state

The state is the source of a great deal of information of potential significance for social researchers. It produces a great deal of statistical information, some of which was touched on in Chapter 10. In addition to such quantitative data, the state is the source of a great deal of textual material of potential interest, such as Acts of Parliament and official reports.

An interesting use of official documents is Turner's (1994) employment of the reports of public inquiries into three disasters, one of which—the fire at the Summerland Leisure Centre, Douglas, Isle of Man, in 1973—is a particular emphasis in his discussion. The report was published in 1974. Turner was primarily interested in the preconditions of the fire—the factors that were deemed by the inquiry to have led to the fire itself and to the way in which the handling of the incident produced such disastrous consequences (fifty deaths). In his initial analysis, which was based on a grounded theory approach, Turner aimed to produce a theoretical account of the fire's preconditions. Turner describes the process for this and the other two public inquiry reports he examined as one of slowly going through the details of the report. He describes the process as follows:

I asked, for each paragraph, what names or 'labels for ideas' I needed in order to identify those elements, events or notions which were of interest to me in my broad and initially very unfocused concern to develop a theory of disaster preconditions. I then recorded each name or concept label on the top of a 5 inch by 8 inch card, together with a note of the source paragraph, and added further paragraph references to the card as I encountered additional instances of the concept identified.   (Turner 1994: 198)

He ended up with 182 of these cards, which provided the raw materials for building his theoretical model. Similar sources were employed by Weick (1990) in his study of the Tenerife plane crash in 1977, in that he used an official report of the Spanish Ministry of Transport and Communication and a further report by the US-based Airline Pilots Association.

Similar kinds of materials but in a different context were employed by Abraham (1994) in connection with his research on the medical drug Opren. The research was concerned with the role of interests and values in scientists' evaluations of the safety of medicines. The author describes his sources as 'publicly available transcripts of the testimonies of scientists, including many employed in the manufacture of Opren, Parliamentary debates, questions and answers in Hansard, ad leaflets, letters, consultation papers and other documentation disposed by the British regulatory authority in respect of its duties under the 1968 British Medicines Act' (Abraham 1994: 720). Abraham's research shows that there were inconsistencies in the scientists' testimonies, suggesting that interests play an important role in such situations. He also uses his findings to infer that the notion of a scientific ethos, which has been influential in the sociology of science, has limited applicability in areas of controversy in which interests come to the surface.

In terms of J. Scott's (1990) four criteria, such materials can certainly be seen as authentic and as having meaning (in the sense of being clear and comprehensible to the researcher), but the two other standards require somewhat greater consideration. The question of credibility raises the issue of whether the documentary source is biased. This is exactly the point of Abraham's (1994) research. In other words, such documents can be interesting precisely because of the biases they reveal. Equally, this point suggests that caution is necessary in attempting to treat them as depictions of reality. The issue of representativeness is complicated in that materials like these are in a sense unique and it is precisely their official or quasi-official character that makes them interesting in their own right. There is also, of course, the question of whether the case itself is representative, but in the context of qualitative research this is not a meaningful question, because no case can be representative in a statistical sense. The issue is one of establishing a cogent theoretical account and possibly examining that account in other contexts. Turner (1994) in fact examined three disasters and noted many common factors that were associated with behaviour in crisis situations.

Official documents deriving from private sources

This is a very heterogeneous group of sources, but one type that has been used a great deal is company documents. Companies (and indeed organizations generally) produce many documents. Some of these are in the public domain, such as annual reports, mission statements, press releases, advertisements, and public relations material in printed form and on the World Wide Web. Other documents are not (or may not be) in the public domain, such as company newsletters, organizational charts, minutes of meetings, memos, internal and external correspondence, manuals for new recruits, and so on. Such materials are often used by organizational ethnographers as part of their investigations, but the difficulty of gaining access to some organizations means that many researchers have to rely on public domain documents alone. Even if the researcher is an insider who has gained access to an organization, it may well be that certain documents that are not in the public domain will not be available to him or her. For his study of ICI, Pettigrew (see Box 2.23, p. 51) was allowed access to company archives, so that, in addition to interviewing, he was allowed to examine 'materials on company strategy and personnel policy, documents relating to the birth and development of various company OD [organizational development] groups, files documenting the natural history of key organizational changes, and information on the recruitment and training of internal OD consultants, and the use made of external OD consultants' (Pettigrew 1985: 41).

Such information can be very important for researchers conducting case studies of organizations using such methods as participant observation or (as in Pettigrew's case) qualitative interviews. Other writers have relied more or less exclusively on documents. The study of the film director Alfred Hitchcock by Kapsis (1989) employed a combination of personal documents (notably correspondence) and official documents, such as production notes and publicity files (Box 18.4).

Such documents need to be evaluated using Scott's four criteria. As with the materials considered in the previous section, documents deriving from private sources like companies are likely to be authentic and meaningful (in the sense of being clear and comprehensible to the researcher), though this is not to suggest that the analyst of documents should be complacent. Issues of credibility and representativeness are likely to exercise the analyst of documents somewhat more.

People who write documents are likely to have a particular point of view that they want to get across. An interesting illustration of this simple observation is provided by a study of company documentation by Forster (1994). In the course of a study of career developments issues in a major British retail company (referred to pseudonymously as TC), Forster carried out an extensive analysis of company documentation relating primarily to human resource management issues, as well as interviews and a questionnaire survey. Because he was able to interview many of the authors of the documents about what they had written, 'both the accuracy of the documents and their authorship could be validated by the individuals who had produced them' (1994: 155). In other words, the authenticity of the documents was confirmed and it would seem that credibility was verified as well. However, Forster also tells us that the documents showed up divergent interpretations among different groupings of key events and processes:

One of the clearest themes to emerge was the apparently incompatible interpretations of the same events and processes amongst the three sub-groups within the company—senior executives, HQ personnel staff and regional personnel managers. . . . These documents were not produced deliberately to distort or obscure events or processes being described, but their effect was to do precisely this. (Forster 1994: 160)

In other words, members of the different groupings expressed through the documents certain perspectives that reflected their positions in the organization. Consequently, although authors of the documents could confirm the content of those

---

Box 18.4 Constructing Alfred Hitchcock: Personal and official documents

The focus of Kapsis's (1989) study of Alfred Hitchcock is the way in which a reputation is fashioned in popular culture. In particular, he emphasizes the way in which Hitchcock's reputation as a director changed in the 1960s and beyond from that of a popular entertainer to that of a celebrated maker of highly significant films. Kapsis's analysis emphasizes the importance of sponsors, such as the influential French director François Truffaut, in the process of re-evaluation of his work, as well as the part played by Hitchcock himself. The main source was the director's personal files, which had been lodged with the Academy of Motion Picture Arts and Sciences. This collection is made up of materials that could be described as

both personal and official documents, as well as other sources:

- scripts, production notes, and publicity files;
- correspondence, especially between Hitchcock and Truffaut and with various arts organizations;
- fifty-two hours of taped interviews with Truffaut;
- speeches delivered between 1960 and 1975;
- newspaper and magazine clippings, especially reviews;
- interviews by Kapsis with various people associated with Hitchcock.

---

documents, the latter could not be regarded as 'free from error and distortion', as J. Scott puts it. Therefore, documents cannot be regarded as providing objective accounts of a state of affairs. They have to be interrogated and examined in the context of other sources of data. As Forster's case suggests, the different stances that are taken up by the authors of documents can be used as a platform for developing insights into the processes and factors that lie behind divergence. In this instance, the documents are interesting in bringing out the role and significance of subcultures within the organization.

Issues of representativeness are likely to loom large in most contexts of this kind. Did Forster have access to a totally comprehensive set of documents? It could be that some had been destroyed or that he

was not allowed access to certain documents that were regarded as sensitive. The case of the documents relating to Alfred Hitchcock is particularly interesting in this regard (see Box 18.4). Hitchcock or possibly others may not have deposited documents that were less than favourable to his image. Since Kapsis's article is concerned with reputation building and particularly with the active part played by Hitchcock and others in the construction of his reputation as a significant film maker, the part played by documents that might have been less than supportive of this reputation would be of considerable importance. This is not to say that such documents necessarily exist but that doubts are bound to surface whenever there is uncertainty about the representativeness of sources.

Mass media outputs

Newspapers, magazines, television programmes, films, and other mass media are potential sources for social scientific analysis. Of course, we have encountered these kinds of source before when exploring content analysis in Chapter 9. In addition to exploring mass media outputs using a quantita-

tive form of data analysis like content analysis, such sources can also be examined so that their qualitative nature is preserved. Typically, such analysis entails searching for themes in the sources that are examined, but see the discussion on analysing documents below for a more detailed examination of this issue.

In Chapter 9, Beharrell's (1993) content analysis of AIDS/HIV in the British press was cited as an illustration of different aspects of content analysis on several occasions. However, in this particular publication, the content analysis served mainly as a backcloth to a detailed investigation of themes in media representations of the risk of heterosexual transmission of HIV. During the period of press coverage that Beharrell investigated, a key component of the British government's health education strategy concerning HIV transmission was to demonstrate the risks associated with heterosexual transmission and especially the heightened risks of unprotected sex. Beharrell shows through an examination of such sources as editorials and articles by specialist medical reporters that three newspapers—the *Sun*, *Daily Mail*, and *Daily Express*—were consistently opposed to the government's campaign. For example, the *Daily Mail*'s editorials criticized the strategy on the grounds that it did not target sufficiently the high-risk groups—homosexuals and intravenous drug users. By contrast, the *Daily Mirror* was broadly supportive of the campaign. For example, a feature article on the occasion of World AIDS Day in 1988 proclaimed: 'And what we must never forget is that there is still no cure or vaccine for AIDS. So the way to stop its spread is through information, education and changes in human behaviour. Only then will there be any hope of controlling this deadly scourge' (*Daily Mirror*, 1 Dec. 1988, quoted in Beharrell 1993: 226). The broadsheet newspapers, such as *The Times*, *The Independent*, and the *Guardian*, were, like the *Daily Mirror*, broadly supportive of the government's strategy of a general educational programme. However, Beharrell also points to internal contradictions in newspapers' reporting, such as references to articles in tabloids like the *Sun* in the summer of 1991 warning of the risks of HIV infection among British tourists going abroad for sun, sea, and sex holidays.

As Beharrell points out, his research shows that an examination of reporting like this brings out the difficulty of referring to the 'press' in an undifferentiated way and even conventional distinctions between tabloids and broadsheets need to be treated with some caution following such evidence. It also

points to some of the contradictions in reporting. A content analysis might have been able to bring out aspects of this set of findings, but the employment of a more fine-grained analysis allows a greater sensitivity to the nature and content of specific themes. Magazines provide similar potential, as the example in Box 18.5 suggests.

Similar observations can frequently be made about films. Aitken (1998) has analysed five British documentary films made between 1929 and 1939. All of the films are about or touch substantially upon work and organizations. As such, they could be regarded as telling us a great deal in a graphic way about these themes in the inter-war years. For example, one of the five films—*Night Mail* (1936)—provides an insight into the Royal Mail train delivery service and concentrates on the operation during one day and night. While a shift in emphasis was apparent over the years the films were made, Aitken notes that they reveal a celebration of manual and craft skills but provide a less enthusiastic or at least ambivalent depiction of administrative routines and organizational structures. As such, the films cannot be regarded as providing a neutral record of work and organizations during this period. Instead, they probably tell us more about the ambivalence towards large corporations during their emergence over this period.

Authenticity issues are sometimes difficult to ascertain in the case of mass media outputs. While the outputs can usually be deemed to be genuine, the authorship of articles is often unclear (for example, editorials, some magazine articles), so that it is difficult to know whether the account can be relied upon as being written by someone in a position to provide an accurate version. Credibility is frequently an issue, but in fact, as the examples used in this section show, it is often the uncovering of error or distortion that is the objective of the analysis. Representativeness is rarely an issue for analyses of newspaper or magazine articles, since the corpus from which a sample has been drawn is usually ascertainable, especially when a wide range of newspapers is employed, as in Beharrel's (1993) investigation. However, it is difficult to know whether the films analysed by Aitken (1998)

Box 18.5 Aberdeen football fanzines

Giulianotti (1997) has written about the fanzines that emerged in connection with Aberdeen football club, which was one of the clubs that were the focus of his ethnographic research (see Box 14.4, p. 296). He shows how the fanzines, some of which were defunct by the time of his analysis, play a role in the creation of a sense of identity among supporters, especially during a period of footballing decline. He shows, for example, that 'the fanzines combine the more traditional sense of cultural differences from the rest of Scotland with the North- East's self-deprecating, often self-defeating humour' (Giulianotti

1997: 231). An illustration of this tendency is through the medium of the sheep. Rival fans insist that Aberdeen supporters have an interest in this creature that extends beyond its potential as a provider of food and wool. This is revealed in the repetitive chant of rival supporters: 'Sheepshagging bastards, You're only [etc.] . . .' (1997: 220). This allegation of bestiality is turned by the supporters upon themselves in their fanzines, so that the sheep is frequently used in cartoons and stories about sheep frequent their pages.

---

are typical. Finally, the evidence is usually clear and comprehensible but may require considerable awareness of contextual factors, such as the need for Giulianotti to be aware of the symbolic significance of sheep to Aberdeen football supporters (see Box 18.5).

Virtual outputs

There is one final type of document that ought to be mentioned—the documents that appear on the Internet. The relative newness of the Internet means that this is an area that is fairly underused by social researchers. However, the vastness of the Internet and its growing accessibility make it a likely source of documents for both quantitative and qualitative data analysis. Aldridge (1998), for example, examined both written consumer guides to personal finance published in the UK and several Internet web sites. Through an analysis of such documents Aldridge extracts a number of themes that he sees as part of the 'promotional culture' in which we live. Examples of such themes are the necessity for members of the public to assume responsibility for their personal finances, particularly in the light of the reductions in welfare provision, and the notion of the professional–client relationship as an uncontentious one in which the client has the ability to ask informed questions.

There is clearly huge potential with the Internet as a source of documents, but J. Scott's criteria need keeping in mind. First, authenticity: anyone could set up a web site, so that such matters as financial advice may be given by someone who is not an authority, though Aldridge selected sites of relatively assured probity. Secondly, credibility: we need to be aware of possible distortions. For example, if we were studying advice about the purchase of shares, it is known that web sites have been set up encouraging people to buy or sell particular stocks held by the web site authors, so that the prices of stocks can be manipulated. Thirdly, given the constant flux of the Internet, it is doubtful whether we could ever know how representative web sites on a certain topic are. Finally, web sites are notorious for a kind of Webspeak, so that it may be difficult to comprehend what is being said without considerable insider knowledge.

The world as text

There is one word that I have done my best to avoid using in the chapter so far—text. The word text is frequently employed as a synonym for a term like 'written document'. We have clearly strayed from this association, in that photographs and films have been touched upon. But, in relatively recent times, the word 'text' has been applied to an increasingly wide range of phenomena, so that theme parks, landscapes, heritage attractions, technologies, and a wide range of other objects are treated as texts out of which a 'reading' can be fashioned (e.g. Grint and Woolgar 1997). Thus, in Barthes's (1972) influential collection of essays, objects as varied as wrestling matches, Citroën cars, and striptease acts are submitted to readings. In a sense, therefore, just about everything can be treated as a text and perhaps as a document.

Readers and audiences—active or passive?

In Chapter 16, mention was made of the interest in audience reception as a prominent area of enquiry in media and cultural studies. Focus group research has played an important role in providing access to the ways in which members of audiences read media and cultural texts, and all of the examples in Table 16.1 (p. 340) except Morgan and Spanish (1985) and Lupton (1996) were concerned with this issue. The key point about such research is whether audiences/ readers are active interpreters of what they see or hear. Do they passively derive the meanings that authors or designers infuse into their texts, or do they resist those meanings and arrive at resistant readings, or do they arrive at a middle point that incorporates both passive and active elements? Much research on this issue suggests, as with Morley's (1980) study, which was briefly referred to in Chapter 16, that audiences frequently come up with alternative readings to those that were intended by authors or designers (see Fenton *et al.* 1998 for a summary of some of this research). Although the idea of the 'active audience' has not gone unchallenged (e.g. McGuigan 1992), the stream of research has been very influential and has placed a question mark over the readings of texts by social scientists. This means that we have to be cautious in concluding that the interpretations offered by social scientists of texts, such as Giulianotti's (1997) study of fanzines or Aitken's (1998) examination of documentary films in the inter-war years, are going to be the same as those of another social scientist, or as those of the readers or audiences of these outputs. The social researcher is always providing his or her own 'spin' on the texts that are analysed. The same is true of all social science data: the conclusions you derive from your questionnaire or ethnographic data are always going to be a reflection of your own personal interpretation. However, the main point being made for the present is that caution is required when reading writers' renditions of texts of all kinds.

Interpreting documents

Although it means straying into areas that are relevant to the next chapter, this section will briefly consider the question of how, if you are not using content analysis, you interpret documents. Three possible approaches are outlined: qualitative content analysis; semiotics; and hermeneutics. In addition to these, discourse analysis, which was covered in Chapter 17, has been employed as an approach for analysing documents.

Qualitative content analysis

This is probably the most prevalent approach to the qualitative analysis of documents. It comprises a searching-out of underlying themes in the materials being analysed and can be discerned in several of the studies referred to earlier, such as Beharrell (1993), Giulianotti (1997), and Aitken (1998). The processes through which the themes are extracted is often (if not invariably) left implicit. The extracted themes are usually illustrated—for example, with brief quotations from a newspaper article or magazine. The procedures adopted by Turner (1994) in connection with his research on the Summerland disaster are an example of the search for themes in texts, although Turner provided greater detail about what he did than is often the case. Altheide (1996) has outlined an approach that he calls *ethnographic content analysis* (which he contrasts with quantitative content analysis of the kind outlined in Chapter 9). Altheide's approach (referred to by him as ECA) represents a codification of certain procedures that might be viewed as typical of the kind of qualitative content analysis on which many of the studies referred to so far are based. He describes his approach as differing from traditional quantitative content analysis in that the researcher is constantly revising the themes or categories that are distilled from the examination of documents. As he puts it:

ECA follows a recursive and reflexive movement between concept development-sampling-data, collection-data, coding-data, and analysis-interpretation. The aim is to be systematic and analytic but not rigid. Categories and variables initially guide the study, but others are allowed and expected to emerge during the study, including an orientation to *constant discovery* and *constant comparison* of relevant situations, settings, styles, images, meanings, and nuances.   (Altheide 1996: 16; emphases in original)

Thus, with ECA there is much more movement back and forth between conceptualization, data collection, analysis and interpretation than is the case with the kind of content analysis described in Chapter 9. Quantitative content analysis typically entails applying predefined categories to the sources; ECA employs some initial categorization, but there is

greater potential for refinement of those categories and the generation of new ones.

Qualitative content analysis as a strategy of searching for themes in one's data lies at the heart of the coding approaches that are often employed in the analysis of qualitative data and as such will be encountered again in the next chapter.

Semiotics

Semiotics is invariably referred to as the 'science of signs'. It is an approach to the analysis of symbols in everyday life and as such can be employed in relation not only to documentary sources but also to all kinds of other data because of its commitment to treating phenomena as texts. The main terms employed in semiotics are:

- the *sign*, that is, something that stands for something else;
- the sign is made up of: a *signifier* and the *signified*;
- the *signifier* is the thing that points to an underlying meaning (the term *sign vehicle* is sometimes used instead of *signifier*);
- the *signified* is the meaning to which the signifier points;
- a *denotative meaning* is the manifest or more obvious meaning of a signifier and as such indicates its function;
- a *sign-function* is an object that denotes a certain function;
- a *connotative meaning* is a meaning associated with a certain social context that is in addition to its denotative meaning;
- *polysemy* refers to a quality of signs—namely, that they are always capable of being interpreted in many ways;
- the *code* is the generalized meaning that interested parties may seek to instil in a sign; a code is sometimes also called a *sign system*.

Semiotics is concerned to uncover the hidden meanings that reside in texts as broadly defined. Consider, by way of illustration, the curriculum vitae

Box 18.6 A semiotic Disneyland

Gottdiener (1982; 1997: 108–15) has proposed that Disneyland in Los Angeles, California, can be fruitfully analysed through a semiotic analysis. In so doing, he was treating Disneyland as a text. One component of his analysis is that Disneyland's meaning 'is revealed by its oppositions with the quotidian—the alienated everyday life of residents of L. A.' (1982: 148). He identifies through this principle nine *sign systems* that entail a contrast between the park and its surrounding environment: transportation; food; clothing; shelter; entertainment; social control; economics; politics; and family. Thus, the first of these sign systems—transportation—reveals a contrast between the Disneyland visitor as pedestrian (walk in a group; efficient mass transportation, which is fun) and

as passenger (car is necessary; poor mass transportation; danger on the congested freeways). A further component of his analysis entails an analysis of the connotations of the different 'lands' that make up the park. He suggests that each land is associated as a signifier with signifiers of capitalism, as follows:

- Frontierland—predatory capital
- Adventureland—colonialism/imperialism
- Tomorrowland—state capital
- New Orleans—venture capital
- Main Street—family capital.   (Gottdiener 1982: 156)

(CV) in academic life. The typical CV that an academic will produce contains such features as: personal details; education; previous and current posts; administrative responsibilities and experience; teaching experience; research experience; research grants acquired; and publications. We can treat the CV as a system of interlocking signifiers that signify at the level of denotative meaning a summary of the individual's experience (its sign function) and at the connotative level an indication of an individual's value, particularly in connection with his or her prospective employability. Each CV is capable of being interpreted in different ways, as anyone who has ever sat in on a short-listing meeting for a lectureship can testify, and is therefore polysemic, but there is a code whereby certain attributes of CVs are seen as especially desirable and that are therefore less contentious in terms of the attribution of meaning. Indeed, applicants for posts know this latter point and devise their CVs to amplify the desired qualities so that the CV becomes an autobiographical practice for the presentation of self, as Miller and Morgan (1993) have suggested.

Box 18.6 provides an illustration of a study from a semiotic perspective of Disneyland as a text. The chief strength of semiotics lies in its invitation to the analyst to try to see beyond and beneath the apparent ordinariness of everyday life and its

manifestations. The main difficulty one often feels with the fruits of a semiotic analysis is that, although we are invariably given a compelling exposition of a facet of the quotidian, it is difficult to escape a sense of the arbitrariness of the analysis provided. However, in all probability this sensation is unfair to the approach, because the results of a semiotic analysis are probably no more arbitrary than any interpretation of documentary materials or any other data, such as a thematic, qualitative content analysis of the kind described in the previous section. Indeed, it would be surprising if we were not struck by a sense of arbitrariness in interpretation, in view of the principle of polysemy that lies at the heart of semiotics.

Hermeneutics

Hermeneutics refers to an approach that was originally devised in relation to the understanding or interpretation of texts and of theological texts in particular. It has been influential in the general formulation of interpretivism as an epistemology (see Chapter 1, where the idea of hermeneutics was briefly encountered) and is more or less synonymous with Weber's notion of *Verstehen*. The central idea behind hermeneutics is that the analyst of a text must seek to bring out the meanings of a text from the perspective of its author. This will entail attention to the social and historical context within which the text was produced. An approach to the analysis of texts like qualitative content analysis can be hermeneutic when it is sensitive to the context within which texts were produced. Hermeneutics is seen by its modern advocates as a strategy that has potential in relation both to texts as documents and to social actions and other non-documentary phenomena.

Phillips and Brown (1993) and Forster (1994) separately identify an approach to the interpretation of company documents that they describe as a *critical hermeneutic* approach. A hermeneutic approach, because of its emphasis on the location of interpretation within a specific social and historical context, would seem to represent an invitation to ensure that the analyst of texts is fully conversant with that context. As such, the approach is likely to entail the collection and analysis of data that will allow an understanding in context to be forged. As noted previously, Forster's study of the company referred to as TC included interviews with senior managers and a questionnaire survey. For their study of the corporate image advertisements of a Canadian company that produces synthetic crude oil, Phillips and Brown also employed a large database of magazine and newspaper articles relating to the company, which also supplied the authors with additional documentary materials. Forster's critical hermeneutic analysis entailed the interrogation of the documents and the extraction of themes from them by reference to his knowledge of the organizational context within which the documents and the people and events within them were located.

Phillips and Brown's somewhat more formal approach entailed the examination of the advertisements in terms of three 'moments'.

- *The social–historical moment*, which involves 'an examination of the producer of the text, its intentional recipient, its referent in the world [i.e. what

it refers to], and the context in which the text is produced, transmitted, and received' (1993: 1558).

- *The formal moment*, which involves 'a formal analysis of the structural and conventional aspects of the text' (1993: 1563). This means that the texts must be examined in terms of the constituent parts of each text and the writing conventions employed. This phase can involve the use of any of several techniques, such as semiotics or discourse analysis (see Chapter 17). Phillips and Brown used the former of these.

- *The interpretation–reinterpretation moment*, which 'involves the interpretation of the results of the first two moments' (1993: 1567); in other words, they are synthesized.

Through this strategy, Phillips and Brown show, for example, the ways in which the corporate image advertisements constitute an attempt to mobilize support for the company's activities from government (and from among the public who were unlikely to be familiar with the company) at a time of intense competition for funding, and to ward off environmental legislation. The approach has points of affinity with the idea of the active audience (see above), in that there is an emphasis on the reception of texts and as such the notion that there may be a plurality of interpretations of them.

The critical hermeneutic approach thus can draw on practices associated with qualitative content analysis and can fuse them with ways of formally approaching texts, such as semiotics. What is crucial is the linkage that is made between understanding the text from the point of view of the author and the social and historical context of its production. Indeed, in many respects, for a hermeneutic approach, the latter is a precondition of the former. Its appeal to qualitative researchers is that it is an approach to the analysis of documents (and indeed other data) that explicitly draws on two central tenets of the qualitative research strategy: an emphasis on the point of view of the author of the text and a sensitivity to context.

Key points

- Documents constitute a very heterogeneous set of sources of data, which include personal documents, official documents from both the state and private sources, and the mass media.

- Such materials can be the focus of both quantitative and qualitative enquiry but the emphasis in this chapter has been upon the latter.

- Documents of the kinds considered may be in printed, visual, digital, or indeed any other retrievable format.

- For many writers, just about anything can be 'read' as a text.

- Criteria for evaluating the quality of documents are: authenticity; credibility; representativeness; and meaning. The relevance of these criteria varies somewhat according to the kind of document being assessed.

- There are several ways of analysing documents within qualitative research. In this chapter we have covered qualitative content analysis, semiotics, and hermeneutics.

Revision questions

- What is meant by a document?
- What are J. Scott's four criteria for assessing documents?

Personal documents

- Outline the different kinds of personal documents.

- How do they fare in terms of J. Scott's criteria?

- What might be the role of personal documents in relation to the life history or biographical method?

- What uses can family photographs have in social research?

Official documents deriving from the state

- What do the studies by Abraham and Turner suggest in terms of the potential for social researchers of official documents deriving from the state?

- How do such documents fare in terms of J. Scott's criteria?

Official documents deriving from private sources

- What kinds of documents might be considered official documents deriving from private sources?

- How do such documents fare in terms of J. Scott's criteria?

Mass media outputs

- What kinds of documents are mass media outputs?
- How do such documents fare in terms of J. Scott's criteria?

Virtual outputs

- Do Internet documents and other virtual outputs raise special problems in terms of assessing them from the point of view of J. Scott's criteria?

The world as text

- Can anything be treated as a text?
- What is the significance of audiences in connection with textual readings by academics?

Interpreting documents

- How does qualitative content analysis differ from the kind of content analysis discussed in Chapter 9?
- What is a sign? How central is it to semiotics?
- What is the difference between denotative meaning and connotative meaning?
- What is a hermeneutic approach to documents?
- What lessons can be learned from the studies by Phillips and Brown and by Forster concerning the potential uses of a hermeneutic approach?

19 Qualitative data analysis

Reader's guide

Because qualitative data deriving from interviews or participant observation typically take the form of a large corpus of unstructured textual material, they are not straightforward to analyse. Moreover, unlike quantitative data analysis, clear-cut rules about how qualitative data analysis should be carried out have not been developed. In this chapter, some general approaches to qualitative data analysis will be examined, along with *coding*, which is the main feature of most of these approaches. The chapter explores:

- *analytic induction* as a general strategy of qualitative data analysis;

- *grounded theory* as a general strategy of qualitative data analysis; this is probably the most prominent of the general approaches to qualitative data analysis; the chapter examines its main features, processes, and outcomes, along with some of the criticisms that are sometimes levelled at the approach;

- *coding* as a key process in grounded theory and in approaches to qualitative data analysis more generally; it is the focus of an extended discussion in terms of what it entails and some of the limitations of a reliance on coding;

- the criticism that is sometimes made of coding in relation to qualitative data—namely, that it tends to fragment data; the idea of *narrative analysis* is introduced as an approach to data analysis that is gaining a growing following and that does not result in data fragmentation;

- the possibility of conducting a secondary analysis of other researchers' qualitative data is examined.

Introduction

One of the main difficulties with qualitative research is that it very rapidly generates a large, cumbersome database because of its reliance on prose in the form of such media as field notes, interview transcripts, or documents. Miles (1979) has described qualitative data as an 'attractive nuisance', because of the attractiveness of its richness but the difficulty of finding analytic paths through that richness. The researcher must guard against being captivated by the richness of the data collected, so that there is a failure to give the data wider significance for the social sciences. In other words, it is crucial to guard against failing to carry out a true analysis. This means that you must protect yourself against the condition Lofland (1971: 18) once called 'analytic interruptus'.

Yet, finding a path through the thicket of prose that makes up your data is not an easy matter and is baffling to many researchers confronting such data for the first time. 'What do I do with it now?' is a common refrain. In large part, this is because, unlike the analysis of quantitative data, there are few well-established and widely accepted rules for the analysis of qualitative data. Although learning the tech-niques of quantitative data analysis may seem painful at the time, they do give you an unambiguous set of rules about how to handle your data. You still have to interpret your analyses, but at least there are relatively clear rules for getting to that point. Qualitative data analysis has not reached this degree of codification of analytic procedures and many writers would argue that this is not necessarily desirable anyway (see Bryman and Burgess 1994*b* on this point). What *can* be provided are broad guidelines (Okely 1994), and it is in the spirit of this suggestion that this chapter has been written.

This chapter has two main sections.

- *General strategies of qualitative data analysis*. In this section, I consider two approaches to data analysis—analytic induction and grounded theory.

- *Basic operations in qualitative data analysis*. This section entails a consideration in particular of *coding* and of an alternative approach in the form of *narrative analysis*.

In the next chapter, the use of computers in qualitative data analysis will be outlined.

General strategies of qualitative data analysis

This section considers two strategies of analysis—analytic induction and grounded theory. They are probably the most frequently cited approaches, though others do exist (e.g. Williams 1976; Hycner 1985). By a general strategy of qualitative data analysis, I simply mean a framework that is meant to guide the analysis of data. As we will see, one of the ways in which qualitative and quantitative data analysis sometimes differ is that, with the latter, analysis invariably occurs after your data have been collected. However, as noted in Chapter 13, general approaches like grounded theory (and analytic induction) are often described as *iterative*—that is, there is a repetitive interplay between the collection and analysis of data. This means that analysis starts after some of the data have been collected and the implications of that analysis then shape the next steps in the data collection process. Consequently, while grounded theory and analytic induction are described as strategies of analysis, they can also be viewed as strategies for the *collection* of data as well.

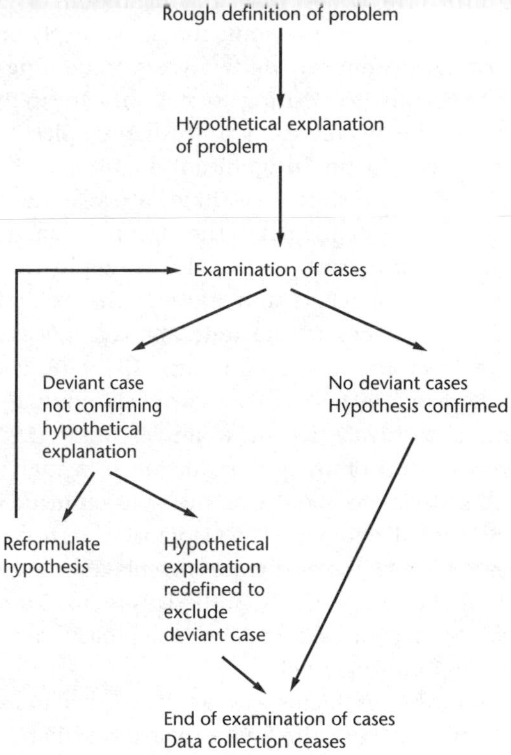

Analytic induction

The main steps in analytic induction are outlined in Figure 19.1. Analytic induction (see Box 19.1) begins with a rough definition of a research problem, proceeds to a hypothetical explanation of that problem, and then continues onto the collection of data (examination of cases). If a case that is inconsistent with the hypothesis is encountered, the analyst *either* redefines the hypothesis so as to exclude the deviant or negative case *or* reformulates the hypothesis and proceeds with further data collection. If the latter path is chosen, if a further deviant case is found, the analyst must choose again between reformulation or redefinition.

As this brief outline suggests, analytic induction is an extremely rigorous method of analysis, because encountering a single case that is inconsistent with a hypothesis is sufficient to necessitate further data

Fig. 19.1 The process of analytic induction

collection or a reformulation of the hypothesis. Nor should the alternative of reformulating the hypothetical explanation be regarded as a soft option, as is shown by Katz's (1982) study of poverty lawyers in Chicago. Katz was interested in finding some characteristics that distinguished those who

Box 19.1 *What is analytic induction?*

Analytic induction is an approach to the analysis of data in which the researcher seeks universal explanations of phenomena by pursuing the collection of data until no cases that are inconsistent with a hypothetical explanation (deviant or negative cases) of a phenomenon are found.

stayed on for some time as lawyers to help the poor (in spite of the lower pay and status associated with such work) from those whose tenure was brief. He writes that 'the definition of the explanandum [the phenomenon to be explained] was changed from staying two years, to desiring to stay two years, to desiring to stay in a frustrating place, to involvement in a frustrating place, to involvement in an insignificant status . . .' (Katz 1982: 200). Each shift necessitated a reanalysis and reorganization of his data. The rigours of analytic induction have not endeared the approach to qualitative researchers and most of the examples used in textbooks to illustrate analytic induction derive from the 1940s and early 1950s (Bryman and Burgess 1994a: 4). Katz's work is unusual in being a relatively recent example. Bloor (1978) used a version of analytic induction in a study of doctors' decisions about whether to recommend an adeno-tonscillectomy. His approach especially diverged from the sequence described in Figure 19.1 in that a specific hypothesis was not formulated. An account using Bloor's approach can be found in Johnson (1998).

Two further problems with analytic induction are worth noting. First, the final explanations that analytic induction arrives at specify the conditions that are *sufficient* for the phenomenon occurring but rarely specify the *necessary* conditions. This means that analytic induction may find out why people of certain characteristics or in certain circumstances become drug addicts (the focus of one major analytic induction study by Lindesmith 1947), but it does not allow us to say why those particular people became addicts rather than others in the same situation with the same characteristics. Secondly, it does not provide useful guidelines (unlike grounded theory) as to how many cases need to be investigated before the absence of negative cases and the validity of the hypothetical explanation (whether reformulated or not) can be confirmed.

Grounded theory

Grounded theory (see Box 19.2) has become by far the most widely used framework for analysing qualitative data. The book that is the chief wellspring of the approach, *The Discovery of Grounded Theory: Strategies for Qualitative Research* by Barney G. Glaser and Anselm L. Strauss (published in 1967), must be one of the most widely cited books in the social sciences. However, providing a definitive account of the approach is by no means a straightforward matter for the following reasons.

- Glaser and Strauss developed grounded theory along different paths after the publication of the above book. Glaser felt that the approach to grounded theory that Strauss was promoting (most notably in Strauss 1987, and Strauss and Corbin 1990) was too prescriptive and emphasized too much the development of concepts rather than of theories (Glaser 1992). However, because of the greater prominence of Strauss's writings, his version is largely the one followed in the exposition below. There is, however, considerable controversy about what grounded theory is and entails (Charmaz 2000).

- Straussian grounded theory has changed a great

Box 19.2 ⛭ *What is grounded theory?*

In its most recent incarnation, grounded theory has been defined as: 'theory that was derived from data, systematically gathered and analyzed through the research process. In this method, data collection, analysis, and eventual theory stand in close relationship to one another' (Strauss and Corbin 1998: 12). Thus, two central features of grounded theory are that it is concerned with the development of theory out of data *and* the approach is *iterative* or *recursive* as it is sometimes called, meaning that data collection and analysis proceed in tandem, repeatedly referring back to each other.

deal over the years. This is revealed in a constant addition to the tool chest of analytic devices that is revealed in his writings.

- Some writers have suggested that grounded theory is honoured more in the breach than in the observance, implying that claims are often made that grounded theory has been used but that evidence of this being the case is at best uncertain (Bryman 1988*a*: 85, 91; Locke 1996; Charmaz 2000). Sometimes the term is employed simply to imply that the analyst has grounded his or her theory in data. Grounded theory is more than this and refers to a set of procedures that are described below. Referencing academic publications is often part of a tactic of persuading readers of the legitimacy of one's work (Gilbert 1977) and this process can be discerned in the citation of grounded theory. Alternatively, researchers sometimes appear to have used just one or two features of grounded theory but refer to their having used the approach without qualification (Locke 1996).

Against such a background, writing about the essential ingredients of grounded theory is not an easy matter.

It is not going to be possible to describe here grounded theory in all its facets; instead, its main features will be outlined. In order to organize the exposition, I find it helpful to distinguish between *tools* and *outcomes* in grounded theory.

Tools of grounded theory

Some of the tools of grounded theory have been referred to in previous chapters. Their location is indicated in the list that follows.

- *Theoretical sampling*—see Box 14.8 (p. 302).

- *Coding*—the key process in grounded theory, whereby data are broken down into component parts, which are given names. It begins soon after the collection of initial data. As Charmaz puts it: 'We grounded theorists code our emerging data as we collect it. . . . Unlike quantitative research that requires data to fit into *preconceived* standardized codes, the researcher's interpretations of data

shape his or her emergent codes in grounded theory' (Charmaz 2000: 515; emphasis in original). In grounded theory, different types or levels of coding are recognized (see Box 19.3).

- *Theoretical saturation*—see Box 14.9 (p. 303). Theoretical saturation is a process that relates to two phases in grounded theory: the coding of data (implying that you reach a point where there is no further point in reviewing your data to see how well they fit with your concepts or categories) and the collection of data (implying that, once a concept or category has been developed, you may wish to continue collecting data to determine its nature and operation but then reach a point where new data are no longer illuminating the concept).

- *Constant comparison*—an aspect of grounded theory that was prominent in Glaser and Strauss (1967) and that is often referred to as a significant phase by practitioners, but that seems to be an implicit, rather than an explicit, element in more recent writings. It refers to a process of maintaining a close connection between data and conceptualization, so that the correspondence between concepts and categories with their indicators is not lost. More specifically, attention to the procedure of constant comparison enjoins the researcher constantly to compare phenomena being coded under a certain category so that a theoretical elaboration of that category can begin to emerge. Glaser and Strauss advised writing a *memo* (see below) on the category after a few phenomena had been coded. It also entails being sensitive to contrasts between the categories that are emerging.

Outcomes of grounded theory

The following are the products of different phases of grounded theory.

- *Concept(s)*—refers to labels given to discrete phenomena; concepts are referred to as the 'building blocks of theory' (Strauss and Corbin 1998: 101). Concepts are produced through *open coding* (see Box 19.3).

Box 19.3 Coding in grounded theory

Coding is one of the most central processes in grounded theory. It entails reviewing transcripts and/or field notes and giving labels (names) to component parts that seem to be of potential theoretical significance and/or that appear to be particularly salient within the social worlds of those being studied. As Charmaz (1983: 186) puts it: 'Codes . . . serve as shorthand devices to *label*, *separate*, *compile*, and *organize* data' (emphases in original). Coding is a somewhat different process from coding in relation to quantitative data, such as social survey data. With the latter, coding is more or less solely a way of managing data, whereas in grounded theory and indeed in approaches to qualitative data analysis that do not subscribe to the approach, it is an important first step in the generation of theory. Coding in grounded theory is also somewhat more tentative than in relation to the generation of quantitative data, where there is a tendency to think in terms of data and codes as very fixed. Coding in qualitative data analysis tends to be in a constant state of potential revision and fluidity. The data are treated as potential indicators of concepts and the indicators are *constantly compared* (see under 'Tools of grounded theory') to see which concepts they best fit with. As Strauss (1987: 25) put it: 'Many indicators (behavioral actions/events) are examined comparatively by the analyst who then "codes"

them, naming them as indicators of a class of events/behavioral actions.'

Strauss and Corbin, drawing on their grounded theory approach, distinguish between three types of coding practice:

- *Open coding*—'the process of breaking down, examining, comparing, conceptualizing and categorizing data' (1990: 61); this process of coding yields concepts, which are later to be grouped and turned into categories.

- *Axial coding*—'a set of procedures whereby data are put back together in new ways after open coding, by making connections between categories' (1990: 96). This is done by linking codes to contexts, to consequences, to patterns of interaction, and to causes.

- *Selective coding*—'the procedure of selecting the core category, systematically relating it to other categories, validating those relationships, and filling in categories that need further refinement and development' (1990: 116). A *core category* is the central issue or focus around which all other categories are integrated. It is what Strauss and Corbin call the storyline that frames your account.

The three types of coding are really different levels of coding and each relates to a different point in the elaboration of categories in grounded theory.

- *Category, categories*—a concept that has been elaborated so that it is regarded as representing real-world phenomena. As noted in Box 14.9 (p. 303), a category may subsume two or more concepts. As such, categories are at a higher level of abstraction than concepts. A category may become a *core category* around which the other categories pivot (see Box 19.3). Box 19.4 provides a good example of the emergence of a core category.

- *Properties*—attributes or aspects of a category.

- *Hypotheses*—initial hunches about relationships between concepts.

- *Theory*—according to Strauss and Corbin (1998: 22): 'a set of well-developed categories . . . that are systematically related through statements of relationship to form a theoretical framework that

explains some relevant social . . . or other phenomenon'. Since its inception, grounded theory writings point to two types or levels of theory: *substantive theory* and *formal theory*. The former relates to theory in a certain empirical instance or substantive area, such as occupational socialization. A formal theory is at a higher level of abstraction and has a wider range of applicability to several substantive areas, such as socialization in a number of spheres, suggesting that higher-level processes are at work. The generation of formal theory requires data collection in contrasting settings.

The different elements can be portrayed in Figure 19.2. As with all diagrams, this is a representation, and it is particularly so in the case of grounded theory, because the existence of different versions of the approach does not readily permit a more definitive

Box 19.4 Categories in grounded theory

Orona's (1997) study of sufferers of Alzheimer's disease and in particular of their relatives exemplifies many features of grounded theory. Orona began her research with an interest in the decision-making process that led relatives to place sufferers in a home. She gradually realized from coding her interview transcripts that this was not a crucial feature for relatives, as she had anticipated, not least because many of them simply felt they had no choice. Instead, she was slowly taken by the significance for relatives of the 'identity loss' sufferers were deemed to experience. This gradually became her core category. She conducted further interviews in order to flesh this notion out and reread existing transcripts in the light of it. The link between indicators and category can be seen in relatives' references to the sufferer as 'gone', 'different', 'not the same person', and as a 'stranger'. Orona was able to unearth four major themes that emerged around the process of identity loss. The theme of 'temporality' was particularly significant in Orona's emerging theoretical rendition. Also, it is difficult to get across diagrammatically the iterative nature of grounded theory—reflections and was revealed in such comments in transcripts as:

It was the *time of the year* when nobody goes in the yard anyway . . .
At the beginning . . .
It got much worse *later on.*
More and more, he was leaning on me.
Before she would never have been like that.
She *used to* love coffee.   (from Orona 1997: 179–80)

In other words, such comments served as indicators that allowed the category 'temporality' to be built up. The issue of temporality was significant in Orona's emerging analysis, because it related to the core category of identity loss. Relatives sought to help sufferers maintain their identities. However, gradually, with the passage of time, crucial events meant that the relatives could no longer deny sufferers' identity loss.

rendition. Also, it is difficult to get across diagrammatically the iterative nature of grounded theory—in particular its commitment to the idea that data collection and analysis occur in parallel. This is partly achieved in the diagram through the presence of arrows pointing in both directions in relation to certain steps. The figure implies the following.

- The researcher begins with a general research problem (step 1).

- Relevant people and/or incidents are theoretically sampled (step 2).

- Relevant data are collected (step 3).

- Data are coded (step 4), which may at the level of open coding generate concepts (step 4a).

- There is a constant movement backwards and forwards between the first four steps, so that early coding suggests the need for new data, which results in the need to theoretically sample, and so on.

- Through a constant comparison of indicators and concepts (step 5) categories are generated (step 5a).

The crucial issue is to ensure that there is a fit between indicators and concepts.

- Categories are saturated during the coding process (step 6).

- Relationships between categories are explored (step 7) in such a way that hypotheses about connections between categories emerge (step 7a).

- Further data are collected via theoretical sampling (steps 8 and 9).

- The collection of data is likely to be governed by the theoretical saturation principle (step 10) and by the testing of the emerging hypotheses (step 11), which leads to the specification of substantive theory (step 11a). See Box 19.5 for an illustration.

- The substantive theory is explored using grounded theory processes in relation to different settings from that in which it was generated (step 12), so that formal theory may be generated (step 12a). A formal theory will relate to more abstract categories, which are not specifically related to the research area in question (for example, chronically ill men, relatives of sufferers of Alzheimer's disease).

Step 12 is relatively unusual in grounded theory, because researchers typically concentrate on a certain setting. One way in which formal theory can be generated is through the use of existing theory and research in comparable settings.

Concepts and categories are perhaps the key elements in grounded theory. Indeed, it is sometimes suggested that, as a qualitative data analysis strategy, it works better for generating categories than theory. In part, this may be because studies purporting to use the approach often generate grounded *concepts* rather than grounded theory as such. Concepts and categories are nonetheless at the heart of the approach, and key processes such as coding, theoretical sampling, and theoretical saturation are designed to guide their generation.

Memos

One aid to the generation of concepts and categories is the *memo*. Memos in grounded theory are notes that researchers might write for themselves and for those with whom they work concerning such elements of grounded theory as coding or concepts. They serve as reminders about what is meant by the terms being used and provide the building blocks for a certain amount of reflection. Memos are potentially

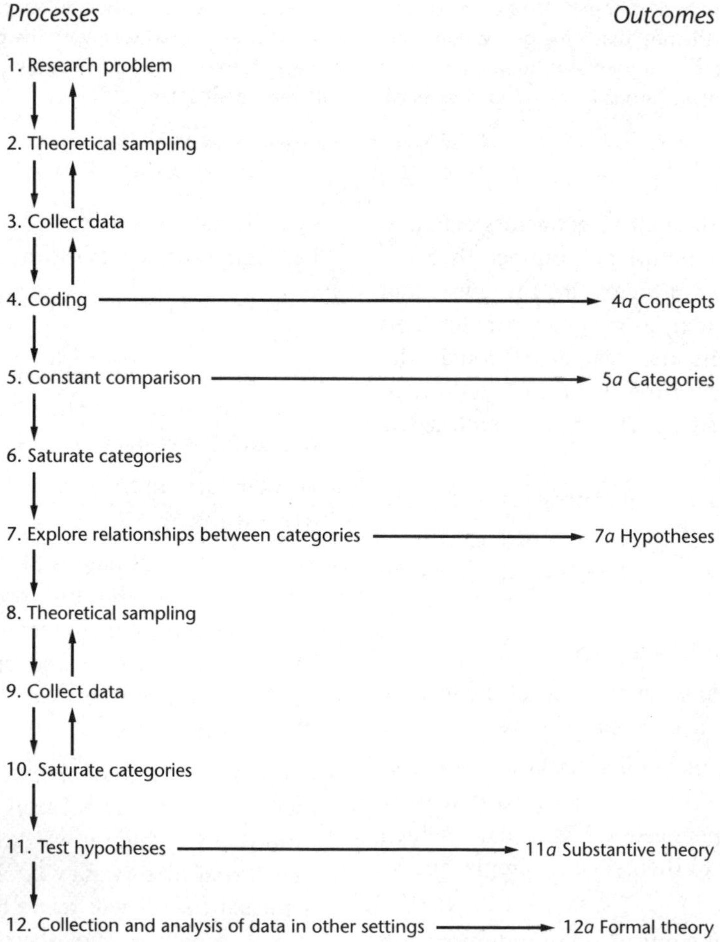

Fig. 19.2 Processes and outcomes in grounded theory

Box 19.5 **Grounded theory in action**

Charmaz's (1997) research is concerned with the identity dilemmas of men who have chronic (but not terminal) illnesses. She outlines very clearly the chief steps in her analysis.

- Interviews with men and a small number of women.

- Exploring the transcripts for gender differences.

- Searching for themes in the men's interviews and published personal accounts (e.g. autobiographies). An example is the notion of 'accommodation to uncertainty', as men find ways of dealing with the unpredictable paths of their illnesses.

- Building 'analytic categories from men's definitions of and taken-for-granted assumptions about their situations' (1997: 39). Of particular significance in her work is the idea of 'identity dilemmas'—that is, the

ways in which men approach and possibly resolve the assault on their traditional self-images in terms of masculinity. She shows that men often used strategies to re-establish earlier selves, so that for many audiences their identity (at least in their own eyes) could be preserved.

- Further interviews designed to refine the categories.

- Rereading personal accounts of chronic illness with a particular focus on gender.

- Reading a new group of personal accounts.

- Making 'comparisons with women on selected key points' (1997: 39).

Charmaz provides a substantive theory that helps to explain the importance of notions of masculinity for the carving-out of an identity for chronically ill men.

---

very helpful to researchers in helping them to crystallize ideas and not to lose track of their thinking on various topics. An illustration of a memo from research in which I was involved is provided in Box 19.6.

Finding examples of grounded theory that reveal all its facets and stages is very difficult, and it is unsurprising that many expositions of grounded theory fall back on the original illustrations provided in Glaser and Strauss (1967). Many studies show some of its ingredients but not others. Box 19.5 provides an illustration by one of Strauss's students that incorporates some key grounded theory features.

Criticisms of grounded theory

In spite of the frequency with which it is cited and the frequent lip-service paid to it, grounded theory is not without its limitations, of which the following can be briefly registered.

- Bulmer (1979) has questioned whether, as prescribed by the advocates of grounded theory, researchers can suspend their awareness of relevant theories or concepts until a quite late stage in the process of analysis. Social researchers are typically sensitive to the conceptual armoury of their

disciplines and it seems unlikely that this awareness can be put aside. Indeed, nowadays it is rarely accepted that theory-neutral observation is feasible. In other words, it is generally agreed that what we 'see' when we conduct research is conditioned by many factors, one of which is what we already know about the social world being studied (in terms of both social scientific conceptualizations and as members of society). Also, many writers might take the view that it is desirable that researchers are sensitive to existing conceptualizations, so that their investigations are focused and can build upon the work of others.

- Related to this first point is that, in many circumstances, researchers are required to spell out the possible implications of their planned investigation. For example, a lecturer making a bid for research funding or a student applying for funding for postgraduate research is usually required to demonstrate how his or her research will build upon what is already known or to demonstrate that he or she has a reasonably tightly defined research question, something which is also frequently disdained in grounded theory.

- There are practical difficulties with grounded

Box 19.6 **A memo**

In the course of research into the bus industry that I carried out with colleagues in the early 1990s (Bryman *et al.* 1996), we noticed that the managers we interviewed frequently referred to the notion that their companies had inherited features that derived from the running of those companies before deregulation. They often referred to the idea of inheriting characteristics that held them back in trying to meet the competitive environment they faced in the 1990s. As such, inheritance is what Strauss (1987) calls an *in vivo code* (one that derives from the language of people in the social context being studied), rather than what he calls *sociologically constructed codes*, which are labels employing the analyst's own terminology. The following memo outlines the concept of inheritance, provides some illustrative quotations, and suggests some properties of the concept.

Memo for Inheritance

Inheritance: many of our interviewees suggest that they have inherited certain company traits and traditions from the period prior to deregulation (i.e. pre-1985). It is a term that many of them themselves employed to denote company attributes that are not of their choosing but have survived from the pre-deregulation period. The key point about inheritance is that the inherited elements are seen by our interviewees as hindering their ability to respond to the changing environment of the post-deregulation era.

Inherited features include:

- expensive and often inappropriate fleets of vehicles and depots;
- the survival of attitudes and behaviour patterns, particularly among bus drivers, which are seen as inappropriate to the new environment (for example, lack of concern for customer service) and which hinder service innovation;

- high wage rates associated with the pre-deregulation era; means that new competitors can enter the market while paying drivers lower wages.

Sample comments

'We *inherited* a very high cost structure because of deregulation. 75% of our staff were paid in terms of conditions affected by [rates prior to deregulation]' (Commercial Director, Company B).

'I suppose another major weakness is that we are very tied by conditions and practices we've *inherited*' (Commercial Director, Company G).

'We have what we've *inherited* and we now have a massive surplus of double decks . . . We have to go on operating those' (Managing Director, Company B).

Managing Director of Company E said the company had inherited staff who were steeped in pre-deregulation attitudes, which meant that 'we don't have a staff where the message is "the customer is number one". We don't have a staff where that is emblazoned on the hearts and minds of everyone, far from it.'

Prepost-deregulation: interviewee makes a contrast between the periods before and after deregulation to show how they've changed. This shows in a sense the *absence* of inherited features and their possible impact; can refer to how the impact of possibly inherited features was negated or offset. For example, *X* referring to the recent end of the 3-week strike: 'there was no way we were going to give in to this sort of thing, this sort of blackmail. We just refused to move and the trade unions had never experienced that. It was all part of the change in culture following deregulation . . .'.

Inheriting constraints: such as staff on high wage rates and with inappropriate attitudes.

Inheriting surplus capacity: such as too many buses or wrong size.

---

theory. The time taken to transcribe tape recordings of interviews, for example, can make it difficult for researchers, especially when they have tight deadlines, to carry out a genuine grounded theory analysis with its constant interplay of data collection and conceptualization.

- It is somewhat doubtful whether grounded theory

in many instances really results in *theory*. As previously suggested, it provides a rigorous approach to the generation of concepts, but it is often difficult to see what theory, in the sense of an explanation of something, is being put forward. Moreover, in spite of the frequent lip-service paid to the generation of formal theory, most grounded theories are substantive in character; in other words, they pertain to the specific social phenomenon being researched and not to a broader range of phenomena (though, of course, they *may* have such broader applicability).

- In spite of the large amount written on grounded theory, but perhaps because of the many subtle changes in its presentation, it is still vague on certain points, such as the difference between concepts and categories. For example, while Strauss and Corbin (1998: 73) refer to theoretical sampling as 'sampling on the basis of emerging *concepts*' (emphasis added), Charmaz (2000: 519) writes that it is used to 'develop our emerging *categories*' (emphasis added). The term 'categories' is increasingly being employed rather than concepts, but such inconsistent use of key terms is not helpful to people trying to understand the overall process.

- Grounded theory is very much associated with an approach to data analysis that invites researchers to fragment their data by coding the data into discrete chunks. However, in the eyes of some writers this kind of activity results in a loss of a sense of context and of narrative flow (Coffey and Atkinson 1996), a point to which I will return below.

- The presence of competing accounts of the ingredients of grounded theory does not make it easy to characterize it or to establish how to use it. This situation has been made even more problematic by Charmaz's (2000) suggestion that most grounded theory is objectivist and that an alternative, constructionist (she calls it *constructivist*) approach is preferable. She argues that the grounded theory associated with Glaser, Strauss, and Corbin is objectivist in that it aims to uncover a reality that is external to social actors. She offers an alternative, constructionist version that 'assumes that people create and maintain meaningful worlds through dialectical processes of conferring meaning on their realities and acting within them . . . Thus, social reality does not exist independent of human action' (Charmaz 2000: 521). Such a position stands in contrast to earlier grounded theory texts that 'imply that categories and concepts inhere within the data, awaiting the researcher's discovery. . . . Instead, a constructivist

approach recognizes that the categories, concepts, and theoretical level of an analysis emerge from the researcher's interaction within the field and questions about the data' (Charmaz 2000: 522). One difficulty here is that the two meanings of constructionism referred to in Box 1.12 (p. 18) seem to be conflated. The first quotation refers to constructionism as an ontological position in relating to social objects and categories; the second is a reference to constructionism in relation to the nature of knowledge of the social world. It is certainly fair to suggest that Glaser, Strauss, and Corbin in their various writings neglect the role of the researcher in the generation of knowledge, but it is not clear that they are indifferent to the notion that social reality exists independently of social actors. Strauss was, after all, the lead of the study referred to on page 17 concerning the hospital as a negotiated order, which was used as an illustration of constructionism (Strauss *et al.* 1973). Also, Orona's (1997) account of her grounded theory analysis of sufferers of Alzheimer's disease is described in a commentary on the research by Strauss and Corbin (1997: 172) as a 'textbook exemplification' of the approach. Yet this study is concerned with the subjective experience of the disease (interpretivism) and with the *construction* of identity in everyday life. However, there is little doubt that there is considerable confusion currently about the nature of grounded theory.

Nonetheless, grounded theory probably represents the most influential general strategy for conducting qualitative data analysis, though how far the approach is followed varies from study to study. What can be said is that many of its core processes, such as coding, memos, and the very idea of allowing theoretical ideas to emerge out of one's data, have been hugely influential. Indeed, it is striking that one of the main developments in qualitative data analysis in recent years—computer-assisted qualitative data analysis—has implicitly promoted many of these processes, because the software programs have often been written with grounded theory in mind (Richards and Richards 1994; Lonkila, 1995).

More on coding

Coding is the starting point for most forms of qualitative data analysis. The principles involved have been well developed by writers on grounded theory and others. Some of the considerations in developing codes, some of which are derived from Lofland and Lofland (1995), are as follows.

- Of what general category is this item of data an instance?

- What does this item of data represent?

- What is this item of data about?

- Of what topic is this item of data an instance?

- What question about a topic does this item of data suggest?

- What sort of answer to a question about a topic does this item of data imply?

- What is happening here?

- What are people doing?

- What do people say they are doing?

- What kind of event is going on?

Steps and considerations in coding

The following steps and considerations need to be borne in mind in preparation for and during coding.

- *Code as soon as possible.* It is well worth coding as you go along, as grounded theory suggests. This may sharpen your understanding of your data and help with theoretical sampling. Also, it may help to alleviate the feeling of being swamped by your data, which may happen if you defer analysis entirely until the end of the data collection period. At the very least, you should ensure that, if your data collection involves recording interviews, you begin transcription at a relatively early stage.

- *Read through your initial set of transcripts, field notes, documents etc.* without taking any notes or considering an interpretation; perhaps at the

end jot down a few general notes about what struck you as especially interesting, important, or significant.

- *Do it again.* Read through your data again, but this time begin to make marginal notes about significant remarks or observations. Make as many as possible. Initially, they will be very basic—perhaps key words used by your respondents, names that you give to themes in the data. When you do this you are *coding*—generating an index of terms that will help you to interpret and theorize in relation to your data.

- *Review your codes.* Begin to review your codes, possibly in relation to your transcripts. Are you using two or more words or phrases to describe the same phenomenon? If so, remove one of them. Do some of your codes relate to concepts and categories in the existing literature? If so, might it be sensible to use these instead? Can you see any connections between the codes? Is there some evidence that respondents believe that one thing tends to be associated with or caused by something else? If so, how do you characterize and therefore code these connections?

- *Consider more general theoretical ideas in relation to codes and data.* At this point, you should be beginning to generate some general theoretical ideas about your data. Try to outline connections between concepts and categories you are developing. Consider in more detail how they relate to the existing literature. Develop hypotheses about the linkages you are making and go back to your data to see if they can be confirmed.

- Remember that *any one item or slice of data can and often should be coded in more than one way.*

- *Do not worry about generating what seem to be too many codes*—at least in the early stages of your analysis; some will be fruitful and others will not—the important thing is to be as inventive and imaginative as possible; you can worry about tidying things up later.

- *Keep coding in perspective*. Do not equate coding with analysis. It is part of your analysis, albeit an important one. It is a mechanism for thinking about the meaning of your data *and* for reducing the vast amount of data that you are facing (Huberman and Miles 1994). You must still interpret your findings, which means attending to issues like the significance of your coded material for the lives of the people you are studying, forging interconnections between codes, and reflecting on the overall importance of your findings for the research questions and the research literature that have driven your data collection.

Turning data into fragments

The coding of such materials as interview transcripts has typically entailed writing marginal notes on them and gradually refining those notes into codes. In this way, portions of transcripts become seen as belonging to certain names or labels. In the past, this process was accompanied by cutting and pasting in the literal sense of using scissors and paste. It entailed cutting up one's transcripts into files of chunks of data, with each file representing a code. The process of cutting and pasting is useful for data retrieval, though it is always important to make sure that you have ways of identifying the origins of the chunk of text (for example, name, position, date). Word processing programs allow this to be done in a way that does not rely on your DIY skills so much (see Box 17.6, p. 363, for an account of this use of word-processing software). Nowadays CAQDAS software is increasingly being used to perform these tasks (see Chapter 20).

There is no one correct approach to coding your data. As Box 19.3 suggests, grounded theory conceives of different types of code. Coffey and Atkinson (1996) point to different levels of coding. These levels can be related to the passage from an interview that was previously encountered in Chapter 15 (see Box 19.7). There are three levels.

- First there is a very basic coding, which, in the passage in Box 19.7, could be in terms of liking or disliking the Disney theme parks. However, such a coding scheme is unlikely to get us very far from an analytical vantage point.

- A second level comprises much more awareness of the content of what is said. Themes reflect much more the language the interviewee uses. We see much more the kinds of issues with which the interviewee is concerned. Examples might be 'developed world', 'black people', and 'black history'.

- A third level moves slightly away from a close association with what the respondent says and towards a concern with broad analytic themes. This is the way that the passage in Box 19.7 has been coded. Here the passage has been coded in terms of such features as whether a response: is uncritically enthusiastic ('uncritical enthusiasm') or is not critical of the Disney Corporation ('not critical of Disney'); reveals comments made about typical visitors ('visitors' ethnicity'); and makes critical comments ('aesthetic critique'; 'ethnicity critique'; 'nationality critique'). Interestingly, the passage also reveals the potential for a code employed by Coffey and Atkinson (1996: 43–5) in relation to one of their examples—namely, the use of a 'contrastive rhetoric'. This occurs when a person makes a point about something by comparing it to something else. This feature occurs when the husband makes a point about the representation of British culture, which in fact he regards as poor, by comparing it to that of China, which he regards as good. The poor showing of Britain is brought out by comparing it in a negative light to China. However, this coding category was not employed in relation to this research.

As Coffey and Anderson (1996) observe, following Strauss and Corbin's account (1990) of grounded theory, codes should not be thought of purely as mechanisms for the fragmentation and retrieval of text. In other words, they can do more than simply manage the data you have gathered. For example, if we ask about the properties and interconnections between codes, we may begin to see that some of them may be dimensions of a broader phenomenon. For example, as shown in the next chapter (see especially Figure 20.1, p. 412), 'ethnicity critique' came to be seen as a dimension of 'ideology critique', along with 'class critique' and 'gender critique'. In this way, we can begin to map the more general or formal properties of concepts that are being developed.

Problems with coding

One of the most commonly mentioned criticisms of the coding approach to qualitative data analysis is the possible problem of losing the context of what

---

Box 19.7 Coded text from the Disney project

Interviewer OK. What were your views or feelings about the presentation of different cultures, as shown in, for example, Jungle Cruise or It's a Small World at the Magic Kingdom or in World Showcase at Epcot?

Wife Well, I thought the different countries at Epcot were wonderful, but I need to say more than that, don't I? — uncritical enthusiasm

Husband They were very good and some were better than others, but that was down to the host countries themselves really, as I suppose each of the countries represented would have been responsible for their own part, so that's nothing — not critical of Disney — aesthetic critique
to do with Disney, I wouldn't have thought. I mean some of the landmarks were hard to recognise for what they were supposed to be, but some were very well done. Britain was OK, but there was only a pub and a Welsh shop there really, whereas some of the other pavilions, as I think they were called, were good ambassadors for the countries they represented. China, for example, had an excellent 360 degree film showing parts of China and I found that very interesting. — content critique

Interviewer Did you think there was anything lacking about the content?

Husband Well I did notice that there weren't many black people at World Showcase, particularly the American Adventure. Now whether we were there on an unusual day in that respect I don't know, but we saw plenty of black Americans in the Magic Kingdom and other places, but very few if any in that World Showcase. And there was certainly little mention of black history in the American Adventure presentation, so maybe they felt alienated by that, I don't know, but they were noticeable by their absence. — visitors' ethnicity — ethnicity critique — visitors' ethnicity

Interviewer	So did you think there were any special emphases?	
Husband	Well thinking about it now, because I hadn't really given this any consideration before you started asking about it, but thinking about it now, it was only really representative of the developed world, you know, Britain, America, Japan, world leaders many of them in technology, and there was nothing of the Third World there. Maybe that's their own fault, maybe they were asked to participate and didn't, but now that I think about it, that does come to me. What do you think, love?	} nationality critique
Wife	Well, like you, I hadn't thought of it like that before, but I agree with you.	

Box 19.8 🔆 *What is narrative analysis?*

Narrative analysis is an approach to the elicitation and analysis of data that is sensitive to the sense of temporal sequence that people, as tellers of stories about their lives or events around them, detect in their lives and surrounding episodes and inject into their accounts. Proponents of narrative analysis argue that most approaches to the collection and analysis of data neglect the fact that people perceive their lives in terms of continuity and process and that attempts to understand social life that are not attuned to this feature neglect the perspective of those being studied. Life history research (Box 15.4, p. 316) is an obvious location for the application of a narrative analysis, but its use can be much broader than this. Mishler (1986: 77), for example, has argued for greater interest in 'elicited personal narratives'. In his view, and that of many others, the answers that people provide, in particular in qualitative interviews, can be viewed as stories that are potential fodder for a narrative analysis. In other words, narrative analysis relates not just to the life span but also to accounts relating to episodes and to the

interconnections between them. Some researchers apply narrative analysis to interview accounts (e.g. Riessman 1993) while others deliberately ask people to recount stories (e.g. R. L. Miller 2000). Coffey and Atkinson (1996) argue that a narrative should be viewed in terms of the functions that the narrative serves for the teller. The aim of narrative interviews is to elicit interviewees' reconstructed accounts of connections between events and between events and contexts. A narrative analysis will then entail a seeking-out of the forms and functions of narrative. R. L. Miller (2000) proposes that narrative interviews in life story or biographical research are far more concerned with eliciting the interviewee's perspective as revealed in the telling of the story of his or her life or family than with the facts of that life. There is a concern with how that perspective changes in relation to different contexts. The interviewer is very much a part of the process in that he or she is fully implicated in the construction of the story for the interviewee.

---

is said. By plucking chunks of text out of the context within which they appeared, such as a particular interview transcript, the social setting can be lost.

A second criticism of coding is that it results in a fragmentation of data, so that the narrative flow of

what people say is lost (Coffey and Atkinson 1996). Sensitivity to this issue has been heightened by a growing interest in narrative analysis since the late 1980s (see Box 19.8). Riessman became concerned about the fragmentation of data that occurs when coding themes when she came to analyse data she had collected through structured interviews on divorce and gender. She writes:

Some [interviewees] developed long accounts of what had happened in their marriages to justify their divorces. I did not realize these were narratives until I struggled to code them. Applying traditional qualitative methods, I searched the texts for common thematic elements. But some individuals knotted together several themes into long accounts that had coherence and sequence, defying easy categorization. I found myself not wanting to fragment the long accounts into distinct thematic categories. There seemed to be a common structure beneath talk about a variety of topics. While I coded one interview, a respondent provided language for my trouble. As I have thought about it since, it was a 'click moment' in my biography as a narrative researcher . . .   (Riessman 1993: p. vi)

Riessman's account is interesting because it suggests several possibilities: that the coding method of qualitative data analysis fragments data; that some forms of data may be unsuitable for the coding method; and that researchers can turn narrative analysis on themselves, since what she provides in this passage is precisely a narrative. Interest in narrative analysis certainly shows signs of growing and in large part this trend parallels the rebirth of interest in the life history approach (see Box 15.4, p. 316). Nonetheless, the coding method is unlikely to become less prominent, because of several factors: its widespread acceptance in the research community; not all analysts are interested in research questions that lend themselves to the elicitation of narratives; the influence of grounded theory and its associated techniques; and the growing use and acceptance of computer software for qualitative data analysis, which frequently invites a coding approach.

Regardless of which analytical strategy you employ, what you must not do is simply say—'this is what my subjects said and did—isn't that incredibly interesting'. It may be reasonably interesting, but your work can acquire significance only when you theorize in relation to it. Many researchers are wary of this—they worry that, in the process of interpretation and theorizing, they may fail to do justice to what they have seen and heard; that they may contaminate their subjects' words and behaviour. This is a risk, but it has to be balanced against the fact that your findings acquire significance in our intellectual community only when you have reflected on, interpreted, and theorized your data. You are not there as a mere mouthpiece.

Secondary analysis of qualitative data

One final point to bear in mind is that this discussion of qualitative data analysis may have been presumed to be solely concerned with the analysis of data in which the analyst has played a part in collecting. However, in recent years, secondary analysis of qualitative data has become a growing focus of discussion and interest. While the secondary analysis of quantitative data has been on the research agenda for many years (see Chapter 10), similar use of qualitative data has only recently come to the fore. The general idea of secondary analysis was addressed in Box 10.1 (p. 196).

There is no obvious reason why qualitative data cannot be the focus of secondary analysis, though it is undoubtedly the case that such data do present certain problems that are not fully shared by quantitative data. The possible grounds for conducting a secondary analysis are more or less the same as those associated with quantitative data (see Chapter 10). With such considerations in mind, Qualidata, an archival resource centre, was created in the UK in 1994. The centre is not a repository for qualitative data (unlike the Data Archive, which does house quantitative data); instead, it is concerned with 'locating, assessing and documenting qualitative data and arranging their deposit in suitable public archive repositories' (Corti *et al.* 1995). It has a very useful website:

http://www.essex.ac.uk/qualidata/

and its online catalogue—Qualicat—can be searched at the following address:

http://www.essex.ac.uk/qualidata/data/catinput.html

Qualidata acknowledges certain difficulties with the reuse of qualitative data, such as the difficulty of making settings and people anonymous and the ethical problems involved in such reuse associated with promises of confidentiality. Also, M. Hammersley (1997) has suggested that reuse of qualitative data may be hindered by the secondary analyst's lack of an insider's understanding of the social context within which the data were produced. This possible difficulty may hinder the interpretation of data but would seem to be more of a problem with ethnographic field notes than with interview transcripts. Such problems even seem to afflict researchers

revisiting their own data many years after the original research had been carried out (Mauthner *et al.* 1998: 742). There are also distinctive ethical issues deriving from the fact that the original researcher(s) may not have obtained the consent of research participants for the analysis of data by others. This is a particular problem with qualitative data in view of the fact that it invariably contains detailed accounts of contexts and people that can make it difficult to conceal the identities of institutions and individuals in the presentation of raw data (as opposed to publications in which such concealment is usually feasible). Nonetheless, in spite of certain practical difficulties, secondary analysis offers rich opportunities not least because the tendency for qualitative researchers to generate large and unwieldy sets of data means that much of the material remains under-explored.

Key points

- **The collection of qualitative data frequently results in the accumulation of a large volume of information.**

- **Qualitative data analysis is not governed by codified rules in the same way as quantitative data analysis.**

- **There are different approaches to qualitative data analysis, of which grounded theory is probably the most prominent.**

- **Coding is a key process in most qualitative data analysis strategies, but it is sometimes accused of fragmenting and decontextualizing text.**

- **Secondary analysis of qualitative data is becoming a more prominent activity than in the past.**

Revision questions

- What is meant by suggesting that qualitative data are an 'attractive nuisance'?

General strategies of qualitative data analysis

- What are the main ingredients of analytic induction?

- What makes it a rigorous method?
- What are the main ingredients of grounded theory?
- What is the role of coding in grounded theory and what are the different types of coding?
- What is the role of memos in grounded theory?
- Charmaz has written that theoretical sampling 'represents a defining property of grounded theory' (2000: 519). Why do you think she feels this to be the case?
- What are some of the main criticisms of grounded theory?

More on coding

- Is coding associated solely with grounded theory?
- What are the main steps in coding?
- To what extent does coding result in excessive fragmentation of data?
- To what extent does narrative analysis provide an alternative to data fragmentation?

Secondary analysis of qualitative data

- How feasible is it for researchers to analyse qualitative data collected by another researcher?

20 Computer-assisted qualitative data analysis: Using NVivo

Reader's guide

One of the most significant developments in qualitative research in the last twenty years is the emergence of computer software that can assist in the use of qualitative data analysis. This software is often referred to as computer-assisted (or computer-aided) qualitative data analysis software (CAQDAS). CAQDAS removes many if not most of the clerical tasks associated with the manual coding and retrieving of data. There is no industry leader among the different programs (in the sense that SPSS holds this position among quantitative data analysis software). This chapter introduces a relatively new entrant that is having a big impact—NVivo. It was developed out of an earlier program—NUD*IST—which is still available. This chapter explores:

- some of the debates about the desirability of CAQDAS;
- how to set up your research materials for analysis with NVivo;
- how to code using NVivo;
- how to retrieve coded text;
- how to create memos;
- basic computer operations in NVivo.

Introduction

One of the most notable developments in qualitative research in recent years has been the arrival of computer software that facilitates the analysis of qualitative data. Computer-assisted qualitative data analysis software, or CAQDAS as it is conventionally abbreviated, has been a growth area in terms of both the proliferation of programs that perform such analysis and the numbers of people using them.

Most of the best-known programs are variations on the code-and-retrieve theme. This means that they allow the analyst to code text while working at the computer and to retrieve the coded text. Thus, if we code a large number of interviews, we can retrieve all those sequences of text to which a code (or combination of codes) was attached. This means that the computer takes over manual tasks associated with the coding process referred to in the previous chapter. Typically, the analyst would

- go through a set of data marking sequences of text in terms of codes (coding); and
- for each code, collect together all sequences of text coded in a particular way (retrieving).

The computer takes over the physical task of writing marginal codes, making photocopies of transcripts or field notes, cutting out all chunks of text relating to a code, and pasting them together. CAQDAS does not automatically do these things: the analyst must still interpret his or her data, code, and then retrieve the data, but the computer takes over the manual labour involved (wielding scissors and pasting small pieces of paper together, for example).

Is CAQDAS like quantitative data analysis software?

One of the comments often made about CAQDAS is that it does not and cannot help with decisions about the coding of textual materials or about the interpretation of findings (Sprokkereef *et al.* 1995; Weitzman and Miles 1995). However, this situation is little different (if at all) from quantitative data analysis software. In quantitative research, the investigator sets out the crucial concepts and ideas in advance rather than generating them out of his or her data. Also, it would be wrong to represent the use of quantitative data analysis software like SPSS as purely mechanical; once the analyses have been performed, it is still necessary to interpret them. Indeed, the choice of variables to be analysed and the techniques of analysis to be employed are themselves areas in which a considerable amount of interpretive expertise is required. Creativity is required by both forms of software.

CAQDAS differs from the use of quantitative data analysis software largely in terms of the environment within which it operates.

No industry leader

With quantitative data analysis, SPSS is both widely known and used. It is not the only statistical software used by social researchers, but it is certainly dominant. It has competitors, such as Minitab, but SPSS is close to being the industry leader. No parallel situation exists with regard to CAQDAS. Up until the early 1990s, The Ethnograph was probably the best known and most widely used CAQDAS. Lee and Fielding (1991: 11) report that, between March 1988 and January 1990, 1,600 copies of the software were sold. However, at that time more and more programs were coming onto the market: ten other programs were referred to in an appendix to the book in which Lee and Fielding's (1991) article appeared, and since then further programs have appeared. Seven years later, the situation had changed. The same authors observed that, in the UK, The Ethnograph 'seems . . . to have lost ground to both NUD*IST and Atlas/it over the last few years. NUD*IST is now probably the package that most people at least know by name' (Fielding and Lee 1998: 15).

NUD*IST (Non-numerical Unstructured Data Indexing Searching and Theorizing) became very popular in the 1990s and has been built upon more recently with the emergence of QSR NUD*IST Vivo, known as NVivo. This software is the one featured in this chapter. It draws upon many features in NUD-*IST, so that, if you have access to NUD*IST, most of what you read in this chapter will be applicable to

you. If you are unsure about which software is likely to meet your needs, demonstration copies of many of the main packages (The Ethnograph, NUD*IST, NVivo, winMax, and ATLAS/it) can be downloaded from either of the distributor's Internet sites:

http://www.scolari.co.uk
http://www.scolari.com

These demonstration copies are full working programs but you cannot save changes to the project work you carry out using them.

Lack of universal agreement about the utility of CAQDAS

Unlike quantitative data analysis, in which the use of computer software is both widely accepted and to all intents and purposes a necessity, among qualitative data analysts its use is by no means universally embraced. There are several concerns.

- Some writers are concerned that the ease with which coded text can be quantified, either within qualitative data analysis packages or by importing coded information into quantitative data analysis packages like SPSS, will mean that the temptation to quantify findings will prove irresistible to many researchers. As a result, there is a concern that qualitative research will then be colonized by the reliability and validity criteria of quantitative research (Hesse-Biber 1995).

- It has been suggested that CAQDAS reinforces and even exaggerates the tendency for the code-and-retrieve process that underpins most approaches to qualitative data analysis to result in a fragmentation of the textual materials on which researchers work (Weaver and Atkinson 1995). As a result, the narrative flow of interview transcripts and events recorded in field notes may be lost.

- It has also been suggested that the fragmentation process of coding text into chunks that are then retrieved and put together into groups of related fragments risks decontextualizing data (Buston 1997; Fielding and Lee 1998: 74). Having an awareness of context is crucial to many qualitative researchers and the prospect of this element being sidelined is not an attractive prospect.

- Catterall and Maclaran (1997) have argued on the basis of their experience that CAQDAS is not very suitable for focus group data because the code and retrieve function tends to result in a loss of the communication process that goes on when this method is used. Many writers view the interaction that occurs in focus groups as an important feature of the method (Kitzinger 1994).

- Stanley and Temple (1995) have suggested that most of the coding and retrieval features that someone is likely to need in the course of conducting qualitative data analysis are achievable through powerful word-processing software. They show how this can be accomplished using Word for Windows. The key point here is that the advantage of using such software is that it does not require a lengthy period of getting acquainted with the mechanics of its operations. Also, of course, if someone already has the necessary word-processing software, the possible cost of a CAQDAS program is rendered unnecessary.

- Researchers working in teams may experience difficulties in coordinating the coding of text when different people are involved in this activity (Sprokkereef *et al.* 1995).

- Coffey *et al.* (1996) have argued that the style of qualitative data analysis enshrined in most CAQDAS software (particularly the more prominent ones such as The Ethnograph, NUD*IST, and NVivo) is resulting in the emergence of a new orthodoxy. This arises because these programs presume and are predicated on a certain style of analysis—one based on coding and retrieving text—that owes a great deal to grounded theory. Coffey *et al.* argue that the emergence of a new orthodoxy is inconsistent with the growing flirtation with a variety of representational modes in qualitative research, partly as a result of the influence of postmodernism (see Chapter 23 for a discussion of these considerations).

On the other hand, several writers have sought to extol the virtues of such packages on a variety of grounds:

- Most obviously, CAQDAS can make the coding and retrieval process faster and more efficient.

- It has been suggested that new opportunities are offered. For example, Mangabeira (1995) has argued on the basis of her experience with The Ethnograph that her ability to relate her coded text to what are often referred to as 'face-sheet variables' (socio-demographic and personal information, such as age, title of job, number of years in school education) offered new opportunities in the process of analysing her data. Thus, CAQDAS may be helpful in the development of explanations.

- It is sometimes suggested that CAQDAS enhances the transparency of the process of conducting qualitative data analysis. It is often noted that the ways in which qualitative data are analysed are unclear in reports of findings (Bryman and Burgess 1994b). CAQDAS may force researchers to be more explicit and reflective about the process of analysis.

- CAQDAS, like Nvivo, invites the analyst to think about codes that are developed in terms of 'trees' of inter-related ideas. This can be a useful feature, in that it urges the analyst to consider possible connections between codes.

- Writers like Silverman (1985) have commented on the tendency towards anecdotalism in much qualitative research—that is, the tendency to use quotations from interview transcripts or field notes but with little sense of the prevalence of the phenomenon they are supposed to exemplify. CAQDAS invariably offers the opportunity to count such things as the frequency with which a form of behaviour occurred or a viewpoint was expressed in interviews. However, as previously noted, some qualitative researchers perceive risks in the opportunity offered for quantification of findings.

To use or not to use CAQDAS? If you have a very small data set, it is probably not worth the time and trouble navigating your way around new software. On the other hand, if you think you may use it on a future occasion, taking the time and trouble may be worth it. If you do not have easy access to CAQDAS, it is likely to be too expensive for your personal purchase, though the afore-mentioned Scolari Internet sites do outline student and educational discounts. It is also worth bearing in mind that learning new software does provide you with useful skills that may be transferable on a future occasion. By and large, I feel it is worthwhile, but you need to bear in mind some of the factors mentioned above in deciding whether to use it.

Learning NVivo

This exposition of NVivo and its functions addresses just its most basic features. There may be features not covered here that you would find useful in your own work, so try to explore it. There is a very good help facility and tutorials have been included to assist learners. In the following account, as in Chapter 12, → signifies 'click once with the left-hand button of your mouse'—that is, select.

On opening NVivo, you will be presented with a welcome screen (known as the **Launch Pad**), offering four options: create a project; open a project; open tutorial project; and exit NVivo. If you are starting a new project, as we will be in the example that follows, select the first of these. You will then be offered the option of opening either a 'typical' or a 'custom' project. First-time users are strongly advised to select the former and this selection was made for this example. You are then presented with a screen offering you an opportunity to give your project a name. I have chosen 'Disney project'. Then, → **Next** >. The details of your Project will then be presented to you, and, if you are happy with them, → **Finish**.

You will then be faced with a window, known as the **Project Pad** (see Plate 20.1), offering several options. My aim is to import into NVivo documents I have created using a standard word processor (Word). This is probably the most common route to creating documents for processing by NVivo. The **Project Pad** can be hidden so that only the menu bar is visible (→ **Windows** and then **Project Pad**). You can access all the functions on the **Project Pad** from the menu bar that is left behind, but when learning NVivo you may find it reassuring to have the **Project Pad** visible.

In order to import word-processed documents, you need to save your project documents as either .txt files (plain text files) or .rtf files (rich text files, which contain the text with some formatting features retained). I chose the latter. To do this if you are working in Word, → **Save As...**. Then in the box at the bottom of the dialog box, which is called **Save as type**, → the downward pointing arrow and select **Rich Text Format**. Doing this will not over-write your existing document as an .rtf document. Instead, two documents will exist: the original Word one and the .rtf one. You may want to give them clearly different names. Then:

1. From the **Project Pad** (Plate 20.1) → **Make a project document** [the **New Document Wizard : Creation** dialog box opens].

2. → **Locate and import readable external text file[s]** → **Next** > [the **Select File to read** dialog box in Plate 20.2 opens].

3. Select the file or files you want to use in your project; more than one can be selected by holding down the Ctrl key and selecting the files.

4. → **Open** [the **New Document Wizard : Obtain Name** dialog box opens].

5. → **Use the source file name as the document name**.

6. → **Finish**.

The selected files will then be copied into your NVivo project and you will be taken back to the **Project Pad** (Plate 20.1). At this point, you can elect to edit any of the documents you have entered into your project by selecting **Browse, Change, Link and Code a Document**. The **Choose Document** dialog box will open. Select the

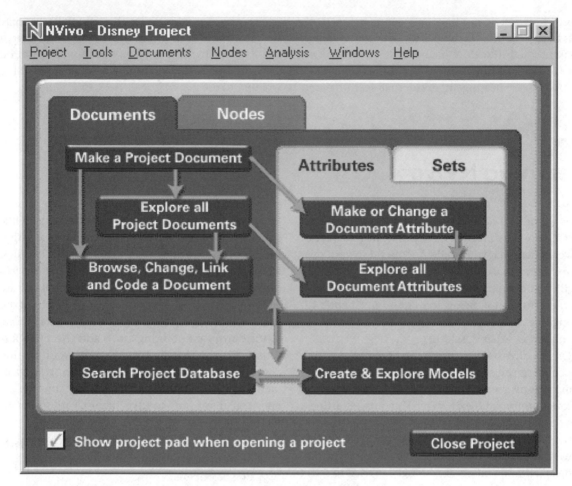

Plate 20.1 The **Project Pad**

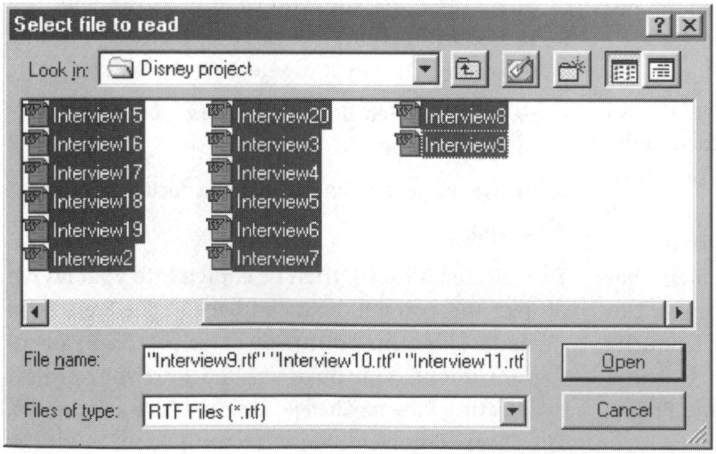

Plate 20.2 The **Select file to read** dialog box

document you want and then → **Open**. This opens the **Document Browser** (Plate 20.3). From the **Document Browser**, you can edit the document as if you were using a word processor.

Coding

Coding your data is obviously one of the key phases in the whole process of qualitative data analysis. For NVivo, coding is accomplished through nodes (see Box 20.1).

There are several ways of going about the coding process in NVivo. The approach I took in relation to the coding of the Disney Project was to follow these steps:

1. I read through the interviews both in printed form and in the **Document Browser** (Plate 20.3).

2. I worked out some codes that seemed relevant to the documents.

3. I went back into the documents and coded them using the **Node Browser** (see below).

An alternative strategy is to code while browsing the documents.

Creating nodes

The codes that I used that were relevant to the passage in Box 19.7 are presented in Figure 20.1. Notice that there are two *free nodes* and three groups of *tree nodes*. With the latter each node point, which is the equivalent of a code, has a unique number. These numbers have been inserted in Figure 20.1. The codes and their associated numbers can be created in the following way.

1. Bring up the **Project Pad** again by exiting the

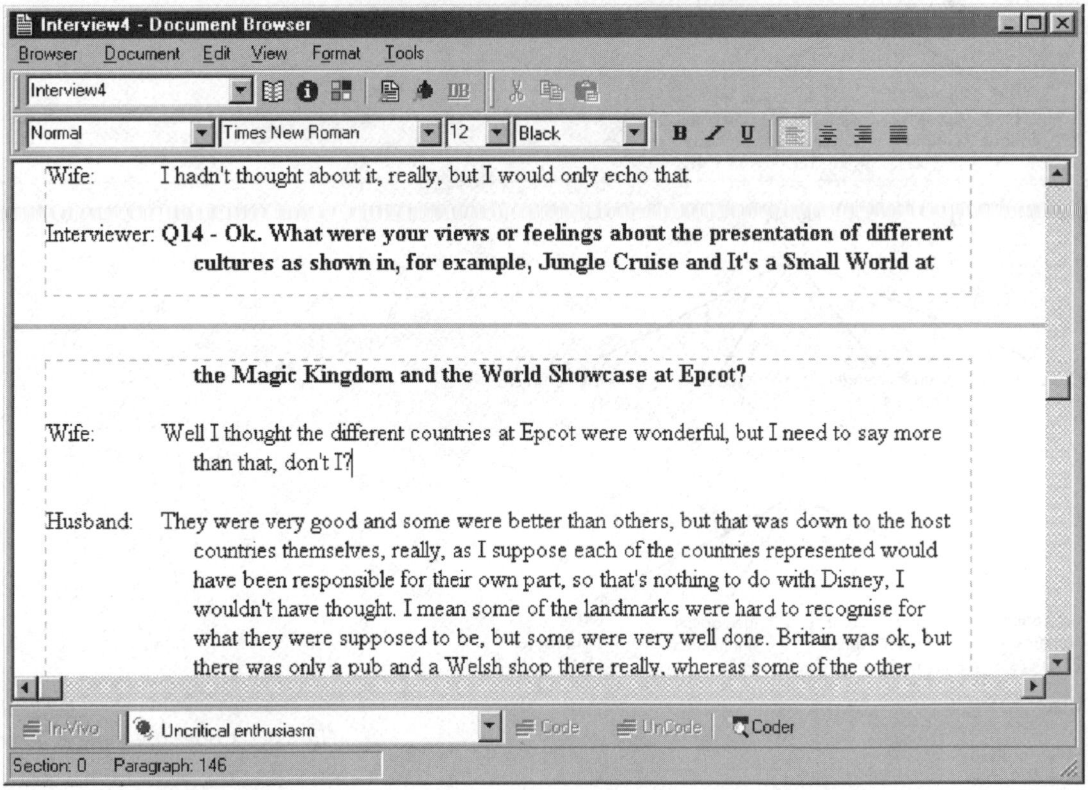

Plate 20.3 The **Document Browser**

Box 20.1 ☼ *What is a node?*

NVivo's help system defines coding as 'the process of marking passages of text in a project's documents with *nodes*' (emphasis added). Nodes are, therefore, the route by which coding is undertaken. In turn, nodes are 'items that you create to represent anything at all in or about your project, and to hold information about it, code text about it, etc. A node belongs to a particular project and is kept inside its database.' When a document has been coded, the node will incorporate references to those portions of documents in which the code appears. Once established, nodes can be changed or deleted. Nodes can be held in any of three ways, but only two are covered in this chapter. First, there are *tree nodes*, whereby nodes are held in a treelike structure, implying connections between them. In this way, you can have groups (trees) of related nodes. The other type covered here are *free nodes*, which are independent of any tree.

Tree codes

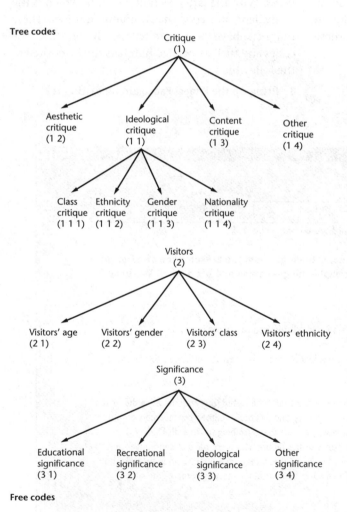

Free codes

Uncritical enthusiasm
Not critical of Disney

Fig. 20.1 Codes used in the Disney project

document browser. You can do this by clicking on the 'close' button.

2. → the tab titled **Nodes**. The **Project Pad** looks just like the one in Plate 20.1, but will refer to nodes rather than to documents.

3. → **Make a Project Node** [opens the **Create Node** dialog box shown in Plate 20.4].

4. • To form a *free node*, make sure the appropriate dialog box is in front of you (see Plate 20.4). If it is not, simply → the **Free** tab.

   • Place the name of the free node in the box to the right of **Title:**, which in Plate 20.4 is *Not critical of Disney*. Note that the box also shows any existing free nodes (Plate 20.4 shows one called *Uncritical enthusiasm*).

   • In the box under **Description** you can place a brief summary of what the node is about. This is not essential but can be useful as a reminder and may form a useful aid to creating memos

(see below on the procedure for creating memos).

   • → **Create**.

5. • To form a *tree node*, make sure the appropriate dialog box is on your screen (see Plate 20.5). To activate it, simply → the **Tree** tab.

   • Make sure you have a good idea of what your Tree Node should look like. Place the starting point of the tree in the box by **Title** (in this case it was **Critique**) and then → **Create**. This Node will then move into the large box under **Tree Nodes:**.

   • As with free nodes, in the box under **Description** you can place a brief summary of what the node is about. This is not essential but can be useful as a reminder and may form a useful aid to creating memos.

   • Then double-click on the new tree node so that it appears in the small box under **Tree Nodes:**. You can then place in the box by **Title:** the name

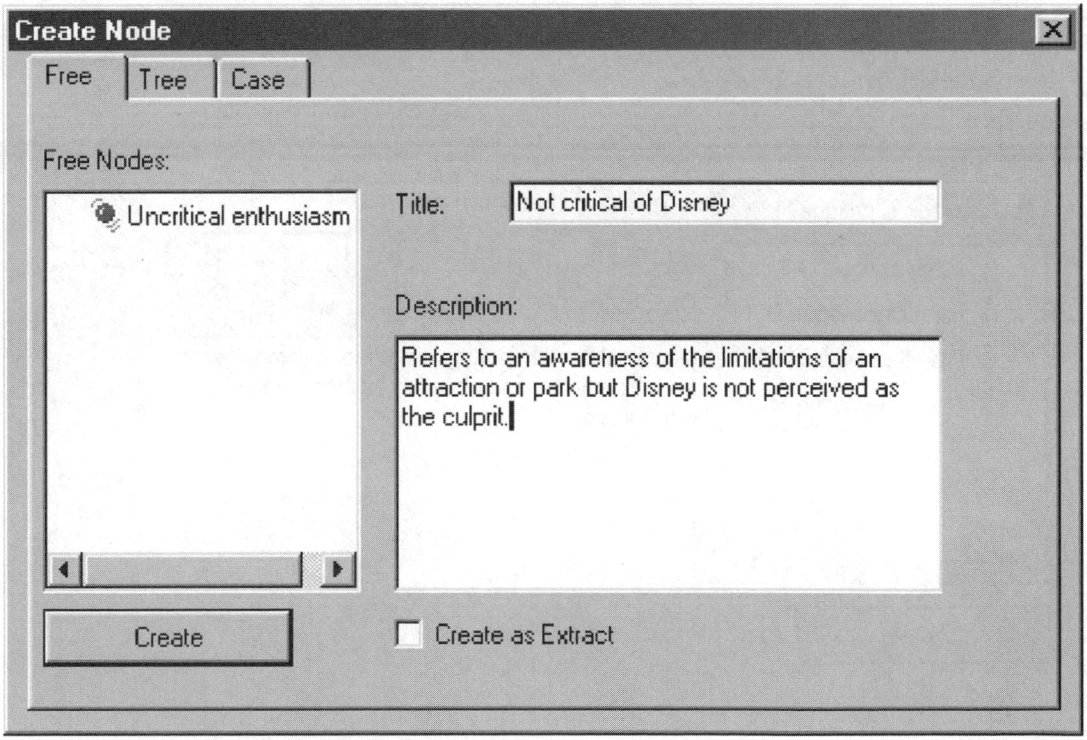

Plate 20.4 The **Create Node** dialog box (free codes)

of the first 'child' (as it is known in NVivo language) of the 'parent'. In this case, the parent is **Critique** and the first child is *Ideological Critique*. Make sure that it is in the box by **Address:** the number is that of the parent (in this case **1**) and the child (**1**, so that it is **1 1**). Carry on doing this until all the children have been dealt with. For 'grandchildren', as we have with the four children of *Ideological Critique*, simply double-click on *Ideological Critique* and follow the same procedure as for the children.

- When each child has been created, remember to → **Create**.

6. When you have finished, close the dialog box. Remember that you can always create new nodes using this procedure or you can add them during coding.

Editing and browsing

At any time, you can browse and edit your nodes. To browse your nodes, from the **Project Pad**, → **Explore All Project Nodes**. The **Node Explorer** dialog box will appear (see Plate 20.6). Selecting any nodes will allow you to see their children or parents and any descriptions you might have provided. Nodes that have already been used at some point in coding documents will appear in **bold**.

From the **Node Explorer** you can delete or change the names of nodes. To delete a node, simply click once on it and then → **Tools** and → **Cut**. To change the name of a Node, click once on the node and then click again after a short pause (i.e. *not* a double-click). The node will then appear in outline and a new name can be provided. When you have carried out some coding, the **Node Explorer** will reveal such

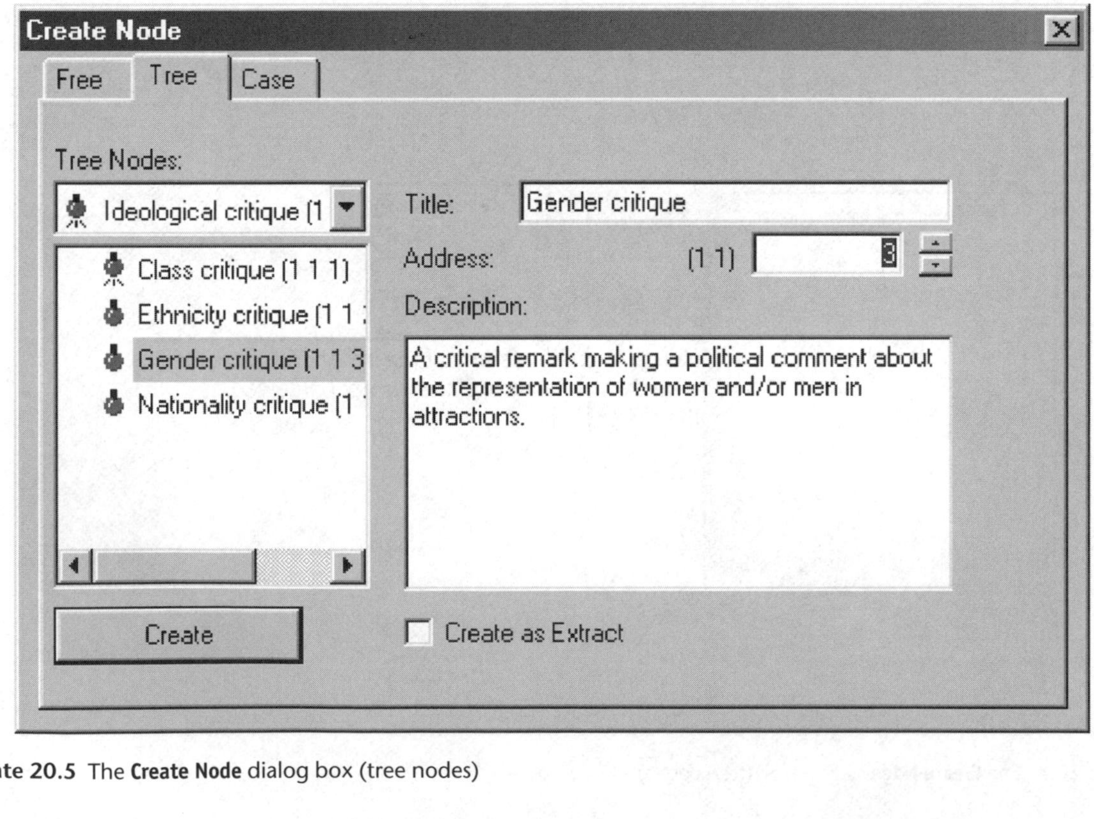

Plate 20.5 The **Create Node** dialog box (tree nodes)

details as the number of occurrences (**Passages**) of that Node.

A child or sibling of a Node can be created by → **Browse, Change, Link and Code a Node** on the **Project Pad** (Plate 20.1). The **Choose Node...** sub-dialog box (see Plate 20.7) will appear. This dialog box also provides useful information about your nodes, but clicking on the 米 button will give you the option of whether to create a child or sibling node for the node that you have selected.

Applying nodes in the coding process

Coding is carried out by applying nodes to segments of text. Once you have set up some nodes (and do remember you can add and alter at any time), follow this procedure:

1. → the **Documents** tab on the **Project Pad** (Plate 20.1).

2. → **Browse, Change, Link and Code a Document** [opens the **Choose Document** dialog box].

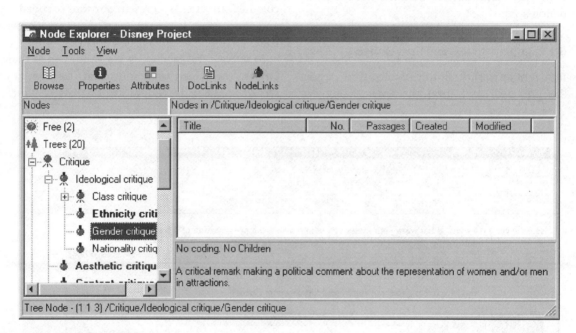

Plate 20.6 The **Node Explorer**

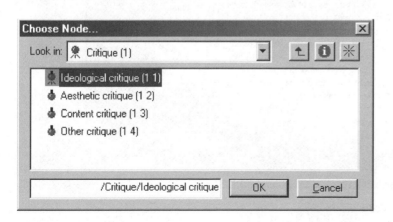

Plate 20.7 The **Choose Node...** sub-dialog box

3. Select the document you want to code, which in this case is **Interview4**, since it contains the passage in Table 19.7 (pp. 400–1) that will be the focus of attention in this account of NVivo's operations, and then ➔ **OK**.

4. When you find a passage that you want to code using one of your nodes, highlight that passage.

5. Then ➔ **Tools** and then ➔ **Coder...** *or* simply ➔ **Coder** on the bar at the bottom of the screen [opens the **Coder** dialog box—see Plate 20.8, which shows the **Document Browser** and the **Coder** dialog box].

6. Select the node you want to apply to the selected (i.e. highlighted) text and then ➔ **Code**.

To *uncode* at any point, simply highlight the passage to be uncoded, and from the **Coder** dialog box ➔ **UnCode** or simply choose **Uncode** from the toolbar at the bottom of the screen.

These instructions apply to the application of *both* free nodes and tree nodes.

Coding stripes

I find it very helpful to be able to see the areas of text that have been coded and the nodes applied to them. NVivo has a very useful aid to this called *coding stripes*. Selecting this facility allows you to see multi-coloured stripes that represent portions of coded text and the nodes that have been used. Overlapping codes do not represent a problem at all.

To activate this facility, ➔ **View** and then ➔ **Coding Stripes**. The screen then splits and the right-hand section contains the coding stripes. Plate 20.9 shows

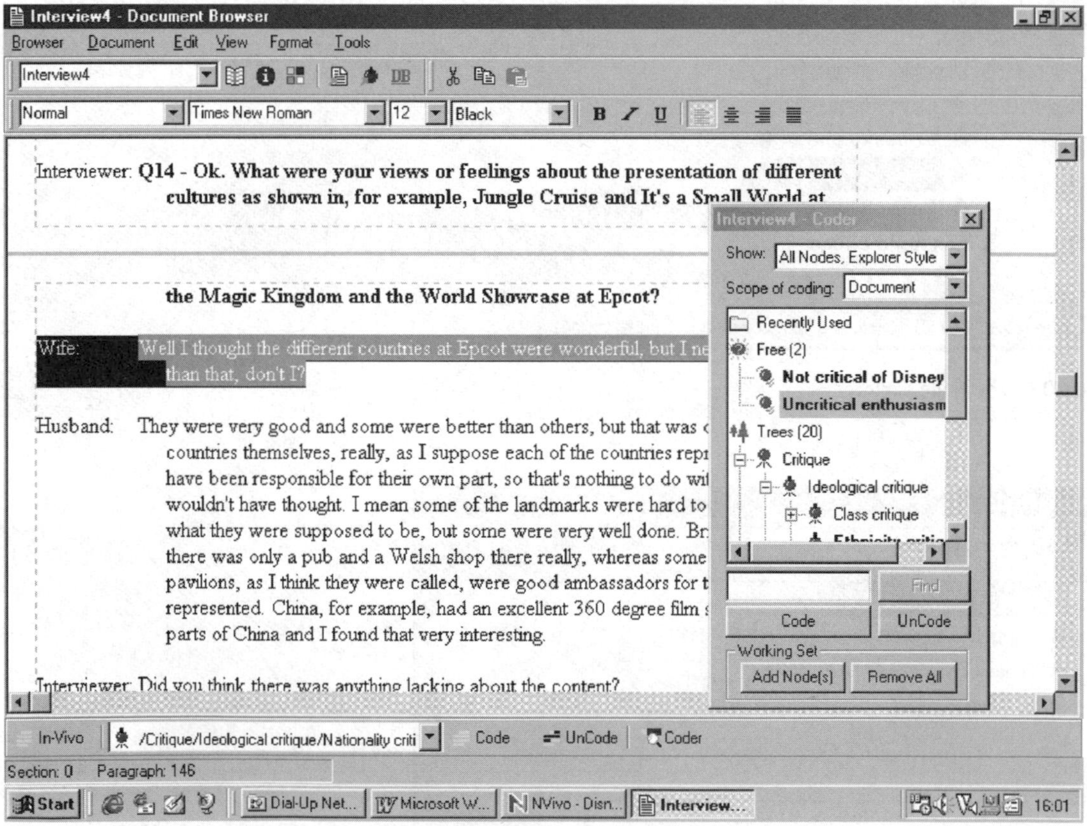

Plate 20.8 The **Document Browser** with the **Coder** dialog box

these stripes. We can see that there is a segment that has been coded with two nodes—***visitors ethnicity*** and ***ethnicity critique***. All the nodes that have been used are clearly displayed and are visible even when the **Coder** dialog box is open.

Speed coding

At the bottom of the Document Browser is the *speed coding* bar (see Plate 20.9). If you are coding a passage or series of passages using recurring nodes, you may find it easier to use this facility. If you click on the

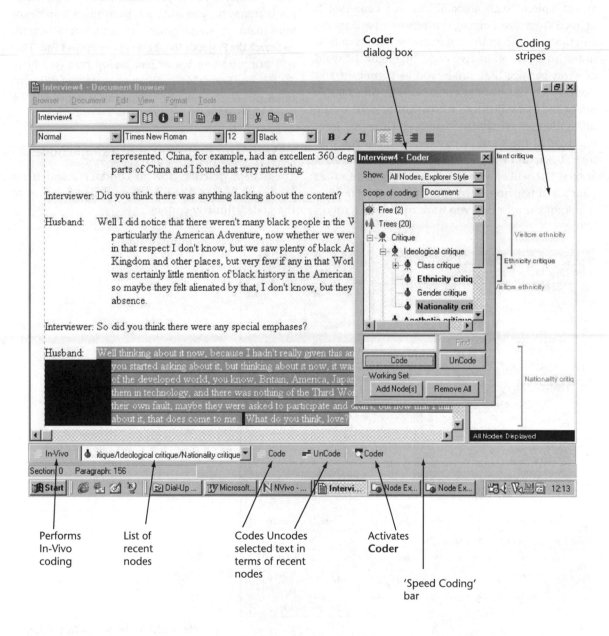

Plate 20.9 The **Document Browser** with coding stripes

downward pointing arrow to the immediate right of the box by it, the most recently used nodes will be displayed. You can then select the appropriate node and then → **Code** to the right of the selected node to code a highlighted section of text.

Another useful facility on this bar is the opportunity to generate *in vivo codes* (see Box 19.6, p. 396, for an example of such a code). This is a code that is derived from the language of research participants and that is found in the interview transcripts or field notes. To create an in vivo code, highlight the word or short passage that strikes you as significant and from which you want to create a node. An example might be 'black history', which can be seen in the unhighlighted passage in Plate 20.9. Once you have highlighted the word or passage, → the **InVivo** button. This action will create a new node entitled *black history*. This will be a free node and NVivo will adjust your list of free nodes accordingly. You then need to highlight the area that you want to code in terms of this new free node and then code it, using either the speed coding bar or the **Coder** dialog box.

Searching text

Once you have coded your data, however preliminary that may be, you will want to conduct searches of your data at some point. To conduct a search, → **Search the Project's Database** on the **Project Pad**. This will bring up the **Search Tool** dialog box (see Plate 20.10). The **Search Tool** facilitates a variety of different types of search, but just three simple types will be presented below.

To search for occurrences of a single node

These steps describe how to conduct a search for sequences of text that have been coded in terms of the node 'ethnicity critique'.

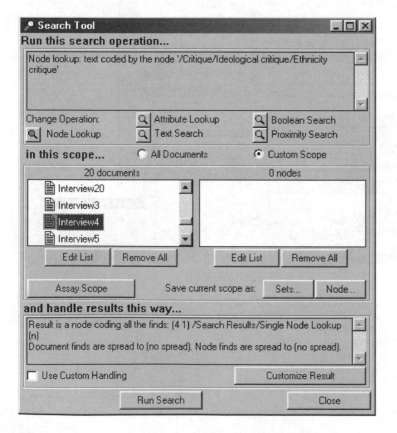

Plate 20.10 The **Search Tool** dialog box

1. While in the **Search Tool** dialog box, ➜ **Node Lookup** under **Change Operation:** [opens the **Single Node Lookup** dialog box shown in Plate 20.11].

2. If you know the name of the node you want to search for, enter it in the window beneath **Search for text coded by this node:** and then ➜ **OK**.

3. If you do *not* know the name of the node, ➜ **Choose** [opens the **Choose Node...** sub-dialog box—see Plate 20.12] and then ➜ the downward pointing arrowhead to the right of the window by **Look in:**. Find the node that you want to use. The node will be listed as either a free or a tree node. If the latter, simply keep clicking on the appropriate branches until you find the node you need. When you have found the node ➜ **OK**.

4. You then need to define the scope of your search. The default in NVivo is **All Documents**. To search particular documents ➜ **Custom Scope** and then choose the documents you want. For this exercise, just 'Interview4' was selected (see Plate 20.10).

5. ➜ **Run Search**.

To search for the intersection of two or more nodes

These steps describe how to conduct a search for sequences of text that have been coded in terms of two nodes: 'aesthetic critique' and 'not critical of Disney'. This type of search is known as a 'Boolean search'. It will locate not text coded in terms of each of the two nodes, but text coded in terms of the two nodes together (that is, where they intersect). The following steps need to be followed:

1. In the **Search Tool** dialog box (Plate 20.10) ➜ **Boolean Search** [opens the **Boolean Search** dialog box shown in Plate 20.13].

2. Make sure that by **Operator:**, the search pattern **Intersection [And]** has been selected.

3. ➜ **Choose Nodes...** [opens the **Choose Nodes...** dialog box which is very similar to the **Choose Node** dialog box shown in Plate 20.12].

4. Select a node and ➜ the **Node** button underneath **Add:**. Do this for the second node and any other nodes.

5. ➜ **OK**, which takes you back to the **Boolean Search** dialog box (Plate 20.13).

6. ➜ **OK**, which takes you back to the **Search Tool** dialog box (Plate 20.10).

7. ➜ **OK**.

To search for specific text

NVivo can also perform searches for specific words or phrases, often referred to as 'strings' in computer jargon. For example, to search for 'Magic Kingdom', the following steps would need to be taken:

1. In the **Search Tool** dialog box (Plate 20.10) ➜ **Text Search** [opens the **Text Search** dialog box shown in Plate 20.14].

2. After **Search for this Text:**, type in the text you want to search for (e.g. *Magic Kingdom*).

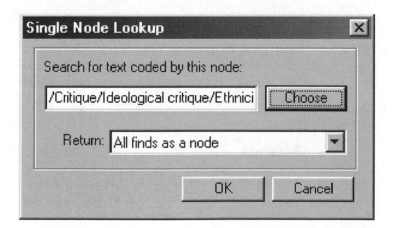

Plate 20.11 The **Single Node Lookup** dialog box

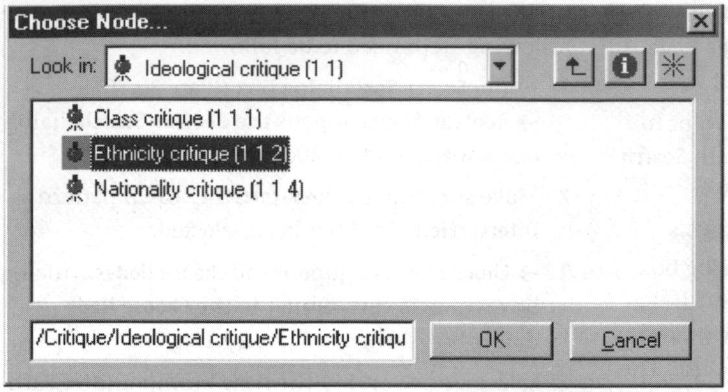

Plate 20.12 The **Choose Node...** sub-dialog box

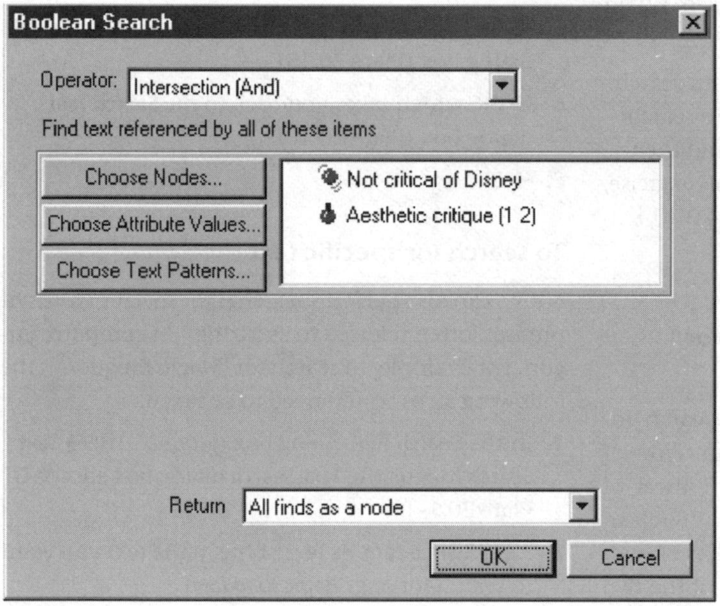

Plate 20.13 The **Boolean Search** dialog box for two or more nodes

3. → **OK**, which takes you back to the **Search Tool** dialog box (see Plate 20.10).

4. → **OK**.

Text searching can be useful for the identification of possible in vivo codes. You would then need to go back to the documents to conduct in vivo coding.

Output

The default is that, for each search you carry out, a node will be created into which the results of your search will be printed. These results can then be inspected using the **Node Browser** and printed. Plate 20.15 shows the results of a search for the node 'ethnicity critique' in Interview4.

Memos

In Chapter 19, it was noted that one feature of the grounded theory approach to qualitative data analysis is the use of memos in which ideas and

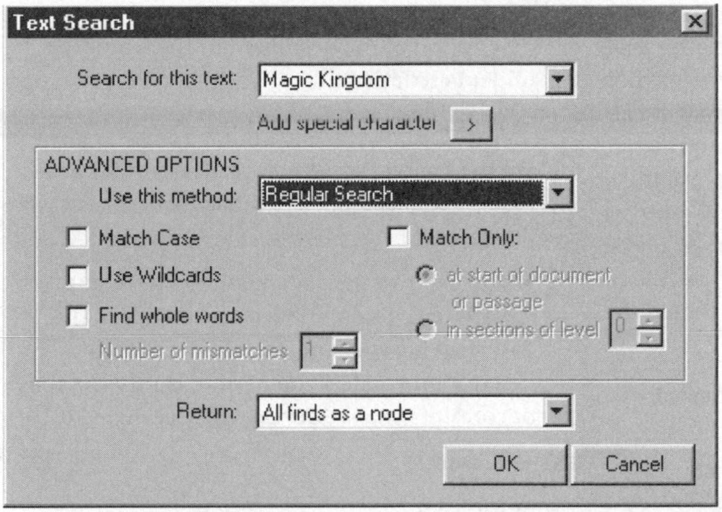

Text Search

Search for this text: Magic Kingdom

Add special character   >

ADVANCED OPTIONS
Use this method: Regular Search

☐ Match Case   ☐ Match Only:
☐ Use Wildcards   ○ at start of document
                              or passage
☐ Find whole words   ○ in sections of level   0
Number of mismatches   1

Return: All finds as a node

OK   Cancel

Plate 20.14 The **Text Search** dialog box

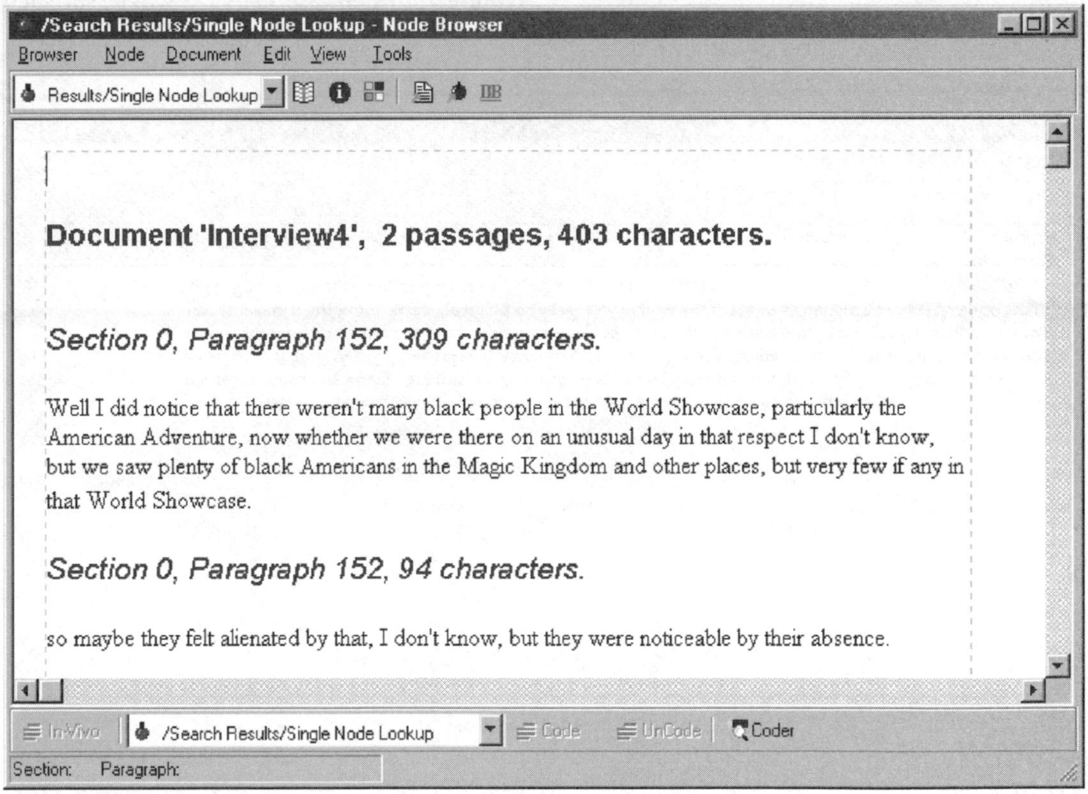

/Search Results/Single Node Lookup - Node Browser

Browser   Node   Document   Edit   View   Tools

Results/Single Node Lookup

Document 'Interview4', 2 passages, 403 characters.

Section 0, Paragraph 152, 309 characters.

Well I did notice that there weren't many black people in the World Showcase, particularly the American Adventure, now whether we were there on an unusual day in that respect I don't know, but we saw plenty of black Americans in the Magic Kingdom and other places, but very few if any in that World Showcase.

Section 0, Paragraph 152, 94 characters.

so maybe they felt alienated by that, I don't know, but they were noticeable by their absence.

InVivo   /Search Results/Single Node Lookup   Code   UnCode   Coder

Section: Paragraph:

Plate 20.15 The **Node Browser** with the results of a node search

illustrations might be stored. Memos can be easily created in NVivo, but it is important to realize that the software makes no distinction between memos and other kinds of document. In other words, when you create a memo, so far as NVivo is concerned, it is indistinguishable from your data (for example, your interview transcripts or field notes) and as such becomes part of your data set. Memos can be created in the **Document Browser** (see Plate 20.16 for an example). The following steps should be followed:

1. On the **Project Pad**, → **Make a Project Document** [opens the **New Document Wizard:Create**].

2. → **Make a new blank document** and → **Create document as a memo**.

3. → **Next**> [opens the **New Document Wizard:Name** dialog box].

4. After **Name:**, type in a name for the document (e.g. **gender critique memo**). You can also provide a brief description of the document in the window under **Description**.

5. → **Finish**.

6. On the **Project Pad**, → **Browse, Change, Link and Code a Document** [opens the **Choose Document** dialog box].

7. → the name of the document you have just created (e.g. **gender critique memo**) [opens the **Document Browser**] and provide the kind of description you feel you need to clarify the code or concepts you are developing (see Plate 20.16).

8. → **Browser**

9. → **Close**

You may find that a brief description is all you require, in which case Steps 1–5 will be sufficient for your needs.

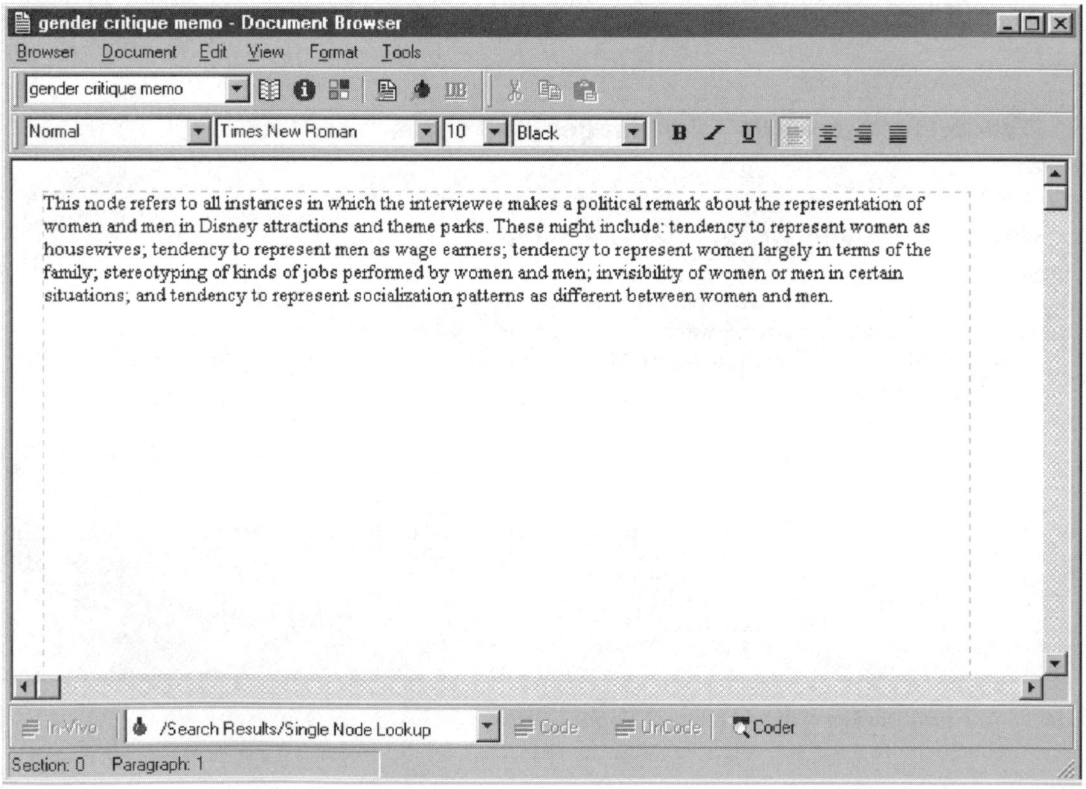

Plate 20.16 The **Document Browser** with a memo

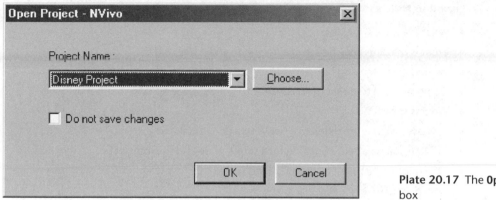

Plate 20.17 The **Open Project** dialog box

Saving an NVivo project

When you have finished working on your data, you will need to save it for future use. To do this, on the **Project Pad → Close Project**. You will then be prompted to save changes to your project. You should → **Yes**. You will then be given the opportunity to exit NVivo or to create or open a project.

Opening an existing NVivo project

To retrieve a project you have created, at the welcome screen, → **Open a Project**. This opens the **Open Project—Nvivo** dialog box. Select the project you want to work on. If you only have one, this will come up as the default as in Plate 20.17. Then → **OK**. The **Project Pad** will then appear (see Plate 20.1).

To import a NUD*IST project (version 3 or 4), from the **Project Pad**, → **Tools** and then → **Import_NUD*IST Project....** You will then be faced with a dialog box requesting that you identify the project you wish to open. When you have located it, → **Open**.

Final thoughts

As with the chapter on SPSS (Chapter 12), a short chapter like this can provide help only with the most basic features of the software. In so doing, I hope that it will have given students who may be uncertain about whether CAQDAS is for them an impression of what the software is like. Doubtless, some readers will decide it is not for them and that the tried-and-tested scissors and paste will do the trick. On the other hand, the software warrants serious consideration because of its power and flexibility.

Revision questions

Is CAQDAS like quantitative data analysis software?

- What are the main points of difference between CAQDAS and quantitative data analysis software like SPSS?
- Why is CAQDAS controversial?
- To what extent does CAQDAS help with qualitative data analysis?

Learning NVivo

- What is a node?
- What is the difference between a free node and a tree node?
- What is in vivo coding?
- Do nodes have to be set up in advance?
- What is speed coding?
- In NVivo, what is the difference between a document and a memo?
- How do you go about searching for a single node and the intersection of two nodes?
- Why might it be useful to diplay coding stripes?
- How do you search for specific text?

Part Four

In Part Four, we will explore areas that transcend the quantitative/qualitative distinction. Chapter 21 invites readers to consider how useful the distinction is. This may seem a contrary thing to do, since the book has been organized around the quantitative/qualitative divide. However, the aim is to show that the distinction is not a hard-and-fast one. Chapter 22 considers the different ways in which quantitative and qualitative research can be combined. Such combinations are referred to as *multi-strategy research*. Chapter 23 examines issues relating to the writing-up of social research and explores some features of good writing in both quantitative and qualitative research. Chapter 24 is concerned with some of the ethical principles that arise in social research and the difficulties of applying them in practice. Chapter 25 has been written to offer advice to students faced with the often daunting prospect of having to produce a dissertation. It will also be helpful to those who have to do mini-projects as part of the coursework requirement associated with modules.

These chapters draw together certain issues from previous parts but also address others that have been raised already but this time in much greater depth. In addition, they offer advice for those students who are confronted with the need to produce a lengthy piece of work, which is an increasingly common requirement.

21 Breaking down the quantitative/qualitative divide

Reader's guide

This chapter is concerned with the degree to which the quantitative/qualitative divide should be regarded as a hard-and-fast one. It shows that, while there are many differences between the two research strategies, there are also many examples of research that transcend the distinction. One way in which this occurs is through research that combines quantitative and qualitative research, which is the focus of the next chapter. The present chapter is concerned with points of overlap between them. This chapter explores:

- aspects of qualitative research that can contain elements of the natural science model;
- aspects of quantitative research that can contain elements of interpretivism;
- the idea that research methods are more independent of epistemological and ontological assumptions than is sometimes supposed;
- ways in which aspects of the quantitative/qualitative contrast sometimes break down;
- studies in which quantitative and qualitative research are employed in relation to each other, so that qualitative research is used to analyse quantitative research and vice versa;
- the use of quantification in qualitative research.

Introduction

With this book structured so far around the distinction between quantitative and qualitative research, it might appear perverse to raise at this stage the prospect that the distinction might be overblown. The distinction has been employed so far for two main reasons.

- There *are* differences between quantitative and qualitative research in terms of research strategy, and many researchers and writers on research methodology perceive this to be the case.
- It is a useful means of organizing research methods and approaches to data analysis.

However, while epistemological and ontological commitments may be associated with certain research methods—such as the often cited links between a natural science epistemology (in particular, positivism) and social survey research, or between an interpretivist epistemology (for example phenomenology) and qualitative interviewing—the connections are not deterministic. In other words, while qualitative interviews may often reveal a predisposition towards or a reflection of an interpretivist and constructionist position, this is not always the case, as an early example suggested (see the discussion of the study by Adler and Adler (1985)

in Chapter 1, p. 21). This means that the connections that were posited in Chapter 1 between epistemology and ontology, on the one hand, and research method, on the other, are best thought of as tendencies rather than as definitive connections. Such connections were implied by the suggestion that within each of the two research strategies—quantitative and qualitative—there is a distinctive mix of epistemology, ontology, and research methods (see Table 1.1, p. 20). However, we cannot say that the use of a structured interview or self-completion questionnaire *necessarily* implies a commitment to a natural scientific model or that ethnographic research *must* mean an interpretivist epistemology. We should not be surprised at this: after all, quantitative research teaches us that it is rarely the case that we find perfect associations between variables. We should not be surprised, therefore, that the practice of social research similarly lacks absolute determinism.

Research methods are much more free-floating than is sometimes supposed. A method of data collection like participant observation can be employed in such a way that it is in tune with the tenets of constructionism, but equally it can be used in a manner that reveals an objectivist orientation. Also, it is easy to under-emphasize the significance of practical considerations in the way in which social research is conducted (though look again at Figure 1.2, p. 22). Conducting a study of drug dealers by mail questionnaire may not be totally impossible, but it is unlikely to succeed in terms of yielding valid answers to questions.

In the rest of this chapter, I will examine a variety of ways in which the contrast between quantitative and qualitative research should not be overdrawn.

The natural science model and qualitative research

One of the chief difficulties with the links that are frequently forged between issues of epistemology and matters of research method or technique is that they often entail a characterization of the natural sciences as necessarily or inherently positivist in orientation. There are three notable difficulties here.

- There is no agreement on the epistemological basis of the natural sciences. As noted in Chapter 1, writers like Harré (1972) and Keat and Urry (1975) have argued that positivism is but one version of the nature of the natural sciences, *realism* being one alternative account (Bhaskar 1975).

- If we assume that the practices of natural scientists are those that are revealed in their written accounts of what they do (and most of the discussions of the nature of the natural sciences do assume this), we run into a problem because studies by social researchers of scientists' practices suggest that there is often a disparity between their work behaviour and their writings. It is useful to recall in this connection the research by Gilbert and Mulkay (1984) cited in Chapter 17 (section on 'Uncovering Interpretative Repertoires') which suggested that the ways in which scientists talked about their work frequently revealed a different set of practices from those inscribed in their articles.

- As Platt (1981) has argued, a term like 'positivist' has to be treated in a circumspect way, because, while it does refer to a distinctive characterization of scientific enquiry (see Box 1.7, p. 12), it is also frequently employed in a polemical way. When employed in this manner, it is rarely helpful, because the term is usually a characterization (a negative one) of the work of others rather than of one's own work.

Quite aside from the difficulty of addressing the natural science model and positivism, there are problems with associating them solely with quantitative research. Further, qualitative research frequently exhibits features that one would associate with a natural science model. This tendency is revealed in several ways:

- *Empiricist overtones.* Although empiricism (see Box 1.4, p. 8) is typically associated with quantitative research, many writers on qualitative research display an equal emphasis on the importance of direct contact with social reality as the springboard for any investigation. Thus, writers on qualitative research frequently stress the importance of direct experience of social settings and fashioning an understanding of social worlds via that contact. The very idea that theory is to be grounded in data (see Chapter 20) seems to constitute a manifesto for empiricism, and it is unsurprising, therefore, that some writers claim to detect 'covert positivism' in qualitative research. Another way in which empiricist overtones are revealed is in the suggestion that social reality must be studied from the vantage point of research participants but that the only way to gain access to their interpretations is through extended contact with them, implying that meaning is accessible to the senses of researchers. The empiricism of qualitative research is perhaps most notable in conversation analysis, which was examined in Chapter 17. This is an approach that takes precise transcriptions of talk as its starting point and applies rules of analysis to such data. The analyst is actively discouraged from engaging in speculations about intention or context that might derive from an appreciation of the ethnographic particulars of the social setting.

- *A specific problem focus.* As noted in Chapter 13, p. 284 in connection with the research by Hammersley *et al.* (1985), qualitative research can be employed to investigate quite specific, tightly defined research questions of the kind normally associated with a natural science model of the research process.

- *Hypothesis- and theory-testing.* Following on from the last point, qualitative researchers typically discuss hypothesis- and theory-testing in connection with hypotheses or theories generated in the course of conducting research, as in analytic induction or grounded theory. However, there is no obvious reason why this cannot occur in relation to previously specified hypotheses or theories. In fact, one of the best-known and most frequently cited articles on participant observation was designed to show how to design a study using this method 'which seeks to discover hypotheses as well as to test them' (Becker 1958: 652). The somewhat infamous research by Festinger *et al.* (1956) on a millenarian religious cult is a classic study that used participant observation, a technique associated with qualitative research, to test a theory. The theory had to do with the ways in which people respond when a belief that they zealously endorse is disconfirmed. The authors argued that it is possible to imagine a number of conditions that, if met, could result in the belief being held *more* fervently than previously after the belief had been shown to be flawed. When the authors learned of a local religious cult which believed that the end of the world was imminent, they felt that this group would provide an ideal opportunity for finding out how people respond to the falsification of a cherished belief. The researchers and some hired observers pretended to be converts and became members of the group. This membership afforded the opportunity for first-hand observation of levels of conviction and commit-

ment among the cult's adherents and therefore for testing the theory. Clearly assuming that the prediction would not in fact come true, the researchers gathered data before the fateful day about members' levels of conviction and behaviour and then afterwards on their adaptation to the thwarted prophecy. It should be noted that this research violates certain ethical principles that will be addressed in Chapter 24.

- *Realism.* Realism (Box 1.8, p. 13) is one way in which the epistemological basis of the natural sciences has been construed. It has entered into the social sciences in a number of ways, but one of the most significant of these is Bhaskar's (1989) notion of *critical realism*. This approach accepts neither a constructionist nor an objectivist ontology and instead takes the view that the 'social world is reproduced and transformed in daily life' (1989: 4). Social phenomena are produced by mechanisms that are real, but that are not directly accessible to observation and are discernible only through their effects. For critical realism the task of social research is to construct hypotheses about such mechanisms and to seek out their effects. Porter's (1993) critical realist ethnography is interesting in this connection (see Box 21.1), because it demonstrates the use of ethnography in connection with an epistemological position that derives from the natural sciences. It also relates to the previous point in providing a further illustration of hypothesis-testing qualitative research.

In addition, writers on qualitative research sometimes distinguish stances on qualitative research that contain elements of both quantitative and qualitative research. R. L. Miller (2000), in connection with an examination of life history interviews (see Box 15.4, p. 316), distinguishes three approaches to such research. One of these, which he calls 'neo-positivist', uses 'pre-existing networks of concepts . . . to make theoretically based predictions concerning people's experienced lives' (R. L. Miller 2000: 12). Therefore, one approach to the life history method, which is associated with qualitative rather than quantitative research, would seem to entail a theory-testing approach to the collection and

Box 21.1 Critical realist ethnography

A critical realist stance was employed by Porter (1993) in connection with an ethnographic study in a large Irish hospital in which the author was employed for three months as a staff nurse. Porter's interest was in the possible role of racism in this setting. He suggests that racism and professionalism were in operation such that the latter tempered the effects of the former in the context of interactions between doctors and nurses. Thus, racism and professionalism were conceptualized as generative structures—that is, mechanisms—that could be productive of certain kinds of effect. Two hypotheses were proposed: racism would play some part in the relationships between white staff and those from 'racialised minorities' and that the 'occupational situation would affect the way in which racism was expressed' (Porter 1993: 599). Porter found that racism was not a significant factor in relation-

ships between members of racialized minorities and the other staff but did manifest itself behind the backs of the former in the form of racist remarks. Racism did not intrude into work relationships, because of the operation of the greater weight given to people's achievements and performance (such as qualifications and medical skills) rather than their ascriptive qualities (that is, 'race') when judging members of professions. The emphasis on values associated with professionalism counteracted the potential role of those associated with racism. Thus, 'racism can be seen as a tendency that is realised in certain circumstances, but exercised unrealised in others' (1993: 607). In terms of critical realism, one possible structural mechanism (racism) was countered by the operation of another structural mechanism (professional ideology).

---

analysis of qualitative data. A further illustration is Charmaz's (2000) suggestion that two approaches to grounded theory can be distinguished: objectivist and constructionist (she uses the term 'constuctivist'). She argues that, in spite of the differences that developed between Glaser (1992) and Strauss

(e.g. Strauss and Corbin 1998), both held to the view of an objective, external reality. In other words, in the eyes of both the major writers on grounded theory, there is a social world beyond the researcher, whose job it is to reveal its nature and functioning.

Quantitative research and interpretivism

Qualitative research would seem to have a monopoly of the ability to study meaning. Its proponents essentially claim that it is only through qualitative research that the world can be studied through the eyes of the people who are studied. As Platt observes (1981: 87), this contention seems rather at odds with the widespread study of attitudes in social surveys based on interviews and questionnaires. In fact, it would seem that quantitative researchers frequently address meanings. An example is the well-known concept of 'orientation to work' associated with the *Affluent Worker* research in the 1960s, which sought to uncover the nature and significance of the meanings that industrial workers bring with them to the workplace (Goldthorpe *et al*. 1968). Similarly,

survey research by Stewart *et al.* (1980: 112) showed that clerks should not be treated as a unitary category and that 'the *meaning* of clerical work will not be the same for all engaged in it' (emphasis added).

The widespread inclusion of questions about attitudes in social surveys suggests that quantitative researchers are interested in matters of meaning. It might be objected that survey questions do not really tap issues of meaning because they are based on categories devised by the designers of the interview schedule or questionnaire. Two points are relevant here. First, in the absence of respondent validation exercises, the notion that qualitative research is more adept at gaining access to the point of view of those being studied than quantitative research is invariably assumed rather than demonstrated. Qualitative researchers frequently claim to have tapped into participants' world views because of, for example, their extensive participation in the daily round of those they study, the length of time they spent in the setting being studied, or the lengthy and intensive interviews conducted. However, the explicit demonstration that interpretative understanding has been accomplished—for example, through respondent validation (see Box 13.3, p. 273)—is rarely undertaken. Secondly, if the design of attitude questions is based on prior questioning that seeks to bring out the range of possible attitudinal positions on an issue, as in the research discussed in Box 7.4 (p. 147), attitudinal questions may be better able to gain access to meaning.

Also, as Marsh (1982) has pointed out, the practice in much survey research of asking respondents the reasons for their actions also implies that quantitative researchers are frequently concerned to uncover issues of meaning. For example, she cites Brown and Harris's (1978) research, which was based on a social survey, on the relationship between critical life events (such as loss of a job, death of husband) and depression. In this research, exploring the meaning of critical life events for respondents was a notable feature of the questioning. As Marsh (1982: 115) puts it, 'it is the *meaning* that these events have for the subjects that gives them their causal force in provoking an onset' (emphasis added). Examples such as these further point to the possibility that the gulf between quantitative and qualitative research is not as wide as is sometimes supposed.

Quantitative research and constructionism

It was noted in Chapter 1 that one keynote of constructionism is a concern with issues of representation, as these play an important role in the construction of the social world. Qualitative content analysis has played an important role in developing just such an understanding, just as discourse analysis has in relation to the social construction of events and meanings in newspaper reports and television programmes. However, it is easy to forget that conventional quantitative content analysis can also be useful in this way.

Lantz and Booth's (1998) research on the social construction of breast cancer (see Box 1.13, p. 19) provides an example of its use. As Box 1.13 makes clear, much of their understanding of the representation of breast cancer derived from a qualitative content analysis, but they also employed a quantitative content analysis as well. For example, a content analysis of the photographs of women linked to each article revealed that 80 per cent are apparently of women who are below the age of 50. Also, 85 per cent of the anecdotes and case stories related to women in this age group. This emphasis on younger women creates the impression that this is the age group that is at risk. This finding allowed Lantz and Booth to make an interesting connection between relative youth and lifestyles and behaviour that are conducive to breast cancer and that therefore is consistent with the 'blame the victim' theme that is conveyed (see Box 1.13, p. 19). In fact, fewer than 20 per cent of new cases of breast cancer are in women under 50 and the mean age at diagnosis is 65. Thus, the quantitative content analysis of the articles in terms of the ages of the women who are focused upon is inconsistent with the actual age of women when first diagnosed with the disease. In this way, content analysis played an important part in revealing the social construction of breast cancer.

More generally, this example shows how quantitative research can play a significant role in relation to a constructionist stance.

Research methods and epistemological and ontological considerations

If we review the argument so far, it is being suggested that

- there are differences between quantitative and qualitative research in terms of their epistemological and ontological commitments, *but*

- the connection between research strategy, on the one hand, and epistemological and ontological commitments, on the other, is not deterministic. In other words, there is a *tendency* for quantitative and qualitative research to be associated with the epistemological and ontological positions outlined in Chapter 1 (for example, in Table 1.1, p. 20), but the connections are not perfect.

However, some writers have suggested that research methods carry with them a cluster of epistemological and ontological commitments such that to elect to use a self-completion questionnaire is more or less simultaneously and inevitably to select a natural science model and an objectivist world view. Similarly, the use of participant observation is often taken to imply a commitment to interpretivism and constructionism. Such a view implies that research methods are imbued with specific clusters of epistemological and ontological commitments and can be seen in comments of the following kind: 'the choice and adequacy of a method embodies a variety of assumptions regarding the nature of knowledge and the methods through which that knowledge can be obtained, as well as a set of root assumptions about the nature of the phenomena to be investigated' (Morgan and Smircich 1980: 491). The difficulty with such a view is that, if we accept that there is no perfect correspondence between research strategy and matters of epistemology and ontology, the notion that a method is inherently or necessarily indicative of certain wider assumptions about knowledge and the nature of social reality begins to founder.

In fact, research methods are much more 'free-floating' in terms of epistemology and ontology than is often supposed. This can be particularly demonstrated by reference to historical and other studies of social research. For example, Snizek (1976) examined 1,434 articles published in sociology journals between 1950 and 1970. He based his analysis on Ritzer's (1975) suggestion that sociology is underpinned by three *paradigms*, a term that will be briefly explored again in Chapter 22 (see Box 22.1, p. 446). Two of the paradigms—the 'social factist' and the 'social definitionist' paradigms—correspond roughly to quantitative and qualitative research respectively. In his analysis, Snizek was unable to uncover an unambiguous pattern linking the grounding of an article in either of these two paradigms with the research methods used. Similarly, Platt's (1986) historical research on American sociology has suggested that the connection that is often forged between functionalism, which itself is often associated with positivism, and the social survey is greatly exaggerated. Her research suggested that 'the two originated independently, and that leading functionalists had no special propensity to use surveys and leading surveyors no special propensity for functionalism' (Platt 1986: 527). Moreover, Platt's general conclusion from her research on the use of research methods in American sociology between 1920 and 1960 is very revealing:

research methods may on the level of theory, when theory is consciously involved at all, reflect intellectual *bricolage* or *post hoc* justifications rather than the consistent working through of carefully chosen fundamental assumptions. Frequently methodological choices are steered by quite other considerations, some of a highly practical nature, and there are independent methodological traditions with their own channels of transmission. . . . In many cases general theoretical/methodological stances are just stances: slogans, hopes, aspirations, not guidelines with clear implications that are followed in practice.   (Platt 1996: 275)

Platt's conclusion again suggests that the notion that research methods reflect or reveal certain assumptions about knowledge and social reality has to be questioned. When the use of research methods in practice is examined, while tendencies may be discernible that link them to certain assumptions, the connections are not absolute.

A further aspect of the way in which research methods are much more autonomous than is sometimes supposed can be seen in the fact that the methods associated with both quantitative and qualitative research are often employed together within a single piece of research. This issue is the focus of Chapter 22.

Problems with the quantitative/qualitative contrast

The contrasts between quantitative and qualitative research that were drawn in Chapter 13 suggest a somewhat hard-and-fast set of distinctions and differences (see in particular Table 13.1, p. 285). However, there is a risk that this kind of representation tends to exaggerate the differences between them. A few of the distinctions will be examined to demonstrate this point.

norms, values, and culture of the group or community in question. In other words, quantitative and qualitative researchers are typically interested in both what people do and what they think, but go about the investigation of these areas in different ways. Therefore, the degree to which the behaviour versus meaning contrast coincides with quantitative and qualitative research should not be overstated.

Behaviour versus meaning

This distinction is sometimes drawn between a focus on behaviour and a focus on meanings. However, quantitative research frequently involves the study of meanings in the form of attitude scales (such as the Likert scaling technique) and other techniques. Qualitative researchers may feel that the tendency for attitude scales to be preformulated and imposed on research participants means that they do not really gain access to meanings (see above). The key point being made here is that at the very least quantitative researchers frequently *try* to address meanings. Also, somewhat ironically many of the techniques with which quantitative research is associated, most notably social survey research based on questionnaires and interviews, have been shown to relate poorly to people's actual behaviour (see, for example, Box 8.3, p. 162). Moreover, looking at the other side of the divide, qualitative research frequently, if not invariably, entails the examination of behaviour in context. Qualitative researchers often want to interpret people's behaviour in terms of the

Theory and concepts tested in research versus theory and concepts emergent from data

A further related point is that the suggestion that theory and concepts are developed prior to undertaking a study in quantitative research is something of a caricature that is true only up to a point. It reflects a tendency to characterize quantitative research as driven by a theory-testing approach. However, while experimental investigations probably fit this model well, survey-based studies are often more exploratory than this view implies. Although concepts have to be measured, the nature of their interconnections is frequently not specified in advance. Quantitative research is far less driven by a hypothesis-testing strategy than is frequently supposed. As a result, the analysis of quantitative data from social surveys is often more exploratory than is generally appreciated and consequently offers opportunities for the generation of theories and concepts. As one American survey researcher has commented in relation to a large-scale survey he conducted in the 1950s, but which has much relevance today: 'There are so many questions which might be asked, so many correlations which can be run, so many ways in which the findings can be organized, and so few rules or precedents for making these choices that a thousand different studies could come out of the same data' (Davis 1964: 232).

The common depiction of quantitative research as solely an exercise in testing preformulated ideas fails to appreciate the degree to which findings frequently suggest new departures and theoretical contributions. Reflecting on his career in social survey research, Glock provides the following example based on his research on the correlates of variation in church involvement in an American sample:

[It] occurred to me and my collaborators that one or both of two things might be happening. The results might simply be a reflection of the fact that women, older persons, the familyless, and the less well-to-do have more time on their hands to become involved in the Church. Alternatively or in addition, it could be that these people become involved as a compensation for being deprived, relative to their counterparts, of access to the rewards of the larger society. The data, having suggested these explanations, did not afford a means to test them . . . Subsequently, I had the opportunity to test the theory with new data . . .   (Glock 1988: 45–6)

Therefore, the suggestion that, unlike an interpretivist stance, quantitative research is solely concerned with the testing of ideas that have previously been formulated (such as hypotheses) fails to recognize the creative work that goes into the analysis of quantitative data and into the interpretation of findings. Equally, as noted above (see page 430), qualitative research can be used in relation to the testing of theories.

Numbers versus words

Even perhaps this most basic element in the distinction between quantitative and qualitative research is not without problems. Qualitative researchers sometimes undertake a limited amount of quantification of their data. Silverman (1984, 1985) has argued that some quantification of findings from qualitative research can often help to uncover the generality of the phenomena being described. While observing doctor–patient interactions in National Health Service and private oncology clinics, Silverman quantified some of his data in order to bring out the differences between the two types of clinic. Through this exercise he was able to show that patients in private clinics were able to have a greater influence over what went on in the consultations. However, Silverman warns that such quantification should reflect research participants' own ways of understanding their social world.

In any case, it has often been noted that qualitative researchers engage in 'quasi-quantification' through the use of terms like 'many', 'often', and 'some' (see below). All that is happening in cases of the kind described by Silverman is that the researcher is injecting greater precision into such estimates of frequency.

Artificial versus natural

The artificial/natural contrast referred to in Table 13.1 (p. 285) can similarly be criticized. It is often assumed that because much quantitative research employs research instruments that are applied to the people being studied (questionnaires, structured interview schedules, structured observation schedules, and so on), it provides an artificial account of how the social world operates. Qualitative research is often viewed as more naturalistic (see Box 2.4, p. 33, on naturalism). Ethnographic research in particular would seem to exhibit this quality, because the participant observer studies people in their normal social worlds and contexts—in other words, as they go about normal activities. However, when qualitative research is based on interviews (such as semi- and unstructured interviewing and focus groups), the depiction 'natural' is possibly less applicable. Interviews still have to be arranged and interviewees have to be taken away from activities that they would otherwise be engaged in, even when the interviewing style is of the more conversational kind. We know very little about interviewees' reactions to and feelings about being interviewed. Phoenix (1994) reports on the responses of interviewees to in-depth interviews in connection with two studies—one concerned with mothers under the age of 20 and the other with the social identities of young people. While many of her interviewees apparently quite enjoyed being interviewed, it is equally clear that they were conscious of the fact that they had been engaged in interviews rather than conversations. This is revealed by the tendency in the replies quoted by Phoenix for some of the interviewees to disclose that they were aware that the experience was out of the ordinary. In the study of social identities, one black young woman is reported as saying that she liked the interview and added: 'I had the chance to explain how I feel about certain things and I don't really get the opportunity to do that much.' And another interviewee said it was a 'good interview' and added: 'I have never talked so much about myself for a long time, too busy talking about kids and their problems' (Phoenix 1994: 61). The interviews were clearly valuable in allowing to surface the perspectives of people whose voices are normally silent, but the point being made here is that the view that the methods associated with qualitative research are naturalistic is to exaggerate the contrast with the supposed artificiality of the research methods associated with quantitative research.

As noted in Chapter 16, focus group research is often described as more natural than qualitative interviewing because it emulates the way people discuss issues in real life. Natural groupings are often used to emphasize this element. However, whether this is how group participants view the nature of their participation is unclear. In particular, when it is borne in mind that people are sometimes strangers, have to travel to a site where the session takes place, are paid for their trouble, and frequently discuss topics they rarely if ever talk about, it is not hard to take the view that the naturalism of focus groups is assumed rather than demonstrated.

In participant observation, the researcher can be a source of interference that renders the research situation less natural than it might superficially appear to be. Whenever the ethnographer is in an overt role, a certain amount of reactivity is possible—even inevitable. It is difficult to estimate the degree to which the ethnographer represents an intrusive element that has an impact on what is found, but once again the naturalism of such research is often assumed rather than demonstrated, although it is admittedly likely that it will be less artificial than the methods associated with quantitative research. However, when the ethnographer also engages in interviewing (as opposed to casual conversations), the naturalistic quality is likely to be less pronounced.

These observations suggest that there are areas and examples of studies that lead us to question the degree to which the quantitative/qualitative contrast is a rigid one. Once again, this is not to suggest that the contrast is unhelpful, but that we should be wary of assuming that in writing and talking about quantitative and qualitative research we are referring to two absolutely divergent and inconsistent research strategies.

The mutual analysis of quantitative and qualitative research

One further way in which the barriers between quantitative and qualitative research might be undermined is by virtue of developments in which each is used as an approach to analyse the other.

A qualitative research approach to quantitative research

There has been a growing interest in the examination of the writings of quantitative researchers using some of the methods associated with qualitative research. In part, this trend can be seen as an extension of the growth of interest among qualitative researchers in the writing of ethnography, which can be seen in such work as Van Maanen (1988) and P. Atkinson (1990). The attention to quantitative research is very much part of this trend because it reveals a concern in both cases with the notion that, not only does the written account of research constitute the presentation of findings but also it is an attempt to persuade the reader of the credibility of those findings. This is true of the natural sciences too; for example, in relation to the research by Gilbert and Mulkay (1984) discussed in Chapter 17, it was shown how the scientists employed an empiricist repertoire when writing up their findings. This writing strategy was used to show how proper procedures were followed in a systematic and linear way. However, Gilbert and Mulkay demonstrated that, when the scientists discussed in interviews how they did their research, it is clear that the process was suffused with the influence of factors to do with their personal biographies.

One way in which a qualitative research approach to quantitative research is manifested is through what Gephart (1988: 9) has called *ethnostatistics*, by which is meant 'the study of the construction, interpretation, and display of statistics in quantitative social research'. Gephart shows that there are a

number of ways in which the idea of ethnostatistics can be realized, but it is with just one of these—approaching statistics as rhetoric—that I will be concerned here. Directing attention to the idea of statistics as rhetoric means becoming sensitive to the ways in which statistical arguments are deployed to bestow credibility on research for target audiences. More specifically, this means examining the language used in persuading audiences about the validity of research. Indeed, the very use of statistics itself can be regarded as a rhetorical device because the use of quantification means that social research can bestow upon itself the appearance of a natural science and thereby achieve greater legitimacy and credibility by virtue of that association (McCartney 1970; John 1992). Some of the rhetorical strategies identified by analysts are presented in Box 23.3 (p. 465). However, the chief point being made here is that the nature of quantitative research can be illuminated by being approached from the vantage point of qualitative research.

A quantitative research approach to qualitative research

In Chapter 9, the research by Hodson (1996), which was based on the content analysis of workplace ethnographies was given quite a lot of attention (see Box 9.4, p. 190). Essentially, Hodson's approach was to apply a quantitative research approach—in the form of content analysis—to qualitative research. This is a form of research that may have potential in other areas of social research in which ethnography has been a popular method and as a result a good deal of ethnographic evidence has been built up. Hodson (1999) suggests that the study of social movements may be one such field; religious sects and cults may be yet another. Hodson's research is treated as a solution to the problem of making comparisons between ethnographic studies in a given area. One approach to synthesizing related qualitative studies is *meta-ethnography*, which is a qualitative research approach to such aggregation (Noblit and Hare 1988). However, whereas the practice of meta-ethnography is meant to be broadly in line with the goals of qualitative research, such as a commitment to interpretivism and a sensitivity to the social context, Hodson's approach is one that largely ignores contextual factors in order to explore relationships between variables that have been abstracted out of the ethnographies.

Certain key issues need to be resolved when conducting analyses of the kind carried out by Hodson. One relates to the issue of conducting an exhaustive literature search for suitable studies for possible inclusion. Hodson chose to analyse just books, rather than articles, because of the limited amount of information that can usually be included in the latter. Even then, criteria for the inclusion of a book needed to be stipulated. Hodson employed three: 'The criteria for inclusion were (a) the book had to be based on ethnographic methods of observation over a period of at least 6 months, (b) the observations had to be in a single organization, and (c) the book had to focus on at least one clearly identified group of workers . . .' (Hodson 1999: 22). The application of these criteria resulted in the exclusion of 279 out of 365 books uncovered. A second crucial area relates to the coding of the studies, which was briefly covered in Box 9.4 (p. 190). Hodson stresses the importance

of having considerable knowledge of the subject area, clear coding rules, and pilot testing the coding schedule. In addition, he recommends checking the *reliability* of coding by having 10 per cent of the documents coded by two people. The process of coding was time-consuming, in that Hodson calculates that each book-length ethnography took forty or more hours to code.

The approach has many attractions, not the least of which is the impossibility of a quantitative researcher being able to conduct investigations in such a varied set of organizations. Also, it means that more data of much greater depth can be used than can typically be gathered by quantitative researchers. It also allows hypotheses deriving from established theories to be tested, such as the 'technological implications' approach, which sees technologies as having impacts on the experience of work (Hodson 1996). However, the loss of a sense of social context is likely to be unattractive to many qualitative researchers.

However, of particular significance for this discussion is the remark that 'the fundamental contribution of the systematic analysis of documentary accounts is that it creates an analytic link between the in-depth accounts of professional observers and the statistical methods of quantitative researchers' (Hodson 1999: 68). In other words, the application of quantitative methods to qualitative research may provide a meeting ground for the two research strategies.

Quantification in qualitative research

As noted in Chapter 13, the numbers versus words contrast is perhaps the most basic in many people's minds when they think about the differences between quantitative and qualitative research. After all, it seems to relate in a most fundamental way to the very terms used to denote the two approaches that seem to imply the presence and absence of numbers. However, it is simply not the case that there is a complete absence of quantification in

qualitative research. As we will see in the next chapter, when qualitative researchers incorporate research methods associated with quantitative research into their investigations, a certain amount of quantification is injected into the research.

Quite aside from the issue of combining quantitative and qualitative research, three observations are worth making about quantification in the analysis and writing-up of qualitative data.

Thematic analysis

In Chapter 19, it was observed that one of the commonest approaches to qualitative data analysis is undertaking a search for themes in transcripts or field notes. However, as Bryman and Burgess (1994*b*: 224) point out, the criteria employed in the identification of themes is often unclear. One possible factor that these authors suggest may be in operation is the frequency of the occurrence of certain incidents, words, phrases, and so on that denote a theme. In other words, a theme is more likely to be identified the more times the phenomenon it denotes occurs in the course of coding. This process may also account for the prominence given to some themes over others when writing up the fruits of qualitative data analysis. In other words, a kind of implicit quantification may be in operation that influences the identification of themes and the elevation of some themes over others.

Quasi-quantification in qualitative research

It has often been noted that qualitative researchers engage in 'quasi-quantification' through the use of terms such as 'many', 'frequently', 'rarely', 'often', and 'some'. In order to be able to make such allusions to quantity, the qualitative researcher should have some idea of the relative frequency of the phenomena being referred to. However, as expressions of quantities, they are imprecise, and it is often difficult to discern why they are being used at all. The alternative would seem to be to engage in a limited amount of quantification when it is appropriate, such as when an expression of quantity can bolster an argument. This point leads directly on to the next section.

Combating anecdotalism through limited quantification

One of the criticisms that is often levelled against qualitative research is that the publications on which it is based are often anecdotal, giving the reader little guidance as to the prevalence of the issue to which the anecdote refers. The widespread use of brief sequences of conversation, of snippets from interview transcripts, and accounts of encounters between people provide little sense of the prevalence of whatever such items of evidence are supposed to indicate. There is the related risk that a particularly striking statement by someone or an unexpected activity may have more significance attached to it than might be warranted in terms of its frequency.

Perhaps at least partly in response to these problems, qualitative researchers sometimes undertake a limited amount of quantification of their data. We can see this feature in Silverman's (1984, 1985) research on oncology clinics, which was referred to above. In their research on concepts of leadership employed by British police officers, Bryman, Stephens, and A Campo (1996) counted the frequency with which certain leadership styles were cited in interview transcripts. This exercise allowed them to demonstrate that the kind of leadership preferred by police officers was different from what was in vogue among theorists of leadership at the time. Gabriel (1998) describes how he studied organizational culture in a variety of organizations by collecting during interviews stories about the organizations in question. Computers and information technology were a particular focus of the stories elicited. Altogether 377 stories were collected in the course of 126 interviews in five organizations. Gabriel shows that the stories were of different types, such as: comic stories (which were usually a mechanism for disparagement of others); epic stories (survival against the odds); tragic stories (undeserved misfortune); gripes (personal injustices); and so on. He counted the number of each type: comic stories were the most numerous at 108; then epic stories (82); tragic stories (53); gripe stories (40); and so on. Themes in the stories were also counted, such as whether they involved a leader, a personal trauma, an accident, and so forth. In all these cases, the types of stories and the themes could have been treated in an anecdotal way, but the use of such simple counting conveys a clear sense of their relative prevalence.

Exercises like these can be used to counter the suggestion that is sometimes made that the approach to presenting qualitative data can be too anecdotal, so that readers are given too little sense of the *extent* to which certain beliefs are held or a certain form of behaviour occurs. All that is happening in such cases is that the researcher is injecting greater precision into estimates of frequency than can be derived from quasi-quantification terms. Moreover, it is not inconceivable that there might be greater use of limited amounts of quantification in qualitative research in the future as a result of the growing incursion of computers into qualitative data analysis (CAQDAS). Most of the major software programs include a facility that allows the analyst to produce simple counts of such things as the frequency with which a word or a coded theme occurs. In many cases, they can also produce simple cross-tabulations—for example, relating the occurrence of a coded theme to gender. Writing when CAQDAS was used far less than it is today, Ragin and Becker concluded their review of the impact of micro-computers on sociologists' 'analytic habits' with the following remark: 'Thus, the microcomputer provides important technical means for new kinds of dialogues between ideas and evidence and, at the same time, provides a common technical ground for the meeting of qualitative and quantitative researchers' (Ragin and Becker 1989: 54). The greater use of quantification by qualitative researchers may turn out to be one of the more significant areas for this 'meeting'.

Key points

- There are differences between quantitative and qualitative research but it is important not to exaggerate them.

- The connections between epistemology and ontology, on the one hand, and research methods, on the other, are not deterministic.

- Qualitative research sometimes exhibits features normally associated with a natural science model.

- Quantitative research aims on occasions to engage with an interpretivist stance.

- Research methods are more autonomous in relation to epistemological commitments than is often appreciated.

- The artificial/natural contrast that is often an element in drawing a distinction between quantitative and qualitative research is frequently exaggerated.

- A quantitative research approach can be employed for the analysis of qualitative studies and a qualitative research approach can be employed to examine the rhetoric of quantitative researchers.

- Some qualitative researchers employ quantification in their work.

Revision questions

The natural science model and qualitative research

- Are the natural sciences positivistic?
- To what extent can some qualitative research be deemed to exhibit the characteristics of a natural science model?

Quantitative research and interpretivism

- To what extent can some quantitative research be deemed to exhibit the characteristics of interpretivism?

Quantitative research and constructionism

- To what extent can some quantitative research be deemed to exhibit the characteristics of constructionism?

Research methods and epistemological and ontological considerations

- How far do research methods necessarily carry epistemological and ontological implications?

Problems with the quantitative/qualitative contrast

- Outline some of the ways in which the quantitative/qualitative contrast may not be as hard and fast as is often supposed.

The mutual analysis of quantitative and qualitative research

- What might some of the implications of Gilbert and Mulkay's concepts of interpretative repertoires be for the qualitative analysis of quantitative research?
- Assess the significance of ethnostatistics.
- Assess the significance of Hodson's research.

Quantification in qualitative research

- How far is quantification a feature of qualitative research?

22 Combining quantitative and qualitative research

Reader's guide

This chapter is concerned with multi-strategy research—that is, research that combines quantitative and qualitative research. While this may seem a straightforward way of resolving and breaking down the divide between the two research strategies, it is not without controversy. Moreover, there may be practical difficulties associated with multi-strategy research. This chapter explores:

• arguments against the combination of quantitative and qualitative research; two kinds of argument are distinguished and are referred to as the embedded methods and paradigm arguments;

- the suggestion that there are two versions of the debate about the possibility of combining quantitative and qualitative research: one that concentrates on methods of research and another that is concerned with epistemological issues;
- the different ways in which multi-strategy research has been carried out;
- the need to recognize that multi-strategy research is not inherently superior to research that employs a single research strategy.

Introduction

Throughout the book so far an emphasis has been placed upon the strengths and weaknesses of the research methods associated with quantitative and qualitative research. One possible response to this kind of recognition is to propose combining them. After all, such a strategy would seem to allow the various strengths to be capitalized upon and the weaknesses offset somewhat. However, not all writers on research methods agree that such integration is either desirable or feasible. On the other hand, it is probably the case that the amount of combined research has been increasing since the early 1980s. Therefore, in discussing the combination of quantitative and qualitative research, this chapter will be concerned with three main issues:

- an examination of the arguments against integrating quantitative and qualitative research;

- the different ways in which quantitative and qualitative research have been combined;
- an assessment of combined research, which asks whether it is necessarily superior to investigations relying on just one research strategy and whether there are any additional problems deriving from it.

In this chapter, I will use the term *multi-strategy research*, which is borrowed from Layder (1993), as a simple shorthand to stand for research that integrates quantitative and qualitative research within a single project. Of course, there is research that, for example, combines structured interviewing with structured observation or ethnography with semi-structured interviewing. However, these instances of the combination of research methods are associated with just one research strategy. By multi-strategy research I am referring to research that combines research methods that cross the two research strategies.

The argument against multi-strategy research

The argument against multi-strategy research tends to be based on either and sometimes both of two kinds of argument:

- the idea that research methods carry epistemological commitments, and

- the idea that quantitative and qualitative research are separate *paradigms*.

These two arguments will now be briefly reviewed.

The embedded methods argument

This first position, which was outlined in Chapter 21, implies that research methods are ineluctably rooted in epistemological and ontological commitments. Such a view of research methods can be discerned in statements like the following:

every research tool or procedure is inextricably embedded in commitments to particular versions of the world and to knowing that world. To use a questionnaire, to use an attitude scale, to take the role of participant observer, to select a random sample, to measure rates of population growth, and so on, is to be involved in conceptions of the world which allow these instruments to be used for the purposes conceived.   (J. A. Hughes 1990: 11)

According to such a position, the decision to employ, for example, participant observation is not simply about how to go about data collection but a commitment to an epistemological position that is inimical to positivism and that is consistent with interpretivism.

This kind of view of research methods has led some writers to argue that multi-strategy research is not feasible or even desirable. An ethnographer may collect questionnaire data to gain information about a slice of social life that is not amenable to participant observation, but this does not represent an integration of quantitative and qualitative research, because the epistemological positions in which the two methods are grounded constitute irreconcilable views about how social reality should be studied. J. K. Smith (1983: 12, 13), for example, argues that each of the two research strategies 'sponsors different procedures and has different epistemological implications' and therefore counsels researchers not to 'accept the unfounded assumption that the methods are complementary'. Smith and Heshusius criticize the integration of research strategies, because it ignores the assumptions underlying research methods and transforms 'qualitative inquiry into a procedural variation of quantitative inquiry' (1986: 8).

The chief difficulty with the argument that writers like Smith present is that, as was noted in Chapter 21, the idea that research methods carry with them fixed epistemological and ontological implications is very difficult to sustain. They are capable of being put to a wide variety of tasks.

The paradigm argument

The paradigm argument is closely related to the previous one. It conceives of quantitative and qualitative research as *paradigms* (see Box 22.1) in which epistemological assumptions, values, and methods are inextricably intertwined and are incompatible between paradigms (e.g. Guba 1985; Morgan 1998*b*). Therefore, when researchers combine participant observation with a questionnaire, they are not really combining quantitative and qualitative research, since paradigms are incommensurable—that is, they are incompatible: the integration is only at a superficial level and within a single paradigm.

The problem with the paradigm argument is that it rests, as with the embedded methods one, on contentions about the interconnectedness of method and epistemology in particular that cannot—in the case of social research—be demonstrated. Moreover, while Kuhn (1970) certainly argued that paradigms are incommensurable, it is by no means clear that quantitative and qualitative research are in fact paradigms. As suggested in Chapter 21, there are areas of overlap and commonality between them.

Box 22.1 🔅 *What is a paradigm?*

Kuhn's (1970) highly influential use of the term *paradigm* derives from his analysis of revolutions in science. A paradigm is 'a cluster of beliefs and dictates which for scientists in a particular discipline influence what should be studied, how research should be done, [and] how results should be interpreted' (Bryman 1988*a*: 4). Kuhn depicted the natural sciences as going through periods of revolution, whereby normal science (science carried out in terms of the prevailing paradigm) is increasingly challenged by anomalies that are inconsistent with the assumptions and established findings in the discipline at that time. The growth in anomalies eventually gives way to a crisis in the discipline, which in turn occasions a revo-

lution. The period of revolution is resolved when a new paradigm emerges as the ascendant one and a new period of normal science sets in. An important feature of paradigms is that they are *incommensurable*—that is, they are inconsistent with each other because of their divergent assumptions and methods. Disciplines in which no paradigm has emerged as pre-eminent, such as the social sciences, are deemed pre-paradigmatic, in that they feature competing paradigms. One of the problems with the term is that it is not very specific: Masterman (1970) was able to discern twenty-one different uses of it by Kuhn. Nonetheless, its use is widespread in the social sciences (e.g. Ritzer 1975; Guba 1985).

Two versions of the debate about quantitative and qualitative research

There would seem to be two different versions about the nature of quantitative and qualitative research, and these two different versions have implications in writers' minds about whether the two can be combined.

- An *epistemological version*, as in the embedded methods argument and the paradigm argument, sees quantitative and qualitative research as grounded in incompatible epistemological principles (and ontological ones too, but these tend not to be given as much attention). According to this version of their nature, multi-strategy research is not possible.

- A *technical version*, which is the position taken by most researchers whose work is mentioned in the next section, gives greater prominence to the strengths of the data-collection and data-analysis techniques with which quantitative and qualitative research are each associated and sees these as capable of being fused. There is a recognition that

quantitative and qualitative research are each connected with distinctive epistemological and ontological assumptions but the connections are not viewed as fixed and ineluctable. Research methods are perceived, unlike in the epistemological version, as autonomous. A research method from one research strategy is viewed as capable of being pressed into the service of another. Indeed, in some instances, as will be seen in the next section, the notion that there is a 'leading' research strategy in a multi-strategy investigation may not even apply in some cases.

The technical version about the nature of quantitative and qualitative research essentially views the two research strategies as compatible. As a result, multi-strategy research becomes both feasible and desirable. It is in that spirit that we now turn to a discussion of the ways in which quantitative and qualitative research can be combined.

Approaches to multi-strategy research

This section will be structured in terms of a classification I developed many years ago of the different ways in which multi-strategy research has been undertaken (Bryman 1988a, 1992). The classification has been changed slightly from the one presented in my earlier publications. Several other ways of classifying such investigations have been proposed by other authors, and two of these are presented in Boxes 22.2 and 22.3.

The logic of triangulation (H1)

The idea of triangulation has been previously encountered in Boxes 10.6 and 13.4 (pp. 209, 274). When applied to the present context, it implies that the results of an investigation employing a method associated with one research strategy are cross-checked against the results of using a method associated with the other research strategy. It is an adaptation of the argument by writers like Webb *et al.* (1966) that confidence in the findings deriving from a study using a quantitative research strategy can be enhanced by using more than one way of measuring a concept.

An illustration of a study using a triangulation approach is an investigation by Hughes *et al.* (1997) of the consumption of 'designer drinks' by young people. The term 'designer drinks' is usually applied to a new range of fortified wines and strong white ciders that became popular in the UK in the 1990s. The authors used two main research methods:

- a qualitative research method: eight focus groups with fifty-six children and young adults with each discussion lasting around two hours;

- a quantitative research method: a questionnaire administered in two parts to a multi-stage cluster sample of 824 12–17 year olds. The first part was conducted by interview and the second, which sought to elicit more sensitive information, was self-administered.

The overall tenor of the results of the combined use of the two research strategies was mutually reinforcing. The qualitative findings showed differences in attitudes towards designer drinks and other forms of alcoholic drink among young people of different ages: the youngest (12–13) tended to adopt a generally experimental approach; the 14 and 15 year olds thought of drinking as a means of having fun and losing inhibitions and felt that designer drinks met their needs well; the oldest group (16 and 17 year olds) were mainly concerned to appear mature and to establish relationships with the opposite sex, and tended to think of designer drinks as immature as they were mainly associated in this age group's mind as targeted at younger drinkers. These connections with age were confirmed by the quantitative evidence, which also corroborated the suggestion from the qualitative evidence that

---

Box 22.2 Hammersley's classification of approaches to multi-strategy research

M. Hammersley (1996) has proposed three approaches to multi-strategy research:

- *Triangulation* (H1). This refers to the use of quantitative research to corroborate qualitative research findings or vice versa.

- *Facilitation* (H2). This approach arises when one research strategy is employed in order to aid research using the other research strategy.

- *Complementarity* (H3). This approach occurs when the two research strategies are employed in order that different aspects of an investigation can be dovetailed.

In the discussion of approaches to multi-strategy research, the three types—H1, H2, and H3—will be referred to.

Box 22.3 Morgan's classification of approaches to multi-strategy research

Morgan (1998b) has proposed four approaches to multi-strategy research. His classification is based on two criteria:

- *The priority decision.* How far is a qualitative or a quantitative method the principal data-gathering tool?

- *The sequence decision.* Which method precedes which? In other words, does the qualitative method precede the quantitative one or vice versa?

These criteria yield four possible types:

		Priority	
		Quantitative	*Qualitative*
Sequence	*Preliminary*	M1	M2
	Follow-up	M3	M4

In the discussion of approaches to multi-strategy research, the three types—M1, M2, M3, and M4—will be referred to whenever possible. This is an interesting approach to take, but the chief difficulty with this scheme is that it relies upon being able to identify both (*a*) that either quantitative or qualitative research had priority in research and (*b*) that one was preliminary to the other. This is not necessarily possible in all cases. Box 22.4 provides an example of a research project that combined quantitative and qualitative research strategies through the use of several methods. However, no single method or research strategy was dominant.

---

the designer drinks were largely associated with a desire to get drunk.

In this research, two features are worth noting: the use of a triangulation strategy seems to have been planned by the researchers and the two sets of results were broadly consistent. However, researchers may carry out multi-strategy research for other purposes, but in the course of doing so discover that they have generated quantitative and qualitative findings on related issues, so that they can treat such overlapping findings as a triangulation exercise. Whether planned or unplanned, when a triangulation exercise is undertaken the possibility of a failure to corroborate findings always exists. This raises the issue of what approach should be taken to inconsistent

results. One approach is to treat one set of results as definitive, as Newby did in connection with his research on Suffolk farm workers. Newby (1977: 127) wrote that, when his survey and participant observation findings were inconsistent, he 'instinctively trusted the latter'. The greater richness and depth of participant observation findings, coupled with the ethnographer's greater proximity to the people studied, frequently inspire greater confidence in such data. However, simply and often arbitrarily favouring one set of findings over another is not an ideal approach to reconciling conflicting findings deriving from a triangulation exercise.

Deacon *et al.* (1998) provide an example of unplanned triangulation in that they gathered data through several quantitative and qualitative research methods (see Box 22.4) but had not intended these to be deployed as part of a triangulation exercise. However, their analysis of their data revealed an inconsistency between some of the quantitative and qualitative data: the former (methods 2 and 3) suggested that journalists and social scientists enjoyed broadly consensual relationships with regard to the reporting of social science research in the media, but the qualitative findings (methods 4 and 5) suggested greater collision of approaches and values. Rather than opt for one set of findings as providing the more accurate view, the data were re-examined. For example, Deacon *et al.* show that a major component of the apparent discrepancy has to do with the tendency for social scientists when answering survey questions about coverage of their own research (method 3) to reply in terms of a feeling of relief that it was not as bad as expected. However, in interviews (method 4), social scientists tend to make much more of what Deacon *et al.* call 'war stories'—that is, memorable and often highly wounding encounters with the media. Such encounters were not being depicted in the interviews as typical, but their general feelings about media coverage of social science research appeared to have been highly influenced by their bruising encounters. Thus, in general, the questionnaires revealed that social scientists were relatively pleased with the reporting of their research, but, when they were encouraged to reflect on specific problems in the past, the drift of their replies became more negative.

Qualitative research facilitates quantitative research (H2, M1)

There are several ways in which qualitative research can be used to guide quantitative research.

- *Providing hypotheses.* Because of its tendency towards an unstructured, open-ended approach to data collection, qualitative research is often very helpful as a source of hypotheses or hunches that can be subsequently tested using a quantitative research strategy. An example is Phelan's (1987) research on incest. She collected data largely through qualitative interviews and conversations with family members attending a treatment programme for incest. After a considerable amount of qualitative data had been collected, she became aware of differences in the meanings of incest for

---

Box 22.4 Research methods used in a study of the reporting of social science research in the mass media

In their research on the reporting of social science research in the British mass media, Fenton *et al.* (1998; see also Deacon *et al.* 1998) employed several quantitative and qualitative methods:

1. content analysis of news and current affairs coverage (local and national newspapers, TV, and radio) (592 items); see Box 9.2 (p. 181) for more on this aspect of the research;

2. mail questionnaire survey of social scientists' views about media coverage and their own practices (674 respondents);

3. mail questionnaire survey of social scientists who had received media coverage as identified in the content analysis (123 respondents);

4. semi-structured interviews with social scientists who had received coverage as identified in the content analysis (20 interviews);

5. semi-structured interviews with journalists identified in the content analysis (34 interviews);

6. semi-structured interviews with representatives of funding bodies and government (27 interviews);

7. tracking of journalists at conferences (3 conferences);

8. focus group analysis of audience reception of media items (13 focus groups); see Box 16.4 and Table 16.1 (pp. 342, 340) for more on this aspect of the research.

natural fathers as against stepfathers. Quantifiable data were collected through interviews with families' counsellors that supported her hypothesis that 'the process of incest in structurally different families may vary' (Phelan 1987: 39).

- *Aiding measurement.* The in-depth knowledge of social contexts acquired through qualitative research can be used to inform the design of survey questions for structured interviewing and self-completion questionnaires. Pope and Mays (1995) point out that semi-structured interviewing took place before a British national survey on sexual attitudes and lifestyles (Wellings *et al.* 1994), so that the most appropriate sexual terms to be used in the survey questions could be decided. The interviews revealed considerable misunderstanding about many terms. Similarly, Carlson *et al.* (1996) used ethnographic data that they had collected on needle sharing among drug injectors to inform the design of questions for a questionnaire survey of 276 users. Laurie and Sullivan (1991) report that, prior to the first wave of data collection for the British Household Panel Study (see Box 2.19, p. 46), qualitative research was conducted through 'depth interviews' and 'group discussions'. One of the main purposes of this phase was 'to clarify terminologies and concepts about intra-household allocative processes in order to aid in the development of questions for the panel questionnaire' (Laurie and Sullivan 1991: 114).

Quantitative research facilitates qualitative research (H2, M2)

One of the chief ways in which quantitative research can prepare the ground for qualitative research is through the selection of people to be interviewed. This can occur in several ways. In the case of the research on the reporting of social science research in the British mass media (see Box 22.4), a content analysis of media content (method 1) was used as a source of data in its own right. However, it also served as a means of identifying journalists who had reported relevant research (method 5). In addition, replies to questions in the general survey of social

scientists (method 2) were used to help identify two groups of social scientists—those with particularly high and those with low levels of media coverage of their research—who would then be interviewed with a semi-structured approach (method 4).

Filling in the gaps (H3, M4)

This approach to multi-strategy research occurs when the researcher cannot rely on either a quantitative or a qualitative method alone and must buttress his or her findings with a method drawn from the other research strategy. Its most typical form is when ethnographers employ structured interviewing or possibly a self-completion questionnaire, because not everything they need to know about is accessible through participant observation. This kind of need can arise for several reasons, such as the need for information that is not accessible to observation or to qualitative interviewing (for example, systematic information about social backgrounds of people in a particular setting), or the difficulty of gaining access to certain groups of people. For her research on the processes whereby people became Moonies (members of the Unification Church) in Britain, Barker (1984) relied mainly on participant observation and in-depth interviewing. However, she also conducted a number of questionnaire surveys of members. Sometimes, this was done to test hypotheses she had begun to formulate (see above on this use of multi-strategy research), but often it was undertaken in order to acquire information on social class backgrounds and religious experiences prior to becoming a Moonie. Such information was not accessible through participant observation.

Static and processual features (H3)

One of the contrasts suggested by Table 13.1 (p. 285) is that, whereas quantitative research tends to bring out a static picture of social life, qualitative research is more processual. The term 'static' can easily be viewed in a rather negative light. In fact, it is very valuable on many occasions to uncover regularities, and it is often the identification of such regularities that allows a processual analysis to proceed. A multi-strategy research approach offers the prospect of being able to combine both elements. For example, both Lacey (1976) and Ball (1981) conducted ethnographic studies of schools, in which the chief purpose was to explore processes of selection and socialization. However, in addition both researchers employed sociometric questionnaires to examine pupils' friendship patterns. Such questionnaires ask respondents to indicate those people with whom they interact and the frequency of interaction. The use of these research instruments allowed the stability of pupils' friendship patterns to be explored.

A further illustration is provided by D. Miller's (1994) study of mass consumption in Trinidad. Miller's main method of data collection was through participant observation, but in addition he conducted questionnaire surveys of forty households in each of the four contrasting communities in which he conducted his ethnographic investigation. The surveys generated information on such issues as the stability of marriages in households, household composition, and the role of ethnicity in marriage. Such data allowed him to establish the structure of Trinidadian society. By contrast, the details of how, for example, mass consumption fits into the everyday life of Trinidadians and how they responded to consumer goods were gleaned from conversations, observations, and interviews with key informants.

investigate a specific set of issues through the more structured approach of quantitative research. An example of this is Milkman's (1997) study of a General Motors car manufacturing plant in the USA.

She was interested in the nature of the labour process in the late twentieth century and whether new factory conditions were markedly different for car workers from the negative portrayals of such work in the 1950s and early 1960s (e.g. Blauner 1964). As such, she was interested in the meaning of industrial work. She employed semi-structured interviews and focus groups with car production workers to elicit data relevant to this aspect of her work. However, in addition she had some specific interests in a 'buyout' plan that the company's management introduced in the mid-1980s after it had initiated a variety of changes to work practices. The plan gave workers the opportunity to give up their jobs for a substantial cash payment. In 1988, Milkman carried out a questionnaire survey of workers who had taken up the company's buyout offer. These workers were surveyed again the following year and in 1991. The reason for the surveys was that Milkman had some very specific interests in the buyout scheme, such as reasons for taking the buyout, how they had fared since leaving General Motors, how they felt about their current employment, and differences between social groups (in particular, different ethnic groups) in current earnings relative to those at General Motors.

Researchers' and participants' perspectives (H3)

Sometimes, researchers want to gather two kinds of data: qualitative data that will allow them to gain access to the perspectives of the people they are studying; and quantitative data that will allow them to explore specific issues in which they are interested. When this occurs, they are seeking to explore an area in both ways, so that they can both adopt an unstructured approach to data collection in which participants' meanings are the focus of attention and

The problem of generality (H3)

As noted in Chapter 21, a problem that is often referred to by critics of qualitative research is that the tendency for findings to be presented in an anecdotal fashion is frequently frustrating, since we are given little sense of the relative importance of the themes identified. Silverman (1984, 1985) has argued that some quantification of findings from qualitative research can often help to uncover the generality of the phenomena being described. In the course of his observational research on doctor–patient interactions in National Health Service and private oncology clinics, Silverman constructed a simple coding frame for recording his observations of interactions in order to bring out the differences between the two types of clinic. Through this exercise he was able to show that patients in private clinics were able to have a greater influence over what went on in the consultations. However, Silverman warns that such quantification should reflect research participants' own ways of understanding their social world. If this occurs, the quantification is more consistent with the goals of qualitative research.

Qualitative research may facilitate the interpretation of the relationship between variables (H3, M3)

One of the problems that frequently confront quantitative researchers is how to explain relationships between variables. One strategy is to look for what is called an intervening variable, which is influenced by the independent variable but which in turn has an effect on the dependent variable. Thus, if we find a relationship between ethnicity and occupation, we might propose that education is one factor behind the relationship implying:

ethnicity → education → occupation.

This sequence implies that the variable ethnicity has an impact on people's education (for example, how much education people of different ethnic groups tend to undergo), which in turn has implications for the kinds of jobs that people of different ethnic groups attain. An alternative approach might be to seek to explore the relationship further by carrying out a qualitative study.

Rank (1989) used official statistics from one state in the USA to establish that women receiving the equivalent of social security benefits had low rates of fertility. Not only was the fertility rate lower than for the equivalent general population; the longer a woman received such benefits, the less likely she was to give birth. Why? Rank carried out fifty interviews

with welfare recipients. The interviews dealt with such issues as 'family dynamics, employment, and the experience of getting on and off welfare' (Rank 1989: 298). Rank explains the relationship between the variables on the basis of these interviews, as follows: 'The economic, social, and psychological costs of becoming pregnant and having a child while on public assistance are perceived as clearly outweighing the benefits. It is argued that the economic and psychological stress that virtually all welfare recipients experience exerts a powerful effect on women's fertility behavior' (Rank 1989: 303). The inclusion of a qualitative research component thus allowed Rank to develop an explanation of his findings about rates of fertility among women receiving benefits.

A further illustration is provided by research on HIV-related risk behaviour among drug injectors by Barnard and Frischer (1995). Data from structured interviews with 503 injectors in Glasgow revealed that 'females report significantly higher levels of needle sharing, sexual activity and AIDS awareness than their male counterparts. Furthermore, women who are co-habiting with sexual partners who are themselves injectors, are particularly likely to report high levels of risk behaviour and also AIDS awareness' (Barnard and Frischer 1995: 357). What are the factors that produced this pattern of relationships between gender, risk behaviour, and co-habitation? Semi-structured interviews with seventy-three injectors in Glasgow were also conducted. The authors suggest that the relationships between these variables 'can be explained by the tendency for women to be in sexual relationships with men who themselves inject and with whom they are unlikely to use condoms' (Barnard and Frischer 1995: 360). Once again, we see an instance of light being shed on relationships between variables derived from quantitative research by a related qualitative one.

Studying different aspects of a phenomenon (H3)

This category of multi-strategy research incorporates two forms I referred to in my earlier work as 'the relationship between "macro" and "micro" levels' and 'stages in the research process', but provides a more general formulation (Bryman 1988*a*: 147–51). The former draws attention to the tendency to think of quantitative research as most suited to the investigation of 'macro' phenomena (such as social mobility, social stratification) and qualitative research as better suited to 'micro' ones (such as small-scale interaction). Table 13.1 (p. 285) suggests this distinction. The category 'stages in the research process' drew attention to the possibility that quantitative and qualitative research may be suited to different phases in a study. However, it now seems to me that these are simply aspects of a more general tendency for quantitative research and qualitative researchers to examine different aspects of their area of interest.

An illustration of the use of multi-strategy research to study different aspects of a phenomenon is the family obligations study by Finch and Mason, which was previously encountered in Boxes 7.6 and 15.10 (pp. 153, 325). This research was concerned with the distribution within families of the obligation to care for relatives. It comprised two main data collection elements: a survey of a sample of nearly 1,000 people by structured interview and semi-structured interviewing with eighty-eight people. A major component of the survey interviewing was the use of the vignette technique described in Box 7.6 (p. 153). The theoretical sampling strategy for the qualitative research element of the study is described in Box 15.10 (p. 325). Mason describes the purpose of integrating quantitative and qualitative research as follows:

From the beginning . . . we were using the two parts of our study to ask different sets of questions about family obligations. Not only were we employing different methods to generate different types of data, but we anticipated that these would tell us about different aspects of family obligations. . . . our view was that an understanding of kin obligations *in practice* would require an analysis of the relationship between the two data sets and the social processes they expressed.   (Mason 1994: 90–1)

What were the two sets of research questions to which Mason refers in this passage? The survey was designed to provide information about the degree to which there was a consensus among members of the sample about '"the proper thing to do" for relatives in a variety of circumstances' (1994: 90). Through the semi-structured interviews, Finch and Mason were 'trying to discover what people actually did in practice for their own relatives, and also the processes by which they came to do it and make sense of it: did a sense of obligation or responsibility have a role in the process? How did people in practice work out what to do for their kin, or ask of their kin?' (Mason 1994: 90).

In such research, then, multi-strategy research is geared to addressing different kinds of research question. The research on the reporting of social science research in the British mass media (Box 22.4) is a further example of a project concerned to use quantitative and qualitative research to answer different research questions.

- Questions about coverage, such as: how much coverage is there of social science research? What gets covered? Where? (method 1).

- Questions about the production of media items, such as: what kinds of attributes do journalists look for when thinking about whether to write an item on social science research? (methods 5 and 7).

- Questions about social scientists' attitudes to the media reporting of research in general (method 2) and to the reporting of their own research (methods 3 and 4). In addition, the research addressed social scientists' practices with regard to media coverage. Method 4 was designed to allow the findings deriving from method 3 to be elaborated and more fully understood.

- Questions about reception, such as: how do readers/viewers interpret media reporting of social science research? (method 8).

- Questions about the communication environment, such as: what are the policies of universities, government departments, and funding bodies concerning the media reporting of research? (method 6).

This form of multi-strategy research entails making decisions about which kinds of research question are best answered using a quantitative research method and which by a qualitative research method and about how best to interweave the different elements, especially since, as suggested in the context of the discussion about triangulation, the outcomes of mixtures of methods are not always predictable.

Solving a puzzle (H3, M3)

The outcomes of research are, as suggested by the last sentence, not always easy to anticipate. Although people sometimes cynically suggest that social scientists find what they want to find or that social scientists just convey the obvious, the capacity of the obvious to provide us with puzzling surprises should never be underestimated. When this occurs, employing a research method associated with the research strategy not initially used can be helpful. One context in which this might occur is when qualitative research is used as a salvage operation, when an anticipated set of results from a quantitative investigation fails to materialize (Weinholtz *et al.* 1995). Box 22.5 provides an interesting illustration of this use of multi-strategy research.

Like unplanned triangulation, this category of multi-strategy research is more or less impossible to plan for. It essentially provides the quantitative researcher with an alternative to either reconstructing a hypothesis or filing the results away (and probably never looking at them again) when findings are inconsistent with a hypothesis. It is probably not an option in all cases in which a hypothesis is not confirmed. There may also be instances in which a quantitative study could shed light on puzzling findings drawn from a qualitative investigation.

Reflections on multi-strategy research

There can be little doubt that multi-strategy research is becoming far more common than when I first started writing about it (Bryman 1988a). Two particularly significant factors in prompting this development are:

- a growing preparedness to think of research methods as techniques of data collection or analysis that are not as encumbered by epistemological and ontological baggage as is sometimes supposed, and

- a softening in the attitude towards quantitative research among feminist researchers, who had previously been highly resistant to its use (see Chapter 13 for a discussion of this point).

Other factors are doubtlessly relevant, but these two developments do seem especially significant. An example of the operation of these factors can be found in an area of research that has been mentioned on several occasions in this book and that has predominantly been studied using qualitative research methods (in particular focus groups, see Chapter 16)—the study of audience reception of media and cultural texts. Some researchers in this area have called for a rethinking of the field's attitude to quantitative research. All of the studies described in Table 16.1 (p. 340), except for Morgan and Spanish (1985) and Lupton (1996), are focus group studies of audience reception. This method, along with other qualitative methods (e.g. Ang 1985), has been the main data-collection approach employed in this field. Yet lingering unease among some practitioners of qualitative research in this area, particularly regarding issues to do with reliability and generalizability of findings, has led to some calls for a consideration of the possible use of quantitative research in tandem with qualitative methods (e.g. Schrøder 1999). However, it is important to realize that multi-strategy research is not intrinsically superior to mono-method or mono-strategy research. It is tempting to think that multi-strategy research is more or less inevitably superior to research that relies on a single method on the grounds that more and more varied findings are

COMBINING QUANTITATIVE AND QUALITATIVE RESEARCH

Box 22.5 Using multi-strategy research to solve a puzzle: The case of displayed emotions in convenience stores

An example of combining quantitative and qualitative research to solve a puzzle is Sutton and Rafaeli's (1988) study of the display of emotions in organizations. Following a traditional quantitative research strategy, based on their examination of studies like Hochschild (1983), Sutton and Rafaeli formulated a hypothesis suggesting a positive relationship between the display of positive emotions to retail shoppers (smiling, friendly greeting, eye contact) and the level of retail sales. In other words, we would expect that, when retail staff are friendly and give time to shoppers, sales will be better than when they fail to do so. Sutton and Rafaeli had access to data that allowed this hypothesis to be tested. The data derived from a study of 576 convenience stores in a national retail chain in the USA. Structured observation of retail workers provided the data on the display of positive emotions, and sales data provided information for the other variable. The hypothesis implied that there would be a positive relationship—that is, stores in which there was a more pronounced display of positive emotions would report superior sales. When the data were analysed, a relationship was confirmed, but it was found to be negative; that is, stores in which retail workers were *less* inclined to smile, be friendly, and so on tended to have better sales than those in which such emotions were in evidence. This was the reverse of what the authors had anticipated that they would uncover. Sutton and Rafaeli (1992: 124) considered restating their hypothesis to make it seem that they had found what they had expected, but fortunately resisted the temptation!

Instead, they conducted a qualitative investigation of four case study stores to help understand what was happening. This involved a number of methods: unstructured observation of interactions between staff and customers; semi-structured interviews with store managers; brief periods of participant observation; casual conversations with store managers, supervisors, executives, and others; and data gathered through posing as a customer in stores. The stores were chosen in terms of two criteria: high or low sales and whether staff typically displayed positive emotions. The qualitative investigation suggested that the relationship between the display of positive emotions and sales *was* negative, but that sales were likely to be a cause rather than a consequence of the display of emotions. This pattern occurred because, in stores with high levels of sales, staff were under greater pressure and encountered longer queues at checkouts. Staff therefore had less time and inclination for the pleasantries associated with the display of positive emotions. The quantitative data were then reanalysed with this alternative interpretation in mind and it was supported.

Thus, instead of the causal sequence being

Display of positive emotions $\longrightarrow$ Retail sales

it was

Retail sales $\longrightarrow$ Display of positive emotions

This exercise also highlights the main difficulty associated with inferring causal direction from a cross-sectional research design (see Box 2.12 and Figure 2.2, pp. 41, 44).

inevitably 'a good thing'. However, four points must be borne in mind.

- Multi-strategy research, like mono-method research, must be competently designed and conducted. Poorly conducted research will yield suspect findings no matter how many methods are employed.

- Just like mono-method or mono-strategy research, multi-strategy research must be appropriate to the research questions or research area with which you are concerned. There is no point collecting more data simply on the basis that 'more is better'.

Multi-strategy research has to be dovetailed to research questions just as all research methods must be. It is, after all, likely to consume considerably more time and financial resources than research relying on just one method.

- Any research project has limited resources. Employing multi-strategy research may dilute the research effort in any area, since resources would need to be spread.

- By no means all researchers have the skills and training to carry out both quantitative and qualitative research, so that their 'trained incapacities' may act as a barrier to integration (Reiss 1968: 351). However, there is a growing recognition of the potential of multi-strategy research, so that this point probably carries less weight than it did when Reiss was writing.

In other words, multi-strategy research should not be considered as an approach that is universally applicable or as a panacea. It may provide a better understanding of a phenomenon than if just one method had been used. It may also frequently enhance our confidence in our own or others' findings, for example, when a triangulation exercise has been conducted. It may even improve our chances of access to settings to which we might otherwise be excluded; Milkman (1997: 192), for example, has suggested in the context of her research on a General Motors factory that the promise that she 'would produce "hard," quantitative data through survey research was what secured [her] access', even though she had no experience in this method. But the general point remains, that multi-strategy research, while offering great potential in many instances, is subject to similar constraints and considerations as research relying on a single method or research strategy.

Key points

- While there has been a growth in the amount of multi-strategy research, not all writers support its use.

- Objections to multi-strategy research tend to be the result of a view that there are epistemological and ontological impediments to the combination of quantitative and qualitative research.

- There are several different ways of combining quantitative and qualitative research and of representing multi-strategy research.

- The outcomes of combining quantitative and qualitative research can be planned or unplanned.

Revision questions

- What is multi-strategy research?

The argument against multi-strategy research

- What are the main elements of the embedded methods and paradigm arguments in terms of their implications for the possibility of multi-strategy research?

Two versions of the debate about quantitative and qualitative research

- What are the main elements of the technical and epistemological versions of the debate about quantitative and qualitative research? What are the implications of these two versions of the debate for multi-strategy research?

Approaches to multi-strategy research

- What are the main differences between Hammersley's and Morgan's classifications of multi-strategy research?
- What are the chief ways in which quantitative and qualitative research have been combined?
- What is the logic of triangulation?
- Traditionally, qualitative research has been depicted as having a preparatory role in relation to quantitative research. To what extent do the different forms of multi-strategy research reflect this view?

Reflections on multi-strategy research

- Why has multi-strategy research become more prominent?
- Is multi-strategy research necessarily superior to single strategy research?

23 Writing up social research

Reader's guide

It is easy to forget that one of the main stages in any research project, regardless of its size, is that it has to be written up. Not only is this how you will convey your findings, but being aware of the significance of writing is crucial, because your audience must be persuaded about the credibility and importance of your research. This chapter presents some of the characteristics of the writing-up of social research. The chapter explores:

- why writing, and especially good writing, is important to social research;
- using examples, how quantitative and qualitative research are composed;
- the influence and implications of postmodernism for writing;
- key issues raised by discussions about the writing of ethnography, an area in which discussions about writing have been especially prominent.

Introduction

The aim of this chapter is to examine some of the strategies that are employed in writing up social research. Initially, we will explore the question of whether quantitative and qualitative research reveal divergent approaches. As we will see, the similarities are frequently more striking and apparent than the differences. However, the main point of this chapter is to extract some principles of good practice that can be developed and incorporated into your own writing. This is an important issue, since many people find writing up research more difficult than carrying it out. On the other hand, many people treat the writing-up stage as relatively unproblematic. But no matter how well research is conducted, others (that is, your readers) have to be convinced about the credibility of the knowledge claims you are making. Good writing is therefore very much to do with developing your style so that it is *persuasive* and *convincing*. Flat, lifeless, uncertain writing does not have the power to persuade and convince. In exploring these issues, we will touch on rhetorical strategies in the writing of social research (see Box 23.1). As P. Atkinson (1990: 2) has observed in relation to social research, 'the conventions of text and rhetoric are among the ways in which reality is *constructed*'.

This chapter will review some of the ways in which social research is written up in a way that will provide some basic ideas about structuring your own written work if you have to produce something like a dissertation. There will be more advice on writing up for a dissertation in Chapter 25.

Two research-based articles that have been published in journals are examined to detect some helpful features. One is based on quantitative research and the other on qualitative research. This raises the question of whether practitioners of the two research strategies employ different writing approaches. It is sometimes suggested that they do, though when I compared two articles based on research in the sociology of work, I found that the differences were less pronounced than I had anticipated on the basis of reading the literature on the topic (Bryman 1999). One difference that I have noticed is that, in journals, quantitative researchers often give more detailed accounts of their research design, research methods, and approaches to analysis than qualitative researchers. This is surprising, because in books reporting their research, qualitative researchers provide detailed accounts of these areas. Indeed, the chapters in Part Three of the

---

Box 23.1   What is rhetoric?

The study of rhetoric is fundamentally concerned with the ways in which attempts to convince or persuade an audience are formulated. We often encounter the term in a negative context, such as 'mere rhetoric' or the opposition of 'rhetoric and reality'. However, rhetoric is an essential ingredient of writing, because when we write our aim is to convince others about the credibility of our knowledge claims. To suggest that rhetoric should somehow be suppressed makes little sense, since it is in fact a basic feature of writing. The examination of rhetorical strategies in written texts based on social research is concerned with the identification of the techniques in those texts that are designed to convince and persuade.

---

book rely heavily on these accounts. Wolcott (1990: 27) has also noticed this tendency: 'Our [qualitative researchers'] failure to render full and complete disclosure about our data-gathering procedures give our methodologically oriented colleagues fits. And rightly so, especially for those among them willing to accept our contributions if we would only provide more careful data about our data.' Being informed that a study was based on a year's participant observation or a number of semi-structured interviews is not enough to gain an acceptance of the claims to credibility that a writer might be wishing to convey.

However, this point aside, in the discussion that follows, although one article based on quantitative research and one based on qualitative research will be examined, we should not be too surprised if they turn out to be more similar than might have been expected. In other words, although we might have expected clear differences between the two in terms of their approaches to writing, the similarities are more noticeable than the differences.

Writing quantitative research: An example

To illustrate some of the characteristics of the way quantitative research is written up for academic journals, I will take the article by Kelley and De Graaf (1997) that was referred to on several occasions in Chapters 1, 2, 3 and 10 (see especially Boxes 1.5 and 3.4, pp. 9, 68). I am not suggesting that this article is somehow exemplary or representative, but rather that it exhibits some features that are often regarded as desirable qualities in terms of presentation and structure. The article is based on a secondary analysis of survey data on religion in fifteen nations and was accepted for publication in one of the most prestigious journals in sociology—the *American Sociological Review*, which is the official journal of the American Sociological Association. The vast majority of published articles in academic journals entail the blind refereeing of articles submitted. This means that an article will be read by two or three peers, who comment on the article and give the editors a judgement about its merits and hence whether it is worthy of publication. Most articles submitted are rejected. With highly prestigious journals, it is common for in excess of 90 per cent of articles to be rejected. It is unusual for an article to be accepted on its first submission. Usually, the referees will suggest areas that need revising and the author (or authors) is expected to respond to that feedback. Revised versions of articles are usually sent back to the referees for further comment and this process may result in the author having to revise the draft yet again. It may even result in rejection. Therefore, an article like Kelley and De Graaf's is not just the culmination of a research process, but is also the outcome of a feedback process. The fact that it has been accepted for publication, when many others have been rejected, testifies to its merits as having met the standards of the journal. That is not to say it is perfect, but the refereeing process is an indication that it does possess certain crucial qualities.

The article has the following components, aside from the abstract:

1. introduction;
2. theory;
3. data;
4. measurement;
5. methods and models;
6. results;
7. conclusion.

Introduction

Right at the beginning of the introduction, the opening four sentences attempt to grab our attention, to give a clear indication of where the article's focus lies, and to provide an indication of the likely significance of the findings. This is what the authors write:

> Religion remains a central element of modern life, shaping people's world-views, moral standards, family lives, and in many nations, their politics. But in many Western nations, modernization and secularization may be eroding Christian beliefs, with profound consequences that have intrigued sociologists since Durkheim. Yet this much touted secularization may be overstated—certainly it varies widely among nations and is absent in the United States (Benson, Donahue, and Erickson 1989: 154–7; Felling, Peters, and Schreuder 1991; Firebaugh and Harley 1991; Stark and Iannaccone 1994). We explore the degree to which religious beliefs are passed on from generation to generation in different nations. (Kelley and De Graaf 1997: 639)

This is an impressive start, because, in just over 100 words, the authors set out what the article is about and its significance. Let us look at what each sentence achieves.

- The first sentence locates the article's research focus as addressing an important aspect of modern society which touches on many people's lives.

- The second sentence notes that there is variety among Western nations in the importance of religion and that the variations may have 'profound consequences'. But this sentence does more than the first sentence: it also suggests that this is an area that has been of interest to sociologists. To support this point, one of sociology's most venerated figures—Émile Durkheim—is mentioned.

- The third sentence suggests that there is a problem with the notion of secularization, which has been a research focus for many sociologists of religion. Several fairly recent articles are cited to support the authors' contention that there is a possibility that secularization is being exaggerated by some commentators. In this sentence, the authors are moving towards a rationale for their article that is more in terms of sociological concerns than pointing to social changes, which are the main concern of the two opening sentences.

- Then in the fourth sentence the authors set up their specific contribution to this area—the exploration of the passing-on of religious beliefs between generations.

So, by the end of four sentences, the contribution that the article is claiming to make to our understanding of religion in modern society has been outlined and situated within an established literature on the topic. This is quite a powerful start to the article, because the reader knows what the article is about and the particular case the authors are making for their contribution to the literature on the subject.

Theory

In this section, existing ideas and research on the topic of religious socialization are presented. The authors point to the impact of parents and other people on children's religious beliefs, but then assert that 'a person's religious environment is also shaped by factors other than their own and their parents' religious beliefs, and hence is a potential cause of those beliefs . . .' (1997: 641). This suggestion is then justified, which prompts the authors to argue that 'prominent among these "unchosen" aspects of one's religious environment is birthplace' (1997: 641). Kelley and De Graaf's ruminations on this issue lead them to propose the first of three hypotheses, which is presented in Box 1.5 (p. 9). This hypothesis stipulates that contextual factors have an impact on religious beliefs. This leads the authors to suggest in two related hypotheses that, in predominantly secular societies, family background will have a greater impact on a person's religious beliefs than in predominantly devout societies, because in the former parents and other family members are more likely to seek to isolate children from secular influences. However, in devout societies this insulation process is less necessary and the influence of national factors will be greater. Thus, we end up with very clear research questions, which have been arrived at by reflecting on existing ideas and research in this area.

Data

In this section, the authors outline the data they drew on for their research. This exposition entails a general outline of the data sets. The quotation on p. 199 is taken from this commentary. The sampling procedures are outlined along with sample sizes and response rates.

Measurement

In this section, Kelley and De Graaf explain how the main concepts in their research were measured. The concepts were: *religious belief* (the questionnaire items used are in Box 3.4, p. 68); *parents' church attendance*; *secular and religious nations* (that is, the scoring procedure for indicating the degree to which a nation was religious or secular in orientation on a five-point scale); *other contextual characteristics of nations* (for example, whether a former Communist nation or not); and *individual characteristics* (for example, age and gender).

Methods and models

This is a very technical section, which outlines the different ways in which the relationships between the variables might be conceptualized and the implications of using different mutivariate analysis approaches for the ensuing findings.

Results

The authors provide a general description of their findings and then consider whether the hypotheses *are* supported. In fact, it turns out the hypotheses are supported. The significance of other contextual characteristics of nations and individual differences are separately explored.

Conclusion

In this final section, Kelley and De Graaf return to the issues that have been driving their investigation. These are the issues they had presented in the Introduction and Theory sections. They begin the section with a strong statement of their findings: 'The religious environment of a nation has a major impact on the beliefs of its citizens: People living in religious nations acquire, in proportion to the orthodoxy of their fellow citizens, more orthodox beliefs than those living in secular nations' (Kelley and De Graaf 1997: 654). They then reflect on the implications of the confirmation of their hypotheses for our understanding of the process of religious socialization and religious beliefs. They also address the implications of their findings for certain theories about religious beliefs in modern society, which were outlined in their Theory section:

Our results also speak to the long-running debate about U.S. exceptionalism (Warner 1993): They support the view that the United States is unusually religious. . . . Our results do not support Stark and Iannaccone's (1994) 'supply-side' analysis of differences between nations which argues that nations with religious monopolies have substantial unmet religious needs, while churches in religiously competitive nations like the United States do a better job of meeting diverse religious needs. (Kelley and De Graaf 1997: 655)

The final paragraph spells out some inferences about the ways in which social changes have an impact on levels of religious belief in a nation. The authors suggest that factors such as modernization and the growth of education depress levels of religious belief and that their impact tends to result in a precipitous rather than a gradual fall in levels of religiosity. In their final three sentences, they go on to write about societies undergoing such change:

The offspring of devout families mostly remain devout, but the offspring of more secular families now strongly tend to be secular. A self-reinforcing spiral of seculariza-tion then sets in, shifting the nation's average religiosity ever further away from orthodoxy. So after generations of stability, religious belief declines abruptly in the course of a few generations to the modest levels seen in many Western nations. (Kelley and De Graaf 1997: 656)

It might be argued that these reflections are some-what risky, because the data from which the authors derive their findings are cross-sectional in research design terms rather than longitudinal. They are clearly extrapolating from their scoring of the fifteen nations in terms of levels of modernization to the impact of social changes on national levels of religi-osity. However, these final sentences make for a strong conclusion, which itself might form a spring-board for further research.

Lessons

What lessons can be learned from Kelley and De Graaf's article? To some extent, these have been alluded to in the course of the above exposition, but they are worth spelling out.

- There is a clear attempt to grab the reader's atten-tion with strong opening statements, which also act as signposts to what the article is about.
- The authors spell out clearly the rationale of their research. This entails pointing to the continued significance of religion in many societies and to the literature on religious beliefs and secularization.

- The research questions are spelled out in a very specific way. In fact, the authors present hypoth-eses that are a highly specific form of research question. As noted in Chapter 3, by no means all quantitative research is driven by hypotheses, even though outlines of the nature of quantitative research often imply that it is. Nonetheless, Kelley and De Graaf chose to frame their research ques-tions in this form.

- The nature of the data, the measurement of con-cepts, the sampling, the research methods employed and the approaches to the analysis of the data are clearly and explicitly summarized in sections 3, 4, and 5.

- The presentation of the findings in section 6 is oriented very specifically to the research questions that drive the research.

- The conclusion returns to the research questions and spells out the implications of the findings for them and for the theories examined in section 2. This is an important element. It is easy to forget that you should think of the research process as closing a circle in which you must return unambiguously to your research questions. There is no point inserting extraneous findings if they do not illuminate your research questions. Digres-sions of this kind can be confusing to readers, who might be inclined to wonder about the signifi-cance of the extraneous findings.

We also see that there is a clear sequential process moving from the formulation of the research ques-tions through the exposition of the nature of the data and the presentation of the findings to the con-clusions. Each stage is linked to and follows on from its predecessor (but see Box 23.2). The structure used by Kelley and De Graaf is based on a common one employed in the writing-up of quantitative research for academic journals in the social sciences. Some-times, there is a separate Discussion section that appears between the Results and the Conclusion. Another variation is that issues of measurement and analysis appear in the same section as the one deal-ing with research methods, but perhaps with distinct subheadings.

Box 23.2 An empiricist repertoire?

At this point, it is worth recalling the discussion in chapter 17 of Gilbert and Mulkay's (1984) research on scientists. The authors drew a distinction between an *empiricist repertoire* and a *contingent repertoire*. The former derived from 'the observation that the texts of experimental papers display certain recurrent stylistic, grammatical and lexical features which appear to be coherently related' (Gilbert and Mulkay 1984: 55–6). We should bear in mind that the same is true of papers written for social science journals. These too display certain features that suggest a certain inevitability to the outcome of the research. In other words, the reader is given a sense that, in following the rigorous procedures outlined in the article, the researchers logically arrived at their conclusions. The contingent repertoire, with its recognition of the role of the researcher in the production of findings, is far less apparent in their published work. Thus, we have to recognize the possibility that the impression of a series of linked stages leading to an inescapable culmination is to a large extent a reconstruction of events designed to persuade referees (who, of course, use the same tactics themselves) of the credibility and importance of one's findings. This means that the conventions about writing up a quantitative research project, some of which are outlined in this chapter, are in many ways an invitation to reconstruct an investigation in a particular way. The whole issue of the ways in which the writing-up of research represents a means of persuading others of the credibility of one's knowledge claims has been a particular preoccupation among qualitative researchers (see below) and has been greatly influenced by the surge of interest in postmodernism. However, in Box 23.3, some of the rhetorical strategies involved in writing up quantitative social research are outlined. Three points are worth making about these strategies in the present context. First, they are characteristic of the empiricist repertoire. Secondly, while the writing of qualitative research has been a particular focus in recent times (see below), some attention has also been paid to quantitative research. Thirdly, when I compared the writing of quantitative and qualitative research articles, I found they were not as dissimilar in terms of rhetorical strategies as is sometimes proposed (Bryman 1998). However, I did find greater evidence of a management metaphor (see Box 23.3), which is also evident in Kelley and De Graaf's article; for example, 'we excluded the deviant cases from our analysis' (1997: 646) and 'we divided the nations into five groups' (1997: 647).

Box 23.3 Rhetorical strategies in writing up quantitative research

The rhetorical strategies used by quantitative researchers include the following.

- There is a tendency to remove the researcher from the text as an active ingredient of the research process in order to convey an impression of the objective nature of the findings—that is, as part of an external reality that is independent of the researcher (Gusfield 1976). Woolgar (1988) refers to this as an externalizing device.

- The researcher surfaces in the text only to demonstrate his or her ingenuity in overcoming obstacles (Bazerman 1987; Bryman 1998).

- Key figures in the field are routinely cited to bestow credibility on the research (McCloskey 1985).

- The research process is presented as a linear one to convey an air of inevitability about the findings arrived at (Gusfield 1976).

- Relatively strict rules are followed about what should be reported in published research and how it should be reported (Bazerman 1987).

- The use of a *management* metaphor is common in the presentation of findings in which the researcher is depicted as ingeniously ' "designing" research, "controlling" variables, "managing" data and "generating" tables' (Bryman 1998: 146). See Shapiro (1985–6) and Richardson (1990) on this point.

Note that the first two are somewhat inconsistent. There is some evidence that disciplines within the social sciences differ in respect of their use of an impersonal style of writing. But it may well also be that it sometimes depends on what the writer is trying to do; for example, sometimes getting across a sense of one's cunning in overcoming practical difficulties can be just as useful as giving a sense of the external nature of the findings. Therefore, sometimes the style of presentation may vary somewhat.

Writing qualitative research: An example

Now we will look at an example of a journal article based on qualitative research. Again, I am not suggesting that the article is exemplary or representative, but that it exhibits some features that are often regarded as desirable qualities in terms of presentation and structure. The article is one that has been referred to in several previous chapters (especially Boxes 2.18, 15.3, and 15.9, pp. 45, 315, 324): a study of vegetarianism by Beardsworth and Keil (1992). The study is based on semi-structured interviews and was published in the *Sociological Review*, a leading British journal.

The structure runs as follows:

1. introduction;
2. the analysis of the social dimensions of food and eating;
3. studies of vegetarianism;
4. the design of the study;
5. the findings of the study;
6. explaining contemporary vegetarianism;
7. conclusions.

What is immediately striking about the structure is that it is not dissimilar to Kelley and De Graaf's (1997). Nor should this be all that surprising. After all, a structure which runs

Introduction → Literature review → Research design/ methods → Results → Discussion → Conclusions

is not obviously associated with one research strategy rather than the other. One difference from quantitative research articles is that the presentation of the results and the discussion of them are frequently rather more interwoven in qualitative research articles. We will see this in the case of Beardsworth and Keil's article. As with Kelley and De Graaf's article, we will examine the writing in terms of the article's structure.

Introduction

The first four sentences give us an immediate sense of what the article is about and where its focus lies:

The purpose of this paper is to offer a contribution to the analysis of the cultural and sociological factors which influence patterns of food selection and food avoidance. The specific focus is contemporary vegetarianism, a complex of inter-related beliefs, attitudes and nutritional practices which has to date received comparatively little attention from social scientists. Vegetarians in western cultures, in most instances, are not life-long practitioners but converts. They are individuals who have subjected more traditional foodways to critical scrutiny, and subsequently made a deliberate decision to change their eating habits, sometimes in a radical fashion. (Beardsworth and Keil, 1992: 253)

Like Kelley and De Graaf's, this is a strong introduction. We can look again at what each sentence achieves.

- The first sentence makes clear that the research is concerned with issues to do with the study of food.

- The second sentence provides us with the specific research focus—the study of vegetarianism—and makes a claim for our attention by suggesting that this is a topic that has been under-researched by sociologists. Interestingly, this is almost the opposite of the claim made by Kelley and De Graaf in their second sentence, in that they point to a line of sociological interest in religion going back to Durkheim. Each is a legitimate textual strategy for gaining the attention of readers.

- Our attention is jolted even more by an interesting assertion that begins to draw the reader into one of the article's primary themes—the idea of vegetarians as converts.

- The fourth sentence elaborates upon the idea of vegetarianism as being for most people an issue of choice rather than a tradition into which one is born.

Thus, after around 100 words, the reader has a clear idea of the focus of the research and has been led to anticipate that there is unlikely to be a great deal of pre-existing social research on this issue.

The analysis of the social dimensions of food and eating

This and the next section review existing theory and research in this area. In this section, the contributions of various social scientists to social aspects of food and eating are discussed. The literature reviewed acts as a backcloth to the issue of vegetarianism. Beardsworth and Keil propose that their review of existing theory and research suggests that 'there exists a range of theoretical and empirical resources which can be brought to bear upon the issue of contemporary vegetarianism' (1992: 255). This point is important, as the authors note once again at the end of the section that vegetarianism has received little attention from social scientists.

Studies of vegetarianism

This section examines aspects of the literature on vegetarianism that has been carried out by social scientists or that has a social scientific angle. The review includes: opinion poll and survey data, which point to the likely percentage of vegetarians in the British population; debates about animal rights; sociological analysis of vegetarian ideas; and one study (Dwyer *et al.* 1974) of vegetarians in the USA carried out by a team of social scientists using social survey research. In the final paragraph of this section, the authors indicate the contribution of some of the literature they have covered.

The design of the study

The first sentence of this section forges a useful link with the preceding one: 'The themes outlined above appear to warrant further investigation, preferably in a manner which allows for a much more richly detailed examination of motivations and experiences than is apparent in the study by Dwyer *et al.*' (Beardsworth and Keil 1992: 260). This opening gambit allows the authors to suggest that the literature in this area is scant and that there are many

unanswered questions. Also, they distance themselves from the one sociological study of vegetarians, which in turn leads them to set up the grounds for preferring qualitative research. The authors then outline:

- who was to be studied and why;
- how respondents were recruited (see Box 15.9, p. 324) and the difficulties encountered;
- the semi-structured interviewing approach (see Box 15.3, p. 315) and the rationale for it;
- the number of people interviewed and the context in which the interviews took place;
- the approach to analysing the interview transcripts, which largely comprised the identification of themes.

The findings of the study

The chief findings are outlined under separate headings: respondents' characteristics; types of vegetarianism; the process of conversion; motivations; nutritional beliefs; social relations; and dilemmas. The presentation of the results is carried out so that there is some discussion of their meaning or significance in such a way as to lead onto the next section, which provides exclusively a discussion of them. For example, in the final sentence in the section reporting findings relating to nutritional beliefs, the authors write:

Just as meat tended to imply strongly negative connotations for respondents, concepts like 'fruit' and 'vegetable' tended to elicit positive reactions, although less frequently and in a more muted form than might have been anticipated on the basis of the analysis of the ideological underpinnings of 'wholefoods' consumption put forward by Atkinson (1980, 1983), or on the basis of the analysis of vegetarian food symbolism advanced by Twigg (1983: 28).   (Beardsworth and Keil 1992: 276)

In this way, the presentation of the results is pointing forward to some themes that are taken up in the following sections and demonstrates the significance of certain findings for some of the previously discussed literature.

Explaining contemporary vegetarianism

This section discusses the findings in the light of the study's research questions in connection with food selection and avoidance. The results are also related to many of the ideas encountered in the two sections dealing with the literature. The authors develop an idea emerging from their research, which they call 'food ambivalence'. This concept encapsulates for the authors the anxieties and paradoxes concerning food that can be discerned in the interview transcripts (for example, food can be construed both as necessary for strength and energy and simultaneously as a source of illness). Vegetarianism is in many respects a response to the dilemmas associated with food ambivalence.

Conclusions

In this section, the authors return to many of the ideas and themes that have driven their research. They spell out the significance of the idea of food ambivalence, which is probably the article's main contribution to research in this area. The final paragraph outlines the importance of food ambivalence for vegetarians, but the authors are careful not to imply that it is the sole reason for the adoption of vegetarianism. In the final sentence they write: 'However, for a significant segment of the population [vegetarianism] appears to represent a viable device for re-establishing some degree of peace of mind when contemplating some of the darker implications of the carefully arranged message on the dinner plate' (Beardsworth and Keil 1992: 290). This sentence neatly encapsulates one of the article's master themes—the idea of vegetarianism as a response to food ambivalence—and alludes through the reference to 'the carefully arranged message' to semiotic analyses of meat and food.

Lessons

As with Kelley and De Graaf's article, it is useful to review some of the lessons learned from this examination of Beardsworth and Keil's article.

- Just like the illustration of quantitative research writing, there are strong opening sentences, which attract our attention and give a clear indication of the nature and content of the article.

- The rationale of the research is clearly identified. To a large extent, this revolves around identifying the sociological study of food and eating as a growing area of research but noting the paucity of investigations of vegetarianism.

- Research questions are specified but they are somewhat more open-ended than in Kelley and De Graaf's article, which is in keeping with the general orientation of qualitative researchers. The research questions revolve around the issue of vegetarianism as a dietary choice and the motivations for that choice.

- The research design and methods are outlined and an indication is given of the approach to analysis. The section in which these issues are discussed demonstrates greater transparency than is sometimes the case with articles reporting qualitative research.

- The presentation and discussion of the findings in sections 5 and 6 are geared to the broad research questions that motivated the researchers' interest in vegetarianism. However, section 6 also represents the major opportunity for the idea of food ambivalence and its dimensions to be articulated. The inductive nature of qualitative research means that the concepts and theories that are generated from an investigation must be clearly identified and discussed, as in this case.

- The conclusion elucidates in a more specific way the significance of the results for the research questions. It also explores the implications of food ambivalence for vegetarians, so that one of the article's major theoretical contributions is clearly identified and emphasized.

In Chapter 25, the implications of the writing practices revealed in this review of the articles by Kelley and De Graaf and Beardsworth and Keil will be returned to in the context of exploring some possible implications for a dissertation or report that you might need to produce.

Postmodernism and its implications for writing

Postmodernism (see Box 13.1, p. 265) is an extremely difficult idea to pin down. In one sense, it can be seen as a form of sensitivity—a way of seeing and understanding that results in a questioning of the taken-for-granted. It questions the very notion of the dispassionate social scientist seeking to uncover a pre-given external reality. Instead, postmodernists view the social scientist's account as only one among many ways of rendering social reality to audiences. The social world itself is viewed as a context out of which many accounts can be hewn. As a result, 'knowledge' of the social world is relative; any account is just one of many possible ways of rendering social reality. As Rosenau (1992: 8) puts it, postmodernists 'offer "readings" not "observations," "interpretations" not "findings" . . .'.

One of the effects of the impact of postmodernism since the 1980s has been a growing interest in the writing of social science. For postmodernists, reporting findings in a journal article is merely one means of getting across a certain version of the social reality that was investigated. Postmodernists mistrust the knowledge claims that are frequently boldly made when findings are reported and instead they adopt an attitude of investigating the bases and forms of those knowledge claims. While the writing of all types of social science is potentially in the postmodernist's firing line, it has been the kinds of text produced by ethnographers that have been a particular focus of attention. This focus has led to a particular interest in the claims to ethnographic authority that are inscribed into ethnographic texts (Clifford 1983). The ethnographic text 'presumes a world out there (the real) that can be captured by a "knowing" author through the careful transcription and analysis of field materials (interviews, notes, etc.)' (Denzin 1994: 296). Postmodernism problematizes such accounts and their authority to represent a reality because there 'can never be a final, accurate representation of what was meant or said, only different textual representations of different experiences' (Denzin 1994: 296).

However, it would be wrong to depict the growing attention being focused on ethnographic writing as exclusively a product of postmodernism. Atkinson and Coffey (1995) have argued that there are other intellectual trends in the social sciences that have stimulated this interest. Writers in the area of theory and research known as the social studies of science have been concerned with the limitations of accepted distinctions between rhetoric and logic and between the observer and the observed (e.g. Gilbert and Mulkay 1984). The problematizing of these distinctions, along with doubts about the possibility of a neutral language through which the natural and social worlds can be revealed, opened the door for an evaluation of scientific and social scientific writing. Some illustrations of these analyses can be discerned in Boxes 23.2 and 23.3. Atkinson and Coffey also point to the antipathy within feminism towards the image of the neutral 'observer-author' who assumes a privileged stance in relation to members of the social setting being studied. This stance is regarded as revealing a position of domination of the observer-author over the observed that is inconsistent with the goals of feminism (see Chapter 13 for an elaboration of this general point). This concern has led to an interest in the ways in which privilege is conveyed in ethnographic texts and how voices, particularly of marginal groups, are suppressed.

The concerns within these and other traditions (including postmodernism) have led to experiments in writing ethnography (Richardson 1994). An example is the use of a 'dialogic' form of writing that seeks to raise the profile of the multiplicity of voices that can be heard in the course of fieldwork. As Lincoln and Denzin (1994: 584) put it: 'Slowly it dawns on us that there may . . . be . . . not one "voice," but polyvocality; not one story, but many tales, dramas, pieces of fiction, fables, memories, histories, autobiographies, poems, and other texts to inform our sense of lifeways, to extend our understandings of the Other . . .'.

Manning (1995) cites, as an example of the postmodern preference for allowing a variety of voices to come through within an ethnographic text, the work of Stoller (1989), who conducted research in Africa. Manning (1995: 260) describes the text as 'periodically' dialogic in that it is 'shaped by interactions between informants or "the other" and the observer'. This postmodern preference for seeking out multiple voices and for turning the ethnographer into a 'bit player' reflects the mistrust among postmodernists of 'meta-narratives'—that is, positions or grand accounts that implicitly make claims about absolute truths and that therefore rule out the possibility of alternative versions of reality. On the other hand, 'mini-narratives, micro-narratives, local narratives are just stories that make no truth claims and are therefore more acceptable to postmodernists' (Rosenau 1992: p. xiii).

Postmodernism has also encouraged a growing reflexivity in considerations about the conduct of social research and the growing interest in the writing of ethnography is very much a manifestation of this trend (see Box 23.4). This reflexivity can be discerned in the way in which many ethnographers have turned inwards to examine the truth claims inscribed in their own classic texts, which is the focus of the next section.

In the end, what postmodernism leaves us with is an acute sense of uncertainty. It raises the issue of how we can ever know or capture the social reality that belongs to others and in so doing it points to an unresolvable tension that will not go away and that is further revealed in the issues raised in the next section, because, to quote Lincoln and Denzin (1994: 582) again: 'On the one hand there is the concern for validity, or certainty in the text as a form of isomorphism and authenticity. On the other hand there is the sure and certain knowledge that all texts are socially, historically, politically, and culturally located. We, like the texts we write, can never be transcendent.' At the same time, of course, such a view renders problematic the very idea of what social scientific knowledge is or comprises.

Box 23.4 　What is reflexivity?

Reflexivity has several meanings in the social sciences. The term is employed by ethnomethodologists to refer to the way in which speech and action are constitutive of the social world in which they are located; in other words, they do more than merely act as indicators of deeper phenomena (see Chapter 17). The other meaning of the term carries the connotation that social researchers should be reflective about the implications of their methods, values, biases, and decisions for the knowledge of the social world they generate. There has been evidence of a growing reflexivity in social research in the form of an industry of books that collect together inside stories of the research process that detail the nuts and bolts of research as distinct from the often sanitized portrayal in research articles. An early volume edited by Hammond (1964) paved the way for a large number of imitators (e.g. Bell and Newby 1977; Bell and Roberts 1984; Bryman 1988) and the confessional tales referred to in Box 23.5 are invariably manifestations of this development. Therefore, the rise of reflexivity largely predates the growing awareness of postmodern thinking since the late 1980s. What distinguishes the reflexivity that has followed in the wake of postmodernism is a greater awareness and acknowledgement of the role of the researcher as part and parcel of the construction of knowledge. In other words, the reflexive attitude within postmodernism is highly critical of the notion that the researcher is someone who extracts knowledge from observations and conversations with others and then transmits knowledge to an audience. The researcher is viewed as implicated in the construction of knowledge through the stance that he or she assumes in relation to the observed and through the ways in which an account is transmitted in the form of a text. This understanding entails an acknowledgement of the implications and significance of the researcher's choices as both observer and writer.

Writing ethnography

The term 'ethnography', as noted in Chapter 14, is interesting, because it refers to both a method of social research and the finished product of ethnographic research. In other words, it is both something that is carried out in doing research and something one reads. Thus, writing seems to be at the heart of the ethnographic enterprise. In recent years, the production of ethnographic texts has become a focus of interest in its own right. This means that there has been a growth of interest not just in how ethnography is carried out in the field but also in the rhetorical conventions employed in the production of ethnographic texts.

Ethnographic texts are designed to convince readers of the *reality* of the events and situations described, and the plausibility of the analyst's explanations. The ethnographic text must not simply present a set of findings: it must provide an 'authoritative' account of the group or culture in question. In other words, the ethnographer must convince us that he or she has arrived at an account of social reality that has strong claims to truth.

The ethnographic text is permeated by stylistic and rhetorical devices whereby the reader is persuaded to enter into a shared framework of facts and interpretations, observations and reflections. Just like the scientific paper and the kind of approach to writing found in reporting quantitative social research, the ethnographer typically works within a writing strategy that is imbued with *realism*. This simply means that the researcher presents an authoritative, dispassionate account that represents an external, objective reality. In this respect, there is very little difference between the writing styles of quantitative and qualitative researchers. Van Maanen (1988) calls ethnography texts that conform to these characteristics *realist tales*. These are the common type of ethnographic writing, though he distinguishes other types (see Box 23.5). However, the *form* that this realism takes differs. Van Maanen distinguishes four characteristics of

realist tales: experiential authority; typical forms; the native's point of view; and interpretive omnipotence.

Experiential authority

Just as in much quantitative research writing, the author disappears from view. We are told what members of a group say and do, and they are the only people directly visible in the text. The author provides a narrative in which he or she is no longer to be seen. As a result, an impression is conveyed that the findings presented are what any reasonable, similarly placed researcher would have found. As readers, we have to accept that this is what the ethnographer saw and heard while working as a participant observer or whatever. The personal subjectivity of the author/ethnographer is essentially played down by this strategy. The possibility that the fieldworker may have his or her own biases or may have become too involved with the people being studied is suppressed. To this end, when writing up the results of their ethnographic work, authors play up their academic credentials and qualifications, their previous experience, and so on. All this enhances the degree to which the author's account can be relied upon. The author/ethnographer can then appear as a reliable witness.

A further element of experiential authority is that, when describing their methods, ethnographers invariably make a great deal of the intensiveness of the research that they carried out—they spent so many months in the field, had conversations and interviews with countless individuals, worked hard to establish rapport, and so on. These features are also added to by drawing the reader's attention to such hardships as the inconvenience of the fieldwork—the danger, the poor food, the disruptive effect on normal life, the feelings of isolation and loneliness, and so on.

Also worth mentioning are the extensive

Box 23.5 Three forms of ethnographic writing

Van Maanen (1988) has distinguished three major types of ethnographic writing.

- Realist tales—apparently definitive, confident, and dispassionate third person accounts of a culture and of the behaviour of members of that culture. This is the most prevalent form of ethnographic writing.

- Confessional tales—personalized accounts in which the ethnographer is fully implicated in the data-gathering and writing-up processes. These are warts-and-all accounts of the trials and tribulations of doing ethnography. They have become more prominent since the 1970s and reflect a growing emphasis on reflexivity in qualitative research in particular. Several of the sources referred to in Chapter 14 are confessional tales (e.g. Armstrong 1993; Hobbs 1993; Giulianotti 1995). However, confessional tales are

more concerned with detailing how research was carried out than with presenting findings. Very often the confessional tale is told in one context (such as an invited chapter in a book of similar tales) but the main findings are written up in realist tale form.

- Impressionist tales—accounts that place a heavy emphasis on 'words, metaphors, phrasings, and . . . the expansive recall of fieldwork experience' (1988: p. 102). There is a heavy emphasis on stories of dramatic events that provide 'a representational means of cracking open the culture and the fieldworker's way of knowing it' (1988: 102). However, as Van Maanen notes, impressionist tales 'are typically enclosed within realist, or perhaps more frequently, confessional tales' (1988: 106).

---

quotations from conversations and interviews that invariably form part of the ethnographic report. These are also obviously important ingredients of the author's use of *evidence* to support points. However, they are a mechanism for establishing the credibility of the report in that they demonstrate the author's ability to encourage people to talk and so demonstrate that he or she achieved rapport with them. The copious descriptive details—of places, patterns of behaviour, contexts, and so on—can also be viewed as a means of piling on the sense of the author being an ideally placed witness for all the findings that have been uncovered.

Typical forms

The author often writes about typical forms of institutions or of patterns of behaviour. What is happening here is that the author is generalizing about a number of recurring features of the group in question to create a typical form that that feature takes. He or she may use examples based on particular incidents or people, but basically the emphasis is upon the general. For example, in A. Taylor's (1993) conclusion to her ethnographic

research on female drug users, which was cited several times in Chapter 14, we encounter findings such as these: 'Yet the control exercised over women through the threat to remove their children highlights a major factor differentiating female and male drug users. Unlike male drug users, female drug users, like many other women, have two careers: one in the public sphere and one in the private, domestic sphere' (A. Taylor 1993: 154). This is meant to portray drug users in general, so that individuals are only important insofar as they represent such general tendencies.

The native's point of view

The point has been made several times that one of the distinguishing features of much qualitative research is the commitment to seeing through the eyes of the people being studied. This is an important feature for qualitative researchers because it is part of a strategy of getting at the meaning of social reality from the perspective of those being studied. However, it also represents an important element in creating a sense of authoritativeness on the part of the ethnographer. After all, claiming that he or she takes the native's point of view and sees through their eyes means that he or she is in an excellent position to speak authoritatively about the group in question. The very fact that the ethnographer has taken the native's point of view testifies to the fact that he or she is well placed to write definitively about the group in question. Realist tales frequently include numerous references to the steps taken by the ethnographer to get close to the people studied and his or her success in this regard. Thus, for her research on female drug users, A. Taylor writes:

Events I witnessed or took part in ranged from the very routine (sitting around drinking coffee and eating junk food) to accompanying various women on visits to DSS [Department of Social Security] offices or to the HIV clinic; I accompanied them when they were in court, and even went flat-hunting with one woman. I went shopping with some, helping them choose clothes for their children and presents for their friends. I visited them in their homes, rehabilitation centres, and maternity wards, sat with them through withdrawals, watched them using drugs, and accompanied them when they went 'scoring' (buying drugs).   (A. Taylor 1993: 16)

Interpretative omnipotence

When writing up an ethnography, the author rarely presents possible alternative interpretations of an event or pattern of behaviour. Instead, the phenomenon in question is presented as having a single meaning or significance, which the fieldworker alone has cracked. Indeed, the evidence provided is carefully marshalled to support the singular interpretation that is placed on the event or pattern of behaviour. We are presented with an inevitability. It seems obvious or inevitable that someone would draw the inferences that the author has drawn when faced with such clear-cut evidence.

These four characteristics of realist tales imply that what the researcher did *qua* researcher is only one part of creating a sense of having figured out the nature of a culture. It is also very much to do with how the researcher represents what he or she did through writing about ethnography. For the postmodernist position, any realist tale is merely one 'spin'—that is one version, that can be or has been formulated in relation to the culture in question.

Key points

- Good writing is probably just as important as good research practice. Indeed, it is probably better thought of as a part of good research practice.

- Clear structure and statement of your research questions are important components of writing up research.

- Be sensitive to the ways in which writers seek to persuade us of their points of view.

- The study of rhetoric and writing strategies generally teaches us that the writings of scientists and social scientists do more than simply report findings. They are designed to convince and to persuade.

- The emphasis on rhetoric is not meant to imply that there is no external social reality; it merely suggests that our understanding of that reality is profoundly influenced by the ways it is represented by writers.

- While postmodernism has exerted a particular influence on this last point, writers working within other traditions have also contributed to it.

- The basic structure of and the rhetorical strategies employed in most quantitative and qualitative research articles are broadly similar.

- We need to get away from the idea that rhetoric and the desire to persuade others of the validity of our work are somehow bad things. They are not. We all want to get our points across and to persuade our readers that we have got things right. The question is—do we do it well? Do we make the best possible case? We all have to persuade others that we have got the right angle on things; the trick is to do it well. So when you write an essay or dissertation, do bear in mind the significance of your writing strategy.

Revision questions

- Why is it important to consider the ways in which social research is written up?

Writing quantitative research: An example

- Read an article based on quantitative research in a British sociology journal. How far does it exhibit the same characteristics as Kelley and De Graaf's article?

- What is meant by rhetorical strategy? Why might rhetorical strategies be important in relation to the writing-up of social research?

- Do Kelley and De Graaf employ an empiricist repertoire?

Writing qualitative research: An example

- Read an article based on quantitative research in a British sociology journal. How far does it exhibit the same characteristics as Beardsworth and Keil's article?

- How far is the structure of Beardsworth and Keil's article different from Kelley and De Graaf's?

Postmodernism and its implications for writing

- Why has postmodernism produced a growth of interest in writing social research?

- What is reflexivity?

Writing ethnography

- How far is it true to say that ethnographic writing is typically imbued with realism?

- What forms of ethnographic writing other than realist tales can be found?

- What are the main characteristics of realist tales?

24 Ethics in social research

Reader's guide

Ethical issues arise at a variety of stages in social research. This chapter is concerned with the concerns about ethics that might arise in the course of conducting research. The professional bodies concerned with the social sciences have been keen to spell out the ethical issues that can arise, and some of their statements will be reviewed in this chapter. Ethical issues cannot be ignored in that they relate directly to the integrity of a piece of research and of the disciplines that are involved. This chapter explores:

- some famous, even infamous, cases in which transgressions of ethical principles have occurred, though it is important not to take the view that ethical concerns arise only in relation to these extreme cases;

- different stances that can be and have been taken on ethics in social research;

- the significance and operation of four areas in which ethical concerns particularly arise: whether harm comes to participants; informed consent; invasion of privacy; and deception;

- some of the difficulties associated with ethical decision-making.

Introduction

Discussions about the ethics of social research bring us into a realm in which the role of values in the research process becomes a topic of concern. They revolve around such issues as:

- How should we treat the people on whom we conduct research?

- Are there activities in which we should or should not engage in our relations with them?

Questions about ethics in social research also bring in the role of professional associations, such as the British Sociological Association (BSA) and the Social Research Association (SRA), which have formulated codes of ethics. The BSA's and SRA's codes will be referred to on several occasions.

Statements of professional principles are frequently accessible from the Internet. Some of the most useful codes of ethics can be found at the following Internet addresses.

British Sociological Association (BSA), *Statement of Ethical Practice*: *http://www.britsoc.org.uk/about/ethic.htm*
Social Research Association (SRA), *Ethical Guidelines*: *http://www.the-sra.org.uk/ethics.htm*
British Psychological Society (BPS), *Code of Conduct, Ethical Principles, and Guidelines*: *http://www.bps.org.uk/about/rules5.cfm*
American Sociological Association (ASA), *Code of Ethics*: *http://www.asanet.org/ethics.htm*

Writings about ethics in social research are frequently frustrating for four reasons.

- Writers often differ quite widely from each other over ethical issues and questions. In other words, they differ over what is and is not ethically acceptable.

- The main elements in the debates do not seem to move forward a great deal. The same kinds of points that were made in the 1960s were being rehashed in the late 1990s and at the start of the present century.

- Debates about ethics have often accompanied well-known, not to say infamous, cases of alleged ethical transgression. Some of them have already been encountered in this book. They include: the study of a religious cult by a group of disguised researchers (Festinger *et al.* 1956); the use of pseudo-patients in the study of mental hospitals (Rosenhan 1973; Box 8.11, p. 172); Rosenthal and Jacobson's (1968) field experiment to study teacher expectations in the classroom (Box 2.5, p. 34); and Holdaway's (1982, 1983) covert ethnography of a police force. The problem with this emphasis on notoriety is that it can be taken to imply that ethical concerns reside only in such extreme cases, when in fact the potential for ethical transgression is much more general than this. See Boxes 24.1 and 24.2 for two cases that have acquired a celebrated status for their notoriety.

- Related to this last point, is that these extreme and notorious cases of ethical violation tend to be associated with particular research methods—notably disguised observation and the use of deception in experiments. Again, the problem with this association of ethics with certain studies (and methods) is that it implies that ethical concerns only or even primarily reside in some methods but not others. As a result, the impression can be gleaned that other methods, such as questionnaires or overt ethnography, are immune from ethical problems.

In this chapter, I will introduce the main ethical issues and debates about ethics. I am not going to try to resolve them, because they are not readily capable of resolution. This is why the ethical debate has scarcely moved on since the 1960s. What *is* crucial is to be aware of the ethical principles involved and of the nature of the concerns about ethics in social research. It is only if researchers are aware of the issues involved that they can make informed decisions about the implications of certain choices. If nothing else, you should be aware of the possible opprobrium that will be coming your way if you make certain kinds of choice. My chief concern lies with the ethical issues that arise in relations between

Box 24.1 The infamous case of the sociologist as voyeur

An investigation that has almost achieved particular notoriety because of its ethics (or lack of them, some might argue) is Humphreys's (1970) uncelebrated study of homosexual encounters in public toilets ('tearoom trade'). Humphreys's research interest was in impersonal sex, and, in order to shed light on this area, he took on the role of 'watchqueen'—that is, someone who watches out for possible intruders while men meet and engage in homosexual sex in public toilets. The style of observation (the sociological bit, that is) was closer to structured than to participant observation. As a result of his involvement in these social scenes, Humphreys was able to collect the details of active participants' car licence numbers. He was then able to track down their names and addresses and ended up with a sample of 100 active tearoom trade participants. He then conducted an interview survey of a sample of those who had been identified and of a further sample that acted as a point of comparison. The interview schedule was concerned with health issues and included some questions about marital sex. In order to reduce the risk of being remembered, Humphreys waited a year before contacting his respondents and also changed his hair style.

Box 24.2 The infamous case of the psychologist as Nazi concentration camp commandant

Milgram (1963) was concerned with the circumstances associated with the use of brutality in the Nazi concentration camps of the Second World War. In particular, he was interested in the processes whereby a person can be induced to cause extreme harm to another by virtue of being ordered to do so. To investigate this issue further, Milgram devised a laboratory experiment. Volunteers were recruited to act out the role of teachers who punished learners (who were accomplices of the experimenter) by submitting them to electric shocks when they gave incorrect answers to questions. The shocks were not, of course, real, but the teachers/volunteers were not aware of this. The level of electric shock was gradually increased with successive incorrect answers, until the teacher/volunteer refused to administer more shocks. Learners had been trained to respond to the rising level of electric shock with simulated but appropriate howls of pain. In the room was a further accomplice of Milgram's who cajoled the teacher/volunteer to continue to administer shocks, suggesting that it was part of the study's requirements to continue and that they were not causing permanent harm, in spite of the increasingly shrill cries of pain. Milgram's study shows that people can be induced to cause very considerable pain to others, and as such he saw it as shedding light on the circumstances leading to the horrors of the concentration camp. This is not the only experiment in which Milgram engaged in ethically dubious practices. Milgram used the 'lost letter technique', which entails deception and a lack of informed consent. As a means of measuring community orientations to political groups and other social institutions, Milgram and his co-researchers deposited unmailed letters in a variety of locations in a city (Milgram et al. 1965). The researchers wanted to create a situation in which a person must decide whether to mail an apparently lost letter. Do finders ignore it or do they find a mail box so that it can reach its destination? Each envelope bore the name of the addressee, a box number address, and a stamp. Four addresses were used: Friends of the Nazi Party; Friends of the Communist Party; Medical Research Associates; and a personal letter. The researchers then kept a record of the proportion of each type of letter that was posted on to each of the four addresses. Letters to the last two addresses were far more likely to be posted on than those to the first two. This technique represents an unobtrusive method that would be categorized as an example of 'contrived observation' (see Boxes 8.5 and 10.6, pp. 163, 209).

Box 24.3 Stances on ethics

Authors on social research ethics can be characterized in terms of the stances they take on the issue. The following stances can be distinguished.

- *Universalism*. A universalist stance takes the view that ethical precepts should never be broken. Infractions of ethical principles are wrong in a moral sense and are damaging to social research. This kind of stance can be seen in the writings of Erikson (1967), Dingwall (1980), and Bulmer (1982). Bulmer does, however, point to some forms of what appears to be disguised observation that may be acceptable. One is retrospective covert observation, which occurs when a researcher writes up his or her experiences in social settings in which he or she participated but not as a researcher. An example would be Van Maanen (1991*b*), who wrote up his experiences as a ride operator in Disneyland many years after he had been employed there in vacation jobs. Even a universalist like Erikson (1967: 372) recognizes that it 'would be absurd . . . to insist as a point of ethics that sociologists should always introduce themselves as investigators everywhere they go and should inform every person who figures in their thinking exactly what their research is all about'.

- *Situation ethics*. E. Goode (1996) has argued for deception to be considered on a case-by-case basis. In other words, he argues for what Fletcher (1966: 31) has called a 'situation ethics', or more specifically as 'principled relativism', which can be contrasted with the universalist ethics of some writers. This argument has two ways of being represented:

  - *The end justifies the means*. Some writers argue that, unless there is some breaking of ethical rules, we would never know about certain social phenomena. Fielding (1982) essentially argues for this position in relation to his research on the National Front, an extreme right-wing organization that was becoming politically influential in the 1970s. Without some kind of disguised observation, this important development and its appeal would not have been studied. This is usually linked to the second form of a situationist argument in relation to social research ethics.

  - *No choice*. It is often suggested that we have no choice but to engage in dissimulation on occasions if we want to investigate the issues in which we are interested. This view can be discerned in the writings of Holdaway (1982) and Homan (Homan and Bulmer 1982).

- *Ethical transgression is pervasive*. It is often observed that virtually all research involves elements that are at least ethically questionable. This occurs whenever participants are not given absolutely all the details on a piece of research, or when there is variation in the amount of knowledge about research. Punch (1994: 91), for example, observes that 'some dissimulation is intrinsic to social life and, therefore, to fieldwork'. He quotes Gans (1962: 44) in support of this point: 'If the researcher is completely honest with people about his activities, they will try to hide actions and attitudes they consider undesirable, and so will be dishonest. Consequently, the researcher must be dishonest to get honest data.'

- *Anything goes* (*more or less*). The writers associated with arguments relating to situation ethics and a recognition of the pervasiveness of ethical transgressions are not arguing for an 'anything-goes' mentality, but for a certain amount of flexibility in ethical decision-making. However, Douglas (1976) has argued that the kinds of deception in which social researchers engage are trivial compared to those perpetrated by powerful institutions in modern society (such as the mass media, the police, and industry). His book is an inventory of tactics for deceiving people so that their trust is gained and they reveal themselves to the researcher. Very few researchers subscribe to this stance. Denzin (1968) comes close to an anything-goes stance when he suggests that social researchers are entitled to study anyone in any setting provided the work has a 'scientific' purpose, does not harm participants, and does not deliberately damage the discipline. The harm-to-participants criterion can also be seen in the case reported in Box 24.4.

researchers and research participants in the course of an investigation. This focus by no means exhausts the range of ethical issues and dilemmas that arise, such as those that might arise in relation to the funding of social research or how findings are used by non-researchers. However, the ethical issues that arise in the course of doing research are the ones that are most likely to impinge on students. Writers on research ethics adopt different stances concerning the ethical issues that arise in connection with relationships between researchers and research participants. Box 24.3 outlines some of these stances.

Ethical principles

Discussions about ethical principles in social research, and perhaps more specifically transgressions of them, tend to revolve around certain issues that recur in different guises but that have been usefully broken down by Diener and Crandall (1978) into four main areas:

- whether there is *harm to participants*;
- whether there is a *lack of informed consent*;
- whether there is an *invasion of privacy*;
- whether *deception* is involved.

We will look at each of these in turn, but it should be appreciated that these four principles overlap somewhat. For example, it is difficult to imagine how the principle of informed consent could be built into an investigation in which research participants were deceived. However, there is no doubt that these four areas form a useful classification of ethical principles in and for social research.

Harm to participants

Research that is likely to harm participants is regarded by most people as unacceptable. But what is harm? Harm can entail a number of facets: physical harm; harm to participants' development; loss of self-esteem; stress; and 'inducing subjects to perform reprehensible acts', as Diener and Crandall (1978: 19) put it. In several studies that we have encountered in this book, there has been real or potential harm to participants.

- In the Rosenthal and Jacobson (1968) study (Box 2.5, p. 34), it is at least possible that the pupils that had not been identified as 'spurters' who would excel in their studies were adversely affected in their intellectual development by the greater attention received by the spurters.

- In the Festinger *et al.* (1956) study of a religious cult, it is quite likely that the fact that the researchers joined the group at a crucial time—close to the projected end of the world—fuelled the delusions of group members.

- Many of the participants in the Milgram experiment (1963) on obedience to authority (Box 24.2) experienced high levels of stress and anxiety as a consequence of being incited to administer electric shocks. It could also be argued that Milgram's observers were 'inducing subjects to perform reprehensible acts'. Indeed, yet another series of studies in which Milgram was involved placed participants in positions where they were being influenced to steal (Milgram and Shotland 1973).

- Many of the participants in Humphreys's (1970) research (see Box 24.1) were married men who are likely to have been fearful of detection as practising homosexuals. It is not inconceivable that his methods could have resulted in some of them becoming identified against their will.

The BSA *Statement of Ethical Practice* enjoins researchers to 'anticipate, and to guard against, consequences for research participants which can be predicted to be harmful' and 'to consider carefully the possibility that the research experience may be a disturbing one'. Similar sentiments are expressed by the SRA's *Ethical Guidelines*, for example, when it is advocated that the 'social researcher should try to minimise disturbance both to subjects themselves and to the subjects' relationships with their environment'.

The issue of harm to participants is further addressed in ethical codes by advocating care over maintaining the confidentiality of records. This means that the identities and records of individuals should be maintained as confidential. This injunction also means that care needs to be taken when findings are being published to ensure that individuals are not identified or identifiable. The case of a study of an American town, Springdale (a pseudonym), by Vidich and Bensman (1968) is instructive in this regard. The research was based on Vidich's participant observation within the town for over two years. The published book on the research was uncomplimentary about the town and many of its leaders and was written in what many people felt was a rather patronizing tone. To make matters worse, it was possible to identify individuals through the published account. The town's inhabitants responded with a Fourth of July Parade in which many of the inhabitants wore badges with their pseudonyms, and an effigy of Vidich was set up so that it was peering into manure. The townspeople also responded by announcing their refusal to cooperate in any more social research. The inhabitants were clearly upset by the publication and to that extent were harmed by it. This example also touches on the issue of privacy, which will be addressed below.

As this last case suggests, the issue of confidentiality raises particular difficulties for many forms of qualitative research. In quantitative research, it is relatively easy to anonymize records and to report findings in a way that does not allow individuals to be identified. However, this is often less easy with qualitative research, where particular care has to be taken with regard to the possible identification of persons and places. The use of pseudonyms is a common recourse, but may not eliminate entirely the possibility of identification. This issue raises particular problems with regard to the secondary analysis of qualitative data (see Chapter 19), since it is very difficult, though by no means impossible, to present field notes and interview transcripts in a way that will prevent people and places from being identified. As Anderson (1998) has suggested, the difficulty is one of being able to ensure that the same safeguards concerning confidentiality can be guaranteed when secondary analysts examine such records as those provided by the original primary researcher.

One of the problems with the harm-to-participants principle is that it is not possible to identify in all circumstances whether harm is likely, though that fact should not be taken to mean that there is no point in seeking to protect them. Kimmel (1988) notes in this connection the example of the Cambridge–Summerville Youth Study. In 1939, an experiment was conducted on boys aged 5–13 who were either identified as likely to become delinquent or who were average in this regard. The 506 boys were equally divided in terms of this characteristic. They were randomly assigned to either an experimental group in which they received preventative counselling or to a no-treatment control group. In the mid-1970s, the records were re-examined and were quite shocking: 'Treated subjects were more likely than controls to evidence signs of alcoholism and serious mental illness, died at a younger age, suffered from more stress-related diseases, tended to be employed in lower-prestige occupations, and were more likely to commit second crimes' (Kimmel 1988: 19).

In other words, the treatment brought about a train of negative consequences for the group. This is an extreme example and relates to experimental research, which is not a research design that is commonly employed in social research (see Chapter 2), but it does illustrate the difficulty of anticipating harm to respondents. The ASA *Codes of Ethics* suggests that, if there is any prospect of harm to participants, informed consent, the focus of the next section, is essential: 'Informed consent must be obtained when the risks of research are greater than the risks of everyday life. Where modest risk or harm is anticipated, informed consent must be obtained.'

Lack of informed consent

The issue of informed consent is in many respects the area within social research ethics that is most hotly debated. The bulk of the discussion tends to focus on what is variously called disguised or covert observation. Such observation can involve covert participant observation (Box 14.3, p. 294), or simple or contrived observation (Box 8.5, p. 163), in which the researcher's true identity is unknown. The principle means that prospective research participants should be given as much information as might be needed to make an informed decision about whether or not they wish to participate in a study. Covert observation transgresses that principle, because participants are not given the opportunity to refuse to cooperate. They are involved whether they like it or not.

Lack of informed consent is a feature of the research in Boxes 24.1 and 24.2. In Humphreys's research informed consent is absent, because the men for whom he acted as a watchqueen were not given the opportunity to refuse participation in his investigation. Similar points can be made about several other studies previously encountered in this book, such as Festinger *et al.* (1956); Rosenthal and Jacobson (1968); Patrick (1973); Rosenhan (1973); Fielding (1981, 1982); and Holdaway (1982, 1983). The principle of informed consent also entails the implication that, even when people know they are being asked to participate in research, they should be fully informed about the research process. As the SRA *Ethical Guidelines* suggests:

Inquiries involving human subjects should be based as far as practicable on the freely given informed consent of subjects. Even if participation is required by law, it should still be as informed as possible. In voluntary inquiries, subjects should not be under the impression that they are required to participate. They should be aware of their entitlement to refuse at any stage for whatever reason and to withdraw data just supplied. Information that would be likely to affect a subject's willingness to participate should not be deliberately withheld, since this would remove from subjects an important means of protecting their own interests.

Similarly, the BSA *Statement* says:

As far as possible sociological research should be based on the freely given informed consent of those studied. This implies a responsibility on the sociologist to explain as fully as possible, and in terms meaningful to participants, what the research is about, who is undertaking and financing it, why it is being undertaken, and how it is to be promoted.

Thus, while Milgram's experimental subjects were volunteers and therefore knew they were going to participate in research, there is a lack of informed consent, because they were not given full information about the nature of the research and its possible implications for them.

However, as Homan (1991: 73) has observed, implementing the principle of informed consent 'is easier said than done'. At least two major points stand out here.

- It is extremely difficult to present prospective participants with absolutely all the information that might be required to make an informed decision about their involvement. In fact, relatively minor transgressions probably pervade most social research, such as deliberately under-estimating the amount of time that an interview is likely to take so that people are not put off being interviewed and not giving absolutely all the details about one's research for fear of contaminating people's answers to questions.

- In ethnographic research, the researcher is likely to come into contact with a wide spectrum of people, and ensuring that absolutely everyone has the opportunity for informed consent is not practicable, because it would be extremely disruptive in everyday contexts. For example, recall the extract from Punch's field notes (1979) from his research on the police in Amsterdam, quoted on p. 301, in which a suspect was apprehended and the ethnographer was represented by the police officers as a fellow police officer. It was not feasible to inform the individual of the fact that Punch was in fact a researcher and to notify him of his rights in relation to the research. Similarly, in the passage from Punch's field notes in Box 14.11 (p. 306), the meandering cyclist could not be given the opportunity for informed consent. Punch was not a disguised participant observer so far as the police were concerned, but *was* disguised in connection with many of those with whom the police had encounters in the course of his fieldwork. Also, even when all research participants in a certain setting are aware that the ethnographer is a researcher, it is doubtful whether they are all similarly (let alone identically) informed about the nature of the research.

In spite of the widespread condemnation of violations of informed consent and the view that covert observation is especially vulnerable to accusations of unethical practice in this regard, studies using the method still appear periodically (e.g. Fielding 1982; S. Taylor 1999). The defence is usually of the 'end-justifies-the-means' kind, which is further discussed below. What is interesting in this present context is that the BSA *Statement* essentially leaves the door ajar for covert observation. The phrase 'as far as possible' regarding informed consent in the last quotation from the *Statement* does this, but they then go even further in relation to covert research:

There are serious ethical dangers in the use of covert research but covert methods may avoid certain problems. For instance, difficulties arise when research participants change their behaviour because they know they are being studied. Researchers may also face problems when access to spheres of social life is closed to social scientists by powerful or secretive interests. However, covert methods violate the principles of informed consent and may invade the privacy of those being studied. Participant or non-participant observation in non-public spaces or experimental manipulation of research participants without their knowledge should be resorted to only where it is impossible to use other methods to obtain essential data. In such studies it is important to safeguard the anonymity of research participants. Ideally, where informed consent has not been obtained prior to the research it should be obtained post-hoc.

While this statement hardly condones the absence of informed consent associated with covert research, it is not unequivocally censorious either. It recognizes that covert research 'may avoid certain

problems' and refers, without using the term, to the possibility of reactivity associated with overt observational methods. It also recognizes that covert methods can help to get over the difficulty of gaining access to certain kinds of setting. The passage entails an acknowledgement that informed consent is jeopardized, along with the privacy principle (see below), but implies that covert research can be used 'where it is impossible to use other methods to obtain essential data'. The difficulty here clearly is how a researcher is to decide whether it is in fact impossible to obtain data other than by covert work. I suspect that, by and large, covert observers typically make their judgements in this connection on the basis of the *anticipated* difficulty of gaining access to a setting or of encountering reactivity problems, rather than as a response to difficulties they have actually experienced. For example, Holdaway (1982: 63) has written that, as a police officer, his only alternatives to covert participant observation were either equally unethical (but less desirable) or 'unrealistic'. Similarly, Homan justified his use of covert participant observation of a religious sect on the grounds that sociologists were viewed very negatively by group members and therefore: 'It seemed probable that the prevalence of such a perception would prejudice the effectiveness of a fieldworker declaring an identity as sociologist' (Homan and Bulmer 1982: 107). The issue of the circumstances in which violations of ethical principles, like informed consent, are deemed acceptable will reappear in the discussion below.

The principle of informed consent is also bound up to some extent with the issue of harm to participants. Erikson has suggested that, if the principle is not followed and if participants are harmed as a result of the research, the investigator is more culpable than if they did not know. For example, he writes: 'If we happen to harm people who have agreed to act as subjects, we can at least argue that they knew something of the risks involved . . .' (Erikson 1967: 369). While this might seem like a recipe for seeking a salve for the sociologist's conscience, it does point to an important issue—namely, that the social researcher is more likely to be vilified if participants are adversely affected when they were not willing accomplices, than when they were. However, it is debatable whether that means that the researcher is any less culpable for that harm. Erikson implies they are less culpable, but this is a potential area for disagreement.

Invasion of privacy

This third area of ethical concern relates to the issue of the degree to which invasions of privacy can be condoned. The right to privacy is a tenet that many of us hold dear, and transgressions of that right in the name of research are not regarded as acceptable. It is very much linked to the notion of informed consent, because, to the degree that informed consent is given on the basis of a detailed understanding of what the research participant's involvement is likely to entail, he or she in a sense acknowledges that the right to privacy has been surrendered for that limited domain. The ASA *Codes of Ethics* makes a direct link: 'Sociologists should take culturally appropriate steps to secure informed consent and to avoid invasions of privacy.' Of course, the research participant does not abrogate the right to privacy entirely by providing informed consent. As we have seen, when people agree to be interviewed, they will frequently refuse to answer certain questions on whatever grounds they feel are justified. Often, these refusals will be based on a feeling that certain questions delve into private realms, which respondents do not wish to make public, regardless of the fact that the interview is in private. Examples might be questions about income, religious beliefs, or sexual activities.

Covert methods are usually deemed to be violations of the privacy principle on the grounds that participants are not being given the opportunity to refuse invasions of their privacy. Such methods also mean that they might reveal confidences or information that they would not have revealed if they had known about the status of the confidant as researcher. The issue of privacy is invariably linked to issues of anonymity and confidentiality in the research process, an area that has already been touched on in the context of the question of whether harm comes to participants. The BSA *Statement* forges this kind of connection: 'The anonymity and privacy of those who participate in the research process should be respected. Personal information concerning research participants should be kept confidential. In some cases it may be necessary to decide whether it is proper or appropriate to record certain kinds of sensitive information.'

Raising issues about ensuring anonymity and confidentiality in relation to the recording of information and the maintenance of records relates to all methods of social research. In other words, while covert research may pose certain kinds of problem regarding the invasion of privacy, other methods of social research are implicated in possible difficulties in connection with anonymity and confidentiality. This was clearly the case with the Springfield research (Vidich and Bensman 1968), which was based on open participant observation. The issue here was that the absence of safeguards concerning the protection of the identity of some members of the community meant that certain matters about them came into the public domain that should have remained private.

Deception

Deception occurs when researchers represent their research as something other than what it is. The two studies by Milgram referred to in Box 24.2 involve deception. In the obedience-to-authority experiment, participants are led to believe they are administering real electric shocks. In the lost-letter study, deception occurs because people who place the lost letters in a mail box, so that they will be sent to their destinations, believe they are sending letters that have been accidentally lost rather than ones that have been deposited for a social psychological experiment. Deception in various degrees is probably quite widespread in such research, because researchers often want to limit participants' understanding of what the research is about so that they respond more naturally to the experimental treatment.

However, deception is by no means the exclusive preserve of social psychology experiments. E. Goode (1996), for example, placed four fake and slightly different dating advertisements in periodicals. He received nearly 1,000 replies and was able to conduct a content analysis of them. Several of the studies we have already encountered entail deception: Rosenthal and Jacobson (1968) deceived teachers into believing that particular children in their charge were likely to excel at school, when they had in fact been randomly selected; Festinger *et al.* (1956) deceived cult members that they were in fact real converts; Rosenhan's (1973) associates deceived admissions staff at mental hospitals that they were mentally ill; and Holdaway (1982) deceived his superiors and peers that he was functioning solely as a police officer.

The ethical objection to deception seems to turn on two points. First, it is not a nice thing to do. While the SRA *Guidelines* recognizes that deception is widespread in social interaction, it is hardly desirable. Secondly, there is the question of professional self-interest. If social researchers became known as snoopers who deceived people as a matter of professional course, the image of our work would be adversely affected and we might experience difficulty in gaining financial support and the cooperation of future prospective research participants. As the SRA *Guidelines* puts it: 'It remains the duty of social researchers and their collaborators, however,

not to pursue methods of inquiry that are likely to infringe human values and sensibilities. To do so, whatever the methodological advantages, would be to endanger the reputation of social research and the mutual trust between social researchers and society which is a prerequisite for much research.' Similarly, Erikson (1967: 369) has argued that disguised observation 'is liable to damage the reputation of sociology in the larger society and close off promising areas of research for future investigators'.

One of the chief problems with the discussion of this aspect of ethics is that deception is, as some writers observe, widespread in social research (see the stance, *Ethical transgression is pervasive*, in Box 24.3). It is rarely feasible or desirable to provide participants with a totally complete account of what your research is about. As Punch (1979) found in the incidents referred to above, he could hardly announce to the youth or the meandering cyclist that he was not in fact a police officer and then launch into a lengthy account of his research. Bulmer (1982), whose stance is predominantly that of a universalist in ethics terms (see Box 24.3), nonetheless recognizes that there are bound to be instances such as this and deems them justifiable. However, it is very difficult to know where the line should be drawn here.

The difficulties of ethical decision-making

The difficulty of drawing the line between ethical and unethical practices can be revealed in several ways. The issue of some members of social settings being aware of the researcher's status and the nature of his or her investigation has been mentioned on several occasions (though see Box 24.4 for an interesting illustration of this issue). Manuals about interviewing are full of advice about how to entice interviewees to open up about themselves. Researchers using Likert scales reword items to identify yeasayers and naysayers. Interviewers frequently err on the low side when asked how long an interview will take. Women may use their identity as

women to influence female interviewees in in-depth interviews to probe into their lives and reveal inner thoughts and feelings, albeit with a commitment to feminist research (Oakley 1981; Finch 1984). Qualitative research is frequently very open-ended, and, as a result, research questions are either loose or not specified, so that it is doubtful whether ethnographers in particular are able to inform others accurately about the nature of their research. Perhaps too some interviewees find the questions we ask unsettling or find the cut and thrust of a focus group discussion stressful, especially if they inadvertently reveal more than they might have intended.

Box 24.4 Ethics and research on prostitution

O'Connell Davidson and Layder (1994) discuss the research into prostitution in which the former author was engaged (and which forms part of the research reported in O'Connell Davidson 1998). She was conducting small-scale ethnographic research on a prostitute (Desiree, a pseudonym), who worked from home, along with her receptionists and clients. While Desiree and her receptionists were fully aware of O'Connell Davidson's status, the clients were not. The authors acknowledge the invasion of the clients' privacy and the lack of informed consent but say they are 'untroubled' by the intrusion O'Connell Davidson's presence represented. This is because the clients were anonymous to her and she was not 'in a position to secure, store or disclose information that could harm them' (1994: 214). Thus, the fact that there was no harm to participants is regarded as the litmus test of the ethical status of the research. In addition, we are given a version of the Ethical transgression is pervasive stance (see Box 24.3): 'Virtually all social research is intrusive and exploitative to some degree' (1994: 215). However, there is an additional and interesting twist to this discussion of ethics. O'Connell Davidson acknowledges her commitment to and sympathy for Desiree and her receptionists. But these sentiments do not extend to the clients:

I have no wish to advance their interests through the research, no personal liking and no real sympathy for them. I have a professional obligation to preserve their anonymity and to ensure that they are not harmed by my research, but I feel no qualms about being less than frank with them, and no obligation to allow them to choose whether or not their actions are recorded.   (O'Connell Davidson and Layder 1994: 215)

In other words, rights of informed consent and of not being deceived are differentially distributed in society according to these authors. In such circumstances, the researcher sets him- or herself up as the judge of which individuals or groups 'deserve' ethical treatment, a view that has far-reaching implications.

There are, in other words, many ways in which there is the potential for deception and, relatedly, lack of informed consent in social research. These instances are, of course, a very far cry from the deceptions perpetrated in the research summarized in Boxes 24.1 and 24.2, but they point to the difficulty of arriving at ethically informed decisions. Ethical codes give advice on patently inappropriate practices, though sometimes leaving some room for manœuvre, as we have seen, but less guidance on marginal areas of ethical decision-making. Indeed, guidelines may even be used by research participants *against* the researcher when they seek to limit the boundaries of a fieldworker's investigation (Punch 1994).

Key points

- This chapter has been concerned with a limited range of issues concerning ethics in social research, in that it has concentrated on ethical concerns that might arise in the context of collecting and analysing data. My concern has mainly been with relations between researchers and research participants. Other ethical issues can arise in the course of social research.

- While the codes and guidelines of professional associations provide some guidance, their potency is ambiguous and they often leave the door open for some autonomy with regard to ethical issues.

- The main areas of ethical concern relate to: harm to participants; lack of   invasion
  informed consent; loss of privacy; and deception.

- Covert observation and certain notorious studies have been particular focuses of
  concern.

- The boundaries between ethical and unethical practices are not clear-cut.

- Writers on social research ethics have adopted several different stances in relation
  to the issue.

- While the rights of research participants are the chief focus of ethical principles,
  concerns about professional self-interest are also of concern.

Revision questions

- Why are ethical issues important in relation to the conduct of social research?
- Outline the different stances on ethics in social research.

Ethical principles

- Does 'harm to participants' refer to physical harm alone?
- What are some difficulties with following this ethical principle?
- Why is the issue of informed consent so hotly debated?
- What are some difficulties with following this ethical principle?
- Why is the privacy principle important?
- Why does deception matter?
- How helpful are notorious studies like Milgram's electric shock experiments and
  Humphreys's study in terms of understanding the operation of ethical principles in social
  research?

The difficulties of ethical decision-making

- How easy is it to conduct ethical research?
- Read one of the ethical guidelines referred to in this chapter. How effective is it in guarding
  against ethical transgressions?

25 Conducting a small-scale project

Reader's guide

The goal of this chapter is to provide advice to students on some of the issues that they need to consider if they have to prepare a dissertation based upon a relatively small-scale project. Increasingly, social science students are required to produce such a dissertation as part of the requirements for their degrees. In addition to needing help with the conduct of research, which it is hoped has been provided by the bulk of this book up to this point, more specific advice on tactics in doing and writing up social research for a dissertation can be useful. It is against this background that this chapter has been written. The chapter explores a wide variety of issues such as:

- advice on timing;
- advice on generating research questions;
- dealing with the existing literature on the subject;
- advice on writing to help you produce compelling findings.

Introduction

This chapter has been written to provide some advice for readers who might be carrying out a small-scale project of their own. Hopefully, the previous twenty-four chapters will have provided helpful information about the choices available to you and how to implement them. But beyond this, how might you go about conducting a small project of your own? I have in mind here the kind of situation that is increasingly common among degree programmes in the social sciences—the requirement to write a dissertation of around 10,000 to 15,000 words. In particular, I have in mind the needs of undergraduate students, but it may be that students on postgraduate degree programmes will also find some of the observations I make helpful. Also, the advice is really concerned with students conducting projects with a component of empirical research in which they collect new data or perhaps conduct a secondary analysis of existing data.

Get to know what is expected of you by your institution

Your institution or department will have specific requirements concerning a wide variety of different features that your dissertation should comprise and a range of other matters relating to it. These include such things as: the form of binding; how it is to be presented; whether an abstract is required; how big the page margins should be; the format for referencing; number of words; perhaps the structure of the dissertation; how much advice you can get from your supervisor; plagiarism; deadlines; how much (if any) financial assistance you can expect; and so on.

The advice here is simple: *follow the requirements, instructions, and information you are given*. If anything in this book conflicts with your institution's guide-lines and requirements, ignore this book! I very much hope this is not something that will occur very much, but if it does, keep to the guidelines your institution gives you.

Start thinking about your research area early on

The chances are that you will be asked to start think-ing about what you want to do research on well before you are due to start work on your dissertation. It is worth giving yourself a good deal of time. As you are doing your various modules, begin to think about whether there are any topics that might interest you and that might provide you with a researchable area.

Identifying research questions

Many students want to conduct research into areas that are of personal interest to them. This is not a bad thing at all and, as I noted in Chapter 1, many social researchers start from this point as well (see also Lofland and Lofland 1995: 11–14). However, you must move on to develop research questions. This recommendation applies to qualitative research as well as quantitative research. I know that I said in Chapter 13 that qualitative research is more open-ended than quantitative research, and that in Chapter 14 I mentioned some notable studies that appear not to have been driven by specific research questions (p. 304). However, totally open-ended research is risky and can lead to the collection of too much data and, when it comes to writing up, to con-fusion about your focus. So, unless your supervisor advises you to the contrary, I would definitely for-mulate some research questions, even if they turn out to be somewhat less specific than the kinds we often find in quantitative research. In other words, what is it about your area of interest that you want to know?

Research questions are, therefore, important. They provide you with a focus that will

• guide your literature search;

• guide you in deciding what data you need to collect;

• guide your analysis of your data;

• guide your writing-up of your data;

• stop you from going off in unnecessary directions and tangents.

Therefore, research questions have many uses and you should resist the temptation of not formulating them or delaying their formulation. But do remem-ber that your research questions must have a clear social scientific (for example, sociological) angle.

Research questions should exhibit the following characteristics.

• They should be clear, in the sense of being intelligible.

• They should be researchable—that is, they should allow you to do research in relation to them. This means that they should not be formulated in terms that are so abstract that they cannot be converted into researchable terms.

• They should have some connection(s) with estab-lished theory and research. This means that there should be a literature on which you can draw to help illuminate how your research questions should be approached. Even if you find a topic that has been scarcely addressed by social scientists, it is unlikely that there will be no relevant literature (for example, on related or parallel topics).

• Your research questions should be linked to each other. Unrelated research questions are unlikely to be acceptable, since you should be developing an argument in your dissertation. You could not very readily construct a single argument in relation to unrelated research questions.

• They should at the very least hold out the prospect of being able to make an original contribution—however small—to the topic.

• The research questions should be neither too large (so that you would need a massive grant to study them) nor too small (so that you cannot make a reasonably significant contribution to your area of study).

If you are stuck about how to formulate research questions (or indeed other phases of your research), it is always a good idea to look at journal articles or research monographs to see how other researchers have formulated them. Also, look at past dissertations for ideas as well. Marx (1997) has suggested a wide range of sources of research questions (see Box 25.1).

Using your supervisor

Most institutions that require a dissertation or similar component allocate students to supervisors. Institutions vary quite a lot in what can be expected of supervisors; in other words, they vary in terms of what kinds of and how much assistance they will give to students allocated to them. Equally, students vary a great deal in how frequently they see their supervisors and in their use of them. My advice here is simple: use your supervisor to the fullest extent that you are allowed and follow the pointers you are given by him or her. Your supervisor will almost certainly be someone who is well versed in the research process and who will be able to provide you with help and feedback at all stages of your research, subject to your institution's strictures in this regard. If your supervisor is critical of your research questions, your interview schedule, drafts of your dissertation, or whatever, try to respond positively. Follow the suggestions that he or she provides, since the criticisms will invariably be accompanied by reasons for

the criticisms and suggestions for revision. It is not a personal attack. Supervisors regularly have to go through the same process themselves when they submit an article to a peer-refereed journal or apply for a research grant or give a conference paper. So respond to criticisms and suggestions positively and be glad that you are being given the opportunity to address deficiencies in your work before it is formally examined.

A further point is that students who get stuck at the start of their dissertations or who get behind with their work sometimes respond to the situation by avoiding their supervisors. They then get caught up in a vicious circle that results in their work being neglected and perhaps rushed at the end. Try to avoid this situation by confronting the fact that you are experiencing difficulties in getting going or are getting behind and seek out your supervisor for advice.

Box 25.1 Marx's sources of research questions

Marx (1997) suggests the following as possible sources of research questions.

- Intellectual puzzles and contradictions.
- The existing literature.
- Replication.
- Structures and functions. For example, if you point to a structure such as a type of organization, you can ask questions about the reasons why there are different types and the implications of the differences.
- Opposition. Marx identifies the sensation of feeling that a certain theoretical perspective or notable piece of work is misguided and exploring the reasons for your opposition.
- A social problem. But remember that this is just a source of a research question; you still have to identify social scientific (for example, sociological) issues in relation to a social problem.

- 'Gaps between official versions of reality and the facts on the ground' (Marx 1997: 113). An example here is something like Delbridge's (1998) fascinating ethnographic account of company rhetoric about Japanized work practices and how they operate in practice.
- The counter-intuitive. For example, when common sense seems to fly in the face of social scientific truths.
- 'Empirical examples that trigger amazement' (Marx 1997: 114). Marx gives, as examples, deviant cases and atypical events.
- New methods and theories. How might they be applied in new settings?
- 'New social and technical developments and social trends' (Marx 1997: 114).
- Personal experience.
- Sponsors and teachers. But do not expect your teachers to provide you with detailed research questions.

Managing time and resources

All research is constrained by time and resources. There is no point in working on research questions and plans that cannot be seen through because of time pressure or because of the costs involved. Two points are relevant here.

- Work out a timetable—preferably in conjunction with your supervisor—detailing the different stages of your research (including the review of the literature and writing-up). The timetable should specify the different stages and the calendar points at which you should start and finish them. Some stages are likely to be ongoing—for example, searching the literature for new references (see below)—but that should not prove an obstacle to developing a timetable.

- Find out what, if any, resources can be put at your disposal for carrying out your research. For example, will you receive help from your institution with such things as travel costs, photocopying, secretarial assistance, postage, stationery, and

so on? Will the institution be able to loan you hardware such as tape recorders and transcription machines if you need to record and transcribe your interviews? Has it got the software you need, such as SPSS or a qualitative data analysis package like NVivo? This kind of information will help you to establish how far your research design and methods are financially feasible and practical. The imaginary 'gym study' that was used in Chapter 12 is an example of an investigation that would be feasible within the kind of time frame usually allocated to undergraduate and postgraduate dissertations. However, it would require such facilities as: typing up the questionnaire, which nowadays students can usually do for themselves with the help of word-processing programs; photocopying covering letters and questionnaires; postage for sending the questionnaires out and for any follow-up letters to non-respondents; return postage for the questionnaires; and the availability of a quantitative data analysis package like SPSS.

Searching the existing literature

Usually, students know a few initial references when they begin on a project. The bibliographies in these references will usually provide you with a raft of further relevant references. Nowadays, online bibliographical databases that are accessible on the Internet are an invaluable source of references. Two that I use regularly are the Social Sciences Citation Index (SSCI) and OCLC FirstSearch. SSCI can be accessed at the following address:

http://wos.mimas.ac.uk

This will take you to the **W**eb **of S**cience home page. Just click on the **WoS** button in the centre of the Screen and after logging in you will be asked to choose between **Full Search** and **Easy Search**. Unless you are very unfamiliar with using the Internet, the former is likely to be preferable. Once you have done this, ➔ **Social Sciences Citation Index**. At this point, you can also narrow down your search to specific years. If you do not elect to do this, your search will cover all years from 1981. To activate your search, ➔ **GENERAL SEARCH**. The **General Search** window will then open. If you are searching for references on a particular topic, insert the key word(s) in **TOPIC** and then ➔ **SEARCH**.

The address for OCLS FirstSearch is:

http://www.oclc.org/oclc/fs/menu/home1.htm

Then ➔ **FirstSearch Logon** to get into FirstSearch.

The output from both databases frequently includes abstracts and references. The SSCI includes only journal articles, but can pick up books, since books reviewed in journals are invariably identified through keyword searches. You will need to experiment with the use of keywords, because this is usually the way in which databases like these are searched, though author searches are also possible. However, you will need to find out whether your institution can give you a user name and password to gain access to these databases.

To search for books, good places to start are the databases of online bookshops. Useful Internet addresses for these are:

http://www.amazon.com
http://www.amazon.co.uk
http://www.bookshop.co.uk

The catalogue of your own institution is an obvious route to finding books, but so too are the catalogues of other universities. Many of these can be found at:

http://www.niss.ac.uk/lis/opacsalpha.html

Another very useful source is the International Bibliography of the Social Sciences at (IBSS), which can be found at:

http://www.lse.ac.uk/ibss

You can go directly to the online IBSS via

http://www.bids.ac.uk

After logging in (you will need a user name and password), ➔ **search** button to the right of **BIDS International Bibliography of the Social Sciences**. You will be given a choice of the **enhanced service** or the **basic service**. Unless you are very unfamiliar with using the Internet, the former is likely to be preferable. If you are searching for a topic, enter the key word(s) by **Search for:**, define the years of your search (the database covers all years since 1951), and then ➔ **search**.

Another useful source is the Resource Guide for the Social Sciences at:

http://www.jisc.ac.uk/subject/socsci/

For all of these online databases, you will need to work out some good keywords that can be entered into the search engines and which will allow you to identify suitable references.

You should explore the existing literature to identify the following issues.

- What is already known about this area?
- What concepts and theories are relevant to this area?

- What research methods and research strategies have been employed in studying this area?

- Are there any significant controversies?

- Are there any inconsistencies in findings relating to this area?

- Are there any unanswered research questions in this area?

This last issue points to the possibility that you will be able to revise and refine your research questions in the process of reviewing the literature.

Why do you need to review the existing literature? The most obvious reason is that you want to know what is already known about your area of interest so that you do not simply 'reinvent the wheel'. Beyond this, using the existing literature on a topic is a means of developing an argument about the significance of your research and where it leads. The simile of a *story* is sometimes used in this context (see below). A competent review of the literature is also at least in part a means of affirming your credibility as someone who is knowledgeable in your chosen area.

When you are reading the existing literature try to do the following.

- Take good notes, including the details of the material you read. It is infuriating to find that you forgot to record the volume number of an article you read and which needs to be included in your Bibliography. This may necessitate a trip to the library on occasions when you are already hard pressed for time.

- Develop critical reading skills. Your review of the literature will need to be critical rather than merely descriptive, so it is worth developing these skills and recording relevant critical points in the course of taking notes. Developing a critical approach is not necessarily one of simply criticizing the work of others. It entails moving beyond mere description and asking questions about the significance of the work. It entails attending to such issues as: How does the item relate to others you have read? Are there any apparent strengths and deficiencies—perhaps in terms of methodology or in terms of the credibility of the conclusions drawn? What theoretical ideas have influenced the item?

In some areas of research, there are very many references. Try to identify the major ones and work outwards from there. Move on to the next stage of your research at the point that you identified in your timetable (see above) so that you can dig yourself out of the library. This is not to say that your search for the literature will cease, but that you need to force yourself to move on. Seek out your supervisor's advice on whether you need to search the literature much more.

Preparing for your research

Do not begin your data collection until you have identified your research questions reasonably clearly. Develop your data collection instruments with these research questions at the forefront of your thinking. If you do not do this, there is the risk that your results will not allow you to illuminate the research questions. If at all possible, conduct a small pilot study to determine how well your research instruments work.

You will also need to think about access and sampling issues. If your research requires you to gain access to or the cooperation of one or more closed settings like an organization, you need to confirm at the earliest opportunity that you have the necessary permission to conduct your work. You also need to consider how you will go about gaining access to people. This issues leads you into sampling considerations, such as the following.

- Who do you need to study in order to investigate your research questions?

- How easily can you gain access to a sampling frame?
- What kind of sampling strategy will you employ (e.g. probability sampling, quota sampling, theoretical sampling, convenience sampling)?

- Can you justify your choice of sampling method?

Also, while preparing for your data collection you should consider whether there are any possible ethical problems associated with your research methods or your approach to contacting people.

Doing your research and analysing your results

This is what the bulk of this book has been about, so it seems superfluous to go over this ground again. Here are some useful reminders of practicalities.

- Keep good records of what you do. A research diary can be helpful here, but there are several other things to bear in mind. For example, if you are doing a social survey by mail questionnaire, keep good records of who has replied, so that you know who should be sent reminders. If participant observation is a component of your research, remember to keep good field notes and not to rely on your memory.
- Make sure that you are thoroughly familiar with any hardware you are using in collecting your data, such as tape recorders for interviewing, and make sure it is in good working order (for example, batteries that are not flat or close to being flat).
- Do not wait until all your data have been collected to begin coding. This recommendation applies to both quantitative and qualitative research. If you

are conducting a questionnaire survey, begin coding your data and entering them into SPSS or whatever package you are using after you have put together a reasonably sized batch of completed questionnaires. In the case of qualitative data, such as interview transcripts, the same point applies, and, indeed, it is a specific recommendation of the proponents of grounded theory that data collection and analysis should be intertwined.

- Remember that the transcription of tapes with recorded interviews takes a long time. Allow at least six hours transcription for every one hour of recorded interview talk, at least in the early stages of transcription.
- Become familiar with any data analysis packages as soon as possible. This familiarity will help you to establish whether you definitely need them and will ensure that you do not need to learn everything about them at the very time you need to use them for your analysis.

Writing up your research

It is easy to neglect the writing stage of your work because of the difficulties that you often encounter in getting your research underway. But—obvious though this point is—your dissertation has to be

written. Your findings must be conveyed to an audience, something that all of us who carry out research have to face. The first bit of advice is . . .

Start early

It is easy to take the view that the writing-up of your research findings is something that you can think about after you have collected and analysed your data. There is, of course, a grain of truth in this view, in that you could hardly write up your findings until you know what they are, which is something that you can know only once you have gathered and analysed your data. However, there are good reasons for beginning writing early on, since you might want to start thinking about such issues as how best to present and justify the research questions that are driving your research or how to structure the theoretical and research literature that will have been used to frame your research questions. A further reason why it is advisable to begin writing earlier rather than later is an entirely practical one: many people find it difficult to get started and employ (probably unwittingly) procrastination strategies to put off the inevitable. This tendency can result in the writing being left until the last minute and consequently rushed. Writing under this kind of pressure is not ideal. How you represent your findings and conclusions is a crucial stage in the research process. If you do not provide a convincing account of your research, you will not do justice to it.

Be persuasive

This point is crucial. Writing up your research is not simply a matter of reporting your findings and drawing some conclusions. Writing up your research will contain many other features, such as referring to the literature on which you drew, explaining how you did your research, and outlining how you conducted your analysis. But above all, you must be *persuasive*. This means that you must convince your readers of the credibility of your conclusions. Simply saying 'this is what I found; isn't it interesting' is not enough. You must persuade your readers that your findings and conclusion are significant and that they are plausible.

Get feedback

Try to get as much feedback on your writing as possible and respond positively to the points anyone makes about what they read. Your supervisor is likely to be the main source of feedback, but institutions vary in what supervisors are allowed to comment on. Provide your supervisor with drafts of your work to the fullest extent that regulations will allow. Give him or her plenty of time to provide feedback. There will be others like you who will want your supervisor to comment on their work, and, if he or she feels rushed, the comments may be less helpful. Also, you could ask others on the same degree programme to read your drafts and comment on them. They may ask you to do the same. Their comments may be very useful, but, by and large, your supervisor's comments are the main ones you should seek out.

Avoid sexist, racist, and disablist language

Remember that your writing should be free of sexist, racist, and disablist language. The British Sociological Association provides very good general and specific advice in this connection which can be found at:

http://www.britsoc.org.uk/about/antisex.htm
http://www.britsoc.org.uk/about/antirace.htm
http://www.britsoc.org.uk/about/ablist.htm

Structure your writing

What lessons might be gleaned from the examination in Chapter 23 of the journal articles by Kelley and De Graaf (1997) and Beardsworth and Keil (1992) for your own research project? It may be that you have to write a dissertation of around 10,000 to 15,000 words for your degree. How might it be structured? The following is typical of the structure of a dissertation.

Title page

You should examine your institution's rules about what should be entered here.

Acknowledgements

You might want to acknowledge the help of various people, such as gatekeepers who gave you access to an organization, people who have read your drafts and provided you with feedback, or your supervisor for his or her advice.

List of contents

Your institution may have recommendations or prescriptions about the form this should take.

An abstract

A brief summary of your dissertation. Not all institutions require this component, so check on whether it is required. Journal articles usually have abstracts, so you can draw on these for guidance on how to approach this task.

Introduction

- You should explain what you are writing about and why it is important. Saying simply that it interests you because of a long-standing personal interest is not enough.

- You might indicate in general terms the theoretical approach or perspective you will be using and why.

- You should also at this point outline your research questions. In the case of dissertations based on qualitative research, it is likely that your research questions will be rather more open-ended than is the case with quantitative research. But do try to identify some research questions. A totally open-ended research is risky and can lead to the collection of too much data, and, when it comes to writing up, it can result in a lack of focus.

- The opening sentence or sentences are often the most difficult of all. Becker (1982) advises strongly against opening sentences that he describes as 'vacuous' and 'evasive'. He gives the example of

'This study deals with the problem of careers', and adds that this kind of sentence employs 'a typically evasive maneuver, pointing to something without saying anything, or anything much, about it. *What* about careers?' (Becker 1982: 51). He suggests that such evasiveness often occurs because of concerns about giving away the plot. In fact, he argues, it is much better to give readers a quick and clear indication of what is going to be meted out to them and where it is going. Kelley and De Graaf's and Beardsworth and Keil's opening sentences do rather well in this regard.

Literature review

This chapter will review the main ideas and research relating to your area of interest. However, you should do more than simply summarize the relevant literature.

- You should, whenever appropriate, be critical in your approach.

- You should use your review of the literature as a means of showing why your research questions are important. For example, if one of your arguments in arriving at your research questions is that, although a lot of research has been done on X (a general topic or area, such as consumption or football hooliganism or the domestic division of labour), little or no research has been done on X_1 (an aspect of X), the literature review is the point where you can justify this assertion. Alternatively, it might be that there are two competing positions with regard to X_1 and you are going to investigate which one provides a better understanding. In the literature review, you should outline the nature of the differences between the competing positions. The literature review, then, allows you to locate your own research within a tradition of research in an area. Indeed, reading the literature is itself often an important source of research questions.

- Bear in mind that you will want to return to much of the literature that you examine in the discussion of your findings and conclusion.

- Do not try to get everything you read into a literature review. Trying to force everything you have read into your review (because of all the hard work involved in uncovering and reading the material) is not going to help you. The literature review must assist you in developing an argument, and bringing in material of dubious relevance may undermine your ability to get your argument across.

- Bear in mind that reading the literature is not something that you should stop doing once you begin designing your research. You should continue your search for and reading of relevant literature more or less throughout your research. This means that, if you have written a literature review before beginning your data collection, you will need to regard it as provisional. Indeed, you may want to make quite substantial revisions of your review towards the end of writing up your work.

- Further useful thoughts about how to develop the literature can be found in Box 25.2. The different ways of construing the literature that are presented in this box are derived from a review of qualitative studies of organizations, but the approaches identified have a much broader applicability, including to quantitative research.

Research methods

The term 'research methods' is meant here as a kind of catch-all for several issues that need to be outlined: your research design; your sampling approach; how access was achieved if relevant; the procedures you used (such as, if you sent out a mail questionnaire, did you follow up non-respondents); the nature of your questionnaire, interview schedule, participant observation role, observation schedule, coding frame, or whatever (these will usually appear in an appendix, but you should comment on such things as your style of questioning or observation and why you asked the things you did); problems of non-response; note-taking; issues of access and cooperation; coding issues; and how you proceeded with your analysis. When discussing each of these issues, you should describe and defend the choices that you made, such as why you used a mail questionnaire rather than a structured interview approach, or why you focused upon that particular population for sampling purposes.

Results

In this chapter you present the bulk of your findings. If you intend to have a separate Discussion chapter, it is likely that the results will be presented with little commentary in terms of the literature or the implications of your findings. If there will be no Discussion chapter, you will need to provide some reflections on the significance of your findings for your research questions and for the literature. Bear these points in mind.

- Whichever approach you take, remember not to include *all* your results. You should present and discuss only those findings that relate to your research questions. This requirement may mean a rather painful process of leaving out many findings, but it is necessary, so that the thread of your argument is not lost.

- Your writing should point to particularly salient aspects of the tables, graphs, or other forms of analysis you present. Do not just summarize what a table shows; you should direct the reader to the component or components of it that are especially striking from the point of view of your research questions. Try to ask yourself what story you want the table to convey and try to relay that story to your readers.

- Another sin to be avoided is simply presenting a graph or table without any comment whatsoever, because the reader is left wondering why you think the finding is important.

- When reporting quantitative findings, it is quite a good idea to vary wherever possible the method of presenting results—for example, provide a mixture of diagrams and tables. However, you must remember the lessons of Chapter 11 concerning the methods of analysis that are appropriate to different types of variable.

- A particular problem that can arise with qualitative research is that students find it difficult to leave out large parts of their data. As one experienced qualitative researcher has put it: 'The major problem we face in qualitative inquiry is not to get data, but to get rid of it!' (Wolcott 1990: 18). He goes on to say that the 'critical task in qualitative research is not to accumulate all the data you

Box 25.2 Presenting the literature in articles based on qualitative research on organizations

Further useful advice on relating your own work to the literature can be gleaned from an examination of the ways in which articles based on qualitative research on organizations are composed. In their examination of such articles, Golden-Biddle and Locke (1993, 1997) argue that good articles in this area develop a story—that is, a clear and compelling framework around which the writing is structured. This idea is very much in tune with Wolcott's (1990: 18) recommendation to 'determine the basic story you are going to tell'. Golden-Biddle and Locke's research suggests the way the author's position in relation to the literature is presented is an important component of storytelling. They distinguish two processes in the ways that the literature is conveyed.

- **Constructing intertextual coherence**—refers to the way in which existing knowledge is represented and organized; the author shows how contributions to the literature relate to each other and the research reported. The techniques used are:
  - *synthesized coherence*—puts together work that is generally considered unrelated; theory and research previously regarded as unconnected are pieced together. There are two prominent forms:
    - the organization of very incompatible references (bits and pieces);
    - connections forged between established theories or research programmes.
  - *progressive coherence*—portrays the building up of an area of knowledge around which there is considerable consensus.
  - *non-coherence*—recognition that there have been many contributions to a certain research programme, but there is considerable disagreement among practitioners.

Each of these strategies is designed to leave room for a contribution to be made.

- **Problematizing the situation**—the literature is then subverted by locating a problem. The following techniques were identified:
  - *incomplete*—the existing literature is not fully complete; there is a gap.
  - *inadequate*—the existing literature on the phenomenon of interest has overlooked ways of looking at it that can greatly improve our understanding of it; alternative perspectives or frameworks can then be introduced.
  - *incommensurate*—argues for an alternative perspective which is superior to the literature as it stands; differs from 'inadequate problematization' because it portrays the existing literature as 'wrong, misguided, or incorrect' (Golden-Biddle and Locke 1997: 43).

The key point about Golden-Biddle and Locke's account of the way the literature is construed in this field is that it is used by writers to achieve a number of things.

- They can demonstrate their competence by referring to prominent writings in the field (Gilbert 1977).
- They develop their version of the literature in such a way to show and to lead up to the contribution they will be making in the article.
- The gap or problem in the literature that is identified corresponds to the research questions.
- The idea of writing up one's research as storytelling acts as a useful reminder that reviewing the literature, which is part of the story, should link seamlessly with the rest of the article and not be considered a separate element.

can, but to "can" (i.e., get rid of) most of the data you accumulate' (Wolcott 1990: 35). You simply have to recognize that much of the rich data you accumulate will have to be jettisoned. If you do not do this, any sense of an argument in your work is likely to be lost. There is also the risk that your account of your findings will appear too descriptive and lack an analytical edge. This is why it is

important to use research questions as a focus and to orient the presentation of your findings to them.

- If you are writing a thesis, for example for an M.Phil. or Ph.D. degree, it is likely that you will have more than one and possibly several chapters in which you present your results. Cryer (1996) recommends showing at the beginning of each chapter the particular issues that are being examined in the chapter. You should indicate which research question or questions are being addressed in the chapter and provide some signposts about what will be included in the chapter. In the conclusion of the chapter, you should make clear what your results have shown and draw out any links that might be made with the next results chapter.

Discussion

In the Discussion, you reflect on the implications of your findings for the research questions that have driven your research. In other words, how do your results illuminate your research questions? If you have specified hypotheses, as Kelley and De Graaf (1997) did, the discussion will revolve around whether the hypotheses have been confirmed or not, and, if not, you might speculate about some possible reasons for and the implications of their refutation. In the case of Beardsworth and Keil's (1992) article, section 6 acts as a discussion section, and it is here that they bring out the main theoretical contribution of their research—the idea of food ambivalence—and explore its implications.

Conclusion

The main points here are as follows.

- A Conclusion is not the same as a summary. However, it is frequently useful to bring out in the opening paragraph of the Conclusion your argument thus far. This will mean relating your findings and your discussion of them to your research questions. Thus, your brief summary should be a means of hammering home to your readers the significance of what you have done. However, the

Conclusion should do more than merely summarize.

- You should make clear the implications of your findings for your research questions.
- You might also suggest some ways in which your findings have implications for theories relating to your area of interest.
- You might also draw attention to any limitations of your research with the benefit of hindsight, but it is probably best not to overdo this element and provide examiners with too much ammunition that might be used against you!
- It is often valuable to propose areas of further research that are suggested by your findings.

Two things to avoid are engaging in speculations that take you too far away from your data, or that cannot be substantiated by the data, and introducing issues or ideas that have not previously been brought up.

Appendices

In your appendices you might want to include such things as your questionnaire, coding frame, or observation schedule, letters sent to sample members, and letters sent to and received from gatekeepers where the cooperation of an organization was required.

References

Include here all references cited in the text. For the format of the References section you should follow whichever one is prescribed by your department. Nowadays, the format is usually a variation of the Harvard method, such as the one employed for this book.

Finally

Remember to fulfil any obligations you entered into, such as supplying a copy of your dissertation, if, for example, your access to an organization was predicated on providing one, and maintaining the

confidentiality of information supplied and the anonymity of your informants and other research participants.

Glossary

Terms appearing elsewhere in the Glossary are in **bold**.

Action research An approach in which the action researcher and a client collaborate in the diagnosis of a problem and in the development of a solution based on the diagnosis.

Ad libitum **sampling** A sampling approach in **structured observation** whereby whatever is happening at the moment that observation is due to occur is recorded.

Adjacency pair The tendency for certain kinds of activity in talk to be characterized by linked phases.

Analytic induction An approach to the analysis of qualitative data in which the researcher seeks universal explanations of phenomena by pursuing the collection of data until no cases that are inconsistent with a hypothetical explanation (deviant or negative cases) of a phenomenon are found.

Arithmetic mean Also known simply as the **mean**, this is the everyday average—namely, the total of a distribution of values divided by the number of values.

Behaviour sampling A sampling approach in **structured observation** whereby an entire group is watched and the observer records who was involved in a particular kind of behaviour.

Biographical method See **life history method**.

Bivariate analysis The examination of two variables in a single analysis, as in **contingency tables** or **correlation**.

CAQDAS An abbreviation of computer-assisted (or -aided) qualitative data analysis software.

Case study A **research design** that entails the detailed and intensive analysis of a single case. The term is sometimes extended to include the study of just two or three cases for comparative purposes.

Causality A concern with establishing causal connections between variables, rather than mere **relationships** between them.

Cell The point in a table, such as a **contingency table**, where the rows and columns intersect.

Census The enumeration of an entire **population**. Unlike a **sample**, which comprises a count of *some* units in a population, a census relates to *all* units in a population. Thus, if a **mail questionnaire** is posted to every person in a town or to all members of a profession, the research should be characterized as a census.

Chi-square test Chi-square (χ^2) is a test of **statistical significance**, which is typically employed to establish how confident we can be that the findings displayed in a **contingency table** can be generalized from a **probability sample** to a **population**.

Closed question A question employed in an **interview schedule** or **self-completion questionnaire** that presents the respondent with a set of possible answers to choose from. Also called **fixed-choice question** and **pre-coded question**.

Cluster sample A sampling procedure in which at an initial stage the researcher samples areas (i.e. clusters) and then samples units from these clusters, usually using a **probability sampling** method.

Code, coding In **quantitative research**, codes act as tags that are placed on data about people or other units of analysis. The aim is to assign the data relating to each **variable** to groups, each of which is considered to be a category of the variable in question. Numbers are then assigned to each category to allow the information to be processed by the computer. In **qualitative research**, coding is the process whereby data are broken down into component parts, which are given names.

Coding frame A listing of the codes used in relation to the analysis of data. In relation to answers to a structured interview schedule or questionnaire, the coding frame will delineate the categories used in relation to each question. It is particularly crucial in relation to the coding of **open questions**. With **closed questions**, the coding frame is essentially incorporated into the pre-given answers, hence the frequent use of the term **pre-coded question** to describe such questions.

Coding manual In **content analysis**, this is the statement of instructions to coders that outlines all the possible categories for each dimension being coded.

Coding schedule In **content analysis**, this is the form onto which all the data relating to an item being coded will be entered.

Comparative design A **research design** that entails the comparison of two or more cases in order to illuminate existing theory or generate theoretical insights as a result of contrasting findings uncovered through the comparison.

Concept A name given to a category that organizes observations and ideas by virtue of their possessing common features.

Concurrent validity One of the main approaches to establishing **measurement validity**. It entails relating a measure to a criterion on which cases (e.g. people) are known to differ and that is relevant to the **concept** in question.

Connotation A term used in **semiotics** to refer to the principal and most manifest meaning of a **sign**. Compare with **denotation**.

Constant An attribute in terms of which cases do not differ. Compare with **variable**.

Constructionism, constructionist An **ontological** position (often also referred to as **constructivism**) that asserts that social phenomena and their meanings are continually being accomplished by social actors. It is antithetical to **objectivism** and **essentialism**.

Constructivism See **constructionism**.

Content analysis An approach to the analysis of documents and texts that seeks to quantify content in terms of predetermined categories and in a systematic and replicable manner. The term is sometimes used in connection with qualitative research as well—see **qualitative content analysis**.

Contingency table A table, comprising rows and columns, that shows the **relationship** between two **variables**. Usually, at least one of the variables is a **nominal variable**. Each cell in the table shows the frequency of occurrence of that intersection of categories of each of the two variables and usually a percentage.

Continuous recording A procedure in **structured observation**, whereby observation occurs for extended periods, so that the frequency and duration of certain types of behaviour can be carefully recorded.

Convenience sample A sample that is selected because of its availability to the researcher. It is a form of **non-probability sample**.

Conversation analysis The fine-grained analysis of talk as it occurs in interaction in naturally occurring situations. The talk is recorded and **transcribed** so that the detailed analyses can be carried out. The analysis is concerned with uncovering the underlying structures of talk in interaction and as such with the achievement of order through inter-action. Conversation analysis is grounded in **ethnomethodology**.

Correlation An approach to the analysis of relationships between **interval/ratio variables** and/or **ordinal variables** that seeks to assess the strength and direction of the relationship between the variables concerned. **Pearson's r** and **Spearman's rho** are both methods for assessing the level of correlation between variables.

Covert research A term frequently used in connection with **ethnographic** research in which the researcher does not reveal his or her true identity. Such research violates the ethical principle of **informed consent**.

Cramér's V A method for assessing the strength of the relationship between two variables, at least one of which must have more than two categories.

Critical realism A **realist** epistemology that asserts that the study of the social world should be concerned with the identification of the structures that generate that world. Critical realism is critical because its practitioners aim to identify structures in order to change them, so that inequalities and injustices may be counteracted. Unlike a **positivist** epistemology, critical realism accepts that the structures that are identified may not be amenable to the senses. Thus, whereas **positivism** is **empiricist**, critical realism is not.

Cross-sectional design A **research design** that entails the collection of data on more than one case (usually quite a lot more than one) and at a single point in time in order to collect a body of quantitative or quantifiable data in connection with two or more variables (usually many more than two), which are then examined to detect patterns of association.

Deductive An approach to the relationship between theory and research in which the latter is conducted with reference to hypotheses and ideas inferred from the former. Compare with **inductive**.

Denotation A term used in **semiotics** to refer to the meanings of a **sign** associated with the social context within which it operates that are supplementary to and less immediately apparent than its **connotation**.

Diary A term that in the context of social research methods can mean different things. Three types of diary can be distinguished: diaries written or completed at the behest of a researcher; personal diaries that can be analysed as a **personal document**, but that were produced spontaneously; and diaries written by social researchers as a log of their activities and reflections.

Dependent variable A **variable** that is causally influenced by another variable (i.e. an **independent variable**).

Dichotomous variable A variable with just two categories.

Dimension Refers to an aspect of a **concept**.

Discourse analysis An approach to the analysis of talk and other forms of discourse that emphasizes the ways in which versions of reality are accomplished through language.

Distribution of values A term used to refer to the entire data relating to a **variable**. Thus, the ages of members of a **sample** represent the distribution of values for that variable for that sample.

Ecological fallacy The error of assuming that inferences about individuals can be made from findings relating to aggregate data.

Ecological validity A concern with the question of whether social scientific findings are applicable to people's everyday, natural social settings.

Empiricism An approach to the study of reality that suggests that only knowledge gained through experience and the senses is acceptable.

Epistemology, epistemological A theory of knowledge. It is particularly employed in this book to refer to a stance on what should pass as acceptable knowledge. See **positivism**, **realism**, and **interpretivism**.

Essentialism A position that has close affinities with naive **realism**. Essentialism suggests that objects have essences that denote their authentic nature. Compare with **constructionism**.

Eta A test of the strength of the **relationship** between two **variables**. The **independent variable** must be a **nominal variable** and the **dependent variable** must be an **interval variable** or **ratio variable**. The resulting level of correlation will always be positive.

Ethnographic content analysis See **qualitative content analysis**.

Ethnography, ethnographer Like **participant observation**, a research method in which the researcher immerses him- or herself in a social setting for an extended period of time, observing behaviour, listening to what is said in conversations both between others and with the field-worker, and asking questions. However, the term has a more inclusive sense than participant observation, which seems to emphasize the observational component. Also, the term 'an ethnography' is frequently used to refer to the written output of ethnographic research.

Ethnomethodology A sociological perspective concerned with the way in which social order is accomplished through talk and interaction. It provides the intellectual foundations of **conversation analysis**.

Evaluation research Research that is concerned with the evaluation of real-life interventions in the social world.

Experiment A **research design** that rules out alternative explanations of findings deriving from it (i.e. possesses **internal validity**) by having at least (*a*) an experimental group, which is exposed to a treatment, and a control group, which is not, and (*b*) **random assignment** to the two groups.

External validity A concern with the question of whether the results of a study can be generalized beyond the specific research context in which it was conducted.

Face validity A concern with whether an **indicator** appears to reflect the content of the concept in question.

Facilitator See **moderator**.

Field stimulation A study in which the researcher directly intervenes in and/or manipulates a natural setting in order to observe what happens as a consequence of that intervention.

Field notes A detailed chronicle by an **ethnographer** of events, conversations, and behaviour, and the researcher's initial reflections on them.

Frequency table A table that displays the number and/or percentage of units (e.g. people) in different categories of a variable.

Focal sampling A sampling approach in **structured observation** whereby a sampled individual is observed for a set period of time. The observer records all examples of whatever forms of behaviour are of interest.

Focus group A form of group interview in which: there are several participants (in addition to the **moderator/ facilitator**); there is an emphasis in the questioning on a particular fairly tightly defined topic; and the emphasis is upon interaction within the group and the joint construction of meaning.

Generalization, generalizability A concern with the **external validity** of research findings.

Grounded theory An approach to the analysis of qualitative data that aims to generate theory out of research data by achieving a close fit between the two.

Hermeneutics A term drawn from theology, which, when imported into the social sciences, is concerned with the theory and method of the interpretation of human action. It emphasizes the need to understand from the perspective of the social actor.

Hypothesis An informed speculation, which is set up to be tested, about the possible relationship between two or more variables.

Independent variable A **variable** that has a causal impact on another variable (i.e. a **dependent variable**).

Index See **scale**.

Indicator A measure that is employed to refer to a **concept** when no direct measure is available.

Inductive An approach to the relationship between theory and research in which the former is generated out of the latter. Compare with **deductive**.

Informed consent A key principle in social research ethics. It implies that prospective research participants should be given as much information as might be needed to make an informed decision about whether or not they wish to participate in a study.

Inter-coder reliability The degree to which two or more individuals agree about the **coding** of an item. Inter-coder reliability is likely to be an issue in **content analysis**, **structured observation**, and when **coding** answers to **open questions** in research based on **questionnaires** or **structured interviews**.

Internal reliability The degree to which the indicators that make up a **scale** are consistent.

Internal validity A concern with the question of whether a finding that incorporates a causal relationship between two or more variables is sound.

Interpretative repertoire A collection of linguistic resources that are drawn upon in order to characterize and assess actions and events.

Interpretivism An **epistemological** position that requires the social scientist to grasp the subjective meaning of social action.

Interval variable A **variable** where the distances between the categories are identical across its range of categories.

Intervening variable A **variable** that is affected by another variable and that in turn has a causal impact on another variable. Taking an intervening variable into account often facilitates the understanding of the relationship between two variables.

Interview guide A rather vague term that is used to refer to the brief list of memory prompts of areas to be covered that is often employed in **unstructured interviewing** or to the somewhat more structured list of issues to be addressed or questions to be asked in **semi-structured interviewing**.

Interview schedule A collection of questions designed to be asked by an interviewer. An interview schedule is always used in a **structured interview**.

Intra-coder reliability The degree to which an individual differs over time in the **coding** of an item. Intra-coder reliability is likely to be an issue in **content analysis**, **structured observation**, and when **coding** answers to **open questions** in research based on **questionnaires** or **structured interviews**.

Key informant Someone who offers the researcher, usually in the context of conducting an **ethnography**, perceptive information about the social setting, important events, and individuals.

Life history interview Similar to the **oral history interview**, but the aim of this type of **unstructured interview** is to glean information on the entire biography of each respondent.

Life history method Also often referred to as the **biographical method**, this method emphasizes the inner experience of individuals and its connections with changing events and phases throughout the life course. The method usually entails **life history interviews** and the use of **personal documents** as data.

Likert scale A widely used format developed by Rensis Likert for asking attitude questions. Respondents are typically asked their degree of agreement with a series of statements that together form a **multiple-indicator** or **-item** measure. The scale is deemed then to measure the intensity with which respondents feel about an issue.

Longitudinal research A **research design** in which data are collected on a **sample** (of people, documents, etc.) on at least two occasions.

Mail questionnaire A form of **self-completion questionnaire** that is sent to respondents and usually returned by them by mail.

Mean See **arithmetic mean**.

Measure of central tendency A statistic, like the **arithmetic mean**, **median**, or **mode**, that summarizes a **distribution of values**.

Measure of dispersion A statistic, like the **range** or **standard deviation**, that summarizes the amount of variation in a **distribution of values**.

Measurement validity The degree to which a measure of a concept truly reflects that concept. See also **face validity** and **concurrent validity**.

Median The mid-point in a **distribution of values**.

Missing data Data relating to a case that are not available, for example, when a respondent in **social survey** research does not answer a question. These are referred to as 'missing values' in **SPSS**.

Mode The value that occurs most frequently in a **distribution of values**.

Moderated relationship A **relationship** between two **variables** is said to be moderated when it holds for one category of a third variable but not for another category or other categories.

Moderator The person who guides the questioning of a **focus group**. Also called a **facilitator**.

Multiple-indicator measure A measure that employs more than one **indicator** to measure a **concept**.

Multi-strategy research A term used to describe research that combines **quantitative** and **qualitative research**.

Multivariate analysis The examination of three or more **variables** in a single analysis.

Narrative analysis An approach to the elicitation and analysis of data that is sensitive to the sense of temporal sequence that people, as tellers of stories about their lives or events around them, detect in their lives and surrounding episodes and inject into their accounts.

Naturalism A confusing term that has at least three distinct meanings: a commitment to adopting the principles of natural scientific method; being true to the nature of the phenomenon being investigated; and a style of research that seeks to minimize the intrusion of artificial methods of data collection.

Negative relationship A **relationship** between two **variables**, whereby as one increases the other decreases.

Nominal variable Also known as a **categorical variable**, this is a variable that comprises categories that cannot be rank ordered.

Non-manipulable variable A **variable** that cannot readily be manipulated either for practical or for ethical reasons and that therefore cannot be employed in an **experiment**.

Non-probability sample A sample that has not been selected using a random selection method. Essentially, this implies that some units in the population are more likely to be selected than others.

Non-response A source of **non-sampling error** that occurs whenever some members of a sample refuse to cooperate, cannot be contacted, or for some reason cannot supply the required data.

Non-sampling error Differences between the **population** and the **sample** that arise either from deficiencies in the sampling approach, such as an inadequate **sampling frame** or **non-response**, or from such problems as poor question wording, poor interviewing, or flawed processing of data.

Null hypothesis A **hypothesis** of no relationship between two variables.

Objectivism An **ontological** position that asserts that social phenomena and their meanings have an existence that is independent of social actors. Compare with **constructionism**.

Observation schedule A device used in **structured observation** that specifies the categories of behaviour that are to be observed and how behaviour should be allocated to those categories.

Official statistics Statistics compiled by or on behalf of state agencies in the course of conducting their business.

Ontology, ontological A theory of the nature of social entities. See **objectivism** and **inductivism**.

Open question A question employed in an **interview schedule** or **self-completion questionnaire** that does not present the respondent with a set of possible answers to choose from. Compare with **closed question**.

Operational definition The definition of a **concept** in terms of the operations to be carried out when measuring it.

Operationism, operationalism A doctrine, mainly associated with a version of physics, that emphasizes the search for **operational definitions** of **concepts**.

Oral history interview A largely **unstructured interview** in which the respondent is asked to recall events from his or her past and to reflect on them.

Ordinal variable A variable whose categories can be rank ordered (as in the case of **interval** and **ratio variables**), but the distances between the categories are not equal across the range.

Paradigm A term deriving from the history of science, where it was used to describe a cluster of beliefs and dictates that for scientists in a particular discipline influence what should be studied, how research should be done, and how results should be interpreted.

Participant observation Research in which the researcher immerses himself or herself in a social setting for an extended period of time, observing behaviour, listening to what is said in conversations both between others and with the fieldworker, and asking questions. Participant observation usually includes interviewing key informants and studying documents and as such is difficult to distinguish from **ethnography**. In this book, participant observation is employed to refer to the specifically observational aspect of ethnography.

Pearson's r A measure of the strength and direction of the **relationship** between two **interval/ratio variables**.

Personal documents Documents such as **diaries**, letters, and autobiographies that are not written for an official purpose. They provide first-person accounts of the writer's life and events within it.

Phenomenology A philosophy that is concerned with the question of how individuals make sense of the world around them and how in particular the philosopher should bracket out preconceptions concerning his or her grasp of that world.

Phi A method for assessing the strength of the **relationship** between two **dichotomous variables**.

Population The universe of units from which a **sample** is to be selected.

Positive relationship A **relationship** between two **variable**s, whereby as one increases the other increases as well.

Positivism An **epistemological** position that advocates the application of the methods of the natural sciences to the study of social reality and beyond.

Postal questionnaire See **mail questionnaire**.

Postmodernism A position that displays a distaste for master-narratives and for a **realist** orientation. In the context of research methodology, postmodernists display a preference for qualitative methods and a concern with the modes of representation of research findings.

Pre-coded question Another name for a **closed question**. The term is often preferred, because such a question removes the need for the application of a **coding frame** to the question after it has been answered. This is because the range of answers has been predetermined and a numerical **code** will have been pre-assigned to each possible answer. The term is particularly appropriate when the codes appear on the **questionnaire** or **interview schedule**.

Probability sample A sample that has been selected using **random sampling** and in which each unit in the population has a known probability of being selected.

QSR NVivo A **CAQDAS** package that derives from but goes beyond NUD*IST (Non-numerical Unstructured Data Indexing Searching and Theorizing).

Qualitative content analysis An approach to documents that emphasizes the role of the investigator in the construction of the meaning of and in texts. There is an emphasis on allowing categories to emerge out of data and on recognizing the significance for understanding the meaning of the context in which an item being analysed (and the categories derived from it) appeared.

Qualitative research Qualitative research usually emphasizes words rather than quantification in the collection and analysis of data. As a **research strategy** it is **inductivist**, **constructivist**, and **interpretivist**, but qualitative researchers do not always subscribe to all three of these features. Compare with **quantitative research**.

Quantitative research Quantitative research usually emphasizes quantification in the collection and analysis of data. As a **research strategy** it is **deductivist** and **objectivist** and incorporates a natural science model of the research process (in particular, one influenced by **positivism**), but quantitative researchers do not always subscribe to all three of these features. Compare with **qualitative research**.

Quasi-experiment A **research design** that is close to being an **experiment** but that does not meet the requirements fully and therefore does not exhibit complete **internal validity**.

Questionnaire A collection of questions administered to respondents. When used on its own, the term usually denotes a **self-completion questionnaire**.

Quota sample A **sample** that non-randomly samples a **population** in terms of the relative proportions of people in different categories. It is a type of **non-probability sample**.

Random assignment A term used in connection with **experiments** to refer to the random allocation of research participants to the experimental group and the control group.

Random sampling Sampling whereby the inclusion of a unit of a **population** occurs entirely by chance.

Range The difference between the maximum and the minimum value in a **distribution of values** associated with an **interval** or **ratio variable**.

Ratio variable An **interval variable** with a true zero point.

Reactivity, reactive effect A term used to describe the response of research participants to the fact that they know they are being studied. Reactivity is deemed to result in untypical behaviour.

Realism An epistemological position that acknowledges a reality independent of the senses that is accessible to the researcher's tools and theoretical speculations. It implies that the categories created by scientists refer to real objects in the natural or social worlds. See also **critical realism**.

Reflexivity A term used in research methodology to refer to a reflectiveness among social researchers about the implications for the knowledge of the social world they generate of their methods, values, biases, decisions, and mere presence in the very situations they investigate.

Relationship An association between two variables whereby the variation in one variable coincides with variation in another variable.

Reliability The degree to which a measure of a concept is stable.

Replication, replicability The degree to which the results of a study can be reproduced. See also **internal reliability**.

Representative sample A **sample** that reflects the population accurately, so that it is a microcosm of the **population**.

Research design This term is employed in this book to refer to a framework for the collection and analysis of data. A choice of research design reflects decisions about the priority being given to a range of dimensions of the research process (such as **causality** and **generalization**).

Research strategy A term used in this book to refer to a general orientation to the conduct of social research (see **quantitative research** and **qualitative research**).

Respondent validation Sometimes called *member validation*, this is a process whereby a researcher provides the people on whom he or she has conducted research with an account of his or her findings and requests feedback on that account.

Response set The tendency among some respondents to **multiple-indicator measures** to reply in the same way to each constituent item.

Rhetoric A concern with the ways in which appeals to convince or persuade are devised.

Sample The segment of the population that is selected for research. It is a subset of the **population**. The method of selection may be based on **probability sampling** or **non-probability sampling**.

Sampling error Differences between a **random sample** and the **population** from which it is selected.

Sampling frame The listing of all units in the **population** from which a **sample** is selected.

Scale A term that is usually used interchangeably with **index** to refer to a **multiple-indicator measure** in which the score a person gives for each component **indicator** is used to provide a composite score for that person.

Scan sampling A sampling approach in **structured observation** whereby an entire group of individuals is scanned at regular intervals and the behaviour of all of them is recorded at each occasion.

Secondary analysis The analysis of data by researchers who will probably not have been involved in the collection of those data for purposes that may not have been envisaged by those responsible for the data collection. Secondary analysis may entail the analysis of either quantitative data or qualitative data.

Self-administered questionnaire See **self-completion questionnaire**.

Self-completion questionnaire A **questionnaire** that the respondent answers without the aid of an interviewer. Sometimes called a **self-administered questionnaire**.

Semiotics The study/science of **signs**. An approach to the analysis of documents and other phenomena that emphasizes the importance of seeking out the deeper meaning of those phenomena. A semiotic approach is concerned to uncover the processes of meaning production and how signs are designed to have an effect upon actual and prospective consumers of those signs.

Semi-structured interview A term that covers a wide range of types. It typically refers to a context in which the interviewer has a series of questions that are in the general form of an **interview guide** but is able to vary the sequence of questions. The questions are frequently somewhat more general in their frame of reference from that typically found in a **structured interview** schedule. Also, the interviewer usually has some latitude to ask further questions in response to what are seen as significant replies.

Sensitizing concept A term devised by Blumer to refer to a preference for treating a **concept** as a guide in an investigation, so that it points in a general way to what is relevant or important. This position contrasts with the idea of an **operational definition**, in which the meaning of a concept is fixed in advance of carrying out an investigation.

Sign A term employed in **semiotics**. A sign is made up of a signifier (the manifestation of a sign) and the signified (that idea or deeper meaning to which the signifier refers).

Simple observation The passive and unobtrusive observation of behaviour.

Simple random sample A **sample** in which each unit has been selected entirely by chance. Each unit of the **population** has a known and equal probability of inclusion in the sample.

Snowball sample A **non-probability sample** in which the researcher makes initial contact with a small group of people who are relevant to the research topic and then uses these to establish contacts with others.

Social survey A **cross-sectional design** in relation to which data are collected predominantly by **self-completion questionnaire** or by **structured interview** on more than one case (usually quite a lot more than one) and at *a single point in time* in order to collect a body of quantitative or quantifiable data in connection with two or more **variables** (usually many more than two) which are then examined to detect patterns of **relationship**.

Spearman's rho (ρ) A measure of the strength and direction of the **relationship** between two **ordinal variables**.

SPSS Originally, short for Statistical Package for the Social Sciences, SPSS is a widely used computer program that allows quantitative data to be managed and analysed.

Spurious relationship A **relationship** between two **variables** is said to be spurious if it is being produced by the impact of a third variable on each of the two variables that form the spurious relationship. When the third variable is controlled, the relationship disappears.

Standard deviation A measure of dispersion around the **mean**.

Standard error of the mean An estimate of the amount that a sample mean is likely to differ from the population mean.

Statistical inference See **statistical significance (test of)**.

Statistical significance (test of) Allows the analyst to estimate how confident he or she can be that the results deriving from a study based on a randomly selected **sample** are generalizable to the **population** from which the

sample was drawn. Such a test does not allow the researcher to infer that the findings are of substantive importance. The **chi-square test** is an example of this kind of test. The process of using a test of statistical significance to generalize from a sample to a population is known as **statistical inference**.

Stratified random sample A **sample** in which units are **randomly sampled** from a **population** that has been divided into categories (strata).

Structured interview A research interview in which all respondents are asked exactly the same questions in the same order with the aid of a formal **interview schedule**.

Structured observation Often also called **systematic observation**, structured observation is a technique in which the researcher employs explicitly formulated rules for the observation and recording of behaviour. The rules inform observers about what they should look for and how they should record behaviour.

Survey research See **social survey**.

Symbolic interactionism A theoretical perspective in sociology and social psychology that views social interaction as taking place in terms of the meanings actors attach to action and things.

Systematic observation See **structured observation**.

Systematic sample A **probability sampling** method in which units are selected from a **sampling frame** according to fixed intervals, such as every fifth unit.

Text A term that is used either in the conventional sense of a written work or in more recent years to refer to a wide range of phenomena. For example, in arriving at a **thick description**, Geertz refers to treating culture as a text.

Theoretical sampling A term used mainly in relation to **grounded theory** to refer to sampling carried out so that emerging theoretical considerations guide the selection of cases and/or research participants. Theoretical sampling is supposed to continue until a point of **theoretical saturation** is reached.

Theoretical saturation In **grounded theory**, the point when emerging **concepts** have been fully explored and no new insights are being generated. See also **theoretical sampling**.

Thick description A term devised by Geertz to refer to detailed accounts of a social setting that can form the basis for the creation of general statements about a culture and its significance in people's social lives.

Time sampling A sampling method in **structured observa-**

tion, which entails using a criterion for deciding when observation will occur.

Transcription, transcript The written translation of a tape-recorded **interview** or **focus group session**.

Triangulation The use of more than one method or source of data in the study of a social phenomenon so that findings may be cross-checked.

Trustworthiness A set of criteria advocated by some writers for assessing the quality of **qualitative research**.

Turn taking The notion from **conversation analysis** that order in everyday conversation is achieved through orderly taking of turns in conversations.

Univariate analysis The analysis of a single **variable** at a time.

Unobtrusive methods Methods that do not entail the awareness among research participants that they are being studied and that are therefore not subject to **reactivity**.

Unstructured interview An interview in which the interviewer typically only has a list of topics or issues, often called an **interview guide**, that are typically covered. The style of questioning is usually very informal. The phrasing and sequencing of questions will vary from interview to interview.

Validity A concern with the integrity of the conclusions that are generated from a piece of research. There are different aspects of validity. See, in particular, **measurement validity**, **internal validity**, **external validity**, and **ecological validity**. When used on its own, **validity** is usually taken to refer to **measurement validity**.

Variable An attribute in terms of which cases vary. See also **dependent variable** and **independent variable**. Compare with **constant**.

References

Abraham, J. (1994), 'Bias in Science and Medical Knowledge: The Opren controversy', *Sociology*, 28: 717–36.

Adler, P., and Adler, P. A. (1985), 'From Idealism to Pragmatic Detachment: The Academic Performance of College Athletes', *Sociology of Education*, 58: 241–50.

Adler, P. A. (1985), *Wheeling and Dealing: An Ethnography of an Upper-Level Drug Dealing and Smuggling Community* (New York: Columbia University Press).

Aitken, I. (1998), 'The Documentary Film Movement: The Post Office Touches All Branches of Life', in J. Hassard and R. Holliday (eds), *Organization-Representation: Work and Organization in Popular Culture* (London: Sage).

Aldridge, A. (1998), 'Reproducing the Value of Professional Expertise in Post-Traditional Culture: Financial Advice and the Creation of the Client', *Cultural Values*, 2: 445–62.

Allison, G. T. (1971), *Essence of Decision: Explaining the Cuban Missile Crisis* (Boston: Little, Brown).

Aitheide, D. L. (1980), 'Leaving the Newsroom', in W. Shaffir, R. A. Stebbins, and A. Turowetz (eds), *Fieldwork Experience: Qualitative Approaches to Social Research* (New York: St. Martin's Press).

—— (1996), *Qualitative Media Analysis* (Thousand Oaks, Calif.: Sage).

Altschuld, J. W., and Lower, M. A. (1984), 'Improving Mailed Questionnaires: Analysis of a 96 Percent Return Rate', in D. C. Lockhart (ed.), *Making Effective Use of Mailed Questionnaires* (San Francisco: Jossey-Bass).

Andersen, M. (1981), 'Corporate Wives: Longing for Liberation or Satisfied with the Status Quo?', *Urban Life*, 10: 311–27.

Anderson, P. (1998), 'Confidentiality and Consent in Qualitative Research', *Network: Newsletter of the British Sociological Association*, 69: 6–7.

Ang, I. (1985), *Watching Dallas: Soap Opera and the Melodramatic Imagination* (London: Methuen).

Arber, S., and Gilbert, G. N. (1989), 'Transitions in Caring: Gender, Life Course and the Care of the Elderly', in B. Bytheway, T. Keil, P. Allatt, and A. Bryman (eds), *Becoming and Being Old: Sociological Approaches to Later Life* (London: Sage).

Armstrong, G. (1993), 'Like that Desmond Morris?', in D. Hobbs and T. May (eds), *Interpreting the Field: Accounts of Ethnography* (Oxford: Clarendon Press).

—— (1998), *Football Hooligans: Knowing the Score* (Oxford: Berg).

Arnold, H. J., and Feldman, D. C. (1981), 'Social Desirability Response Bias in Self-Report Choice Situations', *Academy of Management Journal*, 24: 377–85.

Aronson, E., and Carlsmith, J. M. (1968), 'Experimentation in Social Psychology', in G. Lindzey and E. Aronson (eds), *The Handbook of Social Psychology* (Reading, Mass.: Addison-Wesley).

Asch, S. E. (1951), 'Effect of Group Pressure upon the Modification and Distortion of Judgments', in H. Guetzkow (ed.), *Groups, Leadership and Men* (Pittsburgh: Carnegie Press).

Atkinson, J. M., and Drew, P. (1979), *Order in Court: The Organization of Verbal Interaction in Judicial Settings* (London: Macmillan).

Atkinson, P. (1981), *The Clinical Experience* (Farnborough: Gower).

—— (1990), *The Ethnographic Imagination: Textual Constructions of Society* (London: Routledge).

—— and Coffey, A. (1995), 'Realism and its Discontents: On the Crisis of Cultural Representation in Ethnographic Texts', in B. Adam and S. Allan (eds), *Theorizing Culture: An Interdisciplinary Critique after Postmodernism* (London: UCL Press).

Bahr, H. M., Caplow, T., and Chadwick, B. A. (1983), 'Middletown III: Problems of Replication, Longitudinal Measurement, and Triangulation', *Annual Review of Sociology*, 9: 243–64.

Ball, S. J. (1981), *Beachside Comprehensive: A Case Study of Secondary Schooling* (Cambridge: Cambridge University Press).

—— (1984), 'Beachside Reconsidered: Reflections on a Methodological Apprenticeship', in R. G. Burgess (ed.), *The Research Process in Educational Settings: Ten Case Studies* (London: Falmer Press).

Barker, E. (1984), *The Making of a Moonie: Choice or Brainwashing?* (Oxford: Blackwell).

Barnard, M., and Frischer, M. (1995), 'Combining Quantitative and Qualitative Approaches: Researching HIV-Related Risk Behaviours among Drug Injectors', *Addiction Research*, 2: 351–62.

Barthes, R. (1972), *Mythologies* (London: Jonathan Cape).

Bauman, Z. (1978), *Hermeneutics and Social Science: Approaches to Understanding* (London: Hutchison).

Baumgartner, R. M., and Heberlein, T. A. (1984), 'Applying Attitude Theories to the Return of Mailed Questionnaires', in D. C. Lockhart (ed.), *Making Effective Use of Mailed Questionnaires* (San Francisco: Jossey-Bass).

Bazerman, C. (1987), 'Codifying the Social Scientific Style: The APA *Publication Manual* as a Behaviorist Rhetoric', in J. S. Nelson, A. Megill, and D. N. McClosky (eds), *The Rhetoric of the Human Sciences* (Madison: University of Wisconsin Press).

—— (1988), *Shaping Written Knowledge: The Genre and Activity of the Experimental Article in Science* (Madison: University of Wisconsin Press).

Beardsworth, A. (1980), 'Analysing Press Content: Some Technical and Methodological Issues', in H. Christian (ed.), *Sociology of Journalism and the Press* (Keele: Keele University Press).

—— and Keil, T. (1992), 'The Vegetarian Option: Varieties, Conversions, Motives and Careers', *Sociological Review*, 40: 253–93.

—— —— (1996), *Sociology on the Menu: An Invitation to the Study of Food and Society* (London: Routledge).

—— Bryman, A., Ford, J., and Keil, T. (n.d.) ' "The Dark Figure" in Statistics of Unemployment and Vacancies: Some Sociological Implications', discussion paper, Department of Social Sciences, Loughborough University.

Bechhofer, F., Elliott, B., and McCrone, D. (1984), 'Safety in Numbers: On the Use of Multiple Interviewers', *Sociology*, 18: 97–100.

Becker, H. S. (1958), 'Problems of Inference and Proof in Participant Observation', *American Sociological Review*, 23: 652–60.

—— (1963), *Outsiders: Studies in the Sociology of Deviance* (New York: Free Press).

—— (1967), 'Whose Side are We On?', *Social Problems*, 14: 239–47.

—— (1970), 'Practitioners of Vice and Crime', in R. W. Habenstein (ed.), *Pathways to Data* (Chicago: Aldine).

—— (1982), 'Culture: A Sociological View', *Yale Review*, 71: 513–27.

—— and Geer, B. (1957*a*), 'Participant Observation and Interviewing: a Comparison', *Human Organization*, 16: 28–32.

—— —— (1957*b*), ' "Participant Observation and Interviewing": A Rejoinder', *Human Organization*, 16: 39–40.

Beckford, J. A. (1985), *Cult Controversies: The Societal Response to the New Religious Movements* (London: Tavistock).

Beharrell, P. (1993), 'AIDS and the British Press', in J. Eldridge (ed.), *Getting the Message: News, Truth and Power* (London: Routledge).

Belk, R. W., Sherry, J. F., and Wallendorf, M. (1988), 'A Naturalistic Inquiry into Buyer and Seller Behavior at a Swap Meet', *Journal of Consumer Research*, 14: 449–70.

Bell, C. (1969), 'A Note on Participant Observation', *Sociology*, 3: 417–18.

—— and Newby, H. (1977), *Doing Sociological Research* (London: George Allen & Unwin).

—— and Roberts, H. (1984), *Social Researching: Politics, Problems, Practice* (London: Routledge & Kegan Paul).

Bellaby, P., and Bellaby, F. (1999), 'Unemployment and Ill Health: Local Labour Markets and Ill Health in Britain 1984–1991', *Work, Employment and Society*, 13: 461–82.

Belson, W. A. (1981), *The Design and Understanding of Survey Questions* (Aldershot: Gower).

Berelson, B. (1952), *Content Analysis in Communication Research* (New York: Free Press).

Beynon, H. (1975), *Working for Ford* (Harmondsworth: Penguin).

Bhaskar, R. (1975), *A Realist Theory of Science* (Leeds: Leeds Books).

—— (1989), *Reclaiming Reality: A Critical Introduction to Contemporary Philosophy* (London: Verso).

Billig, M. (1991), *Ideology and Opinions: Studies in Rhetorical Psychology* (Cambridge: Cambridge University Press).

—— (1992), *Talking of the Royal Family* (London: Routledge).

—— Condor, S., Edwards, D., Gane, M., Middleton, D., and Radley, A. (1988), *Ideological Dilemmas: A Social Psychology of Everyday Thinking* (London: Sage).

Blauner, R. (1964), *Alienation and Freedom* (Chicago: University of Chicago Press).

Blaxter, M. (1990), *Health and Lifestyles* (London: Routledge).

Bloomfield, B. P., and Vurdubakis, T. (1994), 'Re-Presenting Technology: IT Consultancy Reports as Textual Reality Constructions', *Sociology*, 28: 455–77.

Bloor, M. (1978), 'On the Analysis of Observational Data: A Discussion of the Worth and Uses of Inductive Techniques and Respondent Validation', *Sociology*, 12: 545–52.

—— (1997), 'Addressing Social Problems through Qualitative Research', in D. Silverman (ed.), *Qualitative Research: Theory, Method and Practice* (London: Sage).

Blumer, H. (1954), 'What is Wrong with Social Theory?', *American Sociological Review*, 19: 3–10.

—— (1956), 'Sociological Analysis and the "Variable" ', *American Sociological Review*, 21: 683–90.

—— (1962), 'Society as Symbolic Interaction', in A. M. Rose (ed.), *Human Behavior and Social Processes* (London: Routledge & Kegan Paul).

Bogdan, R., and Taylor, S. J. (1975), *Introduction to Qualitative Research Methods: A Phenomenological Approach to the Social Sciences* (New York: Wiley).

Bottomore, T. B., and Rubel, M. (1963), *Karl Marx: Selected Writings in Sociology and Social Philosophy* (Harmondsworth, Middx.: Penguin).

Bradburn, N. A., and Sudman, S. (1979), *Improving Interview Method and Questionnaire Design* (San Francisco: Jossey-Bass).

Bridgman, P. W. (1927), *The Logic of Modern Physics* (New York: Macmillan).

Braverman, H. (1974), *Labor and Monopoly Capital: The Degradation of Work in the Twentieth Century* (London: Monthly Review Press).

Brayfield, A., and Rothe, H. (1951), 'An Index of Job Satisfaction', *Journal of Applied Psychology*, 35: 307–11.

Briggs, C. L. (1986), *Learning How to Ask: A Sociolinguistic Appraisal of the Role of the Interview in Social Science Research* (Cambridge: Cambridge University Press).

Brown, G. W., and Harris, T. W. (1978), *The Social Origins of Depression: A Study of Psychiatric Disorder in Women* (London: Tavistock).

Bryman, A. (1974), 'Sociology of Religion and Sociology of Elites', *Archives de Sciences Sociales des Religions*, 38: 109–21.

—— (1988a), *Quantity and Quality in Social Research* (London: Routledge).

—— (1988b), *Doing Research in Organizations* (London: Routledge).

—— (1989a), *Research Methods and Organization Studies* (London: Routledge).

—— (1989b), 'The Value of Re-Studies in Sociology: The Case of Clergy and Ministers, 1971 to 1985', *Sociology*, 23: 31–54

—— (1992), 'Quantitative and Qualitative Research: Further Reflections on their Integration', in J. Brannen (ed.), *Mixing Methods: Qualitative and Quantitative Research* (Aldershot: Avebury).

—— (1994), 'The Mead/Freeman Controversy: Some Implications for Qualitative Researchers', in R. G. Burgess (ed.), *Studies in Qualitative Methodology, Volume 4* (Greenwich, Conn.: JAI Press).

—— (1995), *Disney and his Worlds* (London: Routledge).

—— (1998), 'Quantitative and Qualitative Research Strategies in Knowing the Social World', in T. May and M. Williams (eds), *Knowing the Social World* (Buckingham: Open University Press).

—— (1999), 'Global Disney', in P. Taylor and D. Slater (eds), *The American Century* (Oxford: Blackwell).

—— and Burgess, R. G. (1994a), 'Developments in Qualitative Data Analysis: An Introduction', in A. Bryman and R. G. Burgess (eds), *Analyzing Qualitative Data* (London: Routledge).

—— —— (1994b), 'Reflections on Qualitative Data Analysis', in A. Bryman and R. G. Burgess (eds), *Analyzing Qualitative Data* (London: Routledge).

—— —— (1999), 'Introduction: Qualitative Research Methodology—A Review', in A. Bryman and R. G. Burgess (eds), *Qualitative Research* (London: Sage).

—— and Cramer, D. (2001), *Quantitative Data Analysis with SPSS Release 10 for Windows: A Guide for Social Scientists* (London: Routledge).

—— Haslam, C., and Webb, A. (1994), 'Performance Appraisal in UK Universities: A Case of Procedural Compliance?', *Assessment and Evaluation in Higher Education*, 19: 175–88.

—— Gillingwater, D., and McGuinness, I. (1996), 'Industry Culture and Strategic Response: The Case of the British Bus Industry', *Studies in Cultures, Organizations and Societies*, 2: 191–208.

—— Stephens, M., and A Campo, C. (1996), 'The Importance of Context: Qualitative Research and the Study of Leadership', *Leadership Quarterly*, 7: 353–70.

Brynin, M. (1994), 'Stability of Voting Intentions', in N. Buck, J. Gershuny, D. Rose, and J. Scott (eds), *Changing Households: The BHPS 1990 to 1992* (Colchester, Essex: ESRC Research Centre on Micro-Social Change).

Buchanan, D. R. (1992), 'An Uneasy Alliance: Combining Qualitative and Quantitative Research Methods', *Health Education Quarterly*, 19: 117–35.

Buckle, A., and Farrington, D. P. (1984), 'An Observational Study of Shoplifting', *British Journal of Criminology*, 24: 63–73.

—— —— (1994), 'Measuring Shoplifting by Systematic Observation', *Psychology, Crime and Law*, 1: 133–41.

Bulmer, M. (1979), 'Concepts in the Analysis of Qualitative Data', *Sociological Review*, 27: 651–77.

—— (1980), 'Why Don't Sociologists Make More Use of Official Statistics?', *Sociology*, 14: 505–23.

—— (1982), 'The Merits and Demerits of Covert Participant Observation', in M. Bulmer (ed.), *Social Research Ethics* (London: Macmillan).

—— (1984), 'Facts, Concepts, Theories and Problems', in M. Bulmer (ed.), *Social Research Methods* (London: Macmillan).

Burawoy, M. , *Manufacturing Consent* (Chicago: University of Chicago Press).

Burgess, R. G. (1983), *Inside Comprehensive Education: A Study of Bishop McGregor School* (London: Methuen).

—— (1984), *In the Field* (London: Allen & Unwin).

—— (1987), 'Studying and Restudying Bishop McGregor School', in G. Walford (ed.), *Doing Sociology of Education* (Lewes: Falmer).

Burrell, I., and Leppard, D. (1994), 'Fall in Crime a Myth as Police Chiefs Massage the Figures', *Sunday Times*, 16 Oct., 1, 5.

Business Week (1973), 'The Public Clams up on Survey Takers', 15 Sept.: 216–20.

Buston, K. (1997), 'NUD*IST in Action: Its Use and its Usefulness in a Study of Chronic Illness in Young People', *Sociological Research Online, 2,* http://www.socresonline.org.uk/socresonline/2/3/6.html

Butcher, B. (1994), 'Sampling methods—an Overview and Review', *Survey Methods Centre Newsletter*, 15: 4–8.

Calder, B. J. (1977), 'Focus Groups and the Nature of Qualitative Marketing Research', *Journal of Marketing Research*, 14: 353–64.

Camerer, C. F. (1997), 'Taxi Drivers and Beauty Contests', *Engineering and Science*, 60: 11–19.

Campbell, D. T. (1957), 'Factors Relevant to the Validity of Experiments in Social Settings', *Psychological Bulletin*, 54: 297–312.

Carlson, R. G., Siegal, H. A., Wang, J., and Falck, R. A. (1996), 'Attitudes toward Needle "Sharing" among Injection Drug Users: Combining Qualitative and Quantitative Research Methods', *Human Organization*, 55: 361–9.

Catterall, M., and Maclaran, P. (1997), 'Focus Group Data and Qualitative Analysis Programs: Coding the Moving Picture as well as Snapshots', *Sociological Research Online, 2,* http://www.socresonline.org.uk/socresonline/2/1/6.html.

Cavendish, R. (1982), *Women on the Line* (London: Routledge & Kegan Paul).

Chamberlayne, P., Bornat, J., and Wengraf, T. (2000), 'Introduction: The Biographical Turn', in P. Chamberlayne, J. Bornat, and T. Wengraf (eds), *The Turn to Biographical Methods in Social Science: Comparative Issues and Examples* (London: Routledge).

Charles, N., and Kerr, N. (1988), *Women, Food and Families* (Manchester: Manchester University Press).

Charlton, T., Gunter, B., and Coles, D. (1998), 'Broadcast Television as a Cause of Aggression?: Recent Findings from a Naturalistic Study', *Emotional and Behavioural Difficulties*, 3: 5–13.

—— Coles, D., Panting, C., and Hannan, A. (1999), 'Behaviour of Nursery Class Children before and after the Availability of Broadcast Television: A Naturalistic Study of Two Cohorts in a Remote Community', *Journal of Social Behavior and Personality*, 14: 315–24.

Charmaz, K. (1983), 'The Grounded Theory Method: An Explication and Interpretation', in R. M. Emerson (ed.), *Contemporary Field Research: A Collection of Readings* (Boston: Little, Brown).

—— (1991), *Good Days, Bad Days: The Self in Chronic Illness and Time* (New Brunswick, NJ: Rutgers University Press).

—— (1997), 'Identity Dilemmas of Chronically Ill Men', in A. Strauss and J. M. Corbin (eds), *Grounded Theory in Practice* (Thousand Oaks, Calif.: Sage).

—— (2000), 'Grounded Theory: Objectivist and Constructivist Methods', in N. K. Denzin and Y. S. Lincoln (eds), *Handbook of Qualitative Research*, 2nd edn. (Thousand Oaks, Calif.: Sage).

Chattoe, E., and Gilbert, N. (1999), 'Talking about Budgets: Time and Uncertainty in Household Decision Making', *Sociology*, 33: 85–103.

Cicourel, A. V. (1964), *Method and Measurement in Sociology* (New York: Free Press).

—— (1968), *The Social Organization of Juvenile Justice* (New York: Wiley).

—— (1982), 'Interviews, Surveys, and the Problem of Ecological Validity', *American Sociologist*, 17: 11–20.

Clairbom, W. L. (1969), 'Expectancy Effects in the Classroom: A Failure to Replicate', *Journal of Educational Psychology*, 60: 377–83.

Clifford, J. (1983), 'On Ethnographic Authority', *Representations*, 1: 118–46.

—— and Marcus, G. E. (1986), *Writing Culture: The Poetics and Politics of Ethnography* (Berkeley and Los Angeles: University of California Press).

Cloward, R. A., and Ohlin, L. E. (1960), *Delinquency and Opportunity: A Theory of Delinquent Gangs* (New York: Free Press).

Coffey, A. (1999), *The Ethnographic Self: Fieldwork and the Representation of Reality* (London: Sage).

—— and Atkinson, P. (1996), *Making Sense of Qualitative Data: Complementary Research Strategies* (Thousand Oaks, Calif.: Sage).

—— Holbrook, B., and Atkinson, P. (1996), 'Qualitative Data Analysis: Technologies and Representations', *Sociological Research Online, 2,* http://www.socresonline.org.uk/socresonline/1/1/4.html.

Cohen, S. (1973), *Folk Devils and Moral Panics: The Creation of the Mods and Rockers* (London: Paladin).

Coleman, C., and Moynihan, J. (1996), *Understanding Crime Data: Haunted by the Dark Figure* (Buckingham: Open University Press).

Coleman, J. S. (1958), 'Relational Analysis: The Study of Social Organization with Survey Methods', *Human Organization*, 16: 28–36.

Collins, M. (1997), 'Interviewer Variability: A Review of the Problem', *Journal of the Market Research Society*, 39: 67–84

Collins, R. (1994), *Four Sociological Traditions*, rev. edn. (New York: Oxford University Press).

Conger, J. A., and Kanungo, R. N. (1998), *Charismatic Leadership in Organizations* (Thousand Oaks, Calif.: Sage).

Cook, T. D., and Campbell, D. T. (1979), *Quasi-Experimentation: Design and Analysis for Field Settings* (Boston, Mass.: Houghton Mifflin).

Corti, L. (1993), 'Using Diaries in Social Research', *Social Research Update*, 2.

—— Foster, J., and Thompson, P. (1995), 'Archiving Qualitative Research Data', *Social Research Update*, 10.

Coxon, A. P. M. (1994), 'Diaries and Sexual Behaviour: The Use of Sexual Diaries as Method and Substance in Researching Gay Men's Response to HIV/AIDS', in M. Boulton (ed.), *Challenge and Innovation: Methodological Advances in Social Research on HIV/AIDS* (London: Taylor & Francis).

Cramer, D. (1998), *Fundamental Statistics for Social Research* (London: Routledge).

Crapanzano, V. (1986), 'Hermes' Dilemma: The Masking of Subversion in Ethnographic Description', in J. Clifford and G. E. Marcus (eds), *Writing Culture: The Poetics and Politics of Ethnography* (Berkeley and Los Angeles: University of California Press).

Croll, P. (1986), *Systematic Classroom Observation* (London: Falmer Press).

—— and Moses, D. (1985), *One in Five: The Assessment and Incidence of Special Educational Needs* (London: Routledge & Kegan Paul).

Cryer, P. (1996), *The Research Student's Guide to Success* (Buckingham: Open University Press).

Czarniawska, B. (1998), *A Narrative Approach to Organization Studies* (Thousand Oaks, Calif.: Sage).

Dale, A. (1987), 'The Effect of Life Cycle on Three Dimensions of Stratification', in A. Bryman, B. Bytheway, P. Allatt, and T. Keil (eds), *Rethinking the Life Cycle* (London: Macmillan).

—— Arber, S., and Proctor, M. (1988), *Doing Secondary Analysis* (London: Unwin Hyman).

Daniel, W. W. (1968), *Racial Discrimination in Britain* (Harmondsworth: Penguin).

Davies, C. A. (1999), *Reflexive Ethnography: A Guide to Researching Selves and Others* (London: Routledge).

Davies, R. B., Elias, P., and Penn, R. (1994), 'The Relationship between a Husband's Unemployment and his Wife's Participation in the Labour Force', in D. Gallie, C. Marsh, and C. Vogler (eds), *Social Change and the Experience of Unemployment* (Oxford: Oxford University Press).

Davis, J. A. (1964), '*Great Books and Small Groups*: An Informal History of a National Survey', in P. Hammond (ed.), *Sociologists at Work* (New York: Basic Books).

Deacon, D., and Golding, P. (1994), *Taxation and Representation: The Media, Political Communication and the Poll Tax* (London: John Libbey).

—— Bryman, A., and Fenton, N. (1998), 'Collision or Collusion? A Discussion of the Unplanned Triangulation of Quantitative and Qualitative Research Methods', *International Journal of Social Research Methodology*, 1: 47–63.

—— Fenton, N., and Bryman, A. (1999), 'From Inception to Reception: The Natural History of a News Item', *Media, Culture and Society*, 21: 5–31.

—— Pickering, M., Golding, P., and Murdock, G. (1999), *Researching Communications: A Practical Guide to Methods in Media and Cultural Analysis* (London: Arnold).

Delamont, S. (1976), 'Beyond Flanders' Fields: The Relationship of Subject-Matter and Individuality in Classroom Style', in M. Stubbs and S. Delamont (eds), *Explorations in Classroom Observation* (Chichester: Wiley).

—— and Hamilton, D. (1984), 'Revisiting Classroom Research: A Continuing Cautionary Tale', in S. Delamont (ed.), *Readings on Interaction in the Classroom* (London: Methuen).

Delbridge, R. (1998), *Life on the Line: The Workplace Experience of Lean Production and the 'Japanese' Model* (Oxford: Oxford University Press).

Denzin, N. K. (1968), 'On the Ethics of Disguised Observation', *Social Problems*, 15: 502–4.

—— (1970), *The Research Act in Sociology* (Chicago: Aldine).

—— (1994), 'Evaluating Qualitative Research in the Poststructural Moment; the Lessons James Joyce Teaches us', *International Journal of Qualitative Studies in Education*, 7: 295–308.

—— and Lincoln, Y. S. (1994), 'Introduction: Entering the Field of Qualitative Research', in N. K. Denzin and Y. S. Lincoln (eds), *Handbook of Qualitative Research* (Thousand Oaks, Calif.: Sage).

Denzin, N. K., and Lincoln, Y. S. (2000), *Handbook of Qualitative Research*, 2nd edn. (Thousand Oaks, Calif.: Sage).

Dickinson, H. (1993), 'Accounting for Augustus Lamb: Theoretical and Methodological Issues in Biography and Historical Sociology', *Sociology*, 27: 121–32.

Diener, E., and Crandall, R. (1978), *Ethics in Social and Behavioral Research* (Chicago: University of Chicago Press).

Dillman, D. A. (1983), 'Mail and Other Self-Administered Questionnaires', in P. H. Rossi, J. D. Wright, and A. B. Anderson (eds), *Handbook of Survey Research* (Orlando, Fl.: Academic Press).

Dingwall, R. (1980), 'Ethics and Ethnography', *Sociological Review*, 28: 871–91.

Ditton, J. (1977), *Part-Time Crime: An Ethnography of Fiddling and Pilferage* (London: Macmillan).

Dohrenwend, B. P. (1966), 'Social Status and Psychiatric Disorder: An Issue of Substance and an Issue of Method', *American Sociological Review*, 31: 14–34.

Douglas, J. D. (1967), *The Social Meanings of Suicide* (Princeton: Princeton University Press).

—— (1976), *Investigative Social Research: Individual and Team Field Research* (Beverly Hills, Calif.: Sage).

Duncombe, J., and Marsden, D. (1993), 'Love and Intimacy: The Gender Division of Emotion and "Emotion Work"', *Sociology*, 27: 221–41.

Dunning, E., Murphy, P., and Williams, J. (1988), *The Roots of Football Hooliganism: An Historical and Sociological Study* (London: Routledge).

Durkheim, E. (1938), *The Rules of Sociological Method*, trans. S. A. Solavay and J. H. Mueller (New York: Free Press).

—— (1952), *Suicide. A Study In Sociology*, trans. J. A. Spaulding and G. Simpson (London: Routledge & Kegan Paul).

Dwyer, J. T., Mayer, L. D. V. H., Dowd, K., Kandel, R. F., and Mayer, J. (1974), 'The New Vegetarians: The Natural High?', *Journal of the American Dietetic Association*, 65: 529–36.

Dyer, W. G., and Wilkins, A. L. (1991), 'Better Stories, not Better Constructs, to Generate Better Theory: A Rejoinder to Eisenhardt', *Academy of Management Review*, 16: 613–19.

Edley, N., and Wetherell, M. (1997), 'Jockeying for Position: The Construction of Masculine Identities', *Discourse and Society*, 8: 203–17.

Edwards, R. (1979), *Contested Terrain* (New York: Basic Books).

Eisenhardt, K. M. (1989), 'Building Theories from Case Study Research', *Academy of Management Review*, 14: 532–50.

Elliott, C., and Ellingworth, D. (1997), 'Assessing the Representativeness of the 1992 British Crime Survey: The Impact of Sampling Error and Response Biases', *Sociological Research Online*, 2, *http://www.socresonline.org.uk/socresonline/2/4/3.html.*

Elliott, H. (1997), 'The Use of Diaries in Sociological Research on Health Experience', *Sociological Research Online*, 2, *http://www.socresonline.org.uk/socresonline/2/2/7.html.*

Erikson, K. T. (1967), 'A Comment on Disguised Observation in Sociology', *Social Problems*, 14: 366–73.

Faraday, A., and Plummer, K. (1979), 'Doing Life Histories', *Sociological Review*, 27: 773–98.

Fenton, N., Bryman, A., and Deacon, D. (1998), *Mediating Social Science* (London: Sage).

Ferrie, J., Shipley, M. J., Marmot, M. G., Stansfeld, S., and Smith, G. D. (1998), 'The Health Effects of Major Organizational Change and Job Insecurity', *Social Science and Medicine*, 46: 343–54.

Festinger, L., Riecken, H. W., and Schachter, S. (1956), *When Prophecy Fails* (New York: Harper & Row).

Fielding, N. (1981), *The National Front* (London: Routledge & Kegan Paul).

—— (1982), 'Observational Research on the National Front', in M. Bulmer (ed.), *Social Research Ethics* (London: Macmillan).

—— and Lee, R. M. (1998), *Computer Analysis and Qualitative Research* (London: Sage).

Filmer, P., Phillipson, M., Silverman, D., and Walsh, D. (1972), *New Directions in Sociological Theory* (London: Collier-Macmillan).

Finch, J. (1984), '"It's great to have someone to talk to": The Ethics and Politics of Interviewing Women', in C. Bell and H. Roberts (eds), *Social Researching: Politics, Problems, Practice* (London: Routledge & Kegan Paul).

—— (1987), 'The Vignette Technique in Survey Research', *Sociology*, 21: 105–14.

—— and Hayes, L. (1994), 'Inheritance, Death and the Concept of the Home', *Sociology*, 28: 417–33.

—— and Mason, J. (1990), 'Decision Taking in the Fieldwork Process: Theoretical Sampling and Collaborative Working', in R. G. Burgess (ed.), *Studies in Qualitative Methodology*, 2: 25–50.

Fine, G. A. (1996), 'Justifying Work: Occupational Rhetorics as Resources in Kitchen Restaurants', *Administrative Science Quarterly*, 41: 90–115.

Flanders, N. (1970), *Analyzing Teacher Behavior* (Reading, Mass.: Addison-Wesley).

Fletcher, J. (1966), *Situation Ethics* (London: SCM Press).

Foddy, W. (1993), *Constructing Questions for Interviews and Questionnaires: Theory and Practice in Social Research* (Cambridge: Cambridge University Press).

Forster, N. (1994), 'The Analysis of Company Documentation', in C. Cassell and G. Symon (eds), *Qualitative Methods in Organizational Research* (London: Sage).

Foster, J. (1995), 'Informal Social Control and Community Crime Prevention', *British Journal of Criminology*, 35: 563–83.

Fowler, F. J. (1993), *Survey Research Methods*, 2nd edn. (Newbury Park, Calif.: Sage).

—— and Mangione, T. W. (1990), *Standardized Survey Interviewing: Minimizing Interviewer-Related Error* (Beverly Hills, Calif.: Sage).

Fox, J., and Fogelman, K. (1990), 'New Possibilities for Longitudinal Studies of Intergenerational Factors in Child Health and Development', in D. Magnusson and L. R. Bergman (eds) *Data Quality in Longitudinal Research* (Cambridge: Cambridge University Press).

Frean, A. (1998), 'Children Read More after Arrival of TV', *The Times*, 29 April: 7.

Frey, J. H., and Oishi, S. M. (1995), *How to Conduct Interviews by Telephone and in Person* (Thousand Oaks, Calif.: Sage).

Gabriel, Y. (1998), 'The use of stories', in G. Symon and C. Cassell (eds), *Qualitative Methods and Analysis in Organizational Research* (London: Sage).

Gallie, D. (1978), *In Search of the New Working Class: Automation and Social Integration within the Capitalist Enterprise* (Cambridge: Cambridge University Press).

Gallup, G. (1947), 'The Quintamensional Plan of Question Design', *Public Opinion Quarterly*, 11: 385–93.

Galton, M., Simon, B., and Croll, P. (1980), *Inside the Primary Classroom* (London: Routledge & Kegan Paul).

Gans, H. J. (1962), *The Urban Villagers* (New York: Free Press).

—— (1968), 'The Participant-Observer as Human Being: Observations on the Personal Aspects of Field Work', in H. S. Becker (ed.), *Institutions and the Person: Papers Presented to Everett C. Hughes* (Chicago: Aldine).

Garfinkel, H. (1967), *Studies in Ethnomethodology* (Englewood Cliffs, NJ: Prentice-Hall).

Geertz, C. (1973*a*), 'Thick Description: Toward an Interpretive Theory of Culture', in C. Geertz, *The Interpretation of Cultures* (New York: Basic Books).

—— (1973*b*), 'Deep Play: Notes on the Balinese Cockfight', in C. Geertz, *The Interpretation of Cultures* (New York: Basic Books).

Gephart, R. P. (1988), *Ethnostatistics: Qualitative Foundations for Quantitative Research* (Newbury Park, Calif.: Sage).

Giddens, A. (1984), *The Constitution of Society* (Cambridge: Polity).

Gilbert, G. N. (1977), 'Referencing as Persuasion', *Social Studies of Science*, 7: 113–22.

—— and Mulkay, M. (1984), *Opening Pandora's Box: A Sociological Analysis of Scientists' Discourse* (Cambridge: Cambridge University Press).

Gill, R. (1996), 'Discourse Analysis: Practical Implementation', in J. T. E. Richardson (ed.), *Handbook of Qualitative Research Methods for Psychology and the Social Sciences* (Leicester: BPS Books).

—— (2000), 'Discourse Analysis', in M. W. Bauer and G. Gaskell (eds), *Qualitative Researching with Text, Image and Sound* (London: Sage).

Ginn, J., and Arber, S. (1995), 'Exploring Mid-Life Women's Employment', *Sociology*, 29: 73–94.

Giulianotti, R. (1995), 'Participant Observation and Research into Football Hooliganism: Reflections on the Problems of Entrée and Everyday Risks', *Sociology of Sport Journal*, 12: 1–20.

—— (1997), 'Enlightening the North: Aberdeen Fanzines and Local Football Identity', in G. Armstrong and R. Giulianotti (eds), *Entering the Field: New Perspectives on World Football* (Oxford: Berg).

Glaser, B. G. (1992), *Basics of Grounded Theory Analysis* (Mill Valley, Calif.: Sociology Press).

—— and Strauss, A. L. (1967), *The Discovery of Grounded Theory: Strategies for Qualitative Research* (Chicago: Aldine).

Glasgow University Media Group (1976), *Bad News* (London: Routledge & Kegan Paul).

Glock, C. Y. (1988), 'Reflections on Doing Survey Research', in H. J. O'Gorman (ed.), *Surveying Social Life* (Middletown, Conn.: Wesleyan University Press).

Glucksmann, M. (1994), 'The Work of Knowledge and the Knowledge of Women's Work', in M. Maynard and J. Purvis (eds), *Researching Women's Lives from a Feminist Perspective* (London: Taylor & Francis).

Goffman, E. (1956), *The Presentation of Self in Everyday Life* (New York: Doubleday).

—— (1963), *Stigma: Notes on the Management of Spoiled Identity* (Harmondsworth: Penguin).

Gold, R. L. (1958), 'Roles in Sociological Fieldwork', *Social Forces*, 36: 217–23.

Golden-Biddle, K., and Locke, K. D. (1993), 'Appealing Work: An Investigation of how Ethnographic Texts Convince', *Organization Science*, 4: 595–616.

—— —— (1997), *Composing Qualitative Research* (Thousand Oaks, Calif.: Sage).

Goldthorpe, J. H., Lockwood, D., Bechhofer, F., and Platt, J. (1968), *The Affluent Worker: Industrial Attitudes and Behaviour* (Cambridge: Cambridge University Press).

Goode, E. (1996), 'The Ethics of Deception in Social Research: A Case Study', *Qualitative Sociology*, 19: 11–33.

Goode, W. J., and Hatt, P. K. (1952), *Methods of Social Research* (New York: McGraw Hill).

Gottdiener, M. (1982), 'Disneyland: A Utopian Urban Space', *Urban Life*, 11: 139–62.

—— (1997), *The Theming of America: Dreams, Visions and Commercial Spaces* (Boulder, Colo.: Westview Press).

Greene, J. C. (1994), 'Qualitative Program Evaluation: Practice and Promise', in N. K. Denzin and Y. S. Lincoln (eds), *Handbook of Qualitative Research* (Thousand Oaks, Calif.: Sage).

—— (2000), 'Understanding Social Programs through Evaluation', in N. K. Denzin and Y. S. Lincoln (eds), *Handbook of Qualitative Research*, 2nd edn. (Thousand Oaks, Calif.: Sage).

Greising, D. (1998), *I'd Like the World to Buy a Coke: The Life and Leadership of Robert Goizueta* (New York: Wiley).

Grele, R. J. (1998), 'Movement without Aim: Methodological and Theoretical Problems in Oral History', in R. Perks and A. Thomson (eds), *The History Reader* (London: Routledge).

Griffin, J. H. (1961), *Black Like Me* (Boston: Houghton Mifflin).

Grint, K., and Woolgar, S. (1997), *The Machine at Work: Technology, Work and Organization* (Cambridge: Polity).

Guba, E. G. (1985), 'The Context of Emergent Paradigm Research', in Y. S. Lincoln (ed.), *Organization Theory and Inquiry: The Paradigm Revolution* (Beverly Hills, Calif.: Sage).

—— and Lincoln, Y. S. (1994), 'Competing Paradigms in Qualitative Research', in N. K. Denzin and Y. S. Lincoln (eds), *Handbook of Qualitative Research* (Thousand Oaks, Calif.: Sage).

Gubrium, J. F., and Holstein, J. A. (1997), *The New Language of Qualitative Method* (New York: Oxford University Press).

Gusfield, J. (1976), 'The Literary Rhetoric of Science: Comedy and Pathos in Drinking Driving Research', *American Sociological Review*, 41: 16–34.

Halfpenny, P. (1979) 'The Analysis of Qualitative Data', *Sociological Review*, 27: 799–825.

Hall, W. S., and Guthrie, L. F. (1981), 'Cultural and Situational Variation in Language Function and Use— Methods and Procedures for Research', in J. L. Green and C. Wallatt (eds), *Ethnography and Language in Educational Settings* (Norwood, NJ: Ablex).

Hammersley, B. (1999), 'Changing Faces with a Pandora's Box of Tricks', *The Times* (Interface section), 22 Nov.: 10–11.

Hammersley, M. (1989), *The Dilemma of Qualitative Method: Herbert Blumer and the Chicago Tradition* (London: Routledge).

—— (1992a), 'By what Criteria should Ethnographic Research be Judged?', in M. Hammersley, *What's Wrong with Ethnography* (London: Routledge).

—— (1992b), 'Deconstructing the Qualitative– Quantitative Divide', in M. Hammersley, *What's Wrong with Ethnography* (London: Routledge).

—— (1996), 'The Relationship between Qualitative and Quantitative Research: Paradigm Loyalty versus Methodological Eclecticism', in J. T. E. Richardson (ed.), *Handbook of Research Methods for Psychology and the Social Sciences* (Leicester: BPS Books).

—— (1997), 'Qualitative Data Archiving: Some Reflections on its Prospects and Problems', *Sociology*, 31: 131–42.

—— and Atkinson, P. (1995), *Ethnography: Principles in Practice*, 2nd edn. (London: Routledge).

—— Scarth, J., and Webb, S. (1985), 'Developing and Testing Theory: The Case of Research on Pupil Learning', in R. G. Burgess (ed.), *Issues in Educational Research: Qualitative Methods* (London: Falmer).

Hammond, P. (1964), *Sociologists at Work* (New York: Basic Books).

Hansen, A. (1995), 'Using Information Technology to Analyze Newspaper Content', in R. M. Lee (ed.), *Information Technology for the Social Scientist* (London: UCL Press).

Hantrais, L. (1996), 'Comparative Research Methods', *Social Research Update*, 13.

Harré, R. (1972), *The Philosophies of Science* (Oxford: Oxford University Press).

Haslam, C., and Bryman, A. (1994), 'The Research Dissemination Minefield', in C. Haslam and A. Bryman (eds), *Social Scientists Meet the Media* (London: Routledge).

Heap, J. L., and Roth, P. A. (1973), 'On Phenomenological Sociology', *American Sociological Review*, 38: 354–67.

Heath, C. (1997), 'The Analysis of Activities in Face to Face Interaction Using Video', in D. Silverman (ed.), *Qualitative Research: Theory, Method and Practice* (London: Sage).

Heritage, J. (1984), *Garfinkel and Ethnomethodology* (Cambridge: Polity).

—— (1987), 'Ethnomethodology', in A. Giddens and J. H. Turner (eds), *Social Theory Today* (Cambridge: Polity).

Hesse-Biber, S. (1995), 'Unleashing Frankenstein's Monster? The Use of Computers in Qualitative Research', *Studies in Qualitative Methodology*, 5: 25–41.

Hirsch, J. (1981), *Family Photographs* (New York: Oxford University Press).

Hobbs, D. (1988), *Doing the Business: Entrepreneurship, the Working Class and Detectives in the East End of London* (Oxford: Oxford University Press).

—— (1993), 'Peers, Careers, and Academic Fears: Writing as Field-Work', in D. Hobbs and T. May (eds), *Interpreting the Field: Accounts of Ethnography'* (Oxford: Clarendon Press).

Hochschild, A. R. (1983), *The Managed Heart* (Berkeley and Los Angeles: University of California Press).

Hodges, L. (1998), 'The Making of a National Portrait', *The Times Higher*, 20 Feb.: 22–3.

Hodson, R. (1996), 'Dignity in the Workplace under Participative Management', *American Sociological Review*, 61: 719–38.

—— (1999), *Analyzing Documentary Accounts* (Thousand Oaks, Calif.: Sage).

Holbrook , B., and Jackson, B. (1996), 'Shopping Around: Focus Group Research in North London', *Area*, 28:136–42.

Holdaway, S. (1982), ' "An inside job": A Case Study of Covert Research on the Police', in M. Bulmer (ed.), *Social Research Ethics* (London: Macmillan).

—— (1983), *Inside the British Police: A Force at Work* (Oxford: Blackwell).

Holsti, O. R. (1969), *Content Analysis for the Social Sciences and Humanities* (Reading, Mass.: Addison-Wesley).

Homan, R. (1991), *The Ethics of Social Research* (London: Longman).

—— and Bulmer, M. (1982), 'On the Merits of Covert Methods: A Dialogue', in M. Bulmer (ed.), *Social Research Ethics* (London: Macmillan).

Houghton, E. (1998), 'Sex is Good for You', *Guardian* (G2 section), 20 Jan., 14–15.

Howell, J. M., and Frost, P. J. (1989), 'A Laboratory Study of Charismatic Leadership', *Organizational Behavior and Human Decision Processes*, 43: 243–69.

Huberman, A. M., and Miles, M. B. (1994), 'Data Management and Analysis Methods', in N. K. Denzin and Y. S. Lincoln (eds), *Handbook of Qualitative Research* (Thousand Oaks, Calif.: Sage).

Hughes, J. A. (1990), *The Philosophy of Social Research*, 2nd edn. (Harlow: Longman).

Hughes, K., MacKintosh, A. M., Hastings, G., Wheeler, C., Watson, J., and Inglis, J. (1997), 'Young people, Alcohol, and Designer Drinks: A Quantitative and Qualitative Study', *British Medical Journal*, 314: 414–18.

Humphreys, L. (1970), *Tearoom Trade: Impersonal Sex in Public Places* (Chicago: Aldine).

Hutchby, I., and Wooffitt, R. (1998), *Conversation Analysis* (Cambridge: Polity).

Hycner, R. H. (1985), 'Some Guidelines for the Phenomenological Analysis of Interview Data', *Human Studies*, 8: 279–303.

Jacobs, J. (1967), 'A Phenomenological Study of Suicide Notes', *Social Problems*, 15: 60–72.

Jagger, E. (1998), 'Marketing the Self, Buying an Other: Dating in a Post Modern, Consumer Society', *Sociology*, 32: 795–814.

Janis, I. L. (1982), *Groupthink: Psychological Studies of Policy Decisions and Fiascos*, 2nd edn. (Boston: Houghton-Mifflin).

Jayaratne, T. E., and Stewart, A. J. (1991), 'Quantitative and Qualitative Methods in the Social Sciences: Current Feminist Issues and Practical Strategies', in M. M. Fonow and J. A. Cook (eds), *Beyond Methodology: Feminist Scholarship as Lived Research* (Bloomington, Ind.: Indiana University Press).

Jenkins, G. D., Nader, D. A., Lawler, E. E., and Cammann, C. (1975), 'Standardized Observations: An Approach to Measuring the Nature of Jobs', *Journal of Applied Psychology*, 60: 171–81.

John, I. D. (1992), 'Statistics as Rhetoric in Psychology', *Australian Psychologist*, 27: 144–9.

Johnson, P. (1998), 'Analytic Induction', in G. Symon and C. Cassell (eds), *Qualitative Methods and Analysis in Organizational Research* (London: Sage).

Jowell, R., Brook, L., Prior, G., and Taylor, B. (1992), *British Social Attitudes 1991 Survey* (London: Social and Community Planning Research).

Kamin. L. J. (1974), *The Science and Politics of IQ* (New York: Wiley).

Kapsis, R. E. (1989), 'Reputation Building and the Film Art World: The Case of Alfred Hitchcock', *Sociological Quarterly*, 30: 15–35.

Katz, J. (1982), *Poor People's Lawyers in Transition* (New Brunswick: Rutgers University Press).

Keat, R., and Urry, J. (1975), *Social Theory as Science* (London: Routledge & Kegan Paul).

Kelley, J., and De Graaf, N. D. (1997), 'National Context, Parental Socialization, and Religious Belief: Results from 15 Nations', *American Sociological Review*, 62: 639–59.

Kelly, A. (1985), 'Action Research: What Is It and What Can It Do?', in R. G. Burgess (ed.), *Issues in Educational Research: Qualitative Methods* (London: Falmer Press).

Kelly, L. , Burton, S., and Regan, L. (1994), 'Researching Women's Lives or Studying Women's Oppression? Reflections on what Constitutes Feminist Research', in M. Maynard and J. Purvis (eds), *Researching Women's Lives from a Feminist Perspective* (London: Taylor & Francis).

Kimmel, A. J. (1988), *Ethics and Values in Applied Social Research* (Newbury Park, Calif.: Sage).

King, N. (1994), 'The Qualitative Research Interview', in C. Cassell and G. Symon (eds), *Qualitative Methods in Organizational Research* (London: Sage).

Kirk, J., and Miller, M. L. (1986), *Reliability and Validity in Qualitative Research* (Newbury Park, Calif.: Sage).

Kitsuse, J. I., and Cicourel, A. V. (1963), 'A Note on the Use of Official Statistics', *Social Problems*, 11: 131–9.

Kitzinger, J. (1993), 'Understanding AIDS: Researching Audience Perceptions of Acquired Immune Deficiency Syndrome', in J. Eldridge (ed.), *Getting the Message: News, Truth and Power* (London: Routledge).

—— (1994), 'The Methodology of Focus Groups: The Importance of Interaction between Research Participants', *Sociology of Health and Illness*, 16, 1994: 103–21.

Knights, D., and Willmott, H. (1990), *Labour Process Theory* (London: Macmillan).

—— —— and Collinson, D. (1985), *Job Redesign: Critical Perspectives on the Labour Process* (Aldershot: Gower).

Kohn, M. L., Naoi, A., Schoenbach, C., Schooler, C., and Slomczymski, K. M. (1990), 'Position in the Class Structure and Psychological Functioning in the United States, Japan, and Poland', *American Journal of Sociology*, 95: 964–1008.

Krueger, R. A. (1988), *Focus Groups: A Practical Guide for Applied Research* (Newbury Park, Calif.: Sage).

—— (1998), *Moderating Focus Groups* (Thousand Oaks, Calif.: Sage).

Kuhn, T. S. (1970), *The Structure of Scientific Revolutions*, 2nd edn. (Chicago: University of Chicago Press).

Kvale, S. (1996), *InterViews: An Introduction to Qualitative Research Interviewing* (Thousand Oaks, Calif.: Sage).

Lacey, C. (1976), 'Problems of Sociological Fieldwork: A Review of the Methodology of "Hightown Grammar" ', in M. Hammersley and P. Woods (eds), *The Process of Schooling* (London: Routledge & Kegan Paul).

Lantz, P. M., and Booth, K. M. (1998), 'The Social Construction of the Breast Cancer Epidemic', *Social Science and Medicine*, 46: 907–18.

LaPiere, R. T. (1934), 'Attitudes vs. Actions', *Social Forces*, 13: 230–7.

Laurie, H., and Sullivan, O. (1991), 'Combining Quantitative and Qualitative Data in the Longitudinal Study of Household Allocations', *Sociological Review*, 39: 113–30.

Law, J., and Williams, R. J. (1982), 'Putting Facts Together: A Study of Scientific Persuasion', *Social Studies of Science*, 12: 535–58.

Layder, D. (1993), *New Strategies in Social Research* (Cambridge: Polity).

—— Ashton, D., and Sung. J. (1991), 'The Empirical Correlates of Action and Structure: The Transition from School to Work', *Sociology*, 25: 447–64.

Lazarsfeld, P. (1958), 'Evidence and Inference in Social Research', *Daedalus*, 87: 99–130.

Leake, J. (1998), 'Police Figures Hide Poor Clear-up Rate', *The Times*, 21 June, 1. 5.

LeCompte, M. D., and Goetz, J. P. (1982), 'Problems of Reliability and Validity in Ethnographic Research', *Review of Educational Research*, 52: 31–60.

Lee, R. M. (2000), *Unobtrusive Methods in Social Research* (Buckingham: Open University Press).

—— and Fielding, N. G. (1991), 'Computing for Qualitative Research: Options, Problems and Potential', in N. G. Fielding and R. M. Lee (eds), *Using Computers in Qualitative Research* (London: Sage).

Leidner, R. (1993), *Fast Food, Fast Talk: Service Work and the Routinization of Everyday Life* (Berkeley and Los Angeles: University of California Press).

Levitas, R., and Guy, W. (1996), 'Introduction', in R. Levitas and W. Guy (eds), *Interpreting Official Statistics* (London: Routledge).

Lewis, O. (1961), *The Children of Sánchez* (New York: Vintage).

Liebow, E. (1967), *Tally's Corner* (Boston, Mass.: Little, Brown).

Lincoln, Y. S., and Denzin, N. K. (1994), 'The Fifth Moment', in N. K. Denzin and Y. S. Lincoln (eds), *Handbook of Qualitative Research* (Thousand Oaks, Calif.: Sage).

—— and Guba, E. (1985), *Naturalistic Inquiry* (Beverly Hills, Calif.: Sage).

Lindesmith, A. R. (1947), *Opiate Addiction* (Bloomington, Ind.: Principia Press).

Livingstone, S., and Lunt, P. (1994), *Talk on Television: Audience Participation and Public Debate* (London: Routledge).

Locke, K. (1996), 'Rewriting *The Discovery of Grounded Theory* after 25 Years?', *Journal of Management Inquiry*, 5: 239–45.

Lofland, J. (1971), *Analyzing Social Settings: A Guide to Qualitative Observation and Analysis* (Belmont, Calif.: Wadsworth).

—— and Lofland, L. (1995), *Analyzing Social Settings: A Guide to Qualitative Observation and Analysis*, 3rd edn. (Belmont, Calif.: Wadsworth).

Lonkila, M. (1995), 'Grounded Theory as an Emergent Paradigm for Computer-Assisted Qualitative Data Analysis', in U. Kelle (ed.), *Computer-Aided Qualitative Data Analysis* (London: Sage).

Lucas, R. (1997), 'Youth, Gender and Part-Time Work: Students in the Labour Process', *Work, Employment and Society*, 11: 595–614.

Lunt, P. K., and Livingstone, S. M. (1992), *Mass Consumption and Personal Identity* (Buckingham: Open University Press).

Lupton, D. (1996), *Food, the Body and the Self* (London: Sage).

Lynd, R. S., and Lynd, H. M. (1929), *Middletown: A Study in Contemporary American Culture* (New York: Harcourt, Brace).

—— —— (1937), *Middletown in Transition: A Study in Cultural Conflicts* (New York: Harcourt, Brace).

McCall, M. J. (1984), 'Structured Field Observation', *Annual Review of Sociology*, 10: 263–82.

McCartney, J. L. (1970), 'On Being Scientific: Changing Styles of Presentation of Sociological Research', *American Sociologist*, 5: 30–5.

McClosky, D. N. (1985), *The Rhetoric of Economics* (Brighton: Wheatsheaf).

McGuigan, J. (1992), *Cultural Populism* (London: Routledge).

McKee, L., and Bell, C. (1985), 'Marital and Family Relations in Times of Male Unemployment', in B. Roberts, R. Finnegan, and D. Gallie (eds), *New Approaches to Economic Life* (Manchester: Manchester University Press).

McKeganey, N., and Barnard, M. (1996), *Sex Work on the Streets* (Buckingham: Open University Press).

McPhail, C., and Rexroat, C. (1979), 'Mead vs. Blumer: The Divergent Methodological Perspectives of Social Behaviorism and Symbolic Interactionism', *American Sociological Review*, 44: 449–67.

Madriz, M. (2000), 'Focus Groups in Feminist Research', in N. K. Denzin and Y. S. Lincoln (eds), *Handbook of Qualitative Research*, 2nd edn. (Thousand Oaks, Calif.: Sage).

Malbon, B. (1999), *Clubbing: Dancing, Ecstasy and Vitality* (London: Routledge).

Malinowski, B. (1967), *A Diary in the Strict Sense of the Term* (London: Routledge & Kegan Paul).

Malkin, A. R., Wornian, K., and Chrisler, J. C. (1999), 'Women and Weight: Gendered Messages on Magazine Covers', *Sex Roles*, 40: 647–55.

Mangabeira, W. (1995), 'Qualitative Analysis and Microcomputer Software: Some Reflections on a New Trend in Sociological Research', *Studies in Qualitative Methodology*, 5: 43–61

Mangione, T. W. (1995), *Mail Surveys: Improving the Quality* (Thousand Oaks, Calif.: Sage).

Manning, P. K. (1995), 'The Challenge of Postmodernism', in J. Van Maanen (ed.), *Representation in Ethnography* (Thousand Oaks, Calif.: Sage).

Marsh, C. (1982), *The Survey Method: The Contribution of Surveys to Sociological Explanation* (London: Allen & Unwin).

—— and Scarbrough, E. (1990), 'Testing Nine Hypotheses about Quota Sampling', *Journal of the Market Research Society*, 32: 485–506.

Marshall, G., and Rose, D. (1989), 'Reply to Saunders', *Network: Newsletter of the British Sociological Association*, 44: 4–5.

—— —— Newby, H., and Vogler, C. (1988), *Social Class in Modern Britain* (London: Unwin Hyman).

Martin, P., and Bateson, P. (1986), *Measuring Behaviour: An Introductory Guide* (Cambridge: Cambridge University Press).

Marx, G. T. (1997), 'Of Methods and Manners for Aspiring Sociologists: 37 Moral Imperatives', *American Sociologist*, 102–25.

Mason, J. (1994), 'Linking Qualitative and Quantitative Data Analysis', in A. Bryman and R. G. Burgess (eds), *Analyzing Qualitative Data* (London: Routledge).

—— (1996), *Qualitative Researching* (London: Sage).

Masterman, M. (1970), 'The Nature of a Paradigm', in I. Lakatos and A. Musgrave (eds), *Criticism and the Growth of Knowledge* (Cambridge: Cambridge University Press).

Matza, D. (1969), *Becoming Deviant* (Englewood Cliffs, NJ: Prentice-Hall).

Mauthner, N. S., Parry, O., and Backett-Milburn, K. (1998), 'The Data are Out There, or Are They? Implications for Archiving and Revisiting Qualitative Data', *Sociology*, 32: 733–45.

Maynard, M. (1994), 'Methods, Practice and Epistemology: The Debate about Feminism and Research', in M. Maynard and J. Purvis (eds), *Researching Women's Lives from a Feminist Perspective* (London: Taylor & Francis).

—— (1998), 'Feminists' Knowledge and the Knowledge of Feminisms: Epistemology, Theory, Methodology and Method', in T. May and M. Williams (eds), *Knowing the Social World* (Buckingham: Open University Press).

Mead, M. (1928), *Coming of Age in Samoa* (New York: Morrow).

Meltzer, B. N., Petras, J. W., and Reynolds, L. T. (1975), *Symbolic Interactionism: Genesis, Varieties and Criticism* (London: Routledge & Kegan Paul).

Menard, S. (1991), *Longitudinal Research* (Newbury Park, Calif.: Sage).

Merton, R. K. (1967), *On Theoretical Sociology* (New York: Free Press).

—— Fiske, M., and Kendall, P. L. (1956), *The Focused Interview: A Manual of Problems and Procedures* (New York: Free Press).

Midgley, C. (1998), 'TV Violence has Little Impact on Children, Study Finds', *The Times*, 12 Jan.: 5.

Mies, M. (1993), 'Towards a Methodology for Feminist Research', in M. Hammersley (ed.), *Social Research: Philosophy, Politics and Practice* (London: Sage).

Miles, M. B. , 'Qualitative Data as an Attractive Nuisance', *Administrative Science Quarterly*, 24: 590–601.

Milgram, S. (1963), 'A Behavioral Study of Obedience', *Journal of Abnormal and Social Psychology*, 67: 371–8.

—— and Shotland, L. (1973), *Television and Antisocial Behavior: Field Experiments* (New York: Academic Press).

—— Mann, L., and Harter, S. (1965), 'The Lost Letter Technique: A Tool of Social Research', *Public Opinion Quarterly*, 29: 437–8.

Milkman, R. (1997), *Farewell to the Factory: Auto Workers in the Late Twentieth Century* (Berkeley and Los Angeles: University of California Press).

Millen, D. (1997), 'Some Methodological and Epistemological Issues Raised by Doing Feminist Research on Non-Feminist Women', *Sociological Research Online*, 2, *http://www.socresonline.org.uk/socresonline/2/3/3.html*.

Miller, D. (1994), *Modernity: An Ethnographic Approach: Dualism and Mass Consumption in Trinidad* (Oxford: Berg).

—— Jackson, P., Thrift, N., Holbrook, B., and Rowlands, M. (1998), *Shopping, Place and Identity* (London: Routledge).

—— and Reilly, J. (1995), 'Making an Issue of Food Safety: The Media, Pressure Groups, and the Public Sphere', in D. Maurer and J. Sobal (eds), *Food and Nutrition as Social Problems* (New York: Aldine de Gruyter).

Miller, D. Disney (1956), *The Story of Walt Disney* (New York: Dell).

Miller, N., and Morgan, D. (1993), 'Called to Account: The CV as an Autobiographical Practice', *Sociology*, 27: 133–43.

Miller, R. L. (2000), *Researching Life Stories and Family Histories* (London: Sage).

Mintzberg, H. (1973), *The Nature of Managerial Work* (New York: Harper & Row).

Mishler, E. G. (1986), *Research Interviewing: Context and Narrative* (Cambridge, Mass.: Harvard University Press).

Mitchell, J. C. (1983), 'Case and Situation Analysis', *Sociological Review*, 31: 186–211.

Morgan, D. L. (1998*a*), *Planning Focus Groups* (Thousand Oaks, Calif.: Sage).

—— (1998*b*), 'Practical Strategies for Combining Qualitative and Quantitative Methods: Applications for Health Research', *Qualitative Health Research*, 8: 362–76.

—— and Spanish, M. T. (1985), 'Social Interaction and the Cognitive Organization of Health-Relevant Behaviour', *Sociology of Health and Illness*, 7: 401–22.

Morgan, G., and Smircich, L. (1980), 'The Case for Qualitative Research', *Academy of Management Review*, 5: 491–500.

Morley, D. (1980), *The 'Nationwide' Audience: Structure and Decoding* (London: British Film Institute).

Morrison, D. E. (1998), *The Search for a Method: Focus Groups and the Development of Mass Communication Research* (Luton: University of Luton Press).

Moser, C. A., and Kalton, G. (1971), *Survey Methods in Social Investigation* (London: Heinemann).

Newby, H. (1977), 'In the Field: Reflections on the Study of Suffolk Farm Workers', in C. Bell and H. Newby (eds), *Doing Sociological Research* (London: Allen & Unwin).

Nichols, T., and Beynon, H. (1977), *Living with Capitalism: Class Relations and the Modern Factory* (London: Routledge).

Noblit, G. W., and Hare, R. D. (1988), *Meta-Ethnography:*

Synthesizing Qualitative Studies (Newbury Park, Calif.: Sage).

Nordenmark, M., and Strandh, M. (1999), 'Towards a Sociological Understanding of Mental Well-Being among the Unemployed: The Role of Economic and Psychosocial Factors', *Sociology*, 33: 577–98.

Norris, C. (1993), 'Some Ethical Considerations on Field-work with the Police', in D. Hobbs and T. May (eds), *Interpreting the Field: Accounts of Ethnography'* (Oxford: Clarendon Press).

Oakley, A. (1981), ' Interviewing Women: A Contradiction in Terms', in H. Roberts (ed.), *Doing Feminist Research* (London: Routledge & Kegan Paul).

—— (1998), 'Gender, Methodology and People's Ways of Knowing: Some Problems with Feminism and the Paradigm Debate in Social Science', *Sociology*, 32: 707–31.

O'Connell Davidson, J. (1998), *Prostitution, Power and Freedom* (Cambridge: Polity).

—— and Layder, D. (1994), *Methods, Sex and Madness* (London: Routledge).

Okely, J. (1994), 'Thinking through Fieldwork', in A. Bryman and R. G. Burgess (eds), *Analyzing Qualitative Data* (London: Routledge).

Oppenheim, A. N. (1966), *Questionnaire Design and Attitude Measurement* (London: Heinemann).

—— (1992), *Questionnaire Design, Interviewing and Attitude Measurement* (London: Pinter).

Orona, C. J. (1997), 'Temporality and Identity Loss due to Alzheimer's disease', in A. Strauss and J. M. Corbin (eds), *Grounded Theory in Practice* (Thousand Oaks, Calif.: Sage).

Pahl, J. (1990), 'Household Spending, Personal Spending and the Control of Money in Marriage', *Sociology*, 24: 119–38.

Parker, M. (2000), *Organizational Culture and Identity* (London: Sage).

Patrick, J. (1973), *A Glasgow Gang Observed* (London: Eyre-Methuen).

Pawson, R., and Tilley, N. (1997), *Realistic Evaluation* (London: Sage).

Pendergrast, M. (1993), *For God, Country and Coca-Cola: The Unauthorized History of the World's Most Popular Soft Drink* (London: Weidenfeld & Nicolson).

Penn, R. , Rose, M. , and Rubery, J. (1994), *Skill and Occupational Change* (Oxford: Oxford University Press).

Peräkylä, A. (1997), 'Reliability and Validity in Research Based on Transcripts', in D. Silverman (ed.), *Qualitative Research: Theory, Method and Practice* (London: Sage).

Pettigrew, A. (1985), *The Awakening Giant: Continuity and Change in Imperial Chemical Industries* (Oxford: Blackwell).

—— (1997), 'What is a Processual Analysis?', *Scandinavian Journal of Management*, 13: 337–48

—— and Whipp, R. (1991), *Managing Change for Competitive Success* (Oxford: Blackwell).

Phelan, P. (1987), 'Comparability of Qualitative and Quantitative Methods: Studying Child Sexual Abuse in America', *Education and Urban Society*, 20: 35–41.

Phillips, D. L. (1973), *Abandoning Method* (San Francisco: Jossey-Bass).

Phillips, N., and Brown, J. L. (1993), 'Analyzing Communications in and around Organizations: A Critical Hermeneutic Approach', *Academy of Management Journal*, 36: 1547–76.

Phoenix, A. (1994), 'Practising Feminist Research: The Intersection of Gender and "Race" in the Research Process', in M. Maynard and J. Purvis (eds), *Researching Women's Lives from a Feminist Perspective* (London: Taylor & Francis).

Pinch, T., and Clark, C. (1986), 'The Hard Sell: "Patter Merchanting" and the Strategic (Re)production and Local Management of Economic Reasoning in the Sales Routines of Market Pitchers', *Sociology*, 20: 169–91.

Platt, J. (1981), 'The Social Construction of "Positivism" and its Significance in British Sociology, 1950–80', in P. Abrams, R. Deem, J. Finch and P. Rock (eds), *Practice and Progress: British Sociology 1950–1980* (London: George Allen & Unwin).

—— (1983), 'The Development of the "Participant Observation" Method in Sociology: Origin Myth and History', *Journal of the History of the Behavioral Sciences*, 19, 379–93.

—— (1986), 'Functionalism and the Survey: The Relation of Theory and Method', *Sociological Review*, 34: 501–36.

—— (1996), *A History of Sociological Research Methods in America 1920–1960* (Cambridge: Cambridge University Press).

Plummer, K. (1983), *Documents of Life: An Introduction to the Problems and Literature of a Humanistic Method* (London: Allen & Unwin).

Podsakoff, P. M., and Dalton, D. R. (1987), 'Research Methodology in Organizational Studies', *Journal of Management*, 13: 419–44.

Poland, B. D. (1995), 'Transcription Quality as an Aspect of Rigor in Qualitative Research', *Qualitative Inquiry*, 1: 290–310.

Pollert, A. (1981), *Girls, Wives, Factory Lives* (London: Macmillan).

Polsky, N. (1967), *Hustlers, Beats and Others* (Chicago: Aldine).

Pope, C., and Mays, N. (1995), 'Reaching the Parts Other Methods Cannot Reach: An Introduction to Qualitative Methods in Health and Health Services Research', *British Medical Journal*, 311: 42–5.

Porter, S. (1993), 'Critical Realist Ethnography: The Case of Racism and Professionalism in a Medical Setting', *Sociology*, 27: 591–609.

Potter, J. (1996), *Representing Reality: Discourse, Rhetoric and Social Construction* (London: Sage).

—— (1997), 'Discourse Analysis as a Way of Analysing Naturally Occurring Talk', in D. Silverman (ed.), *Qualitative Research: Theory, Method and Practice* (London: Sage).

—— and Wetherell, M. (1987), *Discourse and Social Psychology: Beyond Attitudes and Behaviour* (London: Sage).

—— —— (1994), 'Analyzing Discourse', in A. Bryman and R. G. Burgess (eds), *Analyzing Qualitative Data* (London: Routledge).

—— —— and Chitty, A. (1991), 'Quantification Rhetoric—Cancer on Television', *Discourse and Society*, 2: 333–65.

Powell, G. N., and Butterfield, D. A. (1997), 'Effect of Race on Promotions to Top Management in a Federal Department', *Academy of Management Journal*, 40: 112–28.

Psathas, G. (1995), *Conversation Analysis: The Study of Talk-in-Interaction* (Thousand Oaks, Calif.: Sage).

Punch, M. (1979), *Policing the Inner City: A Study of Amsterdam's Warmoesstraat* (London: Macmillan).

—— (1994), 'Politics and Ethics in Qualitative Research', in N. K. Denzin and Y. S. Lincoln (eds), *Handbook of Qualitative Research* (Thousand Oaks, Calif.: Sage).

Rafaeli, A., Dutton, J., Harquail, C. V., and Mackie-Lewis, S. (1997), 'Navigating by Attire: The Use of Dress by Female Administrative Employees', *Academy of Management Journal*, 40: 9–45.

Ragin, C. C., and Becker, H. S. (1989), 'How the Microcomputer is Changing our Analytic Habits', in G. Blank *et al.* (eds), *New Technology in Sociology: Practical Applications in Research and Work* (New Brunswick, NJ: Transaction Publishers).

Rank, M. R. (1989), 'Fertility among Women on Welfare: Incidence and Determinants', *American Sociological Review*, 54: 296–304.

Raz, A. E. (1999), *Riding the Black Ship: Japan and Tokyo Disneyland* (Cambridge, Mass.: Harvard University Press).

Reed, M. (2000), 'The Limits of Discourse Analysis in Organizational Analysis', *Organization*, 7: 524–30.

Reiner, R. (2000), 'Crime and Control in Britain', *Sociology*, 34: 71–94.

Reinharz, S. (1992), *Feminist Methods in Social Research* (New York: Oxford University Press).

Reiss, A. J. (1968), 'Stuff and Nonsense about Social Surveys and Participant Observation', in H. S. Becker, B. Geer, D. Riesman, and R. S. Weiss (eds), *Institutions and the Person: Papers in Memory of Everett C. Hughes* (Chicago: Aldine).

—— (1976), 'Systematic Observation of Natural Phenomena', in H. W. Sinaiko and L. A. Broedling (eds), *Perspectives on Attitude Assessment: Surveys and their Alternatives* (Champaign, Ill.: Pendleton).

Richards, L., and Richards, T. (1994), 'From Filing Cabinet to Computer', in A. Bryman and R. G. Burgess (eds), *Analyzing Qualitative Data* (London: Routledge).

Richardson, L. (1990), 'Narrative and Sociology', *Journal of Contemporary Ethnography*, 19: 116–35.

—— (1994), 'Writing: A Method of Inquiry', in N. K. Denzin and Y. S. Lincoln (eds), *Handbook of Qualitative Research* (Thousand Oaks, Calif.: Sage).

Riessman, C. K. (1993), *Narrative Analysis* (Newbury Park, Calif.: Sage).

Ritzer, G. (1975), 'Sociology: A Multiple Paradigm Science', *American Sociologist*, 10: 156–67.

Robinson, W. S. (1951), 'The Logical Structure of Analytic Induction', *American Sociological Review*, 16: 812–18.

Rojek, C. (1995), *Decentring Leisure: Rethinking Leisure Theory* (London: Sage).

Rosaldo, R. (1986), 'Ilongot Hunting as Story and Experience', in V. W. Turner and E. M. Bruner (eds), *The Anthropology of Experience* (Urbana, Ill.: University of Illinois Press).

Rosenau, P. M. (1992), *Post-Modernism and the Social Sciences: Insights, Inroads, and Intrusions* (Princeton: Princeton University Press).

Rosenhan, D. L. (1973), 'On Being Sane in Insane Places', *Science*, 179: 350–8.

Rosenthal, R., and Jacobson, L. (1968), *Pygmalion in the Classroom: Teacher Expectation and Pupils' Intellectual Development* (New York: Holt, Rinehart & Winston).

Rosnow, R. L., and Rosenthal, R. (1997), *People Studying People: Artifacts and Ethics in Behavorioral Research* (New York: W. H. Freeman).

Rubin, H. J., and Rubin, I. S. (1995), *Qualitative*

Interviewing: The Art of Hearing Data (Thousand Oaks, Calif.: Sage).

Rubinstein, J. (1973), *City Police* (New York: Ballantine).

Sacks, H., Schegloff, E. A., and Jefferson, G. (1974), 'A Simplest Systematics for the Organization of Turn-Taking in Conversation', *Language*, 50: 696–735.

Salancik, G. R. (1979), 'Field Stimulations for Organizational Behavior Research', *Administrative Science Quarterly*, 24: 638–49.

Samuel, R. (1976), 'Oral History and Local History', *History Workshop Journal*, 1: 191–208.

Sanjek, R. (1990), 'A Vocabulary for Fieldnotes', in R. Sanjek (ed.), *Fieldnotes: The Making of Anthropology* (Ithaca, NY: Cornell University Press).

Sarsby, J. (1984), 'The Fieldwork Experience', in R. F. Ellen (ed.), *Ethnographic Research: A Guide to General Conduct* (London: Academic Press).

Saunders, P. (1989), 'Left Write in Sociology', *Network: Newsletter of the British Sociological Association*, 44: 3–4.

Schegloff, E. A. (1997), 'Whose Text? Whose Context?', *Discourse and Society*, 8: 165–87.

Schlesinger, P., Dobash, R. E., Dobash, R. P., and Weaver, C. K. (1992), *Women Viewing Violence* (London: British Film Institute).

Schrøder, K. C. (1999), 'The Best of Both Worlds? Media Audience Research between Rival Paradigms', in P. Alasuutari (ed.), *Rethinking the Media Audience* (London: Sage).

Schuman, H., and Converse, J. (1971), 'The effects of Black and White Interviewers on Black Responses in 1968', *Public Opinion Quarterly*, 35: 44–68.

—— and Presser, S. (1981), *Questions and Answers in Attitude Surveys: Experiments on Question Form, Wording, and Context* (San Diego, Calif.: Academic Press).

Schutz, A. (1962), *Collected Papers I: The Problem of Social Reality* (The Hague: Martinus Nijhof).

Scott, A. M. (1994), *Gender Segregation and Social Change: Men and Women in Changing Labour Markets* (Oxford: Oxford University Press).

Scott, J. (1990), *A Matter of Record* (Cambridge: Polity).

Seale, C. (1999), *The Quality of Qualitative Research* (London: Sage).

Seeman, M. (1959), 'On the Meaning of Alienation', *American Sociological Review*, 24: 783–91.

Shapiro, M. (1985–6), 'Metaphor in the Philosophy of the Social Sciences', *Cultural Critique*, 2: 191–214.

Sharf, B. F. (1999), 'Beyond Nettiquette: The Ethics of

Doing Naturalistic Discourse Research on the Internet', in S. Jones (ed.), *Doing Internet Research: Critical Issues and Methods for Examining the Net* (Thousand Oaks, Calif.: Sage).

Shaw, C. R. (1930), *The Jack-Roller* (Chicago: University of Chicago Press).

Silverman, D. (1984), 'Going Private: Ceremonial Forms in a Private Oncology Clinic', *Sociology*, 18: 191–204.

—— (1985), *Qualitative Methodology and Sociology: Describing the Social World* (Aldershot: Gower).

—— (1993), *Interpreting Qualitative Data: Methods for Analysing Qualitative Data* (London: Sage).

—— (1994), 'Analysing Naturally-Occurring Data on AIDS Counselling: Some Methodological and Practical Issues', in M. Boulton (ed.), *Challenge and Innovation: Methodological Advances in Social Research on HIV/AIDS* (London: Taylor & Francis).

—— (2000), *Doing Qualitative Research: A Practical Handbook* (London: Sage).

Skeggs, B. (1994), 'Situating the Production of Feminist Ethnography', in M. Maynard and J. Purvis (eds), *Researching Women's Lives from a Feminist Perspective* (London: Taylor & Francis).

—— (1997), *Formations of Class and Gender* (London: Sage).

Smith, J. K. (1983), 'Quantitative versus Qualitative Research: An Attempt to Clarify the Issue', *Educational Researcher*, 12: 6–13.

—— and Heshusius, L. (1986), 'Closing down the Conversation: The End of the Quantitative–Qualitative Debate among Educational Enquirers', *Educational Researcher*, 15, 4–12.

Smith, T. W. (1995), 'Trends in Non-Response Rates', *International Journal of Public Opinion Research*, 7: 157–71.

Snizek, W. E. (1976), 'An Empirical Assessment of "Sociology: A Multiple Paradigm Science" [Ritzer, 1975]', *American Sociologist*, 11: 217–19.

Snyder, N., and Glueck, W. F. (1980), 'How Managers Plan—the Analysis of Managers' Activities', *Long Range Planning*, 13: 70–6.

Spradley, J. P. (1979), *The Ethnographic Interview* (New York: Holt, Rinehart & Winston).

Sprokkereef, A., Larkin, E., Pole, C. J., and Burgess, R. G. (1995), 'The Data, the Team, and The Ethnograph', *Studies in Qualitative Methodology*, 5: 81–103.

Squire, C. (2000), 'Situated Selves, the Coming-out Genre and Equivalent Citizenship in Narratives of HIV', in P. Chamberlayne, J. Bornat, and T. Wengraf (eds), *The*

Turn to Biographical Methods in Social Science: Comparative Issues and Examples (London: Routledge).

Stacey, J. (1988), 'Can there be a Feminist Ethnography?', *Women's International Studies Forum*, 11: 21–7.

Stacey, M. (1960), *Tradition and Change: A Study of Banbury* (London: Oxford University Press).

Stake, R. E. (1995), *The Art of Case Study Research* (Thousand Oaks, Calif.: Sage).

Stanley, L., and Temple, B. (1995), 'Doing the Business? Evaluating Software Packages to Aid the Analysis of Qualitative Data Sets', *Studies in Qualitative Methodology*, 5: 169–97.

Stewart, S., Prandy, K., and Blackburn, R. M. (1980), *Social Stratification and Occupations* (London: Macmillan).

Stirling Media Research Institute and Violence Research Centre (Manchester University) (1998), *Men Viewing Violence* (London: Broadcasting Standards Commission).

Stoller, P. (1989), *The Taste of Ethnographic Things* (Philadelphia: University of Pennsylvania Press).

Strauss, A. (1987), *Qualitative Analysis for Social Scientists* (New York: Cambridge University Press).

—— and Corbin, J. M. (1990), *Basics of Qualitative Research: Grounded Theory Procedures and Techniques* (Newbury Park, Calif.: Sage).

—— —— (1997), 'Commentary [on Orona, 1997]', in A. Strauss and J. M. Corbin (eds), *Grounded Theory in Practice* (Thousand Oaks, Calif.: Sage).

—— —— (1998), *Basics of Qualitative Research: Techniques and Procedures for Developing Grounded Theory* (Thousand Oaks, Calif.: Sage).

—— Schatzman, L., Ehrich, D., Bucher, R., and Sabshin, M. (1973), 'The Hospital and its Negotiated Order', in G. Salaman and K. Thompson (eds), *People and Organizations* (London: Longman).

Sudman, S., and Bradburn, N. M. (1982), *Asking Questions: A Practical Guide to Questionnaire Design* (San Francisco: Jossey-Bass).

Sullivan, O. (1996), 'Time Co-ordination, the Domestic Division of Labour and Affective Relations: Time Use and the Enjoyment of Activities within Couples', *Sociology*, 30: 79–100.

Sutton, R. I. (1992), 'Feelings about a Disneyland Visit: Photography and the Reconstruction of Bygone Emotions', *Journal of Management Inquiry*, 1: 278–87.

—— and Rafaeli, A. (1988), 'Untangling the Relationship between Displayed Emotions and Organizational Sales: The Case of Convenience Stores', *Academy of Management Journal*, 31: 461–87.

—— —— (1992), 'How we Untangled the Relationship between Displayed Emotion and Organizational Sales: A Tale of Bickering and Optimism', in P. J. Frost and R. Stablein (1992), *Doing Exemplary Research* (Newbury Park, Calif.: Sage).

Taylor, A. (1993), *Women Drug Users: An Ethnography of an Injecting Community* (Oxford: Clarendon Press).

Taylor, S. (1999), 'Covert Participant Observation: Unguarded Moments in Organizational Research', *Notework: The Newsletter of the Standing Conference on Organizational Symbolism*, May: 8–18.

Thompson, C. (1996), 'Is the End of AIDS in Sight?', *Sunday Times Magazine*, 30 June: 22–8.

Thompson, P. (1989), *The Nature of Work*, 2nd edn. (London: Macmillan).

Thompson, T. L., and Zerbinos, E. (1995), 'Gender Roles in Animated Cartoons: Has the Picture Changed in 20 Years?', *Sex Roles*, 32: 651–73.

Tourangeau, R., and Smith, T. W. (1996), 'Asking Sensitive Questions: The Impact of Data Collection Mode, Question Format, and Question Context', *Public Opinion Quarterly*, 60: 275–304.

Trow, M. (1957), 'Comment on "Participant Observation and Interviewing: A Comparison"' *Human Organization*, 16: 33–5.

Turnbull, P. (1973), *The Mountain People* (London: Cape).

Turner, B. A. (1994), 'Patterns of Crisis Behaviour: A Qualitative Inquiry', in A. Bryman and R. G. Burgess (eds), *Analyzing Qualitative Data* (London: Routledge).

Tyler, S. A. (1986), 'Post-Modern Ethnography: From Document of the Occult to Occult Document', in J. Clifford and G. E. Marcus (eds), *Writing Culture: The Poetics and Politics of Ethnography* (Berkeley and Los Angeles: University of California Press).

Van Maanen, J. (1978), 'On Watching the Watchers', in P. Manning and J. Van Maanen (eds), *Policing: The View from the Street* (Santa Monica, Calif.: Goodyear).

—— (1988), *Tales of the Field: On Writing Ethnography* (Chicago: University of Chicago Press).

—— (1991*a*), 'Playing Back the Tape: Early Days in the Field', in W. B. Shaffir and R. A. Stebbins (eds), *Experiencing Fieldwork: An Inside View of Qualitative Research* (Newbury Park, Calif.: Sage).

—— (1991*b*), 'The Smile Factory: Work at Disneyland', in P. J. Frost, L. F. Moore, M. R. Louis, C. C. Lundberg and J. Martin (eds), *Reframing Organizational Culture* (Newbury Park, Calif.: Sage).

—— and Kolb, D. (1985), 'The Professional Apprentice: Observations on Fieldwork Roles in two Organizational

Settings', *Research in the Sociology of Organizations*, 4: 1–33.

Vidich, A. R., and Bensman, J. (1968), *Small Town in Mass Society* (Princeton: Princeton University Press).

Von Wright, G. H. (1971), *Explanation and Understanding* (London: Routledge).

Waddington, D. (1994), 'Participant Observation', in C. Cassell and G. Symon (eds), *Qualitative Methods in Organizational Research* (London: Sage).

Wall, R. (1989), 'The Living Arrangements of the Elderly in Europe in the 1980s', in B. Bytheway, T. Keil, P. Allatt, and A. Bryman (eds), *Becoming and Being Old: Sociological Approaches to Later Life* (London: Sage).

Walsh, D. (1972), 'Sociology and the Social World', in P. Filmer, M. Phillipson, D. Silverman, and D. Walsh, *New Directions in Sociological Theory* (London: Collier-Macmillan).

Warde, A. (1997), *Consumption, Food and Taste* (London: Sage).

Wardhaugh, J. (1966) ' "Homeless in Chinatown": Deviance and Social Control in Cardboard City', *Sociology*, 30: 701–16.

Weaver, A., and Atkinson, P. (1995), *Microcomputing and Qualitative Data Analysis* (Aldershot: Avebury).

Webb, E. J., Campbell, D. T., Schwartz, R. D., and Sechrest, L. (1966), *Unobtrusive Measures: Nonreactive Measures in the Social Sciences* (Chicago: Rand McNally).

Weber, M. (1947), *The Theory of Social and Economic Organization*, trans. A. M. Henderson and T. Parsons (New York: Free Press).

Weick, K. E. (1990), 'The Vulnerable System: An Analysis of the Tenerife Air Disaster', *Journal of Management*, 16: 571–93.

Weinholtz, D., Kacer, B., and Rocklin, T. (1995), 'Salvaging Quantitative Research with Qualitative Data', *Qualitative Health Research*, 5: 388–97.

Weitzman, E. A., and Miles, M. B. (1995), *Computer Programs for Qualitative Data Analysis* (Thousand Oaks, Calif.: Sage).

Wellings, K., Field, J., Johnson, A., and Wadsworth, J. (1994), *Sexual Behaviour in Britain: The National Survey of Sexual Attitudes and Lifestyles* (Harmondsworth: Penguin).

Westergaard, J., Noble, I., and Walker, A. (1989), *After Redundancy: The Experience of Economic Insecurity* (Cambridge: Polity).

Wetherell, M. (1998), 'Positioning and Interpretative Repertoires: Conversation Analysis and Post-Structuralism in Dialogue', *Discourse and Society*, 9: 387–412.

Whyte, W. F. (1955), *Street Corner Society*, 2nd edn. (Chicago: University of Chicago Press).

Widdicombe, S. (1993), 'Autobiography and Change: Rhetoric and Authenticity of "Gothic" Style', in E. Burman and I. Parker (eds), *Discourse Analytic Research: Readings and Repertoires of Text* (London: Routledge).

Wilkinson, P. , and Whitworth, D. (1998), 'Fat is Fanciable, Says the Body of Evidence', *The Times*, 7 Jan. , 3.

Wilkinson, S. (1998), 'Focus Groups in Feminist Research: Power, Interaction, and the Co-Production of Meaning', *Women's Studies International Forum*, 21: 111–25.

—— (1999a), 'Focus Group Methodology: A Review', *International Journal of Social Research Methodology*, 1: 181–203.

—— (1999b), 'Focus Groups: A Feminist Method', *Psychology of Women Quarterly*, 23: 221–44.

Williams, R. (1976), 'Symbolic Interactionism: Fusion of Theory and Research', in D. C. Thorns (ed.), *New Directions in Sociology* (London: David & Charles).

Willis, P. (1977), *Learning to Labour* (Farnborough: Saxon House).

Winch, P. (1958), *The Idea of a Social Science and its Relation to Philosophy* (London: Routledge & Kegan Paul).

Winkler, C. (1995), 'The Ethnography of the Ethnographer', in C. Nordstrom and A. C. G. M. Robben (eds), *Fieldwork under Fire: Contemporary Studies of Violence and Survival* (Berkeley and Los Angeles: University of California Press).

Wolcott, H. F. (1990), *Writing up Qualitative Research* (Newbury Park, Calif.: Sage).

Wolf, D. R. (1991), 'High Risk Methodology: Reflections on Leaving an Outlaw Society', in W. B. Shaffir and R. A. Stebbins (eds), *Experiencing Fieldwork: An Inside View of Qualitative Research* (Newbury Park, Calif.: Sage).

Woolgar, S. (1988), *Science: The Very Idea* (Chichester: Ellis Horwood).

Yin, R. K. (1984), *Case Study Research: Design and Methods* (Beverly Hills, Calif.: Sage).

Zimmerman, D. H., and Wieder, D. L. (1977), 'The Diary: Diary-Interview Method', *Urban Life*, 5: 479–98.

Zukin, S. (1982), *Loft Living: Culture and Capital in Urban Change* (Baltimore, MD: Johns Hopkins University Press).

Name Index

A

Abraham, J. (1994) 375
Adler, P. and Adler, P. A. (1985) 21, 51, 428
Adler, P. A. (1985) 24
Aitken, I. (1998) 378–9, 380, 381
Aldridge, A. (1998) 379
Allison, G. T. (1971) 48
Altheide, D. L. (1980) 307; (1996) 180, 381
Andersen, M. (1981) 327
Anderson, P. (1998) 480
Ang, I. (1985) 371
Arber, S. and Gilbert, G. N. (1989) 198
Armstrong, G. (1993) 277, 278, 296, 297, 298, 301, 304, 305, 331, 472; (1998) 282
Arnold, H. J. and Feldman, D. C. (1981) 124
Aronson, E. and Carlsmith, J. M. (1968) 38
Asch, S. E. (1951) 349–50
Atkinson, J. M. and Drew, P. (1979) 358
Atkinson, P. (1981) 292, 305–6, 467; (1983) 467; (1990) 437, 460; and Coffey, A. (1995) 469

B

Bahr, H. M., Caplow, T. and Chadwick, B. A. (1983) 51
Ball, S. J. (1981) 47, 451; (1984) 273
Barker, E. (1984) 293, 450
Barnard, M. and Frischer, M. (1995) 452
Barthes, R. (1972) 380
Bauman, Z. (1978) 14
Baumgartner, R. M. and Heberlein, T. A. (1984) 133
Bazerman, C. (1987) 465
Beardsworth, A. (1980) 179, 191; and Keil, T. (1992) 45, 48, 49, 315, 322, 324, 329, 466–8, 495, 496, 499; and Keil (1996) 148; Bryman, A., Ford, J. and Keil, T. 205
Bechhofer, F., Elliott, B. and McCrone, D. (1984) 111
Becker, H. S. (1958) 430; (1963) 98–9; (1967) 22; (1970) 296; (1982) 18, 467; and Geer, B. (1957) 327, 328, 331–2

Beharrell, P. (1993) 67, 179, 181, 182, 189, 378, 381
Belk, R. W., Sherry, J. F. and Wallendorf, M. (1988) 274
Bell, C. (1969) 292, 293; and Newby, H. (1977) 470; and Roberts, H. (1984) 470
Bellaby, P. and Bellaby, F. (1999) 199
Belson, W. A. (1981) 161
Berelson, B. (1952) 178–9, 180
Beynon, H. (1975) 190
Bhaskar, R. (1975) 13, 429; (1989) 13, 430
Billig, M. (1991) 361; (1992) 360, 362; Condor, S., Edwards, D., Gane, M., Middleton, D. and Radley, A. (1998) 363
Blauner, R. (1964) 192, 451
Blaxter, M. (1990) 42, 43, 45
Bloor, M. (1978) 273, 390; (1997) 273, 274
Blumer, H. (1954) 269–70, 280; (1956) 78; (1962) 15
Bogdan, R. and Taylor, S. J. (1975) 14
Bottomore, T. B. and Rubel, M. (1963) 151
Bradburn, N. A. and Sudman, S. (1979) 115
Braverman, H. (1974) 7, 69, 166
Brayfield, A. and Rothe, H. (1951) 134
Bridgman, P. W. (1927) 63, 78
Briggs, C. L. (1986) 124
Brown, G. W. and Harris, T. W. (1978) 432
Bryman, A. (1974) 190; (1988) 54, 55, 78, 79, 284, 391, 446, 447, 453, 454, 470; (1989) 97, 102; (1994) 282; (1995) 5, 371, 374; (1998) 5, 465; (1999) 98–9, 111, 320–1, 460, 465
Bryman, A. and Burgess, R. G. (1994) 283, 388, 390, 408, 439; (1999) 264–5
Bryman, A. and Cramer, D. (2001) 69, 214, 231, 232
Bryman, A., Gillingwater, D. and McGuinness, I. (1996) 315
Bryman, A., Haslam, C. and Webb, A. (1994) 281, 315, 396
Bryman, A., Stephens, M. and A Campo, C. (1996) 179, 331, 439
Brynin, M. (1994) 46

Buckle, A. and Farrington, D. P. (1994) 168, 169
Bulmer, M. (1979) 395; (1980) 208, 210; (1982) 478, 484; (1984) 64
Burawoy, M. (1979) 47
Burgess, R. G. (1983) 47, 51, 293; (1984) 298, 314; (1987) 51, 293, 331
Burrell, I. and Leppard, D. (1994) 73
Business Week (1973) 95–6
Buston, K. (1997) 407
Butcher, B. (1994) 101

C

Calder, B. J. (1977) 336, 339
Camerer, C. F. (1997) 210
Campbell, D. T. (1957) 35, 37
Carlson, R. G., Siegal, H. A., Wang, J. and Falck, R. A. (1996) 450
Catterall, M. and Maclaran, P. (1997) 408
Cavendish, R. (1982) 47, 190, 292
Chamberlayne, P., Bornat, J. and Wengraf, T. (2000) 316
Charles, N. and Kerr, N. (1988) 144, 146, 148
Charlton, T., Gunter, B. and Coles, D. (1998) 39, 166
Charlton, T., Coles, D., Panting, C. and Hannan, A. (1999) 39
Charmaz, K. (1983) 392; (1991) 11; (1997) 10–11, 395; (2000) 302, 390, 397, 431
Chattoe, E. and Gilbert, N. (1999) 322
Cicourel, A. V. (1964) 74, 77, 79, 124, 191; (1968) 355; (1982) 31, 43, 77, 124
Clairborn, W. L. (1969) 36
Clifford, J. (1983) 469
Cloward, R. A. and Ohlin, L. E. (1960) 6
Coffey, A. (1999) 293, 306
Coffey, A. and Atkinson, P. (1996) 397, 399, 401
Coffey, A., Holbrook, B. and Atkinson, P. (1996) 408
Cohen, S. (1973) 170, 184
Coleman, C. and Moynihan, J. (1996) 73, 206, 207, 210
Coleman, J. S. (1958) 99
Collins, M. (1997) 115
Collins, R. (1994) 15

Subject Index

Page numbers in **bold** refer to expositions of subjects in boxes.